PERCEPTION AS BAYESIAN INFERENCE

PERCEPTION AS BAYESIAN INFERENCE

Edited by
DAVID C. KNILL
University of Pennsylvania

WHITMAN RICHARDS
Massachusetts Institute of Technology

CAMBRIDGE
UNIVERSITY PRESS

CAMBRIDGE UNIVERSITY PRESS
Cambridge, New York, Melbourne, Madrid, Cape Town, Singapore, São Paulo

Cambridge University Press
The Edinburgh Building, Cambridge CB2 8RU, UK

Published in the United States of America by Cambridge University Press, New York

www.cambridge.org
Information on this title: www.cambridge.org/9780521461092

© Cambridge University Press 1996

First published 1996
This digitally printed version 2008

A catalogue record for this publication is available from the British Library

ISBN 978-0-521-46109-2 hardback
ISBN 978-0-521-06499-6 paperback

Contents

Contributors

E.H. Adelson
Department of Brain & Cognitive Sciences, Massachusetts Institute of Technology, Cambridge MA 02139

H. Barlow
Physiological Laboratory, Downing St., Cambridge, England CB3 OEH

P.N. Belhumeur
Department of Electrical Engineering, Yale University, New Haven, CT 06520

B.M. Bennett
Department of Mathematics, University of California at Irvine, Irvine, CA 92717

A. Blake
Department of Engineering Science, University of Oxford, Oxford, OXl 3PJ England

H.H. Bülthoff
Max-Planck Institut für biologische Kybernetik, 72076 Tübingen, Germany

J. Feldman
Center for Cognitive Science, Rutgers University, Piscataway, NJ 08855

W.T. Freeman
Mitsubishi Electric Research Laboratories, 201 Broadway, Cambridge, MA 02139

D.D. Hoffman
Department of Cognitive Science, University of California at Irvine, Irvine, CA 92717

A. Jepson
Department of Computer Science, University of Toronto, Toronto, M5S 1A4 Canada

D. Kersten
Department of Psychology, University of Minnesota, Minneapolis, MN 55455

D.C. Knill
Department of Psychology, University of Pennsylvania, Philadelphia, PA 19104

P. Mamassian
Department of Psychology, University of Minnesota, Minneapolis, MN 55455

D.D. Mumford
Department of Mathematics, Harvard University, Cambridge, MA 02138

K. Nakayama
Vision Sciences Laboratory, Department of Psychology, Harvard University, Cambridge, MA 02138

A.P. Pentland
Media Arts & Sciences, Massachusetts Institute of Technology, Cambridge, MA 02139

C. Prakash
Department of Mathematics, California State University, San Bernardino, CA 92407

W. Richards
Media Arts & Sciences, Massachusetts Institute of Technology, Cambridge, MA 02139

S. Richman
Department of Program in Mathematical Behavioral Science, University of California at Irvine, Irvine, CA 92717

R. Rensink
Vision Sciences Laboratory, Department of Psychology, Harvard University, Cambridge, MA 02138

D. Sheinberg
Department of Cognitive & Linguistic Sciences, Brown University, Providence, RI 02912

S. Shimojo
Department of Psychology, University of Tokyo, Komaba, Meguro-ku, Tokyo 153 Japan

A.L. Yuille
Division of Applied Sciences, Harvard University, Cambridge, MA 02138

Preface

By the late eighties, the computational approach to perception advocated by Marr (1982) was well established. In vision, most properties of the 2 1/2 D sketch such as surface orientation and 3D shape admitted solutions, especially for machine vision systems operating in constrained environments. Similarly, tactile and force sensing was rapidly becoming a practicality for robotics and prostheses. Yet in spite of this progress, it was increasingly apparent that machine perceptual systems were still enormously impoverished versions of their biological counterparts. Machine systems simply lacked the inductive intelligence and knowledge that allowed biological systems to operate successfully over a variety of unspecified contexts and environments. The role of "top-down" knowledge was clearly underestimated and was much more important than precise edge, region, "textural", or shape information. It was also becoming obvious that even when adequate "bottom-up" information was available, we did not understand how this information should be combined from the different perceptual modules, each operating under their often quite different and competing constraints (Jain, 1989). Furthermore, what principles justified the choice of these "constraints" in the first place? Problems such as these all seemed to be subsumed under a lack of understanding of how prior knowledge should be brought to bear upon the interpretation of sensory data. Of course, this conclusion came as no surprise to many cognitive and experimental psychologists (e.g. Gregory, 1980; Hochberg, 1988; Rock, 1983), or to neurophysiologists who were exploring the role of massive reciprocal descending pathways (Maunsell & Newsome, 1987; Van Essen *et al.*, 1992). But the contributions of these groups were principally facts and observations; there were no really comprehensive models. Missing was an overarching framework within which a variety of computational and experimental results might fit together and be assimilated. Here, we offer several such frameworks, woven together by Bayesian threads.

Not surprisingly, at roughly the same time, several laboratories saw the need for a well articulated, formal framework for perception that would show how prior knowledge could drive the interpretation of sensory observations. Seeds had already been planted in adjacent fields (e.g., Pearl, 1988; Skilling, 1991), as well as in our own (e.g., Bennett *et al.*, 1989; Clark & Yuille, 1990). The time seemed ripe to bring together a small group to compare several of these new frameworks, and to place the burden upon the authors to show how their proposals might suggest new directions for experimental research. I asked David Knill, who had recently written with Dan Kersten one of the keynote papers, if he would assume the principal role of organizing a meeting, assisted by a committee of myself, Heinrich Bülthoff, and Alan Yuille. Our intent was to choose participants from computer science, mathematics, cognitive science and psychophysics, but to favor those who were already engaged in collaborative studies of human vision from a computational perspective. After an enthusiastic group of participants agreed to meet, David Knill subsequently contacted Dr. John Tangney of AFOSR, who subsequently provided support. The meeting was then held in January 1993 at Chatham Bars Inn, Chatham, Massachusetts. This collection represents a partial distillation of the results of the Chatham meeting.

As mentioned, our main goal was to evaluate whether any of the new formal frameworks for perception could have any practical impact upon the kinds of questions asked by the experimentalists. In the process of this evaluation, we expected that the common ground underlying the different, more theoretical proposals would be revealed. Indeed, the title of the book, "Perception as Bayesian Inference" reflects the unifying theme. However the reader should not be misled into concluding that all contributors accept the hypotheses that biological perceptual systems indeed make strict Bayesian inferences. Rather, the more representative view is that the Bayesian formulation captures the essence common to most of the frameworks, and allows the distinctions to be articulated clearly. Consequently, we begin this collection with a tutorial by Knill *et al.* to aid the newcomer to Bayesian inference. But others may wish to start at the end, reading first the final chapter (12) by Horace Barlow on "Banishing the Homunculus", which provides an entirely different motivation for continuing through this volume. The remainder of the book then reflects the main goals: the first part presents several different frameworks for understanding the perceptual process, whereas the second part is committed more to implications and applications. Finally, we have added commentaries to the contributions that enlarge upon the discussions that took place at the Chatham meeting. These commentaries, then, are probably the most critical indicator of the extent to which we managed to meet our main goal of fleshing out the theoretical frameworks and integrating them with practical psychophysics and computation. Our hope is that we have kindled interest in developing new, more powerful approaches to understanding the perceptual act.

Whitman Richards

References

Bennett, B.M., Hoffman, D.D. & Pratash, C. (1989). *Observer Mechanics: A Formal Theory of Perception.* New York: Academic.

Clark, J.J. & Yuille, A.L. (1990). *Data Fusion for Sensory Information Processing Systems.* Boston, MA: Kluwer Academic.

Gregory, R.L. (1980). Perceptions as hypotheses. In *The Psychology of Vision*, ed. H.C. Longuet-Higgins and N.S. Sutherland, pp. 137-149. London: The Royal Society.

Hochberg, J. (1988). Machines should not see as people do, but must know how people see. *Computer Vision, Graphics & Image Proc.*, **37**, 221-237.

Jain, R. (1989). Environmental models and information assimilation. Tech. Rep. IBM Almaden Res. Labs., June. Also Assimilation Workshop, Univ. Michigan, Ann Arbor, 1990.

Marr, D. (1982). *Vision: A Computational Investigation into the Human Representation and Processing of Visual Information.* San Francisco, CA: W.H. Freeman.

Maunsell, H.R. & Newsome, W.T. (1987). Visual processing in monkey extrastriate cortex. *Ann. Rev. Neurosci.*, **10**, 363-401.

Pearl, J. (1988). *Probabilistic Reasoning in Intelligent Systems.* San Francisco: Morgan Kauffman.

Rock, I. (1983). *The Logic of Perception.* Cambridge, MA: Bradford/MIT Press.

Skilling, J. (1991). Fundamentals of maximum entropy in data analysis. In *Maximum Entropy in Action*, ed. B. Buck and V. Macaulay, chapter 2. London: Oxford Univ. Press.

Van Essen, D.C., Anderson, C. & Fellerman, D.J. (1992). Information processing in the primate visual system: an integrated systems perspective. *Science*, **255**, 419-423.

Acknowledgments

Again, many thanks to David Knill for coordinating and arranging support for the Chatham meeting, and to John Tangney for providing this help under AFOSR-90-0177. Dan Kersten also offered many helpful suggestions at various stages of this enterprise, in addition to the committee that included Heinrich Bülthoff and Alan Yuille. Preparation of this manuscript turned into an unexpectedly long enterprise, and we thank William Gilson for his patience in dealing with various formats.

0

Introduction:
A Bayesian formulation of visual perception

DAVID C. KNILL

Dept. of Psychology, University of Minnesota,

DANIEL KERSTEN

Dept. of Psychology, University of Minnesota

ALAN YUILLE

Division of Applied Sciences, Harvard University

0.1 Overview

Bayesian approaches have enjoyed a great deal of recent success in their application to problems in computer vision (Grenander, 1976-1981; Bolle & Cooper, 1984; Geman & Geman, 1984; Marroquin *et al.*, 1985; Szeliski, 1989; Clark & Yuille, 1990; Yuille & Clark, 1993; Madarasmi *et al.*, 1993). This success has led to an emerging interest in applying Bayesian methods to modeling human visual perception (Bennett *et al.*, 1989; Kersten, 1990; Knill & Kersten, 1991; Richards *et al.*, 1993). The chapters in this book represent to a large extent the fruits of this interest: a number of new theoretical frameworks for studying perception and some interesting new models of specific perceptual phenomena, all founded, to varying degrees, on Bayesian ideas. As an introduction to the book, we present an overview of the philosophy and fundamental concepts which form the foundation of Bayesian theory as it applies to human visual perception. The goal of the chapter is two-fold: first, it serves as a tutorial to the basics of the Bayesian approach to readers who are unfamiliar with it, and second, to characterize the type of theory of perception the approach is meant to provide. The latter topic, by its meta-theoretic nature, is necessarily subjective. This introduction represents the views of the authors in this regard, not necessarily those held by other contributors to the book.

First, we introduce the Bayesian framework as a general formalism for specifying the information in images which allows an observer to perceive the world. Such a specification, however, is only one side of the story of perception, written from a point of view outside an observer's head. It characterizes the information available to observers for perception, not how observers use this information. To characterize how observers use visual information requires a description of how the visual system makes inferences about the world based on image data, and is the point of view most commonly associated with information processing approaches

1

to perception. Secondly, therefore, we re-introduce the Bayesian framework in the context of modeling perceptual inference. By taking both points of view, we hope to highlight the fact that a Bayesian approach provides a useful framework for modeling both information and inference, and that the elements used to model information are equivalent to those used to model perceptual inference. In particular, we will see that explicit models of world structure (i.e. regularities in properties of the world) are needed to completely characterize both the information provided in images for perception and the actual inferences made by the visual system in the course of perception. The information problem demands of us models of the "true" structure of the world, whereas the inference problem demands models of the implicit assumptions about the world which the human visual system relies on for perception.

The introduction is organized into four parts: a qualitative formulation of the general problem of perception as communication, a brief tutorial on the Bayesian formulation of information, a reconceptualization of Bayesian formulations in terms of perceptual inference and a brief discussion of some of the issues involved in modeling visual perception within a Bayesian framework.

0.2 Perception as communication

Formulating visual perception as communication provides a useful metaphor for illustrating the nature of the information processing problem faced by the human visual system. A generic communication system (see figure 0.1a) consists of a *message set*, from which a *transmitter* draws messages, which it codes and sends as signals down a *channel* to a *receiver*, which decodes the signal to determine the message which was sent. Consider how this maps onto visual perception (figure 0.1b). For simplicity of discussion, we will consider the message set as the set of all possible physical configurations of scenes in our world[†]. While there is no identifiable physical transmitter, we can consider the messages (physical scenes) to be coded in the pattern of light reflected from surfaces and projected on a retinal receiving surface. The coding rules are the physical laws of light reflection, refraction and transmittance and the geometric laws of perspective projection. The receiver is the visual system, which processes the pattern of light impingent on the retina

---

[†] One can generalize the notion of "visual messages" to more abstract properties of a scene, such as the moods and intentions of biological organisms. For such abstract messages, we must conceive of the coder as including the processes by which these abstract properties are mapped to physical properties of a scene (e.g. facial expressions), as well as the image formation process which encodes these physical properties. In some sense, then, the set of messages is determined in part by exactly what an observer wants to "perceive". This is not a flaw in the metaphor, but does suggest caution in fixing our notions of what elements of the communication metaphor map to corresponding elements of perception.

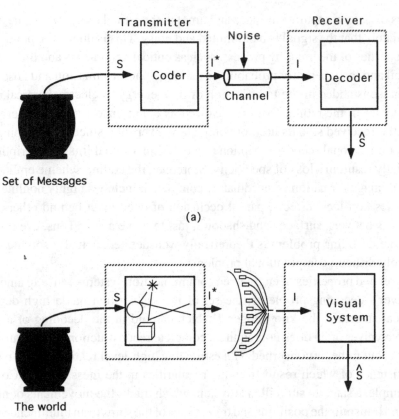

Fig. 0.1 (a) A general communication system model: A transmitter draws a message **S** from a bin according to some probability law, codes it into a signal **I**** and transmits the signal down a noisy channel. A receiver receives the noisy signal, **I** and attempts to decode it to determine the messages sent; that is, to estimate **S**. (b) The analogy with perception – **S** is a description of a particular scene in the world. An imaginary coder codes this description of scene properties in the form of an idealized image, **I****. The visual system receives a noisy, bandlimited version of this image, **I**, which it must use to estimate properties of the scene **S**.

to "decode" the message; that is, it determines as best it can at least some of the properties of the scene which are projected to an image, or set of images.

Communication systems, at the level of abstraction used here, seem simple enough; however, as any communication engineer will tell you, the details of most real systems are quite complex. The code may not be complete (it may not be invertible to uniquely determine the original, coded message) and the physical channel will generally be bandlimited and noisy, so that the signal which arrives at the receiver is a degraded version of the original. The job faced by the receiver is, therefore, highly non-trivial. The same is true in vision. If we take as the received signals patterns of photon capture (in space and time) in the retinal receptor mosaic, we see immediately that the signal is bandlimited and noisy. This is due to the purely physical properties of the imaging process, such as optical aberrations and diffraction at the pupil and the inherently probabilistic nature of photon emission and absorption. More noise is added in the transduction of light energy to electrochemical energy by receptors in the retina. Even if idealized as being uncorrupted by these influences, the received signals are not completely invertible, since the mapping from a three-dimensional scene description to a two-dimensional image description can potentially result in a loss of specificity. Moreover, the coding scheme embodied in physical image formation is inordinately complex: it includes highly nonlinear, and sometimes non-local effects; partial occlusion of one object behind others, interreflections between surfaces and shadows, just to name a few. Thus, even in cases where the decoding problem is theoretically well-defined, actually solving it is an extremely difficult computational problem.

Two related properties of engineered communication systems can help ameliorate a receiver's decoding problems; the set of messages often has a high degree of statistical structure, the knowledge of which can aid in the decoding of a signal; and the receiver often does not require a complete reconstruction of the transmitted message, but rather is concerned with estimating high-level features of the message (the existence of which result from the regularities in the message set). Consider, for example, a satellite surveillance system which tracks the movements of military ships and transmits the positions and trajectories of the ships to an intelligence station on earth. The set of possible messages is the set of possible positions and motions of military ships on the seas' surfaces. The sender is the satellite computer/radio system which codes the information and transmits it to a radio receiver on earth. The signal received by the radio operator on earth will be corrupted by noise; thus, some of the reported ships' coordinates may be in error or may be missing altogether. The set of messages has a very strong structure imposed by the constraints on positioning and movement of military ships. Besides physical constraints (for example, on speed), military ships are often clustered into groups whose motions are very strongly correlated. A well-designed decoding system, when doing error correction on an individual ship's motion, should estimate it based not only on the data transmitted for that ship, but also on the data transmitted for ships in its group. Moreover, the military planners who ultimately will use the information received may only be interested in fleet movements, thus the system could "average" the data for each ship in a group to produce an estimate of the fleet's motion which is more reliable than the estimate of any individual ships' motion.

The same situation holds for visual perception. The world has a tremendous amount of structure. A simple and obvious example is that matter coheres into objects, the shapes of whose surfaces structure the light projected to images. Moreover, these shapes are not arbitrary, first being clustered in different classes (landscapes, plants, rocks, man-made objects, etc.), and within these classes having certain regularities (mountains being fractal, man-made objects tending to be symmetric, etc.). The same holds true for other scene properties; for example, surface material is constrained by natural laws, most objects are rigid, and when they aren't, deform in specific ways (e.g. the articulated motion of animate objects), ballistic movements follow Newton's laws of motion, etc.. This structure helps to make the information in images about scenes more reliable than it would be in a less structured world. It also plays a significant role in determining what scene properties a visual observer might be designed to estimate from images.

The perceptual problem faced by any visual system, like the decoding problem faced by the receiver in a general communication system, requires four basic components (see column 1, table 0.1) for its specification:

(1) The elements of interest in messages – for visual perception these are the properties of scenes the visual system attempts to estimate. As mentioned above, the structure of the environment plays some role in determining this, but so do the functional needs of the organism. An excellent example is the importance of surface properties to perception, which arises in part from the fact that matter coheres into objects and in part from the fact that the surface properties of objects determine in large part how they interact with each other and with observers (e.g. balls roll more easily than cubes).
(2) The structure of the message set; that is, the regularities which messages have – for visual perception this is the structure of scenes in our environment (regularities in object shape, etc.).
(3) The coding scheme used by the transmitter – in the context of visual perception, "the transmitter" encodes scenes as an image signal. While in some absolute sense, one should model the image signal as the pattern of photon capture over time in retinal receptors, many problems in perception are more conducive to high-level descriptions of the signal. This could be in terms of features such as optic flow, image contours or texture gradients, to name a few. In these cases, the coding scheme would map high-level features of a scene to high-level features of an image (e.g. edges of surfaces map to contours along luminance discontinuities in images). Whatever the case, the coding scheme is ultimately based on the physics of light reflection, refraction and transmission and the geometric laws of perspective projection.
(4) The form of signal corruption – again, this depends on what one considers to be the signal for a particular problem. A signal represented as the pattern of photon capture over time in retinal receptors would be "corrupted" by the uncertainty of photon emission and capture. For analyses in which the signal is treated as a collection of higher-level image features, the effects of physical corruption of the image are often considered to be negligible for purposes of the problem at hand or are approximated as noise added to the coding of the high-level features; for example, noise added to the orientations or curvatures of image contours.

Taken together, these four components define what properties of a scene a visual system attempts to estimate in the course of perception and how these scene properties are encoded in images. In a deeper sense, components (2), (3) and (4) specify the information content of images; that is, what images can potentially tell one about the world. Note the role of the second component, the structure of the environment, in the definition of information. It is not a second source of information which is "added" by an observer to image information, but rather it is an integral part of a specification of what information images carry about scenes.

The discussion so far can be thought of as describing a particular way to characterize perceptual problems posed to an observer. We can summarize this in the following statement:

Perceptual problems posed to an observer are characterized by (1) the properties of the world which an observer makes inferences about (e.g. shape), and (2) the information provided by images about those properties, as determined by the prior structure of the world, the coding scheme and the form of image data corruption.

A complete characterization of a communication system also requires specifying how the receiver actually decodes the signals it receives to determine what message was sent; that is, how it solves the decoding problem. Analogously, we are interested in how an observer solves perceptual problems in the act of perception:

An observer's solutions to perceptual problems are characterized by (1) the properties of the world which an observer makes inferences about, (2) the image data actually used by observers as the basis for perceptual inferences and (3) the assumptions about image coding and about the prior structure of the world used by the observer to make inferences.

The quality of an observer's solution of a perceptual problem depends on how well the observers' assumptions about the world and about image coding match the world in which it exists; that is, on the similarity between corresponding elements of the perceptual problem and perceptual solution specifications.

The communication metaphor does not completely capture the difficulty of perception. In prototypical communication systems, both man-made and biological, senders and receivers are designed, or evolve, together; that is, the coding and decoding schemes are designed hand-in-hand to match one another. The classic example of this in the biological domain is human language, for which production and comprehension systems evolved together. Moreover, the coding schemes are often designed to ameliorate the problems imposed by signal corruption in the transmission channel (for example, by adding appropriate forms of redundancy in the code). Visual perception, on the other hand, involves the evolution of an organism's visual system to match the structure of the world and the coding scheme provided by nature. Unlike usual communication systems, the coding scheme (light reflection and perspective projection) has not been designed a-priori to maximize the reliability of the information transmitted about message features of interest to an organism (scene properties), nor to minimize the computational problems of decoding the signals. It simply exists as a property of our environment, and the visual system has to make do with what nature has provided. All of our experience attempting to build artificial vision systems tells us that the computational problems of decoding images are actually quite difficult.

0.3 The Bayesian formulation of the problem of perception

0.3.1 The Bayesian characterization of information

The basic idea behind the Bayesian approach is to characterize the information about the world contained in an image as a probability distribution which characterizes the relative likelihoods of a viewed scene being in different states, given the available image data. The exact form of the distribution, called the "posterior" conditional probability distribution, is determined in part by the image formation process, including the nature of the noise added in the image coding process, and in part by the statistical structure of the world. As we will see shortly, Bayes' rule provides the mechanism for combining these two factors into a final calculation of the posterior distribution. The Bayesian approach distinguishes itself from other statistical formulations of information by taking into account the contributions of both factors to the specification of information. In particular, the approach is notable for its reliance on explicit models of world structure. While this forms the basis for most attacks on the approach, we emphasize that modeling this aspect of visual information is a fundamental necessity, and is always implicitly done, if not explicitly.

Table 0.1 summarizes the Bayesian formalization of the decoding problem posed to the receiver in a communication system. Referring back to our original discussion of the four major components of a model of information, we have for visual perception;

(1) A formal representation of the scene properties of interest – **S**. **S** might include such things as surface shape, object motion, observer motion, the projected time of collision between objects, and so on.

(2) A model of the structure of scenes which defines the *prior* probability distribution, $p(\mathbf{S})$. $p(\mathbf{S})$ embodies the large number of statistical dependencies which exist between scene properties.

(3) A model of image formation, which we write as a function applied to **S**, $\pi(\mathbf{S})$. π can be thought of as an idealized model of image formation which incorporates the laws of light reflection, refraction and emission as well as the laws of perspective projection. More realistically, π could be modeled so as to take into account physical effects of imaging such as blur, optical aberrations in the eye and sampling.

(4) A model of image noise, **N**, which we can think of as being added to the result of the image formation function, $\mathbf{I} = \pi(\mathbf{S}) + \mathbf{N}$. It need not, of course, be strictly additive,

Communication system		Bayesian framework for perception		
Elements of interest in messages		Scene properties of interest **S**		
Information	Structure of the message set	Prior $p(\mathbf{S})$		Posterior $p(\mathbf{S} \mid \mathbf{I})$
	Coding	Image Formation $\pi(\mathbf{S})$	Likelihood $p(\mathbf{I} \mid \mathbf{S})$	
	Noise	Image Noise **N**		

Table 0.1 *Column 1 shows the qualitative components of a communication problem specification. Column 2 shows the corresponding formal components within the Bayesian framework (see text for details of variable and function meanings).*

and, depending on what one is modeling as the input to the visual system, it may involve complex models of noise induced at various stages in neural processing.

Sticking to our metaphor of perception as communication, we say that images, **I**, are signals which provide information about transmitted messages, which are taken to be specific configurations of scene properties, **S**. The posterior conditional probability distribution $p(\mathbf{S} \mid \mathbf{I})$, characterizes this information. If an image uniquely specifies the scene (e.g. their is no uncertainty induced by noise), then the posterior distribution is trivial, being zero for all scene configurations but the one actually being viewed. More commonly, images have some ambiguity, and this is reflected in the "spread" of probability over the space of possible scenes. The posterior distribution depends on the structure of the set of possible scenes ($p(\mathbf{S})$), the image formation function ($\pi(\mathbf{S})$) and the noise added to images (**N**). Bayes' rule specifies a way to partially decompose the posterior into these parts. According to Bayes' rule, the posterior is given by

$$p(\mathbf{S} \mid \mathbf{I}) = \frac{p(\mathbf{I} \mid \mathbf{S})\, p(\mathbf{S})}{p(\mathbf{I})}. \qquad (0.1)$$

For our purposes, we can treat $p(\mathbf{I})$, the probability of occurrence of an image, as a normalizing constant, so we have

$$p(\mathbf{S} \mid \mathbf{I}) \propto p(\mathbf{I} \mid \mathbf{S})\, p(\mathbf{S}). \qquad (0.2)$$

$p(\mathbf{I} \mid \mathbf{S})$, for a given value of **S** (a given scene), is a probability distribution specifying the relative probability of obtaining different images from that scene. It is a function of the image formation function and the corrupting noise (thus incorporating two of the components of information described above). $p(\mathbf{I} \mid \mathbf{S})$ is generally referred to as the likelihood function for $\mathbf{S}$. $p(\mathbf{S})$ we have described above, and is the prior distribution on scene configurations $\mathbf{S}$.

Equation (0.2) is the foundation of the Bayesian approach to visual perception. It shows how to factor out the relative effects on image information of the coding scheme and noise on the one hand, and the prior structure of the environment on the other. Consider what the likelihood function and prior distribution represent for problems of visual perception. The likelihood function reflects the noisiness of the data and the loss of specificity implicit in the projection from three dimensions to two. If the image were uncorrupted by noise and unaffected by optical distortions, then $p(\mathbf{I} \mid \mathbf{S})$ would be non-zero only for those scenes which would project, under perspective projection, to a given image $\mathbf{I} = I$; that is, it would select a set of candidate scene interpretations for a given image[†]. Noise has the effect of spreading the likelihood function over a larger range of possible scenes, making the information provided by an image about scene properties more unreliable. The distribution $p(\mathbf{S})$ is the prior probability of different collections of scene properties actually occurring in our environment. It embodies knowledge of the structure of the environment which constrains the perceptual estimate of scene properties. A good example of a prior constraint is the assumption that object motions tend to be rigid. The rigidity constraint is often hard-wired into structure-from-motion models, leading to an effective assumption that $p(\mathbf{S}) = 0$ for non-rigidly moving objects (Koenderink & van Doorn, 1975; Ullman, 1979; Bennett *et al.*, 1989). Other examples of prior constraints are the smoothness constraints often used in computer vision models (Ikeuchi & Horn, 1981; Julesz, 1971; Marr & Poggio, 1979; Yuille, 1989). Typically, when formulated in probabilistic terms they characterize particular probabilistic models of surfaces (Szeliski, 1989). (See chapter 5, by Yuille and Bülthoff and chapter 8 by Belhumeur for complete discussions of the relationship between smoothness constraints and Bayesian priors).

0.3.2 A tutorial example

In this section, we illustrate the Bayesian formulation of an information processing problem with a simple example for which we can compute the posterior function exactly, but which retains key similarities to real problems in perception. In our example communication system (see figure 0.2), the set of messages consists of four

---

[†] Transactionalist theory, a school of perceptual psychology popularized by Ames with "illusions" such as the Ames' room and Ames' trapezoidal window, referred to the set of scenes which could project to a given image or images as "equivalent configurations" (Ittleson, 1960)

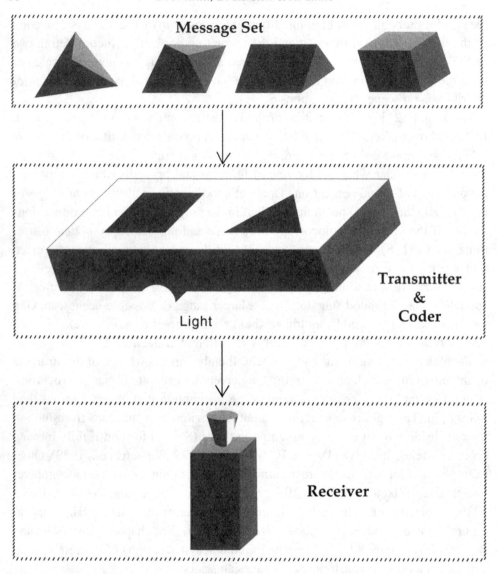

Fig. 0.2 The communication system for the shape sorter example. See text for description.

objects: a tetrahedron, a pyramid, a prism and a cube. Each object is a "message". The tetrahedron has four triangular sides, the pyramid has a square base with four triangular sides, the prism has three square sides and two triangular sides, and the cube has six square sides. Each of the square and triangular sides has the same shape for all the objects. The transmitter selects objects for coding and transmission with the probabilities given in table 0.2. These probabilities form the prior distribution characterizing the structure of the message set, or what we have referred to for vision

Prior distribution of objects $p(\text{object})$	
tetrahedron	0.1
pyramid	0.3
prism	0.4
cube	0.2

Table 0.2.

as the structure of the world. The coding device used by the transmitter has two stages. The first is like the toy for toddlers in which only certain three-dimensional shapes fit through two-dimensional holes. The selected object is dropped in a box and can fall through one of two slots; a triangle slot, whose shape matches the triangular sides of all the objects, or a square slot, whose shape matches the square sides of the objects. The shape of the side of an object which faces down determines which slot an object falls through. For simplicity, we assume that each side of an object has equal probability of facing down. The laws governing this device are crudely analogous to the process of geometric projection in vision; thus, we refer to the "output" of this stage of the coding device (which slot an object falls through) as an object's silhouette. The second stage of the coder sends a color signal to the receiver based on the object's silhouette: red if the silhouette is a triangle, and blue if it is square. The final component of the system is a receiver, which we will take to be a photodetector which is sensitive to the wavelength of light it absorbs. The photodetector signals whether a red or blue light is received.

As a first step in our analysis of the information provided by the signals in this system, let us ignore the color coding and treat the silhouettes as the received signal. The problem for a receiver detecting these silhouettes is that they do not uniquely determine the shapes of the objects selected by the transmitter, since, unlike the child's toy, two of the objects (the pyramid and the prism) can fall through either of the two slots. For a given silhouette, therefore, there is more than one possible message which could have given rise to the silhouette, and the information provided by the silhouette is ambiguous and probabilistic. The information is characterized by the posterior function, $p(\mathbf{S} \mid \mathbf{I}) = p(\textbf{object} \mid \textbf{silhouette})$, where **object** is a random variable specifying the object chosen by the transmitter, and **silhouette** is a random variable specifying the silhouette received as a signal. For now, we are assuming a noiseless signal, so the posterior function is determined by the coding scheme and the prior distribution of objects. Having specified the prior, we turn to a probabilistic specification of the coding scheme.

	Likelihood function $p(\textbf{silhouette} \mid \textbf{object})$			
	Tetrahedron	Pyramid	Prism	Cube
triangle	1.0	0.8	0.4	0.0
square	0.0	0.2	0.6	1.0

Table 0.3 *For a given silhouette, the sum of the likelihood function taken over the objects (within a row) is not 1, reflecting the fact that fixing the signal does not make the likelihood function a probability distribution on set of possible messages. Fixing the message, however, does make it a probability distribution on the set of possible signals, as seen by summing within a column.*

We use the likelihood function, $p(\mathbf{I} \mid \mathbf{S})$, to model the probabilistic properties of the coding scheme. Since we have assumed that each side of an object, when dropped in our imaginary coding box, has an equal probability of facing down, the probability that an object will be coded as a given silhouette is simply the proportion of sides of the object which have that silhouette's shape. A simple calculation gives the probabilities shown in table 0.3.

To obtain the posterior function, we combine the likelihood function and the prior distribution using Bayes' rule, giving

$$p(\textbf{object} \mid \textbf{silhouette}) \propto p(\textbf{silhouette} \mid \textbf{object})\,p(\textbf{object}). \qquad (0.3)$$

Table 0.4 summarizes the results of calculating the posterior function for all possible signals and messages in our example. While both silhouettes allow three possible interpretations of the object selected by the transmitter, a receiver which had to choose one and be correct as often as possible would choose the object with the highest probability conditional on the silhouette received: for a triangle, it would be the pyramid, and for the square, it would be the prism.

We now turn to a consideration of the effects of noise on the posterior and consider the full example system, including the color coder and the photodetector receiver. In vision, we do not directly receive information about the geometrical shape of objects, rather, the signal received by the retina is a more indirectly coded form of the shape information than is given by silhouettes. In a similar way, the transmitter in our full example codes objects in the form of the color of light it transmits. If there is no noise in the coding or in the transduction of light by the photodetector, the posterior for objects conditional on the color signal is equivalent to the one derived for a silhouette signal, with red replacing triangle, and blue replacing square. Suppose, however, that noise is added to the signal, either in the coder or in the photodetector,

Posterior distribution $p(\mathbf{object} \mid \mathbf{silhouette})$		
	Triangle	Square
tetrahedron	0.2	0.0
pyramid	0.48	0.12
prism	0.32	0.48
cube	0.0	0.4

Table 0.4 *For a given silhouette, the sum of the posterior function over the different objects (within a column) is 1, reflecting the fact that fixing the signal, makes the posterior a probability distribution defined over the set of possible messages.*

so that the mapping from silhouettes to received color signals is not one-to-one. We then need to compute a different likelihood function, $p(\mathbf{color} \mid \mathbf{object})$, and hence a different posterior, $p(\mathbf{object} \mid \mathbf{color})$. Assuming the color noise is independent of the process used to select which silhouette matches an object, we can write the likelihood function as

$$
\begin{aligned}
p(\mathbf{color} \mid \mathbf{object}) = \; & p(\mathbf{color} \mid \mathbf{silhouette} = \text{triangle}) \\
& \times \; p(\mathbf{silhouette} = \text{triangle} \mid \mathbf{object}) \\
& + \; p(\mathbf{color} \mid \mathbf{silhouette} = \text{square}) \\
& \times \; p(\mathbf{silhouette} = \text{square} \mid \mathbf{object}), \quad (0.4)
\end{aligned}
$$

where $p(\mathbf{color} \mid \mathbf{silhouette})$ is determined by the color noise. Values of $p(\mathbf{color} \mid \mathbf{silhouette})$ for the noise-free case and an example noisy case are tabulated in table 0.5. If we use the likelihood function obtained in the noisy example, we obtain the posterior function shown in table 0.6. Note that the noise has the effect of making the posterior distribution more similar to the prior distribution of shapes. This reflects the loss of reliability of the signal's information induced by the addition of noise. In the limit, as the noise increases, the posterior distribution approaches the prior distribution showed in table 0.2. In the example we have described, the noise has also changed the peaks of one of the distributions, so that the most likely interpretations given our example noisy color signals are different from those obtained with noise-free data (in fact the most likely interpretations given either signal are the same, suggesting that a receiver which uses the strategy of picking the most likely interpretation will do no better with the information provided by the received signal than without).

Noise-free color signal p(**color** | **silhouette**)		
	Triangle	Square
red	1.0	0.0
white	0.0	1.0

Noisy color signal p(**color** | **silhouette**)		
	Triangle	Square
red	0.6	0.4
white	0.4	0.6

Table 0.5.

Posterior function for noisy color signal p(**object** | **color**)		
	Red	White
tetrahedron	0.12	0.08
pyramid	0.336	0.264
prism	0.384	0.416
cube	0.16	0.24

Table 0.6.

The example illustrates a number of points about the problem of visual perception and the Bayesian approach to characterizing visual information. First, the form of the received signal is not simply related to the form of the messages. Image intensities are a coded form of what we "see" and are as qualitatively different from scene properties as the color signal was from the nature of the objects in our example. Of course, in our example the mapping from messages to signals was quite simple. The same is not true for the mapping from scene properties to image data. Second, both the lack of a one-to-one inverse mapping from images back to scene properties and the presence of image noise make the information provided by images about scenes inherently probabilistic. In our example, not only could different objects fit through different slots in the coder, but noise further increased the ambiguity of the received color signal. If we had included a stellate shaped object in the message set and a similarly shaped slot in the coder, that particular silhouette would provide unambiguous information about the object chosen as a message (since only the stellate-shaped object would fall through it). The addition of noise would impose some ambiguity on the final color signal. While searching for such invariants is a good research strategy, we should not be surprised to find that few exist in images. Finally, just as in the example, the prior structure of the environment plays a crucial role in determining the information provided by images about scene properties. In the example, treating the likelihood function as a characterization of signal information would lead an observer to make irrational inferences (compare tables 0.3 and 0.6) in that the maxima of the likelihood function occur for different objects than the maxima of the posterior distributions.

0.4 Perception as unconscious inference

0.4.1 Bayesian models of inference

We have described the Bayesian framework as a language for specifying what information images provide about the world. From this perspective, the framework provides a way to objectively specify the information content of images for the estimation of scene properties or more generally for the performance of perceptual tasks. Consideration of human perceptual performance, however, generally suggests a somewhat different perspective; namely, the characterization of perception as a process of unconscious inference, as suggested by Helmholtz (1925). From this point of view, Bayesian probability provides a normative model for how prior knowledge should be combined with sensory data to make inferences about the world[†]. Specification of the functions $p(\mathbf{I} \mid \mathbf{S})$ and $p(\mathbf{S})$ form the basis of what would be an "ideal" perceptual inference device. One more element is needed, however, to completely model an inference process: a specification of a decision rule for selecting an estimate of $\mathbf{S}$ based on $p(\mathbf{S} \mid \mathbf{I})$. Common rules applied in the literature include selection of the peak of the distribution (Maximum A-Posteriori, or MAP, estimation) or selection of the mean of the distribution (Minimum Mean Squared-Error, or MMSE, estimation). More general decision rules can be incorporated using cost functions to weight the relative cost of making errors in an inference (see chapter 5, by Yuille & Bülthoff, and chapter 9, by Freeman). A complete functional model of an ideal perceptual inference device, then, consists of a model of the information in images, as characterized by $p(\mathbf{S} \mid \mathbf{I})$, and a model of the decision rule to be applied to this function to make inferences.

We make the jump from building ideal inference devices to modeling human perception by recognizing that one can treat the human visual system as making perceptual inferences on an implicitly assumed model of $p(\mathbf{S} \mid \mathbf{I})$, which we will refer to as $p_h(\mathbf{S} \mid \mathbf{I})$ (Kersten, 1990; Knill & Kersten, 1991). This model incorporates assumptions about image formation and the structure of scenes in our environment. In some sense, one could say that a model of $p_h(\mathbf{S} \mid \mathbf{I})$ (along with a model of perceptual decision rules) characterizes the world to which the human visual system

---

[†] Classical Bayesian inference in the sciences interprets probabilities as degrees of belief. Jaynes (1986) has shown that given some elementary and reasonable assumptions about how degrees of belief should be formulated, one arrives at the probabilistic calculus, or a class of monotonic derivatives of the calculus, as the appropriate way to combine information to modify degrees of belief.

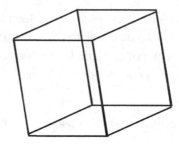

Fig. 0.3 The Necker cube. The line drawing can appear in one of two orientations, depending on which face is seen in front, however, it always appears as a cube.

is "tuned" and in which humans would be ideal perceptual inference makers (see chapter 6, by Knill *et al.*). To demonstrate this, consider the example of the previous section, and assume the presence of an observer viewing the outputs of the light. Our hypothetical observer might implicitly (and incorrectly) assume that each of the four objects was equally likely to fall into the shape sorter. this would lead the observer to "perceive" the shape of objects based on a posterior function which has the same form as the likelihood function (see table 0.3), leading to more mistakes than if the observer assumed the correct prior.

Terms like prior knowledge and inference suggest to many people the view that perception is strongly influenced by cognitive factors. We do not mean to do so here. While we readily acknowledge the possibility of cognitive effects on perception, this is not what we mean in our conception of perception as inference. Much of what we refer to as prior knowledge may be built into low-level, automatic perceptual processes which do not have access to our cognitive database of explicit knowledge about the world. For example, in some contexts, pior knowledge about the world can be implicitly built into relatively simple filters for the estimation of scene properties (Kersten *et al.*, 1987; Knill & Kersten, 1990). More generally, work in neural networks has shown that many network models can be conceived of as particular implementations of Bayesian inference (Golden, 1988; MacKay, 1991). The prior knowledge in these cases is "represented" by the connection strength between cooperative computational elements.

The Necker cube provides a simple example of a probabilistic inference made by the human visual system (see figure 0.3) which is classically "perceptual" and automatic. Though often used to illustrate the bistability of some percepts, the more impressive phenomenon is the obvious one – that we see it as a cube at all. Consideration of the ambiguity imposed by mapping a three-dimensional object onto two dimensions shows that an infinite number of possible polyhedral shapes could have given rise to an image of a Necker cube (just as multiple objects could fall through the square slot in our toy example). The visual system selects as its estimate of the shape the most symmetric of the possibilities – a cube. As simple as it is, this is an impressive demonstration of the visual system's use of prior constraints on object shape (the nature of the prior constraints needed for such a percept to be accurate is discussed in chapter 3, by Richards *et al.*).

0.4.2 *Bayesian theories and levels of explanation*

The information processing approach to modeling perceptual inference typically leads to theories about perceptual *process*; that is, about the architecture and algorithms of the system which makes the inferences. This is true despite Marr's prescription to build computational theories for perceptual problems before modeling the processes which implement the theories (Marr, 1982). One reason for this state of affairs is that most researchers have not had available a formal framework for building computational theories with enough specificity to usefully constrain models of process (more so, that is, than informal statements of principles). Moreover, there is some confusion about the nature of what comprises a computational theory, the term itself being rather vague. Marr was unclear as to whether a computational theory should characterize the problems posed to a perceiving organism or some aspects of an organism's solution to these problems. At various times he seems to have meant it to characterize one or the other (or both). In considering the Bayesian approach as a framework for building what we think of as computational theories, we have found that a new conceptualization of Marr's three-fold heirarchy of levels of explanation (computational / algorithmic / implementation) has naturally emerged which resolves the ambiguity. This is summarized in figure 0.4. In essence, we split the computational level into two components: theories of information and rational theories of inference[†]. The former can be thought of as characterizing the computational problems posed to an observer, while the latter characterizes the computational aspects of an observer's solution to these problems. Below the two computational levels is the impementation level of explanation, which describe properties of the processeses of perception. For our purposes here, we treat this as one level, though it may usefully be partitioned into more, as Marr did. What is notable about the formulation is that the Bayesian framework applies both to the information level of description and to the rational level. By providing a common language for building theories of both types, the framework supports a strong interaction between theoretical analyses of information and the process of modeling human perceptual behavior. Just as importantly, it provides the formal tools with which to build theories at these levels without necessarily having to make recourse to lower levels of explanation. Ultimately, the levels must interact and constrain

[†] We have borrowed the term "rational" to characterize Bayesian theories of inference from a related proposal by Anderson (1991) in the context of explaining cognitive function

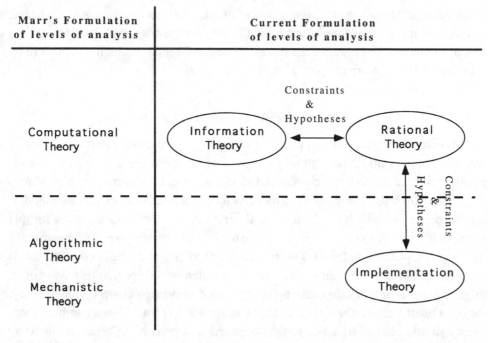

Fig. 0.4 The discussion in the text suggests that Marr's computational level of theory for visual processes really consists of two parallel modes of explanation: theories of the information available for perception and rational theories of the inferences made by the visual system in the course of perception. The Bayesian framework provides the structure for building both types of theory, with the addition of decision criteria for models of inference. Theories of information constrain theories of inference, because they limit the reliability with which inferences can be made. Both types of theories can suggest hypotheses for the other, since, on the one hand, the information and constraints in our world are always available to the visual system to use, and on the other hand, information and constraints employed by the visual system are likely to have evolved to match those available in the world. While we have focused on the two upper levels of theory-building, theories at the implementation level clearly interact strongly with those at the level of rational inference, mutually constraining and informing one another.

one another, but it is important for the development of perceptual models that we be able to build predictive theories of human performance at the rational level. This level suggests its own questions and modes of explanation which cannot be easily characterized at other levels.

0.5 Conclusions

A number of arguments support using the Bayesian framework for modeling perception. First, it provides a normative framework within which to formulate objective theories of the information provided by images in our world for different perceptual tasks[†].The form of the function $p(\mathbf{S}|\mathbf{I})$ which describes our environment provides a theoretical absolute limit on the reliability with which an observer can make perceptual inferences (Kersten, 1990). A function made up of strongly peaked posterior distributions, $p(\mathbf{S}|\mathbf{I} = I)$, supports inferences which are likely to be correct or to be made with small errors, while one composed of broad distributions does not. Secondly, formulation of computational models within the framework requires making explicit many assumptions which are often left implicit. It is, we feel, the natural framework in which to formulate computational descriptions of many problems. In particular, it distinguishes between functionally different aspects of the computational problems facing an observer: The nature of the uncertainty in the data for performing a perceptual task and the prior constraints on scene structure which serve to reduce this uncertainty. Thirdly, the framework provides a means for formalizing experimentally testable hypotheses about functional aspects of human perceptual processing. Building objective theories of the information available for perception and theories of human perceptual performance within the same framework supports a strong degree of cooperation between formal, mathematical analyses and psychophysical experimentation.

We have attempted to introduce the main concepts of a Bayesian framework for modeling perception and have highlighted three of its features: that it provides the tools for a full mathematical description of the problems of perception, that these same tools may be used to build functional models of perceptual performance, and that it suggests a new conceptualization of perception which provides a novel structure for asking questions about perceptual function. We have argued for the usefulness of the framework as a paradigm for investigating and modeling human perception, but have done so at a fairly abstract level, never actually discussing particular applications of the approach to real problems in perception. The success or failure of such applications will be the ultimate test of the framework's usefulness and will help define the domains to which it is best suited. We also have not elucidated many of the specific problems which arise from considering perception within a Bayesian framework. The remaining chapters of the book flesh out these gaps and should leave the reader with a greater appreciation and understanding of the approach and its application to visual perception.

[†] Jaynes (1986) has shown that some basic qualitative criteria on how measures of belief are enough to derive the probabilistic calculus (or some monotonic derivative of it) as the appropriate mechanism for combining and manipulating degrees of belief. We refer the reader to his paper for a proof and discussion and simply not that the criteria he proposes for degrees of belief are exactly those which one would want to apply to measures of information.

References

Anderson, J.R. (1991). The adaptive nature of human categorization, *Psychological Review*, **98**, 409-429.

Bennett, B.M., Hoffman, D.D. & Prakash, C. (1989). *Observer Mechanics*. London: Academic Press.

Bennett, B.M., Hoffman, D.D., Nicola, J.E. & Prakash, C. (1989). Structure from two orthographic views of rigid motion, *Journal of the Optical Society of America, A*, **6**, no. 7, 1052-1069.

Bolle, R.M. & Cooper, D.B. (1984). Bayesian recognition of local 3-D shape by approximating image intensity functions with quadric polynomials, *IEEE Trans. PAMI*, **PAMI-6**, 418-429.

Clark, J.J. & Yuille, A.L. (1990). *Data Fusion for Sensory Information Processing Systems*. Kluwer Academic Press.

Geman, S. & Geman, D. (1984) Stochastic relaxation, Gibbs distributions, and the Bayesian restoration of images, *IEEE Trans. PAMI*, 721-741.

Golden, R. (1988). A unified framework for connectionist systems, *Biological Cybernetics*, **59**, 109-120.

Grenander, U. (1976-1981). *Lectures in Pattern Theory I, II and III: Pattern Analysis, Pattern Synthesis and Regular Structures*. Springer-Verlag.

Helmholtz, H. (1925). *Physiological Optics, Vol. III: The Perceptions of Vision (J. P. Southall, Trans.)*. Optical Society of America, Rochester, NY. (Original publication in 1910).

Ickeuchi, K. & Horn, B.K.P. (1981). Numerical shape from shading and occluding boundaries, *Artificial Intelligence*, **17**, 141-184.

Ittleson, W.H. (1960). *Visual Space Perception*. New York: Springer Publishing Co.

Jaynes, E.T. (1986). Bayesian methods: general background. In *Maximum Entropy and Bayesian Methods in Applied Statistics*, ed. J.H. Justice. Cambridge University Press.

Jepson, A. & Richards, W. (1993). What is a percept? *Dept. of Computer Science Tech. Report RBCV-TR-93-43*.

Julesz, B. (1971). *Foundations of Cyclopean Perception*. University of Chicago Press.

Kersten, D. (1990). Statistical limits to image understanding. In *Vision: Coding and Efficiency*, ed. C. Blakemore. Cambridge Univ. Press.

Kersten, D., O'Toole, A.J., Sereno, M., Knill, D.C. & Anderson, J. (1987). Associative learning of scene parameters from images, *Applied Optics*, **26**, 4999-5006.

Knill, D.C. & Kersten, D. (1990). Learning a near-optimal estimator for surface shape from shading, *Computer Vision, Graphics and image Processing*, **50**, 75-100.

Knill, D. & Kersten, D. (1991). Ideal perceptual observers for computation, psychophysics and neural networks. In *Vision and Visual Dysfunction, Vol. 14: Pattern Recognition by Man and Machine*, ed. R. Watt. New York: MacMillan Press.

Koenderink, J.J. & van Doorn, A.J. (1975). Invariant properties of the motion parallax field due to the movement of rigid bodies relative to an observer, *Optica Acta*, **22**, 773-791.

MacKay, D.J.C. (1991). A practical Bayesian framework for backpropagation networks, *Neural Computation*, 448-472.

Madarasmi, S., Kersten, D. & Pong, T. (1993). The computation of stereo disparity for transparent and opaque surfaces. In *Advances in Neural Information Processing*, ed. G.J. Giles, S.J. Hanson and J.D. Cowan. Morgan Kaufman.

Marr, D. (1982). *Vision: A Computational Investigation into the Human Representation and Processing of Visual Information*. New York: W.H. Freeman.

Marr, D. & Poggio, T. (1979). Cooperative computation of stereo disparity, *Science*, **194**, 283-287.

Marroquin, J.L., Mitter, S. & Poggio, T. (1985). Probabilistic solution of ill-posed problems in computational vision. In *Proceedings Image Understanding Workshop* ed. L. Baumann, pp. 293-309. McLean, VA: Scientific Applications International Corporation.

Szeliski, R. M. (1989). *Bayesian Modeling of Uncertainty in Low-Level Vision*. Norwell, MA: Kluwer Academic Press.

Ullman, S. (1979) The interpretation of structure from motion, *Proc. R. Soc. London, B*, **23**, 405-426.

Yuille, A.L. (1989). Energy functions for early vision and analog networks, *Biological Cybernetics*, **61**, 115-123.

Yuille, A.L. & Clark, J.J. (1993). Bayesian models, deformable templates and competitive priors. To appear in *Spatial Vision in Humans and Robots*, ed. L.Harris and M. Jenkins. Cambridge University Press, Cambridge.

Part one
Bayesian frameworks

1

Pattern theory: A unifying perspective

DAVID MUMFORD

Department of Mathematics, Harvard University

1.1 Introduction

The term "Pattern Theory" was introduced by Ulf Grenander in the 70's as a name for a field of applied mathematics which gave a theoretical setting for a large number of related ideas, techniques and results from fields such as computer vision, speech recognition, image and acoustic signal processing, pattern recognition and its statistical side, neural nets and parts of artificial intelligence (see Grenander, 1976-81). When I first began to study computer vision about ten years ago, I read parts of this book but did not really understand his insight. However, as I worked in the field, every time I felt I saw what was going on in a broader perspective or saw some theme which seemed to pull together the field as a whole, it turned out that this theme was part of what Grenander called pattern theory. It seems to me now that this is the right framework for these areas, and, as these fields have been growing explosively, the time is ripe for making an attempt to reexamine recent progress and try to make the ideas behind this unification better known. This article presents pattern theory from my point of view, which may be somewhat narrower than Grenander's, updated with recent examples involving interesting new mathematics.

The problem that Pattern Theory aims to solve, which I would like to call the 'Pattern Understanding Problem', may be described as follows:

the analysis of the patterns generated by the world in any modality, with all their naturally occurring complexity and ambiguity, with the goal of reconstructing the processes, objects and events that produced them and of predicting these patterns when they reoccur.

These patterns may occur in the signals generated by one of the basic animal senses. For example *vision* usually refers to the analysis of patterns detected in the electromagnetic signals of wavelengths 400-700 nm. incident at a point in space from different directions. *Hearing* refers to the analysis of the patterns present in the oscillations of 60-20,000 hertz in air pressure at a point in space as a function

25

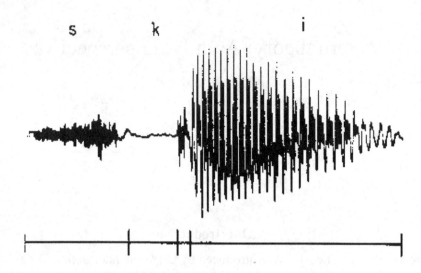

Fig. 1.1 Acoustic waveform for an utterance of the word *SKI*.

of time, both with and without human language. On the other hand, these patterns
may occur in the data presented to a higher processing stage, in so-called cognitive
thought. As an example, *medical expert systems* are concerned with the analysis of
the patterns in the symptoms, history and tests presented by a patient: this is a higher
level modality, but still one in which the world generates confusing but structured
data from which a doctor seeks to infer hidden processes and events. Finally, these
patterns may be temporal patterns occurring in a sequence of motor actions and the
resulting sensations, e.g. a sequence of complex signals 'move-feel-move-feel- etc.'
involving motor commands and the resulting tactile sensation in either an animal
or a robot.

Pattern Theory is one approach to solving this pattern understanding problem. It
contains three essential components which we shall detail in Sections 1.2, 1.3 and
1.4 below. These concern firstly the abstract mathematical setup in which we frame
the problem; secondly a hypothesis about the specific mathematical objects that
arise in natural pattern understanding problems; and thirdly a general architecture
for computing the solution.

Before launching into this description of pattern theory, we want to give two examples of simple sensory signals and the patterns that they exhibit. This will serve
to motivate and make more concrete the theory which follows. The first example
involves speech: Figure 1.1 shows the graph of the pressure $p(t)$ while the word
"SKI" is being pronounced. Note how the signal shows four distinct wave forms:
something close to white noise during the pronunciation of the sibilant 'S', then
silence followed by a burst which conveys the plosive 'K', then an extended nearly

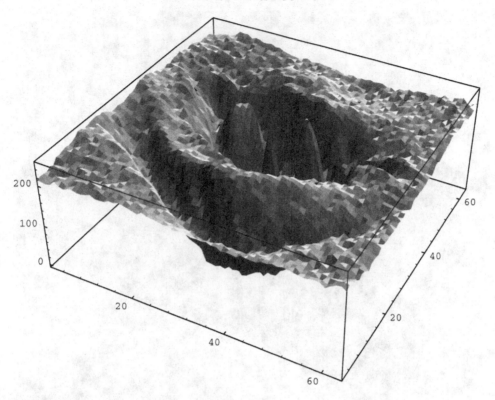

Fig. 1.2a Visual waveform for an image of an eye.

musical note for the vowel 'I'. The latter has a fundamental frequency corresponding to the vibration of the vocal cords, with many harmonics whose power peeks
around three higher frequencies, the formants. Finally, the amplitude of the whole
is modulated during the pronunciation of the word. In this example, the goal of
auditory signal processing is to identify these four wave forms, characterize each
in terms of its frequency power spectrum, its frequency and amplitude modulation,
and then, drawing on a memory of speech sounds, identify each wave form as being produced by the corresponding configurations of the speaker's vocal tract, and
finally label each with its identity as an english phoneme. In addition, one would
like to describe explicitly the stress, pitch and the quality of the speaker's voice,
using this later to help disambiguate the identity of the speaker and the intent of the
utterance.

Figure 1.2a shows the graph of the light intensity $I(x, y)$ of a picture of a human
eye: it would be hard to recognize this as an eye, but the black and white image
defined by the same function is shown in Figure 1.2b. Note again how the domain
of the signal is naturally decomposed into regions where I has different values or
different spatial frequency behavior: the pupil, the iris, the whites of the eyes, the

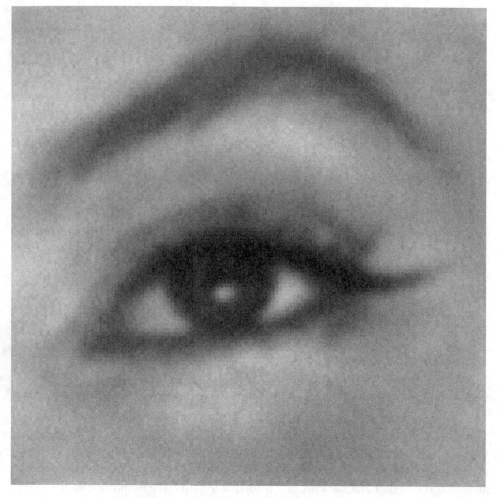

Fig. 1.2b Identical waveform presented using variable intensity.

lashes, eyebrows and skin. These six regions are the six types of visible surface in this image, characterized in real world terms by distinct albedo, texture and geometry. The goal of visual signal processing is again to describe this function of two variables as being built up from simpler signals on subdomains, on which it either varies slowly or is statistically regular, i.e. approximately stationary and hence to describe the distinct 3D visible surface patches. In other words, each surface patch is assumed to have an identifiable 'texture', which may be the result of its particular spatial power spectrum or may result from it being composed of some elementary units, called *textons*, which are repeated with various modifications. These modifications in particular include spatial distortion, contrast modulation and interaction with larger scale structures. This description of the signal may be computed either prior to or concurrent with a comparison of the signal with remembered eye shapes, which include a description of the expected range of variation of eyes, specific descriptions of the eyes of well-known people, etc.

Note that in both of these examples, something rather remarkable happened. The simplest description of the signal as an abstract function, e.g. having subdomains on which it is relatively homogeneous, leads naturally to a description of the true processes and objects that produced the signal. We will discuss this further below, in connection with the idea of 'minimum description length'.

In order to understand what the field of pattern theory is all about, it is necessary to begin by addressing a major misconception – namely that the whole problem is essentially trivial. The history of computer speech and image recognition projects, like the history of AI, is a long one of ambitious projects which attained their goals with carefully tailored artificial input but which failed as soon as more of the complexities of real world data were present. The source of this misconception, I believe, is our subjective impression of perceiving instantaneously and effortlessly the significance of the patterns in a signal, e.g. the word being spoken or which face is being seen. Many psychological experiments however have shown that what we perceive is not the true sensory signal, but a rational reconstruction of what the signal should be. This means that the messy ambiguous raw signal never makes it to our consciousness but gets overlaid with a clearly and precisely patterned version whose computation demands extensive use of memories, expectations and logic. An example of how misleading our impressions are is shown in Figure 1.3: the reader will instantly recognize that it is an image of an old man sitting on a park bench. But ask yourself – how did you know that? His face is almost totally obscure, with his hand merging with his nose; the most distinct shape is that of his hat, which by itself could be almost anything; even his jacket merges in many places with the background because of its creases and the way light strikes them, so no simple algorithm is going to trace its contour without getting lost. However, when you glance at the picture, in your mind's eye, you 'see' the face and its parts distinctly, the man's jacket is a perfectly clear coherent shape, whose creases in fact contribute to your perception of its 3-dimensional structure instead of confusing you. The ambiguities which must, in fact, have been present in the early stages of your processing of this image never become conscious because you have found an explanation of every peculiarity of the image, a match with remembered shapes and lighting effects. In fact, the problems of pattern theory are hard, and although major progress has been made in both speech and vision in the last 5 years, a robust solution has not been achieved!

Fig. 1.3 A challenge image for computers to recognize.

1.2 Mathematical formulation of the problem

To make the field of pattern theory precise, we need to formulate it mathematically. There are three parts to this which all appear in Grenander's work: the first is the description of the players in the field, the fundamental mathematical objects which appear in the pattern understanding problem. The second is to restrict the possible generality of these objects by using something about the nature of the world. This gives us a more circumscribed, more focussed set of problems to study. Finally, the goal of the field being the reconstruction of hidden facts about the world, we aim primarily for algorithms, not theorems, and the last part is the general framework for these algorithms. In this section, we look at the first part, the basic mathematical objects of pattern theory. This formulation of the pattern understanding problem is not unique to pattern theory. It has been introduced many times, e.g. in the hidden Markov models of speech understanding, in work on expert systems, in connectionist analyses of neural nets, etc.

There are two essentially equivalent formulations, one using Bayesian statistics and one using information theory. The statistical approach (see for instance D. Geman, 1991) is this: consider all possible signals $f(\mathbf{x})$ which may be perceived. These may be considered as elements of a space Ω_{obs} of functions $f : \mathcal{D} \to \mathcal{V}$. For instance, speech is defined by pressure $P : [t_1, t_2] \to \mathbf{R}_+$ as a function of time; color vision is defined by intensity I on a domain $\mathcal{D} \subset S^2$ of visible rays with values in the convex cone of colors $\mathcal{V}_{RGB} \subset \mathbf{R}^3$, or these functions may be sampled on a discrete subset of the above domains, or their values may be approximated to finite precision, etc. The first basic assumption of the statistical approach is that nature determines a probability p_{obs} on a suitable σ-algebra of subsets of Ω_{obs}, and that, in life, one observes random samples from this distribution. These signals, however, are highly structured as a result of their being produced by a world containing many processes, objects and events which don't appear explicitly in the signal. This means many more random variables are needed to describe the state of the world. Several chapters in this volume address this point. The second assumption is that the possible states w of the world form a second probability space Ω_{wld} and that there is a big probability distribution $p_{o,w}$ on $\Omega_{\text{obs}} \times \Omega_{\text{wld}}$ describing the probability of both observing f and the world being in state w. Then p_{obs} should be the marginal distribution of $p_{o,w}$ on Ω_{obs}. The mathematical problem, in this setup, is to infer the state of the world w, given the measurement f, and for this we may use Bayes's rule:

$$p(w|f) = \frac{p(f|w) \cdot p(w)}{p(f)} \tag{1.1}$$

leading to the *maximum a posteriori reconstruction of the state of the world*[†]:

$$\text{MAP estimate of } w = \arg\max_{w}[p(f|w) \cdot p(w)] \tag{1.2}$$

To use the statistical approach, therefore, we must construct the probability space $(\Omega_{\text{obs}} \times \Omega_{\text{wld}}, p_{o,w})$ and find algorithms to compute the MAP-estimate.

The information theoretic approach has its roots in work of Barlow (1961) (see also Rissanen, 1989). Assume D and V, hence Ω_{obs} are finite. The idea is that instead of writing out any particular perceptual signal f in raw form as a table of values, we seek a method of encoding f which minimizes its expected length in bits: i.e. we take advantage of the patterns possessed by most f to encode them in a compressed form. We consider coding schemes which involve choosing various

---

[†] Other statistical procedures can be used for estimating the state of the world: e.g. taking the mean of various world variables in the posterior distribution, or minimum risk estimates, etc.

auxiliary variables w and then encoding the particular f using these w (e.g. w might determine a specific typical signal f_w and we then need only to encode the deviation $(f - f_w)$). We write this:

$$\text{length}(\text{code}(f, w)) = \text{length}(\text{code}(w)) + \text{length}(\text{code}(f \text{ using } w)). \qquad (1.3)$$

The mathematical problem, in the information theoretic setup, is, for a given f, to find the w leading to the shortest encoding of f, and moreover, to find the encoding *scheme* leading to the shortest expected coding of all f's. This optimal choice of w is called the *minimum description length* or MDL estimate of w:

$$\text{MDL est. of } w = \arg\min_{w}[\text{len}(\text{code}(w)) + \text{len}(\text{code}(f \text{ using } w))]. \qquad (1.4)$$

Finding the optimal encoding scheme for all the signals of the world is obviously impractical and perhaps even contradictory (recall the problem of the finding the smallest integer not definable in less than twenty words!). What is really meant by MDL is that we seek some approximation to the optimal encoding, using coding schemes constrained in various ways[†]. Pattern theory proposes that there are quite specific kinds of encoding schemes which very often give good results and which may, therefore, be built into our thinking: we shall discuss these in the next section.

There is a close link between the Bayesian and the information-theoretic approaches which comes from Shannon's optimal coding theorem. This theorem states that given a class of signals f, the coding scheme for such signals for which a random signal has the smallest expected length satisfies:

$$\text{len}(\text{code}(f)) = -\log_2 p(f) \qquad (1.5)$$

(where fractional bit lengths are achieved by actually coding several f's at once, and doing this the LHS gets asymptotically close to the RHS when longer and longer sequences of signals are encoded at once). We may apply Shannon's theorem both to encoding w and to encoding f, given w. For these encodings $\text{len}(\text{code}(w) = -\log_2 p(w)$ and $\text{len}(\text{code}(f \text{ using } w) = -\log_2 p(f|w)$. Therefore, taking $\log_2$ of equation (1.2), we get equation (1.4) and find that the MAP estimate of w is the same as the MDL estimate.

There is an additional wrinkle in the link between the two approaches. Why shouldn't the search for optimal encodings of world signals lead you to odd combinatorial coding schemes which have nothing to do with what is actually happening in the world? In the previous paragraph, we have assumed that the encoding scheme for f was based on encoding the true world variables w and using them to encode

---

[†] One could argue that the hypothesis of vengeful sky gods with human emotions was an early MDL hypothesis for the deeper processes of the world, and that modern science only bettered its description length when people sought to describe the quantitative signals of the world with more bits and with much larger samples including those outliers which we call 'experiments'.

f. But one can imagine discovering some strange numerology (like Kepler's hypothesis for spacing the orbits of the planets via the inscribed and circumscribed spheres of the platonic polyhedra) which gave a concise description of some class of signals or measurements but had nothing to do with the true objects or processes of the world. This does not seem to happen in real life! We encountered an example of this in Section 1.1 where we noticed that finding time intervals in which a speech signal had a nearly constant spectrogram, hence was concisely codable, also gave us the time intervals in which the mouth of the speaker was in a particular position, i.e. a specific phoneme was being articulated. Similarly, finding parts of images where the texture was nearly constant usually gives coherent 3D surface patches. In fact, it seems that the search for short encodings leads you *automatically, without prior knowledge of the world* to the same hidden variables on which the Bayesian theory is based. Insofar as this can be relied on, the information-theoretic approach has the great advantage over the Bayesian approach that it does not require that you have a prior knowledge of the physics, chemistry, biology, sociology, etc. of the world, but gives you a way of discovering these facts.

A very simple example may be useful here. Suppose five different bird songs are heard regularly in your back yard. You can assign a short distinctive code to each such song, so that instead of having to remember the whole song from scratch each time, you just say to yourself something like "Aha, song #3 again". Note that in doing so, you have automatically learned a world variable at the same time: the number or code you use for each song is, in effect, a name for a species, and you have rediscovered part of Linnaean biology. Moreover, if one bird is the most frequent singer, you will probably use the shortest code, e.g. "song #1", for that bird. In this way, you are also learning the probability of different values for the variable "song #x", as in Shannon's fundamental theorem. In Section 1.5.4, we will give a more extended example of how this works.

1.3 Four universal transformations of perceptual signals

The above formulation of the pattern understanding problem provides a framework in which to analyze signals, but it says nothing about the nature of the patterns which are to be expected, what distortions, complexities and ambiguities are to be expected, hence what sorts of probability spaces Ω_{obs} are we likely to encounter, how shall we encode them, etc. What gives the theory its characteristic flavor is the hypothesis that the world does not have an infinite repertoire of different tricks which it uses to disguise what is going on. Consider the coding schemes used by engineers for the transmission of electrical signals: they use a small number of well-defined transformations such as AM and FM encoding, pulse coding, etc. to convert information into a signal which can be efficiently communicated. Analogous to this, the world produces sound to be heard, light to be seen, surfaces to be felt, etc. which are all, in various ways, reflections of its structure. (See chapter 2 by Jepson *et al.* for an elaboration.) We may think of these signals as the productions of a particularly perverse engineer, who sets us the problem of decoding this message, e.g. of recognizing a friend's face or estimating the trajectory of oncoming traffic, etc. The second contention of pattern theory is that such signals are derived from the world by *four types of transformations or deformations*, which occur again and again in different guises. In the terminology of Grenander (1976) simple unambiguous signals from the world are referred to as *pure images* and the transformations on them are called *deformations*, which produce the actually observed perceptual signals which he called *deformed images*. The bad news is that these four transformations produce much more complex effects than the coding schemes of engineers, hence the difficulty of decoding them by the standard tricks of electrical engineering. The good news is that these transformations are not arbitrary recursive operations which produce unlearnable complexity.

A very similar situation occurs in the study of the syntax of languages. In the formal study of the learnability of the syntax of language, Gold's theorem gives very strong restrictions on what languages can be learned if their syntax is at all general (see Osherson & Weinstein, 1984, for an excellent exposition). In contrast, Chomsky (1981) has suggested that all languages have essentially the same syntax, with individual languages differing only by the setting of a small number of parameters. In fact, transformational grammar has a very similar structure to pattern theory: each sentence has an underlying deep structure, analogous to Grenander's pure images. It is subjected to a restricted set of transformations, analogous to Grenander's deformations. And finally one observes the spoken surface form of the sentence, analogous to Grenander's deformed image.

The study of perceptual signals suggests a small number of special transformations, or deformations, that the languages in which perceptual signals speak are of very special types. The exact set of these is not completely clear at this point and my choices are not exactly the same as Grenander's. But to make progress, we must make some hypothesis and so I give here a set of four transformations which seem to me to suffice. These are:

(i) *Noise and blur.* These effects are the bread and butter of standard signal processing, caused for instance by sampling error, background noise and imperfections in your measuring instrument such as imperfect lenses, veins in front of the retina, dust and rust. A typical form of this transformation is given by the formula:

$$I \rightarrow (I * \sigma)(x_i) + n_i \qquad (1.6)$$

where σ is a blurring kernel, x_i are the points where the signal is sampled and n_i is some kind of additive noise, e.g. Gaussian, but of course much more complex formulae are possible. Especially significant is that Gaussian noise is usually a poor model of the noise effects, for example when the noise is caused by finer detail which is not being resolved. Rosenfeld calls such an *n clutter*, which conveys what it often represents. The key feature of noise, in whatever guise, is that it has no significant remaining patterns, hence cannot be compressed significantly by recoding. These transformations are part of what Grenander calls *changes in contrast*. When they are present, the unblurred noiseless I should be one of the variables w as getting rid of noise and blur reveals the hidden processes of the world more clearly.

(ii) *Superposition.* Signals typically can be decomposed into simpler components. Fourier analysis is the best studied example of this, in which a signal is written as a linear combination of sinusoidal functions. But the whole development of wavelets has shown that there are many other such expansions, appropriate for particular classes of signals. Most such superpositions have the property that the various components have different scales, but some may combine several on the same scale (e.g. one can superimpose 2D Gabor functions with different orientations; for another example, faces with arbitrary illumination can be approximated by the superposition of about half a dozen 'eigenfaces'.) Most such superpositions are linear, but some may be more complex (e.g. in amplitude modulation, a low frequency signal plus a large enough positive constant is multiplied by a high frequency 'carrier'). In images, local properties such as sharp edges and texture details may be constructed by adding Gabor functions or model step edges with small support, while global properties like slowly varying shading or large shapes may be obtained by adding slowly varying functions with large support. In speech, information is conveyed by the highest frequency formants, by the lower frequency vibration of the vocal cords and the even slower modulation of stress. A typical form of this transformation is given by the formula:

$$I_1, \cdots, I_n \longrightarrow (I_1 + \cdots + I_n) \quad \text{or} \quad \sigma(I_1, \cdots, I_n) \tag{1.7}$$

where $I_1, \cdots, I_n$ represent component signals often in disjoint frequency bands, which can be combined either additively or by some more complex rule σ. The individual components I_k of I should be included in the variables w.

(iii) *Domain warping.* Two signals generated by the same object or event in different contexts typically differ because of expansions or contractions of their domains, possibly at varying rates: phonemes may be pronounced faster or slower, the image of a face is distorted by varying expression and viewing angle. In speech, this is called 'time warping' and in vision, this is modeled by 'flexible templates'. In both cases, a diffeomorphism of the domain of the signal brings the variants much closer to each other, so that this transformation is given by:

$$I \longrightarrow (I \circ \psi) \tag{1.8}$$

where ψ represents a diffeomorphism of the domain of I. These transformations are what Grenander calls *background deformations*. The diffeomorphism ψ should be one of the variables w.

(iv) *Interruptions.* Natural signals are usually analyzed best after being broken up into pieces consisting of their restrictions to subdomains. This is because the world itself is made up of many objects and events and different parts of the signal are caused by different objects or events. For instance, an image may show different objects partially occluding each other at their edges, as in Figure 1.3 where the old man is an object which occludes part of the park bench or as in a tiger seen behind a fragmented foreground of occluding leaves. In speech, the phonemes naturally break up the signal and, on a larger scale, one speaker or unexpected sound may interrupt another. Such a transformation is given by a formula like:

$$I_1, I_2 \longrightarrow (I_1|_{D'}, I_2|_{D-D'}) \tag{1.9}$$

where I_2 represents the background signal which is interrupted by the signal I_1 on a part D' of its domain D, (or I_2 may only be defined on $D - D'$). This type of deformation is called *incomplete observations* by Grenander. The components I_k and the domain D' should be included in the variables w.

What makes pattern theory hard is not that any of the above transformations are that hard to detect and decode in isolation, but rather that all four of them tend to coexist, and then the decoding becomes hard.

1.4 Pattern analysis requires pattern synthesis

Taking the Bayesian definition of the objects of pattern theory, we note that the probability distribution $(\Omega_{\text{obs}} \times \Omega_{\text{wld}}, p_{o,w})$ allows you to do two things. On the one hand, we can use it to define the MAP-estimate of the state of the world; but we can also sample from it, possibly fixing some of the world variables w, using this distribution to construct sample signals f generated by various classes of objects or events. A good test of whether your prior has captured all the patterns in some class of signals is to see if these samples are good imitations of life. For this reason, Grenander's idea was that the analysis of the patterns in a signal and the synthesis of these signals are inseparable problems, using a common probabilistic model: computer vision should not be separated from computer graphics, nor speech recognition from speech generation.

Many of the early algorithms in pattern recognition were purely *bottom-up*. For example, one class of algorithms started with a signal, computed a vector of 'features', numerical quantities thought to be the essential attributes of the signal, and then compared these feature vectors with those expected for signals in various categories. This was used to classify images of alpha-numeric characters or phonemes for instance. Such algorithms give no way of reversing the process, of generating typical signals. The problem these algorithms encountered was that they had no way of dealing with anything unexpected, such as a smudge on the paper partially obscuring a character, or a cough in the middle of speech. These algorithms did

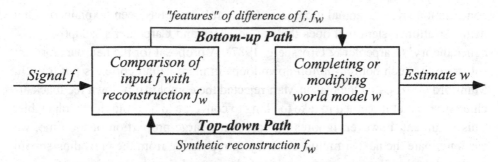

Fig. 1.4 The fundamental architecture of pattern theory.

not say what signals were expected, only what distinguished typical signals in each category.

In contrast, a second class of algorithms works by actively reconstructing the signal being analyzed. In addition to the bottom-up stage, there is a *top-down* stage in which a signal with the detected properties is synthesized and compared to the present input signal. What needs to be checked is whether the input signal agrees with the synthesized signal to within normal tolerances, or whether the residual is so great that the input has not been correctly or fully analyzed. This architecture is especially important for dealing with the fourth type of transformation: interruptions. When these are present, the features of the two parts of the signal get confused. Only when the obscuring signal is explicitly labelled and removed, can the features of the background signal be computed. We may describe this top-down stage as 'pattern reconstruction' in distinction to the bottom-up purely pattern recognition stage. A flow chart for such algorithms is shown in Figure 1.4.

The question of whether the correct interpretation of real world signals can be solved by a purely bottom-up algorithm, or whether it requires an iterative bottom-up/top-down architecture has been widely debated for a long time. The first person, to my knowledge, to introduce the above type of iterative architecture, was Donald MacKay (1956). On the other hand, Marr was a strong believer in the purely feedforward architecture, claiming that one needed merely to develop better algorithms to deal with things like interruptions in a purely feedforward way. A strong argument for the necessity of a top-down stage for the recognition of heavily degraded signals, such as faces in deep shadow, is given in Cavanagh (1991). Neural net theory has gone in both directions: while 'back propagation' nets categorize in an exclusively bottom-up manner (only using feedback in their learning phase), the 'attractive neural nets' with symmetric connections (Hopfield, 1982; D. Amit, 1989) seek not merely to categorize but also to construct the prototype ideal version of the category by a kind of pattern completion which they call 'associative memory'. What these nets do not do is to go back and attempt to compare this reconstruction with the actual input to see if the full input has been 'explained'. One demonstration system that does this is Grossberg and Carpenter's 'adaptive resonance theory' (Carpenter & Grossberg, 1987). A proposal for the neuroanatomical substrate for such bottom-up/top-down loops in mammalian cortex is put forth in Mumford (1991-92). One reason Marr rejected the complex top-down feedback architecture is that it seemed to take too long to converge to be biologically plausible. This argument, however, ignores the fact that a large proportion of the time, we can anticipate the next stimulus, either by extrapolating from the preceding stream of stimuli or by drawing on memories of shapes and sounds. In this situation, the top-down pathway may actively synthesize a guess for the next stimulus even before it arrives, and convergence is fast unless something totally unexpected happens.

The third part of our definition of pattern theory is the hypothesis that no practical feedforward algorithm exists for computing the most likely values of the world variables w from signals f. But that if your algorithm explicitly models the generation process, starting with a guess for w (or a set of guesses), then generating an f_w, then deforming w, combining and extending these guesses, you can solve the problem of computing the most likely w in a reasonable time.

1.5 Examples

In this section, we want to present several examples of interesting mathematics which have come out of pattern theory, in attempting to come to grips with one or another of the above universal transformations. These examples are from vision because this is the field I know best, but many of these ideas are used in speech recognition too.

1.5.1 Pyramids and wavelets

The problem of detecting transformations of analyzing functions that convey information on more than one scale, has arisen in many disciplines. The classical method of separating additively combined scales is, of course, Fourier analysis. But what is usually required is to analyze a function locally simultaneously in its original domain _and_ in the domain of its Fourier transform, and Fourier analysis does not do this. In vision, moving closer or farther from an object by a factor σ changes the image $I(x, y)$ of the object into the new image $I(\sigma x, \sigma y)$, thus any feature which occurs on one scale in one image is equally likely to occur at any other scale in a second image. In computer vision, at least as far back as the early 70's, this problem led to the idea of analyzing an image by means of a 'pyramid', e.g. Uhr, 1972; Rosenfeld & Thurston, 1971. In its original incarnation, the main idea was to compute a series of progressively coarser resolution images by blurring and resampling, e.g. a set of

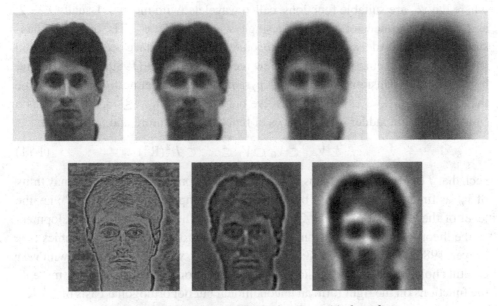

Fig. 1.5 The Gaussian and Laplacian pyramids for a face.

$(2^n \times 2^n)$-pixel images, for $n = 10, 9, \ldots, 1$. Putting these together, the resulting data structure looks like an exponentially tapering pyramid. Instead of running algorithms that took time proportional to the width of the image, one ran the algorithms up and down the pyramid, possibly in parallel at different pixels, in time proportional to log(width). Typical algorithms that were studied at this time are morphological ones, involving for instance linking and marking extended contours, which have nothing to do with filtering or linear expansions. The bottom layer of this so-called *Gaussian pyramid* held the original image, with both high and low frequency components, although it was used only to add local or high-frequency information.

In the early 80's, the idea of using the pyramid to separate band pass components of a signal and thus to expand that signal arose both in computer vision (Burt & Adelson, 1983) (where they *subtracted* successive layers of the Gaussian pyramid, producing what they called the *Laplacian pyramid*) and in petroleum geology (Grossman & Morlet, 1984). Figure 1.5 shows this Laplacian pyramid for a face: note that the high-frequency differences show textures and sharp edges, while the low frequency differences show large shapes. This work led directly to the idea of wavelets and wavelet expansions which now seem to be the most natural way to analyze a signal locally in both space and frequency. Mathematically, the idea is simply to expand an arbitrary function $f(\mathbf{x})$ of n variables as a sum:

$$f(\mathbf{x}) = \sum_{\text{scale } k \in Z} \left[\sum_{\vec{n} \in \text{lattice} L} \sum_{\text{fin.\# of } \alpha} a_{k,\vec{n},\alpha} \psi_\alpha(\lambda^k \mathbf{x} + \vec{n}) \right] \qquad (1.10)$$

where the ψ_α are suitable functions, called wavelets, with mean 0. Usually $\lambda = 2$, and, at least in dimension 1, there is a single α and wavelet ψ_α. The original expansions of Burt and Adelson, which are not quite of this form, have been reinvestigated from a more mathematical point of view recently in Mallat (1989). The basic link between the expansion in (1.10) and pyramids is this: define a space V_m to be the set of f's whose expansions involve only terms with $k \leq m$. This defines a 'multi-resolution ladder' of subspaces of functions with more and more detail:

$$\ldots \subset V_{-1} \subset V_0 \subset V_1 \subset \ldots \subset L^2(\mathbf{R}^n) \qquad (1.11)$$

such that $f(x) \longmapsto f(2x)$ maps V_m isomorphically onto V_{m+1}. Then one may think of V_m as functions which have been blurred and sampled at a spacing 2^{-m}: i.e. the level of the pyramid of $(2^m \times 2^m)$-pixel images. The mathematical development of the theory of these expansions is due especially to Meyer and Daubechies (see Meyer, 1986; Daubechies, 1988; Daubechies, 1990), who showed that (i) with *very* careful choice of ψ, this expansion is even an orthogonal one, (ii) for many more ψ, the functions on the right form an unconditional but not orthogonal basis of $L^2(\mathbf{R}^n)$ and (iii) for even more ψ, the functions on the right form a 'frame', a set of functions that spans $L^2(\mathbf{R}^n)$ and gives a canonical though non-unique expansion of every f.

From the perspective of pattern theory, we want to make two comments on the theory of wavelets. The first is that they fit in very naturally with the idea of minimum description length. Looked at from the point of view of optimal linear encoding of visual and speech signals (i.e. encoding by linear combinations of the function values), the idea of wavelet expansions is very appealing. This was pointed out early on by Burt and Adelson and data compression has been one of the main applications of wavelet theory ever since. Moreover, its further development leads beyond the classical idea of expanding a function in terms of a fixed basis to the idea of using a much larger spanning set which *oversamples* a function space and using suitably chosen subsets of this set in terms of which to expand or approximate the given function (see Coifman, Meyer & Wickerhouser, 1990, where *wavelet libraries* are introduced). Even though the data needed to describe this expansion or approximation is now both the particular subset chosen and the coefficients, this may be a more efficient code. If so, it should lead us to the correct variables w for describing the world (cf. Section 1.2): for example, expanding a speech signal using wavelet libraries, different bases would naturally be used in the time domains during which different phonemes were being pronounced – thus the break up of the signal into phonemes is discovered as a consequence of the search for efficient coding! It also appears that nature uses wavelet type encoding: there are severe size restrictions on the optic nerve connecting the retina with the higher parts of the brain and the visual signal is indeed transmitted using something like a Burt-Adelson wavelet expansion (Dowling, 1987).

The second point is that wavelets, even in their oversampled form, are still just the linear side of pyramid multi-scale analysis. In our description of multi-scale transformations of signals in Section 1.3, we pointed out that the two scales can be combined by multiplication or a more general function σ as well as by addition. To decode such a transformation, we need to perform some local non-linear step, such as rectification or auto-correlation, at each level of the pyramid before blurring and resampling. An even more challenging and non-linear extension is to a *multi-scale description of shapes*: e.g. subsets $S \subset \mathbf{R}^2$ with smooth boundary. The analog of blurring a signal is to let the boundary of S evolve by diffusion proportional to its curvature (see Gage & Hamilton, 1986; Grayson, 1987; Kimia, Tannenbaum & Zucker, 1993). Although there is no theory of this at present, one should certainly have a multi-scale description of S starting from its coarse diffused form – which is nearly round – and adding detailed features at each scale. In yet another direction, face recognition algorithms have been based on matching a crude blurry face template at a low resolution, and then refining this match, especially at key parts of the face like the eyes. This is the kind of general pyramid algorithm that Rosenfeld proposed many years ago (Rosenfeld & Thurston, 1971), many of which have been successfully implemented by Peter Burt and his group at the Sarnoff Laboratory (Burt & Adelson, 1983).

1.5.2 Segmentation as a free-boundary value problem

A quite different mathematical theory has arisen out of the search for algorithms to detect transformations of the 4th kind, interruptions. Evidence for an interruption or a discontinuity in a perceptual signal comes from two sources: the relative homogeneity of the signal on either side of the boundary and the presence of a large change in the signal across the boundary. One approach is to model this as a variational problem: assuming that a blurred and noisy signal f is defined on a domain $D \subset \mathbf{R}^n$, one seeks a set $\Gamma \subset D$ and a smoothed version g of f which is allowed to be discontinuous on Γ such that:

- g is as close as possible to f,
- g has the smallest possible gradient on $D - \Gamma$,
- Γ has the smallest possible $(n - 1)$-volume.

These conditions define a variational problem, namely to minimize the functional

$$E(g, \Gamma) = \mu^2 \int \cdots \int_D (f - g)^2 + \int \cdots \int_{D-\Gamma} \|\nabla g\|^2 + \nu|\Gamma| \qquad (1.12)$$

where μ and ν are suitable constants weighting the three terms and $|\Gamma|$ is the $(n-1)$-volume of Γ. The g minimizing E may be understood as the optimal piecewise smooth approximation to the quite general function f. In Grenander's terms, the function g is the pure image and f is the deformed image; I like to call g a *cartoon* for the signal f. The Γ minimizing E is a candidate for the boundaries of parts of the domain D of f where different objects or events are detected. Segmenting the domain of perceptual signals by such variational problems was proposed independently by S. and D.Geman and by A.Blake and A.Zisserman (see Geman & Geman, 1984, and Blake & Zisserman, 1987) for functions on discrete lattices, and was extended by Mumford & Shah (1989) to the continuous case. In the case of visual signals, the domain D is 2-dimensional and we want to decompose D into the parts on which different objects in the world are projected. When you reach the edge of an object as seen from the image plane, the signal f typically will be more or less discontinuous (depending on noise and blur and the lighting effects caused by the grazing rays emitted by the surface as it curves away from the viewer). An example of the solution of this variational problem is shown in Figure 1.6: Figure 1.6a is the original image of the eye, 1.6b shows cartoon g and 1.6c shows the boundaries Γ. This is a case where the algorithm succeeds in finding the 'correct' segmentation, but it doesn't always work so well. Figure 1.7 gives the same treatment as Figure 1.6, to the 'oldman' image. Note that the algorithm fails to find the perceptually correct segmentation in several ways: the man's face is connected to his black coat and the black bar of the bench and the highlights on the back of his coat are treated as separate objects. One reason is that the surfaces of objects are often textured, hence the signal they emit is only statistically homogeneous. More sophisticated variational problems are needed to segment textured objects (see below).

From a mathematical standpoint, it is important to know if this variational problem is well-posed. It has been proven that E has a minimum if Γ is allowed to be a closed rectifiable set of finite Hausdorff $(n-1)$-dimensional measure and g is taken in a certain space SBV ('special bounded variation', which means that the distributional derivative of g is the sum of an L^2-vector field plus a totally singular distribution supported on Γ) (see DeGiorgi, Carriero & Leaci, 1988; Ambrosio & Tortorelli, 1989; Dal Maso, Morel & Solimini, 1989). Unfortunately, it seems hard to check whether these minima are 'nice' when f is, e.g. whether, when $n=2$, Γ is made up of a finite number of differentiable arcs, though Shah and I have conjectured that this is true. Of course, if the signal is replaced by a sampled version, the problem is finite dimensional and certainly well-posed.

This variational problem fits very nicely into both the Bayesian framework and the information theoretic one. Geman and Geman introduced it, for discrete domains, in the Bayesian setting. The basic idea is to define probability spaces by Gibbs fields. Let $D = \{x_\alpha\}$ be the domain, $\{f_\alpha\}$ and $\{g_\alpha\}$ the values of f and g at x_α. To describe Γ, for each pair of 'adjacent pixels' α and β, let $\ell_{\alpha,\beta} = 1$ or 0 depending on whether or not Γ separates the pixels α and β: these random variables are called

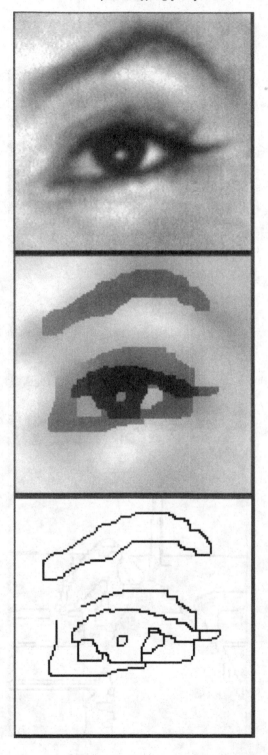

Fig. 1.6 Segmentation of the eye-image via optimal piecewise smooth approximation.

Fig. 1.7 Segmentation of the oldman-image via optimal piecewise smooth approximation.

the *line process*. Then we define an initial probability distribution on the random variables $\{\ell_{\alpha,\beta}\}$ by the formula:

$$p(\{\ell_{\alpha,\beta}\}) = \frac{e^{-\nu(\sum \ell_{\alpha,\beta})}}{Z_1} \qquad (1.13)$$

where Z_1 is the usual normalizing constant. This just means that boundaries Γ get less and less probable, the bigger they are. Next, we put a joint probability distribution on $\{g_\alpha\}$ and on the line process by the formula:

$$p(\{g_\alpha\}, \{\ell_{\alpha,\beta}\}) = \frac{e^{-\sum_{\alpha,\beta \text{ adj}} (1-\ell_{\alpha,\beta}) \cdot (g_\alpha - g_\beta)^2}}{Z_2}. \qquad (1.14)$$

This is a discrete form of the previous E: if adjacent pixels α and β are *not* separated by Γ, then $\ell_{\alpha,\beta} = 0$ and the probability of $\{g_\alpha\}$ goes down as $|g_\alpha - g_\beta|$ gets larger, but if they *are* separated, then $\ell_{\alpha,\beta} = 1$ and g_α and g_β are independent. Together, the last two equations define an intuitive prior on $\{g_\alpha, \ell_{\alpha,\beta}\}$ enforcing the idea that g is smooth except across the boundary Γ. The data term in the Bayesian approach makes the observations $\{f_\alpha\}$ equal to the model $\{g_\alpha\}$ plus Gaussian noise, i.e. it defines the conditional probability by the formula:

$$p(\{f_\alpha\}|\{g_\alpha, \ell_{\alpha,\beta}\}) = \frac{e^{-\mu^2 \cdot \sum_\alpha (f_\alpha - g_\alpha)^2}}{Z_3}. \qquad (1.15)$$

Multiplying (1.12), (1.13) and (1.14) defines a probability space $(\Omega_{\text{obs}} \times \Omega_{\text{wld}}, p_{o,w})$ as in Section 1.2 and taking $-log$ of this probability, we get back a discrete version of E up to a constant. Thus the MAP-estimate of the world variables $\{g_\alpha, \ell_{\alpha,\beta}\}$ is essentially the minimum of the functional E.

This probability space is closely analogous to that introduced in physics in the Ising model. In terms of this analogy, the discontinuities Γ of the signal are exactly the interfaces between different phases of some material in statistical mechanics (specifically in the Ising model of where the magnetic field of the iron atoms are oriented up or down).

From the information-theoretic perspective, we want to interpret E as the bit length of a suitable encoding of the image $\{f_\alpha\}$. These ideas have not been fully developed, but for the simplified model in which Γ is assumed to divide up the domain into pieces $\{D_k\}$ on which the image is approximately a constant $\{g_k\}$, this interpretation was pointed out by Leclerc (1989). We imagine encoding the image by starting with a 'chain code' for Γ: the length of this code will be proportional to its length $|\Gamma|$. Then we encode the constants $\{g_k\}$ up to some accuracy by a constant times the number of these pieces k. Finally, we encode the deviation of the image from these constants by Shannon's optimal encoding based on the assumption that $f_\alpha = g_k +$ Gaussian noise n_α. The length of this encoding will be a constant times the first term in E. (If g is not locally constant, we may go on to interpret the second term in E as follows: consider the Neumann boundary value problem for the laplacian Δ acting on the domain $D - \Gamma$. We may expand g in terms of its eigenfunctions, and encode g by Shannon's optimal encoding assuming these coefficients are independently normally distributed with variances going down with the corresponding eigenvalues. The length will be this second term.)

Many variants of this Gibbs field or 'energy functional' approach to perceptual signal processing have been investigated. Some of these seek to incorporate texture segmentation, e.g. Geman *et al.* (1990) and Lee *et al.* (1992) (which proposes an algorithm that should also segment most phonemes in speech) and others to deal with the asymmetry of boundaries caused by the 3D-world: at a boundary, one side is in front, the other in back (Nitzberg & Mumford, 1990). The 'Hidden Markov Models' used in speech recognition are Gibbs fields are of this type. To clarify the relationship, recall that HMM's are based on modelling speech by a Markov chain whose underlying graph is made up of subgraphs, one for each phoneme and whose states predict the power spectrum of the speech signal in local time intervals. Assuming a specific speech signal f is being modelled, HMM-theory computes the MAP sample of this chain conditional on the observed power spectra. Note that any sample of the chain defines a segmentation of time by the set $\Gamma = \{t_k\}$ of times at which the sample moves from the subchain for one phoneme to another, and each interval $t_k \leq t \leq t_{k+1}$ is associated to a specific phoneme a_k. Let A be the string $\{a_1 a_2, \cdots, a_N\}$. Taking $-log$ of the probability, the MAP estimate of the chain is the pair $\{\Gamma, A\}$ minimizing an energy E of the form:

$$E(A, \Gamma) = \sum_k \text{dist.}(f|_{t_k}^{t_{k+1}}, \text{phoneme } a_k) + \nu|\Gamma| \qquad (1.16)$$

which is clearly analogous to the E's defined above.

Finally, some physiological theories have been proposed in which various areas of cortex (e.g. V1 and V2) compute the segmentation of images by an algorithm analogous to minimizing (1.12) (Grossberg & Mignolla, 1985). It has also been used in computing depth from stereo (see Belhumeur, this volume; Geiger *et al.*, 1992), computing the so-called optical flow field, the vector field of moving objects across the focal plane (Yuille & Grzywacz, 1989; Hildreth, 1984) and many other applications.

We have not mentioned the problem of actually computing or approximating the minimum of energy functionals like E. Four methods have been proposed: in case $n = 1$, we can use *dynamic programming* to find the global minimum fast and efficiently. This applies to the speech applications and is one reason why speech recognition is considerably ahead of image analysis. For any n, Geman & Geman (1984) applied a Monte Carlo algorithm due to Kirkpatrick *et al.* (1983) known as *simulated annealing*. Making this work is something of a black art, as the theoretical bounds on its correctness are astronomical; still it is always an easy thing to try as a first step. A third method, which seems the most reliable at this point, is the *graduated non-convexity* method introduced in Blake & Zisserman (1987). It is based on putting the functional E in a family E_t such that $E = E_0$ and E_1 is a convex functional, hence has a unique local minimum. One then starts with the minimum of E_1 and follows it as $t \rightarrow 0$. The final idea is related to the third and that is to use *mean field theory* as in statistical physics: this often leads to approximations to the Gibbs field which allow us to put E in a family becoming convex in the limit (see Geiger & Yuille, 1989).

1.5.3 *Random diffeomorphisms and template matching*

The third example concerns the identification of objects in an image, putting them in categories such as 'the letter A', 'a hammer' or 'my Grandmother's face'. One of the biggest obstacles in these problems is the variability of the shapes which belong to such categories. This variability is caused, for example, by changes in the orientation of the object and the viewpoint of the camera, changes in individual objects such as varying expressions on a face and differences between objects of the same category such as different fonts for characters, different brands of hammer, etc. If the shapes were not too variable, one could hope to introduce average examples of each letter, of each tool, of the faces of everyone you know – 'templates' for each of these objects – and recognize each such object as it is perceived by comparing it to the various templates stored in memory. Unfortunately, the variations are usually too large for this to work, and, worse than that, some variations occur commonly, while others do not (e.g. faces get wrinkled but never become wavy like water). What we need to do is to explicitly model the common variations and use our knowledge to see if a suitably varied template fits! A large part of this variation can be modelled by domain warping, the third of the transformations introduced in Section 1.3 and this leads one to study *deformable templates*, templates whose parts can be changed in size and orientation and shifted relative to each other. These were first introduced in computer vision by Fischler & Elschlager (1973) who called them 'templates with springs' but the idea is well-known in biology, e.g. in the famous and beautiful book by Thompson (1917) (see Figure 1.8a, showing the deformations between three primate skulls).

Mathematically, we can describe flexible templates as follows. We must construct four things: (i) a standard image I_T on a domain D_T which can be a set of pixels or can also be reduced to a graph of 'parts' of the object, (ii) a space of allowable maps $\psi : D_T \rightarrow D$ or $(D \cup \{\text{missing}\})$, (iii) a measure $E(\psi)$ of the degree of deformation in the map ψ, the 'stretching of the springs' and (iv) a measure of the difference d

Fig. 1.8a Diffeomorphism between primate skulls.

between the standard image I_T and the deformation $\psi^*(I)$ of the observed image I. Here ψ is typically a diffeomorphism, 'missing' is an extra element in the range of ψ to allow certain parts of the standard image to be missing in the observed image and $\psi^*(I)$ is a 'pull-back' of I which may be just the composition of I and ψ if D_T is a set of pixels, or may be some set of local 'features' of I when D_T is a graph of parts. The basic problem is then to compute:

$$\arg\min_{\psi}[d(\psi^*(I), I_T) + E(\psi)], \qquad (1.17)$$

in order to find the optimal match of the template with the observed image.

Figures 1.8b, 1.8c and 1.8d show three examples of such matches. Figure 1.8b from Yamamoto & Rosenfeld (1982) applies these ideas to the recognition of chinese characters or kanji. In this application D_T is a 1-dimensional polygonal skeleton of the outline of the character, and ψ is a piecewise linear embedding of D_T in the domain D of the character image. Figure 1.8c from Y. Amit (1991) applies these ideas to tracing a hand in an X-ray by comparing it with a standard hand. Here ψ is a small deformation of the identity defined by a wavelet expansion of its (x, y)-coordinates and the prior $E(\psi)$ is a weighted L^2-norm of the expansion coefficients. Finally Figure 1.8d from Yuille, Hallinan & Cohen (1992) applies these ideas to the recognition of eyes. Here D_T has two parts, a pair of parabolas representing the outline of the eye and a black circle on a white ground representing the iris/pupil on

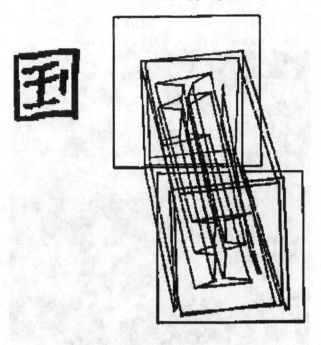

Fig. 1.8b Diffeomorphism between kanji.

the eyeball. ψ is linear on each parabola and on the circle, but the range of the first may *occlude* the range on the second to allow the iris/pupil to be partially hidden. This is incorporated in a careful definition of d.

An interesting mathematical side of this theory is the need for a careful definition and comparative study of various priors on the spaces of diffeomorphisms ψ. One can, for instance, define various measures $E(\psi)$ based (i) on the square norm of the Jacobian, as in harmonic map theory, (ii) on the area of the graph, as in geometric measure theory, (iii) on the stress of the map as in elasticity theory or (iv) on second derivatives of ψ, which give more control over the minima. Mumford (1991) discusses some of these measures, but the best approach is unclear and the restriction of maps to be diffeomorphisms is not always natural. An interesting neurophysiological aside is that the anatomy of the cortex of mammals seems well equipped to perform domain warping. The circuitry of the cortex is based on two types of connections: local connections within disjoint subsets of the cortex known as *cortical areas*, and global connections, called *pathways*, between the two distinct areas. The pathways occur in pairs, setting up maps which are crudely homeomorphisms between the cortical surfaces of the two areas which are inverse to each other. These pathways are not exactly point to point maps, however, because of the multiple synapses of their axons, hence the pair of inverse pathways may be able to shift a pattern of excitation by small amounts in any direction.

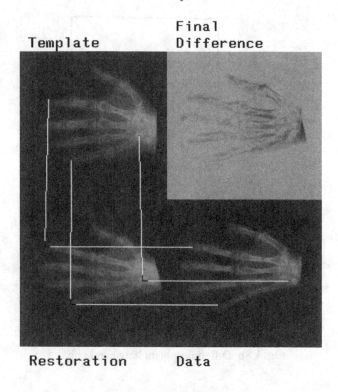

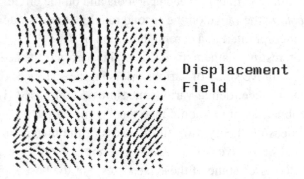

Fig. 1.8c Diffeomorphism between X-rays of hands.

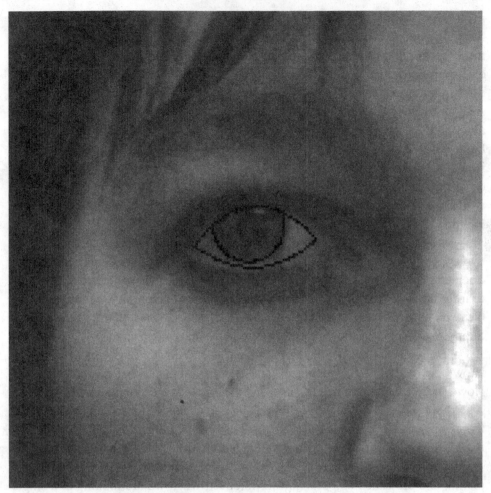

Fig. 1.8d Diffeomorphism from a cartoon eye to a real eye.

1.5.4 *The Stereo correspondence problem via minimum description length*

As described in Section 1.2, there are two approaches to the problems of pattern
theory: the first is to use all the geometry, physics, chemistry, biology and sociology
that we know about the world and try to define from this high-level knowledge
an appropriate probabilistic model $(\Omega_{\text{obs}} \times \Omega_{\text{wld}}, p_{o,w})$ of the world and our observations. The second involves *learning this model* using only the patterns and
the internal structure of the signals that are presented to us. Almost all research to
date in computer vision falls in the first category, while the standard approach to
speech recognition starts with the first but significantly improves on it using the
'EM-algorithm', a learning algorithm in the second category.

However, newborn animals seem to rely as strongly on learning their environment as on a genetically transmitted knowledge of it: it not hard to imagine that a baby growing up in a virtual reality governed by quite unusual physics would learn these just as rapidly as the physics of its ancestral world. Humans can read scanning electron microscope images, which are produced by totally different reflectance rules from normal images. All of this suggests the possibility of discovering universal pattern analysis algorithms which learn patterns from scratch. One of the great appeals of the idea of pattern theory is the hope that the structure of the world can be discovered in this way. It is in this spirit that we present the final example. It is not an extensive theory like the previous three, but illustrates how the minimum description length principle can lead one to uncover the hidden structure of the world in a remarkably direct way. Closely related ideas can be found in Becker & Hinton (1992).

We are concerned with the problem of stereo vision. If we view the world with two eyes or with two cameras separated by a known distance, and either identically oriented or with a known difference of orientations, then we can use trigonometry to infer the 3-dimensional structure of the world: see Figure 1.9. More precisely, the two imaging systems produce two images, I_L and I_R (the left and right images). Suppose a point A in the world visible in both images appears as $A_L \in D_L$ and $A_R \in D_R$ in the domains of the two images. The coordinates of A_L and A_R plus the known geometry of the imaging system give the 3-dimensional coordinates of A. However, to use this, we need to first find the pair of corresponding points A_L and A_R: finding these is called the *correspondence problem*. Notice from Figure 1.9 that the geometry of the imaging system gives us one simplification: all points A in a fixed 3-dimensional plane π, through the centers of the two lenses, are seen as points $A_L \in \ell_L$ and $A_R \in \ell_R$, where ℓ_L and ℓ_R are the intersections of π with the two focal planes, and are called *epipolar lines*. Moreover, when we are looking at a single relatively smooth surface S in the 3-dimensional world, S is visible from the left . and right eye as subdomains $S_L \subset D_L$ and $S_R \subset D_R$ and the corresponding points on these subdomains define a diffeomorphism $\psi : S_L \to S_R$ carrying each epipolar line in the left domain to the corresponding epipolar line in the right. This leads us to a problem like that in the last section. But there is a further twist: at the edges of objects, each of the two eyes can typically see a little further around one edge, producing pixels in one domain D_L or D_R with no corresponding pixel in the other domain. In this way, the domain is often segmented into subdomains corresponding to distinct objects. (See chapter 8 by Belhumeur for further elaboration.)

My claim is that the minimum description length principle alone leads you naturally to discover all this structure, without any prior knowledge of 3-dimensions. The argument is summarized in Figure 1.10. In this figure, I have diagrammatic form. Firstly, in order to represent the essentials concisely, I have used only a single pair of epipolar lines ℓ_L and ℓ_R instead of the full domains D_L and D_R. Secondly,

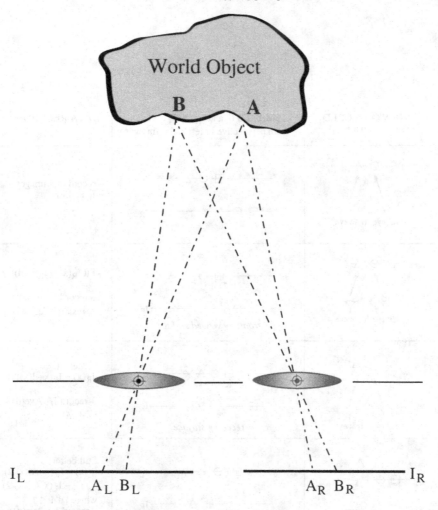

Fig. 1.9 The geometry of stereo vision, in a plane through the centers of the two lenses.

instead of graphing the complex intensity function, we have used small symbols (squares, circles, triangles, stars, etc.) to denote local intensity functions with various characteristics. Thus a square on both lines represents local intensities which are similar functions. On the left, at each stage in Figure 1.10, we see the plane π in the world, with the visible surface points, and the left and right eyes. In the middle, we see the left and right images I_L and I_R which this scene produces, as well as dotted lines connecting corresponding points A_L and A_R. On the right we give a method of encoding the image data.

Stage 0 represents a simple flat object seen from the front: it produces images I_L and I_R, but we assume that our pattern analysis begins with naively encoding the images independently. At stage 1, the same scene is seen, but now the analysis

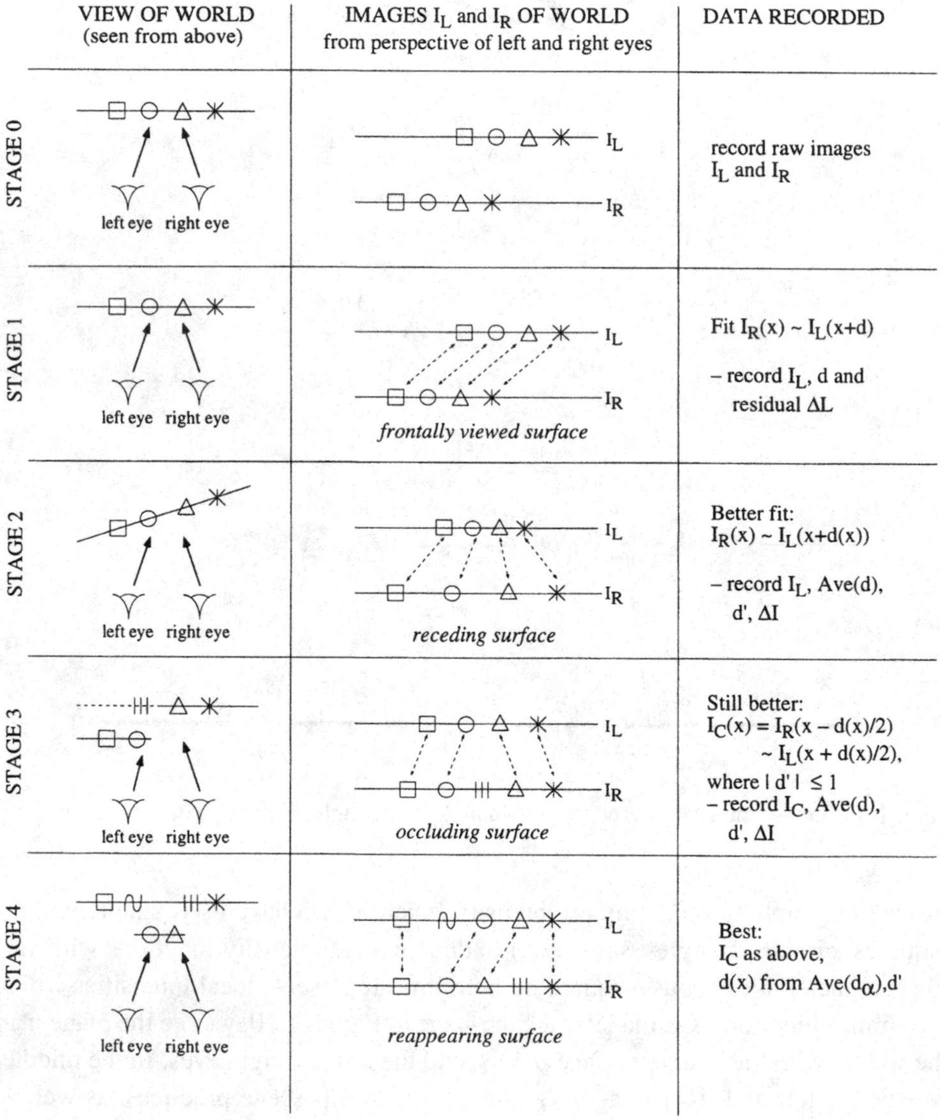
VIEW OF WORLD (seen from above)
IMAGES I_L and I_R OF WORLD from perspective of left and right eyes
DATA RECORDED
STAGE 0
left eye right eye
I_L
I_R
record raw images I_L and I_R
STAGE 1
left eye right eye
I_L
I_R
frontally viewed surface
Fit $I_R(x) \sim I_L(x+d)$
– record I_L, d and residual ΔL
STAGE 2
left eye right eye
I_L
I_R
receding surface
Better fit: $I_R(x) \sim I_L(x+d(x))$
– record I_L, Ave(d), d', ΔI
STAGE 3
left eye right eye
I_L
I_R
occluding surface
Still better: $I_C(x) = I_R(x - d(x)/2) \sim I_L(x + d(x)/2)$, where $|d'| \leq 1$
– record I_C, Ave(d), d', ΔI
STAGE 4
left eye right eye
I_L
I_R
reappearing surface
Best: I_C as above, d(x) from Ave(d_α),d'

Fig. 1.10 Discovering the world via MDL.

uses the much more concise method of encoding only I_L, the fixed translation d by which corresponding points differ and a possible small residual $\Delta I(x) = I_R(x) - I_L(x + d)$. Clearly this is more concise. At stage 2, the scene is more complex: a surface of varying distance is seen, hence the displacement between corresponding points (called the *disparity*) is not constant. To adapt the previous encoding to this situation, one could take a mean value of d and have a bigger residual ΔI. But this residual could be quite big and a better scheme is replace the fixed d by a function $d(x)$ and encode I_L, the mean and derivative $(\bar{d}, d')$ of d and the residual ΔI. Now in stage 3, we encounter a new wrinkle: the scene consists in two surfaces, one occluding the other. Notice that a little bit of the back surface is visible to one eye only. To include this complexity, we go over to a more symmetrical treatment of the two eyes and encode a combined *cyclopean* image $I_C(x)$, where

$$I_C(x) = I_R(x - \frac{d(x)}{2}), I_L(x + \frac{d(x)}{2}) \text{ or their average} \qquad (1.18)$$

depending on whether the point is visible only to the right eye, only to the left eye or to both eyes. To make this representation unique, it is easy to see that we must require that $|d'(x)| \leq 1$. Then we encode the scene via $(I_C, \bar{d}, d', \Delta I)$. In the final stage 4, we introduce the possibility of a surface disappearing behind another *and then reappearing*. The point is that each surface has its own average disparity, and it now becomes more efficient to record d by several means $\bar{d}_\alpha$, one for each surface, and the derivative d'. Thus we see how the search for minimum length encoding leads us naturally, first to the third coordinate of world points, then to smooth descriptions of surfaces in terms of their tangent planes and finally to explicit labelling of distinct surfaces in the visible field.

Although this approach might seem very abstract and impossible to implement biologically, G. Hinton (unpublished) has developed neural net theories incorporating both MDL and feed-back. These might be able to learn stereo exactly as outlined in this section.

1.6 Pattern theory and cognitive information processing

The examples of the last section all concern pattern theory as a theory for analyzing sensory input. The examples come from vision, but most of the ideas could apply to hearing or touch too. The purpose of this section is to ask the question: to what extent is pattern theory relevant to all cognitive information processing, both 'higher level' thinking as studied in cognitive psychology and AI, and the output stages of an intelligent agent, motor control and action planning. I believe that in many ways the same ideas are applicable on a theoretical level and that there is physiological evidence that the same algorithms are applied throughout the cortex.

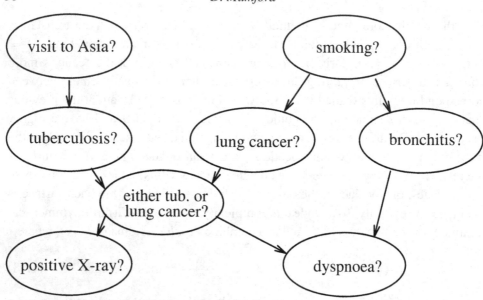

Fig. 1.11 Causal graph in a toy medical expert system.

In the introduction, we gave medical expert systems as another example of pattern theory. In this extension, we considered the data available to a physician – symptoms, test results and the patient's history – as an encoded version of the full state of the world, a 'deformed image' in Grenander's terminology. The full state of the world, the 'pure image', in this case means the diseases and processes present in the patient. Inferring these hidden random variables can and has been studied as a problem in Bayesian statistics, exactly as in Section 1.2: see, for instance, Pearl (1988) and Lauritzen & Spiegelhalter (1988). In particular, describing the probability distribution on all the random variables as a Gibbs field, as in Section 1.5, has been shown to be a powerful technique for introducing realistic models of the probability distribution in the real world. Figure 1.11, from the article Lauritzen & Spiegelhalter (1988), shows a simplified set of such random variables and the graph on which a Gibbs distribution can be based. Whether or not pattern theory extends in an essential way to these types of problems hinges on whether the transformations described in Section 1.3 generate the kind of probability distributions encountered with higher level variables. To answer this, it is essential to look at test cases which are not too artificially simplified (as is done all too often in AI), but which incorporates the typical sorts of complexities and complications of the real world. While I do not think this question can be definitively answered at present, I want to make a case that the four types of transformations of Section 1.3 are indeed encoding mechanisms encountered at all levels of cognitive information processing.

The first class of transformations, noise and blur, certainly occur at all levels of thought. In the medical example, errors in tests, the inadequacies of language in conveying the nature of a pain or symptom, etc. all belong to this category. Uncertainty over facts, misinterpretations and confusing factors are within this class. The simplest model leads to multi-dimensional normal distributions on a vector P of 'features' being analyzed.

The fourth category of transformation, 'interruptions', also are obviously universal. In any cognitive sphere, the problem of separating the relevant factors for a specific event or situation being analyzed from the extraneous factors involved with everything else in the world, is clearly central. The world is a complex place with many, many things happening simultaneously, and highlighting the 'figure' against the 'ground' is not just a sensory problem, but one encountered at every level. Another way this problem crops up is that a complex of symptoms may result from one underlying cause or from several, and, if several causes are present, their effects have to teased apart in the process of pattern analysis. As proposed in Section 1.4, pattern synthesis – actively comparing the results of one cause with the presenting symptoms P followed by analysis of the residual, the unexplained symptoms, is a universal algorithmic approach to these problems.

The second of the transformations, 'multi-scale superposition', can be applied to higher level variables as follows: philosophers, psychologists and AI researchers have all proposed systematizing the study of concepts and categories by organizing them in hierarchies. Thus psychologists (see Rosch, 1978) propose distinguishing *superordinate categories, basic level categories and subordinate categories*: for instance, a particular pet might belong to the superordinate category 'animal', the basic-level category 'dog' and the subordinate category 'terrier'. In AI, this leads to graphical structures called *semantic nets* for codifying the relationships between categories (see Findler, 1979). These nets always include ordered links between categories, called *isa* links, meaning that one category is a special case of another. I want to propose that cognitive multi-scale superposition is precisely the fact that to analyze a specific situation or thing, some aspects result from the situation belonging to very general categories, others from very specific facts about the situation that put it in very precise categories. Thus sensory thinking requires we deal with large shapes with various overall properties, supplemented with details about their various parts, precise data on location, proportions, etc.; cognitive thinking requires we deal with large ideas with various general properties, supplemented with details about specific aspects, precise facts about occurrence, relationships, etc.

Finally, how about 'domain warping'? Consider a specific example first. Associated to a cold is a variety of several dozen related symptoms. A person may, however, be described as having a sore throat, a chest cold, flu, etc.: in each case the profile of their symptoms shifts. This may be modelled by a map from symptom to symptom, carrying for instance the modal symptom of soreness of throat to that of coughing.

The more general cognitive process captured by domain warping is that of making an *analogy*. In an analogy, one situation with a set of participants in a specific relationship to each other is mapped to another situation with new participants in the same relationship. This map is the ψ in Section 1.5, and the constraints on ψ, such as being a diffeomorphism, are now that it preserve the appropriate relationships. The idea of domain warping applying to cognitive concepts seems to suggest that higher level concepts should form some kind of geometric space. At first this sounds crazy, but it should be remembered that the entire cortex, high and low level areas alike, has the structure of a 2-dimensional sheet. This 2-dimensional structure is used in a multitude of ways to organize sensory and motor processes efficiently: in some cases, sensory maps (like the retinal response and patterns of tactile responses) are laid out geometrically. In other cases, interleaved stripes carry intra-hemispheric and inter-hemispheric connections. In still other cases, there are 'blobs' in which related responses cluster. But, in all cases, adjacency in this 2D sheet allows a larger degree of cross-talk and interaction than with non-adjacent areas and this seems to be used to develop responses to related patterns. My suggestion is: is this spatial adjacency used to structure abstract thought too[†]?

To conclude, we want to discuss briefly how pattern theory helps the analysis of motor control and action planning, the output stage of a robot. Control theory has long been recognized as the major mathematical tool for analyzing these problems but it is not, in fact, all that different from pattern theory. In Figure 1.12a, we give the customary diagram of what control theory does. The controller is a black box which compares the current observation of the state of the world with the desired state and issues an updated motor command, which in turn affects the black box called the world. This diagram is very similar to Figure 1.4, which described how pattern analysis and pattern synthesis formed a loop used in the algorithm for reconstructing the hidden world variables from the observed sensory ones. Figure 1.12b presents the modification of Figure 1.4 to a motor task. Here a high-level area or 'black box' is in a loop with a low-level area: the high-level area compares the desired state with an analysis of the error and generates an updated motor command sequence by pattern synthesis. The low-level area, either by actually carrying out an action and observing its consequences, or by internal simulation, finds that it falls short in various ways, and send its pattern analysis of this error back up. Notice that the four transformations of Section 1.3 will occur or should be used in the top-down pattern

[†] I have argued elsewhere that the remarkable anatomical uniformity of the neo-cortex suggests that common mechanisms, such as the 4 universal transformations of pattern theory, are used throughout the cortex (Mumford, 1991-92; 1993). The referee has pointed out that 'the uniformity of structure may reflect common machinery at a lower level. For example, different computers may have similar basic mechanisms at the level of registers, buses, etc., which is a low level of data handling. Similarly in the brain, the apparent uniformity of structure may be at the level of common lower-level mechanisms rather than the level of dealing with universal transformations.' This is a certainly an alternative possibility, quite opposite to my conjectural link between the high-level analysis of pattern theory and the circuitry of the neo-cortex.

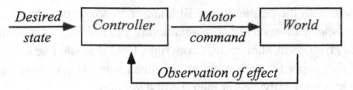

Fig. 1.12a The flow chart of control theory.

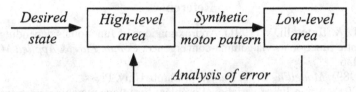

Fig. 1.12b A motor task via pattern theory.

synthesis step. Noise and blur are the inevitable consequences of the inability to control muscles perfectly, or eliminate external uncontrollable interference. Domain warping is the bread-and-butter of control theory – speeding up or slowing down an action by modifying the forces in order that it optimizes performance. Multi-scale superposition is what hierarchical control is all about: building up an action first in large steps, then refining these steps in their parts, eventually leading to detailed motor commands. Finally, interruptions are the terminations of specific control programs, either by success or by unexpected events, where quite new programs take over. In general, we seek to anticipate these and set up successor programs beforehand, hence we need to actively synthesize these as much as possible.

In summary, my belief is that pattern theory contains the germs of a universal theory of thought, one which stands in opposition to the accepted analysis of thought in terms of logic. The extraordinary similarity of the structure of all parts of the human cortex to each other and of human cortex with the cortex of the most primitive mammals suggests that a relatively simple universal principal governs its operation, even in complex processes like language (see Mumford, 1991-92, 1993) where these physiological links are developed): pattern theory is a proposal for what these principals may be.

Acknowledgements

Supported in part by NSF Grant DMS 91-21266, by the Army Center for Intelligent Control ARO DAAl03-92-G-0115 and by the Geometry Center, University of Minnesota, a STC funded by NSF, DOE and Minnesota Technology Inc. This paper is a revised version of a talk given at the first European Congress of Mathematics. It is reprinted here with the permission of Birkhauser-Boston from hte *Proceedings of the First European Congress of Mathematicians, Paris 1992,* a three volume work in the series Progress in Mathematics copyright 1993. I would like to thank the two referees of this paper for their excellent comments and suggestions which have I hope made it significantly clearer than the first version.

References

Ambrosio, L. & Tortorelli, V. (1991). Approximations of functionals depending on jumps by elliptic functionals via gamma-convergence. *Comm. Pure & Applied Math.*, **43**, 999-1036.

Amit, D. (1989). *Modelling Brain Function*, Camb. Univ. Press.

Amit, Y. (1991). A non-linear variational problem for image matching. preprint, Brown Dept. of Applied Math.

Barlow, H. (1961). Possible principles underlying the transformation of sensory messages. In *Sensory Communication*, ed. W. Rosenblith. MIT Press.

Becker, S. & Hinton, G. (1992). Self-organizing neural network that discovers surfaces in random-dot stereograms, *Nature*, **235**, 161-163.

Blake, A. & Zisserman, A. (1987). *Visual Reconstruction*. Cambridge, MA: MIT Press.

Burt, P. & Adelson, E. (1983). The Laplacian pyramid as a compact image code. *IEEE Trans. on Comm.*, **31**, 532-540.

Carpenter, G. & Grossberg, S. (1987). A massively parallel architecture for a self-organizing neural pattern recognition machine. *Comp. Vision, Graphics & Image Proc.*, **37**, 54-115.

Cavanagh, P. (1991). What's up in top-down processing. *Proc. 13th ECVP.*

Chomsky, N. (1981). *Lectures on Government and Binding*. Dordrecht: Foris.

Coifman, R., Meyer, Y. & Wickerhouser, V. (1990). Wavelet analysis and signal processing. Preprint, Yale Univ. Math. Dept.

Dal Maso, G., Morel, J-M. & Solimini, S. (1992). A variational method in image segmentation, *Acta Math.*, to appear.

Daubechies, I. (1988). Orthonormal bases of compactly supported wavelets. *Comm. Pure & Applied Math.*, **49**, 909-996.

Daubechies, I. (1990). The wavelet transform, time-frequency localization and signal analysis. *IEEE Trans. Inf. Theory*, 961-1005.

DeGiorgi, E., Carriero, M. & Leaci, A. (1989). Existence theorem for a minimum problem with free discontinuity set. *Arch. Rat. Mech. Anal.*, **108**, 95-18.

Dowling, J. (1987). *The Retina*. Harvard Univ. Press.

Findler, N. ed. (1979). *Associative Networks*. Academic Press.

Fischler, M. & Elschlager, R. (1973). The representation and matching of pictorial structures. *IEEE Trans. on Computers*, **22**, 67-92.

Gage, M. & Hamilton, R. (1986). The heat equation shrinking convex plane curves. *J. Diff. Geom.*, **23**, 69-96.

Geiger, D. & Yuille, A. (1989). A common framework for image segmentations. Harvard Robotics Lab. Tech Report, 1989.

Geiger, D., Ladendorf, B. & Yuille, A. (1992). Occlusions and binocular stereo. *Proc. European Conf. Comp. Vision*, Springer Lecture Notes in Comp. Sci. **588**.

Geman, D. (1991). Random fields and inverse problems in imaging. Springer Lecture Notes in Mathematics, **1427**.

Geman, S. & Geman, D. (1984). Stochastic relaxation, Gibbs distribution and Bayesian restoration of images. *IEEE Trans. Pattern Anal. Mach. Intell.*, **6**, 721-741.

Geman, S., Geman, D., Graffigne, C. & Dong, P. (1990). Boundary detection by Constrained Optimization. *IEEE Trans. Pattern Anal. and Mach. Int.*, **12**.

Grayson M. (1987). The heat equation shrinks embedded plane curves to round points. *J. Diff. Geom.*, **26**, 285-314.

Grenander, U. (1976-1981). *Lectures in Pattern Theory I, II and III: Pattern Analysis, Pattern Synthesis and Regular Structures.* Springer-Verlag.

Grossberg, S. & Mingolla, E. (1985). Neural dynamics of form perception: Boundary completion, illusory figures and neon color spreading. *Psych. Rev.*, **92**, 173-211.

Grossman, A. & Morlet, J. (1984). Decomposition of Hardy functions into square integrable wavelets of constant shape. *SIAM J. Math. Anal.*, **15**, 723-736.

Hertz, J., Krogh, A. & Palmer, R. (1991). *Introduction to the Theory of Neural Computation.* Addison-Wesley.

Hildreth, E. (1984). *The Measurement of Visual Motion.* Cambridge, MA: MIT Press.

Hopfield, J. (1982). Neural networks and physical systems with emergent collective computational abilities. *Proc. Nat. Acad. Sci.*, **79**, 2554-2558.

Kass, M., Witkin, A. & Terzopoulos, D. (1987). Snakes: active contour models. *IEEE Proc. 1st Int. Conf. Computer Vision*, 259-268.

Kimia, B., Tannenbaum, A. & Zucker, S. (1993). Shapes, shocks and deformations I. *Int. J. Comp. Vision.*

Kirkpatrick, S., Geloti, C. & Vecchi, M. (1983). Optimization by simulated annealing. *Science*, **220**, 671-680.

Lauritzen, S. & Spiegelhalter, D. (1988). Local computations with probabilities on graphical structures and their applications to expert systems. *J. Royal Stat. Soc.B*, **50**, 157-224.

Leclerc, Y. (1989). Constructing simple stable descriptions for image partitioning. *Int. J. Comp. Vision*, **3**, 73-102.

Lee, T.S., Mumford, D. & Yuille, A. (1992). Texture segmentation by minimizing vector-valued energy functionals. *Proc. Eur. Conf. Comp. Vision*, Springer Lecture Notes in Comp. Sci. **1427**.

MacKay, Donald (1956). The epistemological problem for automata. In *Automata Studies*, ed. Shannon & McCarthy, pp. 2235-2251. Princeton Univ. Press.

Mallat, S. (1989). A theory of multi-resolution signal decomposition: The wavelet representation. *IEEE Trans. PAMI*, **11**, 674-693.

Meyer, Y. (1986). Principe d'incertitude, bases hilbertiennes et algèbres d'opérateurs. *Séminaire Bourbaki*, Springer Lecture Notes in Mathematics.

Mumford, D. (1991). Mathematical theories of shape: Do they model perception? *Proc. SPIE*, **1570**, 2-10.

Mumford, D. (1991-92). On the computational architecture of the neocortex I and II. *Biol. Cybernetics.* **65**, 135-145 & **66**, 241-251.

Mumford, D. (1993). Neuronal architectures for pattern-theoretic problems. *Proc. Idyllwild conference on large scale neuronal theories of the brain.* To appear, MIT press.

Mumford, D. & Shah, J. (1989). Optional approximation by piecewise smooth functions and associated variational problems. *Comm. Pure & Applied Math.*, **42**, 577-685.

Nitzberg, M. & Mumford, D. (1990). The 2.1D sketch. *Proc. 3rd IEEE Int. Conf. Comp. Vision*, 138-144.

Osherson, D. & Weinstein, S. (1984). Formal learning theory. In *Handbook of Cognitive Neuroscience*, ed. M. Gazzaniga, pp. 275-292. Plenum Press.

Pearl, J. (1988). *Probabilistic Reasoning in Intelligent Systems*. Morgan-Kaufman.

Perona, P. & Malik, J. (1987). Scale-space and edge detection using anisotropic diffusion. *IEEE Workshop on Computer Vision*, Miami.

Rissanen, J. (1989). *Stochastic Complexity in Statistical Inquiry*. World Scientific.

Rosch, E. (1978). Principles of categorization. In *Cognition and Categorization*, ed. E. Rosch and B. Lloyd. L.Erlbaum.

Rosenfeld, A. & Thurston, M. (1971). Edge and curve detection for visual scene analysis. *IEEE Trans. on Computers*, **C-20**, 562-569.

Thompson, D'Arcy (1917). *On Growth and Form*. Camb. Univ. Press.

Uhr, L. (1972). Layered "recognition cone" networks that preprocess, classify and describe. *IEEE Trans. on Computers*, **C-21**, 758-768.

Yamamoto, K. & Rosenfeld, A. (1982). Recognition of handprinted Kanji characters by a relaxation method. *Proc. 6th Int. Conf. Pattern Recognition*, 395-398.

Yuille, A. & Grzywacz N. (1989). A mathematical analysis of the motion coherence theory. *Int. J. Comp. Vision*, **3**, 155-175.

Yuille, A., Hallinan, P., & Cohen D. (1992). Feature extraction from faces using deformable templates. *Int. J. Comp. Vision*, **6**.

2

Modal structure and reliable inference

ALLAN JEPSON

Department of Computer Science, University of Toronto

WHITMAN RICHARDS

Media Arts & Sciences, Massachusetts Institute of Technology

DAVID C. KNILL

Department of Psychology, University of Minnesota

2.1 Introduction

The world we live in is a very structured place. Matter does not flit about in space and time in a completely unorganized fashion, but rather is organized by the physical forces, biological processes, social interactions, and so on which exist in our world (McMahon, 1975; Thompson, 1952). It is this structure, or regularity, which makes it possible for us to make reliable inferences about our surroundings from the signals taken in from various senses (Marr, 1982; Witkin and Tenenbaum, 1983). In other words, regularities in the world make sense data reliably informative about the world we move around in. But what is the nature of these regularities, and how can they be used for the purposes of perception?

   In this chapter, we consider one class of environmental regularities which arise from what we call the modal structure of the world and which has the effect of making sensory information for certain types of perceptual judgements highly reliable (Bobick and Richards, 1986). Our definition of modal regularities is motivated by careful analyses of some simple examples of reliable perceptual inferences. Given the resulting definition, we then briefly discuss some of the implications for the knowledge required of a perceiver in order for it to make reliable inferences in the presence of such modal structure.

2.2 Modal structure: An example

2.2.1 When can we infer that an object is stationary?

A common perceptual inference is that of whether an object is moving or at rest. How can we make this inference given only the two-dimensional projection of a three-dimensional object? When the image of an object is moving the inference is trivial, since a stationary object cannot give rise to image motion (assuming a stationary observer). What about the case in which the image of an object is not moving? Can we then reasonably infer that the object itself is not moving? Intuitively, this is a common inference which is rarely wrong, so it seems that the answer to the question is a strong "yes". We will show that object motions in the world must have a strong type of regularity to support this inference. We will then generalize the discussion to show that the same type of structure in the world must be present to support a wide variety of similarly reliable inferences.

One explanation for the reliability of inferences like "stationary in the image implies stationary in the world" is that a stationary image would be an "accidental" view of a moving object (Albert & Hoffman, 1991; Lowe, 1985). That is, one would have to be viewing the object head-on (in the direction of the motion), in order to obtain a stationary image of a moving object. Small perturbations of the viewpoint would destroy the stationarity of the image motion when viewing a moving object. Moreover, only two viewpoints of the infinite number of possible viewpoints would have this special property, thus the probability of obtaining a stationary image from a moving object is zero (or, if we allow for some uncertainty in the measurement of image motion, the probability would be small). On the face of it, this argument is attractive and seems perfectly logical. Unfortunately, the inference described is based on the wrong probability distribution; namely, the probability of obtaining a stationary image, given that an object is moving. Typically, this distribution is called the likelihood function, and we can characterize the inference as being within the class of maximum-likelihood criteria for making statistical decisions. The distribution of interest, however, is the posterior distribution: the probability that an object is moving, given that the image is stationary (Jepson & Richards, 1992; Knill & Kersten, 1991). The difference between the two is critical, as we will show.

We begin by formalizing the general viewpoint argument as a statistical decision based on the ratio of likelihood functions, $p(||\mathbf{v}_{image}|| = 0 \,|\, ||\mathbf{v}|| = 0)$ and $p(||\mathbf{v}_{image}|| = 0 \,|\, ||\mathbf{v}|| \neq 0)$, where $\mathbf{v}$ is the 3-dimensional velocity vector of an object, $\mathbf{v}_{image}$ is the 2-dimensional image velocity vector, and $|| \cdot ||$ is the usual 2-norm. The general viewpoint argument says that the assumption of a generic view makes the ratio of the two likelihood functions large, so that one can reliably infer that the object is stationary given a stationary image. The likelihood ratio is given by

$$R_{likelihood} = \frac{p(||\mathbf{v}_{image}|| = 0 \,|\, ||\mathbf{v}|| = 0)}{p(||\mathbf{v}_{image}|| = 0 \,|\, ||\mathbf{v}|| \neq 0)}. \tag{2.1}$$

The numerator is clearly equal to 1, while the denominator, under the generic viewpoint assumption, is equal to 0, so, the argument goes, one should clearly infer that an object is stationary when one detects no image motion. A seeming advantage of this approach is that it does not appear to depend on any knowledge about the world (with the exception of assuming a generic view). It suggests that one can make a rational decision without knowing about the probabilistic structure of object motions in the world; that is, without assuming any constraints on object motion. We will now proceed to show that this is false, and that, if one assumes a generic, relatively unconstrained model of object motion, the inference of object stationarity from image stationarity will be wrong most of the time (and in the limit, all of the time). In fact, with such a model of object motion, one should infer the opposite, that the object is moving.

Our generic model of object motion is that of idealized gas molecules within a container having constant temperature T. Maxwell's distribution provides the probability density for the 3D velocity of a single molecule as

$$p(\mathbf{v}) = \frac{1}{(2\pi cT)^{\frac{3}{2}}} exp(-||\mathbf{v}||^2/(2cT)), \qquad (2.2)$$

where c is a positive constant (Fowler and Guggenheim, 1952). This is just an isotropic Gaussian distribution in three variables, having mean zero and variance cT. Note that the most probable velocity corresponds to the mean, namely $\mathbf{v} = 0$. We define the molecule to be at rest whenever the speed is less or equal to some tolerance $\epsilon > 0$. Given this definition, it follows that the prior probability of the particle being "at rest" is nonzero and roughly proportional to ϵ^3 for small values of ϵ (in our notation, $p(\text{at rest}) = p(||\mathbf{v}|| < \epsilon) = O(\epsilon^3)$). We assume that ϵ is significantly smaller than the standard deviation of the probability distribution, namely $\sqrt{cT}$, since otherwise, being at rest would have no significant meaning.

Suppose our observer has orthographic projection (for simplicity), and can measure the first two components of $\mathbf{v}$ ($\mathbf{v}_{image}$) such that the error in the estimation of the image speed, $||\mathbf{v}_{image}||$, is no larger than $\epsilon > 0$, where we assume some image sensing noise to make the mathematical analysis simpler (we can still examine the limit as $\epsilon \to 0$). Consider the specific case in which the observer measures the image speed to be between 0 and ϵ. Can the observer then infer that the particle is at rest?

The appropriate computation to make is the conditional probability that the particle is at rest, given the data that the image speed has been observed to be less than ϵ. We denote this distribution by $p(||\mathbf{v}_{world}|| < \epsilon \mid ||\mathbf{v}_{image}|| < \epsilon)$. It is just $1 - p(||\mathbf{v}_{world}|| > \epsilon \mid ||\mathbf{v}_{image}|| < \epsilon)$, where the latter term is the conditional probability that the particle is not at rest, given the same observation. As with the likelihood ratio analysis, we find it convenient to compute the ratio of these two probabilities. For small values of ϵ we find

$$\frac{p(||\mathbf{v}_{world}|| < \epsilon \mid ||\mathbf{v}_{image}|| < \epsilon)}{p(||\mathbf{v}_{world}|| > \epsilon \mid ||\mathbf{v}_{image}|| < \epsilon)} = \frac{p(||\mathbf{v}_{world}|| < \epsilon \mid ||\mathbf{v}_{image}|| < \epsilon)}{1 - p(||\mathbf{v}_{world}|| < \epsilon \mid ||\mathbf{v}_{image}|| < \epsilon)}$$

$$\approx \epsilon/\sqrt{2\pi cT} \qquad (2.3)$$

to leading order. Since we have assumed that ϵ is significantly smaller than the standard deviation of the distribution, namely $\sqrt{cT}$, it follows that the above ratio of conditional probabilities is significantly smaller than 1. That is, the odds strongly favour the interpretation that the particle is actually moving, even though the image motion is consistent with it being at rest. This is not a problem with the accuracy of the motion measurements. In fact, the same probability ratio is obtained (to leading order) even if the first two components of the velocity are assumed to be measured within a tolerance of some δ taken significantly smaller than ϵ. The difficulty is that the third component of the velocity is not measured at all, and can vary according to the Gaussian distribution with standard deviation $\sqrt{cT}$. For small values of ϵ this third component will rarely fall sufficiently close to zero for the particle to qualify to be at rest. The odds, therefore, consistently favour the inference that the particle is moving no matter how accurately the image velocity is measured. Moreover, having more time frames in which the image motion is measured to be less than δ can actually decrease the odds that the object is at rest.

Our model of the world is clearly missing something which would allow reliable inferences of object stationarity to be made. Since such inferences in our own world our commonplace and are usually correct, the unconstrained model of object motions just presented does not suffice to characterize our world. Similar results may be obtained for a wide range of normally reliable perceptual inferences, including so called "non-accidental properties" such as the colinearity or cotermination of two line segments (see Table 1). What type structure is needed to make such inferences reliable?

2.2.2 A Bayesian analysis

We wish to explore conditions that must be satisfied in order for an observer to be able to make a reliable inference of, say, a particle being at rest. In fact, it is convenient to approach the problem in a slightly more general fashion. We suppose that, at least in a restricted context C, the occurrence of a world property P can be modeled using the probability $p(P|C)$, and it's absence by $p(not\,P|C)$. Suppose that some measurements are taken of the objects and events in the world. We refer to a particular collection of such measurements as a feature F. Hence a feature will be identified with the set of all world events having measurements specified by F, and thus probabilities such as $p(F|C)$ are well defined. We wish to study the inference that property P occurs in the world, given both that the world context is C and that the measurements F are satisfied. Note that the probabilities $p(P|C)$ and $p(F|C)$ are considered to be objective facts about the world (or at least an idealization of the world), and are *not* statements about the perceiver's model of the world. Here we keep the issue of whether or not a perceiver needs to use any probabilistic model of the world quite separate from our analysis of a good inference.

In the probabilistic formalism a measure of the success of inferring property P

from F is the a posteriori probability of P given the feature F in the context C. A reliable inference makes this probability, namely $p(P|F\&C)$, nearly one, and the probability of an error, namely $p(not\,P|F\&C)$, nearly zero. It is convenient to consider the ratio of these two quantities, that is

$$R_{post} = \frac{p(P|F\&C)}{p(not\,P|F\&C)}. \tag{2.4}$$

We consider the feature F to provide a reliable inference, in the context C, precisely when this probability ratio R_{post} is much larger than one. Below we consider how such a condition can be ensured.

Bayes' rule can be used to break down the probability ratio R_{post} into two components. The first component, $R_{likelihood}$, is a likelihood ratio and relates to the measurement F of property P. The second component is another probability ratio, R_{prior}, and specifies the relative probabilities of occurrence of P and $not\,P$ in context C. The decomposition of R_{post} has the simple form:

$$R_{post} = R_{likelihood} \cdot R_{prior} \ . \tag{2.5}$$

Here the prior probability ratio R_{prior} is given by (compare equation (2.4))

$$R_{prior} = \frac{p(P|C)}{p(not\,P|C)}. \tag{2.6}$$

and the likelihood ratio $R_{likelihood}$ is defined to be

$$R_{likelihood} = \frac{p(F|P\&C)}{p(F|not\,P\&C)}. \tag{2.7}$$

From equation (2.5) we see that the likelihood ratio $R_{likelihood}$ acts as an amplification factor on the prior probability ratio R_{prior}. In words, we obtain a reliable inference only when the product of the likelihood ratio and the prior probability ratio is significantly larger than one.

To be concrete, consider the gas particle observer discussed in the previous section. In this case the context C denotes the fact that we are using Maxwell's distribution for the particle's velocity. The numerator of the likelihood ratio, $p(F|P\&C)$, is the probability of observing F, namely the image speed to be less than ϵ, given that the object is actually at rest. For the measurement accuracy of ϵ, and a particle moving with 3D speed no larger than ϵ, at least half of the measurements will show an image velocity having a speed of less than ϵ. The actual value doesn't matter for our current argument, so long as it is bounded away from zero. The denominator of the likelihood ratio, $p(F|not\,P\&C)$, is the probability that the image velocity is small even though the particle is not at rest. This probability is proportional to the square of the tolerance for the image motion, namely ϵ^2. Thus we find that the likelihood ratio is proportional to $1/\epsilon^2$, and is therefore large for sufficiently small values of ϵ. In other words, the image feature F in this case is much more likely to come from a particle at rest than from a moving particle, as expected from our earlier discussion of the likelihood ratio test.

But equation (2.5) has shown that the likelihood ratio does not provide the whole story, rather it acts as an amplification factor on the prior probability ratio for P versus *not P* in context C. For our gas particle example, property P denotes that the particle has a velocity of magnitude less than ϵ, and the context specifies that the velocity is distributed according to Maxwell's equation. Therefore R_{prior} is simply

$$\frac{p(P|C)}{p(not\,P|C)} = \frac{p(||\mathbf{v}_{world}|| < \epsilon)}{p(||\mathbf{v}_{world}|| > \epsilon)} = \frac{p(||\mathbf{v}_{world}|| < \epsilon)}{1 - p(||\mathbf{v}_{world}|| < \epsilon)} \approx \epsilon^3/(2\pi cT)^{\frac{3}{2}},$$

(2.8)

to leading order. It should now be clear what the problem is with the inference that the particle is stationary, given that it's image is stationary, in this gas particle context. In particular, note that as $\epsilon \to 0$ the prior probability ratio R_{prior} decreases to zero like ϵ^3, while we showed in the previous paragraph that the likelihood ratio $R_{likelihood}$ increases like $1/\epsilon^2$. Thus, even though the likelihood ratio becomes large, it is simply not large enough to amplify the prior probability ratio beyond one. Indeed, in agreement with equation (2.3) above, we find the posterior ratio to be of order ϵ and, for sufficiently small values of ϵ, the odds are therefore strongly against the particle being stationary.

While the above argument puts our conclusions on a solid Bayesian foundation it has not yet answered our basic question of why, when we observe an object to be stationary in the image, can we expect to be able to reliably conclude that the object is actually stationary in the world (still assuming a stationary observer). From equation (2.5) we see there are only two places to look for this answer, the likelihood ratio and the prior probability ratio.

Considering the likelihood ratio first, we might attempt it raise it by considering a more informative feature. For example, suppose we have accurate *stereo* measurements of the velocity of the particle, so that we obtain accurate constraints on all three components of it's motion. Such a system would increase the likelihood ratio to be of order $1/\epsilon^3$, if the measurement accuracy was order ϵ in each component. However, note that the resulting feature is still not necessarily a reliable indicator that the particle is at rest, since we can only conclude from equation (2.5) that the posterior probability ratio, R_{post}, would remain bounded away from zero as $\epsilon \to 0$. In order to get a reliable inference, the measurement accuracy would have to be significantly finer than the tolerance ϵ in our definition of stationarity. This approach of refining the measurements to raise the likelihood ratio does not fit our intuition very well, in which it seems a mere glance at a ball on our desk suffices to assure us that it is stationary. Thus we turn to the second place to look for our answer, namely the prior probability ratio.

2.2.3 A mode for stationary

Recall that the prior probability ratio represents a fact about the world, such as Maxwell's distribution for the velocities of gas particles, and *not* a perceiver's model of it. Therefore, in asking how the priors may help us in reliably inferring that a ball on our desk is at rest, we are asking about the structure of a suitable prior probability distribution for the velocities of balls. In fact, we will show that only a very simple qualitative property of such prior distributions is needed, not a detailed *quantitative* specification.

One obvious property of a prior distribution for velocities of balls is that, unlike gas particles, friction and gravity together provide strong constraints on the ball's motion. In particular, when in contact with a stationary supporting surface, the ball is often at rest (to within some tolerance ϵ). Thus, the prior distribution is more appropriately modeled using the "mixture" distribution

$$p(\mathbf{v}|B) = \pi^0 \delta(\mathbf{v}) + \pi^1 p_1(\mathbf{v}). \tag{2.9}$$

Here $\delta(\mathbf{v})$ is the Dirac delta function which represents a probability distribution concentrated at the point $\mathbf{v} = \vec{0}$, and $p_1(\mathbf{v})$ is some smooth probability distribution over the 3-space representing $\mathbf{v}$. These two 'component distributions' are combined in equation (2.9) using the 'mixture proportions' π^0 and π^1 to form the overall distribution, $p(\mathbf{v}|B)$, for such a ball context, B. Of course, to maintain a valid probability distribution we require that π^0 and π^1 are nonnegative and sum to one. Notice that the distribution $p(\mathbf{v}|B)$ models the property that objects are at rest with probability π^0, which is assumed to be nonzero in context B. This qualitative model for the prior distribution provides an alternative context in which to consider the inference of an object being at rest.

In this new context, the prior probability ratio R_{prior} is easily seen to be

$$\frac{p(P|B)}{p(not\,P|B)} = \frac{p(||\mathbf{v}_{world}|| < \epsilon)}{p(||\mathbf{v}_{world}|| > \epsilon)} = \frac{p(||\mathbf{v}_{world}|| < \epsilon)}{1 - p(||\mathbf{v}_{world}|| < \epsilon)}$$

$$= \pi^0/(1 - \pi^0) + O(\epsilon^3), \tag{2.10}$$

as $\epsilon \to 0$. Note that, to leading order, all that matters here is the fact that being stationary occurs with the positive probability π^0; none of the details of the smooth distribution for velocities contribute to R_{prior} to first order. Also, in contrast to Maxwell's distribution, we now have a significant prior probability ratio, $\pi^0/(1 - \pi^0)$, bounded away from zero.

Next we need to consider the likelihood ratio. A similar argument to the one given above for the derivation of the likelihood ratio for context C shows that

$$R_{likelihood} = \frac{p(F|P\&B)}{p(F|not\,P\&B)} = O(1/\epsilon^2). \qquad (2.11)$$

Together these two equations give us a posterior probability ratio, $R_{post} = O(1/\epsilon^2)$, which is much larger than one for ϵ sufficiently small. Therefore, in the context B we can reliably infer that the object is at rest, given that it was observed to be at rest in an image (assuming the measurement accuracy ϵ is sufficiently small); a mere glance should suffice.

The difference between contexts C and B is simply that in the ball context the property of being at rest is what we call a "modal property". That is, the property $\mathbf{v} = 0$ has nonzero probability in the prior distribution (See Jepson and Richards, 1993, for a formal definition of a "mode".). As we saw above, if a property is modal then the prior probability ratio R_{prior} remains bounded away from zero. Then, given an image feature for which the likelihood ratio $R_{likelihood}$, is known to be large, we might safely conclude that the modal property actually occurs in this instance. It is important to note that this works given fairly weak constraints on the prior distribution; we do not need to have a quantitative model for the prior distribution for the velocity of a ball (nor, in our opinion, can we expect to). Rather we need only assume that:

- The prior distribution is a mixture of two components or 'modes'.
- One component of the mixture, accounting for $1 - \pi^0$ of the probability, is a smooth function of $\mathbf{v}_{world}$.
- The other component, accounting for probability $\pi^0 > 0$, appears as a delta function at $\mathbf{v}_{world} = \vec{0}$.

As we saw above, such prior knowledge is needed to license even apparently innocuous inferences such as "objects which are stationary in the image are stationary in the scene".

2.3 Observability of modes: Key features

The general Bayesian argument presented in the previous section is not limited to inferences about whether or not an object is at rest. A similar argument shows the importance of prior knowledge in other apparently innocuous inferences, involving so called non-accidental properties (Binford, 1981; Lowe, 1985). For example, it can be shown that a nonzero prior for two sticks in the world to form a 'V'-configuration is critical for the reliability of the intuitively plausible inference that a V-configuration observed in an image corresponds to a V-configuration in the

Property	Psychophysical Evidence	A Posteriori Analysis
Straightness	Watt & Andrews, 1982	1
Cotermination	Julesz, 1971; Nakayama & Shimojo, 1992	3,4,6
Circular	Foster & Wagemans, 1993; Lowe, 1985	1,3
Rectangular	Gregory, 1970	7
Parallel	Rock, 1983; Stevens, 1988	5,7
Rigid Body Motion	Ullman, 1979; Wallach & O'Connell, 1953	1,8
Collinearity	Westheimer & McKee, 1977	2,5
Skew Symmetry	Kanade, 1981; Leyton, 1992	*

Table 2.1 *Some familiar "non-accidental" relations often suggested as driving visual perceptual inferences (for acoustic analogs, see Bregman, 1990). The numbers in the third column refer respectively to: (1) Bennett, Hoffman & Prakash, 1989; (2) Albert & Hoffman, 1991; (3) Knill & Kersten, 1991; (4) Jepson & Richards, 1992; (5) Jepson & Richards, 1991; (6) Nakayama & Shimojo, 1992; (7) Richards, Jepson & Feldman, 1994; (8) Reuman & Hoffman, 1986.*

world (Jepson & Richards, 1993). Similarly, two colinear line segments in an image can be treated as reliable indicators that the corresponding 3D line segments are colinear in the world *only* when there is a modal prior probability for them to be colinear in the world. The interested reader is referred to Jepson and Richards (1993) for details. Other examples are listed in Table 1, along with the relevant references.

There are also many examples of modal structures in the world for which a single view may not be enough to obtain a reliable inference. Consider a context consisting of a set of elliptical rings, of various eccentricities, scattered on a planar surface. Suppose there is also a mode for perfectly circular rings. Finally, suppose the slant and tilt of the plane with respect to the viewer is randomly chosen using a smooth distribution. Then, given an orthographic image consisting of just one ellipse, can the perceiver reliably determine the mode, namely elliptical or circular, of the ring that generated this image feature? Clearly the answer is no, since the observation of an ellipse in the image is typical for both elliptical and circular rings. Another example of a modal property which cannot be reliably indentified is provided in Section 2.5.5 below, where we exhibit a context in which (amoungst other things) we cannot tell if a ball is sliding along the floor or moving through the air. It is important to emphasize that modal properties may be important to the perceiver, even though some may not be reliably observable from a single image.

Nevertheless, as we see from Table 1, there are a variety of applications for the Bayesian analysis presented in Section 2.2, and therefore it is useful to summarize the essential properties in a definition. In particular, we assume we have a context C

which specifies the prior probability distribution for world events in the particular situation being studied. Suppose we are interested in whether or not property P holds in the world, given an image feature F with resolution parameter ϵ. Then we have the following definition of a "key feature":

Key Feature Definition: The feature F, with resolution parameter ϵ, is said to be a key feature for property P in the context C if:

$$R_{likelihood} = \frac{p(F|P\&C)}{p(F|not\,P\&C)} \text{ is unbounded as } \epsilon \to 0,$$

$$\tag{2.12}$$

$$R_{prior} = \frac{p(P|C)}{p(not\,P|C)} \text{ remains bounded away from zero as } \epsilon \to 0.$$

In this case, the posterior probability ratio R_{post} is unbounded as $\epsilon \to 0$, and thus, for sufficiently small ϵ, the image feature F provides a reliable indicator for world property P in context C.

The term "key feature" was introduced by Jepson and Richards (1993), with the intent that 'key' referred to unlocking reliable inferences about the world. The essential properties of key features, as listed in the above definition, have also been noted or, in fact, anticipated by a number of other authors. For example, Bennett, Hoffman and Prakash (1989) introduced the notion of an ideal observer, which has the same essential ingredients of a high likelihood ratio and a nonvanishing prior probability ratio. Similarly, Knill and Kersten (1991) discuss a different notion of an ideal observer which rests on these same conditions. (See chapters 5 and 6, this volume.) For example, Knill & Kersten (1991) discuss the inference of the 3D shape of a wire given just one orthographic image. The critical element is the perceiver's prior knowledge of modal structure about the way in which the wires can be bent in the context they treat. Also, in more natural contexts, there is a key feature for the chromaticity of the illuminant (Lee, 1986), and a key feature for rigid 3D motion given perspective projection (Bennett *et al.*, 1989; Jepson & Richards, 1993).

The notion of a key feature is clearly an idealization of both the properties of the world and the sensing process. As we discussed above we need to assume that physical events occur at a variety of scales and, in order to obtain the required sorts of prior distributions involving delta functions, this separation of scales must be assumed to be extreme. This idealization frees us from talking about detection rates, acceptable false target probabilities, and so on. In fact, we view one of the most important contributions of the idea of a key feature to be that, in freeing us from such details, we are left to consider appropriate representations for world structure in a much simpler setting. In the next two sections we illustrate this by describing a suitable representation for a simple domain, along with the use of this representation in determining the reliability of various inferences.

2.4 Modal analysis

We began this paper by saying that the world we live in is a very structured place, and that it is knowledge of this structure which allows us to make reliable inferences from our various sensory signals (Bobick, 1987; Richards & Bobick, 1988). So far we have provided a glimpse into the details of how this might come about. We saw earlier how the essential ingredients of a key feature, namely a large likelihood ratio and a nonzero prior, were both important for obtaining a reliable inference. Moreover we saw how regularities in our world can give rise to these essential ingredients. For example, we showed that the inference that an object is stationary rests on the fact that our world is structured so that objects often *are* stationary. This regularity, trivial as it sounds, is reflected as a mode in the prior probability distribution for the motion of objects in our world. The existence of this mode was shown to be critical in order to obtain a reliable inference that an object being observed is in fact at rest.

In this section we attempt to broaden the picture we have painted so far. In particular, we wish to show how a property space may consist of an embedded set of modes, and how these modes may interact with those occurring in a different property space. The particular example we consider is an idealization of a ball inside a box. The ball can move around inside the box, bounce off of the walls, roll along the floor or simply rest on the floor. Our goal is to illustrate a modal analysis of this context, and to briefly examine how reliable inferences may arise given perceptual data in this more complex domain. In order to keep the analysis simple we keep a strict idealization of the domain, which allows the essential structure of several natural inferences to be clearly exposed.

2.4.1 *Motion modes: A ball in a box*

The position of the ball's center of mass is denoted by $\mathbf{x}(t)$, which is taken to form a continuous trajectory. The velocity of the ball, $\mathbf{v}(t)$, is taken to be piecewise continuous in order to model collisions with the box. For the purpose of this section the critical observation is that the velocity of the ball appears naturally at several scales. In particular, we distinguish small velocities of the ball due to vibrations of the box, air currents, and other small perturbations, from the range of velocities achieved by throwing it, dropping it, or hitting it with a squash racket. We idealize the first distribution as the ball being at rest, that is the single point $\mathbf{v} = \vec{0}$, while the latter corresponds to a range of velocities which occur with the ball in the air. In addition, there is the set of velocities which occur while the ball is rolling on the floor. Here again there is a separation of scales, with the component of the velocity in the direction perpendicular to the floor taken to be negligible.

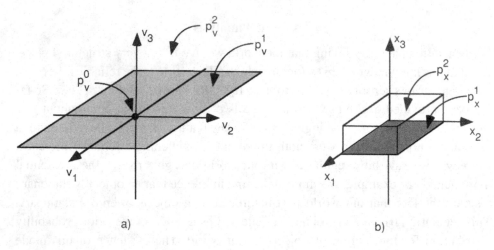

Fig. 2.1.

This notion of a separation of scales between the velocities which occur due to different physical processes does not mean an exclusive separation. In particular, we allow that the ball can momentarily be moving slowly while it is in the air even though this speed is more typical of the ball being on the floor. For example, if the ball bounces nearly vertically, then it will be nearly stationary at the top of it's trajectory. Our point about the separation of scales is that the distribution of velocities of the ball while it is in the air has a broad range and it is the *exceptional situation* which can produce a small velocity. Our idealization is then to take this separation of scales to be extreme. In particular, we take the small motions due to vibrations, etc. to be negligible, and treat the "at rest" state as the single point $\mathbf{v} = \vec{0}$.

The modes in the prior probability distribution on a configuration space correspond to the effects of different physical processes, operating at different scales and existing primarily on different sets within this configuration space. For example, consider the configuration space consisting only of the set of velocities, $\mathbf{v}(t)$, of the ball. Then, as depicted in Figure 2.1a we have a mode for being at rest (i.e. at the point $\mathbf{v} = \vec{0}$, another for rolling or sliding on the floor (i.e. in the plane $v_3 = 0$), and a third mode for velocities which occur during free fall. This third mode is taken to be a smooth distribution over the three dimensional configuration space $\mathbf{v}$. The critical point is that the processes operating at different scales have resulted in modes that exist on sets which have different scales in particular directions. We have idealized this separation of scales to the extreme of changing the *dimension* of the various subsets corresponding to modes in the configuration space. For example, smooth free fall generates velocities smoothly distributed over the 3D configuration space, rolling motion only exists in the 2D subset consisting of $v_3 = 0$, while being at rest occurs only at a single point, namely the origin. Our prior model then is to put smooth probability distributions on each of these sets.

To be concrete, we take the prior distribution for velocities $\mathbf{v}(t)$ to have the form of the mixture model

$$p(\mathbf{v}) = \pi_v^0 p_0(\mathbf{v}) + \pi_v^1 p_1(\mathbf{v}) + \pi_v^2 p_2(\mathbf{v}). \qquad (2.13)$$

Here p_n denotes the *component distribution* associated with the nth mode or process. Each of these component distributions is combined with it's *mixing proportion* π_v^n, and the sum provides the desired prior distribution. The sum of the π_v^n over the n processes should be 1. For processes which exist on sets having a dimension smaller than the full configuration space, such as rolling, the prior distribution is taken to be a smoothly modulated delta function along this set. In particular, for our current example, we have component distributions of the following form

$$p_0(\mathbf{v}) = \delta(\mathbf{v}),$$
$$p_1(\mathbf{v}) = \delta(v_3)q_1(v_1, v_2), \qquad (2.14)$$
$$p_2(\mathbf{v}) \text{ is a bounded function of } \mathbf{v}.$$

Note that p_0 represents the "at rest" mode, p_1 represents rolling or sliding on the floor with $q_1(v_1, v_2)$ some bounded distribution over the plane of horizontal velocities $(v_1, v_2, 0)$. The final mode, for particles on a ballistic trajectory for example, is accounted for by the last component, $p_2(\mathbf{v})$. We assume that both q_1 and p_2 are bounded functions in order to rule out the possibility of additional modal structure not already represented by the delta functions in (2.14).

Given our analysis in the preceding sections, one might expect that these modes play a critical role in making inferences such as whether the ball is at rest or moving at time t. Before considering a Bayesian analysis of such an inference it is useful to first examine a separate configuration space for the ball-in-a-box example which represents spatial properties of the system.

2.4.2 Spatial modes: A ball in a box

The position of the ball's center of mass, $\mathbf{x}(t)$, provides another example of a configuration space for which the prior distribution has a modal structure. Here, we have one mode consisting of a smooth distribution over the inside of the box which corresponds to positions of the ball during free fall. Also, there is a mode on the floor, say $x_3 = 0$, which corresponds to situations in which the ball is rolling or simply at rest on the floor (see Figure 2.1b). Finally, we assume that the collisions are effectively instantaneous[†] so there are no additional modes arranged around the walls and ceiling of the box.

Following our previous example, such a prior distribution can be conveniently written as the mixture model

$$p(\mathbf{x}) = \pi_x^1 p_1(\mathbf{x}) + \pi_x^2 p_2(\mathbf{x}). \tag{2.15}$$

Again the quantities π_x^n provide the mixing proportions for the two modes. The component distributions p_n are given by

$$p_1(\mathbf{x}) = \delta(x_3) q_1(x_1, x_2).$$
$$p_2(\mathbf{x}) \text{ is a bounded function of } \mathbf{x}. \tag{2.16}$$

Note that p_1 represents the both the "at rest" mode and the "rolling" mode, with $q_1(x_1, x_2)$ representing some bounded distribution over the plane of horizontal positions $(x_1, x_2, 0)$. Since there is no special position on the floor for the ball to be at rest we do not have a pure delta function in the spatial domain. Also, no point on the floor should be forbidden, so we take $q_1(x_1, x_2)$ to be a smooth nonzero distribution over the floor. The second mode, $p_2(\mathbf{x})$, accounts for the positions achieved during it's various possible trajectories, and we take it to be a smooth (nonzero) distribution over the interior of the box.

2.4.3 Mode coupling

Given the spatial and motion modes described in the previous sections we need to consider how they can be combined to derive the prior probability for the ball to be at position $\mathbf{x}(t)$ with velocity $\mathbf{v}(t)$ at time t. Our basic point is a simple one, namely that the appropriate joint distribution is *not* just what one obtains by treating the priors for position and velocity independently. Rather, the mixture distributions for position and velocity must be coupled in a nontrivial way (see also Pearl, 1988; Yuille et al., 1994).

To see this, consider the distribution $p_{indep}(\mathbf{x}, \mathbf{v})$ obtained by treating the position $\mathbf{x}$ and velocity $\mathbf{v}$ as independent, that is

$$p_{indep}(\mathbf{x}, \mathbf{v}) = p(\mathbf{x})p(\mathbf{v}). \tag{2.17}$$

Our claim is that this distribution does not provide the correct modal properties. In particular, consider the conditional prior probability density that the ball is at rest, given that it is at position $\mathbf{x}$, for some $\mathbf{x}$ in the interior of the box. Since there is no physical process generating a mode for the ball to be at rest, we should expect the

---

[†] This is yet another form of the argument that processes occur at different scales. Here we are taking the time duration of a collision as negligible compared to the temporal resolution dt of the system.

prior to similar to the one obtained in Section 2.2 for the gas particle (see equation (2.8)). That is, we expect the prior to be roughly

$$p(||\mathbf{v}|| < \epsilon \mid x_3 > 0) = p_2(\vec{0})\epsilon^3 + O(\epsilon^4),$$

with $p_2(\mathbf{v})$ the prior distribution for velocities while the ball is in the air. The actual coefficient $p_2(\vec{0})$ of the leading order term does not matter here; what is significant is that this probability is of order ϵ^3. In contrast, it follows from equation (2.17) that

$$p_{indep}(||\mathbf{v}|| < \epsilon \mid x_3 > 0) = \pi_v^0 + O(\epsilon^2),$$

which is just the mixing proportion, π_v^0, of the rest state to leading order.

The reason for this difference is that the independent combination of the spatial and motion distributions, namely p_{indep}, does not take into consideration the appropriate coupling between the modes in the different configuration spaces. In particular, notice that when the product in (2.17) is written out we obtain six different modes in the resulting mixture model. Some of these modes do not make sense physically. For example, when the ball is above the floor there should be no mode for being at rest (i.e. the mixture proportion π_v^0 should be 0), and no mode for horizontal motion (i.e. $\pi_v^1 = 0$). Also, when the ball is on the floor, there should not be a mode for a general 3D velocity (i.e. $\pi_v^2 = 0$). Together these give the mode coupling conditions

$$\begin{aligned} \pi_v^0 = \pi_v^1 = 0 \text{ whenever } x_3 > 0, \\ \pi_v^2 = 0 \text{ whenever } x_3 = 0. \end{aligned} \qquad (2.18)$$

These coupling conditions can also be incorporated into a mixture model for the joint distribution of $\mathbf{x}$ and $\mathbf{v}$, in which only the physically plausible modes are kept. In particular, an appropriate model is

$$p(\mathbf{x}, \mathbf{v}) = \pi_{x,v}^0 p_0(\mathbf{x}, \mathbf{v}) + \pi_{x,v}^1 p_1(\mathbf{x}, \mathbf{v}) + \pi_{x,v}^2 p_2(\mathbf{x}, \mathbf{v}). \qquad (2.19)$$

Here the three modes, or component processes, are

$$\begin{aligned} p_0(\mathbf{x}, \mathbf{v}) &= \delta(\mathbf{v})\delta(x_3)q_1(x_1, x_2), \\ p_1(\mathbf{x}, \mathbf{v}) &= \delta(v_3)\delta(x_3)q_1(x_1, x_2, v_1, v_2), \\ p_2(\mathbf{x}, \mathbf{v}) &\text{ is a bounded distribution.} \end{aligned} \qquad (2.20)$$

Here $q_1(x_1 x_2)$ is the same as introduced in equation (2.16). Also, we constrain the new distributions $q_1(x_1, x_2, v_1, v_2)$ and $p_2(\mathbf{x}, \mathbf{v})$ to be bounded functions, which eliminates the possibility of further modal structure within this model. Note that the three mixture components in equation (2.19) correspond to the processes at rest on the floor, rolling or sliding on the floor, and moving through the air.

2.4.4 Reliable inferences

Suppose the image feature F_{floor} includes the fact that the image velocity of the ball satisfies $\|\mathbf{v}_{image}(t)\| < \epsilon$, along with some positional information about the ball and the box. In particular we assume that the image feature F_{floor} also shows that the position of the ball in the image is consistent with the ball being on the floor. Should we infer from the observation that the ball is stationary? Let property P denote that the ball is stationary in the world (i.e. $\|\mathbf{v}\| < \epsilon$), given our "ball-in-a-box" context, B. First consider the likelihood ratio $R_{likelihood} = p(F|P\&B)/p(F|not\,P\&B)$. Then $R_{likelihood}$ is of order $1/\epsilon^2$, as follows: The numerator of the likelihood ratio is nonzero, since image motion is typically small when the ball is at rest (property P). On the other hand, in the absence of property P, the image motion will be small only if both coordinates of the image velocity also happen to be small. However, because the prior distribution for $\mathbf{v}$ requires that these components be smoothly distributed, $\|\mathbf{v}_{image}\|$ will be less than ϵ with a probability proportional to ϵ^2. The likelihood ratio is therefore of order $1/\epsilon^2$ as $\epsilon \to 0$, and we see that the first condition of the key feature definition is satisfied, given our observation of no image motion.

Next consider the prior probability ratio $R_{prior} = p(P|B)/p(not\,P|B)$. The mode coupling condition (2.18) allows a mode in which the ball is stationary so long as it is on the floor. Moreover, there is also a spatial mode for the ball to be on the floor. By equation (2.19), the prior $p(P|B)$ is just $\pi_{x,v}^0$ to leading order in ϵ, and therefore the ratio R_{prior} is given by $\pi_{x,v}^0/(1 - \pi_{x,v}^0)$ to leading order. Therefore the second condition of our key feature definition is satisfied, and we can reliably conclude that the ball is at rest. Notice that we can also conclude that the ball must be *on the floor*. In fact, it can be shown that this state in which the ball is on the floor and at rest has the a posteriori probability of $1 - O(\epsilon^2)$, and is therefore a reliable inference for sufficiently small ϵ.

Now consider another image feature F_{air} for the ball-in-a-box where again $\|\mathbf{v}_{image}(t)\| < \epsilon$, but $x_3 > 0$, and hence the ball cannot be on the floor. Then, from the mode coupling condition (18), it follows that there is no mode for the ball to be at rest. Indeed, the prior probability ratio R_{prior} for it to be at rest is only of order ϵ^3. Hence the feature F_{air} does not satisfy the second key feature condition, namely that R_{prior} remain bounded away from zero, as $\epsilon \to 0$. Given the likelihood ratio $R_{likelihood}$ is of order $1/\epsilon^2$, the posteriori ratio R_{post} for property P being correct is only $O(\epsilon)$. Hence the odds strongly favor the conclusion that the ball must be in motion, even though that motion must be special in that it is nearly directed along the line of sight (see Figure 6.4 in Jepson and Richards, 1992, for a different perceptual example of the possible use of such mode coupling conditions).

2.5 Qualitative probabilities

An important property of the modal analysis presented in the previous section is that the conclusions, namely the reliability of the inference that the ball is at rest, do not depend on quantitative details of the various smooth component distributions in the prior probability model (2.19). In fact, all that matters in the limit as $\epsilon \to 0$ is that the mixture proportion for the mode "at rest on the floor" is nonzero (i.e. $\pi^0_{x,v} > 0$), along with various nondegeneracy assumptions which ensure the density functions $q_1(v)$, $p_2(v)$, etc. are smooth and bounded. A perceiver can therefore gain some freedom from knowing precise quantitative details about the appropriate prior distributions, yet still expect to make reliable inferences, at least for contexts that support key features (see also Doyle & Sacks, 1989). Here we illustrate this point by considering inferences about the occurrence of a collision, again using the "ball-in-a-box" context.

2.5.1 *Velocity discontinuities*

Recall that the position of the ball's center of mass, $x(t)$, is taken to form a continuous trajectory but that the velocity of the ball, $v(t)$, is taken to be piecewise continuous. Behind this assumption there is again a separation of scales of various physical processes, just as we had for the distinction of moving versus at rest in the previous section. Here we note that forces on the ball arise naturally at several scales. At one scale we have gravity, aerodynamic effects, and so on. It is assumed that the forces due to effects at this scale are significantly smaller than the typical forces due to collisions. We emphasize again that this separation is not absolute since collisions can, of course, produce small forces, but it is an exceptional collision which produces a force as small as gravity.

The analysis is simplest when we take this separation of scales to be extreme. In particular, over a time interval of duration dt, which is just resolvable by the system, we take the change of velocity due to the gravity and aerodynamic effects to be negligible while collisions can produce significant changes in the velocity. At the resolution determined by dt then, the velocity of the ball may be discontinuous due to collisions with the walls. Otherwise the motion of the ball is well approximated by a constant velocity over each interval $(t, t + dt)$.

Consider then the configuration space made up of the 6D-points, $(v(t), v(t+dt))$. As discussed above, the modes in the prior distribution on this space are meant to correspond to the effects of different physical processes, operating at different scales and existing primarily on different sets within this space. For example, smooth trajectories appear on the 3D surface $v(t) = v(t + dt)$, where we have used the

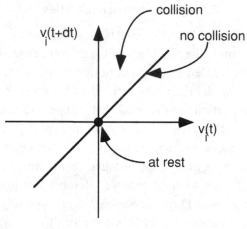

Fig. 2.2.

idealization that the smaller forces produce negligible velocity changes over time intervals of length dt. In Figure 2.2 we depict a 2D slice of the velocity configuration space, and this smooth motion mode is represented simply by the line $v_1(t) = v_1(t + dt)$. The modes we studied in the previous section, namely for the ball to be at rest and for the ball to be rolling or sliding on the floor will also appear in this 6D configuration space.

The large forces due to collisions can generate large changes in the velocity during a time step of dt. We take these collision events as producing a smooth distribution in the configuration space $(\mathbf{v}(t), \mathbf{v}(t + dt))$. In fact, there is additional structure within the set of velocities consistent with a collision occurring between time t and $t + dt$. For example, if the ball can only collide with the stationary box then conservation of energy (neglecting spin) requires that the speed $||\mathbf{v}(t + dt)||$ can be no larger than $||\mathbf{v}(t)||$. In addition, there are further restrictions on the direction of the outgoing trajectory due to the surface normal and spin on the ball. In order to keep our analysis simple we ignore these further regularities and just require that the component of the prior distribution due to collisions is a bounded function of $(\mathbf{v}(t), \mathbf{v}(t + dt))$.

2.5.2 Collisions

In order to make inferences about collisions we need to consider the prior distribution for the ball to be at position $\mathbf{x}(t + dt)$ with velocity $\mathbf{v}(t + dt)$ at time $t + dt$, given that it was at $\mathbf{x}(t)$ with velocity $\mathbf{v}(t)$ at time t. Again it should be clear that the desired distribution cannot be represented with an independent combination of a distribution for the position of the ball with a second distribution for the velocity of the ball at $t + dt$. Instead, we need to take into account further structure about the context, such as the fact that velocity discontinuities only occur when the ball collides with the box.

The desired prior can be broken up into two cases, depending on whether or not a collision occurs during the time interval $(t, t + dt)$. Since we are taking the time duration dt to be short enough such that the velocity of the ball is essentially constant, the ball's trajectory can be initially predicted by the linear model

$$\mathbf{x}_p(\tau) = \mathbf{x}(t) + (\tau - t)\mathbf{v}(t), \tag{2.21}$$

for $\tau \in (t, t + dt)$. This prediction is taken to be accurate so long as this trajectory does not penetrate the walls of the box. Here t, $\mathbf{x}(t)$ and $\mathbf{v}(t)$ are treated as constants, and they together completely specify the trajectory $\mathbf{x}_p(\tau)$. We say that the trajectory $\mathbf{x}_p(\tau)$ *transversally* intersects the box at a point $\mathbf{x}_c$ if the path intersects the box at that point and is not tangent to the box. Thus rolling or sliding motions are non-transversal, while a typical collision is a tranversal intersection. In the cases where no collision occurs during $[t, t + dt)$ we take the prior model to be

$$p(\mathbf{x}(t + dt), \mathbf{v}(t + dt) \mid \mathbf{x}(t), \mathbf{v}(t), noCollision)$$

$$= \delta(\mathbf{x}(t + dt) - \mathbf{x}_p(t + dt))\delta(\mathbf{v}(t + dt) - \mathbf{v}(t)). \tag{2.22}$$

Here the conditional term $noCollision$ refers to the fact that the predicted trajectory $\mathbf{x}_p(\tau)$ does not transversally intersect the box for $\tau \in [t, t + dt)$. The two delta functions in the above equation impose the constraint that the predicted trajectory $\mathbf{x}_p(t + dt)$ is accurate in the absence of collisions. In practice one would need to replace these delta functions with distributions which have nonzero variances. But for simplicity here we are assuming the scale of the errors in the prediction is negligible over a time step of length dt.

In the second case, for which a collision occurs, the predicted trajectory $\mathbf{x}_p(\tau)$ is piecewise linear. The discontinuity occurs at the point of transversal intersection, namely $(\mathbf{x}_c, t_c)$, between the line described in (2.21) and the box. For simplicity we neglect the special cases in which several discontinuities may appear in the time interval $(t, t + dt)$. The predicted trajectory is thus

$$\mathbf{x}_p(\tau) = \begin{cases} \mathbf{x}(t) + (\tau - t)\mathbf{v}(t), & \text{for } \tau \in [t, t_c]; \\ \mathbf{x}_c + (\tau - t_c)\mathbf{v}(t + dt), & \text{for } \tau \in [t_c, t + dt). \end{cases} \tag{2.23}$$

Here we have approximated the impact to be instantaneous, and taken the reflected velocity, $\mathbf{v}(t + dt)$ to be constant after the impact. Clearly, the assumption here is that the reflected velocity points back into the interior of the box or, at least, along the wall from the contact position $\mathbf{x}_c$. Given this predicted trajectory $\mathbf{x}_p(\tau)$, the prior distribution given a collision is taken to be

$$p(\mathbf{x}(t+dt), \mathbf{v}(t+dt) \,|\mathbf{x}(t), \mathbf{v}(t), \, Collision\,)$$

$$= \delta(\mathbf{x}(t+dt) - \mathbf{x}_p(t+dt))p_{refl}(\mathbf{v}(t+dt)|\mathbf{v}(t), \mathbf{x}_c). \qquad (2.24)$$

Here p_{refl} provides the distribution for the reflected velocity, $\mathbf{v}(t+dt)$, given the incoming velocity $\mathbf{v}(t)$ and the point of collision $\mathbf{x}_c$. In order to model relatively unstructured scattering of the ball off of the wall, due to spins or imperfections in the wall, we take p_{refl} to be a smooth bounded function of $\mathbf{v}(t+dt)$, subject to the constraint that $\mathbf{v}(t+dt)$ cannot point out of the box from $\mathbf{x}_c$.

It is also possible to model more specialized structure in the process of the ball bouncing off of the walls. For example, the distribution p_{refl} above could be augmented with a mixture of different modes of reflection. In addition, to the general scattering used in (2.24), we could include a second mode in which the reflected velocity is in the direction of the perfect reflection. A third mode could be added in which the motion immediately after the collision is directed along the planar surface at $\mathbf{x}_c$, as in a rolling or sliding motion. Thus our basic framework in terms of mixture models is sufficiently expressive to capture a wide range of phenomena. However, for our purposes here, it is convenient to keep the model simple and ignore these more detailed structures.

2.5.3 Non-degeneracy conditions

In order to complete the specification of our ball-in-a-box context B, we need to impose some non-degeneracy conditions on the various prior components which we have introduced so far. For example, consider the component distribution $p_2(\mathbf{x}, \mathbf{v})$, introduced in (2.19), which is just the prior probability distribution for the ball to be at location $\mathbf{x}(t)$ with velocity $\mathbf{v}(t)$ during it's free motion through the air. Up to this point we have only required that p_2 is a bounded function of $\mathbf{x}$ and $\mathbf{v}$. But clearly this is too broad a class of distributions, since entirely unintended behaviours can arise by choosing distributions with particular structures. For example, p_2 might be zero within a wide layer all around the inside of the box, in which case the prior probability of a collision would also vanish. To avoid such bogus properties we need to bound the various component distributions from below. Just such a bound was used in Section 2.4.4, where we discussed the inference that the ball was resting on the floor of the box. There we needed to assume that the density $q_1(x)$ was bounded away from zero over the floor of the box. The main point of this section is that such a bound can be conveniently expressed in terms of a single *canonical* distribution.

First consider the component distribution $p_2(\mathbf{x}, \mathbf{v})$. We take the canonical model, $m_{x,v}(\mathbf{x}, \mathbf{v})$ to be a uniform distribution over the inside of the box for all velocities having speed less than some constant v_{max}. That is,

$$m_{x,v}(\mathbf{x}, \mathbf{v}) = \begin{cases} K \text{ for } \mathbf{x} \text{ in the box and } ||\mathbf{v}|| < v_{max}; \\ 0 \text{ otherwise.} \end{cases} \quad (2.25)$$

Here K is a positive normalization constant, which depends on the volume of the box and v_{max}, such that the model distribution $m_{x,v}$ integrates to one. Our nondegeneracy condition on $p_2(\mathbf{x}, \mathbf{v})$ is simply that there exists a positive constant c such that

$$p_2(\mathbf{x}, \mathbf{v}) \geq c m_{x,v}(\mathbf{x}, \mathbf{v}) \quad (2.26)$$

for all values of $\mathbf{x}$ and $\mathbf{v}$. In words, our component density $p_{22}(\mathbf{x}, \mathbf{v})$ must be bounded below by some constant multiple of our canonical model $m_{x,v}(\mathbf{x}, \mathbf{v})$. Such a condition, ensures the prior density p_2 is nonzero at any point $(\mathbf{x}, \mathbf{v})$, with $\mathbf{x}$ in the box and $\mathbf{v}$ having a speed of at most v_{max}. As we show in the next subsection this condition is sufficient to ensure that collisions between the ball and the box do occur with a positive prior probability. Notice that equation (2.26) is a rather loose constraint on the component $p_2(\mathbf{x}, \mathbf{v})$ in that many different distributions satisfy this constraint.

Similarly, to specify context B, we also need to impose a non-degeneracy condition on the conditional prior $p_{refl}(\vec{u}|\mathbf{v}, \mathbf{x}_c)$ used in equation (2.24). In this case we take our canonical model m_{refl} to be

$$m_{refl}(\vec{u}|\mathbf{v}, \mathbf{x}_c) = \begin{cases} K' \text{ for } \vec{n}(\mathbf{x}_c) \cdot \vec{u} \leq 0 \text{ and } ||\vec{u}|| \leq ||\mathbf{v}||; \\ 0 \text{ otherwise.} \end{cases} \quad (2.27)$$

Again K' is a positive normalization factor. Here $\vec{n}(\mathbf{x}_c)$ is an outward pointing normal vector for the side of the box which contains the point of collision $\mathbf{x}_c$. The above model states that the reflected velocity $\vec{u}$ is uniformly distributed in any direction, other than those that penetrate the box, with the speed limited to be no larger than the speed $||\mathbf{v}(t)||$ along the incoming trajectory. Our nondegeneracy condition for the distribution p_{refl} is then simply that there exists a positive constant c such that

$$p_{refl}(\vec{u}|\mathbf{v}, \mathbf{x}_c) \geq c m_{refl}(\vec{u}|\mathbf{v}, \mathbf{x}_c) \quad (2.28)$$

for all $\vec{u}$, $\mathbf{v}$, and $\mathbf{x}_c$.

Finally, non-degeneracy conditions are required for the remaining distributions, $q_1(x_1, x_2)$ and $q_1(x_1, x_2, v_1, v_2)$ in equation (2.20). For $q_1(x_1, x_2)$ we take the canonical distribution, say m_x, to be a uniform distribution over the floor of the box. Recall that the distribution $q_1(x_1, x_2, v_1, v_2)$ models the position and velocity of the ball while it is rolling on the floor. A canonical model distribution, say $m_{x,v}$ similar to the one used in equation (2.25) can be formulated, but with x_3 and v_3 constrained to be zero.

This completes the specification of the context B. In particular the prior distribution in this context B is given by equations (2.19), (2.22), and (2.24). Each of the mixture proportions $\pi^n_{x,v}$ in equation (2.19) are taken to be positive. More-over, the various component distributions q_1, p_2, and p_{refl} must each satisfy a non-degeneracy condition of the form (2.26) and (2.28) using the corresponding canonical distribution m_x, etc. A large class of particular quantitative distributions satisfy these conditions, and it is in this sense that our probabilistic model is qual-itative. The perceiver need not precisely specify the prior distributions, but rather only needs to describe it's modal structure. Our last task is to consider what sort of reliable inferences can be made given only that the prior distribution is in this class of distributions which are consistent with the canonical model, that is, within the context B.

2.5.4 *Key feature for a collision*

As Rubin has pointed out (1986), the observation of a velocity discontinuity in an image can be a reliable indicator of a velocity discontinuity in 3D. For our context B, a velocity discontinuity occurs only if the ball collides transversally with the box. In fact, as we show in this section, the observation of a discontinuity in the image velocity provides a key feature for such a collision.

It is useful to walk through the argument in terms of the Bayesian analysis we presented in Section 2.2 and the key feature definition provided in Section 3. Let the feature F denote the observation of image velocities $\mathbf{v}_{image}(t)$ and $\mathbf{v}_{image}(t + dt)$ such that the norm of the difference satisfies $||\mathbf{v}_{image}(t) - \mathbf{v}_{image}(t + dt)|| > dv$. Here the threshold $dv > 0$ should be taken smaller than the rough scale of velocities which occur while the ball is in the air. That is, given our canonical model, for which speeds at least up to the value v_{max} are known to occur, we should take $dv << v_{max}$. Next, let property P denote the occurrence of a collision of the ball with the box at some time in the interval $(t, t + dt)$. Similarly, let *not P* denote the property that no collision occurs during the same time interval. Finally, suppose the (absolute) error in the measured image velocities is no larger than ϵ.

Consider the likelihood ratio, $p(F|P\&B)/p(F|not P\&B)$, as the measurement resolution ϵ goes to zero. The denominator is just the likelihood of observing the image feature F given that no collision (i.e. *not P*) occurs. In our context B, the change in the 3D velocity over a time interval of duration dt is negligible unless a collision occurs. Given orthographic projection, the same holds true for the exact image velocity. Thus, given *not P*, the observation of a significant change in the observed image velocity (i.e. the observation of F) can only be due to measurement error. Therefore, as the velocity measurement resolution, ϵ, goes to zero it must be the case that $p(F|not P\&B)$ also goes to zero. That is, a smooth 3D trajectory is increasingly unlikely to produce a sudden large jump in the image motion as the measurement resolution becomes finer.

Next consider the numerator in the likelihood ratio, $p(F|P\&B)$, which is just the likelihood of observing the image feature F given a collision occurs. In general this likelihood depends on the nature of the collisions. For example, if all the collisions occurred with the ball moving extremely slowly, then it is possible that the likelihood $p(F|P\&B)$ might vanish since no velocity step will be larger than dv, as is required to trigger the feature F. Therefore, to ensure a positive likelihood we must use the nondegeneracy conditions discussed in the previous section.

In order to check that $p(F|P\&B)$ is bounded away from zero, it is convenient to consider the collisions which *fail* to generate a suitable image feature F. For each choice of incoming velocity, $\mathbf{v}(t)$, the detection of a velocity discontinuity will fail precisely when $||\mathbf{v}_{image}(t) - \mathbf{v}_{image}(t+dt)|| \leq dv$. The set of all reflected velocities $\mathbf{v}(t+dt)$ which satisfy this inequality is a tube through the 3D velocity space, having radius dv, which is aligned with the viewing direction. Since dv is chosen to be much smaller that the maximum speed v_{max} in the canonical model, then for all sufficiently large incoming velocities $\mathbf{v}(t)$, there must be a large region outside the tube in which the canonical density $m_{refl}(\mathbf{v}(t+dt)|\mathbf{v}(t), \mathbf{x}_c)$ is strictly positive. The result then is that, given the canonical model, $p(F|P\&B)$ is strictly positive. And, by our nondegeneracy conditions, the same must hold for any suitable prior. As a result, we have shown that the likelihood ratio is unbounded as ϵ goes to zero.

In order for discontinuities in the image velocity to be a key feature for collisions we need show that the prior probability ratio satisfies the second condition in the key feature definition. That is, the prior probability ratio, $p(P|B)/p(not P|B)$, must be positive (or, more precisely, bounded away from zero as ϵ goes to zero). Here again we need to use the nondegeneracy conditions, this time to argue that a collision during a time interval of duration dt has a positive prior probability. To do this, consider the region close to one wall of the box, say within a distance dx of the wall. Then the canonical model $m_{x,v}(\mathbf{x}(t), \mathbf{v}(t))$ ensures a positive probability for the ball to be in such a region at time t. In order for a collision to occur before time $t+dt$ we also require that the velocity, $\mathbf{v}(t)$, satisfies $\vec{n}_{wall} \cdot \mathbf{v}(t) > dx/dt$, where $\vec{n}_{wall}$ is the outward pointing normal. But with dx chosen sufficiently small (i.e. $dx < v_{max}dt$), there is a positive probability that the ball will also have a velocity such that a transversal impact will occur before time $t+dt$. Thus collisions occur with a strictly positive probability under our canonical model, and therefore the same must be true for any prior consistent with this model. Thus we find $p(P|B)$ is bounded away from zero, which is sufficient to ensure the second requirement in the key feature definition. As a result, a discontinuity in the image velocity is a key feature for a collision in 3D in our ball-in-a-box context B.

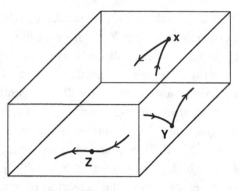

Fig. 2.3.

2.5.5 Reliable inferences

Given that we have a key feature, suppose you observe a velocity discontinuity in the trajectory near the point 'X' in Figure 2.3. Then the calculations in the previous subsection show that the posterior probability ratio, $p(P|F\&B)/p(not\,P|F\&B)$, is large and the odds overwhelmingly favour the conclusion that the ball hit the back wall (or a transparent front one) somewhere near the visual ray through the point X.

In fact, the priors introduced above also sanction the conclusion that, after the collision, the ball bounced away from the wall rather than sliding along it. To show this, consider the set of all collisions which are consistent with the images of the three points $\mathbf{x}(t)$, $\mathbf{x}_c$, and $\mathbf{x}(t + dt)$. The situation in which the ball slides along the wall is uniquely specified by these observations, and a single value of the reflected velocity $\mathbf{v}(t + dt)$ is determined. Alternatively, for bounces in which the ball comes away from the wall, the set of reflected velocities consistent with the observations form a line directed along the visual ray. Including some image noise changes these structures to a small neighbourhood and a tube, respectively. The basic structure is similar to our "at rest"/"moving along the line of sight" distinction we had before. In fact, since our canonical distribution for 3D reflected velocities (namely $m_{refl}(\vec{u}|\mathbf{v}, \mathbf{x}_c)$) does not have a mode directed along the wall, it is much more probable that the observed reflected velocity is away from the wall (i.e. $\mathbf{v}(t + dt)$ lies somewhere in the tube, not just near one end).

As an alternative example, suppose you observe an abrupt stop at X. That is, there is a discontinuity in the image velocity at time t, and that image of the ball remains at rest immediately after this event. The best bet is then that the ball hit the wall and is now coming towards/going away from you. The analysis again provides a tube of possible motions consistent with the ball moving towards or away from the viewer (to within the resolution ϵ). The prior $m_{refl}(\vec{u}|\mathbf{v}, \mathbf{x}_c)$ has no mode at the rest state, and as a result the posterior probability is strongly in favour of motion (nearly) along the line of sight.

Next, suppose you observe a velocity discontinuity in the trajectory near the point Y in Figure 2.3, so the image observations are consistent with the ball bouncing off of the floor. Actually, the same observations are consistent with the ball colliding with the floor and then beginning to roll, or rolling and then suddenly leaving the floor, or, finally, executing a velocity discontinuity as it rolls on the floor. Does our current qualitative probabilistic model have anything to say about the choice between these various possibilities? The latter two interpretations are eliminated by our model since velocity discontinuities do not occur unless the trajectory of the motion is transverse to a surface (i.e. the floor is smooth). We are therefore left with two interpretations, one in which the ball bounces off of the floor, and another in which the ball impacts the floor but then immediately begins rolling. This case is different than the one discussed previously for the collision occurring at the point X, since now there is a mode for rolling or sliding along the floor. Which interpretation, if either, is more probable?

The issue can be resolved using the model for the reflected velocity, $m_{refl}(\vec{u}|\mathbf{v}, \mathbf{x}_c)$, just as for the collision at X treated above. In particular, the majority of collisions (i.e. $1 - O(\epsilon)$ versus $O(\epsilon)$) predicted by this model will be away from the floor. Thus we can reliably infer that the ball is in the air shortly after the collision with the floor. (Note that we cannot apply the prior distribution $p_{x,v}$ to the analysis of the state $(\mathbf{x}(t + dt), \mathbf{v}(t + dt))$ at time $t + dt$, since the conditional distribution p_{refl} shows that this state is not independent of the initial state $(\mathbf{x}(t), \mathbf{v}(t))$.)

Finally, suppose you observe the smooth trajectory through the image point Z at time t, and that $||\mathbf{v}_{image}(t + dt) - \mathbf{v}_{image}(t)|| < \epsilon$ (call this F_{smooth}). The reader is left to check that the two most plausible interpretations are: 1) the ball is moving smoothly (no collision) through the air during $(t, t+dt)$; 2) the ball is rolling/sliding smoothly along the floor during $(t, t + dt)$. In particular, the probability that a collision will give rise to this image observation is $O(\epsilon^2)$. Therefore it is improbable that a collision has occurred (in fact F_{smooth} is a key feature for smooth motion during $(t, t + dt)$). We are therefore left with the above two possibilities. How should we decide between the two?

One way to decide is to seek the most probable category, that is, either the trajectory is in the air or it is on the ground. Our canonical distribution cannot uniquely designate one of these two categories as being necessarily more probable. The result depends on the mixture proportions for the prior probabilities of motion through the air and motion on the ground ($\pi^2_{x,v}$ and $\pi^1_{x,v}$, respectively), which have not been specified. The appropriate conclusion then is that without more information, we cannot decide on the most probable category.

A second way to decide is to seek the most probable *initial state* $(\mathbf{x}(t), \mathbf{v}(t))$, say up to our ubiquitous resolution parameter ϵ. Here, because of the mode for the ball to be rolling on the floor, there is a clear cut winner. The a posteriori probability for the (unique) rolling state is some constant, bounded away from zero. Each of the other states, accounting for 3D velocities in a neighbourhood of radius ϵ, have posterior probabilities of only $O(\epsilon)$. Thus rolling on the floor is the most probable state, even though it is possible that, as a category it is less probable than motion through the air.

This is not a paradox so much as a warning. The reason the category for motion through the air can be more probable is simply that it is made up of lots (i.e. $O(1/\epsilon)$) of states each of which have probability $O(\epsilon)$. While no single state may be very probable, the total probability over the category can be significant. The choice of which method to use to come up with a preferred interpretation depends on the task. For example, we might consider using the maximally probable state if we wish to intercept the ball. While, for purposes of predicting future events such as possible collisions with the floor, we may wish to consider the most probable category instead.

Our point with these examples is not to generate a detailed model of a ball in a box. Rather, we hope it has demonstrated that by using a qualitative model of the prior probability distribution we have been able to make simple back-of-the-envelope calculations to arrive at plausible inferences about events within an interesting natural context.

2.6 Summary

We have argued that for a perceiver to make reliable inferences about it's world, the perceiver should make use of world regularities. The class of regularities stressed are those that give rise to modal structures in the distribution of events. The essential ingredient of modal structure is simply that different physical processes generate effects distributed over significantly different scales. For example, the range of velocities of an object while it is in the air is significantly larger than the range due to small vibrations while the object is at rest on the ground. Similarly, differences of scale occur in the positions objects achieve during free fall versus where they come to rest, and also in the accelerations objects undergo due to gravitational or aerodynamic factors versus those during collisions. Once this basic notion that physical processes generate effects over significantly different scales is understood, then other examples that support reliable inferences become apparent, such as rigid 3D motion, articulated motion, skew or reflectional symmetry, or various patterns and groupings of objects.

We have taken such scale separations to be extreme, by assuming that the variation generated by a particular process is negligible, at least in particular directions.

This assumption frees us from considering many details, such as precisely how concentrated a particular process needs to be in order for a particular sensor measurement to indicate a world event with 95% confidence. Such details can be added when there is sufficient knowledge about the prior distributions and errors in the sensing process. Their inclusion here, however, would simply mask the important role of modal structure in making certain perceptual inferences reliable.

One application of modal structure is to the notion of a key feature, which is a specialization of the so called non-accidental properties. Roughly speaking, the basic criteria for a particular sensor measurement to be a key-feature for some world property are: i) the feature is highly unlikely to occur in the absence of the property, but often occurs in it's presence; and ii) the prior probability of the property occuring is not negligible. A non-accidental property need only satisfy the first condition here, which ensures the likelihood ratio is large. As we have discussed at some length, this condition alone is not sufficient to lead to a reliable inference. Rather, the reliability of the inference that the particular world property occurs depends critically on the second condition, namely that there must be a significant prior probability.

The presence of this condition on the prior probability has serious implications for perceptual systems. For example, consider a frog that reflexively responds to a dark blob that moves faster than a certain speed, but not at all when the blob moves slower than this speed. Clearly this beast is not computing a posteriori odds in the manner suggested by equation (2.5). But equally clearly, in more general contexts, the frog certainly would be better off if it could identify situations in which there was no known process which could cause a dark blob, observed to be at rest in the image, to actually be at rest in the world. This is analogous to our ball observed to be at rest in the image and projected against the back wall of the box. The appropriate inference in this case is that the blob is moving along the line of sight and, hence, such a blob would deserve further scrutiny. The more advanced perceptual system, then, should have the ability to represent the critical information needed to make the appropriate inference. Our notion of a context as a class of prior probability distributions over a configuration space, in which various modes are assumed to have nonzero mixture proportions, gives the advanced perceiver this capability. In particular, the mode coupling conditions were shown to be essential in order for a perceiver to arrive at the most probable conclusion, both when the ball is seen against the floor, and when it is seen against the back wall.

More generally, the context sensitivity of modal properties raises the possibility that a perceptual system may use an explicit representation of modal structure. In particular, instead of making an implicit use of modal structure, such as in the speed threshold of our hypothetical frog discussed above, a perceptual system may attempt to maintain an explicit representation of where and when different physical processes, responsible for different modal structures, are active. This is, after all, the critical ingredient in terms of the modal prior probability distributions discussed in this paper. What would one expect to be able to observe about such a system? Perhaps the primary property is that such a system should be able to rapidly learn about a particular class of novel environments, but should be much slower to learn about others. The environments which are rapidly learnable are ones in which the perceiver already knows the various modes, that is, their locations in configuration space, but does not know which modes have nonzero mixing proportions.

A preliminary psychophysical experiment down these lines has already been done (Feldman, 1992). The results provide some support for the hypothesis that an explicit representation of modal structure is involved in human perception, in that modal properties in a novel domain were shown to be learnable from a single example. Further investigation of how we learn to perceive novel environments promises to shed considerable light on how we represent structure in our world.

Acknowledgements

The first author wishes to thank Richard Mann for many fruitful discussions. This work was supported by CIAR, NSERC Canada, IRIS (Canada).

References

Albert, M.K. & Hoffman, D.D. (1991). Generic visions. Univ. Calif., Irvine, Math. Behav. Sciences Technical Report MBS-91-23. (Sci. Ameri.?)

Ames, A. (1951). Visual perception and the rotating trapezoidal window. *Psych. Monographs*, 65, **329** (entire issue).

Attneave, F. (1982). Pragnanz and soap bubble systems: a theoretical explanation, In *Organization and Representation in Perception*, ed. J. Beck. Hillsdale, NJ: Lawrence Erlbaum.

Attneave, F. (1982). The determination of perceived tridimensional orientation by minimum criteria. *Percept. Psychophys.*, **6**, 391-396.

Binford, T.O. (1981). Inferring surfaces from images. *Artificial Intelligence*, **17**, 205-244.

Bennett, B.M., Hoffman, D.D. & Prakash, C. (1989). *Observer Mechanics: A Formal Theory of Perception*. NY: Academic Press.

Biederman, I. (1987). Recognition-by-components: a theory of human image understanding. *Psychol. Rev.*, 94(2), 115-147.

Binford, T.O. (1981). Inferring surfaces from images. *Art. Intell.*, **17**: 205-244.

Bobick, A. (1987). Natural categorization. MIT Art. Intell. Lab. Tech. Report 1001.

Bobick, A. & Richards, W. (1986). Classifying objects from visual information. MIT Art. Intell. Lab Memo 879.

Bregman, A.S. (1990). *Auditory Scene Analysis: The Perceptual Organization of Sound*. Cambridge, MA: MIT Press.

Clark, J.J. & Yuille, A.L. (1990). *Data fusion for sensory information processing systems*. Boston: Kluwer.

Doyle, J. & Sacks, E.P. (1989). Stochastic analysis of qualitative dynamics. MIT Lab for Comp. Sci. Report TM-418.

D'Zmura, M. & Lennie, P. (1986). Mechanisms of color constancy. *Jrl. Opt. Soc. Am. A,* **3**: 1662-1672.

Fahle, M. (1991). Parallel perception of vernier offsets, curvature, and chevrons in humans. *Vis. Res.,* **31**, 2149-2184.

Feldman J. (1992). Perceptual categories and world regularities. PhD thesis, Massachusetts Institute of Technology, Cambridge, MA.

Feldman, J. (1991). Perceptual simplicity and modes of structural generation. *Proc. 13th Ann. Conf. Cog. Sci.,* August.

Foster, D.H. & Wagemans, J. (1993). Viewpoint in variant Weber fractions and standard contour-curvature discrimination. *Biol. Cyber.,* **70**, 29-36.

Fowler, R. & Guggenheim, E.A. (1952). *Statistical Thermodynamics.* The University Press, Cambridge.

Geisler, W. (1989). Sequential ideal-observer analysis of visual discriminations. *Psychol. Rev.,* **96**, 26-314.

Gershon, R., Jepson, A.D. & Tsotsos, J.K. (1987). Highlight identification using chromatic information. *Proc. IEEE 1st International Conference on Computer Vision, London, England,* pp. 161-170.

Gregory, R.L. (1970). *The Intelligent Eye.* New York: McGraw Hill.

Helmholtz, H. (1963). *Handbook of Physiological Optics.* (Dover reprint of 1925 edition, Ed JPC Southall, 3 volumes).

Helmholtz, H. (1925). *Physiological Optics, Vol. III: The Perceptions of Vision.* (J.P. Southall, trans.) Rochester, NY: Optical Society of America (original publication in 1910.)

Hochberg, J. (1987). Machines should not see as people do, but must know how people see. *Compt. Vision Graphics & Image Proc.,* **37**, 221-237.

Jepson, A. & Richards, W. (1993). *What is a Percept?* University of Toronto, Dept. of Computer Science Tech Report RBCV-TR-93-43. (Also MIT Cognitive Science Memo 43, 1991.)

Jepson A, Richards W, (1993). "What makes a good feature?" To appear in *Spatial Vision in Humans and Robots* ed.L. Harris & M. Jenkin, Cambridge University Press. See also Massachusetts Institute of Technology Artificial Intelligence Lab Memo 1356 (1992).

Jepson, A. & Richards, W. (1992). A lattice framework for integrating vision modules. *IEEE Transactions on Systems, Man and Cybernetics,* **22**, 1087-1096.

Jepson, A. & Richards, W. (1991). *What's a Percept?* (MIT Cognitive Science Memo 43).

Julesz, B. (1971). *Foundations of Cyclopean Perception.* Chicago: Univ. Chicago Press.

Kanade, T. (1981). Recovery of the three-dimensional shape of an object from a single view. *Art. Intell.,* **17**, 409-460.

Kendall, D.G. & Kendall, W.S. (1980). Alignments in two-dimensional random sets of points. *Adv. Appl. Prob.,* **12**: 380-424.

Knill, D.C. & Kersten, D.K. (1991). Ideal perceptual observers for computation, psychophysics and neural networks. In *Pattern Recognition by Man and Machine,* ed. R.J. Watt. London: MacMillan.

Koenderink, J.J. (1990). *Solid Shape.* Cambridge, MA: MIT Press.

Koffka, K. (1935). *Principles of Gestalt Psychology.* NY: Harcourt Brace.

Lee, H.-C. (1986). Method for computing the scene illuminant chromaticity from specular highlights. *Jrl. Opt. Soc. Am. A,* **3**: 1694-1699.

Leyton, M. (1992). *Symmetry, Causality, Mind.* Cambridge, MA: MIT Press.

Lowe, D. (1985). *Perceptual Organization and Visual Recognition.* Boston: Klewer.

McMahon, T.A. (1975). Using body size to understand the structural design of animals. *J. Applied Physiology*, **39**, 619-627.

Marr, D. (1982). *Vision: A Computational Investigation into the Human Representation and Processing of Visual Information*. San Francisco: Freeman.

MacKay, D.M. (1985). The significance of 'feature sensitivity'. In *Models of the Visual Cortex*, eds. D. Rose & V.G. Dobson, Chapt. 5. New York: Wiley.

Nakayama, K. & Shimojo, S. (1992). Experiencing and perceiving visual surfaces. *Science*, **257**: 1357-1363.

Pearl, J. (1988). *Probabilistic Reasoning in Intelligent Systems*. San Mateo, CA: Morgan Kauffman.

Reuman, S. & Hoffman, D. (1986). Regularities of nature: the interpretation of visual motion. In *From Pixels to Predicates*, ed.A. Pentland. Norwood, NJ: Ablex.

Richards, W. & Bobick, A. (1988). Playing twenty questions with nature. In *Computational Processes in Human Vision: An Interdisciplinary Perspective*, ed. Z. Pylyshyn. Norwood, NJ: Ablex Publishing.

Rock, I. (1983). *The Logic of Perception*. Cambridge, MA: MIT Press.

Rubin, J. (1986). Categories of visual motion. Ph.D. Thesis, Dept. of Brain & Cognitive Sciences, Mass. Inst. of Tech., Cambridge, MA.

Shafer, S.A. (1984). Using color to separate reflection components. *Color Res. & Appl.*, **10**: 210-218.

Stevens, K.A. (1988). Line of curvature constraint and the interpretation of 3D shape from parallel surface contours. In *Natural Computation*, ed. W. Richards. Cambridge, MA: MIT Press.

Thompson, D'Arcy (1952). *On Growth and Form*. Cambridge: The University Press.

Ullman, S. (1979). *The interpretation of visual motion*. Cambridge, MA: MIT Press.

Wallach, H. & O'Connell, D.N. (1953). The kinetic depth effect. *Jrl. Expt. Psych.*, **45**, 205-217.

Waltz, D. (1975). Understanding line drawings of scenes with shadows. In *The Psychology of Computer Vision*, ed. P.H. Winston, pp. 19-91. NY: McGraw-Hill,

Watt, R.J. & Andrews, D.P. (1982). Contour curvature analysis: Hyperacuities in the discrimination of shape. *Vis. Res.*, **22**, 449-460.

Westheimer, G. & McKee, S. (1977). Spatial configurations for visual hyperacuity. *Vis. Res.*, **17**, 941-947.

Witkin, A. & Tennenbaum, J.M. (1983). On the role of structure in vision. In *Human and Machine Vision*, ed. J. Beck, B. Hope & A. Rosenfeld. New York: Academic.

Yuille, A.L. & Bülthoff, H.H. (1994). A Bayesian approach to vision: sensor fusion and competitive priors. In *Perception as Bayesian Inference*, ed. W. Richards & D. Knill. Cambridge University Press.

3

Priors, preferences and categorical percepts

WHITMAN RICHARDS

Media Arts & Sciences, Massachusetts Institute of Technology

ALLAN JEPSON

Dept. of Computer Science, University of Toronto

JACOB FELDMAN

Center for Cognitive Science, Rutgers University

3.1 Introduction

Visual perception is the process of inferring world structure from image structure. If the world structure we recover from our images "makes sense" as a plausible world event, then we have a "percept" and can often offer a concise linguistic description of what we see. For example, in the upper panel of Figure 3.1, if asked, "What do you see?", a typical response might be a pillbox with a handle either erect (left) or flat (right). This concise and confident response suggests that we have identified a model type that fits the image observation with no residual ambiguities at the level of the description. In contrast, when asked to describe the two lower drawings in Figure 3.1, there is some hesitancy and uncertainty. Is the handle erect or not? Does it have a skewed or rectangular shape? The depiction leaves us somewhat uncertain, as if several options were possible, but none where all aspects of the interpretation collectively support each other. What then, leads us to the certainty in the upper set and to the ambiguity in the lower pair?

To be a bit more precise about our goal, let us assume that some Waltz-like algorithm has already identified the base of the pillbox and the wire-frame handle as separate 3D parts. Even with this decomposition, there remains an infinity of possible interpretations for any of these drawings. Yet we confidently commit to one interpretation in the case of the upper panel, but otherwise for the lower pair. Our aim, then, is to understand why the image structures in the upper panel support the assertion that they must arise *only* from very particular world structures, whereas the lower two structures seem more ambiguous.

Our analysis will consist of three parts: first we will lay out the domain associated with pillboxes having handles. Then the role of preferences for certain structures will be introduced. The result will be a formal definition for a percept. Finally, because our preferences are associated with structural regularities that have high priors in the assumed context, we recast the perceptual decision process in a Bayesian framework.

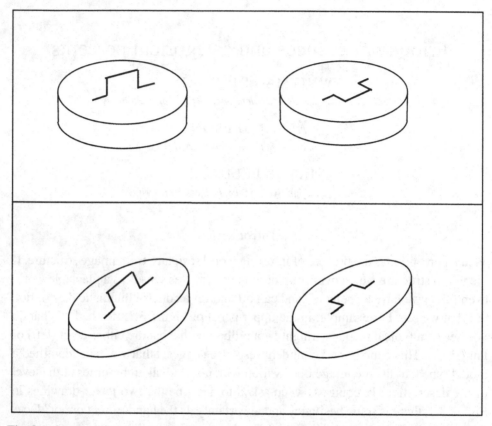

Fig. 3.1 Some pillboxes with handles. In the upper left depiction, most immediately see the handle as rectangular and erect, whereas in the upper right the handle now appears flat. In the two lower panels, both the shape and inclination of the handle are less clear, the percepts exhibiting some multistabilities. Most favor an inclined rectangular handle for the lower left; the lower right drawing, however, yields mixed reports.

3.2 Representations and regularities

Our basic idea is that the structure and parameterizations of our models that describe the world should match the regularities of the image structure as closely as possible. Levesque (1986) and McAllister (1991) call such representations "vivid" because they allow certain kinds of deductions to be made effortlessly (see also Davis, 1991, and Johnson-Laird, 1983).[†] The "vivid" representations we seek are built from image properties that directly point to very specific world properties we know

---

[†] A simple example of a "vivid" representation is the obvious ability to partition a 5 × 6 inch rectangle into 1 inch squares. The partitioning is obvious because the elements (inch-squares) are implicit in the specification of the size of the rectangle.

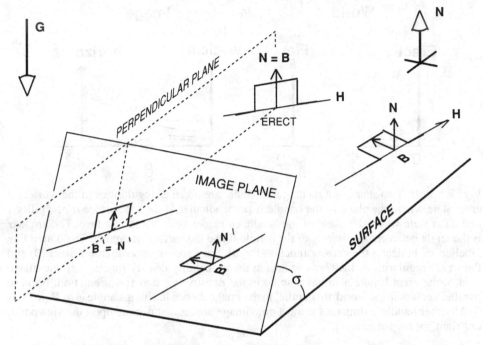

Fig. 3.2 Regardless of the viewing angle σ, an erect rectangular handle will project onto the image plane with its bisector **B** oriented parallel to the projection of the surface normal, **N** (orthographic projection is assumed). However, if the handle is inclined to the surface or lies flat, then the orientation between the bisector and normal can vary over a wide range, depending on σ (see Figure 3.3).

and care about. These criteria place very strong constraints upon the kinds of image structures we should note. In particular, we will see that only certain classes of object properties can lead to "vivid" image structures that support robust deductions about the state of the world.

To clarify this point with respect to the examples chosen here, consider the orthographic projections of two rectangular handles onto the image plane as illustrated in Figure 3.2. The normal to a surface **N** and the visual ray to a point on the surface define a plane perpendicular to the surface at that point. This plane also defines a line in the image. Then the surface normal and any other vector in this plane must project into this image line. The bisector **B** of a rectangular handle perpendicular to the surface is one such vector. We will define such a handle as an erect, rectangular handle. However, if the same rectangular handle is not erect, i.e. is inclined at some angle to this perpendicular plane, then the angle of its projection is less constrained. In particular, the bisector of a flat handle lying in the plane of the surface can project into *any* angle in the image (see Figure 3.3). In a random

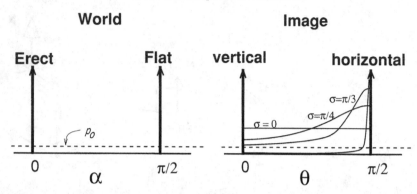

Fig. 3.3 Left: Two states of a rectangular handle are taken as regularities in the world: an erect state where the plane of the handle is perpendicular to the top surface of the pillbox and a flat state where the plane of the handle coincides with this top surface. The angle α is the angle between the bisector of the handle $\mathbf{B}$ and the surface normal $\mathbf{N}$. The dotted line labelled p_o indicates the density function for arbitrary angles, other than the erect (0) and flat ($\pi/2$) regularities which have spikes in the probability density function. In the image (right), the erect handle also has a spike in the density function for orientation, because parallel vectors in the world are parallel in the image, hence the image angle ϕ of $\mathbf{B}'$ to $\mathbf{N}'$ is 0. All other handle inclinations project onto image angles that depend upon the viewpoint, or "slant" of the surface (σ).

world, where both angles and orientations are cast out with equal probability, the image distribution has a broad spectrum (Witkin, 1981). Clearly, if we had to apply these data to infer the handle shape (i.e. its "skew") and its attachment angle, at best we could only make a maximum likelihood judgement that would typically be wrong.[†] In order for the perceiver to develop the inferential leverage needed to strongly disambiguate among many possible configurations of equal likelihood, the world must behave somewhat more regularly (Lowe, 1985; Thompson, 1952; Witkin & Tenenbaum, 1983). In particular, some structures should tend to occur significantly more often than predicted by a uniform distribution over all possible structures.

Consider then a world in which the perceiver *knows* that handles will often be rectangular and will lie either flat, as if freely hinged and resting stably under gravity, or erect, as if firmly attached perpendicular to the surface. In this world, the distribution of handle orientations α, rather than being uniform, will have two "spikes" or "modes", one at each of the two special world configurations as shown in in the left panel of Figure 3.3. In contrast, depending upon the slant of the surface,

[†] Surprisingly, given no other information, the maximum likelihood estimate for the 3D angle is just the image angle itself!

the expected image distribution of the handle bisector will be as in the right panel of Figure 3.3. Now only the "erect" bisector continues to stand out distinctively. In this context, such an image feature is designated a "key" feature because (i) its likelihood of correctly indicating the presence of a particular world property is high (i.e. there are few false targets), and (ii) the associated world configuration has a significant prior probability (see Knill & Kersten, 1991; Jepson & Richards, 1992). This latter condition, though often overlooked, is critical to establishing that a given high-likelihood world interpretation is actually likely to be correct (see previous chapter by Jepson *et al.*). In other words, the configuration ascribed to the world by an inference must actually be one that commonly occurs in the context. Otherwise, the probability of the inference being correct will actually be dominated by the probability of a false target.

The key feature condition entails, in effect, that the perceiver's inferences will be categorically correct just in the case that (a) it is living in a world that tends to behave regularly – i.e. a world that includes certain special configurations – and that further-more (b) the perceiver knows what these special configurations are and can correctly identify them. Such a competence is mandatory for any reasonable perceiver. It is important to keep in mind that there is an underlying hypothesis about these special configurations that drives the perceiver's interest in them: loosely speaking, they are "meaningful" in that such configurations play an important role in the causal forces at work in the perceiver's environment (Feldman, 1992; Leyton, 1992). The perceiver, who presumably has an interest in discovering the rules underlying this causal behavior, is thus well-served to pay special attention to those configurations that express these laws unambiguously. Hence the conclusion states of its percep-tual inference scheme should constitute robust pointers to the underlying laws that actually gave rise to the observed configurations.

To illustrate and to reinforce this point, consider again the upper left panel of Figure 3.1. Our perception is of an erect rectangular handle, which is a configuration associated with a probability spike as in Figure 3.3. However, such a percept is also associated with a particular placement over a center of mass, having a stable construction due to orthogonal bracing (consistent with the method of construction governing many human artifacts that have load-bearing protuberances by which their designers intended them to be lifted: attache cases, trowels, and so forth). Similarly, the flat configuration seen in the upper right panel is associated with a gravitationally stable position of a hinged handle. Notice that the causal explanation behind each of these stable configurations is not necessarily known to the perceiver. Rather, the point is that the perceiver has reason to believe that some such explanation is likely to exist (Mackay, 1978). Conversely, if a causal force (like gravity) *is* known, then the perceiver is justified in placing a high prior on a configuration that this causal force will tend to produce (like the flat handle). One has the sense that our most compelling percepts occur when several such modal observations or regularities are observed and immediately mesh together, creating a distinguished "mode". Then *all* the image structures we observe simultaneously satisfy *all* the various configurations of which we have knowledge and to which we have assigned high priors in the context. Thus, in the upper left panel of Figure 3.1, we consider the handle pose entailed by requiring it to be rectangular, and the handle pose required for it to be perpendicular to the surface and symmetrically positioned, and then find that all are the same pose! Clearly such an effortless recognition of the coincidence of multiple regularities demands a representation based on the regularities themselves. We would claim that such a representation is both "vivid" and meaningful.

3.3 Structure lattice

To set up our representation, we begin by introducing a vehicle called a "structure lattice" that takes our context-sensitive, primitive concepts about structural regularities, and composes them to produce a set of possible configuration states. This is the first of several such lattices we will introduce, the one upon which the later lattices will be built. Each of these lattices displays a partial ordering of the categorical states. (See Moray, 1990, for a related proposal.) In the case of the structure lattice, the ordering is derived by noting that some states are special or limiting cases of others. Later we will impose context-specific preferences upon this collection in order to seek a maximally preferred state.

To illustrate in more detail the role of regularities in creating a representation in which the perceptual categories become obvious, let us propose a context within which alignment and perpendicularity be special regularities between lines (or vectors) that we encounter in our non-random world. For example, assume that object parts have coordinate frames that are often aligned in some manner (Arnold & Binford, 1980). For the pillbox and handle, we have two "parts" and hence two coordinate frames. Let us specify the coordinate frame for the pillbox by its symmetry axis A, and by the feet of the handle H. (See Figure 3.4.) We will assume that the pillbox has been cut at right angles to A, and hence the surface normal N to the top of the pill box will align with the axis A. (Note this assumed axiomatic regularity!) Together, A and H (or henceforth N and H) set up a right-angled Cartesian coordinate frame at the center of the top of the pillbox. Let K be a unit vector orthogonal to N and H, defined by $K = N \times H$. Unfortunately, without knowledge of the actual slant of the surface of the pillbox top, the depiction of K in Figure 3.4 is incompletely specified. Hence we assume here a world consistent with the maximum likelihood

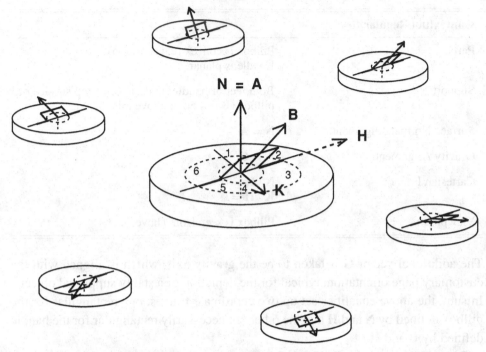

Fig. 3.4 Unit vectors **N** and **H** define the world-based coordinate frame for the pillbox. Vectors **B** and **H** define the handle's coordinate frame. The diagonal line that bisects **N**, **H** defines a third orthogonal axis **K**, that is used to set up an image-based system. (**K** is a maximum likelihood choice.) The dotted ellipses are the projections of circles that can be subdivided into six sectors as discussed in the text. The insets depict handles with bisectors projecting into the various sectors.

rule for slant derived by Kanade (1983), which was observed psychophysically by Stevens (1983) for right-angled coordinate frames. In this case the image projection of **K** will lie on the bisector of the image angle between **N** and **H**, as depicted in Figure 3.4. This additional "maximum likelihood" assumption allows us to relate the world-based Cartesian coordinate frame of **N**, **H** and **K** to its observed image. (Shortly we will explain the role of the numbered sectors marked on the top of the pill box.)

Similarly, in the same context, a coordinate frame for the handle can be defined by its vertical symmetric bisector **B** and by a second vector **H** which is the direction of the feet of the handle. Note that we do not assume that **B** and **H** are perpendicular. However the origins of the two coordinate frames, **B** & **H** and **N** & **H**, are assumed to lie centered on the plane of the top of the pillbox, and coincident with the major axis of the pillbox. We thus are assuming the following:

Contextual Regularities:	
Parts:	Pillbox is convex (e.g.solid top). Handle is planar.
Support:	Both feet of handle lie in plane of top surface of pillbox (**B** lies on or above this plane).
Surface Normal Alignment:	$\mathbf{N} = \mathbf{A}$
Gravity Alignment:	$\mathbf{A} = \mathbf{G}$
Cartesian Frame:	$\mathbf{N} \cdot \mathbf{H} = 0.$ $\mathbf{K} \cdot \mathbf{H} = 0$
Viewpoint:	Pillbox is seen from above.

The additional vector **G** is taken to be the gravity axis, which is aligned with the customary page orientation, typical for the depiction of a stably supported object.[†] In sum, the above equalities set up two coordinate frames, one rectangular for the pillbox defined by **N** and **H** and the other not necessarily rectangular for the handle defined by **B** and **H**.

Given the vectors **N**, **B**, **H** and **K** we can now explore all possible alignments of these vectors. Recall we are proposing that the perceiver is aware of certain "modes" or configurations of structures that occur often in the world. In particular the special regularities we chose were the collinearity of two lines or vectors, such as **B** = **N**, and the perpendicularity of two lines, such as **B** $\perp$ **H**, which corresponds to a rectangular handle, or **B** $\perp$ **N** which defines a flat handle. Hence to generate all these special configurations that are the consequence of these particular relational concepts, we simply enumerate all the alignments of **B** with **N**, **K** and **H**, using either the collinear (=) or perpendicular ($\perp$) relation. The result of this enumeration will then be those special categories that make sense to us, given our chosen relational concepts. We begin first with the three collinear alignments:

Collinear Relation	Category	Notation
B = **N**	erect rectangular handle	*E R*
B = **K**	flat rectangular handle	*F R*
B = **H**	degenerate (infinitely skewed handle)	

If the bisector **B** does not align with either **N**, **K** or **H**, then we define the handle as being either "tilted", which is noted as "*T*", or "skewed", which is noted as "*S*", or both, namely "*T S*". In particular, if the bisector is in the plane determined by **N**

[†] Elsewhere we have explored this preference for supported objects (Jepson & Richards, 1993).

and **K**, then the handle is tilted and rectangular, i.e. "*T R*". Similarly, if the bisector is in the plane containing **N** and **H**, it will be erect and skewed, i.e. "*E S*", while for the flat and skewed state the bisector will be in the **H-K** plane. Thus, excluding the above collinear specializations, we now have the following additional three new cases (alternatively we could have filled out a 4 × 4 table):

Perpendicular Relation	Description	Notation
B ⊥ H	tilted rectangular handle	*T R*
B ⊥ K	erect "skewed" handle	*E S*
B ⊥ N	flat "skewed" handle)	*F S*

Finally, we have the category where none of the relations hold:

Arbitrary Relation	Category	Notation
(none of the above)	tilted, skewed handle	*T S*

Excluding the degenerate case **B** = **H**, we thus have six types of categories for the positioning of the handle, given our conceptualization that part-based structures in the world typically are related by an alignment of some aspect of their individual coordinate frames. Because we can count the number of axes of each frame that are aligned (i.e. either one axis or two), a partial ordering can be placed on these six types of structures. This is illustrated in Figure 3.5 as a graph or lattice. At the top of this lattice, the positioning, *T*, and shape, *S*, of the handle is arbitrary. At the bottom, however, we have two states where the position and shape of the handle are both fixed to be rectangular and either flat or erect (i.e. *F R* and *E R*). In other words, all degrees of freedom of alignments have been removed. In between are the planar alignment states where one degree of freedom of movement is still allowed. For example, the leftmost node *E S* permits the skew of the handle to vary, but it must remain erect. Hence, as we move from top to bottom in this lattice, more and more specialization or restrictions are placed on the configuration. We call this lattice a "structure lattice" because, given this context with the assumed alignment regularity this lattice shows the specialization relations between the categories of structures in the world that will appear in our representation. Elsewhere Feldman (1992) explores conditions that allow such lattices to be built automatically.

3.4 Preference relations

The structure lattice simply enumerates the structural categories that we know about, or can easily infer, given our chosen regularities. Ideally, we would hope that the

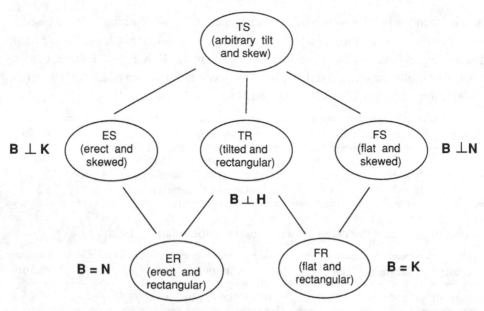

Fig. 3.5 The structure lattice for the pillbox plus handle (i.e. the "state space").

image is consistent with some kind of maximization of these regularities. In other words, given a particular context, we expect certain regularities to appear, but in another context the structures expected might differ. For example, a "flat" handle would not be likely if the pillbox were upside down. This suggests that given a context, there is a preference ordering on the expected regularities. If you will, a ranking is given to the prior probabilities of the structures that are expected in the assumed context. (Later, in Section 3.6.1, we will recast some of these notions in a Bayesian framework.)

A preference ordering differs from the structure ordering introduced in the previous section. The structure lattice simply presents all the categories available to us in the chosen context, ordered with respect to increasing specialization of structure. A preference ordering specifies which kinds of specializations are preferred to others. So, for example, given a choice between handle shapes that are rectangular or skewed, we'll prefer the rectangular version. This preference should not be surprising, because if our representation is to be "vivid", then the chosen parameterization (e.g. rectilinear coordinates) and the preferences (e.g. rectangular) should be tightly coupled. Denote this preference for rectangular over skewed shapes as $R > S$. Similarly, for the attachment angles, our parameterization suggests that the erect "E" and flat "F" angles will be preferred over arbitrary inclinations, or "tilts", "T", hence $E > T$ and $F > T$. However, we have no reason to believe that an *arbitrarily* shaped erect handle "E" will be preferred over one that is flat,

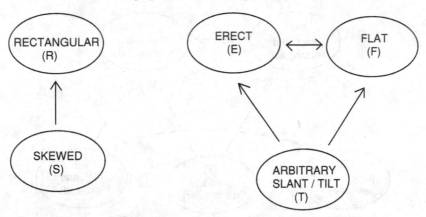

Fig. 3.6 Elemental preference relations for handle shape (left) and handle inclination (right).

"F". Denote this indifference by $E \sim F$. We will designate these three orderings, one for shape and the other two for attachment angle as the "elemental" preference orderings. They can also be cast in the form of a directed graph as in Figure 3.6.

Using the above elemental preference relations, we can now impose a partial order on the states of the base plus handle configurations that we know about, namely the states shown in Figure 3.5. This preference ordering is based on the *consensus* of the elemental preference relations, and is illustrated in Figure 3.7. Note that a state such as ER is to be preferred over TS because both of the elemental preference relations, $E > T$ and $R > S$, favor the same state. However, such a consensus does not always occur. For example, the same two elemental relations are in conflict for the states ES and TR, and as a result these two states remain unordered in the preference ordering. The intuition behind such unordered states is that the perceiver does not have sufficient information to be able to resolve whether ES should be preferred to TR, or vice versa. Thus unordered states represent a total lack of information on the appropriate preference. In addition, we also have a distinct notion of an equal preference between two states, such as occurs between ER and FR, as well as between ES and FS.

In general we cannot expect a consensus ordering to provide a total ordering of the state space, because some conflicts amoungst the elemental preference relations are likely to hold. This is related to Arrow's general impossibility theorem which states that rational choice - i.e. rational voting behaviour - does not guarantee a unique winner (Doyle & Wellman, 1989; Saari, 1994). Somewhat counter-intuitively, the introduction of more elemental preference relations does not lead to a more complete ordering, but rather tends to introduce more conflicts and hence tends to eliminate ordering relations. To counteract this tendency to fracture the state-space, it is often useful to consider priorities amongst the elemental preference relations (Jepson &

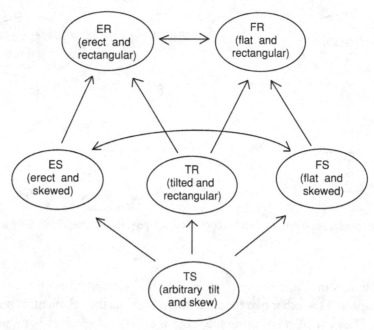

Fig. 3.7 A reordering of the entire "state-space" based on the assumed elemental preference relations.

Richards, 1993). Such priorities can break particular conflicts and thereby enlarge the ordering. Nevertheless, we should expect typical preference orderings to be partial as a consequence of the incomplete knowledge a perceiver has of its current domain. Of particular interest are instances in which the ordering results in several *maximally* preferred explanations of the image structure, where it remains undecided just which maximal state is to be preferred. As we discuss below, this is an intuitive explanation behind the difference in the stability of the percepts in the upper and lower panels of Figure 3.1.

3.5 The pillbox plus handle

To clarify our framework further, we now return to Figure 3.1, and use these images together with the preference relations to impose an ordering on the state space in each case. Not surprisingly, our notion is that the state which is maximally preferred in this ordering will contain our percept.

To set up these examples, we assume that the view is from above and that the world-based Cartesian coordinate frame for the pillbox is consistent with the Kanade-Stevens rule, as depicted in Figure 3.4 (i.e. that the axis **K** is seen as lying along the bisector of the image angle between **N** and **H**). We take this coordinate frame as being the *unique* coordinate system containing the line **H** and the line perpendicular to **N**. Later we will consider cases when this frame itself appears as a preference that may be altered.

3.5.1 A "vivid" representation

We begin by choosing a representation that allows us to effortlessly read off the states of the handle of interest, given a particular image. Figure 3.4 shows the form of this vivid representation, based on the **N**, **K** and **H** coordinates. The added feature is that now we identify the six sectors of unit circle (seen slanted) that lie between the projections of these axes of the coordinate frame. The idea then is to regard the bisector **B** as the arm of a clock, and simply note either the sector it falls in, or whether it is precisely aligned with one of the axes. A simple example is when **B** is aligned with either **N** or **K**. If $\mathbf{B} = \mathbf{N}$, then obviously the erect rectangular handle ER is a possibility, because the handle is ER if and only if $\mathbf{B} = \mathbf{N}$, whereas if the handle is flat and rectangular, then $\mathbf{B} = \mathbf{K}$. Similarly, if **B** falls into one of the six sectors, again we can easily check to see if a state is consistent or not. For example, when the handle is rectangular and tilted forward, **B** must be in the upper quadrant of the **NK** plane and hence its projection must fall into sectors 2 or 3 (see insets to Figure 3.4). Similarly if the handle is erect but skewed, **B** must lie in sectors 1 and 6 (if skewed to the left) or sector 2 (if skewed to the right). The following table captures all the cases (excluding the alignments):

Sector	Possible Categories
1	TR (backward), ES, FS, TS
2	TR (forward), ES, FS, TS
3	TR (forward), FS, TS
4	FS, TS
5	FS, TS
6	ES, FS, TS

Table 3.1 *The possible attachment categories*
for handle pose, given the sector
that the bisector **B** *falls into. (See Figure 3.4.)*

Note that our condition that the handle lies on or above the top of the pillbox constrains TR and ES to require that **B** not fall in sectors 4 and 5.

3.5.2 Case by case analysis

The state space for the two upper drawings in the top panel of Figure 3.1 is given in Table 3.2. Again, we use the notation E, F, R respectively to indicate an erect,

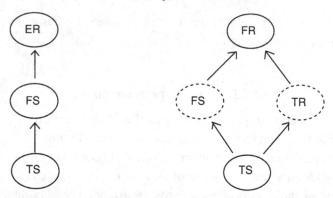

Fig. 3.8 A preference ordering for the two drawings in the upper panel of Figure 1. The two dotted nodes at the right become possibilities if **B** is not precisely aligned with **K**.

flat or rectangular handle, or S and T repectively to indicate either a skewed or "tilted" handle. First consider the possibilities for the "erect" handle depiction in the upper left drawing. The bisector **B** aligns with **N**. Hence ER is an obvious choice. However, **B** can also lie off **N**, but in the plane defined by the visual ray. All of these states correspond to either tilted and skewed (TS) handles, or perhaps a flat and skewed (FS) handle. Note that erect and skewed (ES) is not consistent with the Kanade-Stevens coordinate frame assumption since, from Figure 3.4, we see the only way the handle can be in the **NH** plane (i.e. erect) yet have **B** align with **N** in the image is for **B** to equal **N** (i.e. the ER state). Similar arguments showing that TR and FR states are inconsistent can also be read off of Figure 3.4. These three inconsistent states are indicated by an asterisk in Table 3.2. The remaining three valid states, TS, FS, and ER can now be ordered using consensus amongst the elemental preference relations introduced above. The result is shown in Figure 3.8 left, and is seen to be a total ordering with the erect rectangular handle (ER) as the unique maximal state.

Upper Left Drawing	Handle State	Upper Right Drawing
TS	arbitrary tilt & skew	TS
*	erect, skewed handle	*
FS	flat, skewed handle	(FS)
*	tilted, rectangular	(TR)
*	flat, rectangular	FR
ER	erect, rectangular	*

Table 3.2 *State spaces for the two drawings in the upper panel of Figure 3.1.*

Similarly, for the upper right drawing we first note that the leg of the handle, hence the bisector **B** appears to align with the axis **K** in the Kanade-Stevens coordinate frame for the pillbox. Therefore, FR is obviously in the state space. However, the true 3D orientation of **B** need not be coincident with **K**, but can point anywhere in the plane created by the lines of sight through **K**, and hence TS is also a possibility. Obviously the erect states ES and ER are excluded because **B** lies in sectors 3 and 4 *below* **H**. States TR and FS are marginal, depending on whether **B** is taken to be precisely aligned with **K** or not. If **B** is seen to fall below **K** in the representation depicted in Figure 3.4 (i.e. in sector 4), then TR is not in the state space. But if **B** lies above **K** (in sector 3), then TR is a possibility. In either case, FS is possible. Because of this ambiguity TR and FS are shown parenthetically in Table 3.1, and as dotted nodes in the preference ordering of Figure 3.8 (right). Again, the ordering here follows from the relations $F > T$ and $R > S$, yielding the state FR seen most "vividly" as the maximal node.

For the two more ambiguous drawings in the lower panel of Figure 3.1 we may go through a similar exercise. The allowable states are given in Table 3.3. To review the allowable states, first note that the revision introduced by skewing the handle shape misaligns **B** and **N**, as well as **B** and **K**, i.e. the Kanade-Stevens coordinate frame (Figure 3.4) and hence for both of the lower figures the handle can not be either flat and rectangular or erect and rectangular (as indicated by the * in the last two rows of Table 3.3.) However, for the lower left drawing, state TR is still possible because **B** lies in sector 1 (of Figure 3.4) and hence can be in the plane of **NK**. The TR state is excluded from the lower right drawing, however, because now **B** lies in sector 6 (of Figure 3.4), which would require **B** to fall below the top of the pillbox for the TR state.

Lower Left Drawing	Handle State	Lower Right Drawing
TS	arbitrary tilt & skew	TS
ES	erect, skewed handle	ES
FS	flat, skewed handle	FS
TR	tilted, rectangular	*
*	flat, rectangular	*
*	erect, rectangular	*

Table 3.3 *State spaces for the two drawings in the lower panel of Figure 3.1.*

Figure 3.9 shows the ordering of the states in Table 3.2 using the same elemental preference relations as before. In one case, there are three maximal nodes, namely ES, FS and TR, whereas in the other, there are only two, ES and FS. In both cases, states ES and FS are equally preferred, with the perceiver having no information supporting one over the other. For the bottom left panel of Figure 3.1 however, the additional maximal state TR is unordered with respect to the other two. That is, the perceiver cannot determine if TR is to be more, less, or equally preferred when

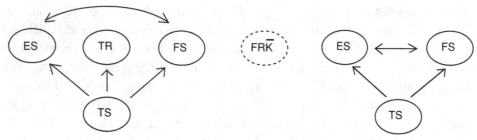

Fig. 3.9 A preference ordering for the two drawings in the lower panel of Figure 3.1. The dotted node in the middle with the FR interpretation appears for both lower panels when the Kanade-Stevens rule is broken, as indicated by the $\overline{K}$. (See Section 3.5.3)

compared to ES and FS. Hence unlike the top panel of Figure 3.1, our perceiver is left with several possible interpretations, given this choice of representation. In the natural world, this is clearly not desirable, and additional evidence might well be sought to distinguish between these choices. Alternately, the context may be revised.

3.5.3 Context revision

A possible weak link in the above treatment is the imposition of the Kanade-Stevens coordinate frame which specified the image direction of axis **K** by using a bisector rule (Figure 3.4). Although this setup creates one particular "vivid" representation where most categorical states can be readily recognized, the choice is clearly a "rule of thumb", and hence a premise or preference. Other choices, equally vivid, are possible. For example why not pick for the unspecified axis **K** the minor axis of the imaged pillbox top? Or perhaps even align **K** with a leg of the handle? Although this latter choice may seem a bit bizarre for the current orientation of Figure 3.1, the choice becomes more plausible for the lower panel if the page is rotated so the handle's feet are near vertical. Still another option is simply to leave the viewpoint uncertain, which is equivalent to letting the image of axis **K** lie anywhere in the sector between the normals to the images of **N** and **H** (see Figure 3.10, bottom left).[†]

To show the effect of including other assumptions about the coordinate frame, consider this last "don't know" option for the orientation of axis **K**. Let the initial Kanade-Stevens viewpoint premise for the axis **K** be designated as K and let $\overline{K}$ denote the relaxed preference that the **K** axis need only lie in the range appropriate for a right-angled system. We take as the elemental preference ordering $K > \overline{K}$ for the customary viewing of Figure 3.1. Clearly in this revised context $\overline{K}$ all the states

---

† If this condition was violated then the three coordinate axes **K**, **N** and **H** would lie in a sector having an angle smaller than 90 degrees, which is not consistent with the axes arising from a right-angled system.

computed previously still reappear. Hence if the original state space included states ER and TR, now designated as ERK and TRK, then the augmented state space will include states $ER\overline{K}$ and $TR\overline{K}$ as well. Of course, our preference ordering $K > \overline{K}$ will still place these original states such as ERK above their counterparts, i.e. $ER\overline{K}$, in the ordering. However, as we shall see shortly, entirely new states may also appear.

To create a vivid depiction of the additional states possible under the relaxed $\overline{K}$ premise, we again use the image sector scheme illustrated in Figure 3.4. The only change is that now three different cases must be considered for each of the panels of Figure 3.1. These three cases correspond to choices of the axis **K** which put the image of the handle bisector **B** into one of the sectors illustrated in Figure 3.4. For example, consider the bottom left panel of Figure 3.1. We need only differentiate the following three separate cases of the positioning of the variable axis **K**. First, **K** may be such that **B** lies in sector 1. This produces precisely the same set of feasible handle states as for the particular choice of the Kanade-Stevens premise, namely $TR\overline{K}, *S\overline{K}$, where the asterisk denotes that all of the possibilities, namely E, F, and T, for the orientation of the handle plane are allowed. Secondly, consider the sub-cases in which the axis **K** is chosen such that **B** lies in sector 6. For this case a rectangular handle is not possible (it would have to go down through the surface of the pillbox), and the allowable states are just $*S\overline{K}$. Finally, consider the intermediate case where **K** is taken to align with **B**. Here a new pose for the handle is allowed, namely $FR\overline{K}$, along with the skewed states $TS\overline{K}$ and $ES\overline{K}$. Thus the state space can again be constructed using the simple rules about the sectors, even though the viewpoint premise $\overline{K}$ does not pick out a unique coordinate system.

Taken together then, for the bottom left panel in Figure 3.1 we see that the relaxation of the coordinate axis premise to $\overline{K}$ produces the states $TR\overline{K}, FR\overline{K}$, and $*S\overline{K}$. These states can be included in the ordering provided in Figure 3.9, with the previous states appended by K to make the viewpoint premise explicit. Considering the elemental preference relation $K > \overline{K}$, we find that the previous local maxima all remain local maxima in the revised context. Moreover, a new local maximum $FR\overline{K}$ is also introduced.

The analysis of revised context for the other panels in Figure 3.1 can be done in a similar way. For the bottom right panel, the situation is much the same as above with a new local maximum, $FR\overline{K}$, appearing and with the states ESK and FSK remaining as local maxima. Interestingly, for the top left panel (**B** = **N**) no new handle configurations appear with the $\overline{K}$ premise and the unique maximal state remains ERK. Finally, for the top right panel of Figure 3.1 (**B** = **K**), two new handle configurations appear in the states space, namely $FS\overline{K}$ and $TR\overline{K}$. However, the revised context still has a unique maximal node, FRK, corresponding to the flat rectangular handle.

Hence the particular context revision of including the relaxed premise $\overline{K}$, which requires simply that the three axes **N**, **H** and **K** are orthogonal, has not resolved the issue of multiple local maxima in the preference orderings for the lower panels. In some sense it has made the ambiguity worse by introducing new possibilities. As previously mentioned, this is not entirely unexpected, because in general the addition of premises cannot reduce the number of local maxima (see Jepson & Richards, 1992). In some scenes, however, especially natural ones that are rich in regularities, a context revision can lead to the observance of new features indicative of additional regularities and a new maximal node will emerge that contains co-occurrences of these regularities. The percept associated with such a node will be "more coherent" and hence less ambiguous. An example of this is treated elsewhere (Jepson & Richards, 1993).

3.5.4 Recapitulation

To summarize, our notion then is that each image is evaluated with respect to the current set of observed regularities. These regularities suggest a context that dictates the form of the model representation. Given this representation and the image, a set of categorical structures can be deduced easily as "vivid" states (i.e. the state space). The context also points to preferences for certain 3D regularities in the representation, which are used to place an ordering on the feasible states or "interpretations". Hopefully there will be a unique global maximum in this ordering that "explains" all the observed regularities, given the image and the preferences (such as in Figure 3.8). If not, or if further regularities are observed in the resultant 3D interpretation, or if additional relevant premises are retrieved from the knowledge base, the context may be revised and the process continued with the aim of insuring that all regularities, both in the image and in the interpretation, are explained by the preferences at hand. Sometimes, as in the lower panel of Figure 3.1, closure is not possible, and several maximal interpretations continue to be evaluated (Figure 3.9). In all cases, the explanation of the image attempts to maximize our preferences for certain world regularities over other states. This leads to the following proposal for defining a "percept":

Proposal: given a context, a percept is an interpretation in the state space that is locally maximal within the associated preference ordering.

Elsewhere (Jepson & Richards, 1993), we have elaborated the consequences of this proposal, and its implications for the machinery that underlies the perceptual process itself. However, of special interest for this collection of papers is the relation between the above Boolean proposal for percepts and one based on versions of utility or probability theory (such as Dempster-Shafer or Pearl's (1988) Bayesian graphs). In the following section, we provide a partial bridge to these alternative approaches.

3.6 Bayesian formulation

Our framework for understanding percepts is based on recognizing that certain image structures point reliably to particular regularities of properties in the world with which we are familiar and expect in certain contexts. In other words, these regularities have high priors in that context. Here, these are the world properties "rectangular angle", R; a "flat" handle F; an "erect" handle E; and the Kanade-Stevens coordinate frame, K. We regard these properties as special, in that their probability density functions are "modal", whereas in contrast, the properties "tilted" T and "skewed" S have broad density functions (see Figure 3.10). The perceiver is assumed to have an internal model for these properties, together with some tolerance for accepting the actual 3D angular values, namely $\delta\tau$ for the tilt angle, $\delta\phi$ for skew and $\delta\psi$ the $\mathbf{K}$ axis. A Bayesian perceiver also has a probabilistic model for the generation of images. (For example, a random selection of a tilt, skew and viewpoint from

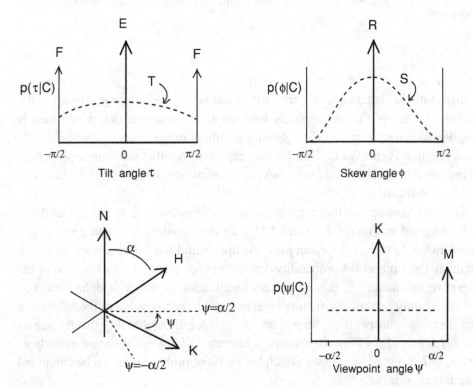

Fig. 3.10 Modal priors for flat (F), erect (E) and tilted (T) handle, as well as for a rectangular shape (R) versus a skewed shape (S). In the lower panel the "modal" probability for the Kanade-Stevens coordinate frame (K) and the frame defined by the major axis of the ellipse (M) are shown. The dotted line represents "other" possibilities. Note that the allowable range for the third rectangular axis is $\pm\alpha/2$ as indicated.

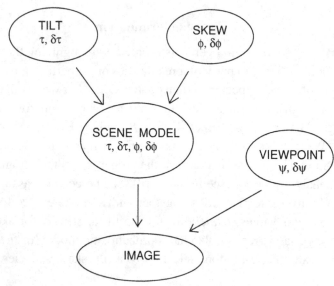

Fig. 3.11 Directed Bayesian graph. The arrows show the conditional dependencies assumed in the text.

the distributions sketched in Figure 3.10 would be one possibility.) Together, the particular values of tilt and skew chosen comprise a scene model, which then is compiled with the "viewpoint" to generate a sample image, as indicated by the directed graph of Figure 3.11. Note that the graph assumes that these three properties are independent, thereby allowing us certain simplifications in the calculation of various probabilities.

Given the assumption that images are generated according to the probabilistic model outlined in Figures 3.10 and 3.11 (call this 'context C'), and given a particular image I, then a Bayesian may attempt to find the interpretation(s) which maximize the a posteriori probability density, $p(\tau, \phi, \psi | I, C)$, as a function of the generative parameters τ, ϕ, and ψ. Our idealization in terms of delta functions presents a minor technical difficulty here, in that the precise value of the height of a delta function is unspecified. So instead we consider the probability that the generative parameters lie within the resolution tolerance of a specified point, namely as $p(\tau, \phi, \psi | I, C)\delta\tau\delta\phi\delta\psi$. As we sketch below, these probabilities can be computed using Bayes' rule.

To simplify the presentation, and to mirror the previous development in terms of preference orderings, we consider the spectial case in which $\psi = 0$, that is, the viewpoint is such that the Kanade-Stevens coordinates apply. Bayes' Rule provides the a posteriori probability density of the tilt and skew, given the image I, the context

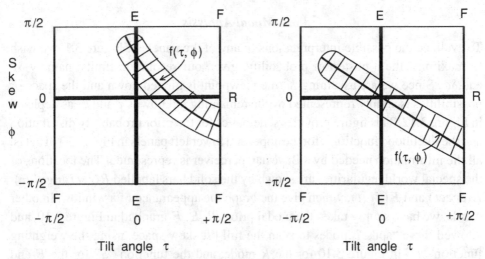

Fig. 3.12 "Projections" of the probability density functions onto the $\tau - \phi$ plane. The priors for the modal properties E, F and R appear as the heavy solid bars that form a window. The heavy diagonal lines labelled $f(\tau, \phi)$ indicate the noise-free possibilities for handle pose for each depiction. The bands about these lines represent the spread of the possibilities for each case: Bottom left panel of Figure 3.1 (left) and top left panel of Figure 3.1 (right).

C, and the viewpoint coordinate frame choice V (which in this case will be $\mathbf{K}$):

$$p(\tau, \phi | I, V, C) = \frac{p(I | \tau, \phi, V, C) p(\tau, \phi | V, C)}{p(I | V, C)} \qquad (3.1)$$

However, referring again to the Bayesian net of Figure 3.11, the assumption of the independence of the chosen viewpoint frame and the tilt and skew of the handle allows us to factor out V from the priors. Hence the priors can be decomposed as follows:

$$p(\tau, \phi | V, C) = p(\tau | C) p(\phi | C) \qquad (3.2)$$

Substituting (2) into (1) we find that:

$$p(\tau, \phi | I, V, C) = \frac{p(I | \tau, \phi, V, C)[p(\tau | C) p(\phi | C)]}{p(I | V, C)}, \qquad (3.3)$$

where the first term on the right hand side is the likelihood of the image given the scene and viewpoint, while the next term in brackets is the prior probability densities. Note that the denominator $p(I | V, C)$, will be a constant scaling factor as long as we consider a particular image I, viewpoint V and context C. Because our concern here is to simply compare various a posteriori probabilities we can safely ignore this constant term.

3.6.1 Modal Analysis

To evaluate the possible interpretations of any of the panels of Figure 3.1, we wish to maximize the a posteriori probability, given our resolution limits, namely $\delta\tau$ and $\delta\phi$. Since we are assuming K, the viewpoint is pinned down and the space of possibilities is simply represented by the remaining unknowns τ and ϕ, as depicted in Figure 3.12. This figure provides schematics for the prior probability distribution and the likelihood functions, for the upper and lower left panels in Figure 3.1. That is, all the information needed by a Bayesian perceiver is represented. The locations of the special world regularities are shown by the solid bars labelled $R(rectangular)$, $E(erect)$ and $F(flat)$, which give the graph the appearance of a window. In other words, we have simply taken the modal priors R, E, F graphed in Figure 3.10, and allowed these "spike" modes to span the full tilt-skew space, using the weighting function "T" in Figure 3.10 for the R mode, and the function "S" for the E and F modes. Each modal prior in Figure 3.12 thus has a smooth distribution over the window, concentrated on either the center cross bar (R) or the three uprights (E, F). In addition, at the three intersections of these bars there are point or "spike" delta functions for the ER or FR combinations. Thus each of the six different structures for the orientation of the handle occur with nonzero probability. (Note that this depiction makes the structure relations represented by Figure 3.5 quite explicit, with the different levels in Figure 3.5 appearing as sets of different dimensions.) In addition to the priors, we have also depicted the likelihood function $p(\tau, \phi|I, V, C)$. For the noise-free case, this function simply picks out a one-parameter family of possible tilts (τ) and skews (ϕ) that are consistent with I, V and C. The family is represented by the lines labelled $f(\tau, \phi)$ in Figure 3.12 for the two cases considered. Finally, the effect of noise in the image measurements is crudely represented by the bands overlaid on these lines. This band represents the extent of support for the "blurred" likelihood function formed by averaging $p(I|\tau, \phi, V, C)p(I)$ over various images having nearly the same measurements. For simplicity we assume this blurred likelihood function is roughly constant within the shaded band and vanishes elsewhere (nothing substantial depends on this assumption). In fact, since we only need to compare probabilities we will ignore this constant.

We now wish to evaluate the a posteriori probabilities for various states. This will simply be the respective probability masses obtained by integrating the product of the prior and likelihood functions over a small patch of size $\delta\tau$ by $\delta\phi$. Since we are assuming simple uniform behavior for the priors, these calculations are conveniently summarized by the category from which the point (τ, ϕ) is taken, that is, TR, TS, etc. Letting the prior for "flat" be designated as π_F, and similarly for E, T, S and R, we calculate the probabilities as shown in Table 3.4. For Table 3.4a, which corresponds to the bottom left image in Figure 3.1, note that zeros appear

Tilt	Skew S	R	Tilt	Skew S	R
E	$\pi_E \pi_S \delta \Phi$	O	E	$\pi_E \pi_S \delta \Phi$	$\pi_E \pi_R$
F	$1/2 \pi_F \pi_S \delta \Phi$	O	F	$1/2 \pi_F \pi_S \delta \Phi$	O
T	$\pi_T \pi_S \delta \tau \delta \Phi$	$\pi_T \pi_R \delta \tau$	T	$\pi_T \pi_S \delta \tau \delta \Phi$	$\pi_T \pi_R \delta \tau$
(A) Bottom Left			(B) Top Left		

Table 3.4 *A posteriori probabilities for the configuration specified by the point (τ, ϕ), for the two left panels of Figure 3.1, as a function of the various categories of tilt and skew for this point.*

for the states ER, FR, which were found to be inconsistent (see Table 3.2) and lie off the band in Figure 3.12. However, consider choosing a point (τ, ϕ) in the intersection of the diagonal band and the regularity R. The segment of length $\delta \tau$ of the line-delta function along R contributes a probability mass of $\pi_T \pi_R \delta \tau$, as listed in Table 3.4a. In addition, there is another additive term of size $\delta \tau \delta \phi$, arising from the smooth distribution function. We have neglected this second, higher order term in Table 3.4a since, for high resolution, it will be dominated by the former modal case. The other entries in Table 3.4 can be obtained in a similar way (the $1/2$ term is included because there are two "flat" possibilities). Notice that for Table 3.4b, the ER entry does not depend on either $\delta \tau$ or $\delta \phi$. This is because the diagonal band now goes through the origin of the window, where there is a delta function in the priors according to the erect and rectangular mode (again we omit the higher order terms in $\delta \tau$ and $\delta \phi$).

Given these a posteriori probabilities, we can now consider choosing the maximum probability states. Assume that both $\delta \tau$ and $\delta \phi$ are much smaller than any of the the modal probabilities π_i. That is, assume that the resolution of the system is sufficiently high. In this regime certain comparisons of probabilities are easy to resolve; we need only count the number of δ's. For example, from Table 3.4b we see that the maximal state for the top left image in Figure 3.1 must come from the category ER, because this is the only category for which the probability does not depend on the resolution (or vanish altogether). This agrees with our preference ordering in Figure 3.8 left. Similarly, we place state TS at the bottom of the Bayesian order. But without more information about the priors, states ES, FS and TR can only be given some intermediate ordering between TS and ER. Note that this probability ordering parallels, but is not identical to, our previous analysis, which assumed noise-free alignments (and hence excluded states ES and TR).

Similarly, from Table 3.4a we obtain an ordering of the states for the bottom left image in Figure 3.1. In particular, for sufficiently fine resolution, and nonzero modal probabilities, any state within TS cannot be maximal but a state in either ES, FS, or TR may be. These latter states are precisely the maximal states computed using the preference ordering (see Figure 3.9 left). To recreate our previous ordering we would need the additional assumption that π_E and $\frac{1}{2}\pi_F$ are to be considered roughly equivalent. Moreover, to eliminate the $ES \sim FS$ indifference and to make the ordering complete, we would need to be able to compare the probabilities $\pi_E \pi_S \delta \phi$ and $\pi_T \pi_R \delta \tau$. Of course, if we had numerical estimates for all these quantities then a total ordering may result, such as $TS \rightarrow FS \rightarrow ES \rightarrow TR$. Clearly when such priors and resolution limits are known precisely, the Bayesian approach will (almost) always yield a unique maximal a posteriori interpretation.

3.6.2 *Context and coordinate frame*

Our Bayesian treatment skirted the issue of the choice of coordinate frame for the pillbox by assuming the Kanade-Stevens coordinate frame. However, as illustrated earlier, a preference ordering of possible states may be sensitive to the choice of assumptions about the coordinate frame. In particular, in addition to the Kanade-Stevens frame premise K, we also examined the premise $\overline{K}$, in which the choice needed only to be consistent with some view of a right-angled frame. Here we consider the Bayesian version of this less restrictive viewpoint choice.

To begin, it is of interest to consider a suitable quantitative prior. A natural default context is the view of a right-angled coordinate frame from a uniformly distributed random viewpoint (see Arnold & Binford, 1980; Freeman, 1994). We take this to be the image independent prior, according to the directed graph of Figure 3.11. However, in order to calculate the effective prior on angle ψ (see Figure 3.10), we need also to consider image information, namely the angle between the images of **N** and **H**. (For notational simplicity we will ignore $p(\psi|C)$, etc., effectively treating this image angle to be part of the context C.)

To simulate the distribution for ψ we randomly generate views of a right-angled coordinate frame. Moreover, we discarded cases in which the angle between a pair of axes (in the image) failed to lie within a particular tolerance of a specified angle (eg. 60 degrees). This gives an approximation for the statistics of randomly viewing the **N**, **H**, and **K** coordinate frame, conditional on the image having a particular angle between **N** and **H**. A histogram was constructed of the deviation, ψ, from the bisector rule. The histogram appears relatively flat across the range $\pm \alpha/2$, with no significant peak or mode at the Kanade-Stevens rule $\psi = 0$. Thus a suitable prior for ψ appears to be a flat distribution, not the modal one pictured in Figure 3.10.

As in Section 3.5.3, where our default frame $\overline{K}$ lay arbitrarily within an appropriate range for a rectilinear frame, we can consider the implications of having a flat prior for ψ, but this time with respect to the Bayesian approach. The critical case turns out to be the bottom left image in Figure 3.1. Recall that the state space for this image, given the unconstrained viewpoint premise $\bar{K}$, consisted of the states FR, TR, and $*S$. In terms of our schematic in Figure 3.12, this means that the likelihood density, for this image given the $\overline{K}$ premise[†] is a broad distribution that intersects all these states (but not ER). The important difference between this distribution and the shaded band depicted in Figure 3.12 (left) is that this extended band now includes the state FR, rather than just the FS state as depicted. Calculations similar to those for Table 3.4 shows that the FR state has a probability proportional to $\frac{1}{2}\pi_F\pi_R$ (as before, we are treating the magnitude of the blurred likelihood as roughly constant, and dropping it). The other terms in Table 3.4a remain the same (after factoring out the lower blurred likelihood contribution). For a sufficiently fine resolutions we see that this FR state dominates, and is the *unique* interpretation which maximizes the a posteriori probability.

Psychophysically the FR state is seldom reported for the bottom left image in Figure 3.1. The most common interpretation is TR, which contains a local maxima in both our preference ordering and our previous "modal" a posteriori probability distribution. How then can the seemingly more "correct" a-modal or flat prior for **K** be reconciled with the perceiver's choice for a modal **K**? One interesting possibility is that the modal prior for the Kanade-Stevens frame is actually 'in the head', even though it does not occur in our random viewpoint context. This is (weakly) supported by psychophysical experiments of Feldman (1992) which indicate the general existence modal priors in the head, and by Stevens (1983) data on the bisector rule. A possible source of such a prior might be from viewing line drawings, where the bisector rule could appear modally as a convention. Alternatively, it may arise as a consequence of a heuristic such as mininum slant (Kanade, 1983). In either case, if our perceptual system is Bayesian, then the priors on the possible viewpoints of Figure 3.1 appear to be biased in favour of the "modal" bisector rule, and moreover this bias is unfair relative to a uniform distribution of viewpoints.

3.7 Preference lattices vs. Bayesian optimizations

One might inquire about the relation between our framework, and other approaches to data interpretation that emphasize probability measures and weighted variables (see several chapters in this volume, as well as Bülthoff & Mallott, 1988; Clark & Yuille, 1990). As previously mentioned, the primary distinction is that we assign values either near zero or one, attempting to choose image features and world regularities that support such extreme measures. Hence we are stressing categorical, as contrasted to metrical judgments about structures in the world. This should be

---

[†] I.e. $p(I|\tau, \phi, \psi, C)p(\psi|C)$ averaged over all feasible angles ψ.

clear from the discussion surrounding key features (Figure 3.2) and our "binary" use of Bayesian probabilities. The advantage of our approach is that when priors are "modal" and are cast in the form of elemental preference relations which are relatively insensitive to context, we can obtain a relatively context-free partial ordering of the states. In other words, the essence of the priors is captured by the preference relations without the need to assume complex relationships based on probability density functions, utility factors, etc. (Arrow, 1963). Although we lose statistical optimality, we gain a robustness over contexts. The use and form of the preferences, then, are more akin to Bennett & Hoffman's Boolean Lebesque logic, than they are to statistical estimation procedures.

To make this advantage still clearer, note that maximal nodes in our preference orderings (i.e. the percepts) represent the transitive closure of the preference relations applied to the set of interpretations in the state space. In order to get a picture of this, imagine that each elementary preference relation is taken to have its own dimension. When the elementary preference relations are binary, the result is that the state space has been laid out at the vertices of a multi-dimensional cube. The edges of the cube correspond to the elementary preference relations and, overall, the preferences all favour moving towards one vertex of the multi-dimensional cube. Two states can be compared if and only if one of them is strictly closer to the optimal vertex. Otherwise the states will remain unordered. This occurs, for example, when one elementary preference relation favors one state and another relation favors the other state. Given this strong restriction on the derived ordering, it should be clear that weights on the preference relations will not change the ordering of the state space. Maximal nodes – i.e. the "percepts" – will continue to remain maximal.

A fully probabilistic approach, on the other hand, would assign a single number, the a posteriori probability, to each state, just as we attempted to do in Section 3.6. In such a scheme, presumably many different factors and weights have been merged into a single number, and now the states indeed can be totally ordered by the magnitude of these numbers, if they are computable. The merging process allows trade-offs between various different effects to be evaluated and resolved, but requires quantitative knowledge about a priori conditional distributions. If these quantities were known, and if the probabilities can be computed correctly, then clearly the fully probabilistic approach is optimal. (See Jepson & Richards, 1992, 1993, for further elaborations.)

3.8 Conclusion

We have attempted to illustrate the tight coupling between image structure, world structure, and representation. If image features are not chosen to satisfy key feature requirements, then not all useful world structures will be reliably and "vividly" inferrable directly from image structure. However, even image structure alone is not a sufficient basis for inferring world structure. The right-angled handle is one such example. Although common in our world, it does not by itself project into a reliable and robust image feature. Yet, the regularity still is an important ingredient in our perceptual reasoning process because it serves to bind together other observable properties in a "Natural Mode". Such modal properties, although not always solutions to key features, still lead to more robust models. The examples in Figure 3.1 illustrate these points. For the upper left panel, the percept is clear and robust because the modal co-occurrance of rectangular and erect appears vividly in the chosen representation. For the other panels the co-occurrences are not explicable. For example in the upper right panel, a co-occurrence between the handle shape and pose results only if the third axis is chosen appropriately. In the lower pair, where there is no such co-occurence, the percept is less clear. Hence the incorporation of modal regularities as an explicit part of the representation appears to us a crucial aspect of perception. Learning such modal correlations that support natural modes and which direct the reconfiguration of the perceiver's representations, are clearly important elements in the acquistion of perceptual knowledge. Elsewhere in this volume Barlow and also Mumford address this issue.

Although our principal aim was to explore the relation between priors, preferences and percepts, a consequence of this is that considerable machinery and issues were introduced along the way. Our intent was not to address these issues directly, because their treatment will depend to a large part upon the hardware and computational abilities of the perceiver. Instead we have attempted to focus upon the competence of a perceiver, not its performance, although in this respect our inclusion of "vivid" representations was clearly a departure. Here we highlight four additional performance issues that clearly loom quite large. These are (i) the richness required of our conceptualization; (ii) the flexibility of the reasoning process; (iii) the choice of the aspects or features of the image that are relevant; and (iv) the indexing to the appropriate context that sets up the state space and preference relations. At the heart of our treatment is the notion that percepts are inductive inferences based on premises and preferences (Gregory, 1970, 1980; Helmholtz, 1963; Rock, 1983) and that this inference process entails reasoning about consistency or plausibility in a conceptualization of the world (see Bennett, Hoffman & Prakash, 1989; Nakayama & Shimojo 1992; also their chapter in this volume). No matter what the logical or illogical form, the reasoning process must be world-based, not image-based. Hence a conceptualization must be indexed, a context chosen right at the outset before the preferred interpretations can be sought.

A considerable amount of work remains to develop and explore the proposed framework in a complete and formal manner. (See Jepson and Richards, 1993, for first steps in this direction.) For example, in this paper we have used the notion of interpretations that are *consistent* with an image. A formal specification of this notion is given in Reiter & Mackworth (1989), and this component itself can be seen to involve considerable machinery. A second formal issue is that the transitive closure of the elementary preference relations must be a partial order. Ascent through this order and the search for locally maximal nodes raise several technical difficulties that we have ignored. A third important issue is to elaborate the means for recognizing and evaluating incoherent interpretations that leave regularities unexplained (Jepson & Richards, 1993; Geffner, 1989; MacKay, 1978). And finally, considerable experimental work needs to be done to determine appropriate sets of preferences and their correlated regularities: i.e. the modes and their associated elemental preference relations.

Acknowledgments

Jacob Feldman was supported by an NSF fellowship and by AFOSR 89-504. Allan Jepson was supported by NSERC Canada, IRIS, and CIAR. Whitman Richards was supported by AFOSR grant 89-504. Technical support was provided by William Gilson. Donald Hoffman, R. Mann, D. Richards, A. Yuille and especially David Knill provided helpful criticisms.

References

Arnold, R.D. & Binford, T.O. (1980). Geometric constraints in stereo vision. *SPIE*, **238**, *Image Processing for Missle Guidance*, pp. 281-292.

Arrow, K.J. (1963). *Social Choice and Individual Values*. New Haven: Yale University Press, 2nd edition.

Barlow, H. (1990). Conditions for versatile learning, Helmholtz's unconscious inferences, and the task of perception. *Vision Res.*, **30**: 1561-1571.

Bennett, B., Hoffman D. & Prakesh, C. (1989). *Observer Mechanics*. London: Academic Press.

Bülthoff, H. & Mallot, H.A. (1988). Integration of depth modules: stereo and shading. *Jrl. Opt. Soc. Am. A*, **5**, 1749-1758.

Clark, J.J. & Yuille, A.L. (1990). *Data Fusion for Sensory Information Processing Systems*. Boston, MA: Kluwer Academic.

Davis, E. (1991). Lucid representations. *NYU Computer Science Dept. Tech Report 565*.

Doyle, J. & Wellman, M.P. (1989). Impediments to universal preference-based default theories. *Proc. First International Conference on Principles of Knowledge Representation and Reasoning, Toronto*, pp. 94-102.

Feldman, J. (1992). Constructing perceptual categories. *Proc. IEEE Conference on Comp. Vis. & Pat. Recog.*, 244-250.

Feldman, J. (1992). Perceptual categories and world regularities. PhD thesis, Massachusetts Institute of Technology, Cambridge, MA.

Feldman, J., Jepson, A. & Richards, W. (1992). Is perception for real? *Proc. Conf. on Cognition and Representation, Center for Cognitive Science Report 92-12, SUNY Buffalo*, pp. 240-267.

Geffner, H. (1989). Default reasoning, minimality and coherence. *Proc. First International Conference on Principles of Knowledge Representation and Reasoning, Toronto*, pp. 137-148.

Gregory, R.L. (1970). *The Intelligent Eye*. New Jersey: McGraw Hill, eg. p. 31.

Gregory, R.L. (1980). Perception as hypotheses. In *The Psychology of Vision*, eds. H.C. Longuet-Higgins & N.S. Sutherland, pp. 137-149. London: The Royal Society.

Helmholtz, H. (1963). *Handbook of Physiological Optics*. Dover reprint of 1925 edition, ed. J.P.C. Southall, 3 volumes.

Jepson, A. & Richards, W. (1993). *What is a Percept?* University of Toronto, Dept. of Computer Science Tech Report RBCV-TR-93-43. (Also MIT Cognitive Science Memo 43, 1991.)

Jepson, A. & Richards, W. (1992). A lattice framework for integrating vision modules. *IEEE Trans. Systems, Man & Cybernetics*, **22**, 1087-1096.

Jepson, A. & Richards, W. (1993). What makes a good feature? To appear in *Spatial Vision in Humans and Robots*, eds. L. Harris & M. Jenkin. Cambridge University Press. See also MIT Artificial Intelligence Lab Memo 1356 (1992).

Johnson-Laird, P. (1983). *Mental Models*. Cambridge, MA: Harvard University Press.

Kahneman, D. & Tversky, A. (1979). On the interpretation of intuitive probability: a reply to Jonathan Cohen. *Cognition*, **7**, 409-411.

Kanade, T. (1983) . Geometrical aspects of interpreting images as a three dimensional scene. *Proc. IEEE*, **71**, 789-802.

Knill, D.C. & Kersten, D.K. (1991). Ideal perceptual observers for computation, psychophysics and neural networks. In *Pattern Recognition by Man and Machine*, ed. R.J. Watt. London: McMillan.

Levesque, H. (1986). Making believers out of computers. *Art. Intell.*, **29**, 289-338.

Leyton. M. (1992). *Symmetry, Causality, Mind*. Cambridge, MA: MIT Press.

Lowe, D. (1985). *Perceptual Organization and Visual Recognition*. Boston, MA: Kluwer Academic.

McAllister, D. (1991). *Observations on Cognitive Judgements*. MIT Artificial Intelligence Lab Memo 1340.

MacKay, D.M. (1978). The dynamics of perception. In *Cerebral Correlates of Conscious Experience*, eds. P.A. Busen & A. Rougent-Buser. Amsterdam: Elsevier.

Marr, D. (1982). *Vision: A Computational Investigation into the Human Representation and Processing of Visual Information*. New York: Freeman.

Moray, N. (1990). A lattice theory approach to the structure of mental models. *Phil. Trans. Royal Soc. Lond. B*, **327**, 577-583.

Nakayama, K. & Shimojo, S. (1992). Experiencing and perceiving visual surfaces. *Science*, **257**, 1357-1363.

Pearl, J. (1988). *Probabalistic Reasoning in Intelligent Systems*. San Mateo, CA: Morgan Kauffman.

Reiter, R. & Mackworth, A. (1989). A logical framework for depiction and image interpretation. *Art. Intell.*, **41**, 125-155. Also *The Logic of Depiction*, University of British Columbia Department of Computer Science Technical Report 87-42, 1987.

Rock, I. (1983). *The Logic of Perception*. Cambridge, MA: MIT Press.

Saari, D.G. (1994). *The Geometry of Voting*. New York: Springer-Verlag.

Stevens, K. (1983). The line of curvature constraint and the interpretation of 3D shape from parallel surface contours. *Proc. 8th Annual Int. Joint Conf. on Art. Intell.*, pp. 1057-1061. (See also Chapt. 9, *Natural Computation*, ed. W. Richards. Cambridge, MA: MIT Press, 1988.)

Thompson, D. (1952). *On Growth and Form*. Cambridge: The University Press.

Witkin, A. (1981). Recovering surface shape and orientation from texture. *Artif. Intell.*, **17**, 17-47.

Witkin, A. & Tenenbaum J. (1983). On the role of structure in vision. In *Human and Machine Vision*, ed. A. Rosenfeld. New York: Academic.

4

Bayesian decision theory and psychophysics

A.L. YUILLE

Division of Applied Sciences, Harvard University

HEINRICH H. BÜLTHOFF

Max-Planck Institut für biologische Kybernetic

4.1 Introduction

4.1.1 The Bayesian decision theory approach to vision

We define vision as perceptual inference, the estimation of scene properties from an image or a sequence of images. Vision is ill-posed in the sense that the retinal image is potentially an arbitrarily complicated function of the visual scene and so there is insufficient information in the image to uniquely determine the scene. The brain, or any artificial vision system, must make assumptions about the real world. These assumptions must be sufficiently powerful to ensure that vision is well-posed for those properties in the scene that the visual system needs to estimate.[†] In this Chapter we argue that Bayesian decision theory provides a natural framework for modeling perceptual inference. We will discuss the theoretical problems that arise, in particular when combining different visual cues, and propose solutions.

How are these assumptions about the world imposed in vision systems? The Bayesian formulation, see also the introductory Chapter to this book, gives us an elegant way to impose constraints in terms of prior probabilistic assumptions about the world. This approach is based on Bayes formula (Bayes, 1783):

$$p(S|I) = \frac{p(I|S)p(S)}{p(I)}. \tag{4.1}$$

Here S represents the visual scene, the shape and location of the viewed objects, and I represents the retinal image. $p(I|S)$ is the *likelihood function* for the scene and it specifies the probability of obtaining image I from a given scene S. It incorporates a model of image formation and of noise and hence is the subject of computer graphics. $p(S)$ is the *prior* distribution which specifies the relative probability of different scenes occurring in the world, and formally expresses the prior assumptions about

---

[†] The issue of precisely which scene properties need be estimated is still an open one. We will briefly discuss this in Section 4.6.

the scene structure including the geometry, the lighting and the material properties. $p(I)$ can be thought of as a normalization constant and it can be derived from $p(I|S)$ and $p(S)$ by elementary probability theory, $p(I) = \int p(I|S)p(S)[dS]$. Finally, the *posterior distribution* $p(S|I)$ is a function giving the probability of the scene being S if the observed image is I.

In words (4.1) states: the probability of the scene S given the image I is the product of the probability of the image given the scene, $p(I|S)$, times the *a priori* probability $p(S)$ of the scene, divided by a normalization constant $p(I)$.

To specify a unique interpretation of the image I we must make a decision based on our probability distribution, $p(S|I)$, and determine an estimate, $S^*(I)$, of the scene. In Bayesian decision theory (Berger, 1985; DeGroot, 1970) this estimate is derived by choosing a loss function which specifies the penalty paid by the system for producing an incorrect estimate.[†] Standard estimators like the *maximum a posteriori* (MAP) estimator, $S^* = \arg\max_S p(S|I)$ (i.e. S^* is the most probable value of S given the posterior distribution $p(S|I)$), correspond to specific choices of loss function. The loss function emphasizes that the interpretation of the image cannot be divorced from the purpose of the visual system.[‡] In Section 4.4 we will illustrate the idea of loss functions by analyzing the generic viewpoint assumption (Binford, 1981; Freeman, 1993; and chapter 9 by Freeman).

The Bayesian framework is sufficiently general to encompass many aspects of visual perception including depth estimation, object recognition and scene under-standing. However, to specify a complete Bayesian theory of visual perception is, at present, completely impractical. Instead we will restrict ourselves to model in-dividual visual cues for estimating the depth and material properties of objects and the ways these cues can be combined. It has become standard practice for computa-tional theories of vision to separate such cues into modules (Marr, 1982) which only weakly interact with each other. From the Bayesian perspective, this modularization is often inappropriate, due to the interdependence between visual cues. Hence we argue in Section 4.3 that the visual cues should be more strongly coupled.

The choice of prior assumptions in the Bayesian framework is very important. Each visual cue, as standardly defined, contains built-in prior assumptions. If these assumptions are being used by the visual system they will inevitably bias perception, particularly for the impoverished stimuli favoured by psychophysicists. Indeed the perceptual biases detected in psychophysical experiments offer clues about the nature of the prior assumptions being used by the visual system.[§] However the prior

---

[†] For other applications of decision theory to vision see (Sperling & Dosher, 1986).
[‡] Decision theory can also be used to couple vision directly to action (Dean & Wellman, 1970).
[§] The human visual system is very good at performing the visual tasks necessary for us to interact effectively with the world. Thus the prior assumptions used must be fairly accurate, at least for those scenes which we need to perceive and interpret correctly.

assumptions used by theorists to model one visual cue may conflict with those used to model another, and consistency should be imposed when cues are combined.[†]

Moreover, the prior assumptions may be context dependent and correspond to the categorical structure of the world. Each visual module, or coupled groups of modules, will have to determine automatically which priors should be used. This can lead to a system of competitive prior assumptions, see Section 4.5. Bayesian Decision Theory (Berger, 1985) standardly deals with both competing models of this type and also complex systems of elementary priors indexed by hyper-parameters.

In this Chapter we first describe in Section 4.2 Bayesian theories for individual cues and argue that several psychophysical experiments can be interpreted in terms of biases towards prior assumptions. Next, in Section 4.3, we describe ways of combining different depth cues and argue that strong coupling between different modules is often desirable. In Section 4.4 we introduce the concept of loss function by analyzing the generic view assumption and argue that this concept is crucial for specifying the purpose of the visual system. Then in Section 4.5 we argue that it is preferable to use competing, often context dependent, priors rather than the single generic priors commonly used. Implications of this approach are described in Section 4.6.

4.2 Bayesian theories of individual visual cues

We now briefly describe some Bayesian theories of individual visual cues and argue that psychophysical experiments can be interpreted as perceptual biases towards prior assumptions. From (4.1) we see that the influence of the prior is determined by the specificity of the likelihood function $p(I|S)$. In principle, as described in Section 4.1, the likelihood function should make no prior assumptions about the scene (though, as we will see, this is often not the case in practice).

In the following we will specifically discuss theories of stereo, shape from shading and shape from texture. All these modules require prior assumptions about the scene geometry, the material properties of the objects being viewed, and, in some cases, the light source direction(s). We will concentrate on the assumptions used by the theories rather than the specific algorithms. A number of theories described here were originally formulated in terms of energy functions (Horn, 1986) or regularization theory (Poggio *et al.*, 1985). Yet the Bayesian approach incorporates, by use of the Gibbs distribution (Paris, 1988), these previous approaches (see also the Appendix).

Let us now look at one specific example. (See chapter 5, section 5.16 for an extensive commentary.) Shape from shading models typically assume that the scene

---

[†] Although it is conceivable that the human visual system uses conflicting prior assumptions for different cues.

consists of a single object with known reflectance function. It is usually assumed that there is a single light source direction $\vec{s}$ which can be estimated and that the reflectance function is Lambertian with constant albedo. This leads to an imaging model $I = \vec{s} \cdot \vec{n} + N$ where $\vec{n}$ denotes the surface normals and N is additive Gaussian noise. In this case the likelihood function can be written as $p(I|S) = (1/Z)e^{-(1/2\sigma^2)(I-\vec{s}\cdot\vec{n})^2}$, where σ^2 is variance of the noise and Z is a normalization factor. The prior model for the surface geometry $p(S)$ typically assumes that the surface is piecewise smooth and biases towards a thin plate or membrane.[†]

Observe that this likelihood function contains the prior assumption that the reflectance function is Lambertian with constant albedo. Moreover, it ignores effects such as mutual illumination and self-shadowing. The model is therefore only applicable for a certain limited class of scenes and only works within a certain *context*[‡](see Figure 4.1). A visual system using this module would require a method for automatically checking whether the context was correct. In this section we will assume that the context is fixed and leave the discussion of context selection to our later Section on competitive priors.[§]

What predictions would models of this type make for psychophysical experiments? Clearly, they would predict that the perception of geometry for shape from shading would be biased by the prior assumption of piecewise smoothness (see Figure 4.2). If we use the models of piecewise smoothness typically used in computer vision then we would find a bias towards frontoparallel surfaces. Such a bias is found in the psychophysical shape from shading experiments by Bülthoff and Mallot (Bülthoff & Mallot, 1988).

Existing shape from texture models also make similar assumptions about the scenes they are viewing. They typically assume that the scene consists of texture elements scattered on piecewise smooth surfaces. The distribution of these elements on the surface is typically assumed to be statistically homogeneous. Therefore the imaging model or likelihood function will assume that these texture elements are generated from a homogeneous distribution on the surface and then projected onto the image plane. Assumptions about the geometry, such as piecewise smoothness, are then placed in the prior.

Once again, the nature of the likelihood term means that the models will only

---

[†] These theories also assume that the occluding boundaries of the object is known. This is helpful for giving boundary conditions.

[‡] Indeed the likelihood functions used in most visual theories often make strong context dependent assumptions. This fact will be briefly illustrated in this Section and we will describe its implications in Sections 4.3 and 4.5.

[§] We also point out that ideal observer theories by necessity also operate within a specific context (see the chapter 6 by Knill & Kersten and chapter 7 by Blake, Bülthoff & Sheinberg). The experimenter chooses a specific visual task and set of stimuli. He then models the performance of an ideal observer, who knows everything about the task and the stimuli, and compares it to that of a human observer. For the human's performance to be anywhere close to that of the ideal observer would require that humans have visual abilities tuned to this context and are able to automatically adapt to them.

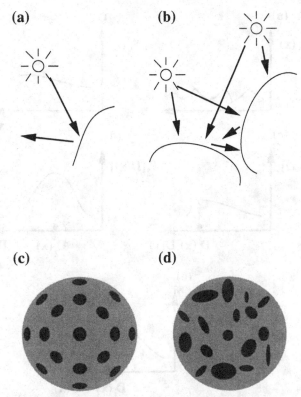

Fig. 4.1 Cues are valid only in certain contexts. In (**a**) we sketch a Lambertian object illuminated by a single light source and no mutual illumination, so standard shape from shading algorithms will work. However, in (**b**) the mutual illumination will prevent shape from shading from working. Similarly, shape from texture is possible for (**c**) but not for (**d**) where the homogeneity assumption for the texture elements is violated. Thus both shading and texture depth cues are only valid in certain contexts.

be appropriate in certain contexts, see Figure 4.1. To become well-posed, shape from texture must make strong assumptions about the world which are only valid for a limited class of scenes. If standard piecewise smoothness priors are used then texture models will also predict biases towards the frontoparallel plane, as observed experimentally (Bülthoff & Mallot, 1988). Stronger predictions can be made by testing the predictions of a specific model, see for example that presented in chapter 7 by Blake, Bülthoff & Sheinberg.

Finally, we consider a model of stereopsis that is a simplified version of one developed in more detail by Belhumeur in chapter 8. Again, this model assumes that the world consists of piecewise smooth Lambertian surfaces. The imaging model is defined by saying that a surface with disparity $d(x)$ and intensity $I(x)$ will be mapped to the left and right images I_L and I_R so that $I_L(x+d(x)/2) = I(x)+N_L(x)$ and $I_R(x - d(x)/2) = I(x) + N_R(x)$, where N_L and N_R are additive Gaussian

128 A.L. Yuille & H.H. Bülthoff

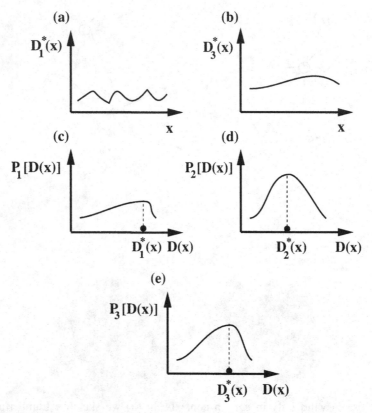

Fig. 4.2 Prior assumption bias perception. (**a**) shows the true depth $D_1^*(x)$ and (**b**) shows the biased depth percept $D_3^*(x)$ after smoothing. In (**c**) we assume that the likelihood function $p_1[D(x)]$ is weakly peaked at the true depth $D_1^*(x)$. The prior in (**d**), however, is peaked at $D_2^*(x)$. The resulting posterior distribution $p_3[D(x)]$ is shown in (**e**) and yields a biased percept $D_3^*(x)$.

noise (Cernushi-Frias *et al.*, 1989). This defines a distribution $P(I_L, I_R | I, d)$ and by introducing a prior $p(I, d)$ and applying Bayes theorem we get

$$p(I, d | I_L, I_R) = \frac{p(I_L, I_R | I, d) p(I, d)}{p(I_R, I_L)}. \tag{4.2}$$

If we assume that the prior $p(I, d)$ is uniform in I then we can integrate out[†] the surface intensity I to compute the marginal distribution

$$p(d | I_L, I_R) = \int p(I, d | I_L, I_R)[dI]$$

$$= (1/Z)e^{-\beta \int (I_L(x+d(x)/2) - I_R(x-d(x)/2))^2 dx} p(d), \tag{4.3}$$

[†] This is possible because our assumptions have made $p(I, d | I_L, I_R)$ a Gaussian in I – which is straightforward to integrate analytically.

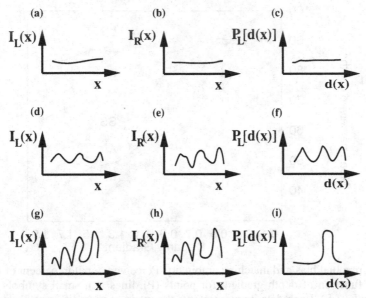

Fig. 4.3 The ambiguity of the likelihood function for binocular stereo. For the intensity profiles of left (**a**) and right (**b**) eye there is considerable matching ambiguity and so the likelihood function $p_L[d(x)]$ is almost flat in (**c**). For the inputs in (**d**) and (**e**) there is less ambiguity, because the bumps in the two images must match, yet there are several possible correspondences and hence the likelihood function has several peaks in (**f**). However, the images in (**g**) and (**h**) are sufficiently structured so that only one match is likely and therefore the likelihood function has only a single peak as shown in (**i**).

where $p(d)$ is the prior for the disparity, Z is a normalization constant, and β is proportional to the inverse of the variance of the noise models.

Such a model, using standard piecewise smoothness priors for $p(d)$, will once again predict the observed biases towards the frontoparallel plane, see (Bülthoff & Mallot, 1988). Moreover, the strength of these biases will depend on the ambiguity of the matching between the images, see Figure 4.3. If the images have little variation then the likelihood function gives little constraint on $d(x)$ (many functions $d(x)$ will have non-zero probability) and the perception is strongly biased towards the prior assumptions on the geometry. Conversely, if the images have a lot of variation then there will be little ambiguity in the matching and so the likelihood function $p(I_L, I_R|d)$ will put strong constraints on the form of $d(x)$ (only one function $d(x)$ will have non-zero probability). If the image variations are periodic or semi-periodic then the likelihood function will have several peaks and there will be matching ambiguity which can result in the well-known wallpaper illusion.

This suggests that the less the matching ambiguity then the weaker the bias towards prior assumptions. Experimental support for this comes from (Bülthoff *et al.*, 1991), see Figure 4.4, who tested the perceived depth gradient between a

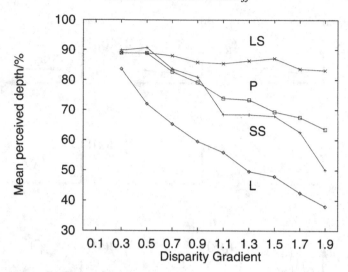

Fig. 4.4 Perceptual bias and matching ambiguity. Perceived depth in percent of displayed depth as a function of depth gradient for points (P), lines (L), small symbols (SS) and large symbols (LS). Each data item represents the mean of nine different disparities (3 – 27 arc min) tested with 10 subjects. The standard errors of the means are in the order of the symbol size. Redrawn from (Bülthoff *et al.*, 1991).

pair of feature points as a function of the dissimilarity between the features. The greater the dissimilarity between features then the less the perceived bias towards the frontoparallel plane. These experiments were consistent with a Bayesian theory (Yuille *et al.*, 1991) which formulated stereo as a surface reconstruction problem and interpreted the experiments as a bias towards prior assumptions which weakens as the likelihood function puts stronger constraints on the disparities.

It seems difficult for other types of stereo theories to explain these experiments. Most theories based on feature matching (e.g. Pollard *et al.*, 1985) obtain depth by trigonometry after matching. They will either match the features correctly, getting one percept, or incorrectly, getting another. There seems to be no mechanism by which they can get the observed differential bias depending on the form of the features.

We stress that Bayesian theories described in this Section are intended as illus-trations and only give qualitative explanations for these experiments. To give a full quantitive explanation would require precise specifications of all the adjustable pa-rameters in the Bayesian theory. Attempts of this type are underway, see work by Yuille & Grzywacz (1989), Grzywacz *et al.* (1989), Watamaniuk *et al.* (1993) on motion perception and by Blake, Bülthoff and Sheinberg (1993) on texture. This is an important research direction but it is not the main focus of this Chapter. Instead our goal is to give an overview of Bayesian theories for visual perception which contrasts them with alternative formulations and focusses on qualitative agreement with experiments.

The main focus of this Section is to give examples af visual modules, to show that it is possible to interpret some psychophysical experiments as biases towards "reasonable" prior assumptions and to stress that the less constraint the likelihood function places on the scene then the stronger the bias. Finally, we emphasize that all these theories make strong contextual assumptions and the visual system must be able to automatically verify whether the context is correct before believing the output of the model.

4.3 Integration of visual cues

It has become standard practice for computational theorists and psychophysicists to assume that different visual cues are computed in separate modules (Marr, 1982) and thereafter only weakly interact with each other. Marr's theory (Marr, 1982) did not fully specify this weak interaction but seemed to suggest that each module separately estimated scene properties, such as depth and surface orientation, and then combined the results in some way.[†] A more quantitive theory, which has experimental support (Bruno & Cutting, 1988; Dosher *et al.*, 1986; Maloney & Landy, 1989), involves taking weighted averages of cues which are mutually consistent and using a vetoing mechanism for inconsistent cues. A further approach by Poggio and collaborators (Poggio *et al.*, 1988) based on Markov Random fields has been implemented on real data.

The Bayesian approach suggests an alternative viewpoint for the fusion of visual information (Clark & Yuille, 1990). This approach stresses the necessity of taking into account the prior assumptions used by the individual modules. These assumptions may conflict or be redundant. In either case it seems that better results can often be achieved by strongly coupling the modules in contrast to the weak methods proposed by Marr or the weighted averages theories (Bruno & Cutting, 1988; Dosher *et al.*, 1986; Maloney & Landy, 1989). See Figure 4.5 for an overview of weak and strong coupling.

To see the distinction between weak and strong coupling suppose we have two sources of depth information f and g. Marr's theory would involve specifying two posterior distributions, $p_1(S|f)$ and $p_2(S|g)$, for the individual modules. Two MAP estimates of the scene S_1^* and $S_2^{*\ddagger}$ would be determined by each module and the results would be combined in some unspecified fashion.

[†] "The principle of modular design does not forbid weak interactions between different modules in a task, but it does insist that the overall organization must, to a first approximation, be modular" (Marr, 1982, page 102.)

[‡] We assume for the moment that all estimates are MAP, $S^* = \arg\max_S p(S|f)$, but alternative estimates will be discussed in Section 6.

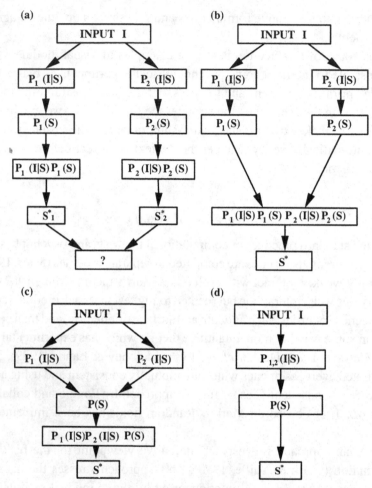

Fig. 4.5 Different types of coupling between modules. (a) shows a form of weak coupling where the two modules act independently, with their own likelihood functions $p(I|S)$ and priors $p(S)$, producing MAP estimators, $S^* = \arg\max_S p(I|S)p(S)$, as outputs which are then combined in an unspecified manner. (b) shows weak coupling where the likelihood functions and priors of the two modules are multiplied together and then the MAP estimator is calculated. Such coupling would yield a weighted combination of cues in some circumstances, see Appendix 2. In (c) the likelihood functions of the modules are combined with a single prior for the combined modules and then the MAP estimator is found. This case is on the borderline between weak and strong coupling. It is weak if the prior $p(S)$ is the same as that used for the individual modules and it is strong otherwise. (d) shows strong coupling where it is impossible to factor the likelihood function of the combined modules into the likelihood functions for the individual modules.

The weighted averages theories are not specified in a Bayesian framework. But one way to obtain them would be to multiply the models together to obtain $p(S|f, g) = p_1(S|f)p_2(S|g)$. If the MAP estimates, S_1^* and S_2^*, from the two theories are similar then it is possible to do perturbation theory and find, to first order, that the resulting combined MAP estimate $S_{1,2}^*$ is a weighted average of S_1^* and S_2^*. (See Appendix to this chapter and section 5.16 of the following chapter by Bennett *et al.*)

Both Marr's and the weighted averages approach would be characterized as weak (Clark & Yuille, 1990) because they assume that the information conveyed by the a posteriori distributions of the two modules is independent. But, as we have argued, the forms of the prior assumptions may cause the information to be dependent or even contradictory.

The Markov Random Field approach by Poggio and collaborators is slightly difficult to classify in our scheme. A specific implementation (Poggio *et al.*, 1988) says that "individual modules are therefore only integrated with each other indirectly, through the brightness constraint", which would mean weak coupling. Yet the system may be improved to include feedback between the modules, which might correspond to strong coupling. This Markov Random Field approach is certainly close in spirit to the one we are advocating.

By contrast the Bayesian approach would require us to specify a combined likelihood function $p(f, g|S)$ for the two cues and a single prior assumption $p(S)$ for the combined system. This will give rise to a distribution $p(S|f, g)$ given by

$$p(S|f, g) = \frac{p(f, g|S)p(S)}{p(f, g)}, \tag{4.4}$$

and in general will not reduce to $p_1(S|f)p_2(S|g)$. A model like (4.4) (which cannot be factorized) is considered a form of strong coupling (Clark & Yuille, 1990). An important intermediate case between weak and strong coupling occurs when the likelihood function can be factored as $p(f, g|S) = p(f|S)p(g|S)$, see Figure 4.5c. If the two individual cues have identical priors and the combined system is given the same prior, i.e. $p(S) = p_1(S) = p_2(S)$, then the coupling is considered weak – though it still differs from Marr's theory or the weighted averages approach. But if the combined prior differs from either of the two individual priors then the coupling is strong. It should be emphasized that it is not unusual for two modules, as formulated by Marr, to have different priors. For example, stereo uses piecewise smoothness and structure from motion uses rigidity. Moreover, because more information is available, the combined prior for two visual modules may not need to be as strong as the priors for the individual modules.[†]

[†] A strict Bayesian would argue that you should never weaken your prior just because more information is available and that the additional information should decrease the dependence on the prior automatically. However, this argument is correct only if the prior is highly accurate. Any visual prior that we can currently imagine is likely to be, at best, a poor approximation and it is sensible to try to reduce the dependence on it.

The need for formulating cue combination by (4.4) may seem obvious to statisticians. Indeed some might argue that the need for strong coupling is only an artifact of incorrect modularization of early vision. We have sympathy for such a viewpoint.

Observe also that there is no need for a veto mechanism between cues in our framework. Such a mechanism is only needed when two cues appear to conflict. But this conflict is merely due to using mutually inconsistent priors when modeling the two cues. If we combine the cues using (4.4) then this conflict vanishes.

In the next two subsections we will consider some examples of cue integration. We will demonstrate that for shading and texture the likelihood function usually cannot be factored and so strong coupling is required. Next we will describe a system for coupling stereo and monocular cues so that the resulting system has no need for a prior.

4.3.1 Examples of strong coupling

We now give two examples where we argue that strong coupling is advantageous. The first example is for a case where the likelihood function of two cues are not independent. The second example shows that when coupling two modules the prior assumptions about the geometry can be significantly altered.

4.3.1.1 Shape from shading and texture

We now consider coupling shading with texture. Firstly, we argue that in this case the likelihood functions are not independent and that strong coupling is usually required. Secondly, we describe an experiment from (Bülthoff & Mallot, 1988), which shows how the integration of shading and texture information gives a significantly more accurate depth perception than that attained by shading and texture independently.

As we discussed in the previous Section, standard theories of shape from shading and texture, in particular their likelihood functions, are only valid in certain contexts. Moreover, these contexts are mutually exclusive. Shape from shading assumes that the image intensity is due purely to shading effects (no albedo variations) while shape from texture assumes that it is due only to the presence of texture.

To couple shading with texture we must consider a context where the image intensity is generated both by shading and textural processes. Such a context may be modeled by a simple reflectance model

$$I(x) = a(x)R(\vec{n}(x)) \tag{4.5}$$

where the texture information is conveyed by the albedo term $a(x)$ and the shading information is captured by $R(\vec{n}(x))$. It is typically assumed that the reflectance function is Lambertian $\vec{s} \cdot \vec{n}$. There are a variety of different texture assumptions

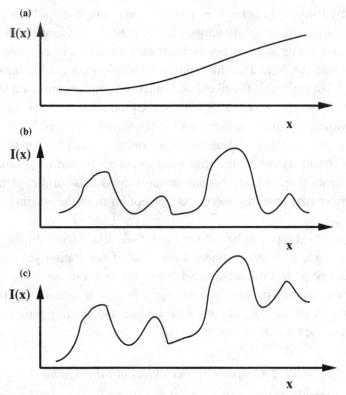

Fig. 4.6 The difficulty of decoupling shading and texture cues. (**a**) shows a typical intensity profile for a Lambertian surface with constant albedo, the context in which shape from shading can be computed. (**b**) shows the intensity profile for a surface with strong albedo variation, the context for shape from texture. (**c**) shows the intensity profile when both cues are present. Separating this profile into its shading in (**a**), and textural components in (**b**), is hard in general. In Bayesian terms this is because the likelihood function for combined shading and texture cannot, in general, be factored into the likelihood functions for the two individual cues.

which typically assume that there are a class of elementary texture elements that are painted onto the surface in a statistically uniform distribution. This will induce a distribution on the albedo, $a(x)$, that depends on the geometry of the surface in space.

Typically texture modules assume that $R(\vec{n}(x)) = 1$, $\forall x$, while shading modules set $a(x) = 1$, $\forall x$. For the coupled system these assumptions are invalid, see Figure 4.6. The shading module has to filter out the albedo $a(x)$, or texture, while the texture information must ignore the shading information $R(\vec{n}(x))$. For some images it may be possible to do this filtering independently (i.e. the texture model can filter out $R(\vec{n}(x))$ without any input from the shading module, and vice versa). In general, however, distinguishing between $R(\vec{n}(x))$ and $a(x)$ is not at all straightforward. Consider an object made up of many surface patches with Lambertian reflectance functions and differing albedos. For such a stimulus it seems impossible to separate the intensity into albedo and shading components *before* computing the surface geometry. Thus we argue that the likelihood functions for the combined shading and texture module usually cannot be factored as the product of the likelihood functions for the individual modules and hence strong coupling is required.[†,‡]

In addition we argue that, because more information is available in the likelihood term of the combined module, the prior assumption on the surface geometry can be weakened. Hence there is both less bias towards the fronto-parallel plane from the priors and more bias towards the correct perception from the shading and texture cues.

In the experiment reported below, see Figure 4.7, shape from shading and shape from texture alone gave strong underestimations of orientation yet the combined cues gave almost perfect orientation. Such a result seems inconsistent with Marr's theory or with coupling by weighted averages. Instead it seems plausible that this is an example of strong coupling between texture and shading with a weak prior towards piecewise smooth surfaces.[§]

4.3.1.2 *Coupling stereo with controlled motion*

Our second example describes theoretical results where the coupling of two cues can significantly reduce the dependence on prior assumptions about the geometry of the scene.

We restrict ourselves to a world consisting of isolated point features in space. The two depth cues are binocular stereo and monocular depth cues obtained by motion parallax from small head or eye movements. This Section is based on work described in Geiger & Yuille (1989).

Consider the two cues independently. For binocular stereo there is the well known correspondence problem, which is illustrated in Figure 4.8. All the assumptions used to make stereo well-posed – the ordering constraint, piecewise smooth surfaces, the disparity gradient limit – will tend to bias the system towards a single depth plane. Although it is true that the disparity gradient limit theories have some ability to

---

[†] A similar point is made by Adelson and Pentland's parable of the painter, the carpenter and the gaffer (lights technician) – see chapter 11 by Adelson & Pentland.

[‡] This is also closely related to the concept of cooperative processes (Knill & Kersten, 1991) where the perception of shape from shading depends very strongly on contour cues or on stereo curvature cues (Buckley *et al.*, 1993), see Chapter by Kersten and Knill.

[§] The only way that these results might be consistent with weak coupling would be if simple filters could decompose the image into texture and shading parts, hence factorizing the likelihood function, and then combining the cues using the same prior used by both modules. This prior would have to be so weak that the likelihood functions of the two modules dominate it.

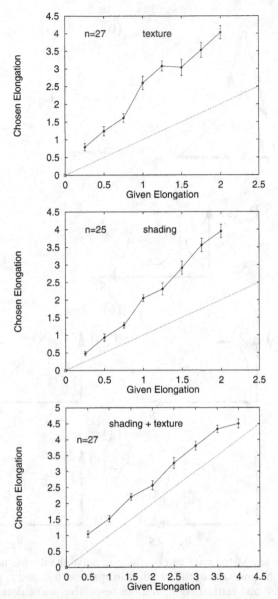

Fig. 4.7 Psychophysical experiments on the integration of shading and texture. In an adjustment task subjects interactively adjusted the shading or texture of a simulated ellipsoid of rotation (seen by one eye) in order to match the form of a given ellipsoid seen with both eyes (in stereo). The ellipsoids were seen end-on so that the outline was the same for both surfaces. Shape from shading and shape from texture individually lead to a strong underestimation of shape, i.e., shading or texture of an ellipsoid with much larger elongation had to be simulated in order to match a given ellipsoid (slope $\gg 1$). If shading and texture are presented simultaneously the shape is adjusted almost correctly (slope $= 1$). Redrawn from (Bülthoff & Mallot, 1990).

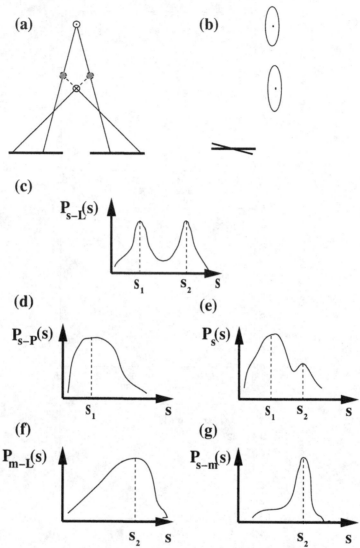

Fig. 4.8 Monocular and stereo cues can combine to solve the double nail illusion. The s variable represents the positions of the two dots in space with s_1 and s_2 denoting the horizontal (frontoparallel) and vertical configurations respectively. The dots are in the vertical configuration s_2. Binocular stereo has a correspondence problem and (a) shows the two possible solutions s_1 and s_2, illustrated by the grey and white ellipses respectively. The monocular cues (b) have no correspondence problem but only yield approximate depth estimates, the sizes of the ellipses show the magnitude of the uncertainty. (c) shows that the stereo likelihood function $p_{s-L}(s)$ has two maxima corresponding to the two possible solutions. A typical prior $p_{s-p}(s)$ for stereo (d) will favour the frontoparallel interpretation s_1. So the stereo module with posterior distribution $p_s(s) \propto p_{s-L}(s) p_{s-p}(s)$ will be biased towards the incorrect solution s_1 shown in (e). The monocular likelihood function $p_{m-L}(s)$ is peaked at the correct interpretation s_2 but the distribution is so broad that there is considerable uncertainty in the estimated position, see (f). However, combining the likelihood functions for the stereo and monocular cues, $p_{s-m}(s)$, yields a sharp peak at the correct solution s_2, see (g).

perceive transparent surfaces they will still be fooled by the double nail illusion, see Figure 4.8.

On the other hand, the monocular depth cues caused by motion parallax will not have a correspondence problem since they will be able to track the feature points. The estimation of depth can then be performed by trigonometry. This estimation, however, is likely to be very inaccurate because the eye/head movements are small, so the baseline for the triangulation is small, and there may be additional uncertainty in the amount of eye/head movement. Nevertheless it is possible to define a probabilistic model for this system to give both the estimated depth values and an estimate of their variability.

Suppose we attempt to weakly couple the stereo and monocular cues for the transparent stimuli shown in Figure 4.8. The monocular cues would give roughly the correct depth estimates but with large variances. By contrast, the prior used by the stereo system would tend to force the data into a single surface, typically as frontoparallel as possible. Thus the monocular estimates would be more accurate than the stereo estimates but they would have larger variance. So if weak coupling is used we would expect the stereo module to override the monocular cues and the system would yield an incorrect answer.

By contrast if we strongly couple the two cues, by multiplying together the likelihood functions for both modules, then the information from the monocular cues will be available to help solve the correspondence problem of stereo hence giving a highly nonlinear interaction between the monocular and the stereo cues. The monocular cues do not need to localize the depths of the features precisely, they only need to be accurate enough to disambiguate the stereo correspondence problem, see Figure 4.8.

This example illustrates several key features of the strong coupling approach: (i) the interaction between modules can become highly nonlinear, (ii) cues that contain little, or inaccurate, information may nevertheless significantly strengthen the performance of another module provided the inaccuracy can be quantified, and (iii) the dependence on priors can be reduced if more cues are available.

This example is atypical of strong coupling because the resulting combined system does not need a prior assumption. We stress that this is only because we are working in a limited context, of isolated feature points, and will not be true in general.

4.3.1.3 Mathematics of monocular and binocular strong coupling

This Section gives mathematical details of the theory for strongly coupling binocular and monocular cues. It can be skipped by readers who are not interested in these details.

Consider a system which has both monocular and binocular depth cues where the scenes consist of isolated feature points. Let there be N feature points, $x_i^l : i = 1, \ldots, N$, visible in the left image and M points, $x_a^r : a = 1, \ldots, M$, visible in the right image. Suppose we have a set of monocular depth values $\{x_i^l, d_i^l, \sigma_i^l : i = 1, \ldots, N\}$ and $\{x_a^r, d_a^r, \sigma_a^r : a = 1, \ldots, M\}$ where the x's are the positions in the two eyes, the d's are the corresponding monocular depth estimates, and the σ's are the standard deviations of these estimates. For details about how these estimates can be derived see Geiger & Yuille (1989). So the monocular depth estimates $f(x)$ are given by Gaussian distributions:

$$p_l(\{f(x_i^l)\}|\{x_i^l\}) = \frac{1}{Z_l} \prod_{i=1}^{N} e^{-(f(x_i^l)-d_i^l)^2/2(\sigma_i^l)^2},$$

$$p_r(\{f(x_a^r)\}|\{x_a^r\}) = \frac{1}{Z_r} \prod_{a=1}^{M} e^{-(f(x_a^r)-d_a^r)^2/2(\sigma_a^r)^2}, \tag{4.6}$$

where Z_l and Z_r are normalization constants (i.e. $Z_l = \prod_{i=1}^{N} \{\sqrt{(2\pi)}\}\sigma_i^l$). For these monocular cues no priors are needed and so the distributions $p_l(\{f(x_i^l)\}|\{x_i^l\})$ and $p_r(\{f(x_a^r)\}|\{x_a^r\})$ correspond to the likelihood functions of the monocular cues. Priors are not needed because we are assuming as context that the scene consists of isolated feature points. It is straightforward to track these features and estimate their depth by motion parallax induced by eye/head movements. This is, however, a big uncertainty in the depth estimates of these points owing to the difficulty in estimating the eye/head movements (see Geiger, 1989).

The binocular stereo system computes depth estimates and standard deviations $\{d_s(x_i^l, x_a^r), \sigma_{ia}\}$ assuming that a point labeled i the left image corresponds to a point labeled a in the right image. Let $\{V_{ia} : i = 1, \ldots, N \; a = 1, \ldots, M\}$ be binary matching elements which can specify the correspondences between the points in the two eyes. In other words we set $V_{ia} = 1$ if we decide that point i matches point a and set $V_{ia} = 0$ otherwise.

For binocular stereo the likelihood function $p_S(\{x_i^l, x_a^r\}|V, f)$ is given by $(1/Z)e^{-\beta E_S(V,f)}$, where Z is a normalization constant and

$$E_S(V_{ai}, f) = \sum_{a,i} \frac{1}{(\sigma_{ia})^2} V_{ai}(d(x_i^l, x_a^r) - f(x_i^l))^2$$

$$+ \lambda \sum_i (1 - \sum_a V_{ia}) + \lambda \sum_a (1 - \sum_i V_{ia}), \tag{4.7}$$

where we require that points in each image have either one or no matches. Hence the terms $\sum_a V_{ia}$ and $\sum_i V_{ia}$ take values of either 0 or 1. The constant λ is therefore a penalty for unmatched points.

For binocular stereo the matching is ambiguous and so prior assumptions on f

or V are needed. Thus the Bayesian theory is of form

$$p_S(V, f | \{x_i^l, x_a^r\}) = p_S(\{x_i^l, x_a^r\} | V, f) p_p(V, f) \tag{4.8}$$

where $p_p(V, f)$ is a prior assumption on V and f. As discussed previously, most standard choices for $p_p(V, f)$ will attempt to reconstruct a piecewise smooth surface (often biased towards the frontoparallel plane).

When strongly coupling the monocular and stereo cues the prior $p_p(V, f)$ becomes unnecessary and can be discarded. The reason is that, in this context of isolated feature points, there will usually be enough information in the likelihood functions to determine the correct matches. Thus the prior required by the stereo system becomes redundant and can be dropped. Observe that this differs from standard Bayesian statistics where the prior is always kept in and its influence merely degrades gracefully as the likelihood function becomes more specific.

When combining the cues we need to express all the cues in one coordinate system. We choose a coordinate system based on the left eye only and use the V variables to perform this transformation. This gives a strongly coupled theory $P_{SC}(V, f | \{x_i^l, x_a^r\}) = (1/Z) e^{-\beta E(V, f)}$ where

$$E(V, f) = \sum_i \frac{1}{(\sigma_i^l)^2} (f(x_i^l) - d_i^l)^2$$

$$+ \sum_{a,i} \frac{1}{(\sigma_a^r)^2} V_{ai} (f(x_i^l) - d_a^r)^2$$

$$+ \sum_{a,i} \frac{1}{(\sigma_{ia})^2} V_{ai} (d(x_i^l, x_a^r)$$

$$- f(x_i^l))^2, \tag{4.9}$$

and V is a normalization constant.

In this case weak coupling will simply correspond to multiplying the distribution p_{SC} by the prior p_p. This gives

$$p_W(V, f | \{x_i^l, x_a^r\}) = \frac{p_{SC}(V, f | \{x_i^l, x_a^r\}) p_p(V, f)}{Z_w}, \tag{4.10}$$

where Z_w is the normalization factor.

Thus the weakly coupled system will show a bias towards the prior assumptions in $p_p(V, f)$ but the strongly coupled system will show no bias.

4.4 Decision theory

In this Section we develop the concept of a loss function which we briefly mentioned in the Introduction. This is a key ingredient of Bayesian Decision theory and, by specifying a penalty for making an incorrect perceptual inference, emphasizes the task dependent nature of vision. We illustrate the importance of the choice of loss function by reformulating Freeman's original Bayesian treatment of the generic viewpoint assumption (Freeman, 1993). We argue that decision theory gives the correct framework for treating this assumption. Freeman and Brainard (Brainard & Freeman, 1994) have independently reached a similar conclusion, making similar choices of Gaussian loss functions, see Freeman's chapter in this book.

Given a Bayesian distribution $p(S|I)$ we must make a decision about the viewed scene. Let the set of allowable decisions be $\mathcal{D} = \{d_\mu : \mu \in \Lambda\}$ (i.e. μ labels a decision d_μ and these labels lie in a set Λ.). These decisions will correspond to the set $\{S\}$ of possible scenes. We introduce a loss function $l(S, d)$, which is the penalty for making a decision d when the true scene is S. The loss function can be used to specify which scenes the visual system considers important or the type of errors that it considers acceptable.

If we have enough visual information to determine the scene S uniquely then the optimal decision corresponds to the d^* which minimizes $l(S, d)$. Typically, however, we will only have a probability distribution $p(S|I)$ for the scene. In this case the Bayes' decision minimizes the expected loss, or *risk*, defined by:

$$R(d) = \int l(S, d) p(S|I)[dS]. \tag{4.11}$$

Conventional statistical estimators can be obtained by an appropriate choice of loss function. If we decide to penalize equally every time we make the incorrect decision and set $l(d, S) = -\delta(S - d)$ (where δ is the Dirac delta function), then we find that $R(d) = -p(d|I)$ and the Bayes decision is the scene d^* that maximizes $p(d|I)$, the maximum a posteriori (MAP) estimator.

The MAP estimator, i.e. the mode of the posterior distribution, is often used in vision but, because it only rewards the system if it attains precisely the right solution, it is suspect to statisticians.[†] If the task requires us only to get precisely the right solution then it should be used, otherwise alternatives are better. One alternative is the minimal variance (MV) estimator whose loss function is $l(S, d) = (S - d)^2$. Thus decisions which are close, but not identical, to the right solution get rewarded. In this case the risk function becomes $R(d) = \int (S - d)^2 p(S|I)[dS]$ and so, by differentiating with respect to d, we see that the optimal decision $d^* = \int Sp(S|I)[dS]$ is simply the mean of the distribution. Some typical loss functions are shown in Figure 4.9.

It should be emphasized that the choice of loss function depends on the visual task that the system is designed to accomplish. To illustrate this we consider Free-

---

[†] "... This means that the mode is hard to find and need not be a good summary of the posterior distribution. It is a Bayes rule, but under a rather perculiar loss function ..." page 95, Ripley (1992).

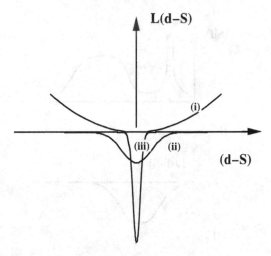

Fig. 4.9 Several standard loss functions. They depend only on the difference between the decision d and the scene S so we write them as functions of $(d - S)$. The quadratic loss function, labeled (i), has $l(d - S) = (S - d)^2$, and its estimator is the mean of the distribution. Curves (ii) and (iii) are the negatives of a Gaussian and a delta function respectively. Observe that the delta function, which corresponds to MAP estimation, only rewards interpretations which are absolutely correct, with $d = S$, while the other two loss functions are more tolerant. Unless the probability distribution $p(S)$ is very sharply peaked it is unrealistic to attempt to estimate S to absolute precision, so MAP estimation is often inappropriate.

man's original formulation of generic viewpoint assumption (Freeman, 1993). This assumption states that the interpretation of the image should not be sensitive to some of the variables, the *generic variables*, which are estimated. Freeman gives an example of shape from shading with unknown light source direction (see chapter 9). Thus the image I is considered to be a function of the surface geometry G and the light source direction S. He defines a Bayesian theory

$$p(G, S|I) = \frac{p(I|G, S)p(G, S)}{p(I)}. \tag{4.12}$$

We must now decide on what we want the system to do. Do we want it to estimate the geometry only and ignore the light source direction? Or do we want to estimate both geometry and source direction simultaneously? If so, how accurate do we want to estimate these variables? Do we want to estimate the light source direction precisely, or do we only need to know them to within a few degrees? Is there sufficient information in $p(G, S|I)$ to provide reliable answers to these questions?

Clearly there are many possible tasks we could ask the system to do and we must choose a loss function suitable for the task. We should also only consider tasks for which we believe that $p(G, S|I)$ contains enough information to accomplish it.

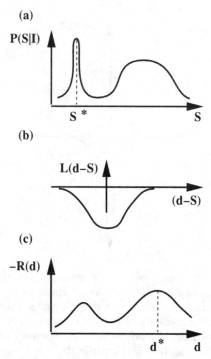

Fig. 4.10 Loss functions can enforce generic viewpoint constraints. The posterior probability $p(S|I)$ in (**a**) has a high narrow peak, at S^*, and a lower broad peak. If we only want to estimate S to within a certain broad tolerance, as in Freeman's original formulation of generic viewpoints, then we should prefer the broad peak to the thin one. Using a negative Gaussian loss function $-G(d - S)$ in (**b**) will introduce the necessary tolerance because the risk, obtained by multiplying $p(S|I)$ by $-G(d - S)$ and integrating, is now minimized near the broad peak $-G(d - S)$. This is demonstrated by plotting the negative of the risk in (**c**). Note that, because the loss function is a function of $(d - S)$, the risk is obtained by convolving the posterior with the loss function.

One possibility is that we should attempt to find the geometry exactly but only estimate the light source direction approximately. Thus we could pick a loss function $l(d_G, d_S, G, S) = -G_{ass}(d_S - S)\delta(d_G - G)$ where G_{ass} is a Gaussian function. This strongly penalizes errors in the geometry, d_G, but is tolerant to errors in the light source direction, d_S.

Such a loss function is consistent with the generic viewpoint assumption. It will effectively prefer fat peaks in the probability distribution of S to thin spikes – see Figure 4.10. Thin peaks clearly do not obey the generic viewpoint assumption since small changes in the estimators lead to very improbable images.[†]

Thus from a decision theoretical standpoint the generic views assumption is

[†] Observe that Freeman's original interpretation (Freeman, 1993) is different but, would lead to a similar interpretation for this example. He proposes integrating out the S variable by doing a saddle point approximation. This yields a *generic viewpoint factor* which would also favour fat peaks to thin ones.

equivalent to saying that some parameters need to be measured very accurately and others need only be estimated roughly. This can be achieved by picking the appropriate loss function.[†]

For another example remember the double nail illusion in the previous Section. Consider a Bayesian theory which tries to estimate the orientation of a line joining the two dots in space. Suppose that the variable we are interested in is the precise orientation of the line. There are two possibilities, frontoparallel and frontoperpendicular, depending on the correspondence between features – and each is equally likely if we use a MAP estimator. Now suppose we are only interested in estimating the orientation of the line to within a few degrees, and use a loss function that only penalizes errors greater than this. Then the frontoparallel interpretation (plus or minus a few degrees) becomes far more likely since it is far more stable with respect to orientation changes, see Figure 4.11.

Finally, we should add that picking the correct loss function is necessary for any Bayesian theory and is far more general than the generic viewpoint assumption. It critically depends on what task the visual system wants to achieve and how badly the system will be penalized if the task is not completed successfully.

4.5 Contexts and competitive priors

As we have seen, the current models for visual cues make prior assumptions about the scene. In particular, the likelihood function often assumes a particular context – for example Lambertian surfaces. The choices of priors and contexts is very important. They correspond to the "knowledge" about the world used by the visual system. In particular, the visual system will only function well if the priors and the contexts are correct.

What types of priors or contexts should be used? The influential work of Marr (Marr, 1982) proposed that vision should proceed in a feedforward way. Low level vision should be performed by vision modules which each used a single general purpose prior[†] such as rigidity for structure from motion and surface smoothness for stereo. Low level vision culminated in the 2-1/2 D sketch, a representation of the world in terms of surfaces. Finally, object specific knowledge was used to act on the 2-1/2 D sketch to perform object recognition and scene interpretation. Because the types of priors suggested for low level vision are general purpose we will refer to them as generic priors.

The question naturally arises whether models of early vision should have one generic prior. It is clear that when designing a visual system for performing a

---

[†] We are grateful for discussions with P. Belhumeur, S. Geman, D. Mumford and B. Ripley which helped clarify these points.

[†] Such priors were called natural constraints by Marr (1982).

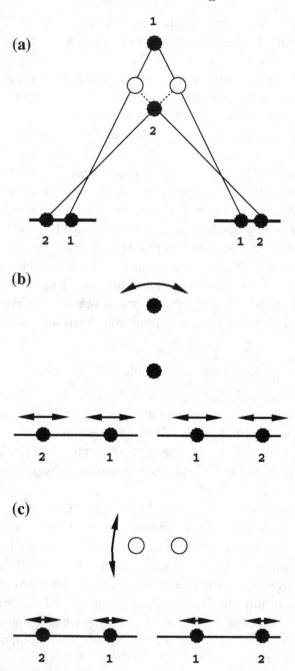

Fig. 4.11 Using the generic viewpoint assumption to "solve" the double nail illusion shown in (**a**). The "black solution" in (**b**), is less stable than the white solution in (**c**). This is because small rotations of the black solution will induce larger changes in the positions of the image points than will corresponding rotations of the white solution. In Bayesian terms the posterior distribution is narrowly peaked about the black solution but broadly peaked about the white solution.

specific visual task the prior assumptions should be geared towards achieving the task. Hence it can be argued (Clark & Yuille, 1990; Yuille & Clark, 1993) that a set of different systems geared towards different tasks and competing with each other is preferable to a single generic prior.

These competitive priors should apply both to the material properties of the objects and their surface geometries. We will first sketch how the idea applies to competing models for prior geometries, then develop the theory more rigorously and give an example of competing priors for material properties.

To make this more precise consider the specific example of shape from shading. Methods based on energy function,[†] such as Horn and Brooks (1986), assume a specific form of smoothness for the surface. The algorithm is therefore biased towards the class of surfaces defined by the exact form of the smoothness constraint. This prevents it from correctly finding the shape of surfaces such as spheres, cylinders and cones.

On the other hand there already exist algorithms that are guaranteed to work for specific types of surfaces. Pentland (1989) designed a local shape from shading algorithm which, by the nature of its prior assumptions, is ensured to work for spherical surfaces. Similarly Woodham (1981) has designed a set of algorithms that are guaranteed to work on developable surfaces, a class of surfaces which includes cones and cylinders.

Thus instead of a single generic prior it would seem more sensible to use different theories, in this case Horn and Brooks, Pentland and Woodham's, in parallel. A goodness of fitness criterion is required for each theory to determine how well it fits the data. These fitness criteria can then be used to determine which theory should be applied.

4.5.1 Theory of competitive priors

More precisely, let $p_1(f), p_2(f), \ldots, p_N(f)$ be the prior assumptions of a set of competing models with corresponding imaging models $p_1(I|f), , p_N(I|f)$. We assume prior probabilities $p_p(a)$ that the ath model is the correct choice, so $\sum_{a=1}^{N} p_p(a) = 1$. This leads to a set of different modules, each trying to find the solution that maximizes their associated conditional probability:

$$p_1(f|I) = \frac{p_1(I|f)p_1(f)}{p_1(I)},$$

$$\vdots$$

$$p_N(f|I) = \frac{p_N(I|f)p_N(f)}{p_N(I)}. \tag{4.13}$$

[†] Which can therefore be directly interpreted as Bayesian by using the Gibbs distribution, see the Appendix.

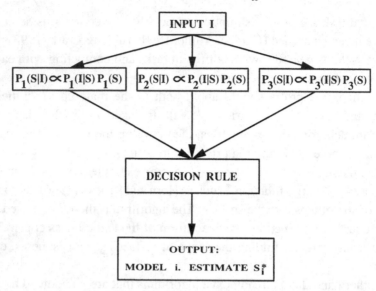

Fig. 4.12 Competitive priors. Three models with different priors compete to explain the input I. The winner is decided by a decision rule. The output is the choice of model i and the estimate given by the winner S_i^*.

Our space of decisions $\mathcal{D} = \{d, i\}$ where d specifies the scene and i labels the model that we choose to describe it. We must specify a loss function $l(d, i : f, a)$, the loss for using model i to obtain scene d when the true model should be a and the scene is f, and define a risk

$$R(d, i) = \sum_a \int l(d, i : f, a) p_a(f|I) p_p(a)[df], \qquad (4.14)$$

where, for example, we might set $l(d, i : f, a) = -\delta(f - d)\delta_{ia}$ (i.e. we are penalized by δ_{ia} for not finding the right model and by $-\delta(f - d)$ for not finding the right surface). Here $\delta(f - d)$ denotes the Dirac delta function and δ_{ia} is the Kronecker delta, where $\delta_{ia} = 1$ if $i = a$ and is 0 otherwise.

The Bayes decision corresponds to picking the model i and the scene d that minimizes the risk, see Figure 4.12.

It is straightforward to adapt this model if a input sequence of images are available as will usually be the case. We simply replace I in the formulae above by the set $\{I_1, I_2, \ldots, I_M\}$ of images. For some scenes a single image may not yield enough information to decide between competing models and yet an image sequence may give the correct result (see Clark *et al.* (1992) for preliminary results showing this). In some situations the system may initially make an incorrect decision which it later corrects as more information becomes available, see Section 4.5.3.

4.5.2 Determining the fitness of prior models for material properties

We now give a specific example for determining the shading model for a surface (Clark & Yuille, 1990). In this example the two competing image formation models are Lambertian reflectance and specular reflectance.

We label the competing models by a and the surface shape by f. Let $p(I|f, a)$ be the probability of generating the image by model a when the surface shape is f. Let $p_p(a)$ be the prior probability that model a is correct.

For simplicity, we initially assume that the surface shape is known (this assumption will be relaxed later in this Section). The problem of deciding which model is most appropriate is now considered as one of deciding, in the presence of noise, whether we have one signal or another (the binary decision problem of statistical communication theory). This involves specifying a *decision rule* $\Delta(i|I)$ which tells us which model i to pick as a function of the input image I.

The optimal Bayesian decision rule, $\Delta(i|I)$ for this problem is that which minimizes the expected risk Middleton, 1987):

$$R(\Delta) = \sum_a p_p(a) \int [dI] p(I|f, a) \sum_i l(a, i) \Delta(i|I) \qquad (4.15)$$

This differs from our previous formulation because: (i) we are finding a decision rule $\Delta(i|I)$ for a class of images instead of making a single decision for a single image (these are equivalent – DeGroot, 1970) and (ii) we are not interested in determining the scene so we have fixed the f variable.

We label the possibilities $a = 1, 2$ for whether the surface is Lambertian or specular. $p(I|f, a)$ is the image formation model – hence $p(I|f, 1) = (1/Z)e^{-\int [dx](I - \vec{n} \cdot \vec{s})^2}$ and $p(I|f, 2) = (1/Z)e^{-\int [dx](I - (\vec{h} \cdot \vec{k})^m)^2}$, where $m, \vec{k}, \vec{h}, \vec{s}, \vec{n}$ take their standard meanings for the Phong shading model. The surface normal $\vec{n}$ can be calculated directly from the surface shape f. Let $p_p(1) = p$ and $p_p(2) = q$.

It is straightforward algebra to derive the optimal Bayes rule for this problem. It corresponds to deciding that the image is specular if $\Lambda(I) < K$, and Lambertian otherwise. $\Lambda(I)$ is the *likelihood ratio*, and is given by

$$\Lambda(I) = \left(\frac{p}{q}\right) \left(\frac{p(I|f, 1)}{p(I|f, 2)}\right) \qquad (4.16)$$

and K is a decision threshold given by

$$K = \frac{l(2, 1) - l(2, 2)}{l(1, 2) - l(1, 1)}. \qquad (4.17)$$

Suppose we set $l(1, 1) = l(2, 2) = 0$ (i.e. no cost for correct decision) and $l(1, 2) = l(2, 1)$ (i.e. both possible errors have equal cost), then $K = 1$. The decision rule can be rephrased as: decide specular when $\log \Lambda(I) < 0$ and Lambertian otherwise, where

$$\log \Lambda(I) = \left[\int [dx](I - \hat{n} \cdot \hat{s})^2 - \log p \right]$$
$$- \left[\int [dx](I - (\hat{h} \cdot \hat{k})^m)^2 - \log q \right]. \qquad (4.18)$$

$\log \Lambda(I)$ is a very intuitive quantity because it depends on the difference in energies of the two possible reflectance models. Essentially, we choose the Lambertian model if its energy is lower than that of the specular model, with a correction factor to adjust for the priors p and q.

This discussion has assumed that the surface shape, represented by f, is already known. We now relax this assumption and show how to estimate f and a simultaneously. First we define prior distributions $p(f|a)$ for the surface shape as a function of the model a. The posterior distribution for the model *and* the surface shape is now:

$$p(f, a|I) = \frac{p(I|f, a)p(f|a)p_p(a)}{p(I)}. \qquad (4.19)$$

Our risk function becomes:

$$R(d, i) = \sum_{a=1}^{2} \int l(d, i : f, a)p(f, a|I)[df]. \qquad (4.20)$$

Let us set $l(d, i : f, a) = -\delta(f - d)l(a, i)$, where $l(a, i)$ is the loss function defined above (i.e. l(1,1) = l(2,2) = 0 and $l(0, 1) = l(1, 0) = 1$). Then the risk simplifies to

$$R(d, 1) = -p(d, 1|I),$$
$$R(d, 2) = -p(d, 2|I). \qquad (4.21)$$

To find the optimal decision we calculate $d_1^* = \arg\max_d p(d, 1|I)$ and $d_2^* = \arg\max_d p(d, 2|I)$. Then, if $l(d_1^*, 1) < l(d_2^*, 2)$ we choose model 1 and surface shape d_1^*, otherwise we pick model 2 and shape d_2^*. In other words, we find the best estimate for the surface shape for each of the models and compare the probabilities of these estimates to determine which model is correct.

4.5.3 Psychophysics of competitive priors

It seems that a number of psychophysical experiments, some of which are described in other Chapters, seem to require explanations in terms of competitive priors. In all cases the perception of the stimuli can be made to change greatly by small changes in the stimuli. Some of these experiments would also seem to require strong coupling.

Kersten *et al.* (1991) describe a transparency experiment in which the scene can be interpreted as a pair of rectangles rotating rigidly around a common axis or as two

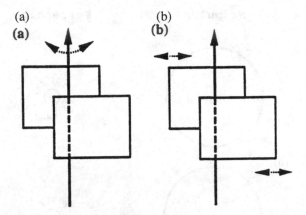

Fig. 4.13 Different types of motion are perceived depending on transparency cues. In (**a**) the two planes are perceived to rotate rigidly together. However in (**b**) they are seen to slide across each other in a periodic motion.

independent rigid rectangles rotating around their own axis (Fig. 4.13). The competitive priors correspond to assuming that the rectangles are coupled together to form a rigid object or that the rectangles are uncoupled and move independently. By adjusting the transparency cues either perception can be achieved. Interestingly, the perception of the uncoupled motion is only temporary and seems to be replaced by the perception of the coupled motion. We conjecture that this is due to the build up of support for the coupled hypothesis over time, as described in Section 4.5.1. The uncoupled interpretation is initially supported because it agrees with the transparency cue. Over a long period of time, however, the uncoupled motion is judged less likely than coupled motion. This hypothesis does require a relative ordering of competing explanations, which could be implemented by prior probabilities (see chapter 3 by Richards *et al.*). It is not hard to persuade oneself that coupled motion is more natural, and hence should have higher prior probability, than uncoupled motion.

Blake and Bülthoff's (1991) work on specular stereo, see Figure 4.14, shows how small changes in the stimuli can dramatically change the perception. In these experiments a sphere is given a Lambertian reflectance function and is viewed binocularly. A specular component is simulated and is adjusted so that it can lie in front of the sphere, between the center and the surface of the sphere, or at the center of the sphere. If the specularity is at the center it is seen as a light bulb and the sphere appears transparent. If the specularity lies in the physical correct position within the sphere (halfway between the center and the surface) then the sphere is perceived as being a glossy, metallic object.[†] If the specularity lies in front of the

---

[†] It is interesting that, before doing the experiment, most people think that the specularity should lie on the convex surface and not behind. You can convince yourself otherwise by looking, for example, at the reflection of a candle appearing inside a wineglass at a candle light dinner.

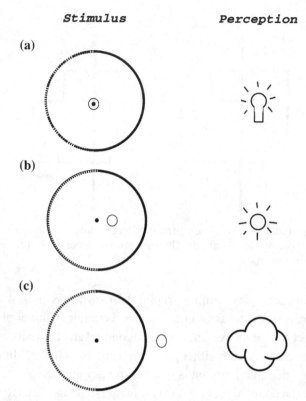

Fig. 4.14 Specular stereo where a hemisphere is viewed binocularly. In (a) the specularity, the white ellipsoid, is adjusted to lie behind the center of the sphere. It is perceived as a light bulb lying behind a transparent sphere. In (b) the specularity lies in approximately the correct position and the hemisphere is perceived to be metallic with the specularity appearing as the image of the light source. If the specularity lies in front of the hemisphere (c), then it is perceived as a cloud floating in front of the hemisphere.

sphere then it is seen as a cloud floating in front of a matte sphere. We can interpret this as saying that there are three competing assumptions for the material of the sphere: (i) transparent, (ii) glossy, (iii) matte. The choice of model depends on the data. In addition if the sphere is arranged so that its Lambertian part has no disparity then the stereo cue for the specularity resolves the concave/convex ambiguity from the shading cues, see Blake & Bülthoff (1991) for details.

Nakayama and Shimojo (Nakayama & Shimojo, 1990; Nakayama & Shimojo, 1992) describe an impressive set of stereo experiments which seem to imply that the visual system attempts to interpret the world in terms of surfaces that can partially occlude each other (see chapter 10 by Nakayama and Shimojo). The visual system often performs significant interpolation in regions that are partially hidden. For example, one can obtain a strong perception of a Japanese flag, see Figure 4.15,

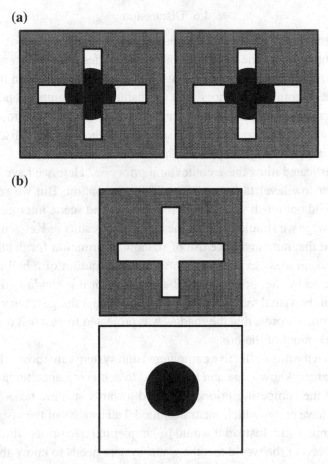

Fig. 4.15 Binocular stereo cues for surfaces occluding each other. The stereo pair (**a**), is perceived as a planar surface, with a cross-shaped hole in its central region, floating above a surface with a circle at its center, see (**b**).

even when the stimulus contains very little information, provided that the missing parts of the flag are occluded by another surface. Nakayama and Shimojo themselves (Nakayama & Shimojo, 1992) argue that their experiments can be described by having a set of competing hypotheses $i = 1, \ldots, N$ about the possible scene and corresponding image formation models $p_i(I|S_i)$. They suggest picking the interpretation j that maximizes $p_j(S_j|I) = p_j(I|S_j)/\{\sum_k p(I|S_k)\}$ – which can be seen as a special case of our competitive prior formulation. They also argue that this is related to the generic viewpoint hypothesis: if a regularity appears in an image then the regularity is due to a regularity in the scene rather than being an accidental result of the viewpoint.

4.6 Discussion

The competitive prior approach assumes that there is a large set of possible hypotheses about scenes in the world and that these scenes must be interpreted by the set of hypotheses, competing priors, that best fit the data. We envision a far larger and richer set of competing priors than the natural constraints proposed in Marr (1982) or the regularizers occurring in regularization theory (Poggio *et al.*, 1985). These priors arise from the categorical structure of the world, as discussed in the Introduction and preceding chapters of this book.

How sophisticated must these contextural priors be? Here we have only considered priors for low level tasks such as surface estimation. But we see no reason why they should not reach up to object recognition and scene interpretation. At an intermediate stage we should mention the interesting results of Kersten *et al.* (1991) which showed that humans make use of shadow information for depth perception (see chapter 6). In these experiments the perceived motion of a ball in a box was strongly affected by the motion of its shadow. But for this shadow information to be meaningful the visual system must have decided that the geometry of the scene was a box. In other words, that the shadow was projected from a ball onto the planar surface at the bottom of the box.

It is clear that the most effective computer vision systems are those which strongly exploit contextural knowledge and are geared to achieving specific tasks. To what extent should the competing priors be geared towards specific tasks? Ideally one would like to have priors which accurately model all aspects of the visual scene, but this may be unrealistic. Instead it would be simpler to have priors which accurately model the aspects of the world that the visual system needs to know about. Though this will mean that the decision rules must be sophisticated enough to prevent the system from constantly hallucinating the things that it desires to see.[†] Building up priors in this task dependent way seems a sensible strategy for designing a visual system, but is there any evidence that biological systems are designed like this? It may be hard to test for humans, since our visual system appears very general purpose, but it is possible that experiments might be designed for animals with simpler visual systems. This emphasize on task dependence is at the heart of recent work on active vision (Blake & Yuille, 1992). By making very specific prior assumptions about certain structures in the scene, and ignoring everything else, it has proven possible to design automatic vehicles capable of driving at high speeds on the Autobahn (Dickmanns *et al.*, 1990). In this case the outputs of the visual system are used directly to control the vehicle, thereby giving another link to decision theory.[‡]

[†] It is tempting to consider the hallucinations induced by sensory deprivation as an example of the prior imposing nonexistent structure on the data.

[‡] Control theory and decision theory are equivalent when applied to such problems as how much to turn the steering wheel of a car.

Decision theory can also be used at a higher level for planning tasks (Dean & Wellman, 1991). We argue that it is also useful for vision itself because, by means of loss functions, it builds in the preferences of the system and hence can incorporate task dependent vision.

Clearly the range of visual tasks that we can achieve is determined by the information, $p(S|I)$, we have about the scene. A cleverly chosen loss function can, at best, allow us to make the most use of the information available. Thus the issue of what visual tasks we can achieve, or what scene parameters we can estimate, is determined by the form of $p(S|I)$, assuming we have exploited all our prior knowledge. It may well be that $p(S|I)$ contains enough information for us to make a reliable decision about whether one object is in front of another, but not enough to decide on the absolute depth values of the objects themselves.

In its current formulation the competitive prior approach leaves many questions unanswered. In particular, how many priors should there be and how can one search efficiently through them. We believe that the answer to the first question is largely empirical and that by building increasingly sophisticated artificial vision systems and by performing more psychophysical experiments it will be possible to determine the priors required. To search efficiently between competing priors seems to require a sophisticated mixed bottom up and top down strategy of the type described in Mumford's Chapter. In such an approach, low level vision is constantly generating possible interpretations while simultaneously high level vision is hypothesizing them and attempting to verify them.

In this Bayesian framework we have said nothing about the algorithms which might be used to make the decisions. In this we are following Marr's levels of explanation (Marr, 1982) where a distinction is made between the high level information processing description of a visual system and the detailed algorithms for computing it. Thus we may hypothesize that a specific visual ability can be modeled by a Bayesian theory without having to specify the algorithm. In a similar style, Bialek (1987) describes various experiments showing that the human visual system approaches optimal performance for certain tasks, such as estimating the number of photons arriving at the retina (Sakitt, 1972), even though precise models for how these computational tasks are achieved is often currently lacking. Certainly the algorithms used to compute a decision may be complex and require intermediate levels of representation. For example, a shape from texture algorithm might require first extracting textural features which are then used to determined surface shape. Thus Bayesian theories certainly do not imply "direct perception" (Gibson, 1979) in any meaningful sense. The issues of when to introduce intermediate levels of representations and of finding algorithms to implement Bayesian theories are important unsolved problems.

Finally, in this Chapter we have been using a broad brush and have not given specific details of many theories. Though much progress has been made existing vision theories are still not as successful as one would like when implemented on real images. Bayesian decision theory gives a framework but there are many details that need to be filled in. For example, the Bayesian approach emphasizes the importance of priors but does not give any prescription for finding them. Although workers in computational vision have developed a number of promising priors for modeling the world, it is an open research task to try to refine and extend these models in order to build systems of the type outlined here. Fortunately the Bayesian framework is able to incorporate learning.[†], see Kersten *et al.* (1987), and the success of (Bayesian) Hidden Markov Models for speech recognition (Paul, 1990) suggests that it may be practical to learn Bayesian theories.[‡]

4.7 Conclusion

In this Chapter we have argued for a framework for Vision based on Bayesian Decision theory. From this perspective, vision consists of specifying priors, likelihood functions and decision rules. Such theories will inevitably causes biases towards the prior assumptions of the theory, particularly for the impoverished stimuli used by psychophysicists.

This approach suggests that when coupling visual cues care must be taken with the dependence between the cues and, in particular, on the prior assumptions which they use. In many cases this will lead to strong coupling between visual cues rather than the weak coupling proposed by other theorists.

We also argue that the prior assumptions used by the visual system must be considerably more complex than the natural constraints and generic priors commonly used. Instead there seems to be evidence for a competing sets of prior assumptions or contexts. This also seems to be a sensible pragmatic way to design a visual system to perform visual tasks. It may be better to design visual systems in terms of modules that are geared towards specific visual tasks in restricted contexts rather than modules based on the traditional concepts of visual cues. This can be incorporated into the Bayesian framework using hyperpriors (or priors with hyperparameters) and decision rules to determine which prior is suitable.

Picking the correct decision rule is also important and is directly tied to the task that the visual system is trying to solve. Certain properties of the visual scene need only be known approximately and undesirable, non-generic, interpretations may result if the decision rule is badly chosen.

[†] Neural network learning is also relevant here.
[‡] It is particularly interesting to ask whether priors can be learnt for new task.

Acknowledgements

We would like to thank Jim Clark, Dan Kersten, David Knill, Whitman Richards, David Mumford, Peter Belhumeur, Ken Nakayama, Andrew Blake and Stuart Geman for helpful discussions. We would also like to thank the four reviewers of this Chapter for their extremely useful comments. One of us, ALY, would like to thank the hospitality of the Isaac Newton Institute for Mathematical Sciences and support from the Brown/Harvard/MIT Center for Intelligent Control Systems with U.S. Army Research Office grant number DAAL03-86-K-0171.

Appendix

Bayesian theory subsumming regularization theory

The Bayesian approach subsumes work based on regularization theory and minimizing energy functions (Horn, 1986; Poggio *et al.*, 1985). In such theories a problem can be made well-posed by adding a regularizing term. Once again we need to estimate a scene S given an input I. The problem is "solved" by minimizing, with respect to S, an energy function

$$E(S; I) = E_{data}(S; I) + E_{regularizer}(S), \qquad (4.22)$$

where $E_{data}(S; I)$ measures the consistency of a scene S with the data I and $E_{regularizer}(S)$ biases the solution to a particular set of scenes.

Minimizing (4.22) is equivalent to maximizing a probability function $p(S|I)$ defined by

$$p(S|I) = \frac{1}{Z} e^{-E(S;I)}, \qquad (4.23)$$

where Z is a normalization constant.

Observe that by substituting (4.22) into (4.23) we can interpret the the data term and the regularizer as corresponding to the likelihood function and the prior of a Bayesian theory respectively. More precisely, $E_{data}(S : I) = -\log p(I|S)$ and $E_{regularizer}(S) = -\log p(S)$. Finding the MAP estimator of $p(S|I)$ corresponds to minimizing $E(S; I)$.

We can also reverse this argument to re-express Bayesian theories in terms of energy minimization. Take the logarithm of both sides of Bayes theorem

$$p(S|I) = \frac{p(I|S)p(S)}{p(I)}, \qquad (4.24)$$

to obtain

$$-\log p(S|I) = -\log p(I|S) - \log p(S) + \log p(I). \qquad (4.25)$$

By comparing to (4.22) we can interpret this as an energy function theory where $-\log p(I|S)$ is the data term and $-\log p(S)$ is the prior. The term $\log p(I)$ is independent of S and so can be ignored. Thus doing MAP on Bayes can be interpreted as minimizing an energy which is the sum of a data term and a regularizer.

Thus regularization theory, in its energy function formulation, is simply a special case of Bayes. But the Bayesian framework is far richer and gives greater insight by making clear the statistical assumptions underlying regularization theory. For example, many regularization theories in vision use quadratic energy functions. From the Bayesian perspective this is equivalent to assuming Gaussian distributions and is only justifiable if this assumption is correct. Similarly regularization theories usually combine sources of evidence by adding together energy terms. This is equivalent to multiplying probability distributions together and is only appropriate if the sources are independent.

Weighted averages from weak coupling

We now show that some forms of weak coupling give a weighted combination of cues to first order approximation provided that the MAP estimates S_1^* and S_2^* of the two cues are similar.

We start with the formula for weak coupling, $p(S|f, g) = p_1(S|f)p_2(S|g)$, and take the logarithm of both sides to obtain

$$\log p(S|f, g) = \log p_1(S|f) + \log p_2(S|g). \qquad (4.26)$$

Performing Taylor series expansions of $\log p_1(S|f)$ and $\log p_2(S|g)$ about their MAP estimators S_1^* and S_2^* gives

$$\begin{aligned}
\log p(S|f, g) = {} & \log p_1(S_1^*|f) - (1/2)(S - S_1^*)^2 w_1 \\
& + \log p_2(S_2^*|f) - (1/2)(S - S_2^*)^2 w_2 \\
& + O\{(S - S_1^*)^3, (S - S_2^*)^3\}, \qquad (4.27)
\end{aligned}$$

where $w_1 = -(d^2 \log p_1(S|f)/dS^2)(S_1^*)$ and $w_2 = -(d^2 \log p_2(S|f)/dS^2)(S_2^*)$. The first order terms in the Taylor expansion vanish because S_1^* and S_2^* are extrema. Moreover w_1 and w_2 are positive since the extrema are maxima. Extremizing $\log p(S|f, g)$, ignoring terms higher than second order, gives

$$S^* = \frac{w_1 S_1^* + w_2 S_2^*}{w_1 + w_2}. \qquad (4.28)$$

If the distributions are Gaussians then the higher order terms in (4.27) vanish and (4.28) is exact. In this case the weights are proportional to the inverse of the variances of the distributions. Thus the sharper the distribution then the more it is weighted.

A consequence of (4.28) is that the combined estimate S^* is a convex combination of S_1^* and S_2^*. Thus if S^* represents a single number, such as depth, it must be bigger than $\min(S_1^*, S_2^*)$ and smaller than $\max(S_1^*, S_2^*)$.

We note that this analysis becomes invalid unless $S_1^* \approx S_2^*$. Also the weighting constants w_1 and w_2 correspond to the Fisher information and are a measure of the reliability of the different cues.

Other forms of weak coupling such as setting $p(S|f, g) \propto p_1(f|S)p_2(g|S)p(S)$ (with $p(S) = p_1(S) = p_2(S)$) might also lead to a weighted combination of cues.[†] We rewrite this as $p(S|f, g) \propto p_1(S|f)p_2(S|g)/p(S)$ and perform a Taylor series expansion of $p_1(S|f)$, $p_2(S|g)$, and $p(S)$. This yields, to first order,

$$S^* = \frac{w_1 S_1^* + w_2 S_2^* - w_3 S_3^*}{w_1 + w_2 - w_3}, \tag{4.29}$$

where S_3^* is the MAP of $p(S)$ and $w_3 = -(d^2 \log P(S)/dS^2)(S_3^*)$. This approximation, however, is less valid than that used to derive (4.28). It requires that not only must S_1^* and S_2^* be similar but also that both of these are close to the estimate given from the prior S_3^*, which is independent of the input data! Moreover, we might expect that the distributions $p(S|f)$ and $p(S|g)$ convey more information than $P(S)$ and hence are sharper. This would imply that w_3 is much less than w_1 and w_2. This casts doubts on our ignoring the higher order terms in the Taylor series expansion since the third order terms in the expansions of $\log p_1(S|f)$ and $\log p_2(S|g)$ may be larger than the second order terms of $\log p(S)$.

References

Bayes, T. (1783). An essay towards solving a problem in the doctrine of chances. *Phil. Trans. Roy. Soc.*, **53**, 370-418.

Berger, J.O. (1985). *Statistical Decision Theory and Bayesian Analysis*. (2nd Edition). New York: Springer-Verlag.

Bialek, W. (1987). Physical limits to sensation and perception. *Ann. Rev. Biophys. Biophys, Chem.*, **16**, 455-78.

Binford, T.O. (1981). Inferring surfaces from images. *Artificial Intelligence*, **17**, 205-244.

Blake, A. & Bülthoff, H. (1991). Shape from specularities: computation and psychophysics. *Philosophical Transactions of the Royal Society of London B* , **331**, 237-252.

Blake, A., Bülthoff, H.H. & Sheinberg, D. (1993). An ideal observer model for inference of shape from texture. *Vision Research*, **33**, 1723-1737.

Blake, A. & Yuille, A.L. (1992). (Eds) *Active Vision*. Cambridge, MA: MIT Press.

Brainard, D.H. & Freeman, W.T. (1994). Bayesian method for recovering surface and illuminant properties from photosensor responses. In *Proceedings of SPIE, Human Vision, Visual Processing and Digital Display V*, ed. B. Rogowitz and J. Allebach, San Jose, CA.

[†] We are grateful to A. Blake for this argument.

Bruno, N. & Cutting, J.E. (1988). Minimodularity and the perception of layout. *J. Exp. Psychology: General*, **117**, 161-170.

Buckley, D., Firsby, J.P. & Freeman, J. (1993). Lightness perception can be affected by surface curvature from stereopsis. Artificial Intelligence Vision Research Unit preprint. Dept. Psychology, University of Sheffield, England.

Bülthoff, H.H. & Yuille, A.L. (1991). Bayesian models for seeing shapes and depth. *Comments of Theoretcial Biology*, **2**, 283-314.

Bülthoff, H. & Mallot, H.A. (1988). Interaction of different modules in depth perception. *J. Opt. Soc. Am.*, **5**, 1749-1758.

Bülthoff, H. & Mallot, H.A. (1990). Integration of stereo, shading and texture. In *AI and the Eye*. A. Blake and T. Troscianko, ed., Chicester: Wiley & Sons.

Bülthoff, H. & Kersten, D. (1989). Interactions between transparency and depth. *Perception*, **18**, A22b.

Bülthoff, H., Little, J. & Poggio, T. (1989). A parallel algorithm for real-time computation of optical flow. *Nature*, **337**, 549-553.

Bülthoff, H., Fahle, M. & Wegmann, M. (1991). Disparity gradients and depth scaling. *Perception*, **20**, 145-153.

Cernushi-Frias, B., Cooper, D.B. Hung, Y-P & Belhumeur, P.N. (1989). Towards a model-based Bayesian theory for estimating and recognizing parameterized 3D objects using two or more images taken from different positions. *IEEE Trans. Pattern Anal. Machine Intell.*, **11**, 1028-1052.

Clark, J.J. & Yuille, A.L. (1990). *Data Fusion for Sensory Information Processing Systems*. Boston/ Dordrecht/ London: Kluwer Academic Press.

Clark, J.J., Weisman, M.J. & Yuille, A.L. (1992). Using Viewpoint Consistency in Active Stereo Vision. *Proceedings SPIE*, Boston, November.

Dean, T.L. & Wellman, M.P. (1991). *Planning and Control*. Morgan Kaufmann.

DeGroot, M.H. (1970). *Optimal Statistical Decisions*. New York: McGraw-Hill.

Dickmanns, E.D., Mysliwetz, B. & Christians, T. (1990). An integrated spatio-temporal approach to automated visual guidance of autonomous vehicles. *IEEE Trans. on Systems, Man and Cybernetics*, **20**(6), 1273-1284.

Dosher, B.A., Sperling, G. & Wurst, S. (1986). Tradeoffs between stereopsis and proximity luminance covariance as determinants of perceived 3D structure. *Vision Research*, **26**, 973–990.

Earman, J. (1992). *Bayes or Bust*. Cambridge, MA: MIT Press.

Freeman, W. (1993). Exploiting the generic view assumption to estimate scene parameters. *Proc. 4th Intl. Conf. Computer Vision*, Berlin, Germany, 347-356.

Geiger, D. & Yuille, A.L. (1989). Stereo and Eye Movement. *Biological Cybernetics*, **62**, 117-128.

Gibson, ? (1979). *The Ecological Approach to Visual Perception*. Houghton Mifflin.

Gregory, R.L. (1978). *Eye and Brain*. 3d edition. New York: McGraw-Hill.

Grzywacz, N.M., Smith, J.A. & Yuille, A.L. (1989). A computational theory for the perception of inertial motion. *Proceedings IEEE Workshop on Visual Motion*, Irvine.

Horn, B.K.P. & Brooks, M.J. (1986). The variational approach to shape from shading. *CVGIP*, (2), 174-208.

Horn, B.K.P. (1986). *Robot Vision*. Cambridge, MA: MIT Press.

Kersten, D., O'Toole, A.J., Sereno, M.E., Knill, D.C. & Anderson, J.A. (1987). Associative learning of scene parameters from images. *Optical Society of America*, **26** (23), 4999-5006.

Kersten, D., Bülthoff, H.H., Schwartz, B. & Kurtz, K. (1991). Interaction between transparency and structure from motion. *Neural Computation*, **4**, 573-589.

Knill, D. & Kersten, D. (1991). Apparent surface curvature affects lightness perception. *Nature*, **351**, 228-230.

Maloney, L.T. & Landy, M.S. (1989). A statistical framework for robust fusion of depth information. *Proceedings of the SPIE: Visual Communications and Image Processing* Part2, 1154-1163.

Marr, D. (1982). *Vision*. San Francisco: W.H. Freeman and Company.

Middleton, D. (1987). *An Introduction to Statistical Communication Theory*. Los Altos, CA: Peninsula Publishing.

Mumford, D. (1992) Pattern Theory: a unifying perspective. Dept. Mathematics Preprint. Harvard University.

Nakayama, K. & Silverman, G.H. (1988). The aperture problem – I. Perception of nonrigidity and motion direction in translating sinusoidal lines. *Vision Research*, **28**, 739-746.

Nakayama, K. & Silverman, G.H. (1988). The aperture problem – II. Spatial integration of velocity information along contours. *Vision Research* **28**, 747-753.

Nakayama, K.& Shimojo, S. (1992). Experiencing and perceiving visual surfaces. *Science*, **257**, 1357-1363.

Nakayama, K. & Shimojo, S. (1990). Towards a neural understanding of visual surface representation. *Cold Spring Harbour Symposia on Quantitative Biology*, Volume LV.

Parisi, G. (1988). *Statistical Field Theory*. Reading, MA: Addison-Wesley.

Paul, D.B. (1990). Speech recognition using hidden markov models. *The Lincoln Laboratory Journal*, **3**, No. 1.

Pentland, A. (1989). Local shading analysis." In *Shape from Shading*, ed. B.K.P. Horn and M.J. Brooks. Cambridge, MA: MIT Press.

Pollard, S.B., Mayhew, J.E.W. & Frisby, J.P. (1985). A stereo correspondence algorithm using a disparity gradient limit. *Perception*, **14**, 449-470.

Poggio, T., Torre, V. & Koch, C. (1985). Computational vision and regularization theory." *Nature*, **317**, 314-319.

Poggio, T., Gamble, E.B. & Little, J.J. (1988). Parallel integration of vision modules. *Science*, **242**, 436-440.

Ramachandran, V.S. & Anstis, S. (1983). Displacement thresholds for coherent apparent motion random dot-patterns. *Vision Research*, **24**, 1719-1724.

Ripley, B.D. (1992). Classification and clustering in spatial and image data. In *Analyzing and Modeling Data and Knowledge*, ed. M. Schader. Springer-Verlag.

Risannen, J. (1983). A universal prior for integers and estimation by minimum description length. *Annals of Statistics*, **11** (2), 416–431.

Sakitt, B. Counting every Quantum." *J. Physiol.*, **284**, 261.

Sperling, G. & Dosher, B.A. (1986). Strategy and optimization in human information processing. In *Handbook of Perception and Performance. Vol. 1.*, ed. K. Boff, L. Kaufman and J. Thomas, pp 1-65. NewYork: Wiley.

Watamaniuk, S.N.J., Grzywacz, N.M. & Yuille, A.L. (1993). Dependence of speed and direction perception on cinematogram dot density. *Spatial Vision*, in press.

Williams, D.W. & Sekuler, R. (1986). Coherent global motion percepts from local stochastic motion. *Nature*, **324**, 253-255.

Woodham, R.J. (1981) Analysing images of curved surfaces. *A.I. Journal*, **17**, No. 1-3, 117-140.

Yuille, A.L. & Grzywacz, N.M. (1988). A computational theory for the perception of coherent visual motion. *Nature*, **333**, 71-74.

Yuille, A.L., Geiger, D. & Bülthoff, H. (1991). Stereo integration, mean field theory and psychophysics. *Network*, **2**, 423-442.

Yuille, A.L. & Clark, J.J. (1993). Bayesian models, deformable templates and competitive priors. To appear in *Spatial Vision in Humans and Robots* ed. L. Harris and M. Jenkin, Cambridge University Press.

5

Observer theory, bayes theory, and psychophysics

BRUCE M. BENNETT

Dept. of Mathematics, University of California at Irvine

DONALD D. HOFFMAN

Dept. of Cogntive Science, University of California at Irvine

CHETAN PRAKASH

Dept. of Mathematics, California State University, San Bernardino, CA

SCOTT N. RICHMAN

Program in Mathematical Behavioral Science, University of California at Irvine

5.1 Introduction

The search is on for a general theory of perception. As the papers in this volume indicate, many perceptual researchers now seek a conceptual framework and a general formalism to help them solve specific problems.

One candidate framework is "observer theory" (Bennett, Hoffman, & Prakash, 1989a). This paper discusses observer theory, gives a sympathetic analysis of its candidacy, describes its relationship to standard Bayesian analysis, and uses it to develop a new account of the relationship between computational theories and psychophysical data. Observer theory provides powerful tools for the perceptual theorist, psychophysicist, and philosopher. For the theorist it provides (1) a clean distinction between competence and performance, (2) clear goals and techniques for solving specific problems, and (3) a canonical format for presenting and analyzing proposed solutions. For the psychophysicist it provides techniques for assessing the psychological plausibility of theoretical solutions in the light of psychophysical data. And for the philosopher it provides conceptual tools for investigating the relationship of sensory experience to the material world.

Observer theory relates to Bayesian approaches as follows. In Bayesian approaches to vision one is given an image (or small collection of images), and a central goal is to compute the probability of various scene interpretations for that image (or small collection of images). That is, a central goal is to compute a conditional probability measure, called the "posterior distribution", which can be written $p(Scene \mid Image)$ or, more briefly, $p(S \mid I)$. Using Bayes rule one writes

$$p(S \mid I) = \frac{p(I \mid S)p(S)}{p(I)}. \tag{5.1}$$

163

This formula gives a method for computing the desired posterior distribution, and is widely referred to in vision research (Geman & Geman, 1984; Marroquin, 1989; Szeliski, 1989; Bülthoff, 1991; Bülthoff & Yuille, 1991; Clark & Yuille, 1990; Geiger & Yuille, 1991; Knill & Kersten, 1991; Yuille *et al.*, 1991; Freeman, 1992; Belhumeur & Mumford, 1992; see also Nakayama & Shimojo, 1992). It provides a powerful approach to understanding and modeling human perceptual capacities. But it has a well-known limitation. For real vision problems the collection of images that might be obtained is very large. (For instance, there are about 10^{15} possible true-color images of 1024 by 1024 pixel resolution.) Therefore $p(I)$ and $p(I \mid S)$ are either 0 or near 0 for most images and the form of Bayes rule given above is either undefined or unstable. We cannot remove this problem by conditioning on large collections rather than on small collections of images, because the task we typically face in image understanding is to interpret a given single image or small collection. In special cases the instability problem can be avoided by the use of energy functionals and Gibbs distributions (Marroquin, *et al.*, 1987; Poggio & Girosi, 1989). What we need, however, is a *general* form of Bayes rule that allows conditioning on events of probability zero and that requires no special assumptions.

Of what practical use is a general form of Bayes rule? Can instabilities that would arise from conditioning on sets of very small measure be avoided by use of this formulation? In many cases, yes. For example, a general (i.e., nondiscrete) formulation frequently permits the calculation of a local value as a limit of more global statistics. The very nature of these statistics is to wash out noise. By contrast, a single local measurement is highly sensitive to noise. Thus we would expect that to calculate the local number as a limit of these statistics provides a much more robust computational strategy. In addition, the existence of general nondiscrete formulations of a theory provides a reliable foundation for the design of discrete approximations; in fact there are many ways to discretize a nondiscrete system. The optimal comparison and selection of these various discretizations is only possible to the degree that the general formulation is well understood.

Observer theory gives a general form of Bayes rule. The result in the noise-free case is a "competence observer" and in the noisy case a "performance observer". The general form of Bayes rule requires two technical tools: regular conditional probability distributions and Radon-Nikodym derivatives. One goal of this paper is to provide an intuitive understanding of these tools and their practical application to problems in vision. After using these tools to derive a new general form of Bayes rule, we apply it to (1) the derivation of posterior distributions of practical use in vision, (2) the development of a theoretical framework for interrelating psychophysical experiments with computational theories, and (3) the analysis of hierarchical and weak coupling as theories of sensor fusion.

5.2 Competence: Some basic ideas

Perception is a process of inference, or informed guessing. From phase and amplitude differences in the acoustic waveforms at the two ears we infer the location of a sound source. From disparities in the images at the two eyes we infer the three-dimensional (3D) shapes and locations of visual objects. From temporal variations in pressure at the finger pads we infer the 3D shapes and identities of haptic objects. As Helmholtz (1925) noted, such inferences are often fast and unconscious (Ittleson, 1960; Gregory, 1973; Rock, 1977; Marr, 1982). Indeed many of these inferences may never have been conscious at any point in our ontogeny or phylogeny. They may be instantiated in low-level neuronal networks, but they are inferences nonetheless.

Perceptual inferences are not deductively valid: the conclusions of perceptual inferences typically go well beyond their premises. The examples just adduced illustrate this point, as do others. Given gradients of shading in a two-dimensional (2D) image as premises, we reach conclusions about the 3D shapes of objects. Given the activity of chemoreceptors in the mouth and nose as premises, we reach conclusions about the safety and palatability of food. These conclusions are not logically dictated by the premises. Indeed, now and then a conclusion is wrong – not due to neurological malfunctions, but due to the nondeductive character of the inferences. The result is a perceptual illusion. We see a 3D shape in a stereogram, when in fact the stereogram is flat. We hear a train rushing by, when in fact we are listening to headphones. Such illusions are not evidence that sense data are incorrigible (Quinton, 1965), but they are powerful evidence that perceptual inferences are not deductively valid (Fodor, 1975).

Perceptual inferences are statistical, but with a unique feature. The inferences typical of statistical decision theory become trivial in the absence of noise. Not so perceptual inferences. Even in the absence of noise and quantization error, perceptual inferences have a nontrivial structure; we call this structure a "competence observer". Even if our corneas and lenses had no optical scatter, our retinas had infinite resolution, and our neurons had no computational limits, still the inferences underwriting stereovision would be nontrivial, and a stereogram could fool the visual system. The role of noise in perceptual inferences must, of course, be carefully studied. But the essential structure of perceptual inferences remains unaltered in the absence of noise. Describing this structure is the proper subject of a competence theory of perception, and a prerequisite to the proper treatment of noise and other issues of performance.

Observer theory captures this structure in its formal definition of a competence observer. A major thesis of observer theory is that the same competence structure lies at the core of every perceptual capacity, and therefore that every perceptual capacity can be described, in its noise-free essence, as an instance of a competence observer. This "observer thesis" cannot be proven, since it states a relationship between a formalism (a competence observer) and an informal concept (a perceptual capacity); but it could, in principle, be disconfirmed by a counterexample, and is therefore an empirical hypothesis. In this regard it resembles the Church-Turing thesis, which states that every effective procedure can be described as some Turing machine. This thesis also cannot be proven, since it states a relationship between a formalism (the Turing machine) and an informal concept (an effective procedure); but it could, in principle, be disconfirmed by a counterexample, and is therefore an empirical hypothesis. Competence observers are proposed to play the same role for the description and analysis of perceptual capacities that Turing machines play for the description and analysis of effective procedures.

To illustrate the intuitions underlying the definition of a competence observer, we consider first the perception of 3D structure from image motion. Experiments by Braunstein and others (Braunstein *et al.*, 1987; Braunstein *et al.*, 1990) indicate that subjects can reliably discriminate visual displays which depict rigid motions of points from displays which depict nonrigid motions, and that subjects can do this with as few as two views of four moving points. For displays depicting rigid motions, subjects report seeing specific 3D interpretations, and can reliably indicate the interpretations they see (Liter *et al.*, 1993). For displays depicting nonrigid motions, subjects generally report seeing no rigid 3D interpretations.

A competence theory of this capacity must account for (i) the ability to discriminate between rigid and nonrigid displays and (ii) the particular 3D interpretations that are reported for the rigid displays. As mentioned before, this account will be idealized, in the sense that it ignores noise and quantization error.

To account for (i) a competence theory must assign (one or more) rigid interpretations not to every display, but only to those displays that depict rigid motions. Most displays do not depict rigid motion. In fact one must carefully program a display to make it depict a rigid motion. Therefore the competence theory must assign no interpretations to most displays. Put more formally, a competence theory for the problem of giving rigid interpretations to motion displays must make sure that the problem is almost surely ill-posed, and must not regularize the problem (Tichonov & Arsenin, 1977; Poggio *et al.* 1985). To regularize the problem (in the sense of Tichonov) would be to require that *every* display have one interpretation, and this would eliminate any ability to discriminate rigid from nonrigid displays. By contrast, making the problem almost surely ill-posed, by requiring that almost all displays have no interpretations, restores the ability to discriminate rigid from nonrigid displays.

To account for (ii) a competence theory must assign one or more 3D interpretations to each display depicting a rigid motion. If subjects see just one 3D interpretation of some rigid display, then the theory should assign that interpretation to the display. If subjects see more than one interpretation, then a complete theory of competence should assign a probability measure supported on these interpretations, giving the appropriate relative frequencies or strengths of the interpretations. For displays in which subjects see just one interpretation, the techniques of (Tichonov style) regularization theory can sometimes be applied. For displays in which subjects see more than one interpretation, more general techniques are required.

5.3 Competence: An example

We now consider one specific computational theory of structure from motion in order to motivate the definition of competence observer and to demonstrate useful computational techniques within the framework of competence observers. There are many accounts of structure from motion that could equally well serve this purpose (e.g., Ullman, 1979; Hoffman and Bennett, 1986), but we consider, for simplicity, the account presented by Bennett *et al.* (1989b). They prove the following "Two-View Theorem":

Theorem 1. *(Two-View Theorem).* Two orthographic views of four noncoplanar points (i) almost surely[†] have no rigid interpretations, but (ii) have a one-parameter family of such interpretations if they have any.

This theorem assumes that the correspondence between points in the two views is known. We can also assume, since the projection is orthographic, that one of the points is taken to be the origin in both views, so that only three points have variable coordinates in each view.

The inference of structure from motion defined by this theorem is as follows. An elementary premise for the inference is two views of three points (plus the origin, which we will no longer mention). The set of all elementary premises is therefore the set of all two views of three points, which is $\Re^{12}$ (i.e., two views × three points per view × two coordinates per point). Here, and throughout the paper, we denote the set of all elementary premises by D. (Here the mnemonic is D for "data", since premises are the data assumed for an inference.) According to the theorem, most of these premises, in fact almost all of these premises, have no rigid 3D interpretations. However there is a small subset of premises which have rigid 3D interpretations. These correspond to displays that depict rigid motion. This subset, which we denote

---

[†] We refer here to Lebesgue measure. "Lebesgue almost surely" means "up to measurable sets of Lebesgue measure zero". Intuitively, a measurable set A is a subset of a space X for which it is meaningful to assign a volume. Lebesgue measure is the standard way to assign volumes to measurable sets of Euclidean spaces. For more on Lebesgue measure see the Appendix, A0.

D_s and call the "special premises", has measure zero in $\Re^{12}$. Thus an element $d \in D_s$ represents two views of three points which have a rigid interpretation. A generically chosen element $d \in D$ represents two views of three points which, almost surely, have no rigid interpretation.

If $d \in D$ is an elementary premise consisting of two views of three points, i.e., of six points in the plane, then an elementary conclusion, c, compatible with d is obtained by adding a depth coordinate to each of these six points, thereby creating a 3D interpretation for d. (Hereafter, in discussing this inference, we use "elementary conclusion" and "3D interpretation" interchangeably.) The depth coordinate of each of these six points in each view can vary independently of the others, so there is, for each $d \in D$, a six-dimensional (6D) space of such conclusions c. Concretely, let d be the set of points $\{(x_{ij}, y_{ij})\}$. (Here, and in the following, $i = 1, 2, 3$ indexes the points and $j = 1, 2$ indexes the views.) Then c is a set of points $\{(x_{ij}, y_{ij}, z_{ij})\}$. We denote the 6D space of all such c by the symbol $[d]$. According to the Two-View Theorem, for almost every $d \in D$ the 6D space $[d]$ contains no rigid 3D interpretations; however, for $d \in D_s$, the 6D space $[d]$ contains a one-dimensional subset of rigid 3D interpretations. This one-dimensional subset can be parametrized by the angle between the image plane and the axis of rotation associated to each rigid 3D interpretation (Bennett *et al.*, 1989b). This angle is called the "slant" of the axis of rotation, and its value varies in the open interval $(0, \pi/2)$.

The set of all elementary conclusions for this inference is simply the union, over all d in D, of the elementary conclusions $[d]$. The set of all elementary conclusions is therefore $\Re^{18}$ (i.e., $\Re^{12} \times \Re^6$). Here, and throughout the paper, we denote the set of all elementary conclusions by C. Almost all elements of C represent nonrigid 3D interpretations. However there is a small subset of elements of C which represent rigid 3D interpretations. This subset, which we denote C_s and call the "special conclusions" or "special interpretations", has measure zero in C. C_s corresponds to a bias or *a priori* assumption of the observer. For purposes of Bayesian analysis, the "prior probabilities" assumed by the observer are probability measures supported in C_s.

The collection of all elementary premises D and the collection of all elementary conclusions C are related by a "rendering function". In this case the rendering function is a map $\pi: C \rightarrow D$ given by $\{(x_{ij}, y_{ij}, z_{ij})\} \mapsto \{(x_{ij}, y_{ij})\}$. From this definition it follows that every 3D interpretation c that is compatible with the image data d actually gets mapped to d by the rendering function π. We can write, therefore, that $\pi(c) = d$ for any c in $[d]$. Equivalently, we can write $\pi^{-1}(d) = [d]$. This structure, plus some extra structure we will discuss shortly, is illustrated in Figure 5.1. A good way to check that one understands this figure and the discussion thus far is to convince oneself that $\pi(C_s) = D_s$.

So far we have an abstract framework that permits inferences. Now we must, so

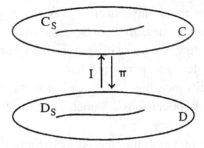

Fig. 5.1 A competence observer: a canonical representation of a class of perceptual inferences.

to speak, breathe life into this framework so that it will in fact perform inferences. We will do this by means of "markovian kernels".[†] Intuitively, given two sets X and Y, a markovian kernel N from X to Y is a device which associates to each element of X a probability measure on Y. If x is an element of X and A is a subset of Y, then we use the notation $N(x, A)$ to denote the probability assigned to A by the probability measure associated, by N, to x. Sometimes we use the notation $N(x, \cdot)$ to denote the whole probability measure associated by N to x. (Since all kernels we discuss in this paper are markovian, we henceforth drop the word "markovian" and call them simply "kernels".)

We model our perceptual inferences by a kernel, $\mathcal{I}$. We call $\mathcal{I}$ an "interpretation kernel" or "inference kernel" because it allows us to estimate conditional probabilities of scene interpretations given images. These probabilities are estimated assuming that there is no noise, i.e., assuming that the 3D interpretation c is in the 6D space $[d]$ iff c is invariably rendered as the two-view display d.

In fact, by definition of a kernel, $\mathcal{I}$ is an infinite collection of distinct probability measures, one probability measure for each two-view display d that depicts a rigid motion. The probability of a set, A, of 3D interpretations given the two-view display d is written $\mathcal{I}(d, A)$ or $\mathcal{I}(A \mid d)$. For purposes of Bayesian analysis, this probability is a posterior probability $\wp(A \mid d)$ under the assumption of no noise. The corresponding prior is a probability measure supported in C_s (the rigid 3D interpretations). The likelihood function associated to any 3D interpretation c, rigid or not, is the conditional probability on images given the scene c. As such this likelihood is the indicator function $1_{\pi(c)}$, i.e., the function which assigns the value 1 to $\pi(c)$ and 0 to all other elements of D. The likelihood function takes this simple form because we are still in the noise-free competence case. We later extend this discussion to the performance case.

A good way to check that one understands the discussion of $\mathcal{I}$ thus far is to convince oneself that $\mathcal{I}(c \mid d) = 0$ if c is not in $[d] \cap C_s$.

[†] For a precise discussion of kernels see the Appendix, sections A1–A4.

The kernel $\mathcal{I}$ expresses an infinite collection of posterior probabilities as a single linear operator (which maps measures on D to measures on C – see Appendix, A3). This is a powerful tool, as we shall see, for interpreting noisy images. And it provides a new way to view perceptual inferences: as logic morphisms between spaces of probability measures, one space of measures representing premises and another representing conclusions (Bennett *et al.*, 1993). We discuss kernels later.

The Two-View Theorem determines a class of kernels $\mathcal{I}$, each of which defines a possible competence observer with the given C, D, C_s, D_s, and π. For each two-view display $d \in D_s$, i.e., for each two views of three points that has a rigid interpretation, the posterior $\mathcal{I}(\cdot \mid d)$ is a probability measure on the 6D space $[d]$. But this probability measure is not supported on the entire 6D space. Instead it is supported on a one-parameter subset of that space, viz., the one-parameter family of rigid 3D interpretations. The Two-View Theorem alone does not provide the information required to select among these posteriors in a principled manner. For example, one candidate posterior gives equal weight to each of the rigid interpretations in the one-parameter family. (A uniform probability density is possible here since the parameter of the family lies in the interval $(0, \pi/2)$.)

We have now described a particular competence theory licensed by the Two-View Theorem. Psychophysical experiments suggest that this theory is psychologically plausible as a competence theory of the ability to discriminate between rigid and nonrigid displays (Braunstein *et al.*, 1987, 1990). But psychophysical experiments also suggest that a uniform posterior is not psychologically plausible in a competence theory of the particular 3D interpretations that are reported for the rigid displays (Liter *et al.*, 1993). Subjects do not give equal probability to all rigid interpretations in the one-parameter family compatible with a given two-view display. Instead, some rigid interpretations are almost always seen, and others are almost never seen. This suggests that the competence theory just discussed must be (1) abandoned or (2) refined to include constraints in addition to rigidity. The second option amounts to finding a more restrictive prior. We consider this later.

5.4 Competence observer: The definition

With a concrete example now in hand, we are ready to consider the abstract definition of a competence observer (see Figure 5.1).

Definition 1. A *competence observer* $\mathcal{O}$ is a collection $(C, D, C_s, D_s, \pi, \mathcal{I})$ with the following properties (see Figure 5.1).

(i) C and D have measurable structures[†] $(C, \mathcal{C})$ and $(D, \mathcal{D})$, respectively. The points of C and D are measurable.

(ii) C_s and D_s are measurable subsets of C and D respectively, i.e., $C_s \in \mathcal{C}$ and $D_s \in \mathcal{D}$. (So C_s and D_s inherit measurable structures $\mathcal{C}_s$ and $\mathcal{D}_s$ respectively.)

(iii) $\pi: C \to D$ is a measurable surjective ("onto") function with $\pi(C_s) = D_s$.

(iv) $\mathcal{I}$ is a kernel on $D_s \times C_s$ such that for each d, $\mathcal{I}(d, \cdot)$ is a probability measure supported in $[d] \cap C_s$. ($[d] = \pi^{-1}(d)$ is called the fiber of π over d.)

C is called the *configuration space* or *conclusion space* of the competence observer. We can think of it as the space of possible scene interpretations. D is called the *data space*. We can think of it as the space of possible image data. C_s is the set of *special configurations*. C_s represents the bias of the observer, and measures on C_s correspond to the priors of Bayesian analysis. D_s is the set of *special premises*. It corresponds to those image data for which the observer is willing to assert nontrivial posterior distributions on possible scene interpretations. (In the terminology of Jepson & Richards (1992), points of D_s correspond to "key features".) π is the *perspective*. It corresponds to a rendering function. $\mathcal{I}$ is the *interpretation kernel*. It is a collection of posterior probabilities, represented as a linear operator.

A competence observer $\mathcal{O}$ "works" as follows. $\mathcal{O}$ receives a premise $d \in D$ and makes a decision: if d is in D_s, then $\mathcal{O}$ gives interpretations in $[d] \cap C_s$ with (posterior) distribution $\mathcal{I}(d, \cdot)$; if d is not in D_s, then $\mathcal{O}$ gives no interpretations, i.e., it remains inert. In other words, $\mathcal{O}$ gives interpretations only for the special premises (premises in D_s), and the interpretations given are only special (interpretations in C_s). It is in this sense that C_s and D_s represent a bias of a perceptual capacity.

There, in a nutshell, is the competence observer. The observer thesis asserts that each competence theory of a perceptual capacity can be written as an instance of a competence observer. If this thesis is correct, the competence observer provides a canonical form for the presentation of competence theories of perceptual capacities. Several examples of perceptual capacities presented in this canonical form can be found in Bennett *et al.* (1989a).

5.5 Competence: The decision

The first thing a competence observer must do is make a decision: act or not. Given a premise d, corresponding perhaps to some image data, the competence observer must decide whether or not d is in D_s. If it is, then the competence observer must

---

[†] A measurable structure on a space X is a collection, $\mathcal{X}$, of subsets of X that includes X and is closed under countable union and complement. The sets in $\mathcal{X}$ are called "events" and correspond intuitively to the possible outcomes of an experiment or observation. For more on measurable structures see Halmos (1950).

act by assigning a posterior distribution $\mathcal{I}(d, \cdot)$. If it is not, then the competence observer does nothing.

We consider this decision first in the noise-free case, and then consider the effects of noise in the next section.

To do so, we return to the Two-View Theorem. In the course of their proof, Bennett *et al.* (1989b) derive a polynomial f on D which vanishes precisely on $D_s \subset D$: for $d \in D_s$, $f(d) = 0$; for $d \in D - D_s$, $f(d) \neq 0$. They did so as follows. Denote the 3D coordinates of feature point i in view j by

$$\vec{a}_{i,j} = (x_{i,j}, y_{i,j}, z_{i,j}), \tag{5.2}$$

where $i = 1, 2, 3$ and $j = 1, 2$. Denote the 2D coordinates of the image of feature point i in view j by

$$\vec{b}_{i,j} = (x_{i,j}, y_{i,j}), \tag{5.3}$$

where again $i = 1, 2, 3$ and $j = 1, 2$. Clearly $\vec{a}_{i,j} = (\vec{b}_{i,j}, z_{i,j})$. Thus from the images we know the $x_{i,j}$ and $y_{i,j}$ coordinates of the feature points, but we do not know the six $z_{i,j}$ coordinates. A necessary condition for points to undergo a rigid motion between the frames is given by the six quadratic polynomial equations

$$\vec{a}_{m,1} \cdot \vec{a}_{n,1} = \vec{a}_{m,2} \cdot \vec{a}_{n,2}, \qquad 1 \leq m, n \leq 3, \tag{5.4}$$

where $\cdot$ indicates the dot (scalar) product of vectors. These equations state that the lengths of the vectors $\vec{a}_{i,j}$ and the angles between them remain constant over the two instants of time. Although there are six quadratic equations in the six unknown $z_{i,j}$'s, the system is nevertheless inconsistent and therefore almost surely has no solutions. That is, for almost any choice of image data $\vec{b}_{i,j}$, equations (5.4) have no solutions, and thus rigid interpretations are impossible. Only for a measure zero set of image data $\vec{b}_{i,j}$ do equations (5.4) have any solutions for rigid interpretations. With some algebraic manipulation, one can show that a necessary and sufficient condition on the image data for equations (5.4) to have a solution is that

$$f = \det \begin{bmatrix} h_{1,1} & h_{1,2} & h_{1,3} \\ h_{2,1} & h_{2,2} & h_{2,3} \\ h_{3,1} & h_{3,2} & h_{3,3} \end{bmatrix} = 0, \tag{5.5}$$

where $h_{m,n} = \vec{b}_{m,2} \cdot \vec{b}_{n,2} - \vec{b}_{m,1} \cdot \vec{b}_{n,1}$. From (5.5) one can show that f is a homogeneous polynomial of sixth degree in the $x_{i,j}$'s and $y_{i,j}$'s, i.e., in the image data (Bennett *et al.*, 1989b).

Having derived f, it is now trivial in the noise-free case to decide if the image data $d \, (= \{\vec{b}_{i,j}\})$ is in D_s, i.e., to decide if the image data have a rigid interpretation. One simply plugs the $\vec{b}_{i,j}$ into the determinant in equation (5.5). If the result is zero, then the image data have a rigid interpretation; otherwise they do not.

5.6 Performance: The decision

If there is noise the decision is not so simple: if the image data d is near D_s, but not in it, we might still decide that d has a rigid interpretation. This decision is often amenable to the well-known tools of statistical decision theory. We will not review these tools here (see, e.g., Savage, 1972). Instead we discuss a class of computational techniques particularly suited to the decisions typical of perceptual capacities.

To make such a decision in a principled way we need (i) a measure of the distance between d and D_s and (ii) the receiver operating characteristic as a function of this distance.

We consider both points, beginning with the measure of distance. For the example of detecting rigid motion, D_s is not a linear or quadric surface to which Euclidean distance is easy to compute. Instead D_s is a sixth degree surface and distance from this surface is hard to compute. However for purposes of our decision we do not need a measure of distance from D_s that is well defined for all points of D. Instead we need a measure that is well defined only nearby D_s (in the Euclidean sense), since it is only for points nearby D_s that we have a difficult decision to make. For this purpose one candidate approach is to use the function f of equation (5.5). This function is zero on D_s and its absolute value increases with increasing Euclidean distance from D_s, at least for points nearby D_s. Here f will have to be normalized for scale: since f is homogeneous of sixth degree, its value nearby a point $d \in D_s$ grows as the fifth power of the size of the corresponding rigid object.

Thus the value of f, suitably normalized, provides a measure of distance from D_s. But this measure of distance will aid our decision only if the receiver operating characteristic (ROC) based on this measure is sufficiently sensitive (Green & Swets, 1966). Recall that the ROC is a vector-valued function. For each distance δ in the domain of the function, there are two corresponding values in its range. These two values are the probability of hits and the probability of false alarms that obtain if δ is used as the decision criterion in the following manner: if $f(d) \leq \delta$ decide that d has a rigid interpretation; otherwise decide that d has no rigid interpretation. Typically an ROC is displayed as a graph of hit probability versus false alarm probability, with the range variable δ left implicit. We do so in this paper.

One could in principle derive the ROC analytically given the function f and a model of the noise, but in practice this is difficult. Instead we ran Monte Carlo simulations as follows. We randomly generated 10,000 nonrigid structures, projected the 3D coordinates of each structure onto two randomly chosen image planes, and computed the 10,000 resulting values of f. We then randomly generated 30,000 different rigid 3D structures (each consisting of three points plus the origin), projected each structure onto two randomly chosen image planes. For 10,000 of these, we randomly perturbed the coordinates of the projected points with 0.05 percent

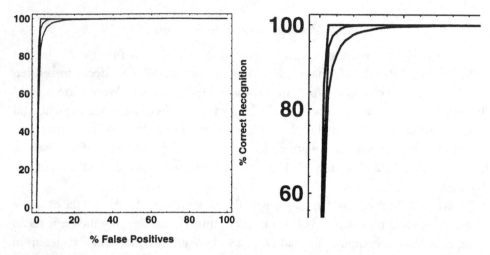

Fig. 5.2 Receiver operating characteristic (ROC) for the function f. Three ROC curves are shown. In order from uppermost to lowest, the ROCs are shown for 0.05%, 1.25%, and 5% gaussian noise in the image coordinates. On the right is shown a magnification of the upper corner of the ROC.

gaussian noise.[†] For another 10,000 we perturbed the coordinates with 1.25 percent gaussian noise. The remaining 10,000 we perturbed with 5 percent gaussian noise. We then computed the 30,000 resulting values of f. Plots of the results as standard ROC curves, shown in Figure 5.2, demonstrate excellent detection properties even with 5 percent noise. In this case it is still possible to pick a decision criterion for which the probability of hits is better than 0.95 and the probability of false alarms is less than 0.03.

This example demonstrates a general approach to the decision problem: (i) Construct a competence observer whose set D_s has measure zero in D; (ii) Find a function which vanishes precisely on D_s; (iii) Analytically, or via Monte Carlo simulations, determine a critical value of this function which gives acceptable hit and false alarm rates for a reasonable model of noise.[‡]

Note that the function f of equation (5.5) can be used to recognize 3D structures. Pick any rigid 3D configuration of points R and any generic view of that configuration. Insert the coordinates from that view into the first frame variables (the $\vec{b}_{i1}$'s). The result is a polynomial f_R of lower degree in just the second frame variables

---

[†] In our Monte Carlo simulations the x and y coordinates of points in the 10,000 nonrigid structures were uniformly distributed within a range of ± 10, so that the expected absolute value of each coordinate was 5. All coordinates in the 30,000 rigid structures were also restricted to a range of ± 10. Thus the phrase "5 percent gaussian noise" means gaussian noise with a standard deviation of 0.25.

[‡] More examples of this approach are contained in Bennett *et al.* (1993a,b). These examples include affine motions and weak perspective projection. Another approach to detecting rigid objects is given by Thompson, *et al.* (1993). Their approach, however, requires an extra step: for each new image to be analyzed one must first estimate a four-dimensional vector r which minimizes the median residual error in a set of linear equations.

(the $\vec{b}_{i2}$'s). Now to determine if a second image depicts a different view of R, insert its coordinates into f_R and compute the resulting value. If the value is small enough (based on the above Monte Carlo results) then decide that the second image depicts R; otherwise decide it does not. This approach allows one to recognize any view of a (transparent) 3D structure after being given only a single view (cf. Basri & Ullman, 1991; Poggio, 1990). For an opaque object, one can recognize any view within one cell of its aspect graph after being given only one view from within that cell.

One can draw a general conclusion from this section. To be able to deal with noise, the definition of competence observer must be augmented with a function $\alpha: D \rightarrow [0, 1]$ which, intuitively, is related to the degree of confidence that each premise should be assigned a special interpretation. Intuitively, we can take $\alpha(d)$ to be the hit rate at the point of the ROC curve corresponding to the parameter value $\delta = f(d)$. This motivates the following definition of performance observer (Bennett *et al.*, 1993).[†]

Definition 2. A *performance observer* is a competence observer $(C, D, C_s, D_s, \pi, \mathcal{I})$ together with a function $\alpha: D \rightarrow [0, 1]$. We call α the *confidence function* of the performance observer.

5.7 Competence: The posterior in the discrete case

In this section we derive a form of the Bayes posterior in the discrete case that will lead naturally to a formulation of the more general case.

Given an image $d \in D$ we want to assign probabilities to possible scene interpretations $c \in C$. Thus we want to compute the conditional probability $\wp(c \mid d)$. For simplicity, and to fix ideas, we consider first the discrete case. In this case we can use Bayes rule:

$$\wp(c \mid d) = \frac{\wp(d \mid c)\mu(c)}{\lambda(d)}. \tag{5.6}$$

Here μ denotes a prior measure on scenes, $\wp(d \mid c)$ is the likelihood function, and λ is a measure on images which expresses the probability that the image d will be acquired, assuming μ is the actual measure on scenes. This expression is well-defined only if $\lambda(d) > 0$. (We discuss shortly how to formulate the problem in the more realistic nondiscrete situation in which $\lambda(d) = 0$.) In the noise-free case the likelihood function $\wp(d \mid c)$ takes, as we have seen, a particularly simple form. It assigns the value 1 to $\pi(c)$, i.e., to the image that would be rendered if the scene

---

[†] Later we give a precise definition of α (Definition 6) and briefly discuss its relationship to standard Bayesian decision methods. Definition 2 is different in form but equivalent in content to the definition given by Bennett *et al.* (1993).

were c, and it assigns the value 0 to all other images. We can write this as

$$\wp(d \mid c) = 1_{\pi(c)}(d),\tag{5.7}$$

where $1_{\pi(c)}(d)$ denotes the indicator function of $\pi(c)$. This, together with our assumption on λ, implies that

$$\lambda(d) = \mu\pi_*(d).\tag{5.8}$$

Here the measure $\mu\pi_*$ is, by definition, the distribution of π with respect to μ defined by $\mu\pi_*(B) = \mu(\pi^{-1}(B))$, where B is any event in $\mathcal{D}$.

For example, for the competence observer defined by the Two-View Theorem, if $c = \{(x_{ij}, y_{ij}, z_{ij})\}$, where $i = 1, 2, 3$ and $j = 1, 2$, then $\wp(d \mid c)$ is 1 for $d = \{(x_{ij}, y_{ij})\}$, and zero otherwise.

Substituting (5.7) into (5.6) gives

$$\wp(c \mid d) = \frac{1_{\pi(c)}(d)\mu(c)}{\lambda(d)},\tag{5.9}$$

but this numerator is equal to $\mu(c)$ if $\pi(c) = d$ and is 0 otherwise, so we can write

$$= \frac{\mu(c \cap \pi^{-1}(d))}{\lambda(d)},$$

which by (5.8) is

$$= \frac{\mu(c \cap \pi^{-1}(d))}{\mu(\pi^{-1}(d))},$$

or

$$= \overline{\mu|_{[d]}}(c),$$

where $\overline{\mu|_{[d]}}$ indicates the normalized restriction of μ to $\pi^{-1}(d)$, i.e., $\overline{\mu|_{[d]}}(c) = \mu(c \cap \pi^{-1}(d))/\mu(\pi^{-1}(d))$. Thus the posterior probability $\wp(c \mid d)$ is the normalized restriction of the prior probability μ to the set $[d]$. Using the observer language of interpretation kernels we can write

$$\wp(c \mid d) = \overline{\mu|_{[d]}}(c) = \mathcal{I}(d, c).\tag{5.10}$$

If we replace the specific scene interpretation c with a measurable set A of scene interpretations, this posterior probability becomes

$$\wp(A \mid d) = \sum_{c \in A} \wp(c \mid d) = \mathcal{I}(d, A).\tag{5.11}$$

Thus for competence observers the posterior distributions contained in the interpretation kernel $\mathcal{I}$ are normalized restrictions of a prior measure μ on C_s. The restriction sets are fibers $[d]$ of the rendering function π. For a competence observer compatible with the Two-View Theorem, $\mathcal{I}(d, \cdot)$ may be taken to be, for example, a uniform probability measure on the set $[d] \cap C_s$; this measure is uniform with respect to the parametrization of $[d] \cap C_s$ by the slant of the axis of rotation.

Note that in this derivation the prior measure μ might be improper, i.e., it might not be a probability measure. The derivation requires, however, that $0 < \mu([d]) < \infty$ for each $d \in D$.

5.8 Competence: The posterior in the continuous case

To generalize the Bayesian results to the nondiscrete case, we must use *regular conditional probability distributions* (Parthasarathy, 1968; Bennett *et al.*, 1989a). Regular conditional probability distributions (rcpd's) are defined precisely in the Appendix, section A5. However here we give a concrete example to illustrate the definition. Let μ be the usual joint gaussian on $\Re^2$ and let π be the projection from $\Re^2$ onto the x-axis. Then the rcpd of μ with respect to π is a kernel $\eta(x, \cdot)$ which assigns to each point x of the x-axis a gaussian measure on the vertical line in $\Re^2$ through that point x.

The intuitions are as follows. Suppose that we are modeling a competence observer $O = (C, D, C_s, D_s, \pi, \mathcal{I})$ and that our prior measure on scene interpretations is a probability measure μ on C_s. If we are given the image data d, our posterior probability distribution, according to equation (5.10), is the normalized restriction of μ to the set $\pi^{-1}(d) = [d]$. That is, the posterior distribution assigns to a set A of scene interpretations the probability $\mu(A \cap [d])/\mu([d])$. But what if the probability (i.e., μ measure) of the set $[d]$ is zero, as it most often is in the continuous case? Then this formulation of the posterior distribution is undefined. Unfortunately, this is precisely the case we need most. In practical situations we are given an image d and must come up with a posterior probability on scene interpretations. This image d, however, is usually just one of a large collection of possible images that we might have been given, and therefore its probability, and the probability of $[d]$, is zero or near zero. To get the desired posterior distributions in this case, what we need is a way to get normalized restrictions of μ to sets $[d]$ of probability zero. Or, to put it slightly differently, we need to be able to condition on sets of probability zero.

This is precisely the power of rcpd's – to condition on sets of probability zero and still get a well-defined probability measure as a result. An rcpd is a kernel. In the case at hand it is denoted m_π^μ, where the superscript indicates the prior probability and the subscript indicates the rendering function.

The application of rcpd's to competence observers is immediate. The interpretation kernel $\mathcal{I}$ just is the rcpd m_π^μ. The probability measures $\mathcal{I}(d, \cdot) = m_\pi^\mu(d, \cdot)$ then correspond to the posterior distributions.

5.9 Performance: The underlying probability space

Now we consider measurement noise. A general model for this noise is a kernel

$$N: C \times \mathcal{D} \rightarrow [0, 1], \tag{5.12}$$

where $\mathcal{D}$ denotes the collection of all measurable subsets[†] of the space D of image data. We interpret this kernel as follows. We fix a scene $c \in C$ and let $B \in \mathcal{D}$ denote a set of images. Then $N(c, B)$ is the probability that the rendered image d is in the set B given that the scene is c. (In the discrete case it is sufficient to know the probabilities when $B = \{d\}$ for all images $d \in D$; for simplicity we denote this $N(c, d)$ instead of $N(c, \{d\})$. It is the probability that d is the image rendered given that the scene is c.) So interpreted, the kernel N is a collection of likelihoods and we would like to write

$$\wp(d \mid c) = N(c, d), \tag{5.13}$$

where $\wp$ is some appropriate probability on perceptual events. In order to do this we must be more explicit and rigorous about the probabilistic setting.

Since each perceptual event is a pair consisting of a scene from C and an image from D, the underlying space for perceptual events is $C \times D$. Our fundamental probability space then is a space $(C \times D, \mathcal{C} \otimes \mathcal{D}, \wp)$.[‡] If we let $A \in \mathcal{C}$ denote a measurable collection of scene interpretations, and $B \in \mathcal{D}$ a measurable collection of images, then $\wp(A \times B)$ denotes the probability of the perceptual event in which the true scene is in the set A and the rendered image is in the set B. We assume we are given a prior probability μ on $C_s \subset C$ and a conditional probability $N: C \times \mathcal{D} \rightarrow [0, 1]$ expressed as a kernel. This conditional probability N reflects the effects of noise as described above and is the "likelihood function" of Bayesian analysis. It follows by definition of conditional probability that in the discrete case $\wp$ assigns to a typical set $A \times B \in \mathcal{C} \otimes \mathcal{D}$ the probability

$$\wp(A \times B) = \sum_{c \in A, d \in B} \wp(c, d) = \sum_{c \in A, d \in B} \mu(c) N(c, d) \tag{5.14}$$

and correspondingly in the continuous case

$$\wp(A \times B) = \int_A \mu(dc) \int_B N(c, dd). \tag{5.15}$$

Thus we may say that in the discrete case

$$\wp(c, d) = \mu(c) N(c, d), \tag{5.16}$$

[†] In the discrete case the σ-algebra is just the collection of all subsets. In the general case the σ-algebra is a nontrivial subcollection.

[‡] The product σ-algebra $\mathcal{C} \otimes \mathcal{D}$ is the σ-algebra generated by all subsets of the form $A \times B$, $A \in \mathcal{C}$, $B \in \mathcal{D}$. In the discrete case the product algebra is (trivially) the collection of subsets of $C \times D$, but in the continuous case $\mathcal{C} \otimes \mathcal{D}$ is nontrivially related to $\mathcal{C}$ and $\mathcal{D}$. See, e.g., Halmos (1950).

while in the continuous case

$$\wp(dc, dd) = \mu(dc)N(c, dd). \tag{5.17}$$

In both cases, we may use the language of kernel multiplication (Appendix, A3) to observe that

$$\wp(A \times B) = \mu(1_A N)(B). \tag{5.18}$$

It follows that the marginal of $\wp$ on C is the prior measure μ on scenes and the marginal of $\wp$ on D is the measure μN on images, i.e., $(\mu N)(B) = \int_C \mu(dc)N(c, B)$. As in the noise-free discrete case, we have assumed that the prior probability on scenes is described by a measure μ on $C_s \subset C$. In the presence of noise, however, we have obtained a different measure λ on images. Recall from (5.8) that in the noise-free case this measure is $\lambda(d) = \mu(\pi^{-1}(d)) = \mu\pi_*(d)$. That is, λ is simply obtained by "pushing down" by π onto D the prior measure μ on $C_s \subset C$. But if there is noise described by a kernel N, then this push down, as we have just seen, must instead be of the form

$$\lambda(d) = (\mu N)(d) = \sum_{c \in C} \mu(c)N(c, d) \tag{5.19}$$

in the discrete case, and of the form

$$\lambda(dd) = (\mu N)(dd) = \int_C \mu(dc)N(c, dd) \tag{5.20}$$

in the continuous case. If $N(c, \cdot)$ is the Dirac measure at $\pi(c)$, i.e., if there is no noise, then equations (5.19) and (5.20) reduce to equation (5.8).

In the discrete case, we can now make sense of equation (5.13) in terms of the above postulated probability measure $\wp$: the correct expression for $\wp(d \mid c)$ is, with our present notation, $\wp(C \times \{d\} \mid \{c\} \times D)$.

5.10 Performance: Derivation of the posterior (standard Bayesian analysis)

We now want the posterior probability, i.e., the conditional probability that the scene is in a set A given that the rendered image is d. In the general case there is a question about the meaning of the posterior probability since the probability of $\{d\}$ might be zero. We will deal with the discrete case first and then use our results to motivate the derivation in the general case.

We now give the discrete posterior distribution in the presence of noise. The result (equation (5.21) below) is a Bayes rule for the perceptual situation. If $A \in C$ is a measurable collection of scene interpretations, and d is an image, the posterior probability given that image is the conditional probability $\wp(A \times D \mid C \times \{d\})$. From now on we shall write this as, simply, $P(A \mid d)$. In what follows we will often abuse notation in this way, e.g., by writing just A instead of $A \times D$, B instead of $C \times B$ etc. In particular, with this notation $\wp(A)$ is the marginal $\mu(A)$, $\wp(B)$ is the marginal $\mu N(B)$, and $P(A \mid d)$ is the posterior we seek. (The exact meaning should be clear from the context, but we caution the reader that the meaning in terms of the underlying probability space be always kept in mind so as to avoid mistakes in computation.)

Theorem 2. *(Discrete Posteriors).* Let the measure μ be the prior distribution on scene interpretations and let the kernel N be the likelihood function. Then the posterior probability that the true scene is in $A \in \mathcal{C}$ given that the rendered image is d, is given by

$$P(A \mid d) \stackrel{\text{def}}{=} \wp(A \times D \mid C \times \{d\}) = \frac{(\mu(1_A N))(d)}{(\mu N)(d)}, \qquad (5.21)$$

whenever $\mu N(d) \neq 0$ and $P(A \mid d) = 0$ otherwise. The posterior satisfies, for any $B \in \mathcal{D}$,

$$\sum_{d \in B} \mu N(d) P(A \mid d) = \wp(A \times B). \qquad (5.22)$$

Moreover, the posterior probability is related to a regular conditional probability distribution as follows: Let $q: C \times D \to D$ be the projection mapping $q(c, d) = d$. Then the rcpd $m_q^\wp$ exists and for any $A \in \mathcal{C}$,

$$P(A \mid d) = m_q^\wp(d, A \times \{d\}) = m_q^\wp(d, A \times D), \qquad (5.23)$$

for μN-almost all d.

Proof. Appendix, A9. ∎

   Equation (5.21) is Bayes rule expressed in kernel notation, and relates the posterior to the prior μ and the noisy likelihood function N. This is a formulation in terms of kernels, equivalent to the usual form. In fact, (5.21) when A is the singleton $\{c\}$ reduces to the familiar form, i.e., $p(c \mid d) = N(d \mid c)\mu(c)/\sum_c N(d \mid c)\mu(c)$. Equation (5.21) itself expands out to $P(A \mid d) = \sum_{c \in A} N(d \mid c)\mu(c)/\sum_c N(d \mid c)\mu(c)$. Thus the likelihood function in Bayesian analysis is a kernel. Equations (5.21)–(5.23) will allow us to generalize from the discrete to the continuous case. One checks that the last equality in equation (5.21) shows that $P(A \mid d)$ is a *markovian kernel* on $D \times C_s$, since μ is supported in C_s. Of course, P naturally extends to a submarkovian kernel on $D \times C$.

   We are now ready for the continuous case. Given the issue of zero probabilities for d, how should we define $P(A \mid d)$? The answer lies in generalizing a property in Theorem 2: In the discrete case, $P(A \mid d)$ is the value of a kernel on $D \times C_s$ (with the usual order of arguments of kernels reversed[†]), satisfying equation (5.22). This motivates

Definition 3. *(General Posterior).* The general posterior $P(A \mid d)$ is any markovian kernel on $D \times C_s$, satisfying

$$\wp(A \times B) = \int_{d \in B} \mu N(\mathrm{d}d) P(A \mid d) = \int_{c \in A, d \in B} \mu N(\mathrm{d}d) P(\mathrm{d}c \mid d). \qquad (5.24)$$

From this and (5.18) it follows that p is a Bayesian posterior for the likelihood N given μ iff

$$(\mu 1_A N)(B) = ((\mu N) 1_B P)(A) \quad (= \wp(A \times B)). \qquad (5.25)$$

It is equivalent to say (by Lemma A39 of the Appendix) the following: For all bounded measurable functions f on C and g on D,

$$\mu f N g = (\mu N) g P f. \qquad (5.26)$$

Notes on Definition 3:

 (i) The notion of Bayes posterior as a relationship between kernels is only meaningful given the prior μ.
 (ii) (5.25) constrains N and P only a.e. μ and μN respectively. This means that we can modify $P(d, \cdot)$ arbitrarily for d in any set of μN measure zero without affecting (5.25). Thus the notion of Bayes posterior is defined only a.e. μ and μN respectively, and this is why, in Definition 3, we said "a" posterior rather than "the" posterior.

By Definition 3, to say that N is the Bayesian posterior for the likelihood P given μN means that the last equation holds, but with the μ on the left replaced by $\mu N P$. Thus we note that Definition 3 is symmetric provided $\mu = \mu N P$. We will prove in Theorem 5 below that this always holds if P is the posterior of N with respect to μ, i.e., that *the relationship of Bayesian posterior is symmetric*. Thus if P is the posterior of N with respect to μ then N is the posterior of P with respect to μN.

Proposition 1. Let $\pi: X \to Y$ be a measurable mapping and μ a measure on X. Then the kernels $\mathcal{I}$ from Y to X and π_* from X to Y are Bayesian posteriors of each other iff $\mathcal{I}$ is the rcpd of μ with respect to π (see Appendix A5 for definition of rcpd, and Appendix A4 for how π_* can be viewed as a kernel). In other words, in the competence case $\mathcal{I}$ and π_* are Bayes posteriors of each other.

Proof. Appendix A36. ∎

[†] Note that a kernel on $D \times C_s$ is normally written with $d \in D$ as its first argument and $A \in C_s$ as its second; in keeping with traditional Bayesian notation, however, we are writing A first and d second in $P(A \mid d)$.

Do the kernels which are the posteriors of Definition 3 exist in general in the continuous case? Indeed so; the appropriate generalization of (5.21) is exhibited in (5.28) below. To see this we need *Radon-Nikodym derivatives,* which we now briefly review.[†]

Definition 4. *(Radon-Nikodym Derivative).* If ν and ρ are measures on some measurable space $(W, \mathcal{W})$ and if, for all $D \in \mathcal{W}$, $\nu(D) = 0$ implies $\rho(D) = 0$, then ρ is said to be *absolutely continuous* with respect to ν, and we write $\rho << \nu$. If $\rho << \nu$, the Radon-Nikodym Theorem states that there exists a measurable function f such that

$$\rho(B) = \int_B f \, \mathrm{d}\nu, \qquad \forall B \in \mathcal{W}, \tag{5.27}$$

as long as ν is a σ-finite measure and ρ is finite. Any function g which differs from f only on a set of ν measure zero also satisfies (5.27), and is also called a Radon-Nikodym derivative of ρ with respect to ν, and denoted $d\rho/d\nu$. Thus the Radon-Nikodym derivative with respect to ν is defined only up to sets of ν-measure zero. The Radon-Nikodym derivative f is sometimes called the *density of ρ with respect to ν.*

The perceptual Bayes rule in the general case now follows:

Theorem 3. *(General Posterior).* Let the measure μ be the prior distribution on scene interpretations and let the kernel N be the likelihood function. Then the posterior probability that the true scene is in $A \in \mathcal{C}$ given that the rendered image is d is given by

$$P(A \mid d) = \frac{\mathrm{d}(\mu(1_A N))}{\mathrm{d}(\mu N)}(d), \qquad \text{a.e. } d \ (\mu N). \tag{5.28}$$

In fact, by definition of Radon-Nikodym derivative (Definition 4), this means that for any $B \in \mathcal{D}$,

$$\int_{d \in B} \mu N(\mathrm{d}d) P(A \mid d) = p(A \times B). \tag{5.29}$$

Let $q: C \times D \to D$ be the projection mapping $q(c, d) = d$. Then we can write $P(A \mid d)$ as a regular conditional probability distribution as follows:

$$P(A \mid d) \overset{\text{def}}{=} \wp(A \times \{d\} \mid C \times \{d\}) = m_q^\wp(d, A \times D). \tag{5.30}$$

Proof. Appendix, A22. ∎

[†] For a detailed discussion of the relationship of Radon-Nikodym derivatives to conditional expectation see, e.g., Chung (1974). See also Grenander (1981) for an application of Radon-Nikodym derivatives to abstract inference.

An important special case of this theorem is when the prior and likelihood have densities. This means that there are measures λ on C and ρ on D, with $\mu(\mathrm{d}c) = f(c)\lambda(\mathrm{d}c)$ and $N(c, \mathrm{d}d) = n(c, d)\rho(\mathrm{d}d)$; we say that $f(c)$ is the "density" of μ (with respect to λ) and $n(c, d)$ is the density of $N(c, \mathrm{d}d)$ (with respect to ρ). (The case most familiar in the perception literature is where C and D are $\Re^n$ and $\Re^m$ for some n and m and λ and ρ are the usual Euclidean volumes.) Then the posterior kernel $P(\mathrm{d}c \mid d)$ also has a density, say $p(c, d)$, with respect to λ, i.e., $P(\mathrm{d}c \mid d) = p(c, d)\lambda(\mathrm{d}d)$. In terms of these densities Bayes Rule says:

$$p(c, d) = \frac{n(c, d)f(c)}{Z(d)}, \qquad (5.31)$$

where $Z(d) = \int n(c, d)f(c)\lambda(\mathrm{d}c)$ is a normalization factor. (Again, the discrete case (5.22) follows upon requiring that λ be counting measure on a finite set.)

Equation (5.28) is of practical importance in computing posteriors in the perceptual situation, as we shall see in the next section. This form of Bayes rule is general. It applies to arbitrary prior probability measures μ. It applies to arbitrary forms of noise N; in particular, it is not restricted to an assumption of gaussian noise. It allows some improper, i.e., infinite, prior measures.[†] And it allows one to condition on images that have probability zero. Thus this form of Bayes rule can be applied to many problems in vision in which a posterior distribution is sought. In section 5.12 we use it to compute a special class of posteriors that often arise in vision research.

Theorem 3 implies that $p(A \mid d) = p(A \cap C_s \mid d)$. One can see this directly from (5.28) by noting that μ is supported on C_s, so that $\mu(1_A N) = \mu(1_{A \cap C_s} N)$.

If the measures involved are all discrete, Theorem 3 specializes to Theorem 23. For in that instance, integrals become sums and Radon-Nikodym derivatives become simply ratios ((5.22) is the analog of (5.29) in the discrete case at hand). Moreover, Theorem 3 also confirms the noise-free or competence case. Here, $N(c, \mathrm{d}d) = \epsilon_{\pi(c)}(\mathrm{d}d)$, i.e., the Dirac kernel at $\pi(c)$. In the proof of Proposition 1 we show that then $\mu N = \pi_* \mu$ and that $\mu 1_A N(B) = \int_B \mu N(\mathrm{d}d)\mathcal{I}(d, A)$. Thus the Radon-Nikodym derivative $P(A \mid d)$ is just the interpretation kernel $\mathcal{I}(d, A)$, as expected.

By Definition 3, $P(\mathrm{d}c \mid d)$ is a markovian kernel. It will be of use later to evaluate integrals of the form $\int P(\mathrm{d}c \mid d)f(c)$, where f is a bounded, measurable function on C. Equation (5.28) tells us what this integral is for $f = 1_A$. We have

---

[†] Improper priors are an issue, e.g., when the measure μN assigns the value infinity to some singleton. The general form of Bayes rule (5.28) will accept any (possibly improper) prior measure μ as long as μN is σ-finite, i.e., as long as there is a measurable partition $\{A_n\}$ of D such that $N(c, A_n)$ is integrable with respect to μ for all n. Note that in this case (5.28) is still defined as a markovian kernel. For more on improper priors, see Hartigan (1983).

184   *B.M. Bennett, D.D. Hoffman, C. Prakash & S.N. Richman*

Corollary 4. For any bounded, measurable function f on C,

$$\int_{c\in C} P(\mathrm{d}c \mid d) f(c) = \frac{\mathrm{d}(\mu(fN))}{\mathrm{d}(\mu N)}(d), \qquad \text{a.e. } d \ (\mu N). \tag{5.32}$$

Proof. Appendix, A24. ∎

We reiterate a key consequence of the foregoing derivations: *In the general case, Bayesian posteriors and likelihoods are kernels.* This is useful for several reasons. First, kernels are well understood mathematical objects whose properties have been extensively investigated. Second, kernels provide a convenient computational tool in the general (i.e., nondiscrete) case. In particular they allow us to compute probabilities of scenes as expectations of functions on the space of images; they also allow us to compute probabilities of images as expectations of functions on the space of scenes.

With the foregoing definitions and characterization of the Bayesian posterior we can prove several important results on the general behavior of these posteriors. For this purpose we will introduce terminology and notation which is simplifying and suggestive.

Definition 5. Let X and Y be measurable spaces. Let μ be a probability measure on X. Let H from X to Y be a markovian kernel. We will denote by $H_\mu^\dagger$ (or just by $H^\dagger$ when there is no confusion about μ) the Bayesian posterior of H for the prior probability μ. We will also refer to $H_\mu^\dagger$ as the *Bayes adjoint* of H for μ, or just the *adjoint* for short when μ is unambiguous. (We remind the reader that the Bayes adjoint is well defined only a.e. μH in the sense of note (ii) after Definition 3.) According to (5.26), $H^\dagger$ is defined by the relation

$$\mu f H g = (\mu H) g H^\dagger f, \tag{5.33}$$

for all bounded measurable functions f on X and g on Y. It is very suggestive to use the following notation. In general, on a measure space X with measure μ and functions f and h, we denote $< f, h >_\mu = \int_X f(x)h(x)\mathrm{d}\mu(x)$. The definition of the Bayes adjoint $H^\dagger$ of H with respect to μ is

$$< f, Hg >_\mu = < H^\dagger f, g >_{\mu H}, \tag{5.34}$$

which is a restatement of (5.26).

Notes on Definition 5:

(i) We recall that the existence of $H^\dagger$ is guaranteed by Theorem 3.
(ii) The adjointness terminology is further justified below by Theorems 5, 6, and 7.

(iii) If $f \in L^2(X, \mu)$ and $g \in L^2(Y, \mu H)$, with $\|f\| = \|g\| = 1$, it is natural to view f and g as *states* on X and Y. The quantity $< f, Hg >_\mu = < H^\dagger f, g >_{\mu H}$ may then be interpreted as a measure of the compatibility of the states f and g, or as the probability of simultaneous occurrence of the two states. A compatibility of numerical value 1 (perfect compatibility) occurs when $f = Hg$, or equivalently, when $g = H^\dagger f$.

Theorem 5. Given X, μ on X, and a kernel H from X to Y,

$$\mu H H^\dagger = \mu. \tag{5.35}$$

Proof. Appendix A37. ∎

Intuitively, $H^\dagger$ reverses the effect of H on the prior μ.

Theorem 6. With X, μ, and H as above,

$$(H_\mu^\dagger)_{\mu H}^\dagger = H. \tag{5.36}$$

Proof. We refer to (5.34) as the definition of the Bayes posterior. Applying this definition first to H and then to $H_\mu^\dagger$, we see that

$$< f, Hg >_\mu = < H^\dagger f, g >_{\mu H} = < f, (H_\mu^\dagger)_{\mu H}^\dagger g >_{\mu H H^\dagger}. \tag{5.37}$$

The right-hand side equals $< f, (H_\mu^\dagger)_{\mu H}^\dagger g >_\mu$ by theorem 5. Comparing this with the left-hand side we are done. ∎

The following theorem is very useful for the study of composite Bayesian inferences.

$$
\begin{array}{ccccc}
\mu & H & \nu = \mu H & K & \lambda = \nu K \\
X & \rightleftarrows & Y & \rightleftarrows & Z \\
& H_\mu^\dagger & & K_\nu^\dagger & \\
& & (HK)_\mu^\dagger & &
\end{array}
$$

Theorem 7. Let X, Y, and Z be measurable spaces. Let H be a markovian kernel from X to Y and K a markovian kernel from Y to Z. Let μ be a probability measure on X. Let $\nu = \mu H$ and $\lambda = \nu K = \mu H K$ on Y and Z respectively. Then

$$K_\lambda^\dagger H_\nu^\dagger = (HK)_\mu^\dagger. \tag{5.38}$$

(This equation holds only a.e. λ, ν, and μ. See note (ii) after Definition 3.)

Proof. (See Appendix A38 for an alternate proof) ∎

$$< f, HKg >_\mu \; = \; < f, (HK)g >_\mu$$
$$= \; < H_\mu^\dagger f, Kg >_{\mu H} \tag{5.39}$$
$$= \; < K_{\mu H}^\dagger H_\mu^\dagger f, g >_{\lambda = \mu HK} .$$

By Definition 5, this means

$$K^\dagger H^\dagger = (HK)^\dagger. \tag{5.40}$$

5.11 Computing posteriors: A class of examples

We now use Theorem 3 and the assumption of simple noise to derive an explicit expression for the posterior distributions in a special class of cases that includes the Two-View Theorem observer and many other observers of interest in computer vision.

Theorem 8. *(Some Useful Posteriors).* Let the set of scene interpretations, C, be a Euclidean space $\Re^j$ and let the set of special scene interpretations, C_s, be a measurable subset of C. Let the set of images, D, be a Euclidean space $\Re^k$ and let the special images, D_s, be a measurable subset of D.[†] Let the rendering function, $\pi: C \to D$, be measurable. Let the prior measure on scene interpretations be μ, and the measure on images be $\lambda \; (= \mu N)$. Let the noise kernel N be constant on fibers of π, and in fact be modeled by independent, identically distributed gaussian random variables with mean zero and standard deviation σ. Thus, for any scene interpretation c and set D of images,

$$N(c, D) = \frac{1}{(\sqrt{2\pi\sigma^2})^m} \int_{D \in \mathcal{D}} \exp\left(\frac{-\|\pi(c) - d\|^2}{2\sigma^2}\right) \lambda(dd), \tag{5.41}$$

where m is the dimension of D. Then the posterior probability that the scene interpretation is in the set A given that the image is d is the following:

$$P(A \mid d) = \frac{d(\mu(1_A N))}{d(\mu N)}(d) = \frac{\int_{C_s \cap A} \exp\left(\frac{-\|\pi(c)-d\|^2}{2\sigma^2}\right) \mu(dc)}{\int_{C_s} \exp\left(\frac{-\|\pi(c)-d\|^2}{2\sigma^2}\right) \mu(dc)}. \tag{5.42}$$

Proof. Appendix, A25. ∎

We now have an explicit form for the posterior distribution $P(d, A)$ for a large class of observers of interest to researchers in computer vision. This class includes the rigid motion observer based on the Two-View Theorem (Theorem 1). If we wish to pick a "best" interpretation on the basis of the posterior distribution we

---

[†] This implies that each of these sets is a standard Borel space and that therefore rcpd's exist (see Appendix A8).

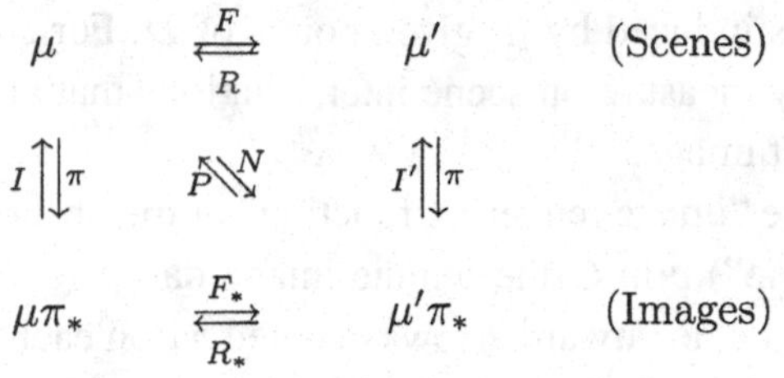

$$\mu \qquad \underset{R}{\overset{F}{\rightleftarrows}} \qquad \mu' \qquad \text{(Scenes)}$$

$$I \big\Updownarrow \pi \qquad P\searrow^{N} \qquad I' \big\Updownarrow \pi$$

$$\mu\pi_* \qquad \underset{R_*}{\overset{F_*}{\rightleftarrows}} \qquad \mu'\pi_* \qquad \text{(Images)}$$

Fig. 5.3 Bayesian observer diagram showing the relationship of observer theory to standard Bayesian analysis.

have several standard options (see, e.g., Papoulis, 1984; Gelb, 1974). For instance, we can choose the interpretation with the maximum posterior probability, the so-called MAP (maximum *a posteriori*) estimator; if the prior is uniform, this is called the maximum likelihood estimate (see Witkin, 1981, for an early use of maximum likelihood estimates in vision).

5.12 The Bayesian observer diagram

So far we have developed several different threads: competence observers, performance observers, and standard Bayesian estimation. Each has its own meaning and applications in the study of perception. Each is also associated with a compound structure embodying various mathematical objects such as measures, mappings, and kernels. It is the purpose of this section to tie these constructs together. We will introduce one diagram, the "Bayesian Observer Diagram" (henceforth "BOD"), which displays their relevant mathematical structures and the precise relationships between them.

The BOD consists of probability measures related by arrows representing kernels. The point here is that kernels operate on measures to produce other measures (Appendix A3). Thus we can move around the diagram by successively applying kernels to a given measure. The BOD diagram is shown in Figure 5.3.

The objects at the corners of the diagram are, as we have noted, probability measures. The measures at the upper corners are probabilities on the conclusion space C. The measures at the lower corners are probabilities on the data space D. Each edge of the diagram consists of arrows in both directions. There are also two arrows in opposite directions along a diagonal of the diagram. These arrows, as mentioned above, represent kernels. The left vertical edge corresponds to a competence observer (Definition 1). The measure μ is a probability measure on conclusions which expresses the prior probability on scenes adopted by the competence observer. $\mathcal{I}$ is the interpretation kernel of the competence observer (i.e., the *noise-free* posterior used by the competence observer). We can also think of $\mathcal{I}$ as describing the conditional probabilities induced by μ, given points of D. For each noise-free image, $\mathcal{I}$ gives a probability measure on scene interpretations that are compatible, via the function π, with that image.

Recall that π is the "image rendering function" of the observer. It assigns to each conclusion (or "scene") c in C the unique image data $\pi(c) = d$, in D, which is compatible with c. The downward arrows denoted π_* on each edge of the BOD are kernels. The kernel π_* assigns to any probability measure ν on C the probability measure $\nu\pi_*$ on D, which is defined as follows. The function π can be thought of as a random variable on C taking values in D; the probability $\nu\pi_*$ is then the usual "distribution" of this random variable.

The kernel F expresses the effect of noise at the level of the conclusion space C. In this sense it associates to any noise-free prior μ of the competence observer a probability measure μ' on C. We can think of μ' as the "fuzzy" analog of μ, for the particular noisy circumstances described by F.

If we view F as the likelihood function for the prior μ, then R is the corresponding Bayesian posterior. Given the meaning of F as a fuzzing kernel, we can think of R as "retracting" noisy interpretations back onto noise-free interpretations. F_* and R_* express the effects of F and R at the level of the data space D.

The right edge of the BOD corresponds to a performance observer (Definition 7). $\mathcal{I}'$ is its interpretation kernel. As in the competence observer of the left edge, we can think of $\mathcal{I}'$ as describing the conditional probabilities induced by μ', given points of D. For each noisy image, $\mathcal{I}'$ gives a probability measure on scene interpretations that are compatible, via the rendering function π, with that image.

The kernel N models noise in the rendering process. Intuitively, $N(c, d)$ gives the probability that the image d is rendered given that the scene is c. Because of noise this probability will in general be nonzero even if d is not $\pi(c)$. In many concrete situations where we can express probability measures as densities with respect to some underlying measure, the density function associated to N is commonly known as the "likelihood function". The kernel P is the Bayesian posterior for the prior μ and the likelihood N. In most cases, the likelihoods and posteriors referred to in the Bayesian literature correspond to N and P. This means that traditional Bayesian analyses refer to just the diagonal of the BOD.

Note that π, F, and N can be specified independently of μ, whereas the definitions of the kernels R, P, R_*, $\mathcal{I}$, and $\mathcal{I}'$ are all contingent on μ.

The BOD is convenient in that it collects and displays all the relevant mathematical structures that figure in both an observer-theoretic and Bayesian analysis of perception. However, the real benefit of the diagram for purposes of conceptualization and analysis follows from the mathematical properties of the diagram itself. In particular, we will prove shortly that one can construct a *consistent* BOD and that every pair of opposite arrows represents Bayes adjoints (with respect to the measures indicated at the appropriate vertices). As a matter of general terminology, any diagram is said to be "consistent" if, whenever it is possible to move an object indicated at a vertex of the diagram by means of two different sequences of arrows which end at the same vertex, then the two results are equal. (Note that consistency is weaker than the general mathematical notion of commutativity of diagrams.)

We now consider the BOD in detail. There are several entities we have already encountered:

(i) *Competence Observer*

    (a) μ on C is the prior probability on scene interpretations.

    (b) $\pi : C \to D$ is the rendering function.

    (c) $\mu\pi_*$ is the distribution on images in the noise-free case.

    (d) $\mathcal{I} : D \times C \to [0, 1]$ is a kernel describing noise-free posterior probabilities. In fact $\mathcal{I}$ is an rcpd of μ.

Thus the left side of the BOD is simply a competence observer with prior probability μ. As we have discussed before, this observer is a canonical description of a perceptual capacity under the assumption that there is no noise. The diagram contains three other entities we have already encountered:

(ii) *Standard Bayesian Analysis*

    (a) $N : C \times \mathcal{D} \to [0, 1]$ is a kernel describing the effect of noise on the image rendering process; it models the likelihoods of standard Bayesian analyses.

    (b) $\mu'\pi_* = \mu N$ is the noisy distribution on images.

    (c) $P : D \times C \to [0, 1]$ is a kernel describing the Bayesian posterior probabilities when there is noise. According to Theorem 3, $P(A \mid d) = [\mathrm{d}(\mu(1_A N))/\mathrm{d}(\mu N)](d)$.

Thus the diagonal of this diagram – $\mu, N, \mu'\pi_*$, and P – describe the Bayesian analysis of perception when there is noise. The prior measure μ on scene interpretations gets pushed down via the likelihood N to a measure $\mu'\pi_*$ ($= \mu N$) on images. The posterior P assigns scene interpretations to these images in a manner consistent with the prior measure μ. The diagram also contains a performance observer, which we now describe:

(iii) *Performance Observer*

    (a) μ' is a probability measure on C such that $\mu'\pi_* = \mu N$, and is not, in general, supported in C_s. This measure describes the actual distribution of scene interpretations perceived by subjects.

    (b) $\mathcal{I}'$ is an rcpd of μ' with respect to the rendering function π.

This right side of the BOD – $\mu', \pi, \mu'\pi_*, \mathcal{I}'$ – together with a significance function α, is a performance observer (Definition 2). The final new entities are the following:

(iv) *Fuzzing and Retraction*

    (a) $F : C \times C \to [0, 1]$ is a kernel given by $F = N\mathcal{I}'$. This kernel "fuzzes up" the ideal prior μ in a way which matches the scene interpretations perceived by subjects in actual noisy circumstances. N and F are both models of noisy circumstances, but F is at the level of scenes and N relates scenes and images. Thus N and F must be compatible in the sense that $N = F\pi_*$.

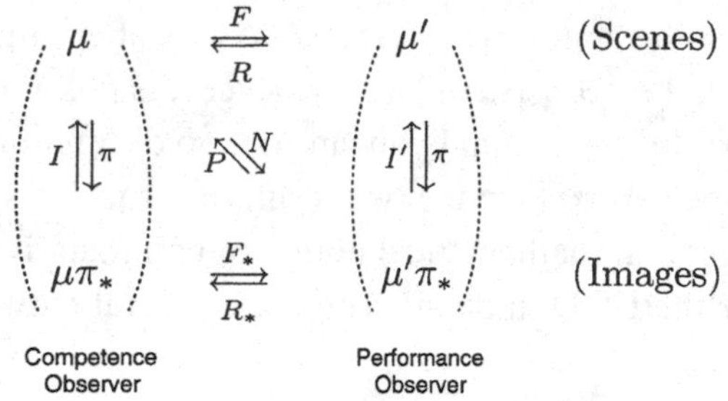

B.M. Bennett, D.D. Hoffman, C. Prakash & S.N. Richman

$$
\left(
\begin{array}{ccc}
\mu & \overset{F}{\underset{R}{\rightleftarrows}} & \mu'
\end{array}
\right)
\quad \text{(Scenes)}
$$

$$
I \, {\Big\Uparrow}{\Big\downarrow}\, \pi \qquad P \overset{N}{\diagdown\!\!\!\diagup} \qquad I' \,{\Big\Uparrow}{\Big\downarrow}\, \pi
$$

$$
\mu\pi_* \quad \overset{F_*}{\underset{R_*}{\rightleftarrows}} \quad \mu'\pi_* \qquad \text{(Images)}
$$

$$
\underset{\text{Competence Observer}}{\qquad\qquad} \qquad \underset{\text{Performance Observer}}{\qquad\qquad}
$$

Fig. 5.4 The two observers in the Bayesian observer diagram.

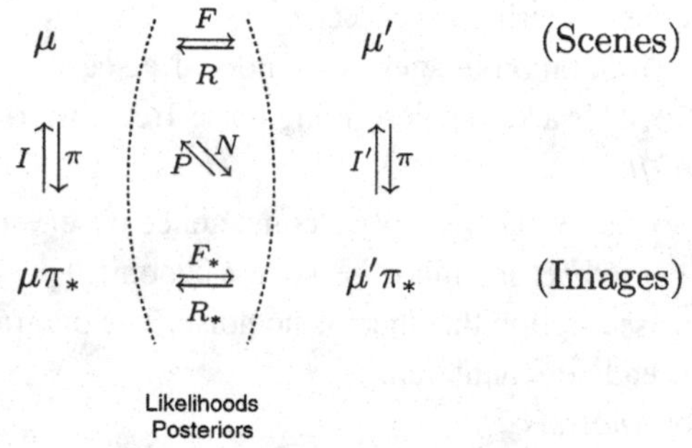

$$
\mu \qquad \left(\begin{array}{c}\overset{F}{\underset{R}{\rightleftarrows}}\end{array}\right) \qquad \mu' \qquad \text{(Scenes)}
$$

$$
I\,{\Big\Uparrow}{\Big\downarrow}\,\pi \qquad P\overset{N}{\diagdown\!\!\!\diagup} \qquad I'\,{\Big\Uparrow}{\Big\downarrow}\,\pi
$$

$$
\mu\pi_* \qquad \left(\begin{array}{c}\overset{F_*}{\underset{R_*}{\rightleftarrows}}\end{array}\right) \qquad \mu'\pi_* \qquad \text{(Images)}
$$

$$
\underset{\substack{\text{Likelihoods}\\ \text{Posteriors}}}{\qquad\qquad}
$$

Fig. 5.5 The Bayesian likelihoods and posteriors in the BOD.

(b) $F_*: D \times \mathcal{D} \to [0, 1]$ is a kernel which is the "pushdown" of F. Thus $F_* = \mathcal{I}F\pi_* = \mathcal{I}N$. This kernel fuzzes up the ideal distribution $\mu\pi_*$ on images to match the actual distribution, $\mu'\pi_*$.

(c) $R: \mathcal{C} \times \mathcal{C} \to [0, 1]$ is a kernel given by

$$
R = F_\mu^\dagger, \tag{5.43}
$$

i.e., R is the Bayes adjoint of F for the prior probability μ. (The dagger notation is as given in Definition 5.) By Theorem 5 we then have $\mu'R = \mu$, i.e., R "retracts" the noisy measure μ' back to the Bayesian prior μ.

(d) $R_*: D \times \mathcal{D} \to [0, 1]$ is a kernel which is the "pushdown" of R. Thus $R_* = \mathcal{I}'R\pi_*$. This kernel "retracts" the noisy distribution on images back to the noise-free distribution, $\mu\pi_*$. In fact we will prove, as part of Theorem 9 below, that R_* is the Bayesian posterior for the likelihood F_* with respect to the prior measure $\mu\pi_*$.

Thus the BOD ties together two observers – competence and performance – and displays their relationship with standard Bayesian estimation. A competence observer is a competence theory of a perceptual capacity in the noise free case. A performance observer is a point at which empirical data makes close contact with the formalism, allowing the competence observer to be constrained by experiments. These two observers are displayed in Figure 5.4. The likelihoods and posteriors of standard Bayesian estimation are highlighted in Figure 5.5.

What are the minimal data that are required to construct a consistent BOD? The minimal data must include the measurable mapping π from C to D, and hence the kernel π_*. We also must have a prior measure on the configuration space. Because of the symmetry of the BOD, this measure can be either μ or μ'. If we choose μ we need a model of "noise" F that allows us to construct μ'. If instead we choose μ', then we need a model R for retracting μ' to μ. Thus there are two possible sets of mathematically minimal data: One is π_*, μ, and F; the other is π_*, μ' and R. This is the essence of the following theorem.

Theorem 9. If the spaces C and D are standard Borel spaces, then given $\{\pi_*, \mu, F\}$ or given $\{\pi_*, \mu', R\}$ one can canonically construct a consistent BOD in which each pair of opposite pointing arrows corresponds to a pair of kernels which are Bayes adjoints of each other.

Proof. See Appendix A40. ∎

This theorem establishes the existence of consistent BODs. One consequence is that we now see from the BOD that, assuming consistency, $\mu N = \mu \pi_* F_*$. Thus, assuming consistency and that the prior μ is a correct model of the situation, we can always view the noise N as "simple noise": N is noise-free projection π_* followed by a noise kernel F_* acting *only* on the image space D. Hence in order to undo the noise N we need only clean up noise in the image space D via the kernel R_*. We can then use $\mathcal{I}$, the noise-free interpretation kernel, to produce our scene interpretations. This observation justifies the noise-free competence observer as an essential aspect of standard Bayesian analysis applied to perception.

5.13 Psychophysical tests of competence theories

Suppose we have a computational model for a visual process. And suppose we wish to test whether this model is psychologically plausible. Then we can first write a description of the model as a competence observer. This observer is the theoretical entity we will evaluate on the basis of psychophysical data. But here we face a problem: the competence observer cannot handle noise, whereas the psychophysical data we collect are doubtless tainted with noise. We must therefore construct a model of performance based on the competence theory we wish to test and the best knowledge we have about the noise likely to obtain. This noise can occur at several levels: (1) in the generation and presentation of stimuli to a subject, (2) in the perceptual processes internal to that subject, (3) in the response processes internal to the subject, and (4) in the response apparatus used by the subject. It is the performance model that we directly test by our psychophysical data and which, in turn, allows us to accept or reject our proposed competence theory. The BOD discussed in the last section deals with the first two levels of noise: in the stimuli and in the subject's perceptual processing. The last two levels, response noise internal and external to the subject, can together be modeled by a "response kernel", M, that maps perceptual conclusions to possible experimental outcomes. Here we shall not concern ourselves with this kernel except to note that it is markovian and does not respect the fibres of the rendering function π. Instead we focus on the BOD and its relation to psychophysical data.

First we note that the Bayesian posterior P does not model what subjects *actually perceive* in noisy displays. The reason is straightforward: P gives positive probabilities only to sets of scene interpretations which have positive probability in the prior probability used to define the competence observer. If the prior probability is supported in C_s then the Bayesian posterior, as we have seen, only leads to interpretations in C_s (see Definition 3 and the remark after Theorem 3). Intuitively, this stipulates that, even when there is noise in the stimuli, one can only see scene interpretations that are strictly compatible with the special interpretations of the competence theory in question. But this is too restrictive. We sometimes perceive scene interpretations that are close to, but not strictly compatible with, the prior of our competence theory. If, for instance, our prior is restricted entirely to rigid motions, and we view a display depicting a nearly, but not exactly, rigid motion, then we should not be straitjacketed into seeing a rigid motion or seeing nothing. We should see a nearly rigid motion. And in fact we do. Thus the Bayesian posterior is too restrictive for the job.

The interpretation kernel $\mathcal{I}'$ of a performance observer, on the other hand, is not too restrictive. It has the flexibility to assign positive probabilities to scene interpretations outside of C_s.

What then is the relation between the Bayesian posterior P and the performance observer's $\mathcal{I}'$ in modeling perceptions under noise? When we perceive a nearly rigid motion we can, in many cases, also visualize a rigid motion that is "close to" the perceived motion. This idealized rigid interpretation is modeled by the Bayesian posterior P, and the "close to" relation by the retraction kernel R. However, the nonrigid motion actually perceived is modeled by $\mathcal{I}'$ of a performance observer. Thus the upper left of the BOD deals with idealized perceptions, the upper right with actual perceptions. This suggests that psychophysical experiments which test subjects' actual perceptions constrain $\mathcal{I}'$ of a performance observer; psychophysical experiments which test subjects' idealized perceptions constrain P of standard Bayesian analysis. The design of the experiment and the instructions to subjects will determine whether the data collected bear most directly on the actual or idealized perceptions of subjects. Here, as in all aspects of experimental design, care must be taken to assure that the appropriate type of data is collected.

How do detection experiments fit into the BOD? Detection experiments constrain

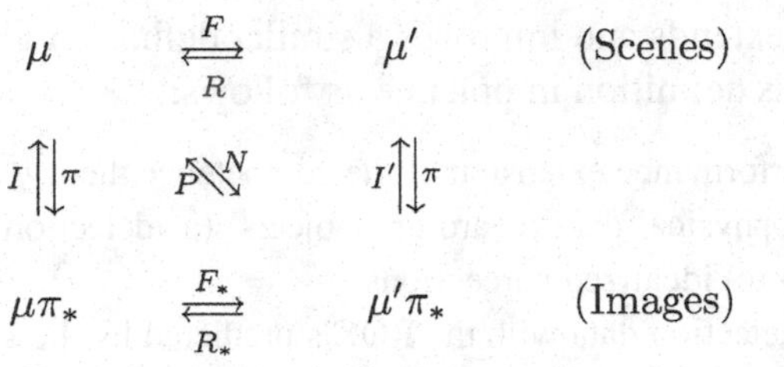

$$\mu \qquad \overset{F}{\underset{R}{\rightleftharpoons}} \qquad \mu' \qquad \text{(Scenes)}$$

$$I \Big\Updownarrow \pi \qquad P \underset{N}{\diagdown\diagdown} \qquad I' \Big\Updownarrow \pi$$

$$\mu\pi_* \qquad \overset{F_*}{\underset{R_*}{\rightleftharpoons}} \qquad \mu'\pi_* \qquad \text{(Images)}$$

Fig. 5.6 Psychophysical experiments which test subjects' actual perceptions constrain $\mathcal{I}'$ of a performance observer; tests of idealized perceptions constrain P of standard Bayesian analysis; detection experiments constrain the significance function α.

the confidence function α of the performance observer on the right of the BOD (see Definition 2 and the immediately preceding discussion). We summarize our discussion in the following hypothesis (see Figure 5.6):

Hypothesis 1. Psychophysical experiments which test subjects' actual perceptions constrain the distributions $\mathcal{I}'(d, \cdot)$ of a performance observer. Psychophysical experiments which test subjects' idealized perceptions constrain the distributions $P(d, \cdot)$ of standard Bayesian analysis. Detection experiments constrain the significance function α of a performance observer.

Which performance observer shall we use to test our competence observer via the BOD? It should be a performance observer that is compatible with the competence observer in the sense that it has the same spaces C, D and rendering function π. Moreover it should be related to the competence observer by the models of noise appropriate to the experimental situation. That is, referring to Figure 5.6, it should be related to the competence observer by maps N and F appropriate to the experimental situation. And finally its significance function α should be appropriate to the experimental situation. A performance observer which is properly related to a competence observer by these criteria we call a *performance extension* of that competence observer. A change in the noise, i.e., a change in N and F, leads to a change in the performance extension. This leads to the following definition.

Definition 6. A performance observer O' is an *extension* of a competence observer O if (1) O and O' satisfy[†] the BOD, with O being the competence observer and O' the performance observer, (2) N and F are proper models of the noise in the experimental situation, and (3) $\alpha(d) = R_*(d, D_s)$, where R_* is the Bayesian posterior for F_* of the BOD, as discussed in section 5.12. (Note that α is the standard Bayesian posterior used for Bayesian classification in the one category case.)

[†] We say that an object or map satisfies a diagram if it permits the diagram to be consistent.

This definition extends and improves a similar definition given by Bennett *et al.* (1993). We use this definition in practice as follows:

  (i) Construct a performance extension of the competence theory.
 (ii) Collect psychophysical data regarding subjects' (a) detection abilities, or (b) actual perceptions, or (c) idealized perceptions.
(iii) Compare the detection data with the ROC's predicted by the significance function α. Compare psychophysical data on the actual perceptions with the relevant measures $\mathcal{I}'(d, \cdot)$ of the performance extension. Compare psychophysical data on the idealized perceptions with the relevant measures $P(d, \cdot)$ of the standard Bayesian analysis.
 (iv) Carry out standard statistical tests to decide if the comparisons in step 3 are satisfactory.
  (v) Conclude that the psychophysical data confirm (disconfirm) the competence theory if the statistical tests in 4 are satisfactory (dissatisfactory).

In many cases our knowledge of the experimental situation leads us to a unique F, and the procedure outlined above can be used without modification. If our knowledge of the experimental situation does not lead us to a unique F then we cannot determine a unique performance extension for the competence observer.

5.14 An example test

We have outlined how, in principle, psychophysical data can be used to test competence theories of perceptual capacities. One practical example of this method applied to a theory of visual surface interpolation is given in Bennett *et al.* (1993). (This example tests $\mathcal{I}'$ of a performance extension.) For another brief practical example, which tests P of standard Bayesian analysis, we return again to the competence theory motivated by the Two-View Theorem (described in section 5.3). Recall that this competence observer takes two distinct orthographic views of four points as a premise. If the two views have no rigid interpretations the competence observer does nothing. If they have a rigid interpretation then they have, in fact, a one-parameter family of interpretations. The Two-View Theorem gives no basis for choosing among the rigid interpretations in the one-parameter family, so we constructed the competence observer to give all the interpretations equal probability.

A psychophysical test of this competence observer was conducted in a series of experiments by Liter *et al.* (1993). In one experiment they showed subjects a two-view display depicting dots in rigid motion. Subjects were simultaneously shown rigid 3D interpretations uniformly sampled from the entire one-parameter family compatible with the two-view display. Subjects selected that 3D interpretation which, up to the resolution of the monitor, best matched their idealized perception of the two-view display. In this way Liter *et al.* obtained psychophysical data relevant to testing hypotheses about the distribution $P(d, \cdot)$ for various two-view displays d.

The noise in the experimental situation was primarily due to roundoff and quantization errors in the displays. The uniform nature of this noise N, together with the assumption of a uniform prior μ on the one-parameter family, led Liter *et al.* to conclude that the posterior P of the subject should also give all interpretations in the one-parameter family equal probability. Thus Liter *et al.* concluded, in effect, that the distributions $P(d, \cdot)$ should be uniform.

They then tested the hypothesis that the subjects' choices reflected a uniform distribution on the one-parameter family. Their data led them to reject this hypothesis and therefore to reject P and, in consequence, to reject the psychological plausibility of both this competence observer and its performance extension. They found instead that subjects' choices were heavily biased towards certain of the rigid interpretations in the one-parameter family and away from others. For instance, subjects seemed to prefer "compact" rigid interpretations, i.e., interpretations in which the 3D structures were about as deep as they were wide. This led Liter *et al.* to suggest that subjects were using constraints in addition to rigidity to guide the interpretation process. Exactly what these constraints are is not yet known, but as hypotheses about the constraints are formulated we can construct competence observers to formalize them and performance observers to submit them to further psychophysical tests. And through a repeated cycling of theory and experiment we can hope eventually to converge on a psychologically plausible competence observer.

The psychophysical studies of Liter *et al.* investigate the posterior P but not the significance function α. This function has been investigated by Braunstein *et al.* (1990). They had subjects observe two-view and multi-view displays, and judge whether or not the displays depicted rigid motion. They found that the ability of subjects to detect rigid motion, as measured by their d' scores, was well above chance. However subjects' performance fell well short of that predicted by the ROC curves developed in section 5.6. This once again suggests that further work is needed to arrive at psychologically plausible competence observers and performance extensions for the perception of structure from motion.

5.15 Summary

The tools of Bayesian estimation provide a powerful approach to understanding and modeling human perceptual capacities. The discrete formulation of Bayes rule is now widely used for this purpose. However in many situations of practical interest to vision researchers the discrete formulation of Bayes rule is inappropriate because it does not allow one to condition on a measure zero event (such as obtaining a specific image out of a continuum of possible images). This paper remedies this defect by deriving a general form of Bayes rule that allows one to compute posterior distributions even when the conditioning event has measure zero. In the noise-free case this general form of Bayes rule is equivalent to the competence observers of observer theory (Bennett *et al.*, 1989a). The consideration of noise leads to the development of performance observers. The relationship between these observers, standard Bayesian estimation, and psychophysical data can be summarized in a single commutative diagram, called the BOD. The BOD provides a useful framework for interrelating psychophysical experiments with computational theories.

Acknowledgements

We thank M. Albert, M. Braunstein, A. Jepson, R. Kakarala, D. Knill, and W. Richards for useful discussions. We thank D. Knill and W. Richards for helpful comments on an earlier draft of this paper. Supported by NSF grant DIR-9014278 and by ONR contract N00014-88-K-0354.

5.16 Postlogue 1: Modularity and coupling

To describe human vision by competence and performance observers is to impose a modularity. We carve the visual system into interacting components and use observer theory to describe each component and its interactions. Observer theory does not tell us a priori how to carve things up. It only provides a language for describing the units that result from such a carving. It is an empirical issue how best things should be carved.

This section gives a brief idea about how observers might be coupled or made to interact. Suppose that we have two competence observers $O_1 = (C_1, D_1, C_{s1}, D_{s1}, \pi_1, \mathcal{I}_1)$ and $O_2 = (C_2, D_2, C_{s2}, D_{s2}, \pi_2, \mathcal{I}_2)$. One way that O_1 and O_2 might be coupled is hierarchically. That is, if the conclusions of O_1 are used as the premises for O_2, then we can create a new observer O which goes from the premises of O_1 directly to the conclusions of O_2. If O_1 infers the 3D positions of feature points given their image motion, and O_2 infers a 3D interpolating surface given the 3D positions of feature points, then O would directly infer a 3D interpolating surface given the image motion of the feature points. Formally, if C_1 and D_2 are the same space, then we can use the definition of kernel product to define a new interpretation kernel $\mathcal{I} = \mathcal{I}_1\mathcal{I}_2$ on $\pi_1(\pi_2(C_{s2})) \cap D_{s1} \times C_2$, where

$$\mathcal{I}(d, A) = (\mathcal{I}_1\mathcal{I}_2)(d, A) = \int_{c \in C_1} \mathcal{I}_1(d, dc)\mathcal{I}_2(c, A). \qquad (5.44)$$

In this case we can write a new competence observer O which is the *hierarchical coupling* of O_1 and O_2 by

$$O = (C_2, D_1, C_{s2} \cap \pi_2^{-1}(\pi_1^{-1}(\pi_1(\pi_2(C_{s2})) \cap D_{s1})), \pi_1(\pi_2(C_{s2})) \cap D_{s1},$$
$$\pi_1 \circ \pi_2, \mathcal{I}), \qquad (5.45)$$

where $\mathcal{I}$ is given by (5.44). This observer has the same effect as first executing observer O_1 and then executing observer O_2.

Another way we might connect O_1 and O_2 is via *weak coupling* as described in chapter 4 (see also Clark & Yuille, 1990; Bülthoff & Yuille, 1991; Knill & Kersten, 1991). We first create the *product observer*

$$O = O_1 \times O_2$$
$$= (C_1 \times C_2, D_1 \times D_2, C_{s1} \times C_{s2}, D_{s1} \times D_{s2}, \pi_1 \times \pi_2, \mathcal{I}_1 \times \mathcal{I}_2) \quad (5.46)$$

where, for $A_1 \in C_1$ and $A_2 \in C_2, \pi_1 \times \pi_2(A_1, A_2) = (\pi_1(A_1), \pi_2(A_2))$, and where, for $d_1 \in D_1$ and $d_2 \in D_2, \mathcal{I}_1 \times \mathcal{I}_2(d_1, d_2; A_1 \times A_2) = \mathcal{I}_1(d_1, A_1)\mathcal{I}_2(d_2, A_2)$. We describe the noise affecting O_1 by a kernel N_1 on $C_1 \times D_1$ and the noise affecting O_2 by a kernel N_2 on $C_2 \times D_2$. We denote the prior distribution on scene interpretations for O_1 by μ_1 and the prior distribution for O_2 by μ_2. We denote their respective posterior distributions by P_1 and P_2. Using this notation we have the following definition and theorem.

Definition 7. *Weak Coupling.* Let $O = O_1 \times O_2$ be a product observer. Let the prior measures for O_1 and O_2 be μ_1 and μ_2 respectively. Let their likelihoods be given by the kernels N_1 and N_2 respectively. Then O is said to be a *weak coupling* of O_1 and O_2 if its prior μ and likelihood N satisfy

$$\mu N(dd_1, dd_2) = \mu_1 N_1(dd_1)\mu_2 N_2(dd_2). \quad (5.47)$$

Theorem 10. *Posterior For Weak Coupling.* Let O be a weak coupling of O_1 and O_2. Let the posterior distributions for O_1 and O_2 be given by the kernels P_1 and P_2. Then P, the posterior distribution of O, is given by

$$P(A_1 \times A_2 \mid d_1, d_2) = P_1(A_1 \mid d_1)P_2(A_2 \mid d_2), \quad (5.48)$$

where $A_1 \times A_2 \in C_1 \times C_2$.

Proof. Appendix A41. ∎

This theorem states that if the sources of noise are independent for two observers, then the posterior distribution associated to the product of the two observers is in fact the product of their individual posteriors. This sometimes, though not always, leads to a linear combination of cues from the two observers. There is evidence that a linear combination rule is sometimes used in human vision (Dosher *et al.*, 1986; Bruno & Cutting, 1988; Maloney & Landy, 1989). Nonlinear combination rules have also been formulated (Bülthoff & Yuille, 1991; Bennett *et al.*, 1993).

5.17 Postlogue 2: Relation to regularization and Gibbs

To illustrate our general Bayesian formalism, we briefly describe a "Gibbsian random field" analysis of shape from shading given by Bülthoff & Yuille (1991) and mentioned in chapter 4. They adopt the Bayesian approach as a way of imposing constraints via a prior probability. Observer theory also calls, as we have seen, for the introduction of prior assumptions via probability measures on a set of special scene interpretations. In Bülthoff and Yuille's paper, as here, the particular model of noise in the perceptual modality determines the likelihood function and Bayes theorem then provides the posterior distribution. We will see that our approach helps to identify some of the issues involved in their analysis and indeed we pose a number of questions regarding the mathematical meaning of their work. We do not present any answers to the questions raised here, preferring to leave that to later research. We conclude here that in order to put their Gibbsian random field theories on a rigorous footing, yet another level of generalization seems to be required – a level beyond that to continuous systems discussed in the present paper.

Even in its nondiscrete form Bayes theorem has not, to our knowledge, been discussed or applied in the vision literature, in spite of the fact that the underlying competence theories are (usually) inherently continuous. Bennett *et al.* (1989a) showed that there is a sense in which continuous systems cannot be modeled to arbitrary precision by discretized versions; a study of the continuous system itself is necessary for its proper understanding.[†] The Bülthoff-Yuille analysis of shape from shading is about such an inherently continuous system and so deserves the approach of this paper.

We now present the Bülthoff-Yuille argument, modifying the language (though not the content) somewhat so as to accord with the notation of this paper. We proceed heuristically, as they and others have, interspersing comments on points of rigor.

From a given light source $\vec{s}$, they wish to infer a surface normal vector field $\vec{n}$, assuming Lambertian reflectance. Here $\vec{n} = \vec{n}(\mathbf{x})$ is a function of the image position $\mathbf{x}$ in the image rectangle R. The constraint they impose is smoothness of the vector field $\vec{n}$. Their prior measure thus assigns higher probabilities to smoother surfaces. They use the prior "density" $c_S^{-1} e^{-\beta E_S(\vec{n})}$ where β is a positive real number, and E_S is an "energy" or "cost" functional on the surface field[‡] – the subscript S refers to the prior constraint of smoothness: $E_S(\vec{n})$ is smaller, and the probability is therefore larger, for smoother fields $\vec{n}(\mathbf{x})$. Bülthoff & Yuille present their analysis in terms of densities; a rigorously correct theory would display full measures. Thus a prior

---

[†] This is a consequence of the fact that discretized approximations need not converge, in some sense, to the required values unless controlled by a knowledge of the actual system.

[‡] The denotation is, respectively, from statistical mechanics or operations research.

measure on the surface normal vector fields would be of the form

$$\wp(d\vec{n}) = c_S^{-1} e^{-\beta E_S(\vec{n})} d\vec{n}, \tag{5.49}$$

where $d\vec{n}$ is some underlying measure on the set of vector fields. Following Horn, they take

$$E_S(\vec{n}) = \lambda \int |S\vec{n}(\mathbf{x})|^2 d\mathbf{x}, \tag{5.50}$$

where λ is another real parameter and S is some appropriate differential operator on the space of vector fields, such that smoother surfaces have lower energy. The quantity c_S is a normalization constant. The prior (5.49), then, is meant to be a measure on the space of *vector fields on R*. This space is infinite-dimensional. Therefore one needs to first ascertain what reasonable measurable structures can be imposed on it, and what bona fide (i.e., σ-finite) measures exist on it. In particular, we need to be able to assert the existence of a measure $d\vec{n}$ which is concentrated on smooth vector fields, in order that a density of the sort they propose makes sense.

Next, they assume a likelihood function that represents Gaussian simple noise applied to the competence theory: Let $I(\mathbf{x})$ be the image intensity at $\mathbf{x} \in R^2$. A Lambertian competence theory requires that $I(\mathbf{x}) = \vec{s} \cdot \vec{n}(\mathbf{x})$. In observer language, the rendering function π takes $\vec{n}$ to $\pi(\vec{n}) = \vec{s} \cdot \vec{n}$, a function on the image rectangle R. Define

$$E_D(I, \vec{n}) = -\int (I(\mathbf{x}) - \vec{s} \cdot \vec{n}(\mathbf{x}))^2 d\mathbf{x}. \tag{5.51}$$

The subscript D stands for data. The likelihood is then the "probability" of the data I, given the scene $\vec{n}$:

$$\wp(dI \mid \vec{n}) = \frac{e^{-\beta E_D(I,\vec{n})} dI}{c_D(\vec{n})}. \tag{5.52}$$

Here β is the same parameter as before and $c_D(\vec{n})$ is the normalization. Note that this noise is not quite the Gaussian noise we discussed in section 5.12 – the underlying space is now an infinite-dimensional space of *functions* and is not some $\mathfrak{R}^n$. But Bülthoff & Yuille assume that this noise behaves similarly to a Gaussian, in that the normalization $c_D(\vec{n})$ is independent of the particular surface field $\vec{n}$. Thus we will write simply c_D for the normalization.

Bayes theorem (3) then tells us that the posterior probability that the surface field belongs to some collection A of surface fields, given the image scalar field I, is

$$\wp(A \mid I) = \frac{\int \wp(d\vec{n}) 1_A(\vec{n}) \wp(dI \mid \vec{n})}{\int \wp(d\vec{n}) \wp(dI \mid \vec{n})} (I) \tag{5.53}$$

$$= \frac{\left[\int_A d\vec{n} \, e^{-\beta(E_D(I,\vec{n}) + \lambda E_S(\vec{n}))}\right] dI}{\left[\int d\vec{n} \, e^{-\beta(E_D(I,\vec{n}) + \lambda E_S(\vec{n}))}\right] dI} (I), \tag{5.54}$$

where the normalizations cancel out and the right hand sides are to be interpreted as Radon-Nikodym derivatives. Now, proceding as in section 5.11 it is clear that

$$\wp(A \mid I) = \frac{\int_A d\vec{n} \; e^{-\beta(E_D(I,\vec{n})+\lambda E_S(\vec{n}))}}{Z}, \tag{5.55}$$

where the normalization Z is

$$Z = \int d\vec{n} \; e^{-\beta(E_D(I,\vec{n})+\lambda E_S(\vec{n}))}, \tag{5.56}$$

an integral over all possible surface fields.

This is the posterior proposed by Bülthoff & Yuille. The discretized versions of the above expressions seem straightforward to implement. In the discrete case the image rectangle R is a finite set of points in $\Re^2$ and there is a finite set of possible unit normal vectors and image intensities at each point. In this case the measures $d\vec{n}$ and dI can be defined as the usual (Lebesgue) uniform measures on finite-dimensional spaces. Let us denote the particular level of discretization by the subscript k, with $k \to \infty$ indicating the limiting passage to the continuum. Then, at level k, the underlying measures are $d\vec{n}_k$ and dI_k. The likelihood is then indeed a Gaussian. However, even in this case it is not clear how the normalizations $c_{D(\vec{n}),k}$ can be independent of the fields $\vec{n}$, considering that the image fields I can never be negative. This assumption is clearly an approximation. How controlled is this approximation as the discretization gets finer?

The question of controlling approximations becomes yet more vexed as we consider the definability of the measures in the limit of the continuum. There is, in fact, no pair of measures that the discretized uniform measures $d\vec{n}_k$ and dI_k can converge to – there is no nontrivial σ-finite *uniform* measure on infinite-dimensional spaces of vector or scalar fields. Perhaps a way out of this impasse is to define the discretized densities in terms of other, possibly *nonuniform*, measures $d\vec{n}_k$ and dI_k. For then the hope is that these measures may be chosen so that the result (5.55) (which indeed holds true at discrete level k), converges as k goes to infinity, to some appropriate kernel $\wp(A \mid I)$, i.e.,

$$\frac{\int_A d\vec{n}_k \; e^{-\beta(E_{D,k}(I,\vec{n})+\lambda E_{S,k}(\vec{n}))}}{Z_k} \longrightarrow \wp(A \mid I). \tag{5.57}$$

It is, after all, the existence of this kernel that we want. But the convergence process needs to be well enough controlled so that $\wp(A \mid I)$ is concentrated on *smooth* vector fields. How do we do this? Are there other ways to define prior measures, likelihoods, and posteriors in this infinite-dimensional situation? What is the structure of Bayesian analysis for random fields? We do not answer these questions here, only referring the reader interested in such questions involving infinite-dimensional integration to Simon (1979).

We make a final remark about regularization and Bayesian observer analysis. The motivation for the Gibbsian random field prior density, given above, was to regularize the situation so as to obtain a unique answer.[†] Probabilistic approaches, such as the Bayes-observer theoretic approach, allow for a consideration of multistability in a most natural fashion: instead of the maximum a posteriori estimate based on a unimodal prior, which leads to a unimodal posterior kernel, choose a *multimodal* prior (or measure on the space of conclusions); this is intended to make manifest the multistability in the posterior.

Appendix

This appendix contains technical definitions and proofs of theorems whose statements appear in the body of the paper.

Definition A0. *(Lebesgue Measure).* Lebesgue measure on $\Re^n$ is a translation invariant measure which assigns to each measurable set $A \subset \Re^n$ a real number equal to its n-volume. Any measurable set of positive codimension in $\Re^n$, i.e., any measurable set whose dimension is strictly less than n, has Lebesgue measure zero in $\Re^n$. The phrase "Lebesgue almost surely" means "except for a set of cases whose total Lebesgue measure is zero". Unless otherwise indicated, the phrases "almost surely", "almost all", "almost every", and "a.e.", mean, in this paper, "except for a set of Lebesgue measure zero". The phrase "a.e. μ" means "except for a set of μ measure zero".

Definition A1. *(Kernels).* Let $(U, \mathcal{U})$, $(V, \mathcal{V})$ be measurable spaces. A *kernel on U relative to V* or a *kernel on* $V \times \mathcal{U}$ is a mapping $N : V \times \mathcal{U} \rightarrow \Re \cup \{\infty\}$, such that

 (i) for every v in V, the mapping $A \rightarrow N(v, A)$ is a measure on U, denoted by $N(v, du)$;
(ii) for every A in $\mathcal{U}$, the mapping $v \rightarrow N(v, A)$ is a measurable function on V, denoted by $N(\cdot, A)$.

N is called *positive* if its range is in $[0, \infty]$ and *markovian* if it is positive and, for all $v \in V$, $N(v, U) = 1$; N is *submarkovian* if $N(v, U) < 1$. If $U = V$ we simply say that N is a *kernel on U*. In the text, *all kernels are positive* unless otherwise stated.

Definition A2. *(Kernel Products).* If N is a kernel on $V \times \mathcal{U}$ and M is a kernel on $U \times \mathcal{V}$, then the *product* $NM(v, D) = \int_U N(v, du)M(u, D)$ is also a kernel on $V \times \mathcal{V}$.

[†] Actually, the question of whether the prior of (5.49) is indeed unimodal (in some reasonable sense) in the continuous limit is moot.

Definition A3. *(Kernels As Linear Operators On Measures).* Let ν be a measure on U, and let M be a kernel from U to V. Then we define νM to be the measure on V given by $\nu M(D) = \int_U \nu(du) M(u, D)$ for measurable sets $D \subset V$.

Remark A4 (Remarks On Kernels). A measurable function g on U yields a new kernel gM by means of $gM(u, D) = g(u)M(u, D)$. A special kind of kernel is the one on V relative to V called the *Dirac kernel at v*. This kernel is denoted $\epsilon(v, dv')$ and defined by $\epsilon(v, B) = 1$ if $v \in B$ and 0 otherwise. For the Dirac kernel the measure in (i) above is the usual Dirac measure $\epsilon_v(dv')$, while the mapping in (ii) above is the "indicator function" $1_B(v)$, which equals 1 if $v \in B$ and 0 otherwise.

As an example of kernels, we consider a measurable map $\pi: U \to V$. If μ is a measure on U, we have defined $\mu\pi_*$ to be the distribution of π with respect to μ, i.e., for a measurable set $B \subset V$, $(\mu\pi_*)(B) = \mu(\pi^{-1}(B))$. However, we can also think of this as the result of a kernel called π_* from U to V operating on μ. In fact, $\pi_*(u, B)$ is $1_{\pi^{-1}(B)}(u)$.

Definition A5. *(Regular Conditional Probability Distribution).* Let $(U, \mathcal{U})$ and $(V, \mathcal{V})$ be measurable spaces. Let $p: U \to V$ be a measurable function and ν a positive measure on $(U, \mathcal{U})$. A *regular conditional probability distribution* (abbreviated *rcpd*) of ν with respect to p is a kernel $m_p^\nu: V \times \mathcal{U} \to [0, 1]$ satisfying the following conditions:

(i) m_p^ν is markovian;
(ii) $m_p^\nu(v, \cdot)$ is supported on $p^{-1}\{v\}$ for $p_*\nu$-almost all $v \in V$;[†]
(iii) If $g \in L^1(U, \nu)$, then

$$\int_U g\, d\nu = \int_V (p_*\nu)(dv) \int_{p^{-1}\{v\}} m_p^\nu(v, du) g(u). \qquad (5.58)$$

In view of (A1)–(A4), condition (iii) may be simply written as the kernel product formula

$$\nu = (p_*\nu)m_P^\nu.$$

In practice it is sufficient to verify (iii) in the case when g is the characteristic function of a measurable subset $A \subset U$, i.e., we may replace (iii') for all $A \in \mathcal{U}$

$$\nu 1_A = (p_*\nu)m_P^\nu 1_A.$$

In the special case that U and V are discrete spaces, integrals become sums and measures become weight functions. Thus, for the discrete situation, the appropriate

---

[†] Again, $p_*\nu(dv)$ is defined by $p_*\nu(B) = \nu(p^{-1}(B))$, $B \in \mathcal{V}$.

version of (iii) above is

$$\sum_U g(u)\nu(u) = \sum_V (p_*\nu)(v) \sum_{p^{-1}\{v\}} m_p^\nu(v,\,u)g(u). \tag{5.59}$$

It is a theorem that if $(U,\,\mathcal{U})$ and $(V,\,\mathcal{V})$ are standard Borel spaces then an rcpd m_p^ν exists for any probability measure ν (Parthasarathy, 1968). In general there will be many choices for m_p^ν any two of which will agree a.e. $p_*\nu$ on V (that is, for almost all values of the first argument). If $p\colon U \to V$ is a continuous map of topological spaces which are also given their corresponding standard Borel structures then one can show that there is a canonical choice of m_p^ν defined everywhere. This is the case typical of image understanding.

Remark A8 (Some Properties Of RCPD's). It is a theorem that if $(U,\,\mathcal{U})$ and $(V,\,\mathcal{V})$ are standard Borel spaces (e.g., euclidean spaces) then an rcpd m_p^ν exists for any probability measure ν (Parthasarathy, 1968). In general the choice for m_p^ν is not unique: any two choices will agree a.e. $p_*\nu$ on V (that is, for almost all values of the first argument of the kernel). If $p\colon U \to V$ is a continuous map of topological spaces which are also given their corresponding standard Borel structures one can show that there is a canonical choice of m_p^ν defined everywhere.

Proof A9 (Proof of Theorem 2). By the definition of conditional probability,

$$P(A \mid d) = \wp(A \times \{d\} \mid C \times \{d\}) = \frac{\wp(A \times \{d\})}{\wp(C \times \{d\})} \tag{5.60}$$

$$= \sum_{c \in A} \frac{\mu(c)N(c,d)}{(\mu N)(d)}$$

$$= \sum_{c \in A} \frac{\mu(c)1_A(c)N(c,d)}{(\mu N)(d)} = \frac{(\mu(1_A N))(d)}{(\mu N)(d)}, \tag{5.61}$$

where we are assuming that $\mu N(d) \neq 0$. Equation (5.22) is now a matter of straightforward computation, left as an exercise.

Next, recall Definition A5 of rcpd's. In the present instance, the set U of Definition A5 is $C \times D$, V is D, ν there is now P, and π is q. Now consider equation (5.59). Take g to be the function $1_A(c)1_B(d)$. With these identifications, equation (5.59) yields

$$\wp(A \times B) = \sum_D \mu N(d) \sum_{C \times \{d\}} m_q^P(d,(c,d'))1_A(c)1_B(d)$$

$$= \sum_{d \in B} \mu N(d) m_q^P(d, A \times \{d\}.)$$

On the other hand, for fixed A, we have

$$\wp(A \times B) = \sum_{d \in B} \wp(A \times \{d\})$$

$$= \sum_{d \in B} \wp(C \times \{d\})\wp(A \times \{d\} \mid C \times \{d\})$$

$$= \sum_{d \in B} \mu N(d)p(A \mid d),$$

where we have used equation (5.14) and the definition, equation (5.21), of P. Thus the two functions of d, $P(A \mid d)$ on the one hand and $m_q^P(d, A \times \{d\})$ on the other, possess the same sums with respect to the measure μN. It is an elementary fact of measure theory that, since the sums over arbitrary B are the same, the two functions must be equal, up to sets of μN-measure 0.

Finally, Definition A5(ii) shows that $m_q^P(d, A \times \{d\}) = m_q^P(d, A \times D)$. ∎

Remark A17 (Variation of equation (5.21)). Equation (5.21) can also be written as

$$P(A \mid d) = \frac{(\mu(1_A N)\mathcal{I})(\pi^{-1}(d))}{(\mu N \mathcal{I})(\pi^{-1}(d))} \qquad (5.62)$$

We can do this since, for any $d \in D, \mathcal{I}(d, \pi^{-1}(B))$ is 1 if $d \in B$ and is 0 otherwise, i.e., $\mathcal{I}(d, \pi^{-1}(B)) = 1_B(d)$. This means that for any measure ν on D we can write

$$\nu(B) = \int \nu(dd)\mathcal{I}(d, \pi^{-1}(B))$$

$$= \nu\mathcal{I}(\pi^{-1}(B))$$

Incidentally, a computation similar to that for equation (5.21) shows that for any subset B of D,

$$P(A \mid B) = \frac{(\mu(1_A N))(B)}{(\mu N)(B)}$$

$$= \frac{(\mu(1_A N)\mathcal{I})(\pi^{-1}(B))}{(\mu N \mathcal{I})(\pi^{-1}(B))} \qquad (5.63)$$

Proof A22 (Proof of Theorem 3). We need to show first that the quantity in the right-hand side of (5.28) exists. Suppose $\mu N(B) = 0$. Then the positivity of μ and of N show that $\mu(1_A N)(B) \leq \mu N(B) = 0$, so the derivative does exist. Next, does the proposed quantity satisfy Definition 3? Yes – immediate, given the definition of Radon-Nikodym derivatives. Finally, is the quantity a markovian kernel? That it is, for fixed A, measurable in d is part of the definition of derivative here. Moreover, the dominated convergence theorem shows that, for any d for which it is defined, $A \to \frac{\mathrm{d}(\mu(1_A N))}{\mathrm{d}(\mu N)}(d)$ is indeed countably additive. This kernel is markovian since

$\frac{\mathrm{d}(\mu(1_C N))}{\mathrm{d}(\mu N)}(d) = \frac{\mathrm{d}\mu N}{\mathrm{d}\mu N}(d) = 1$, for all d. The proof of Theorem 3 is just a transcription of that for the discrete case, with sums over weight functions replaced by integrals over measures. ∎

Remark A23 (Remark on Theorem 3). It follows from Theorem 3 that equation (5.63) still holds in the continuous case.

Proof A24 (Proof of Corollary 4). First, observe that the displayed equation of Corollary 4 holds whenever f is a linear combination of indicator functions. Every non-negative bounded measurable function is an increasing limit of linear combinations of indicator functions. By the Monotone Convergence Theorem, the displayed equation of Corollary 4 holds for non-negative functions, and since every function is a difference of two non-negative functions, it holds for all functions. ∎

Proof A25 (Proof of Theorem 8). Given the assumptions of Theorem 46 we can write, for $B \in \mathcal{D}$,

$$\mu N(B) = \int_C \mu(\mathrm{d}c) N(c, B)$$

$$= \int_{C_s} \left(\frac{1}{(\sqrt{2\pi\sigma^2})^m} \int_B \exp\left(\frac{-\|\pi(c) - d\|^2}{2\sigma^2} \right) \lambda(\mathrm{d}d) \right) \mu(\mathrm{d}c)$$

since μ is supported in C_s. Thus

$$\mu N(\mathrm{d}d) = \frac{1}{(\sqrt{2\pi\sigma^2})^m} \left[\int_{C_s} \exp\left(\frac{-\|\pi(c) - d\|^2}{2\sigma^2} \right) \mu(\mathrm{d}c) \right] \lambda(\mathrm{d}d) \quad (5.64)$$

by Fubini's theorem. A similar derivation shows that

$$\mu(1_A N)(\mathrm{d}d) = \frac{1}{(\sqrt{2\pi\sigma^2})^m} \left[\int_{C_s \cap A} \exp\left(\frac{-\|\pi(c) - d\|^2}{2\sigma^2} \right) \mu(\mathrm{d}c) \right] \lambda(\mathrm{d}d).$$
$$(5.65)$$

μ and λ are of course chosen so that the integrals exist. According to Theorem 3, to find $P(A \mid d)$ we now need to compute the Radon-Nikodym derivative

$$\frac{\mathrm{d}(\mu(1_A N))}{\mathrm{d}(\mu N)}(d).$$

Letting

$$F(d) = \frac{1}{(\sqrt{2\pi\sigma^2})^m} \int_{C_s} \exp\left(\frac{-\|\pi(c) - d\|^2}{2\sigma^2}\right) \mu(dc)$$

and

$$F_A(d) = \frac{1}{(\sqrt{2\pi\sigma^2})^m} \int_{C_s \cap A} \exp\left(\frac{-\|\pi(c) - d\|^2}{2\sigma^2}\right) \mu(dc).$$

Then (5.64) and (5.65) say

$$\mu 1_A N(dd) = F_A(d)\lambda(dd); \quad \mu N(dd) = F(d)\lambda(dd). \tag{5.66}$$

Notice that for nontrivial priors μ, $F(d) > 0 \;\forall d$, so that

$$\mu 1_A N(dd) = \frac{F_A(d)}{F(d)} \cdot \mu N(dd).$$

Hence, recalling Definition 4 of Radon-Nikodym derivative, we have finally

$$\frac{d(\mu(1_A N))}{d(\mu N)}(d) = \frac{\int_{C_s \cap A} \exp\left(\frac{-\|\pi(c) - d'\|^2}{2\sigma^2}\right) \mu(dc)}{\int_{C_s} \exp\left(\frac{-\|\pi(c) - d'\|^2}{2\sigma^2}\right) \mu(dc)}. \tag{5.67}$$

This expression for $P(A \mid d)$ exists generically since the denominator is generically not zero. We will also write this posterior in the form of a kernel, $P(d, A)$. Note that in this derivation we do not have to use a gaussian. We could use any kernel which descends. ∎

Proof A36 (Proof of Proposition 1). Let us assume that $\mathcal{I}$ is the posterior for π_*. We now prove that $\mathcal{I}$ is the rcpd of μ with respect to π. From Definition 3 we have

$$(\mu 1_A \pi_*)(B) = ((\mu\pi_*)1_B \mathcal{I})(A).$$

If we let $B = Y$ we get: for any set A in X

$$\mu 1_A \pi_* 1_Y = \mu\pi_* \mathcal{I} 1_A.$$

But $\pi_* 1_Y = 1_{\pi^{-1}(Y)} = 1_X$, hence

$$\mu 1_A = \mu\pi_* \mathcal{I} 1_A \tag{5.68}$$

which shows that $\mathcal{I}$ is the rcpd of μ with respect to π.

Now let assume that $\mathcal{I}$ is the rcpd of μ with respect to π. We now show that $\mathcal{I}$ is the posterior of π_* with respect to μ. We let A be a measurable subset of X and B a measurable subset of Y. By Definition 3, we want to show that

$$\mu 1_A \pi_* 1_B = \mu\pi_* 1_B \mathcal{I} 1_A.$$

The right hand side is

$$\text{RHS} = \int_{y \in B} \mu \pi_*(dy) \int_X \mathcal{I}(y, dx) 1_A(x)$$

$$= \int_Y \mu \pi_*(dy) \int_X \mathcal{I}(y, dx) 1_{A \cap \pi^{-1}(B)}(x)$$

$$= \mu(A \cap \pi^{-1}(B)).$$

The left hand side is

$$\text{LHS} = \int_X \mu(dx) 1_A(x) \pi_*(x, B)$$

$$= \int_X \mu(dx) 1_A(x) 1_{\pi^{-1}(B)}(x)$$

$$= \mu(A \cap \pi^{-1}(B)).$$

We must also show that under these hypotheses π_* is the posterior of $\mathcal{I}$ with respect to $\mu \pi_*$. But we have remarked after Definition 3 that that definition is symmetric provided that $\mu = \mu NP$, i.e., in this case $\mu = \mu \pi_* \mathcal{I}$. This follows from the definition of rcpd. ∎

Proof A37 (Proof of Theorem 5). For any $A \in \mathcal{X}$ we have

$$\mu H H^\dagger(A) = \int_{y \in Y} \mu H(dy) H^\dagger(y, A)$$

$$= \int_{y \in Y} \mu H(dy) \frac{d\mu(1_A H)}{d\mu H}(y)$$

$$= \int_{y \in Y} \mu 1_A H(dy) \qquad \text{a.e. } \nu \text{ s.t. } \pi_* \nu = \mu H$$

$$= \mu 1_A H(Y)$$

$$= \int_{x \in X} \mu(dx) 1_A(x) H(x, Y)$$

$$= \int_{x \in X} \mu(dx) 1_A(x)$$

$$= \int_A \mu(dx)$$

$$= \mu(A). \qquad \blacksquare$$

Proof A38 (Alternate Proof of Theorem 7). We first prove the following lemma.

■

Lemma A39. Let X and Y be measurable spaces, μ a probability measure on X, and H a markovian kernel from X to Y. The condition

$$(\mu 1_A H)(B) = ((\mu H)1_B H^\dagger)(A)$$

for all measurable $A \subset X$ and $B \subset Y$ (which defines $H^\dagger$) is equivalent to

$$\mu f H g = (\mu H)g H^\dagger f$$

for all bounded measurable functions $f: X \to \Re$ and $g: Y \to \Re$.

Proof. Because kernels act linearly on functions, the first equation immediately implies that the second holds for the case where f and g are simple functions, i.e., finite linear combinations of characteristic functions of sets. Then since every measurable function is a limit of simple functions and since our operator H, being markovian, is bounded we can conclude by, e.g., the Lebesgue dominated convergence theorem.   ■

We want

$$K^\dagger H^\dagger = (HK)^\dagger,$$

where we have suppressed the subscript measures since there is no ambiguity. By Lemma A39 above this means that for every bounded measurable $f: X \to \Re$ and $g: Y \to \Re$

$$\mu f(HK)g = \lambda g K^\dagger H^\dagger f.$$

We now work on the right hand side. Let us temporarily denote $h = H^\dagger f$. Then, noting that $\lambda = \nu K$ the right hand side is

$$RHS = (\nu K)g K^\dagger h$$

which by Lemma A39 is

$$= \nu h K g$$

Here h and Kg are functions on Y, and ν, a measure on Y, operates on their product.
Interchanging the order of multiplication, we write this as

$$= \nu(Kg)h$$

which we recall is

$$= \nu(Kg)H^\dagger f$$
$$= (\mu H)(Kg)H^\dagger f$$

which by Lemma A39 is

$$= \mu f H(Kg)$$
$$= \mu f(HK)g$$

which is the left hand side. ∎

Proof A40 (Proof of Theorem 9). If we are given $\{\pi_*, \mu, F\}$, then we let $\mathcal{I}$ be the canonical rcpd of μ given π. We let $N = F\pi_*$. We let $P = N_\mu^\dagger$. We let $R = F_\mu^\dagger$. We let $\mu' = \mu F$. We let $\mathcal{I}'$ be the canonical rcpd of μ' given π. We let $F_* = \mathcal{I}F\pi_*$. We let $R_* = \mathcal{I}'R\pi_*$. The constructions of $\mu\pi_*$ and $\mu'\pi_*$ are obvious from their names. This is a canonical construction of the BOD. We now show that each pair of opposite pointing arrows corresponds to a pair of kernels which are Bayes adjoints of each other. First, since $\mathcal{I}$ and $\mathcal{I}'$ are defined to be rcpd's of μ and μ' with respect to π, it follows from Proposition 1 that $\mathcal{I}$ and π_* are Bayes adjoints with respect to μ and that $\mathcal{I}'$ and π_* are Bayes adjoints with respect to μ'. (F, R) and (N, P) are, by definition, pairs of Bayes adjoints with respect to μ. Now $N = F\pi_*$ by definition; hence, by Theorem 7, $p = \mathcal{I}'R$. Thus the upper triangle of the BOD is consistent. By definition, $F_* = \mathcal{I}F\pi_* = \mathcal{I}N$. Also $R_* = \mathcal{I}'R\pi_*$ by Definition, and $R_* = P\pi_*$. Hence by Theorem 7, R_* is the Bayes adjoint of F_* with respect to $\mu\pi_*$. Thus all pairs of opposite arrows in the BOD correspond to Bayes adjoints (in either direction, thanks to Theorem 6). For consistency of the BOD we note that $\mu\pi_*F_* = \mu\pi_*\mathcal{I}N = \mu N$, and that $\mu N R_*\mathcal{I} = \mu N P\pi_*\mathcal{I} = \mu$ by two applications of Theorem 5. All other consistency relations follow from the Bayes adjointness of pairs of opposite arrows by Theorem 5 or by the definitions of the various kernels as the appropriate composites.

The construction of the BOD given the minimal data $\{\pi_*, \mu', R\}$ and the proof of its consistency and adjointness is similarly straightforward. ∎

Proof A41 (Proof of Theorem 10). It suffices to show that

$$\int_{B_1 \times B_2} P_1(A_1 \mid d_1) P_2(A_2 \mid d_2) \mu N(\mathrm{d}d_1, \mathrm{d}d_2)$$

$$= \int_{B_1 \times B_2} P(A_1 \times A_2 \mid d_1, d_2) \mu N(\mathrm{d}d_1, \mathrm{d}d_2), \qquad (5.69)$$

for any $B_1 \in \mathcal{D}_1$ and $B_2 \in \mathcal{D}_2$. By Definition 7 of weak coupling, the left hand side of (5.69) becomes

$$LHS = \int_{B_1} P_1(A_1 \mid d_1)\mu_1 N_1(dd_1) \int_{B_2} P_2(A_2 \mid d_2)\mu_2 N_2(dd_2)$$

which by Theorem 3 becomes

$$= \mu_1 1_{A_1} N_1(B_1)\mu_2 1_{A_2} N_2(B_2). \tag{5.70}$$

But by Theorem 3, the right hand side of (5.69) can be written

$$RHS = \mu 1_{A_1 \times A_2} N(B_1 \times B_2)$$

$$= \int_{C_1 \times C_2} \mu_1(dc_1)\mu_2(dc_2) 1_{A_1}(c_1) 1_{A_2}(c_2) N_1(c_1, B_1) N_2(c_2, B_2)$$

which by Fubini's Theorem becomes

$$= \int_{C_1} \mu_1(dc_1) 1_{A_1}(c_1) N_1(c_1, B_1) \int_{C_2} \mu_2(dc_2) 1_{A_2} N_2(c_2, B_2) \tag{5.71}$$

$$= \mu_1 1_{A_1} N_1(B_1)\mu_2 1_{A_2} N_2(B_2) \tag{5.72}$$

which equals (5.70) and we are done. ∎

References

P.N. Belhumeur, P.N. & Mumford, D. (1992). A bayesian treatment of the stereo correspondence problem using half-occluded regions. *Proceedings of the 1992 IEEE Conference on Computer Vision and Pattern Recognition,* 506–512. Los Alamitos, CA: IEEE Computer Society Press.

Bennett, B.M., Hoffman, D.D. & Prakash, C. (1989a). *Observer Mechanics: A Formal Theory of Perception.* New York: Academic Press.

Bennett, B.M., Hoffman, D.D., Nicola, J.E. & Prakash, C. (1989b). Structure from two orthographic views of rigid motion. *Journal of the Optical Society of America, A,* **6,** 1052-1069.

Bennett, B.M., Hoffman, D.D. & Prakash, C. (1993a). Theory of recognition polynomials, (in preparation).

Bennett, B.M., Hoffman, D.D. & Prakash, C. (1993b). Recognition polynomials. *Journal of the Optical Society of America, A,* **10,** 759-764.

Bennett, B.M., Hoffman, D.D. & Murthy, P. (1993). Lebesgue logic for probabilistic reasoning and some applications to perception. *Journal of Mathematical Psychology,* **37,** 1, 63-103.

Bennett, B.M., Hoffman, D.D. & Kakarala, R. (1993). Modeling performance in observer theory. *Journal of Mathematical Psychology,* **37,** 2, 220-240.

Braunstein, M.L., Hoffman, D.D., Shapiro, L., Andersen, G.J. & Bennett, B.M. (1987). Minimum points and views for the recovery of three-dimensional structure. *Journal of Experimental Psychology: Human Perception and Performance,* **13,** 335-343.

Braunstein, M.L., Hoffman, D.D. & Pollick, F. (1990). Discriminating rigid from nonrigid motion: Minimum points and views. *Perception & Psychophysics,* **47,** 3, 205-214.

Bruno, N. & Cutting, J.E. (1988). Minimodularity and the perception of layout. *Journal of Experimental Psychology: General,* **117,** 161-170.

Bülthoff, H.H. & Yuille, A. (1991). Bayesian models for seeing shapes and depth. *Comments Theoretical Biology,* **2**, 4, 283-314.

Bülthoff, H.H. (1991). Shape from X: Psychophysics and computation. In *Computational Models of Visual Processing,* ed. M.S. Landy and J.A. Movshon, pp. 305-330. Cambridge, MA: MIT Press.

Chung, K.L. (1974). *A Course in Probability Theory.* New York: Academic Press.

Clark, J.J. & Yuille, A.L. (1990). *Data Fusion for Sensory Information Processing Systems.* New York: Kluwer Academic Press.

Dosher, B.A., Sperling, G. & Wurst, S. (1986). Tradeoffs between stereopsis and proximity luminance covariance as determinants of perceived 3D structure. *Vision Research,* **26**, 973-990.

Fodor, J. (1975). *The Language of Thought.* New York: Thomas Y. Crowell.

Freeman, W.T. (1992). Exploiting the generic view assumption to estimate scene parameters. *MIT Media Lab Vision and Modeling TR-196.*

Geiger, D. & Yuille, A. (1991). A common framework for image segmentation. *International Journal of Computer Vision,* **6**, 3, 227-243.

Gelb, A. (1974). *Applied Optimal Estimation.* Cambridge, MA: MIT Press.

Geman, S. & Geman, D. (1984). Stochastic relaxation, Gibbs distribution, and the Bayesian restoration of images. *IEEE Transactions on Pattern Analysis and Machine Intelligence,* **6**, 721-741.

Green, D.M. & Swets, J.A. (1966). *Signal Detection Theory and Psychophysics.* New York: Wiley.

Grenander, U. (1981). *Abstract Inference.* New York: Wiley.

Halmos, P.R. (1950). *Measure Theory.* New York: Van Nostrand.

Hartigan, J.A. (1983). *Bayes Theory.* New York: Springer.

von Helmholtz, H. (1925). *Treatise on Physiological Optics.* New York: Dover.

Jepson, A. & Richard, W.A. (1992). What makes a good feature? *MIT AI Memo 1356.*

Knill, D.C. & Kersten, D. (1991). Ideal perceptual observers for computation, psychophysics, and neural networks. In *Pattern Recognition by Man and Machine,* ed. Roger J. Watt. Boca Raton: CRC Press.

Liter, J.C., Braunstein, M.L. & Hoffman, D.D. (1993). Inferring structure from motion in two-view and multi-view displays. *Perception,* **22**, 1441-1465.

Maloney, L.T. & Landy, M.S. (1989). A statistical framework for robust fusion of depth information. In *Visual Communications and Image Processing IV. Proceedings of the SPIE, 1199,* ed. W.A. Pearlman, pp. 1154-1163.

Marroquin, J.L. (1989). A probabilistic approach to computational vision. In *Image Understanding 1989,* ed. S. Ullman and W. Richards. Norwood, New Jersey: Ablex Publishing.

Marroquin, J.L., Mitter, S. & Poggio, T. (1987). Probabilistic solution of ill-posed problems in computational vision. *MIT AI Memo 897.*

K. Nakayama & S. Shimojo. (1992). Experiencing and perceiving visual surfaces. *Science,* 257, 1357–1363.

Papoulis, A. (1984). *Probability, Random Variables, and Stochastic Processes.* New York: McGraw-Hill.

Parthasarathy, K. (1968). *Introduction to Probability and Measure.* New Dehli: Macmillan.

Poggio, T. & Girosi, F. (1989). A theory of networks for approximation and learning. *MIT AI Memo 1140.*

Poggio, T. (1990). 3D object recognition: On a result of Basri and Ullman, *Technical Report IRST 9005-03,* MIT.

Quinton, A.M. (1965). The problem of perception. In *Perceiving, Sensing, and Knowing,* ed. R.J. Schwartz, pp. 497-526. Berkeley, Ca: University of California Press.

Savage, L.J. (1972). *The Foundations of Statistics.* New York: Dover.

Simon, B. (1979). *Functional Integration and Quantum Physics.* New York: Academic Press.

Szeliski, R. (1989). *Bayesian Modeling of Uncertainty in Low-level Vision.* Boston: Kluwer Academic.

Thompson, W.B., Lechleider, P., & Stuck, E.R. (1993). Detecting moving objects using the rigidity constraint. *IEEE PAMI,* **15**, 2, 162-166.

Tikhonov, A.N. & Arsenin, V.Y. (1977). *Solutions of Ill-Posed Problems.* Washington, D.C.: W.H. Winston.

Ullman, S. & Basri, R. (1991). Recognition by linear combinations of models, *IEEE Trans. Pattern Anal. Mach. Intelligence* **13**, 992-1006.

Witkin, A.P. (1981). Recovering surface shape and orientation from texture. *Artificial Intelligence,* **17**, 17-47.

Yuille, A.L., Geiger, D. & Bülthoff, H.H. (1991). Stereo integration, mean field theory and psychophysics. *Network,* **2**, 423-442.

Commentaries

Chapter 1:
A unifying perspective

HORACE BARLOW

The role of redundancy

On reading this very useful survey of pattern theory I was particularly struck by
Mumford's account of the four universal transformations that patterns may undergo.
These cause such a variety of changes and distortions that one doubts if it can really
be true that a single principle, redundancy reduction, leads one back to the pattern
in all these cases. But perhaps it can, for the following reason.

What is a pattern? It is some kind of regularity or self-similarity in a signal or
set of data. If there is no regularity, or no repetition caused by self-similarity, then
surely there is no pattern. But if there is such regularity or repetition, then this is a
form of redundancy, and offers the opportunity for recoding to reduce it. Of course
the pattern element can be completely arbitrary, a sequence of randomly selected
digits for example, but if repeated this element will make a pattern. Thus it seems to
me that the importance of redundancy is almost a tautology and follows simply from
the nature of patterns. However the role of redundancy in perception has certainly
evolved in my own mind since 1956, which was when I first gave a talk about the
idea (Barlow 1960), and it may be worth explaining this.

At first I was simply excited by the fact that the transformations in sensory
messages seemed to be related to their redundant features. Thus temporal adaptation
exploits the relatively slowly varying nature of most sensory messages, while lateral
inhibition exploits their slowly changing spatial properties. I was not smart enough
to predict orientational, directional, and disparity selectivity, but when these were

discovered they obviously fitted in very well. Shannon had shown that redundancy made it possible to compress information, and at first I thought that redundancy reducing codes provided an adequate advantage, because anything that simplifies the horrendously large inflow of information through the senses seemed desirable. I think this was essentially the same line of thought as Attneave (1954) and Watanabe (1960), and maybe it was similar to the much earlier ideas of Ernst Mach (1886) and Karl Pearson (1892) when they wrote about Economy of Thought. But highly compressed representations are not necessarily convenient, and there are a host of other problems with the idea in its initial form.

First, there is usually not a unique redundancy-reducing code, so which one should the brain choose? Second, to apply Shannon's ideas one must be able to attach a cost to a particular way of representing a body of data, and we still have little idea how to assess such costs for neural representations in the brain. Third, judging from the enormous number of neurons available in the cortex to carry the representation of the external world there is no compression to fit the information into a smaller channel, but rather an increase in the capacity of the representational system. Fourth, not all forms of redundancy are a hindrance: those caused by associative structure certainly are, because they interfere with the types of statistical judgement that the brain constantly has to make, but redundancy caused by unequal frequency of use of representational elements is not necessarily harmful. These are the problems, and some of them are considered in chapter 12. Redundancy is still important, because the statistical structure of sensory messages is important, but not simply because it allows compression.

The distribution of output signal amplitudes

This is an aspect of the basis functions chosen for coding that is interesting because it is a property of each individual coding element, rather than of the whole set of basis functions. The aim of a representation is, in most cases, to facilitate some scheme of categorisation. Perceptually we want to know whether a blotchy shape is a face or not, and so on for the countless other hard-to-decide elements of our perception. Now categorisation involves placing a binary boundary at some value of a continuous variable; if the variable exceeds the boundary value the scene belongs to one category, while if it lies below it does not. There is a great disadvantage in making such a category decision at an early level, for it precludes the combination at a later stage of sub-threshold evidence that would enable a better categorisation decision to be made, and I suspect this is one reason why, in most schemes, categorisation is deferred until the latest possible moment. What is found in real brains may help us to understand this issue better.

First, it is pretty clear that steps towards categorisation are taken early in sensory systems. An example of this in vision is the division into "on" and "off" systems, usually assumed to signal "lightness" , or upward deviation in contrast, and "darkness" or downward deviation in contrast. There are many equivalent preliminary categorisations in colour, and also the division into magno- and parvo- systems that correspond roughly to a fast, coarse, movement-and-temporal-change system, and a slower, finer, colour and high-spatial-frequency-luminance system. But although there is this preliminary categorisation, each of these systems continues to transmit graded signals, so that the binary categorisation is being deferred; or to put it another way, subthreshold information, including noise, is still being transmitted centrally, and this allows such information to be summated, thereby achieving greater sensitivity.

How does this relate to the amplitude distributions of sensory messages or of the coefficients of an image coding scheme? I think there is extraordinarily little information about the actual amplitude distirbutions of sensory messages under natural conditions, but it is surely worth looking at this property in artificial image analysis. If the basis functions have been chosen appropriately for subsequent categorisation, then a gaussian distribution of amplitude coefficients is the very last thing one should be looking for, because there is no natural dividing point there. Instead one should hope to find distributions that result from the addition of two parent distributions, corresponding to the two classes of external event that one wishes to separate. If the means of these two distributions are different, such a distribution would be bimodal, while if the means were the same and their variances different they would be long-tailed or kurtotic (see Field, 1993). Thus it would make sense to select basis functions or primitives that yielded such amplitude distributions, for this would facilitate subsequent categorisation. Note again that this does not depend upon other members of the set of basis functions but is a property of each individual coefficient and the statistics of the environment in which it is being used.

References

Attneave, F. (1954) Informational aspects of visual perception. Psychological Review, 61 183-193.

Barlow, H.B. (1960). The coding of sensory messages. In W. H. Thorpe & O. L. Zangwill (Eds.), Current Problems in Animal Behaviour (pp. 331-360). Cambridge: Cambridge University Press.

Field, D.J. (1994) What is the goal of sensory coding. Neural Computation, 16:559-601.

Mach, E. (1886). The Analysis of Sensations, and the Relation of the Physical to the Psychical (Translation of the 1st, revised from the 5th, German Edition by S. Waterlow). Chicago and London: Open Court (Also Dover reprint, New York 1959).

Pearson, K. (1892). The Grammar of Science. London: Walter Scott.

Watanabe, S. (1960) Information-theoretical aspects of Inductive and Deductive Inference. I.B.M. Journal of Research and Development, 4 208-231.

Pattern theory: A unifying perspective

DANIEL KERSTEN

Bayes vs. minimum description length

Mumford's definition of the "Pattern Understanding Problem" is to reconstruct the processes, objects and events that produced the patterns. Pattern Theory provides a framework for achieving this goal. Mumford discusses two means to infer the causes of patterns: by maximum a posteriori Bayesian inference and by finding the Minimum Description Length encoding (MDL). Roughly speaking, these are: seeking the most probable, and seeking the simplest, interpretation of the image data. Discovery by seeking out simple or economical descriptions is a particularly attractive proposal that Mumford deals with at some length. The idea of perceptual processes preferring simple descriptions has been around as least since the Gestaltists promoted the principle. The proposal to prefer likely interpretations has also been around in various forms for some years. Helmholtz was headed in that direction when he sought to explain some illusions in terms of processes in which sense organs seek out "reliable and consistent explanations about objects and their relationships". That the approaches of seeking out the likely, in a Bayesian sense, and the simplest in the information-theoretic sense are formally equivalent is a striking finding of information theory (e.g. Chaitin, 1975). Mumford suggests that, unlike the Bayesian approach, the Minimum Description Length principle provides a way of discovering the world priors from the data. If this turns out to be generally realizable, this would be a truly exciting discovery. However, as Mumford alludes, we may be a long way away. The example of stereopsis did illustrate that shorter descriptions corresponded to an explanation in terms of occluding surfaces. But the tough problem is how to find them. There are a number of examples of applications of MDL in computer vision (e.g. Leclerc, 1990), but they typically assume a model with no fewer a priori constraints than a Bayesian method. Bayesian inference also provides a means to evaluate evidence supporting a prior as a hypothesis, and as such MDL may provide no advantage (MacKay, 1992).

Even if the shortest program can be found, it may not tell one much about the representation of the data that the device under study has discovered. Consider the problem of being presented with a very long sequence of apparently random binary digits produced by a simple maximal length shift register circuit. This number may be most economically represented by the shortest program that could generate it. Finding this program is complicated by the fact that first and second order entropy is maximum – leaving us with the difficult practical problem of finding higher order redundancies. But even if we do succeed, there are many long programs that will generate the data sequence, but the MDL code won't discover these. These longer programs may be analogous to the representations that biological perceptual processes discover. The self- organization of simple cell receptive fields in the cortex can be related to principal components analysis (e.g. Yuille & Kammen, 1989). Here one obtains a Fourier description (assuming stationary statistics). But the particular localization in space and spatial frequency arises as a consequence of an anatomical constraint – limited dendritic spread. Wavelet decomposition is clearly useful for economical coding, but we would like to see algorithms that discover multi-scale analysis over limited spatial regions (i.e. with the right spatial bandwidths), which emerge naturally from trying to describe images concisely. Despite this criticism, I am very sympathetic with the research strategy of trying to understand perception first as a process that finds the scene causes of image data (which do comprise an economical description), and then as a process restricted by functional utility and biological limitation.

Four universal transformations

I particularly liked the four universal transformations inspired by Grenander's work. Most of us who have studied computational vision have thought about how to classify the allowable transformations from world to image, but in the restricted domain of vision, rather than pattern theory in general. It is a useful exercise to try to interpret some of the perceptual transformations studied in human vision in terms of the four fundamental transformations and their combinations. When I did this however, it wasn't always clear to me that the classification was straightforward.

For the sake of argument, consider four fundamental transformations for vision: varying viewpoint, shape, lighting, and material. Varying viewpoint and shape clearly have to do with domain warping together with interruptions when objects occlude. That seemed fine, but how does variable lighting fit in? From the work of Land, Horn and others on lightness algorithms, multi-scale superposition would be a reasonable classification. The problem with this is that human visual perception handles the separation of illumination and reflectance when they have similar spatial scales. Sharp illumination boundaries are quite common (e.g. shadows on sunny days). Reflectance and illumination do have different statistical structure, but it is often not simply characterized by differences in spatial scale. Illumination could be treated as noise to be filtered out. However, illumination variation is not necessarily noise to be discounted and thrown away; it can be useful (e.g. chapter 4).

A second example is inferring surface material when it is transparent. This transformation does fit into the idea of superposition, but here again the spatial scales for the transparent and opaque processes may be identical (Kersten, 1991). One should not really treat transparency as noise, because both surfaces are equally important and may require fairly restrictive priors. Human visual ability to handle transparency may have more to do with our ability to infer occlusion (interruptions) than our ability to discount noise. But then the domains for "interruptions" should not be mutually exclusive as they are for occlusion.

Pattern analysis cannot be done without pattern synthesis. Mumford seems to wish to elevate the theme of the section "Pattern analysis cannot be done without pattern synthesis" to a theoretical necessity rather than just a practical one. Explicitly modeling Bayesian priors can be used for supervised learning of scene from image inferences (Kersten *et al.*, 1987). However, the way in which the priors became internalized in this study was still in a feedforward mechanism. The notion that not just the theory, but also the algorithms should explicitly model the transformations and do the synthesis, is a stronger conjecture that I find attractive. But that is not really argued in a compelling way in this section. This is an interesting issue too because one often hears the argument that, at least for some tasks like entry-level recognition, the brain doesn't have time to reconstruct its current estimate of the input for comparison, which would suggest pattern analysis doesn't necessarily require pattern synthesis followed by a consistency check, at least through feedback. One way around this is to conjecture that certain lower-level inferences which are slower (e.g. subordinate-level object recognition) require feedback to do reliably.

References

Barlow, H. B. (1961). Possible principles underlying the transformation of sensory messages. In *Sensory Communication*, ed. W.A. Rosenblith. Cambridge, MA: MIT Press.

Chaitin, G. J. (1975). A theory of program size formally equivalent to information theory. *Journal of the ACM*, **22**, 329-340.

Leclerc, Y. (1990). Region grouping using the Minimum-Description-Length Principle. *DARPA Image Understanding Workshop Proceedings*, 473-479.

Kersten, D., O'Toole, A. J., Sereno, M. E., Knill, D. C., & Anderson, J. A. (1987). Associative learning of scene parameters from images. *Appl. Opt.*, **26**, 4999-5006.

Kersten, D. J. (1991). Transparency and the cooperative computation of scene attributes. In *Computational Models of Visual Processing*, eds. M. Landy and A. Movshon, (pp. 209- 228). Cambridge, MA: M.I.T. Press.

MacKay, D. J. C. (1992). Bayesian interpolation. *Neural Computation*, **4**(3), 415-447.

Yuille, A. L., Kammen, D. M., & Cohen, D. S. (1989). Quadrature and the development of orientation selective cells by Hebb rules. *Biol. Cyber.*, **61**, 183-194.

Chapter 2:
What do we mean by "The structure of the world"?

DONALD D. HOFFMAN

The first sentence of Jepson, Richards, and Knill's insightful paper reads as follows: "The world we live in is a very structured place." I wish to meditate on this sentence.

What do we mean when we speak of the "structure of the world?" In particular, what do we mean when we, as purveyors of a Bayesian approach to perception, speak of the "structure of the world?"

There is, of course, a strictly mathematical answer to this question. We can say that the structure of the world is a measure, which Bayesians call the prior, on a measurable space. It is through prior measures that the structure of the world is expressed in computations using Bayes formula.

This is surely true and interesting, but misses the real point of my question. Given this mathematical answer, the question is how shall we conceive of the world represented by a prior? Is it a world independent of the observer? Is it a world whose structure we can assess objectively and then compare, favorably or not, with the observer's perceptions? Or is it an observer-dependent world?

I think most of us would vote for a world independent of the observer. We admit this in the terminology we use. We speak of perception as "generating estimates of world properties" (Knill & Kersten, 1995) or as "recovering world properties," as though world properties are objectively out there, independent of the observer, and the task of the observer is to match its perceptions, as best it can, to these properties. Marr speaks of the senses as providing "perception of the real world outside" (Marr, 1982, p. 29). The world is out there, whether we look or not, and the goal of perception is to estimate its structure. This is a view I too have espoused, asserting once that a central problem of perception is how it remains "true to the real world" (Hoffman, 1983, p. 154).

But I now think this is mistaken, and Bayes tells us why. Perception is probabilistic inference. Observers acquire probabilistic premises and reach probabilistic conclusions. What an observer sees, and all it can ever see, are its own probabilistic conclusions. When I look at a table, the 3D shape I see is the conclusion of inferences involving stereo, motion, shading, and texture. The color I see is my conclusion. The temperature, hardness, and smoothness I feel when I touch it are conclusions of my somatosensory inferences. The sound I hear when I tap it is a conclusion of my auditory inferences. In short, the table, and all properties of it that I experience, are my conclusions. What holds for tables holds also for forks, suns, brains, and neurons. These are the products of perception, not the antecedents. In perception, as a Bayesian would put it, we perceive only our posteriors.

This is, of course, not a new idea. But it is sometimes difficult to swallow. As Crick puts it in his *Astonishing Hypothesis* (1994, p. 33), "It is difficult for many people to accept that what they see is a symbolic interpretation of the world – it all seems so like 'the real thing.' But in fact we have no direct knowledge of objects in the world."

So when, as Bayesians, we examine the "external world" to determine what priors we should use, what do we find? We find our own posteriors. And nothing else. All we can ever see in perception is our own posteriors.

Is there nevertheless an observer-independent world out there? I think so. My perceptions are so systematic (I can use group theory to predict what I'll see if I move my head) and intransigent (I can't walk through walls) that I suspect they are due, in part, to something independent of me.

But does this observer-independent world resemble what I see, hear, feel, or smell? That is more than I can know. But I suspect it does not. We all suspect it does not in the case of synesthetics. When we hear of someone who, upon tasting mint, feels as though he were grasping with his hands tall, smooth, cool, columns of glass (Cytowic, 1993) we suspect that there is no relation of resemblance between his perceptions and the observer-independent world with which he might be interacting. But why should we think that the taste of mint that *we* perceive is any more likely to resemble that observer-independent world? Russell (1912, p. 33), when considering this kind of question, argued that we could at least assume that *depth order* (say front to back) as we perceive it, resembles the true order in the observer-independent realm. But he had apparently never seen a Necker cube. The perceived order of its faces changes as we switch from one perceptual conclusion to another. We have no reason to suppose there is a concomitant change in order of an observer-independent realm. And we have no reason to suppose, in any case of perception, that what we perceive bears any resemblance to the observer-independent world.

In sum, for good Bayesian analysis we need appropriate priors (and likelihoods). But when we look we see only our posteriors. What are we to do? Well, what we in fact do is to fabricate those priors (and likelihoods) which best square with our posteriors. And we are happy when the three are finally consistent, via Bayes. Jepson, Richards, and Knill's paper is an excellent example of how to do this.

But if we think that what we are really doing is getting (perhaps through high-tech physical devices) the true properties of the observer-independent world and from these deducing the appropriate priors and likelihoods, we should think again.

References

Crick, F.H.C. (1994). *The Astonishing Hypothesis.* New York: Macmillan.

Cytowic, R.E. (1993). *The Man Who Tasted Shapes.* New York: Putnam.

Hoffman, D.D. (1983). The interpretation of visual illusions. *Scientific American*, **249**, 154-162.

Knill, D.C. & Kersten, D. (1995). Implications of a Bayesian formulation of visual information processing for psychophysics. In *Perception as Bayesian inference*, ed. W. Richards and D. Knill. Cambridge: Cambridge University Press.

Marr, D. (1982). *Vision.* San Francisco: Freeman.

Russell, B. (1912). *The Problems of Philosophy.* Oxford: Oxford University Press.

Chapter 3:
Priors, preferences and categorical percepts

ALAN YUILLE

My comments address the chapter on "Priors, Preferences and Categorical Percepts" by Richards, Jepson and Feldman. They are also relevant to the preceeding, and closely related chapter, on "Modal Structure and Reliable Inference" by Jepson, Richards and Knill. Both chapters contain interesting material which is central to the goals of this book. Most of my comments are motivated by thinking about these issues from the viewpoint of Bayesian decision theory.

I like the concept of modal priors and find it very believable. Nevertheless I think the argument in section 2 of "Modal Structure and Reliable Inference" allows an alternative interpretation. The authors discuss the problem of deciding whether an object is moving or not. They formalize this as a decision problem assuming there are two competing hypotheses – motion and non-motion. They show, using a Bayesian analysis, that this depends critically on the form of the prior assumptions and argue that the prior must contain a strong peak at zero motion. But why should the visual system consider only *two* hypotheses at this stage? Surely it is also plausible that the visual system first tries to determine the velocity of the object, using a large number of competing hypotheses (for example, motion with velocity 0, motion with velocity 1, motion with velocity 2, etc.), and only then decides whether the object is stationary (if the hypothesis "motion with velocity 0" has been chosen) or in motion (if any of the other hypotheses has been chosen). In this scenario the non-motion hypothesis competes with all the other hypotheses on a one to one basis, and will have a good chance of winning if the motion is really zero *without* needing any special help from the prior. By contrast, if there are only two hypotheses (motion and non-motion) then the non-motion hypothesis will have to compete against all the other motion possibilities combined – it will therefore be far less likely to win even if the true motion is zero. The distinction boils down to which *visual task* is the system solving when observing the object. Is it trying only to determine if this motion is stationary? If so, the two hypothesis scenario is correct. Or is it first trying to determine the motion of the object and only then decide if the motion is stationary? (Couldn't one use similar arguments to conclude that an object can never be perceived to travel at a specific speed, say 100 miles per hour? Unless there is a special node in the prior for this speed the authors would have to conclude that the object never travelled at this speed. Can one in this theory, therefore, only determine properties at the modes? This seems okay if one is making discrete decisions, like identifying objects, but would not seem suitable for estimating continuous quantities like speeds. I assume the authors are chiefly concerned with discrete (hence inferential) decisions.)

This argument can be generalized to the other examples of visual inference considered in both chapters. Their way of defining key features is attractive and yet the definition of a key feature F for a property P depends on considering only two hypotheses P and not-P. How would the authors' conclusions about such features, and their prior probabilities, be altered if they considered a larger set of competing feature and property hypotheses, as in the previous paragraph? The issue again would be not how probable the property would be in absolute terms given the presence of the feature but whether it would be more probable than the other features which might be present. Or alternatively, consider a more complex system where key features might interact. For example, a Bayes' net where an observation (which we might think of as a key feature), by itself, may be a clue for a certain event but this clue may be explained away by a second observation. Pearl's book ("Probabilistic Reasoning in Intelligent Systems" J. Pearl. 1988) gives several examples of this type.

"Priors, Preferences and Categorical Percepts" discusses the critical problem of what is a percept. I am curious about the connections, if any, to the ideas on competitive priors discussed in my chapter with Heinrich Bülthoff. From our perspective (or indeed from standard Decision theory) one would attempt to solve problems like pillbox identification, figure 1, by having a set of competing models which would include parameters for the viewpoint, orientation of the handle, etc. One would evaluate the best fit of each model to the data, after adjusting model parameters, using a loss function which would penalize for unusual views (see Freeman's chapter and section (4) of our chapter) and then use a decision rule to select the best model, possibly including a measure of confidence in the choice. It is not clear, a priori, how to specify the loss functions and prior probabilities required by this approach.

By contrast the authors suggest that there is natural, or "vivid", representation system for objects. This leads to the concept of a structured lattice which enumerates the possible structural categories. Preference relations, which are context dependent, determine preferences for interpretation and can be thought of as giving prior probabilities on the structures that are expected to exist in the assumed context. They therefore give a way of formalizing the intuitive notion that one should prefer simple explanations to complicated ones. It is not clear to me how practical it is to construct such lattices in general, but it is an interesting approach and does seem plausible on the examples described in the chapter. If it can be generalized it would avoid the problem, mentioned above, of specifying priors for the possible interpretations.

I am curious about the possibility of formulating these ideas in terms of decision theory. Instead of having highly peaked priors couldn't one instead use a discrete class of decisions, hypotheses, and appropriate loss functions? To what extent would these be distinguishable? One intriguing example is if the human visual system used different loss functions for the same input when attempting different visual tasks. There are intriguing reports (Goodale – personal communication) of situations where perceptual judgements of the size and orientations of objects are incorrect but actions, such as positioning the hand to grasp the object, are carried out correctly. This might be an example where different loss functions are used, by different parts of the brain, for different tasks.

Chapter 4:
Veridicality, utility, and completeness in vision modelling

DANIEL KERSTEN

Alan Yuille and Heinrich Bülthoff's chapter deals with several fundamental issues in vision modeling. For the sake of discussion, consider the following three tensions: veridicality, utility, and completeness. Veridicality asks: how precise should the estimate of a scene parameter be? Utility asks: is the estimate useful for a specific function, such as grasping something with the hand? Completeness asks: how many scene parameters should be estimated together? Veridicality and completeness have to do with the problem of seeking out the causes of the image data. These three tensions manifest themselves in many forms. Completeness is related to questions of modularity – when is it permissible to estimate a scene parameter in isolation from other visual information? And when does it have to be done "cooperatively"? Yuille and Bülthoff very nicely illustrate how the need for strong coupling may arise when scene parameters cannot be estimated in isolation – more complete reconstruction may be needed to get good estimates of some parameters. For example, it may be important to estimate the shape, in order to get the lightness right (see chapters 6, 10 and 11). Decisions about whether to ignore certain aspects of the scene, and do partial reconstruction, are related to what information is useful.

Consider two extremes: complete veridical reconstruction; and, incomplete, approximate, but useful estimates of scene parameters. These two views are often treated as opposing. We have good examples of biological systems making judicious approximations that are not veridical, but work (e.g. Lee & Reddish 1981), and developing specialized perceptual subsystems (e.g. Goodale & Milner, 1992). The trend in computer vision towards purposive vision is also consistent with an emphasis on short-cuts and utility over accurate and complete reconstruction. Yet one is impressed with the phenomenal completeness of the perceived world and with the seemingly unlimited number of visual decisions and plans an observer can potentially make, based on a few glances. The notion of complete reconstruction is closely related to the idea of perception as building a model of the world upon which one plans and subsequently acts (Craik, 1943). A more complete reconstruction is presumed to render greater versatility in the utilization of visual information. What is particularly nice about Yuille and Bülthoff's introduction of Bayesian Decision Theory (BDT) to vision modeling is that it provides a unified framework for dealing with veridicality and utility. Yuille and Büelthoff's analysis of Freeman's genericity results (chapter 9) in terms of risk is a good example of task dependency and BDT. This analysis seems to be on the right track – the precise estimation of light source direction is probably not necessary for most tasks. The task dependency of viewpoint also seems reasonable – estimating viewpoint is important for grasping, but not for naming objects. The cost to BDT is that it introduces more parameters to a model. But one can think up ways of measuring directly and indirectly the precision of human perceptual decisions for these various scene parameters.

A second application of BDT, in which the goal was to selective one of several competing priors, was not as clearly a case of utility. For example, Yuille and Bülthoff show that a risk function can be used for deciding between the competing priors of flat vs. specular surface material in order to estimate shape. Decision theory does provide the mathematical tools for choosing between the two priors, but how does one independently assess whether it is more or less, or just as costly to mistake a specular surface for a flat shaded one? Imagine having two observers who are both required to make the shape estimates, given the same image. The first makes estimates incorporating utility constraints on value – namely, it lives in a context in which specular objects are more valuable than flat-shaded objects. That doesn't mean the observer should estimate the shape of flat shaded objects using a model for specular ones. Further, suppose that the second observer assumes specular objects are more common. It seems possible that the second observer could make the same or similar shape estimates as the first, but for a different reason – because specular objects are more common. One can't distinguish which model is right in the laboratory – they give the same answers. Utility and frequency are intimately tied to the ecological and social context.

So to decide between competing priors, what is the alternative to BDT? One answer is that priors themselves can be treated as hypotheses. This is related to the view of modern Bayesian inference as a formalization of Occam's razor (MacKay, 1992). The idea is that one should prefer the model that can account for the data with the fewest parameters (see Mumford's discussion of the relation between Bayesian and Minimum Description Length approaches). From a Bayesian perspective, the idea is simple. Consider the conditional probability of the image data over hypotheses 1 and 2, corresponding to priors 1 and 2 (e.g. specular and flat). For the sake of concreteness, picture the distributions as unimodal and unidimensional over the data. Because these distributions are normalized, if the first hypothesis is more complex (i.e. has more parameters), crudely speaking, there is a bigger domain over which to spread out the probability. So if the data fall within the domain of the second hypothesis, that hypothesis (i.e. prior) is to be preferred to the first. In the absence of ways to test assumptions about risk, it seems that Occam's razor should be applied to avoid introducing too many parameters.

References

Craik, K.J.W. (1943). *The Nature of Explanation*. Cambridge: Cambridge University Press.

Goodale, M.A., & Milner, D.A. (1992). Separate visual pathways for perception and action. *Trends in Neuroscience*, **15**(1), 20-25.

Lee, D. & Reddish, ?. (1981). Plummeting gannets: a paradigm of ecological optics. *Nature*, **293**(5830), 293-294.

MacKay, D.J.C. (1992). Bayesian interpolation. *Neural Computation*, **4**(3), 415-447.

Chapter 5:
Priors by design

WHITMAN RICHARDS

A claim

My claim is that events become meaningful only when incorporated into a cognitive framework. By framework, I mean some structure that holds knowledge available to the user. A colloquial version of the claim is the expression "to put something into its pigeon-hole". The context would correspond to the structure housing the pigeon-holes. Placing the new fact into one of the holes would correspond to assimilating that event into one's framework for knowledge.

This claim does not prohibit the storing of arbitrary events in a memory. Rather, the insistence is that for such events to be other than meaningless facts, they must be seen as part of a greater design, if you will. The jigsaw puzzle serves as a useful analogy. Each individual piece possesses properties that we note: a curved edge, a splotch of color or texture. But until we begin to visualize the scene, the piece has limited meaning in isolation, – i.e. it is simply one piece of a particular puzzle. Any adequate measure of meaning must anticipate its dependence upon context.

The obvious impact of the claim is that the design of our cognitive frameworks – these houses of "pigeon-holes" if you will – lies at the heart of meaningful perception (and also learning!) This aspect of perception is hardly addressed at all in any of the chapters (including my own!) Instead, much of the focus is on what one might call "inverse optics": using image events to recover facts about world behaviors and properties . The missing part, then, is understanding what makes such world facts meaningful.

If the target of perception is to construct meaningful models of the world, not just to collect facts, then we must consider the nature of the interplay between world structure and our cognitive frameworks for meaningful models. Clearly our cognitive models can not be isomorphic to the grand design that underlies Mother Nature's reality. Hence any meaningful conclusion about the world inferred from our sense data is simply one particular way of assimilating a putative fact into a personal framework that is somewhat arbitrary from Mother Nature's point of view. For example, the scale of space-time may vary drastically between different observers, each of which provides only a small window to the space-time expanse of Mother Nature. The conceptualization of the world held by any observer, then, might be seen in a simple manner as lying intermediate between Mother Nature's grand design and the special world facts inferred from that observer's sense data. These cognitive conceptualizations, or frameworks, act as a sieve or filter of the Grand Design that underlies the behavior of the natural world. Hence they are severely restricted and simple conceptualizations of limited scope.

Priors and probablities

The chapter by Bennett *et al.* probably provides one of the richest and most comprehensive analysis of the details that must be considered if an image event Y is to assert the world event X. But the emphasis is primarily on the probablistic structure linking image events and world events. Certainly there will be uncertainties in our assessment of image facts from which we deduce or infer world facts – not just from noise, but more critically, as the authors recognize, from the reduced dimensionality that arises from the mapping or world events to image events. However, similarly, there will be a different set of uncertainties associated with how closely any chosen model for a world fact indeed matches Mother Nature's model. Capturing these differences seems to me quite difficult; it requires placing measures on knowledge which may not be explicit rule-based "knowing", for example. (The assertion "I know this" can be indeed clearly true, but with no clear explanation for the truth.) Furthermore, if one believes that the range of possible, meaningful cognitive models is limited by the capabilties of our own mental machinery, then this limitation also must be included in our framework that relates how image events are related to (Mother Nature's) world events. It is not enough simply to give these latter limitations a probabalistic structure and then to incorporate them into theoretical frameworks (of Man and Nature) in like manner. We must know specifically just how the structure of our cognitive models (and their underlying assumptions) force particular conclusions about the world. Just as one set of axioms in geometry lead to a special set of conclusions, so will particular cognitive structures lead to particular world descriptions. A law of nature is simply a convenient summary of what we observe, expressed in a framework that makes sense to us. Our cognitive structures, then, dictate to some degree the form of these laws or regularities that we comprehend. If you will, some priors are set by design – by the form of our representations that accommodate lawful knowledge (Eddington, 1939).

A second claim

Meaningful knowledge is confirmed and augmented by design. By this claim I mean that the actual act of designing and building something – a house, an atomic bomb, a new species – is an important confirmation of our knowledge. Such acts of design that can not be shared with others either by construction or communication may simply be unrealistic flights of fancy. The sharing of the knowledge intrinsic to the design reaffirms the cognitive structure that created it. The architect's plan has meaning for designers who conceive buildings. The contractor looks at these plans, and sees a quite different meaning. The architect presumably understands the contractors needs, but at the same time, she has a mental model for the experience of living in the planned house. It is this mental model of design that is confirmed (or not) after the home has been built and one walks through the space. With every such construction (virtual or otherwise), the architect's knowedge is tested.

Cognitive artifacts

The architect, then, might be seen as playing the role of Mother Nature, and the contractor the role of the process that actually constructs new objects, events and things in the world. The presence of the new object, in itself, can augment one's view of the world, changing a host of cognitive frameworks – sometimes in very surprising ways. For example, presumably the architect's grand plan (but not the details) is communicated to the new owner, who has little knowledge of the location of the studs, the electrical wires, etc. The shared, meaningful link between the occupant and the architect is thus principally the living anticipated by and experienced within the layout. To the degree that the new owner adds furniture, paintings, etc. that reinforce the architect's design, the stronger the link. Thus, this process is very analogous to meaningful linguistic communication. The assignment of a probabalistic structure to the architect's plan, to a grammar, to the creation of a new device, to the storyteller's story, seems to me an act that strips away the meaning. It is the design and the experience of the resultant artifact that really matters. These aspects of perception, namely the design and the creation of meaningful cognitive structures, receive little discussion thoughout the book. Yet such structures (and artifacts) seem critical to understanding just what the perceptual act encompasses. Probabilties can not capture the meaning of design nor of the artifacts that they lead to (natural or man-made).

Hence what I seek is a theory of the structure of knowledge – perhaps the categorical structure of our chosen priors, if you will. In terms of Bennett *et al.*, this is the *structure* of the interpretation kernal, not simply its probablity measure. At present, only small steps have been taken toward such constructive theories (Shepard, 1994; Feldman, 1992; Mann & Jepson 1993; Moray, 1990; Talmy, 1988; Richards & Koenderink, 1993).

References

Eddington, A. (1939). *Nature of Physical World*, Oxford University Press.

Bennett, B., Hoffman, D. and Prakash, C. (1992). *Observer Mechanics*. New York: Academic Press.

Feldman, J. (1992). Perceptual categories and world regularities. Ph.D. thesis, Department of Brain & Cognitive Sciences, Massachusetts Institute of Technology.

Mann, R. and Jepson, A. (1993). Non-accidental features in learning, in *Machine Learning in Computer Vision: What, Why, How?*, ed. K. Bowyer and L. Hall, AAAI Press, Raleigh, NC.

Moray, N. (1990). A lattice theory appraoch to the structure of mental modes. *Phil. Trans. Roy. Soc. Lond. B*, **327**: 577-583.

Richards, W. & Koenderink, J.J. (1993). Trajectory Mapping ("TM"): A new non-metric scaling technique. MIT Center for Cognitive Science Occasional Paper #48.

Shepard, R. (1994). Perceptual-cognitive universals as reflections of the world. *Psychonomic Bulletin*, **1**, 2-28.

Talmy, L. (1988). Force dynamics in language and cognition. *Cog. Science*, **12**: 49-100.

A biased view of perceivers

ALAN JEPSON & JACOB FELDMAN

Observers and theorists

The target chapter introduces the notion of an observer as an entity which applies a given Bayesian theory to the task of inferring world properties from sense data. In fact, most of this volume is concerned with observers in one form or another. The basic idea is that the perceptual system uses a model of the current world context, that is, a 'domain theory,' to reduce the ambiguity inherent in the sense data and to select particular interpretations for the state of the world. Example domain theories are: the qualitative probabilistic models used for the motion of a ball in a box in Chapter 2; the preference based scheme for the interpretation of handle shape and orientation discussed in Chapter 3; the Bayesian models for shape from texture and shading used in Chapter 7; and the cost function formulation proposed for the interpretation of shape, illumination, and pigmentation in Chapter 11. In order to include such alternative forms of world models we use the term 'observer' to refer loosely to any entity which applies a *fixed* domain theory to the task of inferring world properties from sensory data.

Our bias is to view the perceptual system as a theorist in its own right, not just an observer. We claim that in order to understand perception we need to understand the way this theorist works, that is: how it selects a theory for a new domain, how it applies a theory to choose particular interpretations for sense data, how it compares different theories, and how it revises and learns theories under the influence of new information. In contrast an observer is concerned with only one of these aspects, namely how a fixed theory is applied.

The distinction between theorist and observer is perhaps blurred by notions such as Yuille's competitive priors (see Chapter 4). Each prior may lead to a single distinct (Bayesian) observer, and the selection of one prior in favor of others can be thought of as a theory selection process. Thus the overall system can be thought of as a theorist. On the other hand, the same sort of process can be captured in a composite model for which the selection of the appropriate prior for a new piece of data is dictated by a new model parameter, a so called 'hyper- parameter.' Thus the system can be also be thought of as an observer. Which one is it? We choose to resolve this issue on pragmatic grounds, deciding in favor of a theorist so long as there is interesting structure within the world model that can be understood in terms of theory selection, revision, comparison, and/or learning; these are just the characteristic tasks of a theorist beyond those of an observer. We would thus consider a system using Yuille's competitive priors, with a well specified means of selecting which prior to use, as a theorist, though it may be a particularly simple form of theorist with only a small set of built-in theories to choose from. Our belief is that the perceptual system is a much more sophisticated theorist than this (see Section below, 'Defining the perceptual theorist'), and therefore the appropriate categorization of such borderline cases is not critical to our argument.

We note in passing that Observer Theory, as it is formulated in the target chapter, has a role to play within many theorists. In particular, if a theorist is to consider Bayesian domain theories then, in order to apply a particular domain theory, the theorist must be able to derive (at least some of) the consequences of the candidate theory. A specific example is the ball-in-a-box model discussed in Chapter 2. There one needs to evaluate the posterior probability of various interpretations, given a prior in the form of a (qualitative) mixture model, complete with Dirac measures. This ability to derive properties of the posterior distribution when the prior probability is a general measure, and the observations are measurable sets, is precisely the domain of Observer Theory. As such, we believe that Observer Theory represents an important part of any rigorous mathematical theory of perception. However, as we explain below, our central point in this commentary is that Observer Theory does not encompass the additional structure of a theorist, and thus it is not sufficient on its own to account for perception.

An indication of the sort of phenomena we are attempting to explain, and which go beyond the scope of Observer Theory, is given by Feldman's experiment (1992). This experiment indicates that humans are capable of generating a novel domain theory from just a single example. In order for a theorist to be able to do this, it must have strong a priori constraints on the forms of theories it will entertain. That is, the system must be sufficiently biased so that, given only a handful of examples, a preferred domain theory can be selected from the set of all possible theories that the system can express. The critical element here is this bias, which can involve restricting the set of concepts the theorist can use, restricting the language for expressing theories, and/or applying a priori preferences for some theories over others (Mitchell, 1980). It is primarily these components which determine how a theorist will revise old domain theories and learn new ones. This is illustrated with a concrete example in the section below, 'Defining the perceptual theorist', but first, as motivation, we consider an alternative hypothesis for the structure of our perceptual systems which is along the lines of Observer Theory.

The homunculus observer

In stark contrast to our proposal for viewing perception as a process of both theory formation and application, one might instead attempt to consider the whole of the perceptual system as just a single observer (as defined in the target chapter). In particular, the transduced stimulus could be taken as the input premises, with the posterior probability distribution for the scene provided over the conclusion space. The capacity for storing and processing information within an Observer Theory framework would not be strained, nor would it be strained if we considered instead the entire past history of stimuli as a possible input space. The basic structural restrictions of an observer, namely that the prior be a positive measure and that various mappings are measurable, easily encompass such a formulation. In other words, Bennett and his coauthors could simply absorb the structure of our proposed perceptual theorist, and therefore presumably the homunculus, into one enormous observer. Let us refer to such an observer as the *homunculus observer*. The critical question is: what, if anything, would be lost in such a change to an observer framework?

Many of the structural elements of our perceiver/theorist would be lost within a homunculus observer formulation. One loss is the ability to make certain assumptions conditional on the *solutions* of other problems that the system may pose. For example, if it can be shown that the ball in Chapter 4 could be stably supported, then one could assume there was a mode for the ball to be at rest. To determine stable support one can check if a particular linear programming problem has a solution (Blum *et al.*, 1970). Such a notion of stable support would constitute a theory fragment in our proposed perceptual theorist. But what would this look like for the homunculus observer? Without a decomposition of this observer, the notion of stable support would show up as structure within the prior distribution μ. Here the prior distribution μ is over all possible scenes (not just all possible scenes for a given image, but *all* possible scenes). For scenes in which an object is being stably supported by another, an omniscient onlooker might notice the regularity that there is also a mode within μ for that object to be at rest. Essentially, the homunculus observer might as well be 'doing the stability test' by table look-up in a table of all possible scenes, a table that might well be infinite. Our point here is simply that some regularities within our world are most efficiently represented in terms of whether or not a particular set of constraints has a solution (or by the character of that solution), and that there may not be a convenient bottom-up way to describe the same regularity.

However, we believe the critical loss is that, without further constraints, the homunculus observer would be unable to learn from visual experience or, equivalently, to draw inductive generalizations from examples. By "learning" here we mean not only the development of new domain theories over a lifetime of observations, but also the generation of new inductive hypotheses during the interpretation of a single scene. The argument is that, in order to learn, the homunculus observer needs to adjust its prior, μ, on the basis of visual data. However, during the course of its lifetime, due to the bandlimited nature of its transducers, it would receive data confined essentially to a finite dimensional set. Given that the prior μ is restricted only to be a probability measure on some infinite dimensional set encompassing all possible scenes, such observational data would provide an insignificant constraint on the choice of μ. The problem in essence is that the perceiver must choose from an infinite space of possible hypotheses on the basis of a data set which is invariably finite (and potentially quite small). Something extra would be needed to bias the homunculus observer to generalize appropriately, for example, from a finite number of samples of stably supported objects to a more general notion of stable support. Thus, one of the primary motivations for considering a perceptual system to be a theorist in its own right is to have it naturally incorporate useful biases for rapid and efficient learning (Feldman, 1992; Mann & Jepson; Mitchell, 1980).

Once the view of the perceptual system as a theorist is taken, then, the critical research questions are what is the overall form of the theories and what are the constraints or biases on the set of available theories. Are there useful general-purpose constraints and biases on the overall form of domain theories such that the theorist can rapidly adapt and learn useful theories about its world? This question can be studied two ways. The first is to study the structure in our world, with the goal being to capture useful world models within a narrowly defined set of domain theories. The second aspect is to study biological perceivers with regards to what sort of domain theories they rapidly learn. We discuss these two aspects in the following two sections.

Defining the perceptual theorist

In order for the notion of the perceptual theorist to be valuable it must be the case that our world is sufficiently structured so that some fairly general purpose biases on the set of available theories are both useful and applicable. Our critique of the homunculus observer rests on just such an assumption about world structure. It is therefore critical to our argument that we indicate that there may indeed be ways to provide suitable general purpose biases. To do this we briefly discuss some recent results on one way in which effective biases might be built into a perceiver/theorist, namely by constraining the very form of the conceptualization, along with the forms of the domain theories to be considered.

The basic idea is that the perceiver/theorist includes a built-in bias for mechanically building domain theories (i.e., world models) in terms of a particular set of categories, which we refer to as the 'latent categorization.' The critical point is that not *all* possible categories are in this latent set, and thus not all subsets can be entertained as hypotheses by the perceiver/theorist. Rather, only certain ones are selected according to this built-in bias. Moreover, we assume that the perceiver/theorist can form qualitative probabilistic domain theories of the general form considered in Chapter 2, but with the constraint that each mode in the prior distribution must

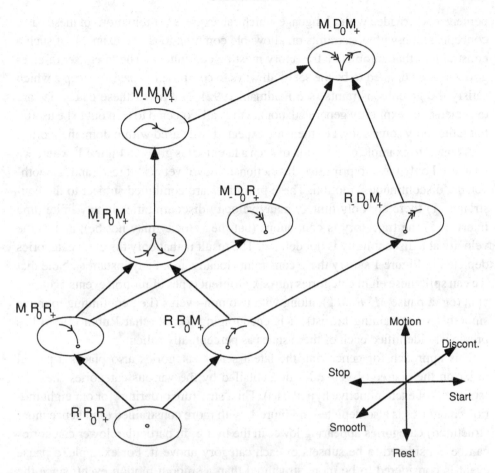

Fig. 5.1 The structure ordering for the motion categories arising from the basic distinctions 'move' versus 'at-rest,' and 'smooth' versus 'discontinuous' motion. Here τ_- and τ_+ are two consecutive open temporal intervals separated by the instant t_0. The notation M_0, R_0, D_0 denote smooth motion, at rest, and a velocity discontinuity, respectively, at the instant t_0. Similarly, the subscripts '$-$' and '$+$' refer to τ_- and τ_+ in place of t_0.

correspond to some category within the latent set. Therefore this specification corresponds to a required reduction in inductive ambiguity and, as we discuss below, makes effective learning and hypothesis formation possible.

For a specific example consider the ball-in-a-box domain described in Chapter 2. An appropriate latent categorization can be constructed from the elementary concepts of smooth motion, being at rest within a ground-based reference frame, abrupt changes in velocity, contact relations between parts or objects, surface normals and the direction of gravity. The idea is that some representation of these basic concepts is built into our novice perceiver, or at least is available at the stage of development in which the perceiver is ready to learn the required models. Moreover, we assume the perceiver is provided with a language which can express combinations of these basic concepts along with constraints on allowable combinations. An example of such a constraint is that an object's trajectory must be continuous. The latent set of categories is then defined to be the set of all ways to compose the basic concepts which satisfy the given constraints (see Feldman, 1992). Not all of these categories are expected to be explicitly generated, nor are they all expected to turn out to be useful, but rather only some subset of them are expected to be used within domain theories.

A concrete example of a portion of such a latent set is given in Figure 1, where we have used only the two primitive distinctions: 'move' versus 'at rest,' and 'smooth' versus 'discontinuous' motion. These primitives are combined subject to the constraints: 1) there are only finitely many velocity discontinuities in any finite time interval; 2) the trajectory is continuous (but the velocity may not be); and 3) the velocity at a discontinuity is not defined. The result is that only the eight categories depicted in Figure 1 satisfy these constraints locally about any instant t_0. Note that we can split these eight categories into six different types of motion events occuring at t_0 (eg. a pause $M_-R_0M_+$), along with two non-events (i.e., continuing to move smoothly or remaining at rest). It is encouraging to note that Rubin (1986) has previously identified each of these states as perceptually salient.

This approach for generating the latent set of categories also places a partial order on the degree of generalization entailed by the various categories (i.e., the 'strength' of each inductive hypothesis). This 'structure ordering' for our eight motion categories is also depicted in Figure 1, with more constrained (and hence more structured) categories appearing lower in the figure. In particular, lower categories can be considered to be subsets of each category above it. For example, a pause event is considered to be more structured than a smooth motion event, since the pause event has the additional constraint that the velocity must be zero at t_0. Similarly, trajectories which have a velocity discontinuity at t_0 (but are smooth in some adjacent open intervals $\tau_\pm$) are the least structured events across t_0, while staying at rest across t_0 is the most structured event.

This latent set and structure ordering can function as an important bias in theory formation. Such a bias can arise, for example, by constraining the available domain theories to take the form of qualitative mixture models where *each mode corresponds to one category* within the latent categorization. Indeed, to take a specific case, the motion of a ball in the air is described by only one of the eight categories in Figure 1, namely the smooth motion era. The appropriate mixture model therefore involves a single component containing only the mode for smooth motion, as desired. Alternatively, consider a model for the motion of a house-fly. We assume our perceptual system cannot distinguish the sharp turns of a fly from a velocity discontinuity. As a result, the motion can be represented with two modes in a qualitative probability distribution, one for smooth motion and one for velocity discontinuities. This simple characterization provides a lot of information about the motion of a fly, namely they do not typically hover, stop, or start while in mid air. Moreover, the basic idea of selecting particular categories and treating them as modes in the qualitative prior distribution also naturally leads to the hypothesis that the discontinuities in a fly's motion appear in some smooth (but unknown) distribution over free space and over time. Such a hypothesis can be uniquely selected given just a single observation of a fly executing an apparent velocity discontinuity in mid-air!

Our proposed constraint on the domain theories, namely that the various modes must be specified in terms of particular categories within the latent set, limits the theorist to a discrete finite set of domain theories. This therefore represents an extremely strong bias on the prior distributions that are to be considered, which we argued above is essential for rapidly learning and revising domain theories. Indeed, because of this bias we conjecture that it is possible, for example, for a novice perceiver constructed along these lines to rapidly learn the modal structure of the ball-in-a-box theory presented in Chapter 2.

Perceptual theorists and psychophysics

Finally, we note that such specific models of theory formation by the perceiver/theorist, as sketched in the previous section, can be used to generate extremely specific predictions for psychophysical experiments. Following the arguments above, such predictions might be generated most readily with respect to how human observers draw inductive generalizations about novel domains. That is, we need to give the perceiver/theorist a task which exercises it's capabilities for learning or revising theories. In fact, a set of such experiments has already been carried out (see Feldman. 1992). The results strongly indicate that human observers can infer the sort of mixture model described above, given just one example. Admittedly this is just a single experiment but, given our biased view of perceivers as entities which build and manipulate qualitative probabilistic theories, we are confident that the reader can make a reliable inference about the nature of perception from just this single example.

References

Blum, M., Griffith, A., & Neumann, B. (1970). A stability test for configurations of blocks. MIT AI Lab. memo 188.

Feldman, J. (1992). Perceptual categories and world regularities. Ph.D. thesis, M.I.T. Dept. Brain & Cognitive Sciences.

Mann, R. & Jepson, A. (1993). Non accidental features in learning, in *Machine Learning in Computer Vision: What, Why, How?*, ed. K. Bowyer and L. Hall. Raleigh, NC: AAAI Press.

Mitchell, T.M. (1980). The need for biases in learning generalizations, Rutgers University Tech. Rep. CBM-TR, 117.

Rubin, J. (1986). Categories of visual motion, Ph.D. thesis, M.I.T. Dept. Brain and Cognitive Sciences.

Part two

Implications and applications

6

Implications of a Bayesian formulation of visual information for processing for psychophysics

DAVID. C. KNILL

Department of Psychology, University of Pennsylvania

DANIEL KERSTEN

Department of Psychology, University of Minnesota

PASCAL MAMASSIAN

Department of Psychology, University of Minnesota

6.1 Introduction

The previous chapters have demonstrated the many ways one can use a Bayesian formulation for computationally modeling perceptual problems. In this chapter, we look at the implications of a Bayesian view of visual information processing for investigating human visual perception. We will attempt to outline the elements of a general program of empirical research which results from taking the Bayesian formulation seriously as a framework for characterizing human perceptual inference. A major advantage of following such a program is that it supports a strong integration of psychophysics and computational theory, since its structure is the same as that of the Bayesian framework for computational modeling. In particular, it provides the foundation for a *psychophysics of constraints*, used to test hypotheses about the quantitative and qualitative constraints used in human perceptual inferences. The Bayesian approach also suggests new ways to conceptualize the general problem of perception and to decompose it into isolatable parts for psychophysical investigation. Thus, it not only provides a framework for modeling solutions to specific perceptual problems; it also guides the definition of the problems.

The chapter is organized into four major sections. In the next section, we develop a framework for characterizing human perception in Bayesian terms and analyze its implications for studying human perceptual performance. The third and fourth sections of the chapter apply the framework to two specific problems: the perception of 3-D shape from surface contours and the perception of 3-D object motion from cast shadow motion. In the fifth section, we compare and contrast the Bayesian approach with other popular approaches within perceptual psychology. We close with a brief discussion of some of the issues which we think Bayesian theories will be faced with as they are applied more generally to problems in visual perception.

6.2 From Bayesian theories to psychophysics

6.2.1 *The Bayesian formulation of information*

Two ideas are central to the Bayesian approach to modeling perception. The first is that one can characterize the information provided by a set of image data about the world in the form of a conditional probability distribution, $p(\mathbf{S} \mid \mathbf{I})$, where $\mathbf{S}$ represents properties of the world, and $\mathbf{I}$ represents the image data (see introductory tutorial for a detailed discussion of this point). The spread of the so-called posterior distribution over the space of possible values of $\mathbf{S}$ roughly corresponds to the reliability of the information provided by a given set of image data about the world[†]. Broad distributions reflect unreliable information, while highly peaked distributions reflect reliable information. The second central idea is expressed by Bayes' rule, which allows us to write the conditional distribution $p(\mathbf{S} \mid \mathbf{I})$ as the normalized product of a likelihood function, $p(\mathbf{I} \mid \mathbf{S})$, and a prior probability distribution, $p(\mathbf{S})$:

$$p(\mathbf{S} \mid \mathbf{I}) = \frac{p(\mathbf{I} \mid \mathbf{S})\,p(\mathbf{S})}{p(\mathbf{I})}, \tag{6.1}$$

where, for most practical purposes, we may consider the denominator $p(\mathbf{I})$ to be a normalizing constant.

The strength of the approach is that it provides a formal means to integrate knowledge about the structure of the world (represented by the prior) with knowledge about how images of the world are formed (represented by the likelihood function) into a specification of the information provided by image data about the world. In other words, it shows how to decompose image information into its two constituent parts: regularities in the properties of the world and how those properties are coded in images[‡].

For an engineer building an artificial vision system, modeling the posterior, $p(\mathbf{S} \mid \mathbf{I})$, is the logical precursor to designing the system. The formulation of the likelihood function and the prior which together specify the posterior distribution amounts to a formal specification of a computational theory (in Marr's sense of the term (Marr, 1982)) for the problems which the system will have to solve. Clearly, such an analysis is also useful for understanding human vision, since a formal char-

---

[†] The spread of a continuous distribution is dependent on the representation; thus, strictly speaking, reliability can only be defined relative to a particular task; for example, estimating surface depth (as opposed to, say, surface curvature).

[‡] Technically speaking, the likelihood function does have incorporated in it prior knowledge about the world. Examples include the geometric laws of perspective projection and the physical laws of light reflection. Often, the prior knowledge built into the likelihood function is "hard" rather than probabilistic, thus it more naturally falls under the purview of the likelihood function than the prior distribution. Sometimes, of course, it actually incorporates probabilistic laws; for example, in the statistical work on shape from texture, prior knowledge about the structure of surface textures is built into the likelihood function. We refer to this form of prior knowledge as "hidden" priors and emphasize the importance of making them explicit in the formulation of the likelihood function.

acterization of the problems posed to the human visual system is an integral part of any understanding of perception (a point emphasized by both Gibson (1950, 1979) and Marr (1982)). The major thesis of this chapter is the extension of the Bayesian approach beyond modeling information to actually modeling human perception by using it to build computational theories of how the human visual system actually solves the perceptual problems it faces. We will argue that it is the joint application of the Bayesian framework to both aspects of visual information processing which makes it so useful for the study of human perception.

6.2.2 The Bayesian formulation of perceptual inference: Ideal observers and ideal worlds

The Bayesian approach to human perception rests on the view of perception as a process of probabilistic inference[†], which naturally leads one to formally model perception within a Bayesian framework. A major advantage of this approach to perception is that it provides a bridge between models of what's in the world and the information about it which is contained in images, and models of what's in a perceiver's head. The first step across this bridge is to specify image information in a form that takes into account the perceptual tasks performed by humans. We do this using the concept of an *ideal observer*.

An ideal observer makes perfect use of the information available to it to make inferences about the world (Kersten, 1990; Knill & Kersten, 1991) or to perform tasks based on this information (e.g. motor control). For simplicity, we will consider tasks which can be characterized as explicitly estimating some world property (e.g. surface shape). An ideal observer for this task is one which estimates the chosen world property as well as possible, given some image data, in the sense that it minimizes a specified average error or cost criterion. (This approach is also used in the following chapter 7 by Blake *et al.* and has been discussed previously by Yuille and Bülthoff in chapter 4.) Built into an ideal observer is complete knowledge of the prior structure of the world properties it is inferring and of the image formation process which maps those properties to the image data available to the observer. A specification of the image data, what world properties the observer attempts to infer, the prior structure of those properties and the likelihood function derived from the image formation process comprise the computational theory of the ideal observer's inference process (see figure 6.1). Predictions about the ideal observer's inferences, such as how reliable they are, can then be made by plugging these elements into an idealized Bayesian inference engine, which estimates scene variables based on a

---

† Probabilistic inference is more general than strict deductive inference, for which the premises logically determine the conclusions. In perception, the premises (the image data) do not uniquely determine the conclusions (percepts of world properties); thus, perceptual inferences are statistically based "guesses".

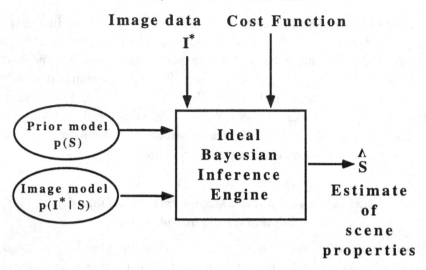

Fig. 6.1 An ideal observer is defined for a set of world properties, **S**, which it infers from image data, **I***. The information available for the inference is characterized by the likelihood function, $p(\mathbf{I}^* \mid \mathbf{S})$, and the prior distribution, $p(\mathbf{S})$, which together define the posterior distribution, $p(\mathbf{S} \mid \mathbf{I}^*)$. The idealized Bayesian inference engine selects estimates of **S** so as to minimize the expected cost, based on the posterior and the specified cost function. "How" it does this is unimportant for this level of analysis.

posterior distribution and a cost function to be minimized. The specification of what scene properties the observer estimates and what cost function it uses to estimate them is the task specification. The other components of the ideal observer characterize the information available for performance of the task. Besides providing an information modeling construct which takes into account the perceptual tasks performed by humans, ideal observers also map neatly onto our intuitive conceptualization of perception as an inference process, thus taking a further step across the bridge from modeling information to modeling perceptual inference.

To make the notion of an ideal observer concrete, consider a simple example world and ideal observer: the world consists entirely of six-sided polyhedra (e.g. cubes), each of constant albedo, or color, and a single light source at infinity which can be placed at any orientation relative to the objects in a scene. A full characterization of scenes in this world includes the shapes and positions of polyhedral objects in a scene and the orientation of the light source. The prior structure of the world is given by the probabilistic laws defining the relative likelihoods of different shapes and positionings of objects in the world, of different light source orientations, and of the observer's viewing position and angle. These laws might capture biases in the processes which create scenes in the world, such as regularities in object pose which result from the influence of gravity and the regularities in object shape which result from the peculiarities of the physical processes and laws which created the

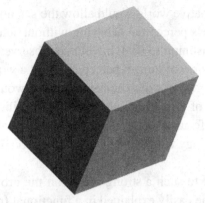

Fig. 6.2 An image of a polyhedron cube in our hypothetical world, which an ideal observer would infer to be a cube.

objects. Let us suppose that the processes which generate objects in this world show a preference for symmetry, so that the closer an object is to being symmetric and the greater the symmetry properties of the object (a cube being more symmetric than a rectangle), the more likely it is to occur in the world. Idealized pin-hole projection of the light reflected from the objects in the world generate grey-level "images" on a flat retina, which we will assume to be sampled at a high enough resolution to allow us to model images as functions mapping real-valued, two-dimensional image coordinates to real-valued, scalar grey-levels (we also assume a non-quantum world in which the retinal receptors register the absolute value of the luminance flux without uncertainty). We can fully characterize the input to the ideal observer as the contours bounding regions of constant intensity in the image and the absolute values of the intensities within these regions. In theory, at least, we could build an ideal observer for estimating object shape in this world. This observer would incorporate all of the knowledge of the world just described. Such an observer, would, for example, estimate that the shape of the object portrayed in figure 6.2 is that of a cube.

Suppose that we actually implemented our example ideal observer, but at some later date moved it to another world (in which skew symmetries, say, were special, instead of regular symmetries). The scientists in that world might well wish to understand this now alien observer's perceptual function. While they would find the observer to be less than ideal in their world, they could, in theory, study the observer's native world, a model of which would provide an almost complete functional characterization of the observer's perception (requiring only the added specification of the perceptual tasks performed by the observer). Because the observer is known to be ideal in its native world, the model of that world would support making predictions about the observers' perceptual behavior. Similarly, the knowledge that the observer is ideal in its native world would allow the scientists to model that world by probing the observer's perceptual behavior, without actually probing the world itself. Applying this reasoning to studying human observers leads to what we will call a *strong* Bayesian view of human perception: that a world exists (or one could theoretically create a world) in which human observers would be ideal. In this view, a Bayesian description of this world, along with a specification of the perceptual tasks which humans perform, provides a complete functional characterization of human perception. By analogy with the ideal observer, we call this world the humans' ideal world.

One may well object to such a strong stance on the grounds that some aspects of perception may not be easily explained in a functional framework but are better described as being due to constraints on the actual processes used by the visual system to subserve perception. In section 5 we will consider how to soften the strong Bayesian position in order to accommodate models of such constraints. For now, however, we will stick to the strong view, since it provides a concrete, unambiguous context for discussing the basic implications of Bayesian approaches to studying human perception.

An ideal observer is defined by four basic elements (some of these are also discussed in the introductory tutorial, table 1):

- The observer's task(s): the properties of the world which the observer infers and the criterion used to weight possible errors (i.e. the cost function).
- The image data available to the observer.
- The likelihood function, which incorporates a model of image formation and noise.
- The prior structure of the observer's world.

A model of an ideal world has the same four elements (though the first one is more naturally considered as an aspect of the observer, rather than the world). The strong Bayesian view suggests a program of research which centers on these four components, and asks the questions:

- What perceptual tasks does the visual system perform; what properties of the world does it infer in the course of perception and what cost criteria does it use to make the inferences?
- What image data does the human perceptual system use as information for perception of these properties?
- What likelihood function is built into perceptual inferences? In particular, what image formation process does the visual system assume when making perceptual inferences, and what uncertainty exists in the image data it uses (e.g. uncertainty induced by sampling and noise in early visual coding)?

- What is the prior structure of the world in which humans are ideal? In other words, what prior knowledge about the world does the visual system use to make perceptual inferences?

These are broad questions, but treating them as the foundational elements of a theory of perception suggests an approach to doing psychophysics which supports the progressive construction of their answers.

6.2.3 *Formalizing a functional approach to psychophysics*

Finding answers to the four questions given above and building towards a complete model of humans' ideal world requires a somewhat different approach than is currently common in computational vision. In particular, we must reject the idea that the primary goal of computational modeling in vision research is to develop *specialized process models*; that is, to construct working solutions for small sub-problems in perception. Adoption of this goal leads to the now familiar approach of specifying problems for limited, well-defined domains (e.g. reflectance estimation in a world of flat surfaces), building computational theories for their solution, implementing these theories in either algorithmic or mechanistic models, and finally using psychophysics to test the predictions of the implemented models. As a paradigm for studying human perception this approach has a number of weaknesses, of which we will highlight two: specifying perceptual problems without empirical support and prematurely implementing models for limited domains.

To specify a perceptual problem, one must assume the answers to two of the questions listed above: What properties of the world are inferred, and what image data are used to make these inferences? Unfortunately, empirical data typically only weakly constrain the answers assumed to these questions. While qualitative observations about human perception may guide the coarse specification of what is inferred perceptually and what image data are used to support these inferences, modelers' intuitions and biases, as well as constraints on the tools available to implement solutions to problems, largely determine the detailed specifications. For example, informal observation suggests that the visual system uses shading (smooth changes in image intensity) as information for the inference of surface shape; however, exactly what properties of shading it uses and what properties of surface shape it infers remain open questions. While these are important elements in our understanding of the perception of shape from shading, they go largely unstudied empirically (though, see Todd & Reichel, 1990), and modeling the processes underlying the perception of shape from shading proceeds by making assumptions about what these properties are (e.g. a 2D map of local surface orientation) (Ikeuchi & Horn, 1981; Pentland, 1982). When comparing psychophysical data to a model's performance, we are therefore uncertain as to which part of the computational theory we should attribute similarities and differences between human data and model data (even assuming a perfect implementation of the theory). Thus, for example, a poor match between human and model performance on a shape discrimination task may result from differences between the human visual system and the model in any of four areas: what properties of shape are actually inferred, what image information is used to make the inferences, what prior assumptions about shape are used, and what model of image formation is assumed.

A second problem with the contemporary computational paradigm results from an emphasis on modeling the algorithms and mechanisms which underly perceptual function. Perceptual theories are necessarily built for toy worlds which result from isolating well-defined visual functions (or tasks) for study. Implementations of these theories in algorithmic or mechanistic models often cannot be easily integrated into more general models of perception. The recent history of research into lightness perception (taken to be the perceptual estimation of surface reflectance, or albedo) illustrates the point. Numerous algorithms and mechanisms have been proposed to explain human lightness perception (Horn, 1973; Hurlbert, 1986; Land & McCann, 1971); however, due to the attempt to isolate lightness perception from other aspects of perception such as the estimation of surface shape, the models deal only with scenes containing flat surfaces. While the models successully explain a range of psychophysical phenomena associated with lightness perception for flat surfaces, recent studies have shown that observers' perceptions of the shapes and spatial layouts of surfaces interact strongly with their perceptions of lightness. Moreover, the processes proposed in the standard lightness models cannot easily accomodate these interactions (Adelson, 1993; Gilchrist, 1977; Knill & Kersten, 1991) (see figure 6.3 and chapter 12 of this book, by Adelson and Pentland). The hypothesized algorithms and mechanisms fail to generalize beyond the specialized sub-domains for which they were built, because, for humans at least, lightness perception interacts with other perceptual functions such as shape perception.

The problem with the lightness work described above is not with using toy worlds for the computational and psychophysical studies of lightness perception; this is a necessary part of doing controlled analyses and experiments. The problem is that the models of the processes which work in those toy worlds do not easily generalize beyond them. Let us, therefore, look at what has the potential to be generalized from the toy world models into a more complete model of lightness perception. The elements which maintain psychological validity in a general context are not the details of the algorithms used, but rather some of the details of the computational theory. An informal summary of this theory is: (1) The system attempts to estimate surface reflectance (what is inferred) from (2) the luminance pattern in images (the image data), (3) luminance patterns in images result from multiplication of a 2D

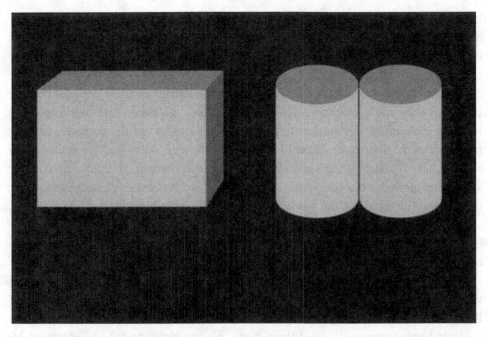

Fig. 6.3 The horizontal luminance profile in (a) and (b) are equivalent, juxtaposed luminance ramps (c), yet the lightness patterns of the two figures appear qualitatively quite different. The effect in (a) is a standard lightness effect demonstrating that the visual system discounts smooth variations in shading as being due to variations in illumination and attributes the step change as being a change in surface albedo. The surface in (b), however, shows that the system can also correctly attribute the shading to the curvature of a surface and the step change in luminance to a discontinuity in surface orientation rather than a change in surface albedo.

surface albedo pattern with a 2D pattern of illumination intensity (a model of image formation) and (4) surface albedo is piece-wise constant while illumination varies smoothly over a surface (a model of the world). In a world of flat surfaces, the problem of lightness estimation reduces to one of factoring the luminance pattern in an image into a piece-wise constant albedo pattern and a smooth illuminant pattern, which, when multiplied together, give back the orginal image. This problem becomes more complicated in the context of general perception, so that algorithms which work for fat surfaces no longer work for curved surfaces; however, the components of the computational theory may well characterize, at least qualitatively, a part of humans' ideal world; and in particular, that part of it which is particularly relevant to lightness perception.

Both of the considerations just discussed argue for directing psychophysical investigations directly at the four questions which define a computational theory for perception; that is, using psychophysics to guide the progressive construction of a model of humans' ideal world. In the remainder of this section, we will discuss how to break the problem into manageable pieces which allow reintegration of models into the general ideal world model. The first step is to limit the domain of consideration. The second is to provide constructs for the partial description of components of an ideal world model (i.e. the prior, likelihood function, and so on).

In order to study any of the elements of the ideal world, we must limit the context in which they are considered. Thus, for example, we might consider exploring humans' prior model of surface reflectance in the context of flat surfaces, or their representation of surface shape in a context in which only shading information is available as data. While such limitations on the domain of study are a major stumbling block for the generalization of specialized process models of perception, they are no obstacle for the generalization of Bayesian models. To illustrate this, we consider again the problem of lightness perception. Limiting the domain of consideration to single flat surfaces is a perfectly reasonable first step, as it avoids a host of very complicated perceptual problems associated with the estimation of shape, spatial layout and so on. From the point of view of modeling the ideal world, this does two things. First, it focuses attention on a particular subclass of image data. Second, it segments the likelihood function and prior model into two parts and considers only one of these parts. We can describe the segmentation by decomposing both the likelihood function and the prior distribution into weighted sums of distributions conditioned on different contexts:

$$p(\text{Image} \mid \text{Refl.}) = p(\text{Context=FLAT}) \, p(\text{Image} \mid \text{Refl., Context=FLAT}) + \quad (6.2)$$

$$p(\text{Context} \neq \text{FLAT}) \, p(\text{Image} \mid \text{Refl., Context} \neq \text{FLAT}) \quad (6.3)$$

and

$$p(\text{Refl.}) = p(\text{Context=FLAT}) \, p(\text{Refl.} \mid \text{Context=FLAT}) + \quad (6.4)$$

$$p(\text{Context} \neq \text{FLAT}) \, p(\text{Refl.} \mid \text{Context} \neq \text{FLAT}) \quad (6.5)$$

where the "FLAT" context is that of scenes containing only one flat surface. $p(\text{Image} \mid \text{Refl., Context=FLAT})$ is the likelihood function for this context and provides a partial description of the "global" likelihood function. Similarly, $p(\text{Refl.} \mid \text{Context} \neq \text{FLAT})$ is the prior for the FLAT context, and is a partial characterization of the global prior. Once we have a reasonable model of the components of the ideal world which characterize the FLAT context, we can flesh out the ideal world by studying it in other contexts. This requires further decomposing the distributions for the more generalized context of non-flat surfaces ($p(\text{Image} \mid \text{Refl., Context} \neq \text{FLAT})$ and $p(\text{Refl.} \mid \text{Context} \neq \text{FLAT})))^{\dagger}$.

[†] Assuming a particular context amounts to assuming strong prior knowledge about the world. This raises an important prescription for psychophysical investigations taking this approach: One must be certain to use stimuli for which one is certain about subjects' percept of the context. As long as what one is taking as a prior context is part of subjects' perceptual model of the stimuli, then one has effectively isolated the desired components of the ideal world for study.

Usually, context limitations in themselves will not suffice to constrain a psychophysical investigation enough to make it practical. We must further focus investigations on highly limited properties of the likelihood and prior models within a given context. That is to say, we cannot generally hope to build experiments which will result in fully parameterized models of these distributions. What we can do is work toward gradually more refined models of the distributions. This leads to what we call a "psychophysics of constraints," in which one generates and tests hypotheses about different characteristics of the likelihood and prior distributions. We use the term constraint to refer to characteristics of the distributions, reflecting the common sense intuition that the distributions embody sets of constraints on scene interpretation. In softening our characterization of ideal worlds from full Bayesian models to a list of the constraints which characterize those worlds, we must be careful not to regress to the fuzzy notion of constraints employed in much computational vision research. Thus, we cannot be satisfied with prior constraints such as the vaguely worded, "preference for smoothness," often applied to many problems in perception. We therefore define what we will call a well-formed constraint:

Well-Formed Constraint: A feature of a probability distribution which unambiguously defines a set of "valid" distributions from the set of possible distributions.

A few examples of Ill-Formed constraints and Well-Formed equivalents should make the definition clear:

Smoothness:

Ill-Formed - Surfaces tend to be smooth.
Well-Formed - The prior distribution on surface orientation is monotonic with the energy function, $E = a\frac{\partial z}{\partial x}^2 + b\frac{\partial z}{\partial y}^2$, where z represents surface depth, x and y are orthogonal image coordinates, and a and b are arbitrary constants.

Symmetry:

Ill-Formed - Texture elements tend to be symmetric.
Well-Formed - The prior distribution on texture element shape concentrates a non-zero percentage of the probability mass in the subspace of symmetric shapes (appropriately defined); that is, it contains modes for symmetric shapes (see Jepson, et. al., this volume, for a formal definition of a mode).

Other constraints could be more general; for example, that surface reflectance and shape are a-priori independent, or that image formation confounds the two so that when conditioned on image data, they become statistically dependent (which would predict the sort of cooperative estimation of shape and reflectance demonstrated in figure 6.3). The important point here is that one needs to specify constraints well enough to make testable predictions about human performance. The problem with ill-formed constraints is that their perceptual implications depend strongly on the details of the algorithms used to implement them, which may vary widely between models.

6.3 Examples

In this section, we discuss two perceptual problems which we have studied within the Bayesian framework. We use these two studies to illustrate two levels of application of the framework; rigorously constructing and testing a Bayesian model (the first example of perceived shape from surface contours), and using the conceptual structure of the framework to guide the initial qualitative explorations of a perceptual phenomenon (the second example of perceived 3D object motion from cast shadow motion). In both cases, the questions we ask center around the image features used by the human visual system for perception and the assumed constraints which define what information those features provide about the world and how the visual system interprets the information.

6.3.1 Surface contours

Image contours are particularly effective sources of information for the perceptual interpretation of surface shape and scene structure. One need merely note the proliferation of line drawings used to represent three-dimensional scenes to be convinced of this. In this example, we consider a particular type of image contour, which we refer to as a surface contour. Surface contours project from intrinsic markings on a surface, such as sharp changes in surface reflectance and surface cracks. We distinguish these from "extrinsic" curves on a surface such as those created at shadow boundaries (which depend on the direction of lighting) and those created along smooth occluding boundaries of a surface, formed where surfaces curve away from the line of sight (which depend on the direction of viewing). We further distinguish surface *markings* from surface *texture*, where surface markings have large spatial extents relative to underlying surface undulations, and surface texture has small spatial extents relative to these undulations. This is ultimately a distinction of scale, and presumably the visual system can treat contours in an image as either surface markings or texture depending on its inferences about the scale of contours relative to the scale of underlying surfaces, though we do not consider this issue here.

Figure 6.4 gives several examples of line drawings which induce strong percepts of surface shape and seem to reflect the perceptual processing of surface contours. Figure 6.5 gives a somewhat more naturalistic display of the phenomenon, in which the perceived shape of a surface is determined by the shapes of contours which

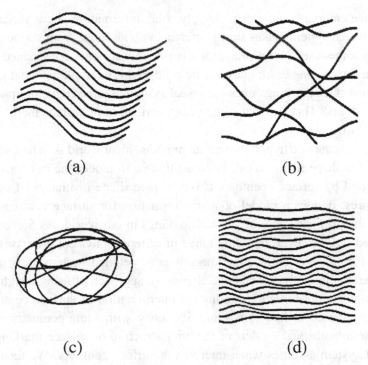

Fig. 6.4 Four examples of line drawings which effectively induce percepts of curved surfaces. The contours in (a), (b) and (c) were all generated by tracing geodesics on different surfaces. The contours in (d) were generated by making parallel, planar slices through a radially defined sine wave surface.

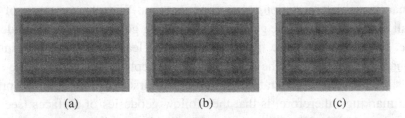

Fig. 6.5 Painting different curved stripes (b, c) over the same shading pattern (a) leads to different percepts of surface shape. The shading pattern is, in fact, consistent with both interpretations, requiring only different interpretations of the illuminant direction. The shape percepts are determined by the shapes of the curved stripes.

appear to project from sharp changes in surface reflectance. As a "cue" for surface shape, surface contours provide a strong example of an image feature which requires a Bayesian analysis to characterize its informativeness, since the information provided by surface contours about surface shape clearly depends on how surface markings are constrained relative to the shapes of the surfaces on which they lie. If all surface markings were generated by weakly constrained physical processes, then surface contours would provide very weak information about surface shape. Since the visual system makes strong inferences about shape from surface contours (at least in some cases), it must assume a reasonably strongly constrained model of surface markings. The basic question we pose in this example is: what prior constraints on surface markings does the visual system assume in its interpretation of surface contours? That is, what is the prior distribution of surface marking shapes in humans' ideal world?

One way to generate hypotheses about humans' ideal world is to first study ideal observers for shape from surface contour; that is, to model the information actually provided by surfaces contours about surface shape in images of our world. This requires, besides a model of image formation for surface contours, a good model of the prior structure of surface markings in our world. As Stevens (1981) has pointed out, however, the wide range of different physical processes that underlie the formation of surface markings makes a detailed study of their properties prohibitive. In our study, we take the alternative approach of using insights gained from phenomenal observations of human interpretation of surface contours, like those demonstrated in figures 6.4 and 6.5, along with some geometric intuition, to generate hypothetical models of the prior structure of surface markings which the visual system assumes when interpreting surface contours. We then perform detailed psychophysical experiments to test the hypotheses.

6.3.1.1 An hypothesis about the assumed structure of surface markings

Figures 6.4 and 6.5 provide the first clues as to the nature of the prior model assumed in human visual interpretations of surface contours. With the exception of figure 6.4d, all of the contours were generated by drawing geodesics of some underlying surface. In interpreting these figures, we seem, at least qualitatively, to interpret their shapes "correctly", in the sense that our percepts of shape match the shapes of the surfaces used to generate the figures. The first cut at an assumed prior on surface markings, therefore, is that they follow geodesics of surfaces (see Knill, 1991; Stevens, 1981). We will consider softening the constraint below, but for now, let us consider its implications.

Geodesics form a special class of curves on a surface, much like straight lines in the plane: they form the shortest path between any pair of points on a surface and, more locally, they have the least amount of curvature afforded by the curvature of the surface on which they lie. By the latter, we mean that at each point on a surface and for each direction through that point, there exists a unique curve which has minimal curvature. In the plane, this is clearly a straight line passing through the specified point in the specified direction. On a curved surface it is a geodesic. The curvature of the geodesic is referred to as the normal curvature of the surface at a point, in a given direction. The magnitude of this curvature, specified locally for every point

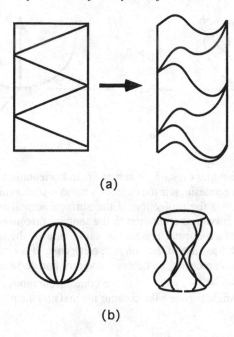

(a)

(b)

Fig. 6.6 Two examples of geodesics. (a) Geodesics of a planar surface are straight lines. If such a surface is folded, straight lines become curved, but remain geodesic. (b) The classic examples of geodesics: great circles on a sphere.

on a surface and for every direction through each point, is an intrinsic property of the surface; thus, we might say that all of the curvature of a geodesic curve is due to the curvature of the underlying surface. Figure 6.6 shows two familiar examples of geodesics. Note that not all curves on surfaces are geodesic, as one can easily "add" curvature to that imposed by the surface. In the plane, this amounts to "drawing" a curved line. On a curved surface, it takes the form of adding what is called geodesic curvature to the surface's normal curvature when generating a curve.[†]

To assume that all surface markings follow geodesics of their underlying surfaces is akin to assuming that all markings on flat surfaces are straight; a highly constraining assumption. Surface contours in a world consisting entirely of geodesic markings would therefore provide strong information about surface shape. Figure 6.7 characterizes the qualitative nature of this information. In words, the sign of curvature of the surface, as it bends in the direction of the contour, is the same as the sign of curvature of the contour (A more quantitative statement of the constraint is given

---

[†] The curvature of a curve on a surface can be dcomposed into orthogonal components, κ_n and κ_g, such that the 3D curvature of the curve is given by $\kappa^2 = \kappa_n^2 + \kappa_g^2$. κ_n is the normal curvature of the surface, and represents the amount of curvature induced by the surface. κ_g is the geodesic curvature of the curve, and represents the amount of curvature of the curve which lies in the surface's tangent plane; that is, which is "added" to the curvature induced by the surface (DoCarmo, 1976).

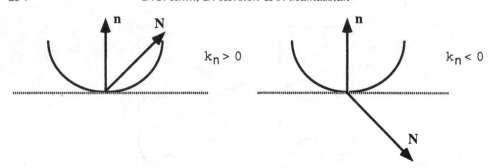

Fig. 6.7 Qualitative constraint on surface curvature and orientation imposed by a contour known to project from a geodesic. **n** is the contour's normal vector (oriented in the direction of contour curvature), **N** is the projection of the surface normal into the image, and κ_n is the surface's normal curvature computed in the tangent direction of the contour. If the contour normal and surface normal are on the same side of the contour, the surface is convex in in the tangent direction of the contour; otherwise, it is concave in that direction. The quantitative relationship between contour curvature and surface curvature is given by $\kappa = -\kappa_n \frac{\sin\theta \sin\sigma (\cos^2\sigma + \sin^2\sigma \cos^2\theta)}{\cos^2\sigma}$, where κ is the contour curvature, σ is the local slant of the surface and θ is the angle between the contour normal and the projected surface normal.

in the caption to figure 6.7). A result of the quantitative version of the constraint is that for at least one class of interesting surfaces; namely, developable surfaces (surfaces which can be generated by folding, without stretching or compressing, a flat surface), any set of two or more surface contours projected from non-parallel geodesics suffices to uniquely determine the shape of the surface "between" the contours (see Knill, 1990, for a partial proof of this statement).

Clearly a strict geodesic constraint does not hold in our world, nor does the visual system assume one; otherwise, we would be constantly misinterpreting the shapes of surfaces (figure 6.4d gives an example in which non-geodesic contours induce an accurate percept of surface shape). We must therefore consider that the human visual system assumes a more general model of the prior on surface markings. To begin the process of formulating a hypothetical model of such a prior, we first express the prior constraints in probabilistic terms. We refer to the prior distribution on surface markings which the human visual system implicitly assumes as $p(\mathbf{C} \,|\, \mathbf{S})$, where $\mathbf{C}$ is some representation of a surface marking, and we have conditioned the prior on surface shape, $\mathbf{S}$, since surface marking shape is inherently dependent on surface shape. The more general prior would be the joint distribution of surface shape and surface marking shape, $p(\mathbf{C}, \mathbf{S})$, but we can write this as $p(\mathbf{S})\, p(\mathbf{C} \,|\, \mathbf{S})$, and we are only concerned here with the marginal on surface marking shape.

We can now easily write the strong geodesic constraint as

$$p(\mathbf{C} \,|\, \mathbf{S}) = \begin{cases} k \;;\; \mathbf{C} \text{ is a geodesic of } \mathbf{S} \\ 0 \;;\; \text{otherwise} \end{cases} \qquad (6.6)$$

where k is the constant density of a uniform distribution over some appropriately parameterized space of geodesics of **S**. Weakening the geodesic constraint amounts to spreading the prior over the space of all possible curves on surfaces (which, for mathematical convenience, we assume to be a finite dimensional, parameterized space of curves). In his dissertation (Knill, 1990), Knill proposed a weaker version of the prior which takes the form of a Gibbs distribution;

$$p(\mathbf{C}\,|\,\mathbf{S}) = \frac{1}{k}exp[-\frac{1}{T}E(\mathbf{C}\,|\,\mathbf{S})] \qquad (6.7)$$

where the energy function, $E(\mathbf{C}\,|\,\mathbf{S})$, reflects a bias towards markings with low variances of geodesic curvature (T captures the degree to which markings tend to vary away from having constant geodesic curvature relative to the scale defined by the length of the curve). The energy function is given by

$$E(\mathbf{C}\,|\,\mathbf{S}) = \frac{\int \kappa_g(s)^2 ds}{L} - (\frac{\int \kappa_g(s)ds}{L})^2, \qquad (6.8)$$

where L is the length of a surface marking, and $\kappa_g(s)$ is the geodesic curvature along the marking, parameterized by arc-length (geodesic curvature is analogous to curvature of a plane curve, and specifies the degree to which a marking locally curves away from being geodesic). The variance measure penalizes variations away from curves with constant geodesic curvature and is generalized from a similar measure for planar curves which gives a bias towards both straight and circular markings. The resulting prior is similar to that obtained by modeling the process which creates surface markings as a random walk, though it is not exactly equivalent (see Belhumeur, chapter 8, and Szeliski, 1987, for a discussion of the relationship between these types of priors and random walk processes). How much the random walk tends to deviate from following a path with constant geodesic curvature is determined by the scale parameter, T.

While the weak version of the prior model has the advantage of assigning non-zero probability density to non-geodesic markings, it suffers from being overly general. It clearly has its maximum for geodesic curves (as well as for curves with constant geodesic curvature), but depending on the value of the scale parameter T, it could be quite broadly distributed around the maxima. This runs counter to our intuitive notion, based on how vividly geodesic contours induce shape percepts, that geodesic surface markings should somehow be special. We therefore follow the suggestion of Jepson, *et. al.* (chapter 2, this volume) to model the prior as a mixture of density functions; in this case, functions which model processes operating at very different scales. A process at one scale (a very low value of T), with a low mean geodesic curvature, generates markings which are, for all practical purposes, geodesic. To avoid fuzziness in the characterization of different scales, we will model this process in the limit as T goes to zero and consider the mean geodesic curvature to be zero, so that the probability density for the markings generated by the process becomes a delta function,

$$p(\mathbf{C} \mid \mathbf{S}, \mathbf{C} \text{ is a geodesic}) = \frac{1}{k_0} \delta\left(\frac{\int \kappa_g(s)^2 ds}{L}\right), \qquad (6.9)$$

which is zero for $\int \kappa_g(s)^2 ds \neq 0$ (non-geodesics) and is normalized by a constant, k_0, so that it integrates to one. The delta function masses the probability density in the space of geodesic surface markings. A second process has a value of T greater than 0 and is modeled by the distribution in (6.7) and (6.8). The mixed prior, then, is a weighted sum of the two models, with the weights corresponding to the probability of a marking having been generated by each of the processes;

$$p(\mathbf{C} \mid \mathbf{S}) = \pi_{geodesic} \frac{1}{k_0} \delta\left(\frac{\int \kappa_g(s)^2 ds}{L}\right) + \pi_{generic} \frac{1}{k_1} exp[-E(\mathbf{C} \mid \mathbf{S})], \qquad (6.10)$$

where $\pi_{geodesic}$ is the probability of a marking being strictly geodesic and $\pi_{generic}$ is the probability of a marking being generated by the pseudo-random walk process.

The assumption of a mixed model like that given in (6.10) is necessary (and sufficient) to explain the particularly reliable inference of surface shape from contour projected from geodesics, as described in more detail in chapter 2. Assuming a mixed prior, when coupled with constraints on surface shape, often allows one to infer which category a set of contours falls in. For example, if one's prior on surface shape includes categories for developable surfaces (i.e. a non-zero percentage of surfaces are developable), then one can make the following inference: if a set of non-parallel contours are consistent with having been projected from geodesics of a developable surface, then they have been projected from geodesics of a developable surface. The basic reasoning is that such a configuration of contours would be accidental (highly unlikely) if generated from the generic, non-geodesic process. Having made this inference, one can then reliably reconstruct the surface shape between the contours, as described above for a strong assumption of geodesicity. Similar reconstructions may be made if contours are not consistent with having come from geodesic markings, since the generic model would also bias the interpretation, but the reliability of the reconstruction would be significantly less (depending on the shapes of the contours and the scale parameter T).

We argue that phenomenal demonstrations like those in figures 6.4 amd 6.5 provide strong evidence for the geodesic component of the mixed prior model. Of course, it may be further conditioned on surfaces being of a certain type, such as developable. In the next section we will present psychophysics directed at testing the psychological validity of the generic, soft-geodesic constraint. We hope that it will provide "case-study" support for directing psychophysics at testing hypotheses about the constraints built into humans' ideal world.

6.3.1.2 Psychophysics

As prescribed earlier in the chapter, we needed to formulate our experimental hypothesis as a well-formed constraint on the prior structure of surface markings assumed by the human visual system. Our hypothesis is

Hypothesis: The visual system assumes a prior distribution on surface marking shape when interpreting contours which is monotonic with the variance of geodesic curvature measure given in (6.8).

This hypothesis is weaker than the explicit form given for the distribution in (6.8); however, it is much easier to test, as will often be the case for such models.

Two major concerns drove the design of the psychophysical experiments: First, it is important to use naturalistic stimuli for the experiment, instead of the simple line drawing figures typically used to demonstrate "shape-from-contour" effects. Second, while prior constraints on surface markings may be most useful for the perception of surface shape, direct measures of perceived shape are difficult to obtain and confound a host of issues; what an appropriate measure of perceived shape is, how other cues in stimuli influence the interpretation of shape and how the visual system's assumed priors on surface shape influence the interpretation, to name a few. In order to satisfy our first concern and avoid the problems raised by the second, we used a contour labelling task, in which subjects were asked to report the physical cause of a set of contours in a stimulus image. In particular, we asked subjects to label closed contours in rendered images of a surface as either reflectance contours on the surface (projected from sharp changes in reflectance on a surface) or the occluding contours of a transparency placed between the surface and the viewer. Figure 6.8 shows two examples of the stimuli used, which elicit each of the two possible interpretations. In both images, the interpretation of the middle darkened patch is formally ambiguous: it could either be a change in reflectance on the vase-like surface or a transparent surface floating over the vase-like surface, though we see the patches unambiguously. The experimental hypothesis makes a clear prediction about how humans would label such patches: all other things being equal, lower values of the variance of geodesic curvature measure for the contours bounding an image patch will lead to higher proportions of reflectance contour judgements; higher values will lead to higher proportions of transparency judgements.

Two experiments were done to investigate the effects of contour shape on contour labeling. In the first experiment, a variety of surfaces and patch shapes were used. The experiment consisted of two conditions: in one, patches defined by sets of either four or five vertices were bounded by geodesics connecting the vertices. The geodesics connecting the vertices on a given surface were computed and projected

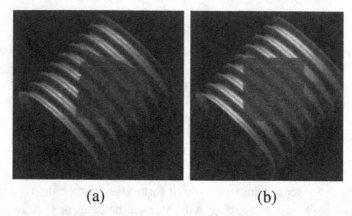

(a)   (b)

Fig. 6.8 Two examples of stimuli used in the experiments described in the text. (a) A patch with bounding contours consistent with having projected from geodesics on the vase-like surface tends to appear as being "on" the surface. (b) A patch with straight bounding contours tends to appear as a transparent surface between the vase-like surface and the viewer. These are similar to the stimuli used in the first experiment described in the text, with the only exception being that the shading within the patches is generated by scaling the shading from the underlying surface by a constant AND adding a constant luminance across the patch. The addition of the constant luminance has the effect of increasing the bias towards a transparency interpretation.

into a stimulus image to form the boundaries of a patch, which was then "colored" by scaling the shading pattern of the surface within the patch by a constant multiplicative factor of 0.3 (see figure 6.9a). In the second condition, the same surfaces and sets of vertices were used, but the vertices were connected by straight lines in the image to form the patch boundaries (see figure 6.9b). Subjects were asked to indicate whether the patch in a stimulus image appeared as a change in reflectance on the surface or as a transparency placed between the surface and themselves. Figure 6.10 summarizes the results of the experiment, averaged over all surfaces and all patch shapes (as defined by vertex configurations).

The data clearly show that patches with geodesic boundaries were more often interpreted as reflectance boundaries than patches with straight boundaries. This does not, however, necessarily support a conclusion that subjects are assuming a prior on surface markings like the one hypothesized. Treating the task as a statistical decision, we see that subjects' decisions would be based not only on prior assumptions about the shapes of reflectance boundaries on surfaces, but also on prior assumptions about the shapes of thin surface boundaries (to test the hypothesis that a patch is a transparent surface). The visual system typically displays a strong bias towards straightness of such boundaries (as well as of other types of edges in the world). This is evidenced by the common inference that a straight contour in an image indicates a straight edge in the world. Thus, one could explain the results by a model in

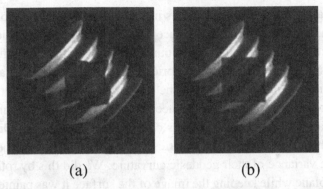

(a)   (b)

Fig. 6.9 Example stimuli used for experiment 1. Both patches have the same four vertices, but are connected in one case by contours which project from geodesics of the vase-like surface (a), and in the other case by straight contours (b). Other surface shapes and vertex configurations were also used in the experiment. The different surface and patch combinations were presented twelve times apiece in random order. The data are averaged over twelve subjects.

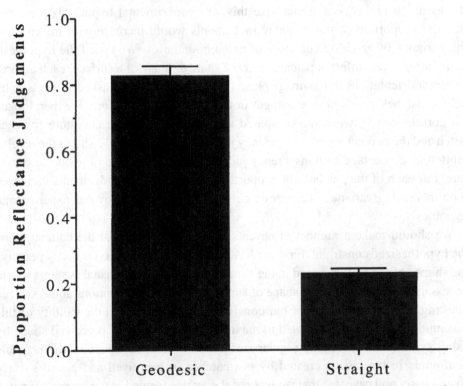

Fig. 6.10 Results from experiment 1, averaged over all surface and patch vertex configurations. The proportion of times subjects judged a patch to be a reflectance change on a surface was significantly greater when the patch boundaries were the shapes of geodesics on underlyng surfaces than when they were straight.

which the straight boundaries of patches in the second condition strongly bias the interpretation toward a transparent surface (since a straight edge could not lie on a curved surface), while the reflectance boundary judgements for the first, geodesic condition, result simply from a strong prior bias to see the patches as reflectance changes, in the absence of evidence to the contrary.

The first experiment highlights the need to control for the influence of priors assumptions about non-surface contours on subjects' judgements. One way to do this is to fix the shapes of patch boundaries in the image, while independently manipulating the variance of their geodesic curvature. We did this by rotating a patch in the image plane while keeping the image of the surface it was painted over fixed. The rotations left the shapes of the image contours the same, but changed where they lay relative to the surface; thus, deprojecting the contours onto the surface resulted in curves on the surface with different values for the variance of curvature measure as a function of the patch rotation angle (see figure 6.11). In the extreme case, we generated a patch with geodesic boundaries before rotating it in the image plane, so that at a zero degree rotation the variance was zero, but at other rotations it was much higher. For stimuli like this, our experimental hypothesis predicted that the proportion of transparency judgements would increase with increases in the variance of geodesic curvature of patch boundaries. We tested the hypothesis by painting three different patches over the shaded image of a surface, each at three different orientations in the image plane (see figure 6.11), and asked subjects to label the patches as reflectance changes or transparencies, as before. We then looked for correlations between the computed variances of geodesic curvature for each patch and the percentage of transparency judgements. Figure 6.12 shows the results, plotted as percentage of transparency judgements vs. variance of geodesic curvature. For each of the patches, the proportion of transparency judgements increased with increasing variance of geodesic curvature, as predicted by our experimental hypothesis.

We should make a number of caveats to the conclusion that the data supports the hypothesized constraint. First, we have assumed that subjects correctly perceive the shapes of the surfaces used in the stimuli. Since subjects' visual systems would necessarily use the *perceived* shape of surfaces to apply assumptions about surface marking shape, the strength of our conclusion is dependent on the validity of this assumption. While we attempted to maximize the accuracy of perceived shape by using symmetric and highly regular surfaces, we must be aware of the possible confounds in the results created by mismatches in perceived and actual surface shape. A second caveat is that we ignored the angles formed at the corners of patch boundaries in the analysis. A number of researchers have suggested that the visual system assumes that corners of surface markings tend toward being perpendicular (though the particular bias may be dependent on the number of sides in a figure).

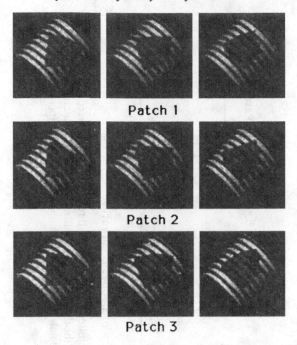

Patch 1

Patch 2

Patch 3

Fig. 6.11 Stimuli used for experiment 2. Three different patch shapes were used, each oriented at three different angles. The experiment incorporated a further manipulation not discussed in the text. The shading within patches was generated by first multiplying the surface shading by a factor of 0.3, as in the first experiment, and then adding one of three constant luminance values to the resulting shading pattern; 0, 38 or 76, expressed in pixel grey levels (on a scale of 0-255). Results for each patch and orientation condition were calculated by averaging transparency ratings across the three values of added luminance. The luminance manipulation was done for two reasons: First, adding a constant luminance within the patches decreased the bias toward seeing the patches as reflectances changes on the surface, which subjects informally reported to be quite high in the first experiment; second, the luminance manipulation masked the main manipulation of patch rotation, as evidenced by subjects' reports that they thought we were looking for an effect of luminance on transparency judgements (none of the twelve subjects picked up on the main patch rotation manipulation).

Such assumptions could conceivably have played a role in the labelling task used here, though we suspect their influence was small.

6.3.1.3 Discussion

The experiments described above, along with the various phenomenal demonstrations presented, provide evidence that the visual system assumes a mixed prior model of surface markings, with one component enforcing a strict geodesic constraint and another enforcing a weaker version of the constraint. We suspect that the model includes other components as well, such as one enforcing a strict constraint

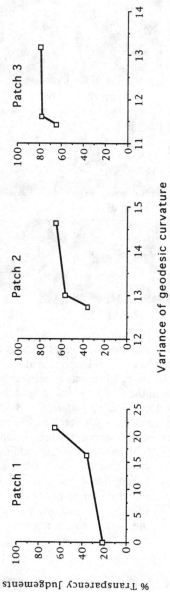

Fig. 6.12 Results from experiment 2, plotted for each of the three patch shapes used. The three points in each graph correspond to the three different rotations used for each patch. The proportion of times subjects judged a patch to be a transparency increased with increases in the variance of geodesic curvature.

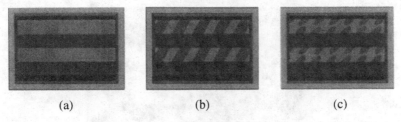

(a)　　　　　　　　　　(b)　　　　　　　　　　(c)

Fig. 6.13 The corner formed by reflectance contours at intersections with surface creases determines the perceived shape of the surface. This works for contours which are straight between the creases (b), as well as for contours which are curved (c).

that markings on cylindrical surfaces (e.g. those in figure 6.4a) follow planar cuts of the surfaces, and in particular, are in symmetry planes of the surfaces (e.g., cuts perpendicular to the axis of a cylindrical tube). As with the other components of the model, this component would be weighted by the proportion of surface markings which match the constraint. We have also argued that the visual system assumes prior constraints on the shapes of surface markings at intersections with surface creases which are analogous to those on markings on smooth regions of a surface (see figures 6.13) (Knill, 1991). In general, such intersections will result in tangent discontinuities in a surface marking (forming corners). We hypothesize that the visual system assumes that some non-zero percentage of markings follow a strict constraint that they bend in the same direction as the surface at intersections with creases. Such a constraint arises naturally in the world for any surface which is folded into a crease. Surface markings, curved or straight, which were on such a surface before folding will follow the constraint where they intersect the crease created by the fold.

6.3.2 *Moving cast shadows*

In our second example, we consider how the visual system uses cast shadow information for the perception of the spatial layout of objects (Kersten, *et al.*, 1994). At least since the time of Da Vinci, it has been known that the relative displacement between an object and its cast shadow in an image provides a source of visual information about the spatial layout of objects (daVinci, 1970; Yonas, 1978). We specifically consider the problem of how the visual system uses the motion of an object's cast shadow to make inferences about the three-dimensional motion of the object. The work was initially motivated by the phenomenal discovery that one could dramatically alter the perceived motion of an object simply by changing the motion of its cast shadow in an image. The effects we obtained were easily as strong, phenomenally, as the perception of motion in depth induced by the changing size of an object or the perception of static depth from stereo. We describe some of

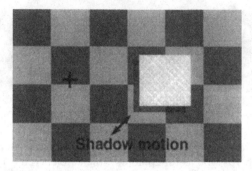

Fig. 6.14 Observers looked at a fixation mark (+) placed on a checkerboard plane subtending 6.6 x 10 deg of visual angle. Viewing distance was 500 mm. At 4.1 deg to the right of the fixation point, a foreground square was superimposed over a sharp shadow of the same size. In a 500 msec animated sequence, the shadow oscillated for one cycle through a 0.34 deg displacement from the foreground square. The foreground square remained stationary throughout the animation. Observers were asked to indicate whether the foreground square appeared to oscillate in depth or appeared to be stationary. Both dark and light (lighter than the background surface) shadows were used. On 78% of the trials using dark shadows, observers reported seeing the foreground square as oscillating in depth–toward and away from the viewer. On only 40% of the trials using light shadows did subjects report seeing the square oscillating in depth. In a different experiment, 19 out of 20 subjects reported seeing the motion effect when a penumbra was added to the shadow.

these below. The main purpose of this section is to demonstrate how the qualitative application of the Bayesian approach helped frame the questions we asked about the phenomena in question, even though we have not yet reached the point of building a complete Bayesian model of the phenomena. Along the way, we will try to highlight some of the research questions which remain to be answered to flesh out such a model.

6.3.2.1 The phenomena

We describe two simple phenomena which illustrate the perceptual effects of cast shadow motion. Figure 6.14 schematically shows a simple animation in which the shadow of a square over a checkered background moves back and forth relative to the square, while the square itself remains stationary. Despite the fact that the square is stationary in the image and does not change size, it typically appears to move towards and away from the checkered background in depth. When presented with an animation using a dark, sharp-edged shadow, most observers report seeing the square move in depth (in an experiment involving other conditions as well, 78% of reports from 20 subjects indicate the effect). When the boundary of the shadow is changed to a fuzzy penumbra, almost all observers reported reported seeing the motion effect (in a seperate experiment, 19 out of 20 subjects report seeing motion in depth). We should point out that the perceptual effect is one of continuous motion,

Fig. 6.15 Ball-in-box animation. The left panel shows the condition in which the image of the ball diverges from that of the shadow. The shadow and ball's initial positions are indicated schematically with outlines. The ball's trajectory is diagonal, where as the shadow's trajectory is horizontal. The right panel illustrates the condition in which both the ball and shadow start at the lower left at the beginning of the animation, and finish in the upper right hand corner at the end of the animation. For this second case, both ball and shadow trajectories are diagonal. Observers report seeing the ball in the first condition as rising above the floor in a plane roughly aligned with the front of the open box. In the second condition, they report the ball as seeming to slide along the ground plane of the box, from front to back. Along with this percept, they also see the ball as increasing in size as it recedes in depth, further demonstrating the strength of the motion-in-depth effect.

of the kind often associated with low-level motion mechanisms, not the sort of jerky motion often reported for motion displays which purportedly do not stimulate low-level motion mechanisms (e.g. isoluminant motion displays).

In a second series of demonstrations, which also formed the basis of the experiments we will report, we generated animations of a ball moving inside an open box, as shown schematically in figure 6.15. The ball followed the same straight, diagonal path in the image in all of the animations, but we varied the motion path of the ball's cast shadow. All observers report a striking difference in their percepts of the ball's three dimensional motion for different shadow motions. In one animation, we were even able to induce the percept of a ball bouncing back and forth in depth by giving the shadow a non-linear motion path (see figure 6.17). Observers typically find it hard to believe that the two-dimensional image motion of the ball is the same in all the animations, and remark on the strength of the effect.

6.3.2.2 Ideal observer analysis

Before asking questions about how the human visual system interprets cast shadow motion, we first outline a simple, primarily qualitative, ideal observer analysis to highlight the issues we wish to explore experimentally. The analysis is not complete, but rather will generate many questions which we can explore experimentally when applying them to an investigation of humans' ideal world for shadow perception. Since the properties of cast shadows are dependent on so many scene properties (the shape of the casting object, the shape of the surface on which the shadow is cast, etc.), a full ideal observer analysis for the interpretation of 3D motion from cast shadow motion would require a compete model of a very complex environment. In order to isolate some of the key features of the problem, we simplify the domain somewhat to one similar to the ball-in-the-box environment shown in figure 6.15. In this domain, the casting object is a ball and the surface on which the shadow is cast is planar. We will also assume that the orientation of the planar surface relative to the observer is known. We will further assume that the lighting is composed of an ambient term and a point source at infinity, a reasonable approximation for many natural scenes. It would seem that the first issues to be resolved in the ideal observer analysis would be what the visual system infers about an object's 3D motion and what image features it uses to make its inferences; however, we will delay considering these questions until we analyze how cast shadows are formed and how the relevant scene properties might be constrained, which will provide clues to the answers. Thus, we take as the first step in our analysis a specification of the image formation process which forms cast shadows. We follow this with a disussion of the prior structure of the world which partially determines the information content of shadows. Finally, we discuss what an observer might infer about object motion from cast shadow motion and what image features it could use to make such inferences.

Image formation

We briefly summarize two aspects of cast shadow formation: its geometric properties; in particular, how cast shadows are positioned in images, and its photometric properties; in particular, how the luminance changes within a shadow relative to its surround. The position of a cast shadow relative to the object casting it is determined by the position of the object, the direction of illumination and the position and orientation of the surface on which the shadow is cast. The geometric variables of interest in the image are the visual angle between an object and its cast shadow (ϕ) and the relative orientation of the object and the shadow θ, taken relative to the horizontal. We obtain for ϕ,

$$\phi = cot^{-1}(\frac{d}{h}\frac{sin\tau_L sin\sigma_L sin\sigma_S + cos\sigma_L cos\sigma_S}{sin\sigma_L} - tan\,\sigma_L), \qquad (6.11)$$

where h is the height of the ball above the planar surface (which we assume to be oriented parallel to the horizontal, as shown in figure 6.15), d is the distance from the ball to the viewer, σ_L and τ_L parameterize the illuminant direction (σ_L is the slant of the illuminant away from the viewer and τ_L is its tilt relative to the horizontal in the image plane), and σ_S is the orientation of the planar surface, expressed as the slant of the surface normal away from the viewing direction. We obtain an even simpler expression for the orientation of the shadow relative to the casting object, as it is given by the tilt of the light source, $\theta = \tau_L$.

A further geometric property of a cast shadow is its shape, which is a function of the shape of the casting object, and the relative positions and orientations of the light source, object and shadowed surface. While these relations are not geometrically complex, characterizing them in full would require an exhaustive analysis of the variety of objects which could exist in the scene. Suffice it to say that assuming the cast shadow to be small relative to the viewing distance, the shadow of a ball on a planar surface would be approximately elliptical.

Turning to the photometric constraints on shadows, we note that the luminance pattern within a shadow is darker than the surround by an amount proportional to the relative intensities of the point and ambient sources. If the surface on which a shadow was cast were curved, one would find that the contrast within the shadow would also be diminished, due to the removal of shading variations caused by the surface curvature and the point source of light. If the light source were an extended source at a finite distance from the object, the boundary of the shadow would be a fuzzy penumbra, whose spatial extent would be determined by the size and shape of the light source and the distances between the light source and the object and between the object and the shadowed surface.

Prior structure of scenes

Since cast shadow properties depend on the properties of the casting object, the light source and the shadowed surface, priors on all of these play a role in determining the information provided by cast shadow motion about 3D object motion. We will make a variety of simplifying assumptions about these, and try to limit them to ones which hold for the types of displays we use in experiments; that is, that they correspond to the way scenes are perceived in the animations, whether due to prior assumptions on the part of the observer or to reliable inferences they make based on non-shadow information, such as the shape of the projected box. The remainder of the prior specifications will become hypotheses about the ideal world for human processing of shadow information; that is, hypotheses about the prior assumptions made by humans when interpreting 3D object motion from shadow information.

We have assumed that the shadowed surface is planar with known orientation and will further assume that it is known to be stationary relative to the viewer. The latter assumption does not matter if the motion of the shadow casting object is perceived in the shadowed surface's frame of reference. We also assume that the shape of the shadow casting object is known (e.g. a ball), though not its size; thus, the only prior structure on the object which we need to worry about is the prior on changes in size over time (shrinking or growing). This prior certainly contains a "mode" for rigid objects (non-deforming); that is, a non-zero percentage of objects do not change size over time. We will not specify the prior on changes in object size more quantitatively than this, since it is not important for the qualitative analysis we present here. It would, however, be important for studying interactions between "looming" information and shadow information in the perception of motion in depth. The prior on objects' 3D motions is clearly important, since this is the domain of perceptual inference we are considering. The world in which we live has strong constraints on object motions: the prior has modes for stationary objects resting on surfaces, objects rolling along surfaces, as well as constraints on object motions in free space and on motions caused by collisions with other surfaces. (See Jepson *et al.*, chapter 2.) We will not attempt to model these priors, but will consider below how such priors built into human visual processing can play a role in the perception of 3D motion.

Finally, we must specify a prior on the illuminant, both on illuminant direction and motion. A commonly cited constraint on illumination is that it comes from above in a viewer-centered coordinate system. This is a rather weak constraint, and as with object motion constraints we will consider what light source position constraints might be built into visual processing of shadows. Constraints on light source motion have not until now been seriously considered, as they don't play a significant role in most perceptual phenomena. They are clearly important for the interpretation of cast shadow motion under normal viewing conditions, where cast shadow motion is ubiquitous. A natural constraint is that the light source position (or illuminant direction) remains fixed on the time scale over which object motions occur (or can be detected by the human visual system). We call this the stationary light source constraint and hypothesize that the visual system assumes such a constraint when interpreting cast shadow motion.

What is perceived

We now turn to the component of the ideal observer specification which depends on what humans actually "do" in perception: what is it about an objects' 3D motion that humans perceive. Two general issues must be resolved to answer this question: Is the perception of object motion viewer-centered or scene-centered (e.g. relative to the box in figure 6.15), and is the perception of 3D motion quantitative or qualitative, or how finely does the visual system represent object motion? We suspect that the answers to these questions vary depending on task and available information, but that humans can in some situations perceptually estimate with some degree of accuracy both viewer and scene-centered measures of object motion. For example, cast shadow information provides direct information about scene-centered motion; that is, motion relative to a shadowed surface; thus we would predict that subjects would be good at tasks involving the perception of object motion relative to another surface when only cast shadow information is provided. Viewer-centered estimates of the motion would either have to be coupled with estimates of the orientation and shape of the shadowed surface (increasing the potential for error) or would have to come from other sources of image information, such as the changing size of an object's image.

A further issue involving what observers perceive when interpreting cast shadow information is how the perception of object motion is coupled with the perception of other scene properties. We have already seen how it could potentially be coupled with the perception of a shadowed surface's shape and orientation to make estimates of viewer-centered motion. Another scene property on which the perception of object motion from shadow motion should depend is the illuminant direction, since the the image formation process confounds object position and motion with illuminant position and motion. Finally, the perceptual use of shadow information depends on labelling a shadow as a shadow, and thus should interact with this perceptual labeling. Some of the psychophysics we present in the next section are aimed at gaining insights into these interactions.

What image features are used

We can isolate a number of different image features which provide information for the interpretation of object motion from shadow motion. The component which is directly related to object position in 3D is the distance between the object and the cast shadow; the change in this distance over time provides direct information about 3D object motion. We use the term "direct" to distinguish the distance feature from images features like the orientation of the shadow relative to the object, which specifies the tilt of the light source in the image plane, and while providing information useful for the interpretation of 3D motion, does so indirectly by constraining the interpretation of a different scene property on which the information provided by the distance feature depends (light source tilt). The shape of the shadow provides information about the relative orientations of the object, the light source and the shadowed surface. The photometric properties of the shadow provide information primarily for labelling the shadow as a shadow.

Since the perceptual interpretation of object motion can (and ideally should) be coupled with the interpretation of other scene properties, other image features not directly related to shadows, but which provide information about these scene properties, provide indirect information for the interpretation of object motion from shadow motion. The changing size of an object's image provides direct information about its 3D motion, independent of the shadow information, the shading on the object provides information about its shape and the illuminant direction, and the texture, shading and outlines of the shadowed surface provide information about its orientation and shape. Of course, other useful information may be available as well, for example, the cast shadows of other objects provide fruther constraint on the illuminant direction. In general, then, at the same time as we consider how the interpretation of object motion from shadow motion is coupled with the interpretation of other scene properties, we must consider issues of how multiple sources of information interact in the interpretation.

6.3.2.3 Psychophysics

The discussion of the four components of an ideal observer for estimating 3D object motion from shadow motion raised a host of questions which can be asked about the same components of humans' ideal world; that is, about how humans actually use cast shadow information in the perception of 3D object motion. We now turn to some psychophysical experiments we have performed which shed light on these questions. As we go through the experiments, we will discuss what they have to say about the various issues raised above.

In the introductory discussion of the phenomenon, we described in part the first experiment (see figure 6.14), in which the motion of a square's cast shadow induced a perceived motion of the square in depth, despite the fact that the square itself remained stationary and did not change in size. The obvious conclusion from this experiment is that the human visual system does in fact use the changing distance between an object and its cast shadow as information for the 3D motion of the object. It also suggests that this information can override the information provided by the object's image motion, or lack thereof. However, since both pieces of information depend on prior constraints on the scene (for the shadow motion, a stationary light source constraint, and for the lack of object image motion, object stationarity and rigidity constraints), another way to phrase the result is that the stationary light source constraint is, in some sense, stronger than and outweighs the prior constraints on object motion and rigidity. We will see further evidence for the latter interpretation later. Another result of the experiment was that the motion effect was significantly stronger for dark shadows than for shadows made artificially lighter than the surround. This suggests that the visual system enforces to some degree photometric constraints or labelling shadows,though the fact that the effect didn't disappear indicates that they are not applied as strongly as one might expect for an ideal observer.

In a second experiment, we modified the ball-in-the-box demonstration (see figure 6.15) to obtain quantitative measures of subjects' percepts of the ball's 3D object motion. During the presentation of animations on a computer display like those in the original demonstration, subjects' adjusted the height along the right wall of the box (using the computer's mouse) to the perceived position of the ball at the peak of its 3D trajectory above the floor of the box. Animations were made for shadows moving along different trajectories, from one following a horizontal path (as in figure 6.15a) to one following a path parallel to the ball's (as in figure 6.15b).

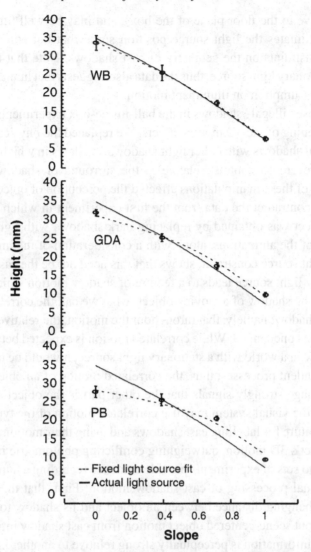

Fig. 6.16 Data for three subjects in the ball-in-a-box experiment. The graphs plot subjects' estimates of the height on the wall to which the ball moved at the rightmost point of its trajectory as a function of the slope of the shadow trajectory (0 - horizontal, 1 - same diagonal trajectory as the ball). The solid lines show the predicted data curves for a model which knows the light source direction used to render the scene (determining the shading on the ball and the elliptical shape of the shadows). Dashed lines show the data curves produced by a similar model with the light source direction chosen to best fit subjects' data.

The data shown in figure 6.16 clearly shows an ability of subjects to make reliable estimates of the ball's 3D motion, answering to some extent the question about what humans are capable of inferring from cast shadow motion. Moreover, the estimates are reasonably close to what would be predicted by a model which knew the position of the light source used to generate the shading on the ball (10 degrees from the vertical relative to the floor plane of the box), and may be well fitted by a model which mis-estimates the light source position somewhat but enforces the image formation constraints on the geometry of cast shadows. Note that the predictions assume a stationary light source, thus the data also suggests that humans may impose such a prior assumption on illuminant motion.

When we use "illegal" shadows in the ball-in-the-box experiments or demos, we find no weakening of the 3D motion effects. We replaced the physically realizeable dark, elliptical shadows with either light shadows, shadows in which the luminance pattern had reveresed contrast relative to the surround or shadows with square shapes. None of these manipulations affected the perception of object motion. This may seem to contradict the data from the first experiment in which some weakening of the effect was obtained by replacing dark shadows with light ones. Closer examination of the animations, along with a consideration of the implications of a stationary light source constraint, shows that this need not be the case. Assumption of a stationary light source leads to a feature of shadow motion which reliably signals that it is the shadow of a moving object: what we call the correlated motion of the ball and shadow; namely, that throughout the motion, the relative orientation of the two remains unchanged. While correlated motion is expected between an object and its shadow in a world with a stationary light source, it would be highly accidental for independent processes; thus, the correlated motion of an object and another part of the image strongly signals that the other part is the object's shadow. This suggests that the visual system may use correlated motion of the type we describe as a trigger feature for labelling cast shadows and using their motion as information about an object's 3D motion, outweighing conflicting photometric information.

The first two sets of experiments provide evidence regarding a number of aspects of human visual processing of cast shadow motion: First, that the visual system can use the changing distance between an object and its shadow to make reliable inferences about scene-centered object motion from cast shadow information. Second, that this information is perceptually strong relative to another known effective source of information for 3D object motion, the changing size of an object. Third, that the visual system may assume a stationary light source constraint to interpret shadow motion, and, as one result, may rely on correlated motion as an image feature to perceptually relate an object with its shadow. Finally, that while the visual system may enforce some photometric constraints on shadow labelling, these constraints are outweighed by the information provided by correlated motion. We now turn to a more in-depth consideration of issues surrounding the role of illuminant direction in these phenomena.

First, we consider whether the visual system can account for a moving illuminant when appropriate information is provided in an image. To do this, we modified some of the ball-in-a-box demos so that information was provided to indicate that

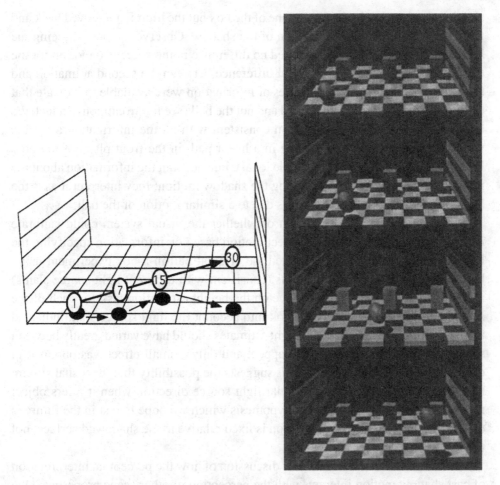

Fig. 6.17 The left panel shows schematically positions 1,7,15, and 30 of the image of a football and its cast shadow during the course of the animation. The shadows were generated by changing the slant of the light source as the football (indicated by a circle) moved. The right panel shows, from the top, actual image frames 1, 7, 15, and 30 of a 30 frame sequence in which the reader should be able to see the image data from the shading and cast shadows that the illumination direction is changing as the ball moves from left to right. If the visual system could take this information accurately into account, it would conclude that the football is moving along a linear trajectory in the fronto-parallel plane. It does not; rather the percept is of a football starting near the observer (frame 1), moving slightly forward (frame 7), moving back in depth (frame 15), and then towards the observer again (frame 30).

the relative motion of the ball and its shadow was caused by illuminant motion, and not motion of the ball in depth. Figure 6.17 illustrates one of the more striking of these demos, in which non-linear motion of the ball's cast shadow induces the percept that the ball bounces back and forth in depth (and up and down relative to the floor of the box). We created a version of the animation which the ball was simulated as moving in the front plane of the box but the illuminant moved back and forth, creating the bouncing motion of the shadow. Observers reported seeing the ball bouncing as before, and reported no difference in the perceived motion for the two types of animation. The critical difference between the second animation and the original is that numerous sources of information were available to indicate that the illuminant was bouncing around and not the ball (see figure caption). In fact, the only interpretation of object motion consistent with all the information available would be that the ball was moving in a linear path in the front plane of the box. Human observers are clearly not able to take into account the information about the moving illuminant when interpreting the shadow motion; they interpret it as if the bouncing motion of the shadow was due to a similar motion of the ball.

We also considered the question of whether the visual system could calibrate its quantitative estimates of 3D object motion based on information specifying the light source direction. We performed the original ball-in-a-box experiment using balls with different shading patterns (consistent with different light source slants) and measured subjects' performance on the height estimation task for each of the shading conditions. If observers took into account the light source slant indicated by the shading on the ball, their height estimates should have varied greatly between shading conditions. This did not happen, and only a small effect was obtained in one condition (see figure 6.18). This suggests the possibility that the visual system has strong biases towards a particular light source direction when it infers object motion from shadow motion. An hypothesis which we hope to test in the future is that the assumed light source position is fixed relative to the shadowed surface, not to the viewer.

We close this section with a brief discussion of how the perceptual interpretation of cast shadow motion interacts with the perception of other scene properties. One such interaction is found between perceived 3D motion and perceived object size. For ball-in-a-box animations in which the ball is made to appear to recede in depth along the floor of the box, subjects report seeing the ball (whose image size is constant throughout the animation) grow in size, consistent with the constraints of perspective projection. This suggests that the shadow information can mitigate a constraint on object rigidity, though perhaps indirectly through the resulting percept of motion in depth. A case in which such an interaction is not found is that of illuminant properties. For example, in the moving light source demonstrations, observers report clearly seeing the illuminant as moving, while their reports of perceived object motion do not reflect this percept.

We have considered here only a few of the questions raised in the ideal observer analysis of moving cast shadow information. Our hope is that the questions so raised and the context of the Bayesian framework will lead to more and richer studies of the phenomena associated with cast shadows.

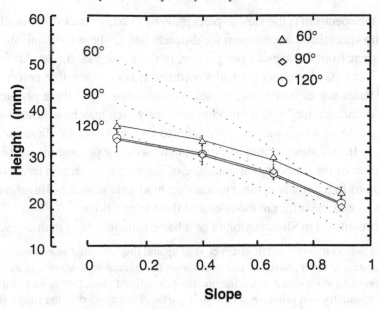

Fig. 6.18 Perceived height above the checkerboard floor of the ball under various illumi-nation slants. 40 subjects were split into 3 groups (13, 13 and 14). Each group was shown animations with four different shadow trajectory slopes in which the ball had a different shading pattern, corresponding to being illuminated by a light source from one of three angles above the checkerboard: 60 deg, 90 deg and 120 deg (the viewing direction was 21.8 deg above the checkerboard). All light sources were at infinity. The data predicted for an observer which accurately estimates the light source positions and uses these to mediate its inference of 3D object motion from cast shadow motion are shown by the dotted lines. The mean height estimates for the three groups of subjects are shown by the open symbols connected by solid lines. Subjects' mean response curves cluster around what be predicted for a single intermediate light source position. Error bars indicate plus or minus 1 S.E. of the mean.

6.4 Beyond the strong Bayesian view

At the end of the last example, we saw a case in which humans could maintain inconsistent perceptual interpretations of a scene property. In particular, humans can perceive a light source as moving, while at the same time interpreting cast shadow motion as if the light source were stationary. While the interpretation of the cast shadow information may not include an explicit estimation of light source motion, it behaves as if implicitly assuming a fixed light source. Inconsistencies like this suggest that the strong Bayesian view presented earlier in the chapter be modified somewhat, a point we take up briefly in this section.

The strong Bayesian view is at one extreme along a spectrum of views of percep-tion, holding that the world model built into visual processing is internally consistent and that perceptual behavior is itself consistent with this model. At the other extreme of the spectrum is the view of perception as a "bag of tricks" (Ramachandran, 1988) with specialized mechanisms for different tasks. These mechanisms need not be consistent from a Bayesian perspective, in the sense that the worlds for which they are ideal may have inconsistent structures. It is our view that perceptual processing stands somewhere between these two extremes; that there undoubtedly is some modularization of visual function, some of which may have "Bayesian" consistency, some of which may not. We refer to this as a "weak" Bayesian view of perception. In this view, a complete functional model of perception must include a specification of the functional architecture of the visual system, in terms of the organization of functionally distinct processing modules, as well as Bayesian models of processing in the different modules and their interactions.

Marr considered modularization to be a basic principle of system design

...the idea that a large computation can be split up and implemented as a collection of parts that are as nearly independent of one another as the overall task allows, is so important that I was moved to elevate it to a principle, the principle of modular design ... Information about the geometry and reflectance of visible surfaces is encoded in the image in various ways and can be decoded by processes that are almost independent (Marr, 1982).

Marr refers to a form of modularity which is at least approximately supported by the information and task demands of perceptual inferences; that is, which is supported by a Bayesian analaysis; however, the last sentence in the quote illustrates the ease with which one can prematurely segment visual functions into modules. As our previous analysis showed, surface geometry and reflectance cannot in theory be decoded *in a consistent way* by modular processes, and that the human visual system does not seem to estimate these surface properties independently, but does so cooperatively. The lesson behind the example is that on the theoretical end, one should carefully analyze different information processing tasks before deciding that they should be modularized. Moreover, when modeling human perception, one should directly test for modularity before relying on it to build models. We must also allow for the possibility of modularity in cases where it is not supported by a Bayesian analysis and where it may involve the application of inconsistent assumptions abut the world. This may require one to step out of the Bayesian framework to characterize the modular structure and the interactions between modules, while still characterizing the functional properties of the individual modules within a Bayesian framework.

The type of modularity we have discussed in the context of surface shape and reflectance perception is that of task modularity; for example, modularity in the estimation of different scene properties. Another form of potential modularity is in the processing of different image features or "cues" for the estimation of scene properties. The most commonly cited example of this is in the domain of shape and spatial layout perception. The last twenty years have seen a proliferation of models for the perception of "shape-from-X", where X might be shading, texture, stereo or any other source of image information about surface shape. Many of these features do not, however, provide independent information about shape. For those which are not independent, modular processing is non-ideal. Moreover, to the extent that any two information sources are processed independently, the different underlying modules may impose different or competing assumptions about the world and the image formation process. Thus, while it may be possible to develop accurate Bayesian models to explain how the human visual system processes each information source in isolation, it may be impossible to develop a consistent Bayesian model for human visual processing of them together. One is then left with the need to model some aspects of the interaction between the modules which process the different sources of information. We will not go into the variety of ways in which one could create such hybrid Bayesian/process models, but we refer the reader to chapter 4, by Yuille and Bülthoff, who consider this issue in some detail.

A final form of modularity which we would like to mention is in the serial processing of image data. A purely Bayesian model of perception would have to take as the sensory signal the luminance flux at the retina. Besides providing an impractical starting point for the analysis and modeling of many perceptual functions, it rests on an unrealistic view of high-level constraints being built into the lowest level sensory processes. To give an example where this may not be the case, consider hypothesized processes of edge-detection (Marr & Hildreth, 1992; Watt & Morgan, 1984; Zucker *et al.*, 1989). The visual system may well perform some form of edge detection and contour estimation which has only weak, if any, interactions with higher-level perceptual processes which make use of contour data. While one could model the early processes in a Bayesian framework, incorporating prior constraints on image contour structure, and at the same time build Bayesian models of the higher-level processes which use contour data, the two may not be entirely consistent, so that one has to characterize the interactions between the low and high level modules in order to fully characterize the visual processing of contour information.

6.5 Relations to other approaches

The Bayesian approach to perception has its roots in a number of historical trends in perceptual theory. In fact, we would argue that it brings together the strongest elements of a variety of approaches and in so doing builds on their similarities rather than their differences. Depending on philosophical preference, one can view the Bayesian framework as the natural extension and formalization of Helmholtz's notion of unconscious inference (Helmholtz, 1925), Gestalt ideas of Praegnanz (Koffka, 1935), Gibson's ecological optics (Gibson, 1979) and contemporary information processing ideas (Gregory, 1973; Marr, 1982; Rock, 1977). In this section, we develop these connections further, in the context of the dual roles of the Bayesian framework described earlier in the chapter; modeling visual information and modeling perceptual inference. First, we compare and contrast the Bayesian formulation of visual information with others which are currently popular; in particular, cue theory and ecological optics. Second, we relate the Bayesian formulation of perceptual inference to other theoretical notions of visual processing.

6.5.1 Contrasting views of information

Critical to the study of perception is the definition of a set of basic building blocks for the description of visual information. These building blocks, or "foundational" elements, for characterizing information should meet several criteria: (1) They should be well-defined and logically consistent; (2) They should relate properties of a system's input, on the one hand, to what in the environment those properties provide information "about", on the other hand (a point emphasized by James Gibson (Gibson, 1979)); (3) They should be free of unstated prior assumptions about both the environment and the system which processes the information they describe; (4) They should support descriptions of a wide a range of types of information; and (5) They should provide a useful language for specifying theories and experimentally testable hypotheses about the perceptual use of visual information.

In this section, we evaluate the two most prominent constructs used to characterize visual information, cues and invariants, as well as the conceptualization of information which falls out of a Bayesian view of information processing, in the context of these five criteria.

6.5.1.1 Cues

When considering the problem of how the visual system could acurately infer 3-dimensional scene properties (particularly depth) from the 2-dimensional projections of scenes onto a pair of retinal images, many researchers have taken the view that images contains cues, or hints, which the visual system uses to estimate 3-dimensional scene properties. Traditional cues for depth and shape include retinal size, interposition, linear perspective, aerial perspective, binocular disparity and motion parallax. Other cues which have begun to receive significant attention are texture gradients, shading and contours (e.g. occluding contours). Non-image based sources of information are also often referred to as cues; for example, the classic cues of accomodation and convergence. What one immediately notices about this list is the lack of significant common features among the definitions of the different "cues". This equivocality of definition is a major problem with the cue concept. As Ittleson, himself a proponent of the study of cues, notes,

The most obvious drawback to the descriptions is their lack of consistency. Some cues are described primarily in terms of the attributes of the physical object, some in terms of the light energy, some with reference to physiological excitation and some entirely in terms of psychological factors. This heterogeneity is not accidental. It reflects a basic property of the cue concept. A cue is not something that can be pointed to; rather it represents a complex interrelationship between a number of aspects that must be taken into account in the definition of the cue (Ittleson, 1960).

In other words, the cue construct violates the first criterion for a descriptor's usefulness: it is not well-defined.

A number of the features of cues listed by Ittleson illustrate how the cue concept also violates the third criterion given. First is his observation that some cues are defined in terms of "psychological" factors. By this, we take him to be referring to the prior knowledge of scene structure which an observer must use in interpreting a cue. Put differently, many cues require that the environment have a certain type of structure for them to be informative. Unfortunately, the assumptions about scene structure are confounded with characteristics of the image formation process in the definition of the cues, and thus are left implicit. This is exemplified in the definition of texture gradients as a cue for surface orientation and shape (Gibson, 1950). Texture gradients, of texture element density and shape, provide no constraint on surface shape by themselves. These gradients only have "meaning"; that is, provide information about surface shape, if one assumes something about the structure of the elements. The typical assumptions are that they are isotropic (uniformly distributed in the local planar orientation of the surface) and homogeneous (their distribution has the same statistical structure over a surface) (Blake & Marinos, 1990; Blake *et al.*, 1990; Witkin, 1981). Linear perspective is an even more striking example. In fact, the term linear perspective, properly used, describes the geometric mapping of scene properties to images, not a property of an image. The term, however, serves as a short-hand to mean the convergence of lines in an image. Taken as a cue for the shape of a polyhedral object, or the orientation of a planar surface, the convergence of such lines by itself no more determines the inference than does texture by itself. An assumption about the spatial layout of the edges which project to those lines must be made in order to reliably infer surface shape or orientation.

Ittleson also notes that many image cues are defined at least partly in terms of some scene property; that is, they include an assumption that some inference about the scene which projects to an image feature must have already been made in order to interpret that feature. Good examples of this are the different "types" of contour which appear in an image and are treated as cues for surface shape or orientation; for example, smooth occluding contours, surface marking contours and polyhedral edge contours. Each of these provide different information about surface shape; thus, their physical cause must be determined prior to, or in cooperation with, the inference of surface shape. The contour labelling experiments described in section 3 of this chapter illustrate the fact that perceived surface shape can affect contour labelling, much as contour labelling affects shape perception.

Finally, we note that a study of cues leads naturally to an assumption of modular processing in the visual system. This view is reflected in the types of question commonly used to frame problems of "cue integration"; for example, "How do different modules interact in generating perceptual estimates of a scene property (e.g. depth)?" As we noted in section 4, assumptions of modularity unnecessarily limit the scope of inquiry into visual information processing and should be treated as hypotheses about the organization of processing mechanisms, open to empirical investigation.

6.5.1.2 Gibsonian invariants

As an alternative to cue theories, James Gibson proposed that information for the perception of functionally important properties of scenes is unambiguously repre-sented in the image (or what he referred to as the "ambient optic array") in the form of invariant relations between properties of the image and scene properties (Gibson, 1979). An extreme statement of Gibson's position is that a complete functional de-scription of visual perception merely requires a list of available invariants (a theory of competence) and a list of the invariants actually used by the visual system (a theory of performance).

An image property has an invariant relationship to some scene property if it unambiguously determines the value of that scene property. An example of this is the time to contact variable, optical *tau*, which specifies the time at which an observer and a surface, moving together at constant relative velocity, will collide (Lee, 1981). The concept of invariants has much to recommend it as a foundational conception of information. The notion of an invariant is well defined (criterion 1). The specification of individual invariants requires an explicit description of the relationship an image property and the scene property about which it provides information (criterion 2). As usually defined; namely, as resulting simply from the laws of physics and projective geometry, they do not hide any implicit assumptions about the visual system or about the environment (criterion 3). Finally, they certainly provide a language for developing formal theories and testable hypotheses (criterion 5).

Unfortunately, the notion of invariants fails the fourth criterion; which requires that they afford the description of a general range of information types. We have noted that, as Gibson conceived them, invariants may be derived from the laws of physics and of projective geometry. This seems to obviate the need to assume prior constraints on scene structure; however, taking into account such constraints can lead to invariant relations not simply derivable from the image formation process (see chapter 4 for examples). Moreover, the condition that usable information unambiguously determine scene properties for those properties to be perceived is far too strong for a practical system. We will consider each of these points in turn by placing the notion of invariants in the Bayesian framework.

In probabilistic terms, one would say that an image property I has an invariant relationship to a scene property S if one can write the conditional distribution, $p(\mathbf{S}|\mathbf{I} = I)$ as a Dirac delta function supported at one value of $\mathbf{S}$. This differs somewhat from the traditional definition of an invariant in that the former can result from properties of the prior distribution, $p(\mathbf{S})$, whereas the latter is assumed to depend only on the image formation process. Jepson, et. al., this volume, describe how categorical structure in the environment can lead to invariant relationships between image properties and scene properties. To summarize one of the examples given there; suppose that the prior probability density of object motions has some proportion of its mass clustered in the subspace of zero motion (i.e. stationary objects occur in the environment with non-zero probability). One can then infer, with probability approaching 1, that if an object is stationary in an image, then it is stationary in the world. We could therefore say that the image motion of an object has an invariant relationship to the stationarity of the object in the world (though not to the quantitative estimate of world motion for non-stationary objects). Invariants such as this, which result from categorical structure in the environment, can only be derived through an explicit recognition of the categorical structure, something not taken into account in Gibson's formulation. We will therefore refer to them as probabilistic invariants.

It seems a simple matter to generalize the traditional notion of invariants to include probabilistic invariants, leaving the basic concept the same. This, however, still leaves us with a major limitation of the invariant concept, resulting from the requirement that image properties unambiguously imply scene properties. Such a strict invariance between image properties and scene properties is too strong a condition to determine what scene properties the visual system infers from images. Functional requirements play a strong role in determining what types of inference the system attempts to make, whether they can be made exactly or not. Even when the information provided by images only supports the inference of a scene property to within some limits on expected errors, such a degree of reliability may be all that is required for the functional needs of an observer. Furthermore, in real visual systems, many sources of uncertainty contribute to the likelihood function. These sources of uncertainty place absolute limits on the reliability with which any scene property can be inferred, and preclude the possibility of most inferences being unambiguous.

A final problem with attempting to explain all perceptual phenomena through a listing of invariants is that such a program of research limits one to investigating those image properties and scene properties which provide independent information about scene properties, leaving one with the same sort of modularity assumptions imposed by structuring theories in terms of cues.

6.5.1.3 The Bayesian view of information

Cues and invariants are a useful short-hand for characterizing visual information, but they should not be used as anything more than that, at least, not without testing the modularity assumptions on which they are based. Shading is a classic example of a source of visual information which requires a richer set of conceptual tools for its description. While often referred to as a cue for shape, shading (smooth variations in luminance in an image) is a function of a host of different scene properties: shape, illumination and surface albedo, to name a few. In order to fully characterize the information provided by shading about shape, one would have to embed it in a description of how shading constrains the interpretation of all of these scene properties. In a probabistic framework, this takes the form of a conditional distribution on all of these properties, given a shading pattern. This distribution is, of course, too complex to serve as the basis for building theories and generating testable hypotheses about visual processing, which leads us to Bayes' rule for splitting this conditional distribution into a prior distribution and a likelihood function. If we further decompose these distributions into a list of constraints which characterize different properties of the distributions, we obtain a construct, the well-formed constraint (see section 2), which is a useable building block for formal descriptions of visual information. Importantly, a study of constraints does not rely on assumptions of modularity; though, as we noted in section 4, models of human visual processing must necessarily combine specifications of constraints with a specification of the organizational strcture of visual processing, to allow for the possibility of non-ideal modularization of visual function.

Though constraints are the foundational elements for descriptions of information within a Bayesian framework, other higher level elements which can be derived from sets of constraints are also important. Specification of enough constraints will often enable one to derive probabilistic laws relating image properties back to scene properties (constraints on the posterior distribution). If the constraints are of an appropriate nature, these relationships may be at least approximately invariant (e.g. contour straightness → 3D edge straightness in a world in which straight edges occur with non-zero probability). Thus, there is an important place in the Bayesian lexicon of image information for Gibson's invariants and their generalizations, probabilistic invariants.

We close this section with a consideration of how well the Bayesian conceptualization of information meets our usefulness criteria. Certainly, it is well-defined (criterion 1). Specification of information constraints on both the image formation process and the structure of the environment provides a characterization of what image properties tell us about scenes (criterion 2). The definitions of Bayesian constraints do not rely on any assumptions about human visual processing nor do they rely on implicit assumptions about environmental structure, since these are made explicit through specifications of prior constraints (criterion 3). The formulation appears to be quite general in its ability to characterize information (criterion 4). Finally, the Bayesian framework provides the same structure and language for developing models of information and of functional aspects of perceptual inference, a critical element in the attempt to relate computational analyses of problems in vision to human perceptual performance (criterion 5).

6.5.2 Bayesianism: Ecological Gestaltism

The Bayesian view of perception as statistical inference has the familiar ring of Helmholtz's idea that perception is a process of unconscious inference (Helmholtz, 1925). The idea of unconscious inference and its derivatives (e.g. perception as problem solving (Rock, 1977)) imbues much of the modern, information processing approach to perception. As we have discussed in this chapter, the Bayesian framework provides a natural set of tools for formalizing this theoretical approach. The framework does, however, shift emphasis from how one constructs a model of the world from sense data to the constraints the system explicitly or implicitly imposes when generating estimates of world properties. This brings to mind a cooperative, constraint satisfaction network which resolves percepts of the world and is thus reminiscent of Gestalt theories.

The central concept in Gestalt theory is that of Praegnanz, that "psychological organization will be as good as the prevailing conditions allow" (Koffka, 1935). In the domain of perception, Gestaltists argue that percepts are organized according to various Praegnanz principles of "goodness" or "simplicity". Koffka identified goodness with minimum/maximum principles; such as maximum symmetry, minimum variation of form, and so on. Numerous attempts have been made to formalize Praegnanz principles; notable among these being the minimization of 'changes' in scene properties (Hochberg & McAlister, 1953), the minimal coding ideas of Leeuwenburg (Leeuwenburg, 1971), and the idea of relating Praegnanz principles to energy minimization in physical systems (Attneave, 1982). All of these have natural analogues in the specification of the prior structure of scenes used in Bayesian forulations of perception. Chapters 2 and 8 of this book formally develop the mathematical relations between the last two of these principles and probabilistic laws. Interestingly, Mach (Mach, 1897), who predated both Gestalt and modern information processing approaches to perception, explicitly recognized the relationship between Praegnanz principles, which he called efficiency principles, and probabilistic laws as far back as the 19th century. Thus, this is not a new idea (as few in perception really are).

Gibson criticized Gestalt theory for focusing on the constructive role played by the visual system at the cost of disregarding the relationship between the observer and the environment (Gibson, 1982). Attneave and Frost explicitly recognized this drawback to the Gestalt programme of research, noting that "A Praegnanz principle assumes a teleological system . . . in which simplicity has the status of a final cause or goal-state." (Attneave, 1982). Gibson, however, went too far in rejecting Gestalt ideas and stressing the importance of image invariants. The Bayesian approach, on the other hand, embraces Gestalt principles by explicitly relating them to the environment and incoporating them in a framework which recognizes the functional goals of perception. It is for this reason that we refer to the Bayesian framework as a form of ecological Gestaltism. From one point of view, Bayesian theories characterize information about the world, hence its ecological nature, from another, they characterize the constraints or principles which govern the formation of percepts, giving them a Gestalt character. This allows the Gestaltist in us to turn to studies of the world to find ideas for organizing principles which the visual system might apply in perceptual processing, and also allows the ecological psychologist in us to relate perceptual organization principles to the environment in which observers are embedded.

References

Adelson, E. H. (1993). Perceptual organization and the judgment of brightness. *Science*, **262**, 2042-2044.

Anderson, J.R. (1991). The adaptive nature of human categorization. *Psychological Review*, **98**, 409-429.

Attneave, F. & Frost, R. (1969). The determination of perceived tridimensional orientation by minimum criteria. *Perception & Psychophysics*, **6**, 391- 396.

Attneave, F. (1982). Pragnanz and soap bubble systems: a theoretical explanation. In *Organization and Representation in Perception*, ed. Beck. Hillsdale, NJ: Erlbaum.

Barlow, H. B. (1991). Vision tells you more than "What is Where." in *Representations of Vision*, ed. A. Gorea. Cambridge University Press.

Blake, A. & Marinos, C. (1990). Shape from texture: estimation, isotropy and moments. *Artificial Intelligence*, **45**, 323-380.

Blake, A., Bülthoff, H.H. & Sheinberg, D. (1990). Shape from texture: Ideal observers and human psychophysics. *Vision Research*, **33**, 1723-1737.

Bobick, A. (1987). Natural object categorization. MIT AI Lab Tech. Report 1001.

Cavanagh, P. & Leclerc, Y.G. (1989). Shape from Shadows. *Journal of Experimental Psychology, Human Perception and Performance*, **15**, 3-27.

Cavanagh, P. (1991). What's up in top-down processing? In *Representations of Vision: Trends and tacit assumptions in vision research*, ed. A. Gorea, pp. 295-304.

Do Carmo, M.P. (1976). *Differential Geometry of Curves and Surfaces*. Englewood Cliffs, NJ: Prentice-Hall.

Gibson, J.J. (1950). *The Perception of the Visual World*. Boston, MA: Houghton Mifflin.

Gibson, J.J. (1979). *The Ecological Approach to Vision*. Boston, MA: Houghton Mifflin.

Gilchrist, A.L. (1977). Perceived Lightness Depends on Perceived Spatial Arrangement. *Science*, **195**, 185-187.

Gibson, E. (1982). Contrasting emphases in Gestalt theory, information processing and the ecological approach to perception. In *Organization and Perception*, ed. Beck. Hillsdale, NJ: Erlbaum.

Gilchrist, A. (1980). When does perceived lightness depend on perceived spatial arrangement? *Perception & Psychophysics*, **28**, 527-538.

Gregory, R.L. (1973). *Eye and Brain: The Psychology of Seeing*. New York: McGraw-Hill.

Helmholtz, H. (1925). *Physiological Optics, Vol. III: The Perceptions of Vision (J.P. Southall, trans.)*. Optical Society of America, Rochester, NY. (Original publication in 1910).

Hochberg, J. & McAlister, E. (1953). A quantitative approach to figural "goodness". *Journal of Experimental Psychology*, **46**, 361-364.

Horn, B.K.P. (1973). On Lightness. (A.I. Memo No. 295). M.I.T.

Hurlbert, A. (1986). Formal connections between lightness algorithms. *J. Opt. Soc. Am. A*, **3**, 1684-1693.

Ikeuchi, K. & Horn, B.K.P. (1981). Numerical shape from shading and occluding contours. *Artificial Intelligence*, **17**, 141-184.

Ittleson, W.H. (1960). *Visual Space Perception*. New York: Springer.

Kersten, D. (1990). Statistical limits to image understanding. In *Vision: Coding and Efficiency*, ed. C. Blakemore. Cambridge Univ. Press.

Kersten, D.J. (1991). Transparency and the cooperative computation of scene attributes. In *Computational Models of Visual Processing*, ed. M. Landy and A. Movshon, eds., Cambridge, MA: MIT Press.

Kersten, D., Mamassian, P. & Knill, D.C. (1994). Moving cast shadows and the perception of relative depth. CogSci Memo No. 6, Max Planck Institute for Biological Cybernetics, Tübingen, Germany.

Knill, D.C. & Kersten, D. (1991). Apparent surface curvature affects lightness perception. Nature, **351**, 228-230.

Knill, D. & Kersten, D. (1991). Ideal perceptual observers for computation, psychophysics and neural networks. In *Vision and Visual Dysfunction, Vol.14: Pattern Recognition by Man and Machine*, ed. R. Watt. New York: MacMillan.

Knill, D.C. (1991). Perception of surface contours and surface shape: from computation to psychophysics. *Journal of the Optical Society of America, A*, **9**, 1449-1464.

Knill, D.C. (1990). The role of cooperative processing in the perception of surface shape and reflectance. PhD Dissertation, Brown University.

Koffka, K. (1935). *Principles of Gestalt Psychology*. New York: Harcourt, Brace and Co.

Land, E.H. & McCann, J. (1971). Lightness and retinex theory. *J. Opt. Soc. Am.*, **61**, 1-11.

Lee, D. (1981). Plummeting gannets: a paradigm of ecological optics. *Nature*, **293**, 197-198.

Leeuwenburg, E. (1971). A perceptual coding language for visual and auditory patterns. *American Journal of Psychology*, **84**, 307-349.

Mach, E. (1897). *Contributions to the Analysis of the Sensations*. (C.M. Williams, trans.). Chicago: Open Court Publishing.

Marr, D. & Hildreth, E. (1980). Theory of edge detection. *Proc. Royal Society of London, B*, **290**, 199-218.

Marr, D. (1982). *Vision: A Computational Investigation into the Human Representation and Processing of Visual Information*. New York: W.H. Freeman.

Pentland, A.P. (1982). Local shading analysis. SRI Technical Note 272.

Ramachandran, V.S. (1988). Perception of shape from shading. *Nature*, **331**, 163-166.

Rock, I. (1977). In defense of unconscious inference. In *Stability and Constancy in Visual Perception: Mechanism and Processes*, ed. W. Epstein. New York: John Wiley and

Sons.

Stevens, K. A. (1981). The visual interpretation of surface contours, *Artif. Intell.*, **17**, 47-73.

Szeliski, R. (1987). Regularization uses fractal priors. *Proceedings, AAAI-87*, Seattle, Washington, 749-754.

Todd, J. T. & Reichel, F. (1990). Ordinal structure in the visual perception and cognition of smoothly curved surfaces. *Psychological Review*, **96**, 643-657.

Turvey, M.T. (1977). Contrasting orientations to the theory of visual information processing. *Psychological Review*, **84**, 67-88.

da Vinci, L. (1970). *The Notebooks of Leonardo da Vinci, Vol. 1*. New York: Dover Press.

Watt, R.J. & Morgan, M.J. (1984). Spatial filters and the localization of luminance changes in human vision. *Vision Research*, **24**, 1387-1397.

Witkin, A. (1981). Recovering surface shape and orientation from texture. *Artificial Intelligence*, **17**, 17-45.

Yonas, A. (1978). Development of sensitivity to information provided by cast shadows in pictures. *Perception*, **7**, 333-341.

Zucker, S.W., Dobbins, A. & Iverson, L. (1989). Two stages of curve detection suggest two styles of visual computation. *Neural Computation*, **1**, 68-81.

7

Shape from texture: Ideal observers and human psychophysics

ANDREW BLAKE

Department of Engineering Science, University of Oxford, Parks Rd, Oxford OX1 3PJ, UK

HEINRICH H. BÜLTHOFF

Max-Planck Institute, Spemannstr. 38, D-740

DAVID SHEINBERG

Department of Cognitive and Linguistic Sciences, Brown University

7.1 Introduction

Texture cues in the image plane are a potentially rich source of surface information available to the human observer. A photograph of a cornfield, for example, can give a compelling impression of the orientation of the ground plane relative to the observer. Gibson (1950) designed the first experiments to test the ability of humans to use this texture information in their estimation of surface orientation. Since that time, various authors have proposed and tested hypotheses concerning the relative importance of different visual cues in human judgements of shape from texture (Cutting & Millard, 1984; Todd & Akerstrom, 1987). This work has generally relied on a cue conflict paradigm in which one cue is varied while the other is held constant. This is potentially problematic, since surfaces with conflicting texture cues do not occur in nature. It is possible that in a psychophysical experiment our visual system might employ a different mechanism to resolve the cue conflict condition. We show in this paper that the strength of individual texture cues can be measured and compared with an ideal observer model without resorting to a cue conflict paradigm.

Ideal observer models for estimation of shape from texture have been described by Witkin (1981), Kanatani & Chou (1989), Davis *et al.* (1983), Blake & Marinos (1990), Marinos & Blake (1990). Given basic assumptions about the distribution and orientation of texture elements, an estimate of surface orientation can be obtained, together with crucial information about reliability of the estimate. The estimated reliability constitutes a theoretical best performance from the given visual information. This is the sense in which the model is a statistical "ideal observer" and is similar to the approach used by Barlow (1980) in the context of detecting symmetry in random-dot patterns and by Kersten (1990) for the computation of scene descriptions. (See also the introductory tutorial and chapter 6 for further details.)

7.1.1 Texture cues for shape

In this paper, we primarily address the perception of statistical textures, as opposed
to the regular patterns used in some previous studies (Stevens, 1981; Stevens &
Brookes, 1988; Buckley *et al.*, 1989; Buckley & Frisby, 1991). We assume a texture model in which independent elements – texels – can be isolated. Voorhees &
Poggio (1988) have shown that such an assumption is computationally plausible.
Furthermore we assume *oriented* texels, elements with an in-built direction that is
a material property, not an artifact of projection. Thin line elements, for instance,
meet this requirement because the direction of the projected line in the image is
a *viewpoint-invariant* feature. Whatever the vantage point, the image line-element
direction is the projection of a fixed direction on the surface, namely the direction
of the surface line-element. Ellipses, however, do not meet this requirement. They
have no obvious viewpoint-invariant features in the image-plane. For instance, the
direction of the major axis of the projected ellipse is not viewpoint-invariant, since
it is a function both of the shape and orientation of the original ellipse and also of
the viewpoint.

Following Cutting & Millard (1984) we acknowledge three textural cues to shape:
compression, density, and perspective (see also Table 1). In the following, we describe these three cues; more formal definitions are deferred until Section 7.2.

7.1.2 Compression

Compression has traditionally referred to the ratio of the width to the length of
individual texture elements. This could, in principle, be a local cue for surface
orientation if the shape of a texel were known *a priori*. Recent psychophysical evidence, however, has shown that human observers can estimate shape from texture
without prior knowledge of texel shape. Nevertheless, such judgements were accurate only when the orientation of the compressed elements was consistent with
projective geometry (Todd & Akerstrom, 1987).

In our model, compression refers solely to the tendency of texel orientations to
align perpendicular to surface orientation (e.g., the horizon for planar surfaces).
More precisely, the compression cue is defined to be the spatial distribution of
observed texel orientations in the image plane. This definition can therefore apply
equally well to surfaces textured by elements with no measurable area (e.g., line
elements). The only necessary assumption for this model is that the distribution of
element orientations is isotropic. Based on this assumption, we can compute the
maximum information available in the projected texture pattern resulting from this
cue, without needing to specify how it is extracted by the human observer.

7.1.3 Density

We define the density cue as the spatial distribution of observed texel centres in the image plane. The density cue is observable under perspective projection and also, generally, under orthographic projection (see Horn (1986) for definitions of perspective and orthographic projection). The exception in the latter case is that, on a planar surface, the density cue provides no information about shape (i.e. the orientation of the planar surface). In order to use the density as a cue for surface orientation, it is necessary to make some assumption about the prior, statistical distribution of texture elements over the object surface. The natural default is a prior assumption of homogeneity: that the probability density function for the positions of texel centres on the surface is uniform, but of unknown magnitude. Any observed gradients of image density (Gibson, 1979) must then be due to projective effects and hence be dependent on local surface orientation relative to the line of sight. In the case of a plane under orthographic projection, the homogeneity assumption also leads to a uniform probability density for the positions of texel centres in the *image*. The orientation of the plane affects only the magnitude of the density, which does not serve as a cue given the assumption that the magnitude of the surface density is *a priori* unknown.

In contrast, when compression is spatially uniform, it *is* an observable cue. Even in the absence of any gradients of compression, the *degree* of compression is a valid cue to shape which has however been neglected (Cutting & Millard, 1984). It is a valid cue because, unlike density, for which the prior assumption is that it has some uniform but unknown value, compression is assumed, under the isotropy assumption, to be uniform and of known value: there is zero compression *a priori*, on the surface. Any texel compression observed in the image therefore indicates that the surface is slanted relative to the image plane, even when that compression is spatially uniform.

7.1.4 Perspective

Texture gradients due to perspective are a result of the scaling of texels inversely with distance from the viewer. This scaling effect is additional to the effect of compression. In the limit of orthographic projection this cue disappears because distance from the viewer to points on a viewed surface is approximately constant. However, the perspective cue is difficult to model statistically because of the lack of any uniquely natural prior assumption about texel size (unlike the other two cues for which homogeneity and isotropy were the natural default assumptions).

Given that we cannot model the perspective cue statistically, how can this cue be eliminated experimentally? There are two ways to do this. First we can use a small field of view so that, approaching the limit of orthographic projection, inverse depth scaling is minimal. Second we can use thin line elements as texels, randomly orientated, for which perspective scaling cannot directly be measured[†].

The properties of the three texture cues are summarised in Table 7.2.

7.1.5 *Integration of texture cues*

Each texture cue present in a particular image offers an "opinion" about surface shape. These opinions, each with their own reliability measure, must somehow be merged to form a joint opinion and associated reliability. Interactions between cues may either be *consistent* or *contradictory*. For example, consider viewing a golf ball with both eyes. There will be consistent depth information from stereo, shading and texture cues. Viewing an image of the same golf ball in a photograph, however, puts the stereo cues (which give constant depth for the entire photograph) into *conflict* with shading and texture, hence the cues are now contradictory. Psychophysicists have attempted to deal with the first case by taking weighted linear combinations with some success (Dosher *et al.*, 1986; Bruno & Cutting, 1988). The case of conflicting cues seems to require significant nonlinearity and is usually assumed to require a different, and independent, mechanism. For example, this case is explicitly excluded in the statistical framework for fusion of depth information proposed by Maloney & Landy (1989).

7.2 The ideal observer model

In this section we outline the framework for constructing ideal observer models for inference of shape from statistical texture. The following assumptions are made:

Parametric surfaces:

> Visible surfaces are of the form
>
> $$z = f(X, Y; \mathbf{a})$$
>
> where $\mathbf{a} = (a_1, a_2, .., a_M)$ is a set of continuous parameters specifying a particular member of a certain family of surfaces and X, Y are image coordinates. An example is the two-parameter family of paraboloids of the form $z = a_1 X^2 + a_2 Y^2$. A world coordinate frame (x, y, z) is defined with (x, y) parallel to (X, Y).

[†] Of course, if we somehow first measured the distribution of texel shape, using a textured surface of known orientation (e.g., looking down at the pebbles on a beach) this prior knowledge could be used in a statistical model.

Cues	Geometric Transformation	Statistical assumption	Ortho-Proj. curved surface	Ortho-Proj. planar surface	Persp-Proj. all surfaces
Compression		isotropy	Cue	Cue	Cue
Density		homogeneity	Cue	No Cue	Cue
Perspective (Scaling)		non-general	No Cue	No Cue	Cue

Table 7.1.

Imaging projection:

The surface is observed in a monocular view. In this paper, for the purposes of modelling, we assume that the field of view is restricted sufficiently that image projection is well approximated by the orthographic limit. This will simplify the mathematics of the ideal observer model.

Surface texture:

The texture is assumed to consist of a set of discrete, statistically independent texels, each generated in the tangent plane to the surface at a particular point. It is assumed that each texel is sufficiently small that it can be considered planar.

Texel observation:

The subject makes a set of observations

$$\mathbf{w} = (w_1, w_2, ..., w_N)$$

of N visible texels. Each observation w_n consists of a number of measurements of the texel in the *projection* of the surface onto the image. In this paper we will consider $w_n = (X_n, Y_n, \alpha_n)$ where X, Y denote image coordinates of the texel centre and α denotes a texel orientation defined relative to the X axis.

Prior distribution of texels:

We assume that *a priori* distributions for the w_n are known. In principle, any prior knowledge, either general or specific, is usable. Specific distributions might be known in experiments where subjects were trained on a particular texture. Having observed numerous fronto-parallel planar instances of the texture they might learn prior distributions for texture position, orientation and shape. In this paper we consider general assumptions: first, that texel position is uniformly distributed over the area of the surface (*homogeneity*), and second, that texel orientation is uniformly distributed on the surface[†] (*isotropy*). Note that the homogeneity assumption implies that the probability density for texel position is uniform over the surface, but that the magnitude of that density is *a priori* unknown.

Posterior distributions of texels:

The posterior (image) distributions of texel position, X, Y, and orientation, α, depend on the prior distributions and also on the biasing effects of projection. The posterior distribution itself is not, of course, observable. Instead the subject sees a sample, $\mathbf{w}$, of texels from that distribution. The posterior distribution of position is the *density* cue. The posterior distribution of orientation is the *compression* cue.

[†] More precisely, a texel at a particular point on the surface must lie in the tangent plane there, and the probability density function for its orientation in that plane is uniform.

The ideal observer model uses the sample, **w**, of image texels to estimate which surface from the allowed family of surfaces generated that particular sample of texels in the image. In the related psychophysical task, the subject observes **w** and is asked to estimate, by means of an adjustment task, the surface parameter **a**.

7.2.1 The maximum likelihood principle

The applicability of Bayesian (MAP) estimation as a model for "shape from texture" was first noted by Witkin (1981). He applied it to the problem of estimating the orientation of an isotropically textured plane under orthographic projection[†]. Maximum Likelihood Estimation (MLE) differs from Bayesian estimation in that it depends only on texel distributions (compression, density) not on the prior distribution of surface orientation. In the planar case, for instance, this means that it is no longer necessary to attempt the difficult task of modelling the probability distribution for the orientation of planes (including possible bias towards ground planes etc.). *Asymptotically*, in the limit that many texels are visible, the two kinds of estimator are identical. That is, provided sufficiently many texels are visible, the prior distribution of surface orientation becomes negligible in comparison to the prior distribution (e.g., isotropy and homogeneity) of texel observables.

An MLE estimator can be regarded in either of the following two senses. It can be treated as an ideal observer model, appealing to standard results (Rao, 1973) showing that asymptotically the MLE is a best estimator in the sense of achieving the minimum possible variance – the so-called "Cramer-Rao lower bound". This is the principal sense in which we use MLE models in this paper, as a laboratory standard of statistical efficiency against which to compare experimental results. Alternatively the MLE can be regarded as a candidate biological model for visual perception of shape. It has been shown (Blake & Marinos, 1990), in the case of orthographic views of planes, the MLE for planar orientation can be reduced to the calculation of a certain second moment of texel orientations. This can be represented as a linear network with oriented edge-detectors at the input and units value-coded for tilt at the output. Biological embodiment of the MLE need not therefore be ruled out on grounds of excessive complexity.

7.2.2 Maximum likelihood estimator for shape

An MLE for shape is constructed by means of a *Log-Likelihood Function* $L(\mathbf{w}|\mathbf{a})$ which is the logarithm of the probability of having observed a particular set of

---

[†] A good review of MAP, MLE and other relevant statistical concepts including the "Cramer-Rao lower bound" is given by Papoulis (1990).

texels **w** *given* that the surface parameter was **a**. The value **â** that maximises L is the estimated shape. In turn L is constructed as a sum over all visible texels:

$$L(\mathbf{w}|\mathbf{a}) = \sum_{n=1}^{N} \log p(w_n|\mathbf{a}),$$

where $p(w|\mathbf{a})$ is the posterior probability of having observed a particular individual texel w, given that the surface parameter had the value **a**.

What is of particular interest is the case that each texel observation w_n contains more than one independent component. How are the individual components combined? We model a texel observable as $w = (X, Y, \alpha)$ which includes the density cue in terms of texel position (X, Y) and the compression cue in terms of orientation α. The effect of the two cues can be factorised:

$$p(w|\mathbf{a}) = p_D(X, Y|\mathbf{a})p_C(\alpha|X, Y, \mathbf{a}),$$

where p_D and p_C are posterior distributions for *single* cues, density and compression respectively. Now the log-likelihood L splits additively into two components

$$L(\mathbf{w}|\mathbf{a}) = L_D(\mathbf{w}|\mathbf{a}) + L_C(\mathbf{w}|\mathbf{a}),$$

where

$$L_D(\mathbf{w}|\mathbf{a}) = \sum_{n=1}^{N} \log p_D(X_n, Y_n|\mathbf{a})$$

and

$$L_C(\mathbf{w}|\mathbf{a}) = \sum_{n=1}^{N} \log p_C(\alpha_n|X_n, Y_n, \mathbf{a}).$$

The two components L_C and L_D are log-likelihoods for the two cues treated individually over the visible texture.

7.2.3 Fisher information

The Fisher Information contained in the observable texture **w** on the parameter **a** is defined to be (Rao, 1973)

$$\mathcal{I}(\mathbf{a}) = -E\left[\partial^2 L(\mathbf{w}|\mathbf{a})/\partial \mathbf{a}^2\right] \tag{7.1}$$

where $E[..]$ denotes expected value[†]. It measures information in the sense that $(1/N)\mathcal{I}^{-1}$ is a lower bound (Cramer-Rao) on the variance[‡] of *any* unbiased estimator

---

[†] $\partial/\partial\mathbf{a}$ denotes differentiation with respect to each of the components of the vector **a**. For instance, given a scalar function f, its derivative is defined to be the following vector: $\partial f/\partial\mathbf{a} = (\partial f/\partial a_1, .., \partial f/\partial a_M)$.

[‡] When **a** has more than one component, $\mathcal{I}$ is a matrix and $\mathcal{I}^{-1}$ denotes the matrix inverse. In this paper we consider cases in which **a** is a single parameter and hence $\mathcal{I}$ is a scalar.

of **a**. Asymptotically, the maximum likelihood estimator **â** reaches this bound and hence a "best" estimator.

In the two-cues case, Fisher Information $\mathcal{I}$, like the log-likelihood L, is additive so that:

$$\mathcal{I}(a) = \mathcal{I}_D(\mathbf{a}) + \mathcal{I}_C(\mathbf{a}) \tag{7.2}$$

Since Fisher Information is an expected value, it is calculated by integrating over all possible values of observable features. For instance, for the density cue,

$$\mathcal{I}_D(\mathbf{a}) = -N \int_{\text{image}} p_D(X, Y|\mathbf{a})(\partial^2 \log p_D(X, Y|\mathbf{a})/\partial \mathbf{a}^2) \, dX \, dY. \tag{7.3}$$

Similarly, for the compression cue,

$$\mathcal{I}_C(\mathbf{a}) = -N \int_{\text{image}} \int_0^{2\pi} p_D(X, Y|\mathbf{a}) p_C(\alpha|X, Y, \mathbf{a})$$
$$(\partial^2 \log p_C(\alpha|X, Y, \mathbf{a})/\partial \mathbf{a}^2) \, d\alpha \, dX \, dY. \tag{7.4}$$

In each case, as expected, Fisher Information is proportional to the number N of visible texels. Hence the variance bound is inversely proportional to N, a familiar statistical property.

Later, in the experimental section of the paper, we compare variances of subjects' responses against theoretical lower bounds for density alone, compression alone, and both together. These bounds are based on $\mathcal{I}_D$, $\mathcal{I}_C$ and $\mathcal{I}$ respectively. For instance, a subject whose variance is significantly less than that computed from $\mathcal{I}_D$ cannot have been using the density cue alone. A subject whose variance is significantly below the one computed from $\mathcal{I}$ must have used extraneous information other than what was contained in the texture cues.

7.2.4 The role of statistical information in cue combination

Given that $\mathcal{I}_D$ and $\mathcal{I}_C$ are natural measures of the information present in density and compression cues it seems reasonable that they should be used when cues are combined to indicate relative reliability. In fact the optimal combination – in the sense of having the lowest overall variance – does indeed mix estimates based on each of the two cues individually, in the ratio of their respective information measures (Rao, 1973). Thus, given estimates $\hat{\mathbf{a}}_D$, $\hat{\mathbf{a}}_C$ from individual cues, assumed unbiased, the best combined estimate from both cues is

$$\hat{\mathbf{a}} = \frac{\hat{\mathbf{a}}_C \, \mathcal{I}_C(\mathbf{w}|\hat{\mathbf{a}}_C) + \hat{\mathbf{a}}_D \, \mathcal{I}_D(\mathbf{w}|\hat{\mathbf{a}}_D)}{\mathcal{I}_C(\mathbf{w}|\hat{\mathbf{a}}_C) + \mathcal{I}_D(\mathbf{w}|\hat{\mathbf{a}}_D)}. \tag{7.5}$$

If we hypothesise that human vision approaches this optimal strategy for cue combination we can make certain predictions about psychophysical performance.

For instance, we can predict theoretically when one cue should be stronger than another and look for corresponding experimental results. (See chapter 4 in this volume for additional discussion of cue integration.)

7.3 Theoretical predictions

The previous section reviewed the calculation of Fisher Information and the consequent bounds on estimator variance *given* the posterior probability density functions p_C and p_D. These functions depend on the family of textured surfaces being viewed. In this section we show first how to construct the functions given a family of surfaces. Then we can compute Fisher Information functions for the cases of parabolic cylinders viewed orthographically and planes viewed in perspective. These are used to predict performance in terms of variance in subjects' responses in estimation tasks and to predict the relative dominance of the compression and density cues under various conditions.

7.3.1 *Slant and tilt*

It transpires that the probability density functions p_C and p_D can be defined concisely in terms of *slant* σ and *tilt* τ. Slant and tilt are used commonly to parameterise the orientation of a planar surface (see e.g. Witkin (1981)). They are simply polar coordinates for the direction of the plane normal, relative to the line of sight. Slant is the angle by which the surface dips away from the frontal plane and tilt is the direction in which the dip takes place (Marr, 1982). For a non-planar surface $z = f(X, Y, \mathbf{a})$, the tangent plane at each point on the surface has its own slant and tilt. They can be evaluated from the local surface gradient

$$\nabla f = (\partial f/\partial X, \partial f/\partial Y). \tag{7.6}$$

Slant is given by:

$$\sec \sigma = \sqrt{1 + (\partial f/\partial X)^2 + (\partial f/\partial Y)^2} \tag{7.7}$$

and tilt is defined by:

$$\tan \tau = \frac{\partial f/\partial Y}{\partial f/\partial X}. \tag{7.8}$$

7.3.2 *Posterior probability function for the density cue*

The probability density function $p_D(X, Y, \mathbf{a})$ for the density cue is relatively simply derived. Applying the homogeneity assumption, the probability of finding a texel within some small patch of the image is proportional to the backprojected area of patch on the surface $z = f(X, Y, \mathbf{a})$. Assuming orthographic projection

$$p_D(X, Y, \mathbf{a}) = \frac{\sec \sigma}{A} \tag{7.9}$$

where the normalising constant is

$$A = \iint_{\text{image}} \sec \sigma \, dX \, dY, \tag{7.10}$$

the total visible surface area. This expression for p_D, for a particular family of surfaces, can now be inserted into equation (7.3) to compute the Fisher Information function $\mathcal{I}_D(\mathbf{a})$ associated with the density cue.

7.3.3 Posterior probability function for the compression cue

The compression cue is a little more complex, involving the biasing of the texel direction *away* from the gradient direction of the surface. Witkin (1981) shows that the biased posterior probability distribution p_C is then given by:

$$p_C(\alpha|\sigma, \tau) = \frac{1}{2\pi} \frac{\sec \sigma}{\sin^2(\alpha - \tau) + \sec^2 \sigma \cos^2(\alpha - \tau)}. \tag{7.11}$$

Now σ, τ, representing local surface gradient, are functions of the surface parameter α, and of position on the surface which is a function of image location X, Y. Thus p_C can be used in equation (7.4) to compute the Fisher Information $\mathcal{I}_C(\mathbf{a})$ associated with the compression cue.

7.3.4 Parabolic cylinders in a narrow field of view

The preceding equations (7.3) and (7.4) form, together with equations (7.9) and (7.11), a procedure to evaluate the Fisher information functions $\mathcal{I}_C$ and $\mathcal{I}_D$. Using MATHEMATICA, a functional programming language, a surface family is defined by defining the form of the function $f(..)$ which is then passed as a parameter to the procedure that evaluates $\mathcal{I}_C, \mathcal{I}_D$. Because the language includes symbolic calculus, the formulae (7.3) and (7.4) for cue-information can be programmed directly, with the integrals and partial derivatives left in symbolic form.

Experiments in the following section relate to a family of textured parabolic cylinders (Fig. 7.1) with vertical axes. These are surfaces of the form $z = f(X, Y; e)$ where[†]

$$f(x, y; e) = e(1 - X^2), \quad -1 \le X \le 1. \tag{7.12}$$

[†] Note, that e (elongation) is a single real number in this specially simple case of the family of parabolic cylinders. Thus the parameter vector $\mathbf{a}$ mentioned earlier reduces now to a vector with one component e only. From here on therefore we refer to e in place of $\mathbf{a}$.

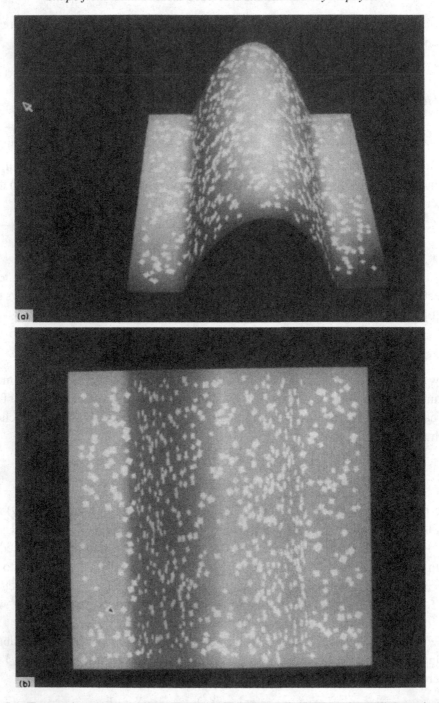

Fig. 7.1 Textured parabolic cylinders (a), viewed perpendicularly to the cylinder axis (b), are used to test subjects' variance of response and cue-integration performance. The family is indexed by the parameter *e* which specifies the "elongation" of the parabolic cylinder (c) – see also text.

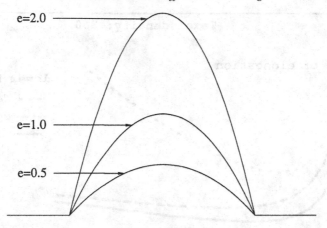

e=2.0

e=1.0

e=0.5

Fig. 7.1 (*continued*)

The z-axis points towards the viewer so that the surfaces appear convex. The parameter e is the "elongation", controlling surface relief. Values of the parameter fall, for practical reasons, in the range $0 \leq e \leq 2.5$ as in Fig. 7.1b.

Having defined a surface family, we can finally compute Fisher Information functions for the two texture cues, both separately and jointly. The results are shown in Fig. 7.2, plotted as lower bounds on the *standard deviations* of subjects' responses (in units of elongation), as a function of the true elongation e of the presented stimulus. Following the definition of the Cramer-Rao bound in the previous section, the plotted lower-bounds on standard deviation are $1/\sqrt{\mathcal{I}_D(e)}$, $1/\sqrt{\mathcal{I}_C(e)}$, and $1/\sqrt{\mathcal{I}_D(e) + \mathcal{I}_C(e)}$ for density, compression and both, respectively.

A number of predictions can be made on the basis of the graphs of Fig. 7.2.

  (i) Under the earlier hypothesis that cues might be integrated linearly, weighted in proportion to their statistical information, it is natural to define "dominance" of one cue over another to be the ratio of respective information measures (or, equivalently, the inverse square of the C.R. lower bounds on standard deviation). Fig. 7.2c shows that compression dominates density ($\mathcal{I}_C/\mathcal{I}_D > 1$) for the family of parabolic cylinders.

 (ii) The dominance of compression over density is least pronounced for zero elongation (planar), becoming more pronounced as elongation e increases.

(iii) Since predicted standard deviations are significantly higher for the density cue alone than for the other two conditions, it should be possible to test experimentally whether or not the compression cue may have been used. If standard deviations of responses fall below the lower bound for density alone some further information must have been used.

(iv) One might not expect to be able to distinguish from standard deviations of responses whether or not the density cue is being used. This is because the "compression only" and "both cues" curves in Fig. 7.2a,b are relatively close throughout the experimentally practicable range of elongations.

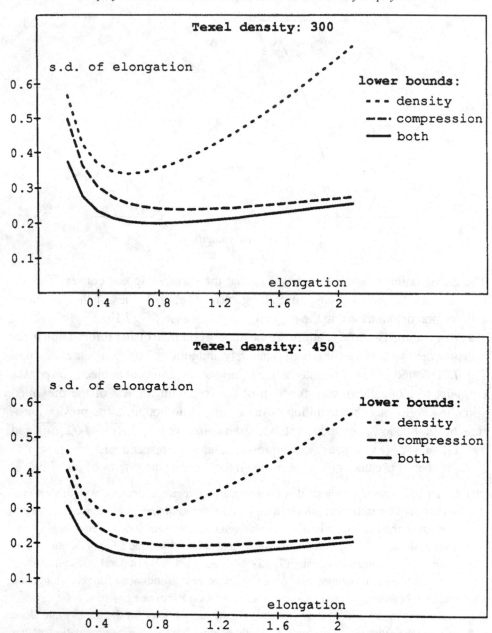

Fig. 7.2 The theory of Maximum Likelihood Estimation and Fisher Information is used to generate lower bounds on subjects' standard deviation in estimating the "elongation" of textured parabolic cylinders. a,b) Predictions are shown for density cue only, compression cue only and both cues together. This is done for two texture densities, $\rho = 300, 450$, the difference between them being simply due to the $1/\sqrt{\rho}$ scaling of the standard deviations. c) The information ratio $\mathcal{I}_C/\mathcal{I}_D$ measures the strength of the compression cue relative to the density cue. Compression is always stronger, its dominance over density becoming more pronounced as elongation e increases.

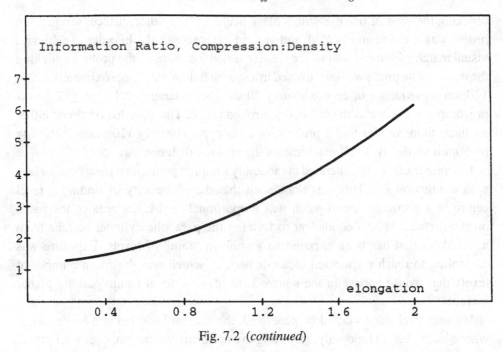

Fig. 7.2 (*continued*)

7.4 Psychophysical results

Two types of experiments have been performed to test hypotheses arising from the ideal observer model for perception of textured parabolic cylinders. First, we have measured the standard deviations of observers' judgements of shape. These have been compared with ideal observer predictions. Second, following Cutting & Millard (1984) and Todd & Akerstrom (1987) we have measured responses to stimuli in which the compression and density cues are in conflict. We compare our results (Sheinberg *et al.*, 1990) with predicted cue-dominance based on statistical information for the ideal observer. In each case stimuli were generated using real-time graphics and their shape was estimated by the method of adjustment, after Bülthoff & Mallot (1988, 1990).

7.4.1 Stimulus generation

A Stardent GS1000 graphics mini-supercomputer was used for stimulus generation and display, together with a pair of electro-optic shutter glasses (StereoGraphics Corp.) for stereoscopic viewing. Subjects viewed a pair of computer generated surfaces (Fig. 7.1), arranged side by side. Each surface was defined in terms of vertically oriented parabolic cylinders, resting against a similarly textured, planar background. One surface was the textured stimulus, and was seen monocularly by blocking the view of one eye with a black occluder. The other surface, serving as a *probe*, was textured and shaded, and viewed stereoscopically. In order to achieve a visual match with the stimulus, the subject varied the shape of the probe by clicking the mouse. The probe was constructed in a *square* field of view approximately 120×120mm. A sequence of approximately 30 surfaces, spanning $0.1 \le e \le 2.5$, was precomputed for use as the subject-controlled probe. The stimulus occupied either a square field, similar to the probe's, or a *slit* approximately 120mm horizontally by 50mm vertically. In all experiments the viewing distance was 95cm.

Discrete texels were generated at randomly sampled points on a parabolic surface with elongation e_D. This was done such that the probability of finding a texel centre in a particular small patch was proportional to dA, the area of the patch on the surface. This is equivalent to forming the parabolic cylinder surface from a flat sheet that has been exposed to a uniform "rain" of texels. Exposure was controlled to reach a specified mean density, ρ, which was the mean number of texels that would appear in the square field of view for a fronto-parallel planar surface.

Various texel shapes could be generated, the standard one being a line element whose length varied randomly, according to a uniform distribution, over a 2:1 range. This was done to remove the possibility of the projected element length acting as a deterministic shape cue.[†] The line element was defined in 3D to lie on the surface of a parabolic cylinder with elongation e_C. Element orientation was selected randomly, distributed uniformly in the tangent plane to the parabolic cylinder. Note that, in the case of the stimulus, e_C and e_D could be set independently. Choosing them to be unequal was the mechanism for generation of conflicting density and compression cues. For the probe, however, texture cues never conflicted and also were consistent with shading and stereoscopic cues.

Once the 3D texels were selected, by random sampling as above, they were projected onto the stereoscopic image. This is done in such a way (Bülthoff & Mallot, 1988) that the projection remains correct regardless of fixation point, given that the subject's head is located in a fixture (Fig. 7.3).

Experiment 1

The aim of the first experiment was to compare measured standard deviations in adjusted elongation e against the ideal observer model presented in the theoretical section. Stimuli were generated at random from the family of parabolic cylinders described earlier, with elongations lying in the range $0 \le e \le 2$. Texture cues

---

[†] There remains however a possibility that the uniform distribution might be used by the observer as a prior distribution from which a statistical shape cue could be obtained. This possibility is yet to be investigated theoretically and experimentally.

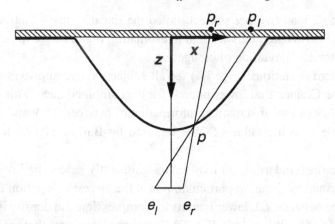

Fig. 7.3 Imaging geometry. Projection onto the $x - z$ plane. Viewing distance is 95cm. Nodal points of left and right eyes are e_L, e_R respectively, separated by 6.5cm. A point p is image onto the screen at p_l for the view from the left eye and at p_r for the view from the right eye.

were consistent, so that $e_C = e_D$, and there was no shading cue – texels were superimposed on a plain-coloured background. Shape judgements are harder to make in the absence of shading but with the benefit that shape information is purely textural. Stimuli for a variety of texel densities and parabolic elongations were presented in random order. A typical experiment involved two densities and four elongations each presented 32 times, split across 4 sessions. The relatively large numbers of presentations (total of 1440 measurements) were required to achieve significant measurements of standard deviation.

Results are shown in Fig. 7.4 for five subjects: ISA and GFB were naive, AB, HHB, DLS were not[†] A reduced field *horizontal slit* was used for the stimuli since statistical efficiency is likely to be impaired by an excessively large field of view. Measured standard deviations with confidence intervals are plotted against the predictions of the ideal observer model. The predictions are essentially those based on the Cramer-Rao lower bounds shown in Fig. 7.2. There is one important difference however. Cramer-Rao bounds apply to *unbiased* estimators. Subjects' responses prove not to be wholly unbiased however. Means often show some regression towards fronto-parallel, a phenomenon that was demonstrated by Bülthoff *et al.* (1988-1991). Thus data analysis includes a linear fit for mean adjusted elongation versus true elongation, whose slope is defined to be the *bias* β. Lower bounds on standard deviations must then be multiplied by β. Note that the linear fit was checked by a χ^2 test and sessions which failed the test were rejected (11 sessions out of 45,

---

[†] Naivity was not a major issue in our experiments because it is not possible to purposefully manipulate standard deviations without also affecting the mean. Systematic changes in standard deviation are then neutralised by our bias correction procedure (see text).

and never more than two per subject, failed the linearity test). Statistical error in the linear fit is also taken into account in estimating β and hence in deriving lower bounds on standard deviation of elongation.

The standard deviations (Fig. 7.4) for all subjects range approximately from 1 to 2 times the Cramer-Rao lower bounds for the combined cues. This corresponds to an efficiency of use of statistical information of between 25% and 100% which is comparable with the value of 25% reported by Barlow (1980) for symmetry detection.

In some cases standard deviations were significantly below the lower bound for density information alone. In particular, it is at the largest elongation $e = 2.0$, that the difference between s.d. lower bounds for compression and density is greatest. In that case, 3 out of 5 subjects (AB, ISA, DLS) register data points that are significantly (at the 99% level) below the lower bound for the density cue. This is true for both texture densities $\rho = 300, 450$. The most likely conclusion is that at least some subjects are able to use the compression cue.

Experiment 2

In order to use subjects' standard deviations as a psychophysical measure of the strength of shape cues we have to assume that our method is sensitive enough to record standard deviations below the Cramer-Rao lower bounds of the individual shape cues. Therefore we tested the sensitivity of our experimental paradigm in a control experiment. Subject HHB repeated the experiment with stereo and shading cues added back to the stimulus (Fig. 7.5). Under these circumstances we would predict that standard deviations could fall below the Cramer-Rao lower bounds for texture cues alone. From Fig. 7.5 it is apparent that standard deviations are greatly reduced relative to the standard experiment and fall below the Cramer-Rao lower bounds for texture cues. Recall that standard deviations below the lower Cramer-Rao lower bounds are only possible if cues other than the ones modelled in the Ideal Observer are employed. This control demonstrates the obvious fact that we can use other cues if they are available, and it also shows that the method is sensitive enough to record small standard deviations. Therefore possible limitations of measuring standard deviations close to the Cramer Rao lower bounds are ruled out.

Experiment 3

Another possible methodological limitation was the use of line elements as texels – a limitation imposed by our Ideal Observer model. As an additional control we used circular texels instead of the standard line elements. The circles project to ellipses in the image so that, in principle, it is possible to estimate surface slant deterministically

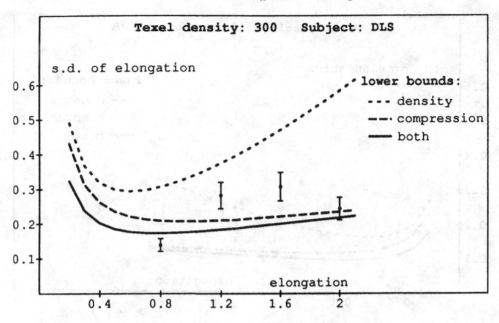

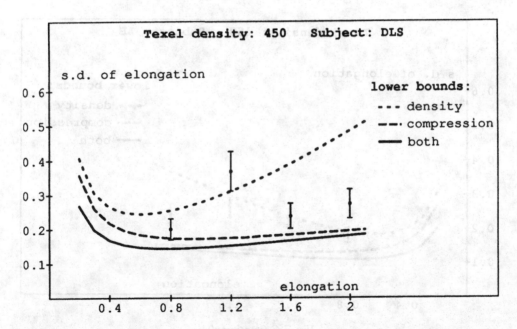

Fig. 7.4 Results of standard deviation measurements for judgements of the elongation of textured parabolic surfaces are shown by dots and error bars. They are plotted against theoretical predictions based on Fig. 7.2, which have been adjusted to take account of bias in subjects' mean responses. Results are shown for two densities $\rho = 300, 450$.

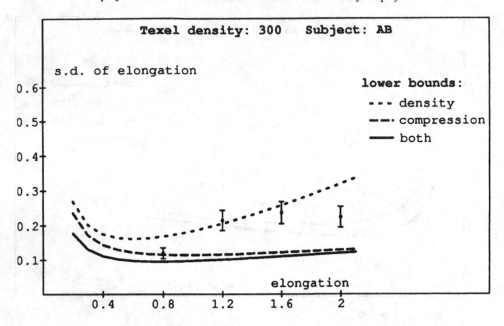

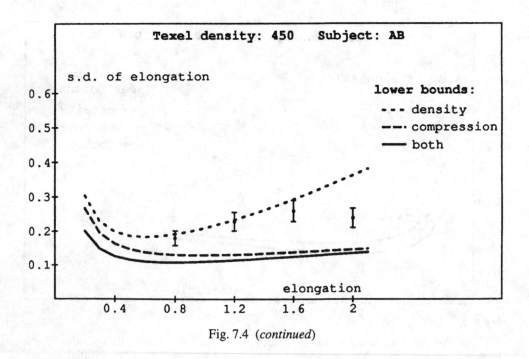

Fig. 7.4 (*continued*)

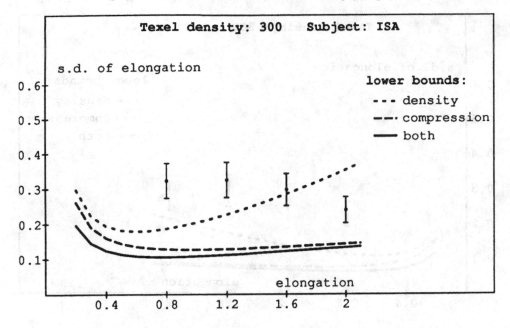

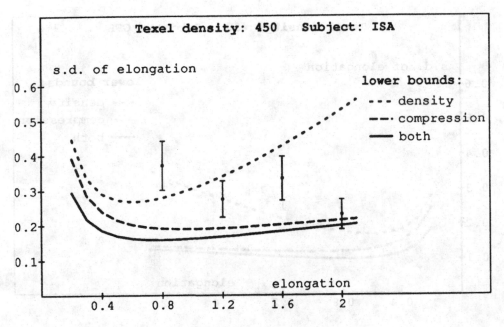

Fig. 7.4 (*continued*)

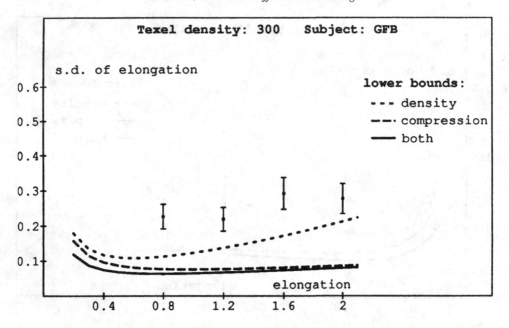

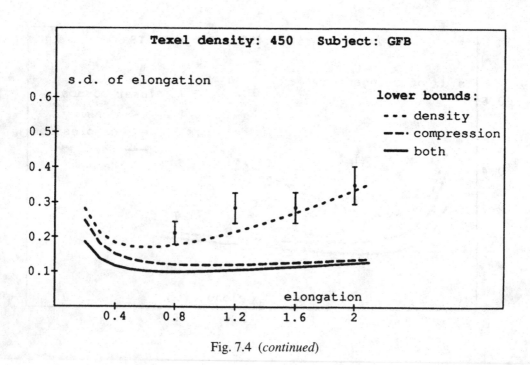

Fig. 7.4 (*continued*)

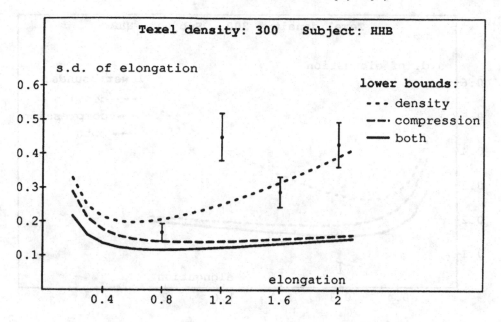

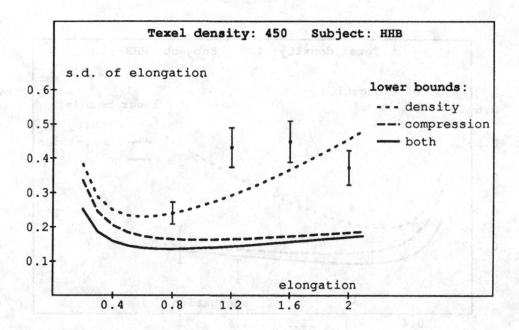

Fig. 7.4 (*continued*)

310   *A. Blake, H.H. Bülthoff & D. Sheinberg*

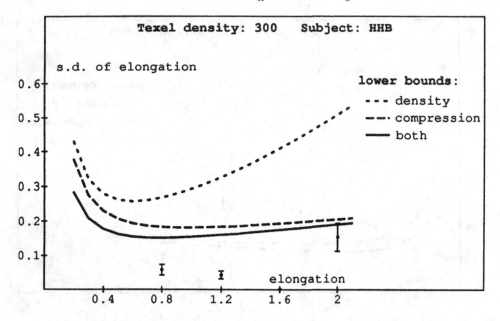

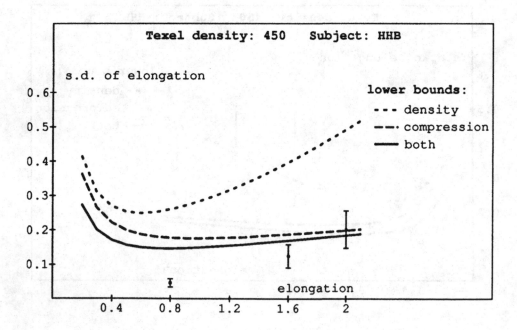

Fig. 7.5 Results for a control in which the stimulus is shaded and viewed stereoscopically. Recorded standard deviations are considerably reduced compared with the same subject in Fig. 7.4.

for each pixel. In other words the Ideal Observer for circular shapes should be exact. If the human visual system could fully use the elliptical shape cue, one would expect a great reduction in standard deviations of estimated elongations. Results of this control (Fig. 7.6) show that standard deviations *are* somewhat reduced but only by a factor of 2 or less, a lesser factor than in the previous experiment (Fig. 7.5).

Experiment 4

In order to compare our results with the cue conflict paradigm used in previous studies of shape from texture, we used our stimuli in a cue conflict experiment. Note that our technique of generating texture and shading on virtual surfaces allows us independent control of different shape cues by mapping texture compression or density on different surfaces. We presented monocularly viewed stimuli in a square field of view, with shading. All experiments were done with line element texels at a density of $\rho = 300$ with the following three conditions randomly interleaved: 1) consistent shading, density and compression, 2) consistent shading and density with "flat" compression, and 3) consistent shading and compression with "flat" density. "Flat" density or compression denote cues constructed with elongation $e_D = 0$, $e_C = 0$ respectively (i.e. consistent with a plane). Each of 9 conditions (3 elongations each with flat density, flat compression or consistent cues) are presented 6 times, with random ordering, to each subject. The pooled results of seven subjects (Fig. 7.7) show that the compression cue dominates the density cue and that the relative dominance increases with increasing elongation.

7.5 Discussion

Experiments 1 and 2 indicate that the human visual system is able to use texture compression as a cue to shape because the variance of subjects' shape judgements was often lower than that predicted by the ideal observer using the density cue alone. A significant virtue of our approach is that, unlike previous experiments (Cutting & Millard, 1984; Todd & Akerstrom, 1987) these results have been achieved without resorting to cue conflict.

Our experiment was not sufficiently sensitive however to demonstrate that *both* density and compression cues are being used. In seems unlikely that a sufficiently sensitive experiment could reasonably have been achieved with parabolic cylinders, because Cramer-Rao bounds for compression alone and for both cues together are so similar. Not all subjects gave conclusive results concerning compression. In the case of a subject like GFB, whose standard deviations never fall significantly below the Cramer-Rao bound for density, it is possible either that both cues are used but with relatively low efficiency, or (less plausibly) that one of the cues is used alone.

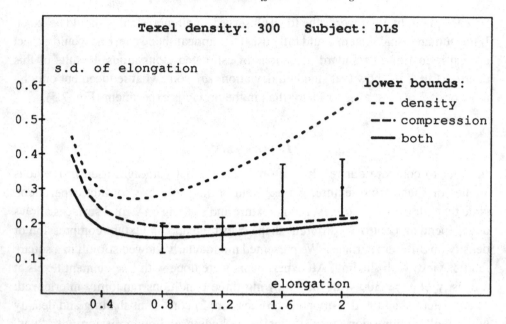

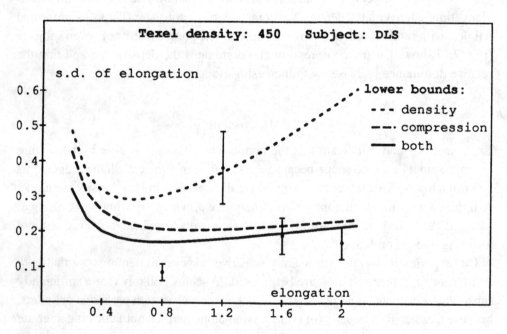

Fig. 7.6 The basic experiment of Fig. 7.4 is repeated here for circular shapes instead of line elements. Both subjects show a consistent but modest reduction in standard deviation.

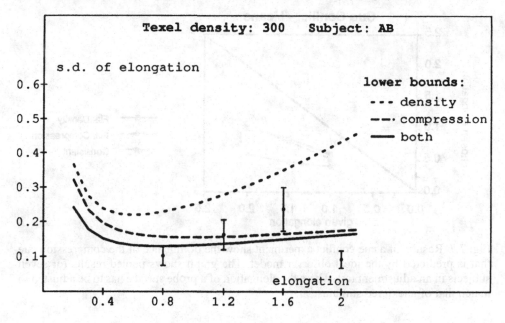

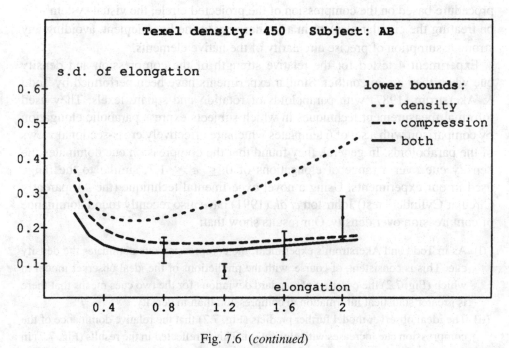

Fig. 7.6 (*continued*)

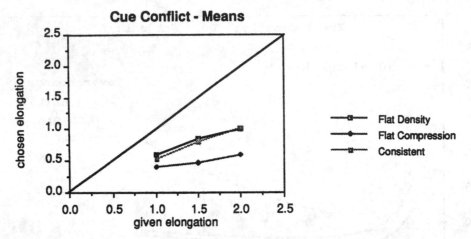

Fig. 7.7 Results of a cue conflict experiment show the dominance of the compression cue that is predicted by the ideal observer model. The graph shows pooled results for seven subjects in an adjustment task where the elongation of a probe surface has to be adjusted to match that of a textured stimulus.

In the case of circular elements in Experiment 3 standard deviations are reduced but only modestly. It is reasonable to infer that, rather than applying a deterministic procedure based on the compression of the projected circle, the visual system may be treating the circular element in a similar way to the line-element, avoiding any strong assumption of precise circularity of the native elements.

Experiment 4 tested for the relative strength of the compression and density cue when they are in conflict. Similar experiments have been performed by Todd & Akerstrom (1987) with paraboloids of rotation and square texels. They used informal measurement techniques in which subjects express parabolic elongation by comparison with a set of 6 templates which are effectively cross-sectional views of the paraboloids. In general, they found that the compression cue dominates the density cue over a range of elongations of $0 \le e \le 1.7$, similar to the range used in our experiments. Using a novel experimental technique (the "Apparently Circular Cylinder" test) Johnston *et al.* (1991) have also recently found dominance of compression over density. Our results show that:

(i) As in Todd and Akerstrom's experiment, the compression cue dominates the density cue. This is consistent, of course, with the predictions of the ideal observer model in which (Fig. 7.2) the ordering of standard deviations for the two cues means that there is greater statistical information in compression than in density.

(ii) The ideal observer model further predicts (Fig. 7.2) that the relative dominance of the compression cue increases with elongation. This is reflected in the results (Fig. 7.7) in which the ratio of subjects' adjusted elongations for zero compression and zero density respectively is seen to increase with the elongation of the surface used to generate the stimulus. This increase is statistically significant at the 95% level.

(iii) Some considerable regression towards the fronto-parallel is evident. Significant regression towards fronto-parallel was also present in experiment 1, for which shading cues were absent. This phenomenon has been studied previously by Bülthoff & Mallot (1990).

7.5.1 Fisher information for planar surfaces

The experimental results for parabolic cylinders were for a *small field of view* and consequently predictions were based on the limiting case of orthographic projection. In that case it was found n that the compression cue always dominates the density cue. However, when the field of view is larger so that perspective effects are significant, this need no longer be the case. In the case of planar surfaces we show below that, indeed, when the field of view is large, the density cue dominates.

The analysis of Fisher Information can be extended, in principle, for perspective projection, to cover the case of a field of view that is wide enough that the orthographic limit does not apply. In the case of the density cue and a planar surface of variable slant σ, this has been done elsewhere (Marinos & Blake, 1990). The result is that the Fisher Information is simply

$$\mathcal{I}_D(\sigma) = 9 \frac{NM}{A} \sec^4 \sigma. \tag{7.13}$$

Here M is a moment of inertia of the *backprojected* area of the image plane, about an axis through the back-projected image centre and orthogonal to the tilt direction; A is the magnitude of the backprojected area. Approximating the backprojected area orthographically and assuming a square field of view of angular extent $\pm\theta$ gives

$$M \approx \frac{1}{3} A \tan^2 \theta$$

so that, approximately,

$$\mathcal{I}_D(\sigma) = 3N \sec^4 \sigma \tan^2 \theta. \tag{7.14}$$

This approximation holds good roughly when $\frac{\pi}{2} - 2\theta > \sigma > \theta$. An exact solution, free of any orthographic approximation, for $\mathcal{I}_D(\sigma)$ has also been found using the symbolic algebra facilities in MATHEMATICA. Owing to the length of the algebra[†] the formula is not reproduced here. However it has been used to confirm the accuracy of the approximation (7.14) and will also be used for comparison with $\mathcal{I}_C(\sigma)$.

The Fisher Information on slant $\mathcal{I}_C(\sigma)$ in the compression cue has been computed using a mixture of symbolic algebra and numerical integration (see below). An

---

[†] MATHEMATICA code is available from the authors upon request.

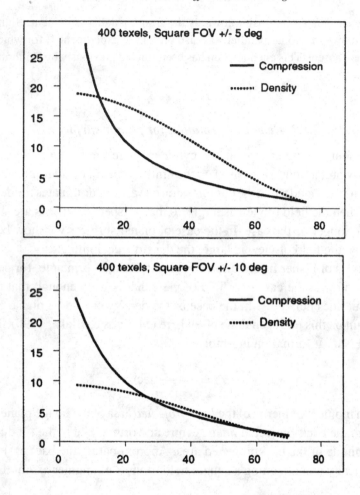

Fig. 7.8 Graphs show Cramer-Rao lower bounds on standard deviation for estimation of planar slant from compression and density cues respectively. Variation with slant σ is shown for four different fields of view: $\theta = 5°, 10°, 20°, 30°$. Notice that the density cue is dominant (smaller s.d.) for larger fields of view, whereas for smaller fields of view compression dominates. Standard deviations are shown for the case that $N = 400$ texels are visible, and scale as $1/\sqrt{N}$.

orthographic approximation[‡] is also available (Blake & Marinos, 1990):

$$\mathcal{I}_C = \frac{1}{2} N \tan^2 \sigma. \tag{7.15}$$

and this is also valid for $\frac{\pi}{2} - 2\theta > \sigma > \theta$.

[‡] Whilst $\mathcal{I}_C$ is approximated orthographically, in the case of $\mathcal{I}_D$ orthographic approximation simply yields $\mathcal{I}_D = 0$ because planar density gradients vanish in the orthographic limit. Instead, only the trapezoidal backprojected area was approximated orthographically, as a rectangle, for the purposes of calculating M.

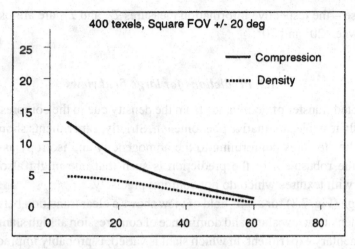

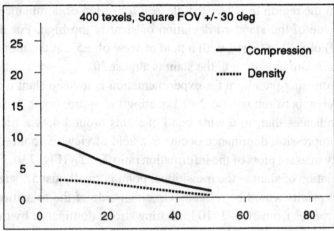

Fig. 7.8 (*continued*)

The exact forms of $\mathcal{I}_C(\sigma)$ and $\mathcal{I}_D(\sigma)$ are used to plot Cramer-Rao lower bounds on standard deviation, in Fig. 7.8. For $N = 400$ visible texels, the plots show bounds $1/\sqrt{N\mathcal{I}_C(\sigma)}$ and $1/\sqrt{N\mathcal{I}_D(\sigma)}$ on standard deviations for the compression and density cues respectively. Dependence on slant σ is shown for various sizes of field of view. The case of a small field of view approaches the orthographic limit in which the density cue vanishes (equation (7.14)) and hence the compression cue tends to dominate (its s.d. is lower). With larger fields of view, perspective effects contribute strongly and the density cue dominates uniformly, throughout the range of slants. Dominance of density over compression is predicted by the approximate equations (7.14) and (7.15) for fields of view exceeding about $\pm 10°$. This is consistent with the graphs (Fig. 7.8) which show that $\theta = 10°$ is close to the critical case – the respective information measures $\mathcal{I}_C$ and $\mathcal{I}_D$ are almost equal for slants between 20° and 70°.

7.5.2 Predictions for large field views

The predicted transfer of dominance from the density cue to the compression cue is a potentially testable, qualitative phenomenon. Strictly, experiments should be done with "needle" textures conforming to the homogeneity and isotropy assumptions. However the robustness of the prediction is such that one might also expect to observe it with textures which do not conform precisely.

The graph (Fig. 7.8) for a ±5° field of view shows a clear transition between dominance of density at low slant, and dominance of compression at high slant. However a complementary experiment, in which slant is varied, is probably impractical. This is because, in the region in where the clearest transition of dominance occurs, the numerical value of the standard deviation of slant is too high. For a practicable number (400) of visible texels, with a field of view of ±5°, at the transitional slant of 10°, the *standard deviation* in the slant is almost 20°.

A more promising paradigm for experimentation is to keep slant fixed and vary the field of view between 0° and 20°. Equating the approximate formulae (7.15) and (7.14) indicates that, in a wide band of slants around 45°, a transition from density to compression dominance occurs at a field of view of about ±10°. This is shown clearly in exact plots of the information ratio $\mathcal{I}_C/\mathcal{I}_D$ (Fig. 7.9). For $\sigma = 45°$, standard deviation of slant at the transitional point is small, just 5°, suggesting that experimental results would be reliable. On either side of the transition, the information ratio ranges from 10 to 1/10 indicating strong dominance by the respective cues. Again, this suggests a robust experimental effect.

7.6 Conclusion

The first conclusion is that experimental results are consistent with the ideal observer model, with typical statistical efficiencies of 25-100%. In most cases standard deviation increases with eccentricity of the cylinders, as predicted by computed Fisher Information in the ideal observer model. The second conclusion is that, for a number of subjects, reliability is too good to result from density effects alone. It must be that other information, most likely information about compression, is used. For the first time (as far as we know), this has this been shown *without resorting to texture cue conflicts*, that is, within the scope of "normal" surface viewing.

Having established plausibility for the idea that the visual system can estimate statistical information in texture cues, we return to the question of cue integration. Predictions for cue combination under orthographic projection agree with our own

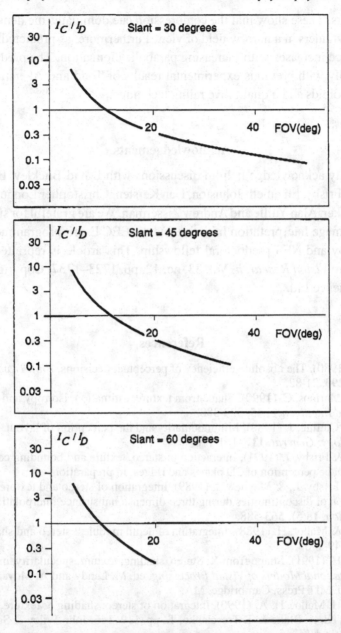

Fig. 7.9 These graphs show the ratio of Fisher Information $\mathcal{I}_C/\mathcal{I}_D$ in compression and density cues respectively, as a function of field of view. The ideal observer weights the cues according to this ratio. A clear transition is predicted at a field of view of 10°, relatively independent of slant. On either side of the transition, the respective cues dominate strongly, by up to a factor of 10.

recent results. These show that the compression cue dominates the density cue, for parabolic cylinders in a narrow field of view. Furthermore, as predicted, the degree of dominance increases with increasing parabolic elongation. The predictions also agree broadly with previous experimental results of Todd and Akerstrom (1987), using paraboloids and a qualitative rating technique.

Acknowledgements

We gratefully acknowledge helpful discussions with David Buckley, Bruce Cumming, John Frisby, Elizabeth Johnston, Dan Kersten, Christopher Longuet-Higgins, Andrew Parker, Alan Yuille and Andrew Zisserman. We are grateful for support from the SERC Image Interpretation Initiative and the EEC Esprit programme. DLS was supported by and NFS predoctoral fellowship. This article is reprinted with permission from *Vision Research,* Vol. 33, no. 12, pp. 1723–1737, Copyright 1993 by Elsevier Science Ltd.

References

Barlow, H. (1980). The absolute efficiency of perceptual decisions, *Phil. Trans. R. Soc. Lond.*, **290**, 71-82.

Blake, A. & Marinos, C. (1990). Shape from texture: estimation, isotropy and moments, *J. Artificial Intelligence*, **45**, 323-380.

Bruno, N. & Cutting, J. (1988). Minimodularity and the perception of layout, *J. Exp. Psychology: General*, **117**, 161-170.

Buckley, D. & Frisby, J. (1991). Interaction of stereo, texture and bounding contour cues in the shape perception of 3D planes and ridges. In preparation.

Buckley, D., Frisby, J., & Mayhew, J. (1989). Integration of stereo and texture cues in the formation of discontinuities during three-dimensional surface interpolation, *Perception*, **18**(5), 563-588.

Bulthoff, H. & Mallot, H. (1988). Integration of depth modules: stereo and shading, *JOSA A*, **5**, 1749-1758.

Bülthoff, H. H. (1991). Shape from X: Stereo, shading, texture, specularity, in *Computational Models of Visual Processing*, ed. M. Landy and A. Movshon, pp. 305-330. MIT Press, Cambridge, MA.

Bülthoff, H. H. Mallot, H. A. (1990). Integration of stereo, shading & texture, in *AI and the Eye*, ed. A. Blake & T. Troscianko, T., pp. 119–146. John Wiley & Sons, Chichester, UK.

Cutting, J. & Millard, R. (1984). Three gradients and the perception of flat and curved surfaces, *J. of Experimental Psychology, General*, **113**(2), 198-216.

Davis, L., Janos, L., & S.M., D. (1983). Efficient recovery of shape from texture, *IEEE Trans. Pattern Analysis and Machine Intell.*, **5**(5), 485-492.

Dosher, B., Sperling, G., & Wurst, A. (1986). Tradeoffs between stereopsis and proximity luminance covariance as determinants of perceived 3d structure, *Vision Research*, **26**, 973-990.

Gibson, J. (1950). *The Perception of the Visual World*. Boston: Houghton Mifflin.

Gibson, J. (1979). *The Ecological Approach to Visual Perception*. Boston: Houghton Mifflin.

Horn, B. (1986). *Robot Vision*. New York: McGraw-Hill.

Johnston, E., Cumming, B., & Parker, A. (1991). Effects of texture gradients on the perception of curved surfaces presented stereoscopically. In preparation.

Kanatani, L. & Chou, T. (1989). Shape from texture: general principle, *Artificial Intelligence*, **38**, 1-48.

Kersten, D. (1990). Statistical limits to image understanding. In *Vision: Coding and Efficiency*, ed. C. Blakemore, C. Cambridge University Press.

Marinos, C. & Blake, A. (1990). Shape from texture: the homogeneity hypothesis, *Proc. 3rd Conf. Computer Vision*, pp. 350-354.

Marr, D. (1982). *Vision*. San Francisco: Freeman.

Papoulis, A. (1990). *Probability and Statistics*. New Jersey: Prentice-Hall.

Rao, C. (1973). *Linear Statistical Inference and Its Applications*. New York: John Wiley and Sons.

Sheinberg, D., Bülthoff, H., & Blake, A. (1990). Shape from texture, *Perception*, **19**, 87b.

Stevens, K. (1981). The visual interpretation of surface contours, *J. Artificial Intelligence*, **17**, 47-73.

Stevens, K. & Brookes, A. (1988). Integrating stereopsis with monocular interpretations of planar surfaces, *Vision Res.*, **28**(3), 371-386.

Todd, J. & Akerstrom, R. (1987). Perception of three-dimensional form from patterns of optical texture, *J. of Experimental Psychology: Human Perception and Performance*, **13**(2), 242-255.

Voorhees, H. & Poggio, T. (1988). Computing texture boundaries from images, *Nature*, **333**, 364-367.

Witkin, A. (1981). Recovering surface shape and orientation from texture, *Artificial Intelligence*, **17**, 17-45.

8

A computational theory for binocular stereopsis

PETER N. BELHUMEUR

Division of Applied Sciences, Harvard University

8.1 Introduction

It has been known since at least the time of Leonardo da Vinci that encoded within a pair of stereo images is information detailing the scene geometry (Leonardo, 1989).[†] The animal brain has known this for millions of years and has developed as yet barely understood neuronal mechanisms for decoding this information. Hold your hand inches in front of your face and, with both eyes focused, stare at your fingers – they appear vividly in three-dimensions (3-D). In fact everywhere you gaze, you are aware of the relative depths of the observed objects.

Stereo vision is not the only clue to depth; there is a whole host of monocular clues which humans bring to bear in determining depth, evidenced by the fact that if you close one eye, it is still relatively simple to determine 3-D spatial relations. Nevertheless, monocular clues are less exact and often ambiguous. Otherwise, why would the mammalian anatomy have bothered to narrow the visual field in order to reposition the eyes for stereo vision? As a simple demonstration of the precision of stereo vision, try to touch the tips of two pencils with your arms outstretched, one pencil in each hand. With one eye closed, the task is frustratingly difficult; with both eyes open, the relative depths of the tips of the pencils are clear, and the task becomes as simple as touching your nose. Naturally, the precision in depth perception that the human visual system displays here is also used unconsciously to solve a multitude of daily tasks.

In the last thirty years, researchers have tried, with mixed success, to computationally reconstruct the scene geometry in a pair of stereo images. First, in the 1960s photogrammetrists tried to automate the process of constructing topological surveys. Later, with the advent of robotics and the birth of the field of robot vision, engineers and computer scientists needed stereo depth information to solve problems ranging from the automation of factory assembly lines to the development of

---

[†] A stereo pair consists of two images of the same scene viewed from slightly different directions.

autonomous land vehicles. Unfortunately, like most problems in computer vision, the stereo problem has proven to be more difficult than originally anticipated – so much so that many researchers temporarily abandoned so-called "passive" stereo algorithms (which construct depth from a pair of stereo images) in favor of more reliable "active" laser range finders. Yet the performance of computational stereo algorithms has steadily improved. Recent advances have, in some cases, produced results almost on par with those of the human visual system (Cochran & Medioni, 1992; Geiger *et al.*, 1992; Grimson, 1981; Jones & Malik, 1992; Pollard *et al.*, 1985b; Yang *et al.*, 1993).

In this introduction, we begin by discussing the complications researchers have encountered in trying to find a computational solution to the stereo problem. Throughout this discussion, we attempt to provide motivation for the contributions of this chapter by interleaving aspects of the solution that we feel have been largely overlooked – namely, methods for properly handling occluded regions, salient features in the scene geometry, and global 3-D structures. We then give an overview of our approach to the stereo problem, providing a section by section breakdown of the material presented in this chapter.

8.1.1 Complications in solving the correspondence problem

In the literature, binocular stereo vision algorithms construct a depth map of the 3-D surfaces captured in a pair of images taken from slightly different viewpoints. These surfaces are estimated by first matching pixels in the images that correspond to the same point on a 3-D surface, and then computing the point's depth as a function of its displacement (or *disparity*) in the two images.[†] The task of matching points between the two images is known as the *correspondence problem*. This problem is made difficult by several known complications:

- **Noise:** Due to quantization error, imperfect optics, noise in the imaging system, lighting variation between images, specular reflection, etc., the feature values for corresponding points in the left and right images often differ.
- **Indistinct Image Features:** Many images contain large regions of constant luminance and, therefore, are effectively featureless in these regions. Even with near perfect measurements and minimal lighting variations between images, the matching is still ambiguous for a great number of pixels.
- **Salient 3-D Features:** Most stereo scenes contain salient features in the 3-D scene geometry (i.e. discontinuities in depth at object boundaries, discontinuities in surface orientation, and steeply sloping surfaces) which must be preserved to

---

[†] We use the expression "matching a pixel or point" to mean matching a feature located at that point. The features might be image luminance, edges, or even a set filter responses.

produce accurate reconstructions. Many of the methods used to minimize the first two complications smooth over the salient features in the scene geometry.

- **Half-Occlusion:** Due to the phenomenon of occlusion, there are almost certainly whole regions of *half-occluded* points which appear in only one image and, consequently, have no match at all. In fact this problem is twofold: first, there is the problem of incorrectly matching half-occluded points to mutually visible points and getting wildly inaccurate depth estimates; second, even if a point can be identified as unmatched, what depth should be assigned to it?

For years people have offered solutions to the correspondence problem without adequately addressing all of these complications. Many have convincingly argued that the complications caused by noise and indistinct image features could be minimized by enforcing constraints on the estimated disparities. In the early area-based algorithms, the disparity was assumed to be nearly constant (i.e. the disparity gradient was close to 0). For camera set-ups with parallel optical axes, this assumption is equivalent to assuming that the observed surfaces are nearly fronto-parallel. The disparity was determined by correlating a window of points in left image with a window in the right image, and then choosing – for each point in the left image – the disparity which gave rise to the best correlation (Gennery, 1980). Others (Julesz, 1971; Marr, 1976a) integrated a type of smoothness (flatness) constraint into matching process, again biasing toward reconstructions with constant disparity. Poggio *et al.* (1985) and Matthies (1992) elaborated on this idea to impose smoothness as soft constraint in an energy/cost functional that gracefully biased toward depth maps where the disparity gradient was small. Pollard *et al.* (1985b) proposed a clever and somewhat less restrictive assumption about the nature of the observed surfaces: the disparity gradients within a window should not exceed some pre-chosen threshold.

Yet while algorithms using smoothness constraints proved effective in handling the first two complications, their performance deteriorated at salient features in the scene geometry. Discontinuities in depth at object boundaries ("breaks") or discontinuities in surface orientation ("creases") were either smoothed over or caused the algorithm to produce erratic results.

Marroquin *et al.* (1987) and Yuille (1989b) maintained that if a smoothness prior is used to influence the matching, there must be some mechanism for suspending the smoothing at the boundaries of objects. Here the suggestion was that "line processes" (i.e. binary random processes) used to solve the image segmentation problem (Blake & Zisserman, 1987; Geman & Geman, 1984; Mumford & Shah, 1985) should be used to explicitly represent discontinuities in depth. While this observation was a significant theoretical step toward preserving the boundaries of objects, it overlooked two important complications. First, no prescription was given for preserving the other salient features in the scene geometry – namely, steeply sloping surfaces and discontinuities in surface orientation. Second, what makes stereo different from the segmentation problem is that in addition to identifying boundaries across which smoothing should be suspended due to a discontinuity, algorithms must also identify whole regions of half-occlusion caused by the discontinuity.

Surprisingly, few of the "classical" papers on stereo vision properly handled the implicit relation between discontinuities in depth and the resulting unmatched regions (Baker & Binford, 1981; Marr & Poggio, 1979; Ohta & Kanade, 1985).[†] These algorithms were forced either to constrain their environments so that occlusion was uncommon, or to accept solutions which smoothed over the depth discontinuities or produced spurious matches for the pixels which did not match anything. In fact, only recently have researchers begun to rigorously address occlusion (Belhumeur & Mumford, 1992; Geiger *et al.*, 1992; Jones & Mallik, 1992; Marroquin *et al.*, 1987).

Finally, while much progress has been made toward developing local priors – priors which enforce local constraints on the scene geometry – little treatment has been given to developing "global" priors (as an exception see Madarasmi *et al.*, 1993). Not even the most carefully considered local priors can properly model global 3-D structures in the scene geometry. Yet most stereo scenes contain global 3-D structures.[‡] For example, the fact that surfaces tend to disappear and reappear behind foreground surfaces (Mutch & Thompson, 1985) is not a coincidence, but rather a result of the global 3-D structure of the scene. To take advantage of this, researchers need to develop prior models that impose global constraints on the scene geometry.

8.1.2 A computational theory for stereopsis

In this chapter we develop, within a Bayesian framework, our computational theory for stereopsis. This theory attempts to explain the process by which the information detailing the 3-D geometry of object surfaces is encoded in a pair of stereo images. We attempt to design our model by making *explicit* all of our assumptions about the nature of image coding and the structure of the world. In designing computer vision models, most researchers skip this step and, consequently, have no way of testing whether the underlying competence theories are correct. By first building a formal theory of competence for stereopsis, we can isolate our assumptions and analyze their validity.

Bayesian approaches to computer vision are not new: Besag (1974) and Grenander (1981) were among of the first to adapt these techniques from statistics and apply them to vision. Others have followed their lead and expanded significantly on

---

[†] Both Baker & Binford (1981) and Ohta & Kanade (1985) mention the fact that discontinuities in depth cause problems, but neither includes a mechanism for explicitly identifying the unmatched pixels and preventing them from interfering with the algorithm.

[‡] We use the term "global" to mean highly non-local, i.e. existing on the scale greater than one-tenth of the observed scene.

these ideas (Cernuschi *et al.*, 1989; Clark & Yuille, 1990; Cohen *et al.*, 1984; Cross & Jain, 1983; Geiger & Girosi, 1991; Geman & Geman, 1984; Kato *et al.*, 1993 Marroquin *et al.*, 1987; Matthies, 1992; Szeliski, 1989). In vision, the Bayesian paradigm seeks to extract scene information from an image, or sequence of images, by balancing the content of the observed image with prior expectations about the content of the observed scene. While this method is general and can be applied to a wide range of vision problems, in this chapter we apply it only to stereopsis.

For our purposes, we wish to infer the quantities in the scene geometry S given the left and right images by I_l and I_r. Within the Bayesian paradigm, one infers S by considering $p(S \mid I_l, I_r)$, the *a posteriori* probability of the state of world given the measurement. Note that by Bayes' theorem, we have

$$p(S \mid I_l, I_r) = \frac{p(I_l, I_r \mid S)p(S)}{p(I_l, I_r)}.$$

The first term in the numerator of the RHS, sometimes referred to as the "image formation model," is a measure of how well S matches the observed images. The second term in the numerator, usually referred to as the "prior model," is a measure of how probable a particular S is *a priori* – before the images are observed. Although for the results presented throughout this chapter we display the *maximum a posteriori* (MAP) estimate $\hat{S} = \arg\max_S p(S \mid I_l, I_r)$, we could have chosen other estimators (e.g. the posterior mean).[†] Yet, in order to avoid confusing the development of our computational theory, we will avoid discussing implementation issues. For discussion of this see Belhumeur (1993b).

For notational convenience, we define the "energy" functional

$$E[S] = -\log(p(I_l, I_r \mid S)p(S))$$
$$= E_D + E_P$$

where

$$E_D = -\log(p(I_l, I_r \mid S))$$
$$E_P = -\log(p(S)).$$

In the pages to follow, E_D will be referred to as the "data term," and E_P will be referred to as the "prior term." (See Yuille *et al.*, chapter 4.)

While this framework seems like fertile ground for the seeds of computer vision algorithms, many past approaches suffered because algorithms were developed that relied on overly simplistic or not well considered prior models. Often in the computer vision literature, people estimate "low level" image quantities, be they

[†] For a discussion of these see Besag (1974) and the chapter by Yuille and Bulthoff.

depth, luminance, texture, etc., by choosing the fit which minimizes some pre-chosen functional. While fitting methods of this type have in some cases proven very effective and, subsequently, become quite popular in the field of computer vision, there is often a tendency to employ these energy functionals without considering *fully* the underlying assumptions.

Other more rigorous approaches have developed energy functionals within the Bayesian framework; yet, for "reasons of mathematical and computational conve-nience" (Geman, 1988), most of these approaches develop priors relying on the machinery of Markov random fields (MRF's) and Gibbs distributions to define the joint prior distribution of a finite set of random variables. While this method for constructing prior distributions is general, it can also be abused. By this we mean that it allows one to ignore what underlying continuous-time stochastic process may have given rise to the finite set of random variables of interest. We intend to argue from the perspective of stereo vision that, in developing a Bayesian formulation of a vision problem, one must be careful both in the choice of the random variables to be estimated and in the assumed relations between these random variables.

8.1.3 *The contributions of this work*

In the sections to follow we develop our computational theory, highlighting a number of important features that have been overlooked in previous theories. In Section 8.2, we derive our image formation model. We introduce a definition of half-occluded regions and derive simple equations relating the disparity function to the unmatched points. In particular, we show that the disparity function alone contains enough information to determine the half-occluded regions. We use these relations to derive a model for image formation in which the occluded regions are explicitly represented and computed.

In Section 8.3, we derive our prior model. We argue that in order to properly address the before mentioned complications, a stereo model should handle – as ran-dom variables – all of the quantities in the scene geometry. These quantities should include not simply depth, but also surface orientation, discontinuities in depth at ob-ject boundaries, and surface creases. In the past, some algorithms have found these quantities by post-processing, in a second pass, the depth map obtained from a stereo matching algorithm (Blake & Zisserman, 1987). More recently, Wilde (1991) pro-posed post-processing the disparity, not the depth, to obtain the scene geometry. In general, the problem with these approaches is that the matching process is separated from the process of identifying these quantities. For example, it is unclear how an algorithm using smoothing as a second pass would be able to distinguish between discontinuities due to object boundaries and discontinuities due to false matches.

We propose that depth, surface orientation, occluding contours, and creases should be estimated simultaneously.[†] To accomplish this, we develop a class of energy functionals that implicitly assumes a prior model that is constructed from the sums of Brownian motion processes and compound Poisson processes. Furthermore, we demonstrate that the prior assumptions which produce this class of energy functionals accurately model the scene geometry for stereo images. This class of energy functionals, which includes the *weak string*, the *weak rod*, and the *weak rubber band*, is commonly used in computer vision (Blake & Zisserman, 1987; Geman & Geman, 1984; Harris, 1989; Marroquin *et al.*, 1987; Mumford & Shah, 1985).

Finally, we extend our prior model to consider global structures. Since most stereo scenes contain either background continuation (large background surfaces continuing behind smaller foreground surfaces) or transparency continuation (small opaque patches on a transparent surface), highly non-local interactions are often present in the scene geometry (see also Mutch & Thompson, 1985, and Madarasmi *et al.*, 1993). The local prior models developed in the middle stage of this chapter are unable to capture the probabilistic subtleties of global 3-D structures. Therefore, we develop a hybridized prior which balances the local properties of the scene geometry with the global properties. To do this, the previous estimate of the scene geometry is analyzed for global structure, and the results are used to influence the current estimate by iteratively adapting the prior model.

Throughout the chapter, we attempt to provide motivation for our theory by investigating the human visual system's handling of occluded regions, salient features in the scene geometry, and global 3-D structures. Through a collection of psychophysical demonstrations, we suggest that the visual system may be more ambitious in solving the correspondence problem than previously believed. In particular, we conjecture the following points: when solving the correspondence problem the visual system uses half-occluded regions as a positive clue to determining depth, rather than a hindrance Lawson & Gulick, 1967; Nakayama & Shimojo, 1990; see also chapter 10); it may explicitly represent boundaries of foreground objects and surface discontinuities; and, in a search for global 3-D structures, it may actively group regions separated by foreground occlusion or transparency into common disparity structures.

8.2 The image formation model

Although all of the concepts can be derived for more general configurations, in deriving our model for image formation, we choose the simplest possible geometry:

[†] Note that the quantities in our scene geometry are exactly those which Marr termed the "$2\frac{1}{2}$-D sketch" (Marr, 1982). Yet Marr argued that low level modules for stereo, motion, shape contours, shading, and texture combine their output to form the $2\frac{1}{2}$-D sketch. Here we argue that computational stereo models should have these quantities explicitly represented.

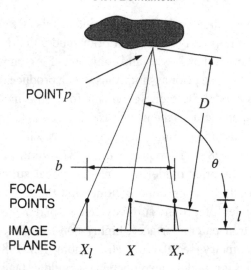

POINT p

b

FOCAL
POINTS

IMAGE
PLANES X_l X X_r

D

θ

l

Fig. 8.1 **Camera Geometries:** The figure shows the left and right image planes, plus an imaginary cyclopean image plane. Both the disparity and distance functions are defined relative to the cyclopean image plane.

pinhole cameras with parallel optical axes. To get a symmetric representation, we define disparity relative to an imaginary cyclopean image plane placed halfway between the left and right cameras (Julesz, 1971). Here we derive explicit relations between disparity and depth, as well as disparity and half-occlusion, showing that the disparity function exactly determines the half-occluded regions in the left and right image planes. We then use these relations to derive our image formation model.

8.2.1 The relation between disparity and distance

Let us assume that we have two pinhole cameras whose optical axes are parallel and separated by a distance B. The cameras each have focal length L, with F_l the focal point of the left image, and F_r the focal point of the right. A point P on the surface of an object in 3-D space, visible to both cameras, is projected through the focal points and onto the image planes. Each image plane has a 2-D coordinate system with its origin determined by the intersection of its optical axis with the image plane. Furthermore, let us restrict the placement of F_l and F_r so that the line segment connecting them, the baseline, is parallel to the image planes and perpendicular to the optical axes. The brightness of each point projected onto the image planes creates image luminance functions I_l and I_r in the left and right planes, respectively. Next, let us create an imaginary cyclopean image plane in the same manner, placing its focal point on the baseline half-way between the original two focal points (see Fig. 8.1).

We look now at a horizontal plane through the baseline. It intersects the three image planes in what are called epipolar lines, which we denote by X_l, X_r, and X, with coordinates $x_l \epsilon X_l$, $x_r \epsilon X_r$, and $x \epsilon X$, respectively. The coordinates of the epipolar lines run right to left, so that when a point in the world moves from left to right, its coordinates in the image planes increase.

When the same point is visible from all three eyes it is easy to check that $x = (x_l + x_r)/2$. Thus, we can relate the coordinates of points projected onto all three image planes by a positive disparity function $d(x)$ via

$$x_l = x + d(x) \text{ and } x_r = x - d(x).$$

The disparity $d(x)$ can be related to the distance $D(x)$ from the middle focal point to a point P on the surface of an object by

$$d(x) = \frac{LB}{2D(x)\sin\theta}$$

where θ is the angle that a directed line segment through the middle focal point to the point P makes with the baseline; B is the length of the baseline; and L is the focal length. If we assume that $\theta \cong \pi/2$, as done throughout this chapter, then the equation simplifies to

$$d(x) = \frac{LB}{2D(x)}.$$

Therefore, with known camera geometries (L, B) and the resulting relations, we can talk about disparity and distance interchangeably.

8.2.2 A psychophysical demonstration of half-occlusion

The development of the camera geometry has assumed that none of the points in either the left or right images are half-occluded, i.e. visible in one camera, but not in the other. Yet, the vast majority of the millions of images we view everyday contain half-occluded regions. Examine the stereo pair in Fig. 8.2. Here we see the left and right stereo images of an English bulldog sitting in an overgrown garden patch.[†] To the left and right of the dog are half-occluded regions – regions seen in only one of two images. In fact, if you look closely, you can see that to the left and right of *every* foreground leaf or stem are half-occluded regions! For most stereo algorithms, this is an extremely difficult stereo pair from which to recover the scene geometry. Yet the human brain recovers the scene geometry with ease: when the images are fused,

---

[†] To view this and following stereograms in 3-D, place a stereopticon exactly between the left and right images and wait for the images to merge. In lieu of a stereopticon, uncross your eyes until the images appear to fuse.

Fig. 8.2 **Bulldog in garden patch:** The stereo pair contains left and right images of an English bulldog sitting regally in an overgrown garden patch. To the left and right of *every* foreground object are half-occluded regions. Yet the human visual system has no difficulty recovering the scene geometry.

the outline of the dog, the leaves, the stems, the flowers, and the picket fence all appear vividly in 3-D. Clearly the human visual system somehow manages to make sense of the many half-occluded regions.

There is psychophysical evidence that the human visual system actually exploits half-occlusion as a positive clue to determining depth, rather than a hindrance. Psychologists have recently constructed striking demonstrations that the human visual system uses unmatched regions to determine depth both with and without confirming evidence from matched regions. Nakayama & Shimojo (1990) as well as Lawson & Gulick (1967), have produced stereograms that demonstrate the formation of a subjective occluding contour induced by the addition of unpaired dots. And, Anderson (1992) "strength of contrast" of unmatched regions plays a role in disambiguating the correspondence of matchable regions.[†]

Following in this vein of inquiry, we have created stereograms which demonstrate that the presence of unpaired regions alone can dramatically alter the perceived depth. Figure 8.3 shows a triptych of stereograms. When the top stereogram is fused, there is no percept of depth; the circles appear in the same plane as the page. The middle stereogram is the same as the top one, except left-eye-only and right-eye-only regions have been added. When the middle stereogram is fused, the circles pop out of the page. The unpaired regions are perceived as being in the occluded shadow of the circles. Consequently, the circles are pulled forward out

---

[†] "Strength of contrast" as used here means a measure of how much the unmatched region differs in luminance from the possible matched regions.

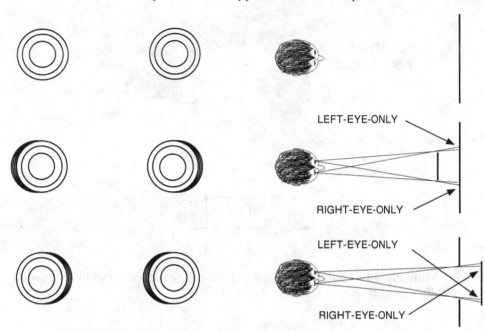

Fig. 8.3 **Half-occlusion demo:** When the top stereogram is fused, there is no percept of depth. The middle stereogram is the same as the top one, except left-eye-only and right-eye-only regions have been added. When the middle stereogram is fused, the unpaired regions in the left and right images cause the circles to pop out of the plane of the page. When the bottom circles are fused, the unpaired regions cause the circles to recede into the page. To the right of each of the three stereograms is a diagram of the perceived depth.

of the plane of the page (as diagrammed in the figure). This explanation is borne out by the bottom stereogram. Here the unpaired regions have been switched in the images. When the bottom stereogram is fused, the circles recede behind the page. The unpaired regions are now perceived as being in the occluded shadow of an imaginary oblong circular hole. Consequently, the circles are pushed back behind the page. What is surprising about this demonstration is that the human visual system uses unmatched regions to determine depth without any confirming evidence from matched regions.

The above demonstration indicates that the human visual system uses unpaired regions as positive clues to determining depth. For the last thirty years, computer vision researchers have ignored the importance of these regions for solving the stereo problem. To get their algorithms to work acceptably, many were forced to constrain their data so that occlusion was uncommon. Yet clearly most real world scenes are filled with half-occluded regions. We argue that, like the human visual system, computer vision systems must take advantage of the clues provided by half-occlusion.

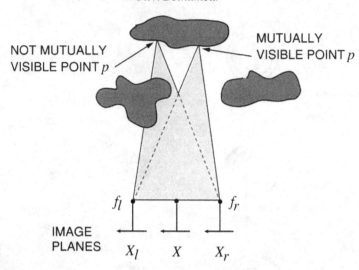

NOT MUTUALLY
VISIBLE POINT p

MUTUALLY
VISIBLE POINT p

f_l f_r

IMAGE
PLANES X_l X X_r

Fig. 8.4 **Mutually visible points :** A mutually visible point has no object within the triangle specified by P, F_l, and F_r.

8.2.3 *The relation between disparity and half-occlusion*

Suppose a surface point is not mutually visible to all three eyes.[†] How are we to define $d(x)$ and $D(x)$? And, furthermore, how are we to identify the point as not mutually visible? The simplest thing to do is to let $D(x)$ be the distance from the cyclopean focal point to the nearest surface point, and define $d(x) = LB/2D(x)$. Thus, the disparity is defined for every point, whether mutually visible or not, along the cyclopean epipolar line. But, if the patch of surface at this point is occluded from the perspective of the left or right eye, the image values $I_l(x - d(x))$ and $I_r(x + d(x))$ will not be related to the light reflected off of this patch. Therefore, to make the distinction between visible and occluded points we state the following definition:

Definition 1. A point P is *mutually visible* to both eyes if the triangle formed by P, F_l and F_r is free of obstructing objects (see Fig. 8.4).

Note that according to this definition, if any object is contained within the triangle formed by P, F_l, and F_r, then the point P is not considered *mutually visible* – even though the point may be visible to all three eyes. The reason for this will be explained shortly.

To determine from the disparity function when a point is mutually visible, it is

---

[†] We use the word "eye" interchangeably with "camera."

convenient to introduce a morphologically filtered version $d^*(x)$ of $d(x)$:

$$d^*(x) = \max_a (d(x+a) - |a|).$$

Graphically, d^* is constructed by taking the graph of d, and letting each peak cast shadows at $45°$ to the left and right. Thus $|d^*(x) - d^*(y)| \leq |x - y|$, and $|(d^*)'(x)| \leq 1$. To interpret d^* in terms of occlusion, we state the following lemma. $d^*(x) = d(x)$ if and only if the point P visible to the cyclopean eye in direction x is mutually visible to the left and right eyes.

Thus the function $d^*(x)$ tracks the mutually visible points. Let us define the *half-occluded points* as the points which are not mutually visible. More formally, we state the following definition:

Definition 2. The *half-occluded points* $O \subset X$ are the closure of the set of points x such that $d^*(x) > d(x)$.

Half-occluded regions are most commonly formed by a foreground surface partially occluding a background surface such that there is a region on the background surface visible to both the left and the right eyes.[†] Half-occluded points will generally be the unmatched pixels, unless the ordering constraint is violated and a point p is visible from both eyes even though some smaller object lies in the triangle formed by P, the left focal point, and the right focal point. (This unusual possibility, usually is referred to as the "double nail illusion.") The most common way for unmatched pixels to arise is for $d(x)$ to jump discontinuously as it tracks points on one surface to points on a new surface. Here $|d'(x)|$ is infinite, so near such a point we must have $d^*(x) > d(x)$. Note that by defining $O = \{x \mid d^*(x) > d(x)\}$, we are implicitly enforcing the ordering constraint.

Figures 8.5 and 8.6 show an example of how half-occluded regions are formed. The figures contain a cartoon scene of a spherical human head in front of a flat black board on which the letters "A B C D E F" are written. Figure 8.5 shows a horizontal cross section of this scene projected into the left, right, and cyclopean image planes. Lines have been drawn through the focal points, tangential to the foreground sphere, to show the half-occluded regions on the background blackboard. Figure 8.6 shows a sketch of this scene as perceived in each of the image planes. The dashed line drawn through the face and letters marks the horizontal cross section from Fig. 8.5. In both figures, we make explicit the relation between $d^*(x)$ and $d(x)$.

For our derivations to follow, we must define the above quantities in the discrete setting. Let us take the fixed interval $[-a, a]$ of the cyclopean epipolar line X and

---

[†] Half-occluded regions can be formed by two foreground surfaces partially occluding a background surface such that there is no region on the background surface visible to both the left and the right eyes. We do not consider this type of half-occlusion in this chapter.

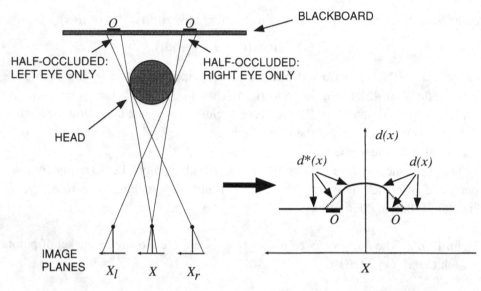

Fig. 8.5 **Half-occlusion – overhead view:** The figure illustrates a horizontal cross section of a spherical head in front of a flat blackboard, as well as graphs of the corresponding $d^*(x)$ and $d(x)$. To the left and right of the foreground sphere are half-occluded regions labeled O.

sample it at n evenly spaced points represented by the vector $\mathbf{x} = (x_1, \ldots, x_n)$ such that $x_1 = -a$, $x_{i+1} - x_i = \delta$, and $x_n = a$. Let the disparities at the sampled points be represented by the vector $\mathbf{d} = (d_1, \ldots, d_n)$. So, the index set $\mathcal{I} = \{1, \ldots, n\}$. We define $O \subset \mathcal{I}$ such that $O = \{i \mid d_j - d_i > |j - i| \text{ for some } j\}$. Finally, we discretize – *with sub-pixel fineness* – the set of possible disparity values. Thus, $d_i \in \{0, \frac{1}{k}, \frac{2}{k}, \ldots, 1, 1+\frac{1}{k}, \ldots, d_{\max}\}$ for some k specifying the disparity resolution.

It is important to note that neither Marroquin *et al.* (1987) or Geiger *et al.* (1992) use sub-pixel resolution for the disparity values – i.e. they choose the disparity values from the set of integers. Yet, unless one uses sub-pixel resolution, it is not possible to distinguish between jumps in the disparity along a sloping surface and jumps in disparity at the boundaries of objects. Because of this, these methods will *falsely* assume that the jumps along sloping surfaces produce half-occluded points. To see this note that if the disparity only has integer values, then $|d_{i+1} - d_i| = 0$, $1, \ldots, d_{\max}$. Yet, as pointed out in the preceding paragraph, all surfaces visible to both the left and right eyes have $|d_{i+1} - d_i| \leq 1$!

8.2.4 *Deriving the model for image formation*

The purpose of the data term is to enforce agreement between the observed images and the estimated scene geometry. Keeping within the Bayesian framework, we

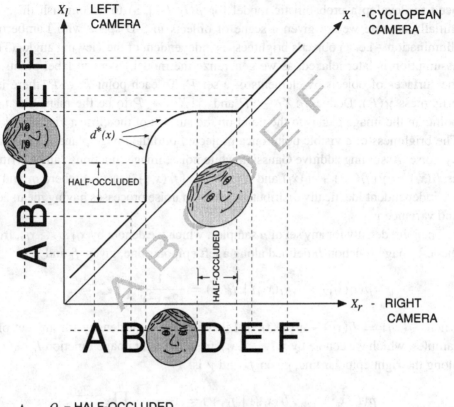

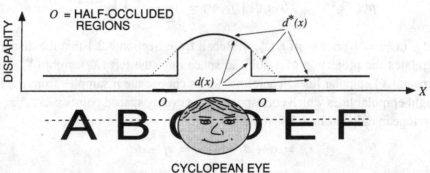

Fig. 8.6 **Half-occlusion – frontal view:** The scene is a frontal view of that depicted in Fig. 8.5. A sketch is drawn illustrating how the scene is perceived in each image plane. The dashed line through the letters and the face mark the horizontal cross section from Fig. 8.5. The epipolar lines X_l, X_r, and X have been flipped so that the image does not appear inverted.

need to develop a probabilistic model for $p(I_l, I_r \mid S)$ to accomplish this. We initially assume we are given a scene of objects in 3-D space with Lambertian illumination – i.e. an object's brightness is independent of the viewing angle. (This assumption is later relaxed, as we generalize the model.) We can label points on the surfaces of objects by elements of a set $\mathcal{P}$. To each point $P \in \mathcal{P}$, there is a brightness $\gamma(P)$. Define $f_l: X_l \to \mathcal{P}$ and $f_r: X_r \to \mathcal{P}$ to be the maps that take points in the image planes to the point on the surface of the closest visible object. The brightness of a visible point once projected into the image plane is corrupted by noise. Assuming additive Gaussian white noise, image functions can be written as $I_l(x_l) = \gamma(f_l(x_l)) + \eta_l(x_l)$ and $I_r(x_r) = \gamma(f_r(x_r)) + \eta_r(x_r)$ where η_l and η_r are independent identically distributed Gaussian noise processes having mean zero and variance ν^2.

The joint density for any set of n samples, which we denote by $x_{l1}, \ldots, x_{ln}$, from the left image function I_l defined along a left epipolar line, given f_l and γ is

$$p(I_l(x_{l1}), \ldots, I_l(x_{ln}) \mid f_l, \gamma) = \frac{1}{(2\pi\nu^2)^n} \prod_{i=1}^{n} e^{-\frac{\xi_l^2(x_{li})}{2\nu^2}}.$$

where $\xi_l(x_{li}) = I_l(x_{li}) - \gamma(f_l(x_{li}))$. Likewise, the joint density for any set of n samples, which we denote by $x_{r1}, \ldots, x_{rn}$ from the right image function I_r defined along the right epipolar line, given f_r and γ is

$$p(I_r(x_{r1}), \ldots, I_r(x_{rn}) \mid f_r, \gamma) = \frac{1}{(2\pi\nu^2)^n} \prod_{i=1}^{n} e^{-\frac{\xi_r^2(x_{ri})}{2\nu^2}}.$$

where $\xi_r(x_{ri}) = I_r(x_{ri}) - \gamma(f_r(x_{ri}))$. Recall from Section 8.2.1 that the disparity $d(x)$ relates the projection of a point in space onto the left (X_l), right (X_r), and cyclopean (X) epipolar lines. Therefore, let us choose the n samples from the left and right epipolar lines which correspond to the evenly spaced points $x_1, \ldots, x_n$ on the cyclopean epipolar line. So we define

$$x_{li} = x_i + d_i \text{ and } x_{ri} = x_i - d_i.$$

with $\mathbf{x_l} = (x_{l1}, \ldots, x_{ln})$ and $\mathbf{x_r} = (x_{r1}, \ldots, x_{rn})$. (Note that for non-constant disparities, neither the points $x_{l1}, \ldots, x_{ln}$, nor the points $x_{r1}, \ldots, x_{rn}$ are evenly spaced along their respective epipolar lines.) With the above notation and the fact that η_l and η_r are independent, we can write, as in Cernuschi *et al.* (1989), the combined joint density as

$$p(I_l(\mathbf{x_l}), I_r(\mathbf{x_r}) \mid f_l, f_r, \gamma, \mathbf{d}) = \frac{1}{(2\pi\nu^2)^n} \prod_{i=1}^{n} e^{-\frac{\xi_l^2(x_{li}) + \xi_r^2(x_{ri})}{2\nu^2}}.^{\dagger}$$

---

† Note that even though the image functions I_l and I_r are discrete we obtain a continuous I_l and I_r by linear interpolation.

However, the brightness function γ is unknown. Therefore, let us approximate γ with its maximum likelihood estimator (MLE)

$$\hat{\gamma}(f_l(x_{li})) = \hat{\gamma}(f_r(x_{ri})) = \frac{I_l(x_{li}) + I_r(x_{ri})}{2}.$$

So, for a point x_i we have

$$\xi_l^2(x_{li}) + \xi_r^2(x_{ri}) \simeq \frac{(I_l(x_{li}) - I_r(x_{ri}))^2}{2}.$$

Now if the point x_i is mutually visible we can compute this quantity from the data. But what if x_i is half-occluded ($x_i \in O$)? Differing from Cernuschi *et al.* (1989), let us approximate the the squared difference $(I_l(x_{li}) - I_r(x_{ri}))^2/2$ by its expected value v^2. With these approximations and a few algebraic manipulations, Eq. 8.2.4 can be rewritten as

$$p(I_l(\mathbf{x_l}), I_r(\mathbf{x_r}) \mid \hat{\gamma}, \mathbf{d}) = \frac{1}{(2\pi v^2)^n} e^{-E_D} \qquad (8.1)$$

where

$$E_D = \frac{1}{4v^2} \sum_{I-O} (I_l(x_i + d_i) - I_r(x_i - d_i))^2 + \sum_O \frac{1}{2}$$

is the data term for our model.

In its current form, this approach relies heavily on the validity of the Lambertian assumption. Many have argued that this is inferior to matching other image features such as edges or texture. (See preceding chapters 6 and 7 for a discussion of features for recovering surface shape.) Therefore let us generalize Eq. 8.1 so that the data term compares, as opposed to simply image intensity, other, possibly more viewpoint invariant, features (e.g. edges, texture, filtered intensity, etc.). In doing this we rewrite Eq. 8.1 by replacing the intensity functions I_l and I_r with general feature functions F_l and F_r. Furthermore, since much of the analysis and, certainly, all of the notation is cleaner if we use a continuous form of the data term as opposed to a discrete form, let us write this down in the continuous form as

$$E_D = \frac{1}{4v^2} \int_{X-O} (F_l(x + d) - F_r(x - d))^2 dx + \int_O \frac{1}{2} dx$$

where X is the interval $[-a, a]$; $O \subset X$ is the collection of half-occluded regions; and F_l and F_r are functions representing the features along the left and right epipolar lines.

8.3 The prior model

This section derives our prior model for our Bayesian estimator, arguing that to capture the quantities in the scene geometry – namely depth, surface orientation, object boundaries, and surface creases – one should *explicitly* represent these quantities as random variables or continuous-time random processes in the prior model. The derivation is broken up into four stages, or worlds, each succeeding world considering additional complications in the scene geometry. Before we derive our prior model, however, we consider three psychophysical demonstrations of how the human visual system handles object surfaces. We use these demonstrations as motivation for the individual stages in the design of our prior model.

8.3.1 Psychophysical demonstrations

In the literature on computer and human vision, most researchers consider the "solution to the stereo problem" as simply a reconstruction of the disparity at each of the mutually visible points in the images. We conjecture that the human visual system may be more ambitious in solving the stereo problem than previously believed. By this we mean that, using binocular stereo, the visual system may reconstruct not simply the disparity, but also other quantities in a local representation of the scene geometry.[†] If, as Marr (1982) claimed, the visual system's low-level goal is to create a $2\frac{1}{2}$-D sketch of the scene geometry (i.e representations of depth, object boundaries, surface orientation, and creases), then why should the part of the brain responsible for stereo reconstructions not have these quantities explicitly represented? Marr (1982) further conjectured that the scene geometry is constructed as a post-processing step "from a number of different and probably independent processes that interpret disparity, motion, shading . . ." Yet due to the implicit relation between object boundaries and half-occlusion, there seems to be little sense in separating the process of identifying object boundaries from the process of determining the half-occluded regions. One might conjecture that these determinations happen simultaneously.

Reexamine the stereogram of the bulldog from Fig. 8.2. Notice that when we fuse the stereogram, we do not simply perceive a rough reconstruction in depth, but rather a very precise reconstruction in which both depth and surface orientation are spatially dense, and the boundaries of the objects and surface creases are well defined. In this figure, the half-occluded regions are so prevalent, and the reconstruction so precise, that it is difficult to imagine that the human visual system does not take advantage of the occluded regions in locating the object boundaries.

One might argue that object boundaries are aligned according to luminance edges in the images, after the correspondence problem has been solved. Yet while luminance edges help locate discontinuities in depth, they are by no means essential. The standard floating square random dot stereogram Julesz, 1971) shown in Fig. 8.7

[†] We call this representation "local" because it contains no information about the global structure of objects within the scene.

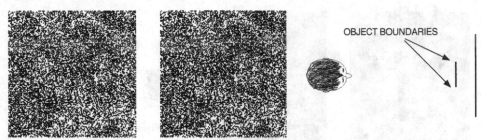

Fig. 8.7 **Object boundaries:** When the random dot stereogram is fused, we see the sharp discontinuity in depth at the boundary of the foreground square, even though there are no monocular clues. To the right is a horizontal cross section of the perceived depth.

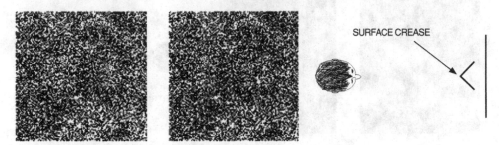

Fig. 8.8 **Surface creases:** When the random dot stereogram is fused, we see the sharp vertical crease of the foreground "roof top," even though there are no monocular clues. To the right is a horizontal cross section of the perceived depth.

has no monocular clues, but when fused we perceive sharp discontinuities in depth at the boundary of the foreground square.

In fact, the same is true for creases. While luminance edges may help locate creases, they are by no means essential. The random dot stereogram shown in Fig. 8.8 again has no monocular clues, but when fused we perceive not only the discontinuities in depth, but also the steeply sloping sides and sharp vertical crease of the foreground "roof top."

Furthermore, we conjecture that in addition to local smoothness constraints, the human visual system may have constraints which bias in favor of global 3-D structures in the images. In particular, we speculate that points are actively grouped into common disparity structures, and that this grouping is invariant to occlusion and transparency. Others researchers have also begun to speculate about global behavior (see for instance Nakayama & Shimojo (1992) and Madarasmi *et al.* (1993). As evidence, we refer to two closely related phenomena: background and transparency continuation.

Background continuation, the more common of the two phenomena, is caused by a foreground object partially occluding a background object such that the background

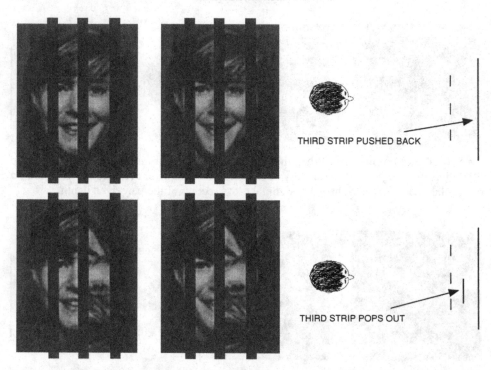

Fig. 8.9 **Background Continuation:** When the top stereogram is fused, most viewers perceive the four background sections continuing behind the vertical strips, even though the correct disparity for the third background section should place it in front of the other three sections. When the bottom stereogram is fused, all viewers correctly perceive that the third section pops out of the plane.

object is visible on both sides of the foreground object. Look around you, and you will see larger background objects disappearing behind smaller foreground occluding objects. In these scenes, you perceive the background object continuing behind the foreground object, even though you can not actually see behind the occluding object.

Examine the stereogram in Fig. 8.9. Here we have placed a woman behind foreground vertical strips. When the top stereogram is fused, most viewers perceive the background plane continuing behind the foreground strips, even though the plane is interrupted by partial occlusion. In fact, the tendency to see background continuation is so strong that the percept in the top stereogram is incorrect. Due to a manipulation of the image, the correct disparity for the third (from the left) background section should place it well in front of the other three background sections. What in the human visual system causes this erroneous percept? Is it simply a desire to link up background surfaces?

Unfortunately, the answer is not so simple. Examine the bottom stereogram.

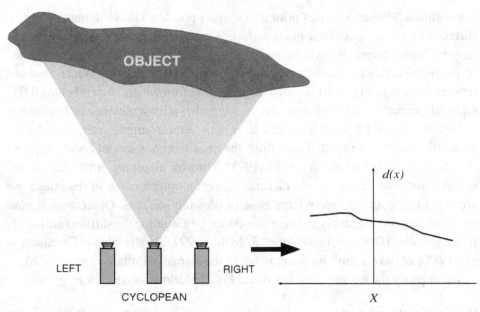

Fig. 8.10 **World I scene:** A scene in World I has only one object. The figure shows a horizontal cross-section of a scene and the corresponding disparity function.

Here we have kept everything the same as above, except we have vertically flipped the third background section. When fused, all viewers correctly perceive the third background section in front of the other three background sections, so much so that there is no percept of continuation. We speculate that the visual system rejects the background continuation because there is too much monocular evidence against this interpretation.

8.3.2 World I – Smoothness

In this section we take the first of four steps toward developing a prior for the disparity function on the surface of objects: here we assume a simple world in which the scenes captured in a stereo pair contain only one object. On the surface of this object, we further assume that the 2-D distance function of the cyclopean coordinate system is everywhere continuous; so, a particular epipolar line has both a distance function D and a disparity function d which are also everywhere continuous.[†] Figure 8.10 shows a hand rendered scene from World I and the corresponding disparity d.

For this world, we assume the disparity function d is a sample path of scaled Brownian motion, with the scaling of the process determined by the expected surface

---

[†] Because the relation between disparity and depth is known, we do not explicitly represent the depth, but rather the disparity in the derivation of the prior model.

"smoothness." We choose this prior as a starting point, acknowledging that not all surfaces – especially not man-made surfaces – are well approximated by Brownian motion. Nevertheless, Brownian motion is a weak prior considering a large class of possible surfaces – the whole space of continuous functions. While the hand rendered scene in Fig. 8.10 shows a disparity function which is well behaved (i.e. relatively smooth), a Brownian motion sample path is almost nowhere differentiable. To get an idea of the jaggedness in a Brownian motion sample path, consider the graph of a stock price plotted over time: the most common model for stock prices is geometric Brownian motion Hull (1993). Thus by assuming Brownian motion as our prior distribution for the disparity along an epipolar line in the image, we are considering an extremely large class of possible surfaces. Other models have *implicitly* imposed arguably stronger constraints by assuming the surfaces are locally fronto-parallel (Gennery,1980; Jones & Malik, 1992) locally planar Cernuschi *et al.* (1985), or have a limit on the gradient of the disparity Pollard *et al.*, 1985b).

We quantify the assumptions for World I in the following definition:

Definition. World I: The disparity d has as its prior distribution the Brownian motion stochastic process $Z(x) = \theta + b^{\frac{1}{2}} B(x)$ where $\theta \sim \mathcal{N}(0, \gamma)$; $B(x)$ is standard Brownian motion; b is fixed; $x \in [-a, a]$; and, θ and B are independent.

With these prior assumptions we want to find a measure for evenly spaced samples of the disparity along the cyclopean epipolar line. Let us take the samples $\mathbf{d} = (d_1, \ldots, d_n)$ corresponding to the points $\mathbf{x} = (x_1, \ldots, x_n)$. As in Section 8.2.3, let the sample period be $\delta = x_{i+1} - x_i$, and the index set be $I = \{1, \ldots, n\}$. With these definitions and notation, we make the following claim:

Claim. Given the assumptions in Definition World I, letting $\gamma \to \infty$, and ignoring constant terms, the functional $E_P[\mathbf{d}]$ is given by

$$E_P[\mathbf{d}] = \frac{1}{2b\delta} \sum_{I - \{n\}} (d_{i+1} - d_i)^2.$$

(For proofs of the claims in this chapter see Belhumeur, 1993a).)

We can combine the data term derived in the previous section with this prior term to get the Bayesian estimator for World I written in its continuous form as

$$E[d] = E_D + E_P \tag{8.2}$$

where

$$E_D = \int_X \big(F_l(x + d) - F_r(x - d) \big)^2 dx$$

$$E_P = \lambda^2 \int_X (d')^2 \, dx$$

where X is the interval $[-a, a]$; F_l and F_r are functions representing the features along the left and right epipolar lines; d' is the derivative of the disparity d; and λ is a constant determined by the parameters ν^2 and b. In this formulation we leave out the half-occluded regions, because the discontinuities in depth (also referred to as occluding contours) are not represented.

In this 1-D formulation the solutions along the epipolar lines are obtained independently of one another. Clearly these solutions are not independent: there are strong smoothness constraints binding epipolar lines (Baker & Binford, 1981; Marr & Poggio, 1976a; Ohta & Kanade, 1985). While we could apply the method used earlier in this section to derive 2-D prior terms for our model, we instead take a simpler route: we *heuristically* extend to 2-D the properties evident in the 1-D models. The matching will now be done the points (x, y) in a 2-D image plane $X \subset \mathcal{R}^2$. We write down the 2-D model as follows:

$$E[d] = E_D + E_P$$

where

$$E_D = \iint_X (F_l(x + d, y) - F_r(x - d, y))^2 dx\, dy$$

$$E_P = \lambda^2 \iint_X \|\nabla d\|^2 dx\, dy$$

and where F_l and F_r are 2-D functions representing the features in the right and left images; and λ is a preset constant. Note that this model is nearly identical to the one suggested by Poggio *et al.* (1985).

At this point, we should make clear that we do not intend to provide a detailed discussion of the nature of Brownian motion surface priors. A discussion of this type would fill an entire book. Therefore, we take the easy way out and refer the reader to Szeliski (1989). Szeliski (1989) provides a detailed discussion of surface priors, including the observation that using the surface prior E_P in the above equation is equivalent to assuming that the underlying surface is fractal. Furthermore, he demonstrates how these priors can, in theory, be generalized as fractional dimensional processes.

Nevertheless, the question remains – how does this prior help us reconstruct the geometry of the observed scene? The answer is simply that the prior constrains the set of possible solutions in such a way that flat and continuous reconstructions are favored over those that are steeply jagged and discontinuous. Thus, the strength of this model is that the implicit smoothing helps eliminate the ambiguity in the matching caused by both the inaccuracy of the measurements and large regions of constant intensity. The E_D term forces the reconstruction to agree with the features in the data. The E_P term biases toward smooth reconstructions with the degree of the bias given by the constant λ.

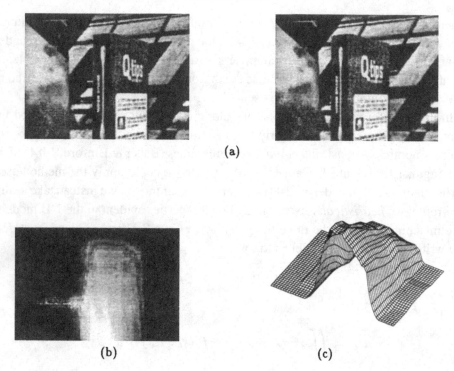

Fig. 8.11 **World I Result:** (a) Qtips box – left and right (b) Image of depth. (c) Wire frame of depth.

The weakness of this model is that it does not accurately model real world scenes; most scenes actually contain several surfaces, with the disparity function discontinuous at the objects' boundaries. Not only does this model have no way of suspending the smoothing at boundaries of objects, but it also has no way of identifying and suspending the matching of half-occluded regions. In short, it flattens steeply sloping surfaces; it smoothes over surface creases; and it smoothes over discontinuities in depth at the boundaries of objects.[†]

To demonstrate these drawbacks, Figure 8.11a shows a stereo pair of a Qtips box stood on end with its long vertical crease protruding toward the cameras. The box stands in front of a flat background. When fused the viewer clearly sees the sharp discontinuities in depth at the boundaries of the foreground Qtips box. The reader might correctly guess that if we applied the above model to this stereo pair, the sharp discontinuities in depth would be smoothed over. The rest of Fig. 8.11 contains the results obtained by minimizing the 2-D version of the above energy functionals:

[†] This prior has two additional weaknesses which are not discussed in this chapter. First, the surface prior is viewpoint dependent. (This is a complication which we have, so far, avoided.) Second, the prior does not enforce a lower bound on the disparity d, but the horizon gives one (i.e. $d \geq 0$).

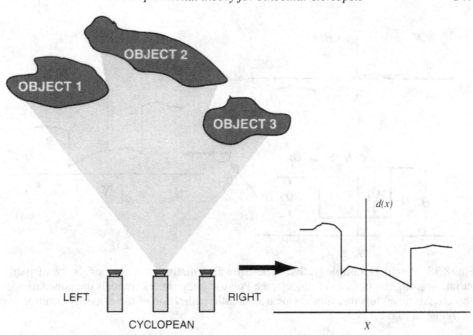

Fig. 8.12 **World II scene:** A scene in World II may have multiple objects. The figure shows a horizontal cross-section of a scene and the corresponding disparity function.

Fig. 8.11b is an image of the depth map in which light corresponds to near and dark to far and Fig. 8.11c is a wire frame view of the depth map. (Note that this result and the others displayed throughout this chapter our MAP estimates.) Notice that the boundaries of the Qtips box are lost and, as assumed by the prior model, the depth reconstruction looks like a single continuous surface.

8.3.3 World II – Object boundaries

In this section we assume a slightly more complicated world than World I: here we consider the possibility of more than one object in a scene. Figure 8.12 shows a scene from World II and the corresponding disparity d. Notice that, as in the actual world, the distance function along the surface of an object is often smooth, but jumps discontinuously at the boundaries of the objects. So, a particular epipolar line has a distance function and, therefore, a disparity function which is not continuous, but rather piecewise continuous. We argue, as Geman & Geman (1984) has for the segmentation problem and Yuille (1989b) has for the stereo problem, that in order to capture this phenomenon it is necessary to introduce a new set of random variables that explicitly represents the discontinuities in disparity at the boundaries of objects.

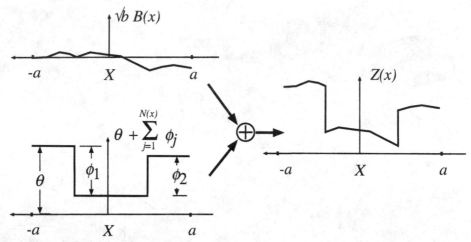

Fig. 8.13 **World II sample paths:** The Brownian motion process models the disparity variation along the surfaces of objects; the Poisson jump process models the boundaries of objects. Summed together they create a stochastic realization of the disparity function for the scene in Fig. 8.12.

For this world we assume the disparity function d is a sample path of the sum of a scaled Brownian motion process and a compound Poisson process with i.i.d. uniform random variables.[†]

As in World I, we use the scaled Brownian motion process as a prior model for the contour of objects' surfaces, with the scaling of the process determined by the expected surface smoothness. But now we use the jumps in the Poisson process to model the objects' boundaries, with the jump rate of the process determined by the expected size of objects. We quantify the assumptions for World II in the following definition:

Definition. World II: The disparity d has as its prior distribution the stochastic process $Z(x) = \theta + b^{\frac{1}{2}} B(x) + \sum_{j=1}^{N(x)} \phi_j$ where $\theta \sim \mathcal{N}(0, \gamma)$; $B(x)$ is standard Brownian motion; b is fixed; $N(x)$ is a Poisson process with jump parameter ϑ; the ϕ_j are i.i.d. $\mathcal{U}[-\Delta, \Delta]$; $x \in [-a, a]$; and, θ, B, and the ϕ_j are all independent.

Figure 8.13 shows a stochastic realization of the quantities in the scene geometry **S** for the scene in Fig. 8.12.

As for World I, we want to find a measure for the evenly spaced samples of the disparity and jumps along the cyclopean epipolar line. Let us take the samples

---

[†] Although we choose uniform random variables to model the jumps in disparity at the boundaries of objects, we could customize our prior by choosing random variables that model particular types of scenes. For example, we might have different random variables to model the jumps in disparity for leaves on a tree, parts on a assembly line, and cars on a highway.

$\mathbf{d} = (d_1, \ldots, d_n)$ corresponding to the points $\mathbf{x} = (x_1, \ldots, x_n)$. As in Section 8.2.3, let the sample period be $\delta = x_{i+1} - x_i$, and the index set be $I = \{1, \ldots, n\}$. Furthermore, let us introduce the vector $\mathbf{l} = (l_1, \ldots, l_{n-1})$ where l_i represents the number of of jumps in the Poisson process $N(x)$ between x_i and x_{i+1}. With these definitions and notation, we state the following claim: Given the assumptions in Definition World II letting $\gamma \to \infty$, and ignoring constant terms, the functional $E_P[\mathbf{d}, \mathbf{l}]$ is well approximated by

$$E_P[\mathbf{d}, B] = \frac{1}{2b\delta} \sum_{I-B-\{n\}} (d_{i+1} - d_i)^2 + \sum_B \frac{1}{2} \log(\frac{2\Delta^2}{\pi b \vartheta^2 \delta^3})$$

where the set of discontinuities $B = \{i \mid l_i = 1\}$ (also known as the "break" points).[†]

We can combine the data term derived in the previous section with this prior term to get the Bayesian estimator for World II written in its continuous form as

$$E[d, B] = E_D + E_P \tag{8.3}$$

where

$$E_D = \int_{X-O} \left(F_l(x+d) - F_r(x-d)\right)^2 dx + \int_O \alpha_O \, dx$$

$$E_P = \lambda^2 \int_{X-B} (d')^2 dx + \alpha_B |B|$$

and where X is the interval $[-a, a]$; O is the set of half-occluded regions; F_l and F_r are functions representing the features along the left and right epipolar lines; B is the set of discontinuities in d; $|B|$ is the cardinality of the set B; α_O is a constant determined by v^2; λ is a constant determined by v^2 and b; and α_B is a constant determined by v^2, b, and ϑ.[‡]

As for World I, we can extend this model to 2-D as follows

$$E[d, B] = E_D + E_P$$

where

$$E_D = \iint_{X-O} \left(F_l(x+d, y) - F_r(x-d, y)\right)^2 dx \, dy + \iint_O \alpha_O \, dx \, dy$$

$$E_P = \lambda^2 \iint_{X-B} \|\nabla d\|^2 \, dx \, dy + \alpha_B |B|$$

and where F_l and F_r are 2-D functions representing the features in the right and left images; $O \subset X$ are the 2-D half-occluded regions; B is a collection of contours

[†] If we assume that $\vartheta \delta << 1$ and $b\delta << \Delta^2$, then for practical implementation purposes we need only consider the cases when there is at most one jump in the interval between x_i and x_{i+1}. Thus, we restrict $l_i \in \{0, 1\}$.

[‡] The form of this prior term is precisely that used in the weak string energy functional (Blake & Zisserman, 1987; Geman & Geman, 1984; Mumford 1985).

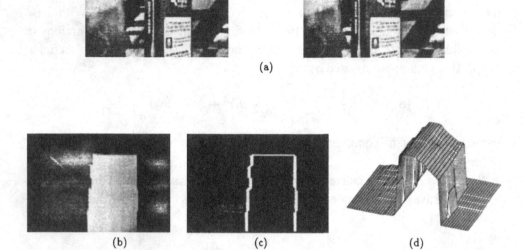

Fig. 8.14 World II Result: (a) Qtips box – left and right (b) Image of depth. (c) Occluding contours. (d) Wire frame of depth.

across which d is discontinuous; $|B|$ is the total length of the collection contours in B; and α_O, λ, and α_B are preset constants.

The strength of this model is that the disparity estimates, the discontinuities, and half-occluded regions are inseparably linked. All of these quantities are found simultaneously. The E_D term forces the reconstruction to agree with the features in the data, but only for mutually visible points $(X - O)$. For half-occluded points (O), we take a penalty α_O which is proportional to variance of the noise in the images. The E_P term biases toward smooth reconstructions with the degree of the bias given by the constant λ. Note, however, that the E_P term allows the smoothing to be suspended at the breaks (B) in the disparity. For break points, we take a penalty α_B.

Demonstrating the effectiveness of this model, Figure 8.14 contains the results obtained by minimizing the 2-D version of the above energy functionals on the stereo pair in Fig. 8.11: Fig. 8.14b is an image of the depth map in which light corresponds to near and dark to far; Fig. 8.14c is a map of the occluding contours; and Fig. 8.14d is a wire frame view of the depth map. Notice that the discontinuities in depth (occluding contours) of the Qtips box are accurately reconstructed.

While this result is encouraging, it also deceptive in that, on closer inspection, we see that the depth on the surface of the Qtips box is rounded off. The steeply sloping surfaces and the sharp vertical crease of the box are largely lost. In other words,

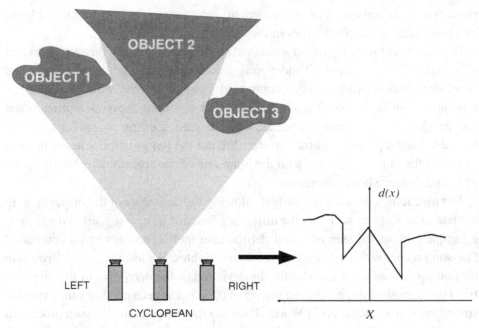

Fig. 8.15 **World III scene:** A scene in World III may have multiple objects as well as steeply sloping surfaces with creases. The figure shows a horizontal cross-section a scene and the corresponding disparity function.

while the model performs well on the large regions of constant luminance, the sharp discontinuities in depth, and the half-occluded regions to the left and right of the foreground box, the model fails to accurately preserve both the steep gradient of the sides of the box and the long vertical crease. If the energy functional's smoothing parameter λ is decreased in an effort to better preserve the crease of the box and the disparity gradient, the results become more erratic.

8.3.4 World III – Surface slope and creases

In this section, we assume an even more complicated world: here not only do we consider more than one object in a scene, but we also consider that surfaces of objects may be steeply sloping and may have creases. Figure 8.15 shows a scene from World III and the corresponding disparity d. For this world, we need a prior model for the disparity which respects not only the possibility of an object beginning or ending, but also the possibility of steeply sloping surfaces and discontinuities in surface orientation (as Harris, 1989, did for the segmentation problem). In World II, we were able to consider multiple objects in a scene by introducing random variables which explicitly represented the discontinuities in disparity at the boundaries of objects. We argue that this method can again be applied to introduce a new random process to represent the slope of the disparity, and a new set of random variables to represent creases (discontinuities in the slope).

For this world we introduce a smoothed slope function m (by this we mean that m is a smoothed version of d') and assume it is a sample path of the sum of a scaled Brownian motion process and a compound Poisson process with i.i.d. uniform random variables. We use the scaled Brownian motion process as a prior model for the slope of the objects' surfaces, with the scaling of the process determined by the expected planarity of the surfaces. We use the jumps in the Poisson process to model the objects' creases, with the jump rate of the process determined by the expected distance between creases.

Next we reintroduce the disparity d allowing the derivative of the disparity d' to deviate from slope m such that the difference function $d(x) - \int_{-a}^{x} m(u)\,du$ is itself a sample path of the sum of a scaled Brownian motion process and a compound Poisson process with i.i.d. uniform random variables. We use the scaled Brownian motion process as a prior model for the deviation of the derivative of the disparity from the smoothed slope, with the scaling of the process determined by the expected smoothness of surfaces. As in World II, we use the jumps in the Poisson process to model the objects' boundaries, with the jump rate of the process determined by the expected size of objects. We quantify the assumptions for World III in the following definition:

Definition. World III: The disparity $d(x)$ has as its prior distribution the stochastic process $Z(x) = Z_d(x) + \int_{-a}^{x} Z_m(u)\,du$. The stochastic process $Z_d(x) = \theta_d + b_d^{\frac{1}{2}} B_d(x) + \sum_{j=1}^{N_d(x)} \phi_{d_j}$ where $\theta_d \sim \mathcal{N}(0, \gamma_d)$; $B_d(x)$ is standard Brownian motion; b_d is fixed; $N_d(x)$ is a Poisson process with jump parameter ϑ_d; the ϕ_{d_j} are i.i.d. $\mathcal{U}[-\Delta_d, \Delta_d]$; and $x \in [-a, a]$. The smoothed slope m has as its prior distribution the stochastic process $Z_m(x) = \theta_m + b_m^{\frac{1}{2}} B_m(x) + \sum_{j=1}^{N_m(x)+N_d(x)} \phi_{m_j}$ where $\theta_m \sim \mathcal{N}(0, \gamma_m)$; B_m is standard Brownian motion; b_m is fixed; $N_m(x)$ is a Poisson process with jump parameter ϑ_m; the ϕ_{m_j} are i.i.d. $\mathcal{U}[-\Delta_m, \Delta_m]$; and $x \in [-a, a]$. Finally, $\theta_d, \theta_m, \phi_{d_j}, \phi_{m_j}, B_d, B_m, N_d,$ and N_m are all independent.

Figure 8.16 shows a stochastic realization of the quantities in the scene geometry **S** for the scene in Fig. 8.15.

As for the previous worlds, we want to find a measure for evenly spaced samples of the disparity, slope, breaks, and creases along the cyclopean epipolar line. Let us take the samples of disparity $\mathbf{d} = (d_1, \ldots, d_n)$ and slope $\mathbf{m} = (m_1, \ldots, m_n)$ corresponding to the points $\mathbf{x} = (x_1, \ldots, x_n)$. As in Section 8.2.3, let the sample period be $\delta = x_{i+1} - x_i$, and the index set be $I = \{1, \ldots, n\}$. Furthermore, let us introduce the vectors $\mathbf{l_d} = (l_{d_1}, \ldots, l_{d_{n-1}})$ where l_{d_i} represents the number of jumps

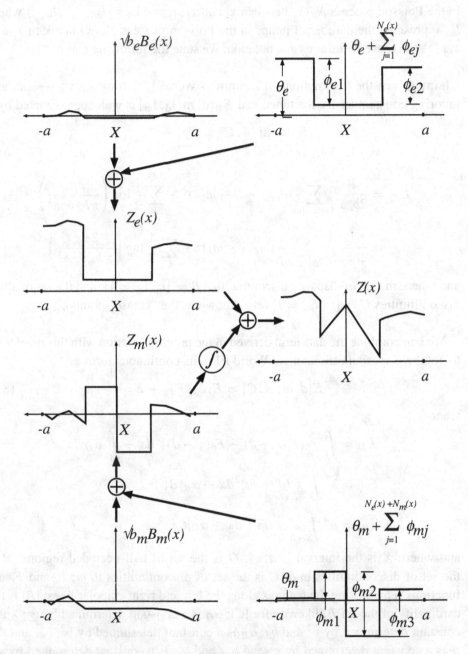

Fig. 8.16 World III sample paths: Along the surfaces of objects, the Brownian motion processes model both the variation of m and the deviation of d from $\int m$. The Poisson jump processes model the boundaries of objects and surface creases. Summed together they create a stochastic realization of the disparity function for the scene in Fig. 8.15

in the Poisson process $N_d(x)$ between x_i and x_{i+1}, and $\mathbf{l_m} = (l_{m_1}, \ldots, l_{m_{n-1}})$ where l_{m_i} represents the number of jumps in the Poisson process $N_m(x)$ between x_i and x_{i+1}. With these definitions and notation, we state the following claim:

Claim. Given the assumptions in Definition World III letting $\gamma_d, \gamma_m \to \infty$, and ignoring constant terms, the functional $E_P[\mathbf{d}, \mathbf{m}, \mathbf{l_d}, \mathbf{l_m}]$ is well approximated by

$$E_P[\mathbf{d}, \mathbf{m}, B, C] = E_{P_d} + E_{P_m}$$

where

$$E_{P_d} = \frac{1}{2b_d\delta} \sum_{I-B-\{n\}} (d_{i+1} - d_i - m_i\delta)^2 + \sum_B \frac{1}{2} \log\left(\frac{2\Delta_d^2}{\pi b_d \vartheta_d^2 \delta^3}\right)$$

$$E_{P_m} = \frac{1}{2b_m\delta} \sum_{I-B-C-\{n\}} (m_{i+1} - m_i)^2 + \sum_C \frac{1}{2} \log\left(\frac{2\Delta_m^2}{\pi b_m \vartheta_m^2 \delta^3}\right)$$

and where the set of disparity discontinuities $B = \{i \mid l_{d_i} = 1\}$; and the set of slope discontinuities $C = \{i \mid l_{m_i} = 1\}$ (also known as the "crease" points).[†]

We can combine the data term derived in the previous section with this prior term to get the Bayesian estimator for World III in its continuous form as

$$E[d, m, B, C] = E_D + E_{P_d} + E_{P_m} \qquad (8.4)$$

where

$$E_D = \int_{X-O} \left(F_l(x+d) - F_r(x-d)\right)^2 dx + \int_O \alpha_O \, dx$$

$$E_{P_d} = \lambda^2 \int_{X-B} (d'-m)^2 dx + \alpha_B|B|$$

$$E_{P_m} = \mu^4 \int_{X-B-C} (m')^2 dx + \alpha_C|C|$$

and where X is the interval $[-a, a]$; O is the set of half-occluded regions; B is the set of discontinuities in d; C is the set of discontinuities in m; F_l and F_r are functions representing the features along the left and right epipolar lines; $|B|$ is the cardinality of the set B, likewise for $|C|$; α_O is a constant determined by ν^2; λ is a constant determined by ν^2 and b_d; α_B is a constant determined by ν^2, b_d, and ϑ_d; μ is a constant determined by ν^2 and b_m; and α_C is a constant determined by ν^2, b_m, and ϑ_m.[‡]

[†] If we assume that $\vartheta_d\delta$, $\vartheta_m\delta \ll 1$, $b_d\delta \ll \Delta_d^2$, and $b_m\delta \ll \Delta_m^2$, then as for World II we need only consider the cases when there is at most one jump in the interval between x_i and x_{i+1}. Thus, we restrict $l_{di}, l_{mi} \in \{0, 1\}$.

[‡] The form of this prior term is precisely that used in the weak rubber band energy functional (Belhumeur, 1993b; Harris, 1989).

As for Worlds I and II, we extend this model to 2-D. To do this, we introduce horizontal and vertical slope functions $m(x, y)$ and $n(x, y)$, with $\mathbf{m} = (m, n)$, and write the model as follows

$$E[d, \mathbf{m}, B, C] = E_D + E_{P_d} + E_{P_m}$$

where

$$E_D = \iint_{X-O} \left(F_l(x + d, y) - F_r(x - d, y)\right)^2 dx\, dy + \iint_O \alpha_O\, dx\, dy$$

$$E_{P_d} = \lambda^2 \iint_{X-B} \|\nabla d - \mathbf{m}\|^2\, dx\, dy + \alpha_B|B|$$

$$E_{P_m} = \mu^4 \iint_{X-B-C} \|\nabla m\|^2 + \|\nabla n\|^2\, dx\, dy + \alpha_C|C|$$

and where F_l and F_r are 2-D functions representing the features in the right and left images; $O \subset X$ are the 2-D half-occluded regions; B is a collection of contours across which d is discontinuous; C is a collection of contours across which either m or n is discontinuous; $|B|$ is the total length of the collection contours in B, likewise for $|C|$; and α_O, λ, α_B, μ, and C are preset constants.

Note that the estimated quantities for World III are exactly those in Marr's $2\frac{1}{2}$-D sketch (Marr, 1982). However, the point we make here is that these quantities should be estimated simultaneously, not in a post-processing step, as Marr suggested. (In chapter 4, Yuille & Bülthoff emphasize the same point, as do several other contributors.)

By incorporating the surface gradient $\mathbf{m}$ we are able to create smoothing terms E_{P_d} and E_{P_m} that do not over bias toward fronto-parallel disparity. The E_{P_d} term biases toward reconstructions in which ∇d is close to the smoothed surface gradient $\mathbf{m}$, with the degree of bias given by the parameter λ. The E_{P_m} term biases toward smooth reconstructions of the surface gradient $\mathbf{m}$, with the degree of bias given by the parameter μ. For any planar disparity function, $E_{P_d} + E_{P_m} = 0$, while for the World I and II energy functionals $E_P \neq 0$. This improvement allows the model to reconstruct surfaces with strong disparity gradients. While there is some evidence that the human visual system is biased toward fronto-parallel surfaces (Bulthoff *et al.*, 1991c), this bias must be much more subtle than simply the (squared first derivative of the disparity) bias in E_P. Specifically, the E_P from World II favors surfaces that are globally fronto-parallel but locally very rough, over surfaces that are globally slightly slanted but locally very smooth (Blake, 1987). This bias is correctly reversed for the smoothing terms E_{P_d} and E_{P_m}. Note that although we could achieve this property by smoothing using only the second derivative of disparity, in Belhumeur (1993a) we present detailed arguments for why this is, in fact, inferior.

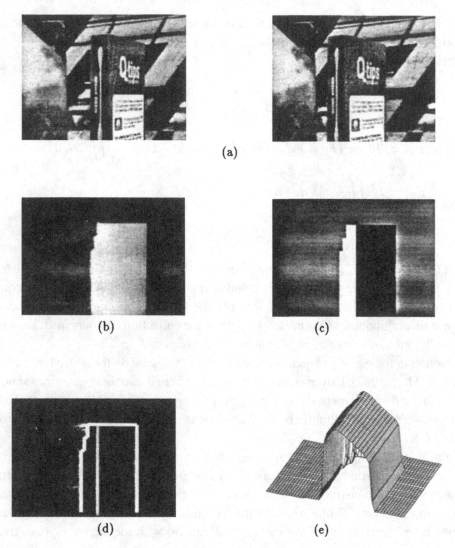

Fig. 8.17 **World III Result:** (a) Qtips box – left and right (b) Image of depth. (c) Image of slope. (d) Occluding contours and creases. (e) Wire frame of depth.

Furthermore, by incorporating the set of creases C, we are able suspend the smoothing term E_{P_m} at creases, while enforcing the term E_{P_d}. This allows the surface gradient **m** to jump discontinuously at the creases, while keeping the disparity continuous. For creases, we take a penalty α_C. This improvement allows the model to reconstruct not only discontinuities in disparity at object boundaries, but also the discontinuities in slope at creases in objects.

Figure 8.17 shows the results produced by minimizing the 2-D version of the above energy functionals on the stereo pair shown in Fig. 8.11. In addition to depth and occluding contours, these results contain surface orientation and creases: Fig. 8.17b is an image of the depth; Fig. 8.17c is an image of the horizontal slope; Fig. 8.17d is an image of the occluding contours (white) and the creases (grey); and Figure 8.17e is a wire frame of the depth. Here the sharp disparity gradients and the long vertical crease of the Qtips box are, for the most part, perfectly preserved.

8.3.5 World IV – Global structures

The three previously developed prior models all share the same drawback: they have no way of modeling the global structures in the scene geometry. For all three worlds, we assumed that the disparity function was constructed from Brownian motion and compound Poisson processes. But note that both Brownian motion and Poisson processes are Markov processes – processes with the property that the conditional distribution of the future, given the present states of the process, does not depend on the past (Bhattacharya & Waymire, 1990). While one can develop increasingly complicated prior models using Markov processes as done for Worlds I-III, these models are limited in that they only allow local interactions of the random variables.

This limitation is unrealistic for several reasons. Most notably, since occluded objects tend to disappear and reappear behind foreground objects (Madarasmi *et al.*, 1993; Mutch & Thompson, 1985) a phenomenon that we call "background continuation," global interactions must also be present.[†] Look around you; in almost any scene you will see background objects continuing behind smaller foreground objects. As an example of background continuation, let us once again revisit the scene captured in Fig.'s 8.5 and 8.6. If we look at a horizontal cross section of the scene (see Fig. 8.18), we see that the corresponding disparity function $d(x)$ is divided by the boundaries of the foreground sphere into three piecewise smooth regions. Although our Markov prior models assume that the disparity in these regions is independent, we see from the figure that this is clearly incorrect: the fact that the disparity is the same for the planar regions to the left and right of the foreground sphere is not a coincidence, but rather a result of the global structure of the scene.

A less common, but closely related phenomenon "transparent continuation" is caused by foreground objects which are, in some regions, opaque and, in other regions, transparent. These types of scenes have proven to be difficult for computational stereo models, even though the human visual system handles these correctly. (See chapter 10 by Nakayama & Shimojo for further examples.)

It seems that the prior models developed in the previous three worlds can not properly model stereo scenes of this type. Yet, what considerations should be made in choosing the new prior model? Recall that in Section 8.1.2 we derived the priors

---

[†] We use the term "global" to mean highly non-local, i.e. existing on the scale greater than one-tenth of observed scene.

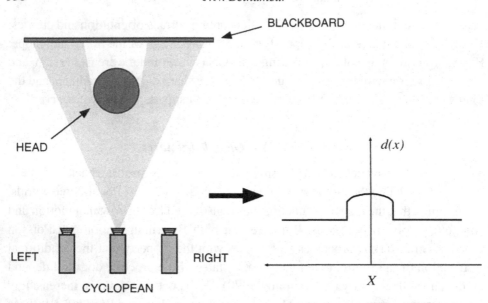

Fig. 8.18 **World IV Scene:** A scene in World IV has background objects continuing behind foreground objects. The figure illustrates a horizontal cross section of a spherical head in front of flat blackboard, as well as a graph of the corresponding disparity $d(x)$. A Markov process can not model the probabilistic subtleties of continuing background surface.

from the bottom up. The random processes we chose to model the scene geometry allowed only for very local interactions between the random variables. Still, the algorithms implied by these models still produced reliable results. How are we to incorporate long range interactions of the random variables without ignoring the progress we have made already?

What is needed is a prior model that balances local smoothness with global structure. (See also chapters 4, 6 and 11.) In this section, we take a small step toward this goal by suggesting a Bayesian feedback model in which the prior is iteratively adapted using information from the from previous estimates. Here the previous estimate is analyzed for global structure, and the results of this analysis are used to adjust specific terms in the prior, unlike Worlds I-III where all of the terms are fixed.

Recall the definition of World II: here we assumed that the jumps of the compound Poisson process were given by i.i.d. uniform random random variables – i.e. that within some fixed range $[-\Delta, \Delta]$ all jumps in disparity were equally likely and independent of one another. Yet, as we tried to demonstrate in Fig. 8.18, due to background and transparency continuation, the jumps in disparity are not actually independent. To model this phenomenon, we intend to iteratively shape the distributions of the jumps by using the results of the previous estimates.

Thus, for World IV we re-use the assumptions of World II, but add the generalization that the jumps in the Poisson process are generated by unknown distributions. For the initial estimate, we set these distributions to be the same as World II – i.i.d. uniform random variables. We then use the results of the this first pass to shape the distributions for the second estimate. This process repeats until the estimates converge. The details of how this distribution is reshaped are beyond the scope of this chapter; however, the reader may refer to Belhumeur (1993a).

Note that the Bayesian estimator for World IV is nearly identical to that of World II, except the penalty for breaks is now a function of the break's location in the image and the disparities on either side of the break. Thus, the model rewards jumps for which there is much evidence and penalizes jumps for which there is little evidence.

$$E_D = \int_{X-O} (F_l(x+d) - F_r(x-d))^2 dx + \int_O \alpha_O \, dx$$

$$E_P = \lambda^2 \int_{X-B} (d')^2 dx + \sum_B \alpha_B(x, d)$$

and where X is the interval $[-a, a]$; O is the set of half-occluded regions; F_l and F_r are functions representing the features along the left and right epipolar lines; B is the set of discontinuities in d; α_O is a constant determined by v^2; λ is a constant determined by v^2 and b; and α_B is a function of x and d determined by the results of the previous estimate. (This modification could be done to World III as well, but for simplicity we have only modified World II.)

As for each of the previous worlds, we can extend this model to 2-D as follows

$$E[d, B] = E_D + E_P$$

where

$$E_D = \iint_{X-O} (F_l(x+d, y) - F_r(x-d, y))^2 dx \, dy + \iint_O \alpha_O \, dx \, dy$$

$$E_P = \lambda^2 \iint_{X-B} \|\nabla d\|^2 dx \, dy + \int_B \alpha_B(x, y, d) ds$$

and where F_l and F_r are 2-D functions representing the features in the right and left images; $O \subset X$ are the 2-D half-occluded regions; B is a collection of contours across which d is discontinuous; s is the length along the contours B; and α_O, λ, and α_B are preset constants.

To illustrate the potential of this feedback method, we choose a stereo pair with transparency. Figure 8.19a shows a stereo pair of small pieces of paper stuck to a transparent Plexiglas window. The window is placed in front of a planar background which falls away from the viewer as you move from left to right. When the stereogram is fused, the viewer clearly sees the pieces of paper floating *within the*

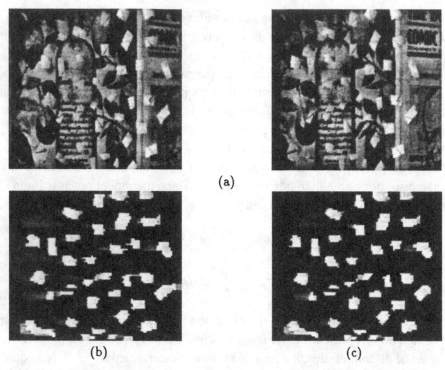

Fig. 8.19 (a) Transparent surface – left and right (b) Image of depth without feedback. (c) Image of depth with feedback.

same invisible plane, several inches in front of the background plane. Figure 8.19b contains the results obtained by minimizing the 2-D form of the World II energy functional. In this result no feedback was used. While the result is fairly accurate, notice that in the transparent regions between many of the foreground pieces of paper, the depth reconstruction degenerates. This negative result is due to the fact that there is not enough information in the small background regions to independently determine the depth. (See chapters 10 and 11 for related effects.) And, the local priors are unable to propagate the background depths into the small transparent regions between the pieces of paper. However, Fig. 8.19c contains the results obtained by minimizing the World IV energy functional. For this example, the break penalty $\alpha_B(x, d)$ simply biased in favor of planar structures in the scene geometry. Note that, except in two or three places, this feedback corrects the previous mistakes.

8.4 Conclusion

In the preceding pages of this chapter, we presented a computational theory for reconstructing the scene geometry from a pair of stereo images. Our intent was to show that one could construct a theory piece by piece – making explicit all of the underlying assumptions. In this way we were able to isolate the effects of each individual assumptions. Throughout, we tried to apply the knowledge gleaned from psychophysical demonstrations to the construction of our theory. To demonstrate its effectiveness, we selected two positive results. First, we presented a result from a stereo pair with large half-occluded regions, steeply sloping surfaces, and pronounced discontinuities in both depth and surface orientation (see Fig. 8.17). Second, we presented a result from a stereo pair with a partially transparent foreground surface (see Fig. 8.19).

While our model performs well on these and many other stereograms, much work remains before we can claim that it is a general purpose stereo model. At present, all of the parameters for our model must be specified in advance. Even though there exists a wide range of parameter values that will produce the presented results, how does one choose these parameters? Ideally, the model should be responsible for determining the proper choices. A possible method for doing this is Wahba's (1990) "generalized cross-validation." Nevertheless, we decided not to include a discussion on how to automate the choice for these parameters and, instead, left this as an area for future research.

Furthermore, the prior models themselves are not general purpose. There are many stereo scenes which would not be accurately modeled by the priors for World I, II, or III. For example, the priors described herein would not be the method of choice for finding the depth in a stereo scene made up of the leafless branches of a tree. Rather, our method is best applied to a scene of several objects with relatively smooth surfaces – the clutter of a desktop for example. We could develop a prior model which would work well for the denuded branches of a tree, but it would almost certainly not be the method of choice for a messy desktop.

Finally, while it may seem that our computational model is limited to stereo vision, we suggest that many of the ideas presented in this chapter can be adapted, or generalized, to other applications. The phenomenon of half-occlusion is not limited to stereo vision, both the problems of object tracking and determining optical flow fields are complicated by occlusion. Move your hand back and forth in front of your eyes, and you will see background objects disappearing behind your hand and then reappearing as your hand moves by. Yet, little of the vision literature on the analysis of motion addresses this complication. Although we have not yet investigated this in depth, it would seem that the prescription given in this chapter for handling half-occluded regions in stereo images should apply equally well for motion images.

Our prior models have clear applications outside of the context of binocular stereopsis. Our prior models are themselves generalizations to stereo vision of the "energy based" approaches used for image segmentation (Blake & Zisserman, 1987; Geman & Geman, 1984; Mumford & Shah, 1985). The key to the success of these models is that discontinuities in the signal to be estimated are explicitly represented in the energy functionals. For example, our energy functional for stereo matching represents the discontinuities in the disparity and the discontinuities in surface orientation, while the weak string energy functional represents the discontinuities in the image luminance. Naturally, these ideas can be further adapted to other areas of vision.

References

Anderson, B. (1992). Personal communication. Technical report, Harvard University.

Baker, H.H. & Binford, T.O. (1981). Depth from edge and intensity based stereo. *IJCAI*, 631-636.

Belhumeur, P.N. (1993a) A Bayesian approach to the stereo correspondence problem. PhD thesis, Harvard University.

Belhumeur, P.N. (1993b). Bayesian models for reconstructing the scene geometry in a pair of stereo images. *Proc. Conf. on Information Sciences and Systems*, Johns Hopkins University.

Belhumeur, P.N. & Mumford, D. (1992). A Bayesian treatment of the stereo correspondence problem using half-occluded regions. *IEEE Comp. Soc. Conf. on Comp. Vison and Pattern Recognition*, pp. 506-512.

Besag, J. (1974). Spatial interaction and statistical analysis of lattice systems. *J. Roy. Stat. Soc. Lond. B.*, **36**, 192-225.

Bhattacharya, R. & Waymire, E. (1990). *Stochastic Processes with Applications*. New York: John Wiley & Sons.

Blake, A. & Zisserman, A. (1987). *Visual Reconstruction*. Cambridge, MA: MIT Press.

Bülthoff, H., Fahle, M. & Wegmen, M. (1991). Disparity gradients and depth scaling. *Perception*, **20**, 145-153.

Cernuschi-Frias, B., Belhumeur, P.N. & Cooper, D.B. (1985). Estimating and recognizing parameterized 3-D objects using a moving camera. *Proc. Conf. Computer Vision and Pattern Recognition*, 167-171.

Cernuschi-Frias, B., Cooper, D.B., Hung, Y.P. & Belhumeur, P.N. (1989). Toward a model-based Bayesian theory for estimating and recognizing parameterized 3-D objects using two or more images taken from different positions. *IEEE Trans. Pattern Analysis and Machine Intelligence*, pp. 1028-1052.

Clark, J.J. & Yuille, A.L. (1990). *Data Fusion for Sensory Information*. Boston: Kluwer Academic Press.

Cochran, S.D. & Medioni, G. (1992). 3-D surface description from binocular stereo. *IEEE Trans. Pattern Analysis and Machine Intelligence*, pp. 981-994.

Cohen, F.S., Cooper, D.B., Silverman, J.F. & Hinkle, E.B. (1984). Simple parallel hierarchical relaxation algorithms for segmenting textured images based on noncausal Markovian random field models. *Proc. 7th Int. Conf. on Pattern Recognition, Montreal, Canada*,k pp. 1104-1107.

Cross, G.C. & Jain, A.K. (1983). Markov random field texture models. *IEEE Trans. Pattern Analysis and Machine Intelligence*, **5**, 25-39.

Geiger, D. & Girosi, F. (1991). Parallel and deterministic algorithms from MRF's: surface reconstruction. *IEEE Trans. Pattern Analysis and Machine Intelligence*, **13**(5), 401-412.

Geiger, D., Ladendorf, B. & Yuille, A. (1992). Occlusions in binocular stereo. *Proc. European Conf. on Computer Vision, Santa Margherita Ligure, Italy.*

Geman, S. (1988). Experiments in Bayesian image analysis. In *Bayesian Statistics*, ed. J.M. Bernando, M.H. DeGroot, D.V. Lindley and A.F.M. Smith. Oxford Univ. Press.

Geman, S. & Geman, D. (1984) Stochastic relaxation, Gibbs distribution and the Bayesian restoration of images. *IEEE Trans. Pattern Analysis and Machine Intelligence*, **6**, 721-741.

Gennery, D.B. (1980). Modelling the environment of an exploring vehicle by means of stereo vision. PhD theis, Stanford University.

Grenander, U. (1981). *Lectures on Pattern Theory*. Springer-Verlag.

Grimson, W.E.L. (1981). *From Images to Surfaces*. Cambridge, MA: MIT Press.

Harris, J.G. (1989). The coupled depth/slope approach to surface reconstruction. Technical Report MIT AI Lab TR-908.

Leonard da Vinci (1989). *Leonardo On Painting*. Ed. M. Kemp. Yale University Press.

Hull, J. (1993). *Options, Futures, and Other Deriviative Securities*. Englewood Cliffs, NJ: Prentice Hall.

Jones, D. & Malik, J. (1992). A computational framework for determining stereo correspondence from a set of linear spatial filters. *Proc. European Conf. on Computer Vision, Santa Margherita Ligure, Italy.*

Julesz, B. (1971). *Foundations of Cyclopean Perception*. Univ. Chicago Press.

Kato, Z., Berthold, M. & Zerubia, J. (1993). Multiscale Markov random field models for parallel image classification. *Proc. 4th Int. Conf. on Computer Vision*, pp. 253-257.

Lawson, R.B. & Gulick, W.L. (1967). Stereopsis and anomalous contour. *Vis. Res.*, **7**, 271-291.

Madarasmi, S., Kersten, D. & Pong, T. (1993). *The Computation of Stereo Disparity for Transparent and for Opaque Surfaces*, eds. C.L. Giles, S.J. Hanson and J.D. Cowan.

Marr, D. (1982). *Vision*. San Francisco, CA: Freeman.

Marr, D. & Poggio, T. (1976). Cooperative computation of stereo disparity. *Science*, **194**, 283-287.

Marr, D. & Poggio, T. (1979) A computational theory of human stereo vision. *Proc. Roy. Soc. Lond.*, **204**, 301-328.

Marroquin, J., Mitter, S. & Poggio, T. (1987). Probabilistic solutions of ill-posed problems in computational vision. *J. of the Am. Stat. Soc.*, **82**(397), 76-89.

Matthies, L. (1992). Stereo vision for planetary rovers: stochastic modeling to near real-time implementation. *Int. Jrl. of Computer Vision*, **8**(1), 71-91.

Mumford, D. & Shah, J. (1985). Boundary detection by minimising functionals. *Proc. Conf. Computer Vision and Pattern Recognition*, **22**.

Mutch, K.M. &f Thompson, W.B. (1985). Analysis of accretion and deletion at boundaries in scenes. *IEEE Trans. Pattern Analysis and Machine Intelligence*, **7**(2), 133-138.

Nakayama, K. & Shimojo, S. (1990). Da Vinci stereopsis: depth and subjective occluding from unpaired image points. *Vis. Res.*, **30**, 1811-1825.

Nakayama, K. & Shimojo, S. (1992). Experiencing and perceiving visual surfaces. *Science*, **257**, 1357-1363.

Ohta, Y. & Kanade, T. (1985). Stereo by intra- and inter-scan line search using dynamic programming. *IEEE Trans. Pattern Analysis and Machine Intelligence*, **7**(2), 139-154.

Poggio, T., Torre, V. & Koch, C. (1985). Computational vision and regularisation theory. *Nature*, **317**, 314-319.

Pollard, S.B., Mayhew, J.E.W. & Frisby, J.P. (1985). PMF:A stereo correspondence algorithm using a disparity gradient. *Perception*, **14**, 449-470.

Szeliski, R. (1989). *A Bayesian Modeling of Uncertainty in Low-level Vision*. Boston, MA: Kluwer Academic Press.

Wahba, G. (1990). Spline models for observational data. In *CBMS-NSF, Regional Conference Series in Applied Mathematics*. Philadelphia.

Wilde, R. (1991). Direct recovery of three-dimensional scene geometry from binocular stereo disparity. *IEEE Trans. Pattern Analysis and Machine Intelligence*, pp. 761-774.

Yang, Y., Yuille, A. & Lu, J. (1993). Local, global, and multilevel stereo matching. *Proc. Conf. Computer Vision and Pattern Recognition*. New York.

Yuille, A. (1989) Energy functions for early vision and analog networks. *Biol. Cyber.*, **61**, 115-123.

9

The generic viewpoint assumption
in a Bayesian framework

WILLIAM T. FREEMAN

Mitsubishi Electric Research Laboratories

9.1 Introduction

A task of visual perception is to find the scene which best explains visual observations. Figure 9.1 can be used to illustrate the problem of perception. The visual data is the image held by two cherubs at the right. Scattered in the middle are various geometrical objects – "scene interpretations" – which may account for the observed data. How does one choose between the competing interpretations for the image data?

One approach is to find the probability that each interpretation could have created the observed data. Bayesian statistics are a powerful tool for this, e.g. Geman & Geman (1984), Jepson & Richards (1992), Kersten (1991), Szeliski (1989). One expresses prior assumptions as probabilities and calculates for each interpretation a posterior probability, conditioned on the visual data. The best interpretation may be that with the highest probability density, or a more sophisticated criterion may be used. Other computational techniques, such as regularization (Poggio *et al.*, 1985; Tikhonov & Arsenin, 1977), can be posed in a Bayesian framework (Szeliski, 1989). In this chapter, we will apply the powerful assumption of "generic view" in a Bayesian framework. This will lead us to an additional term from Bayesian theory involving the Fisher information matrix. (See also chapter 7 by Blake *et al.*.) This will modify the posterior probabilities to give additional information about the scene.

The generic view assumption (Biederman, 1985; Binford, 1981; Koenderink & van Doorn, 1979; Lowe & Binford, 1985a; Malik, 1987; Nakayama & Shimojo, 1992; Richards *et al.*, 1987) postulates that the scene is not viewed from a special position. Figure 9.2 shows an example. The square in (a) could be an image of a wire-frame cube (b) viewed from a position where the line segments of the front face hide those behind them. However, that would require a very special viewpoint, and given the image in (a), one should infer a square, not a cube; Hochberg (1978) and Nakayama & Shimojo (1992) discuss this example. The generic view assumption has been invoked to explain perceptions involving stereo and transparency

W.T. Freeman

Fig. 9.1 This image can describe one approach to the problem of perception. Starting from the visual image, held by the cherubs at the right, one wants to find the probability that each of various models or scene interpretations (on the ground in the middle) could have generated that visual data. (Etching by Samuel Wale, *Putti engaged in the study of geometry and perspective*, from J. Kirby's *The Perspective of Architecture* London, 1761.)

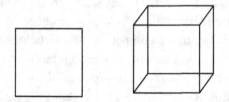

Fig. 9.2 An example of use of the generic view assumption for binary decisions. the image (a) could be of a square, or it could be an "accidental view" of the cube in (b). since a cube would require a special viewing position to be seen as the image in (a), we reject that possible interpretation for (a).

(Nakayama & Shimojo, 1992), linear shape from shading (Pentland, 1990), and feature or object identification (Biederman, 1985; Dickenson *et al.*, 1992; Jepson & Richards, 1992; Koenderink & van Doorn, 1979; Lowe & Binford, 1985a; Malik, 1987; Richards *et al.*, 1987). Typically, researchers assume a view is either generic, and therefore admissible, or accidental, and therefore rejected. Some have pointed out that it should be possible to quantify the degree of accidentalness or have done so in special cases (Dickenson *et al.*, 1992; Jepson & Richards, 1992; Leclerc & Bobick, 1991; Lowe & Binford, 1985a; Malik, 1987; Nakayama & Shimojo, 1992; Witkin, 1981).

In this chapter we take a quantitative approach, in a complementary fashion to the categorical use of the generic viewpoint assumption. Rather than assign categories to views of geometrical objects, we assign probabilities to views of continuous surfaces. This approach will let us make parametric decisions about candidate scene interpretations. We discuss the relationship to aspect graphs in Section 9.5.

In our approach, we divide parameters into two groups, *generic* parameters and *scene* parameters. Generic parameters are parameters we do not need to estimate precisely. Viewpoint is one example; others are object orientation and lighting position. Scene parameters are what we desire to estimate, and can be reflectance function, shape, lighting direction and velocity. We relax this split into two types of parameters in the formulation of Section 9.7.

We will exploit the known distributions of the generic variables to modify the probability of given scene parameters. We will used an established approximation from Bayesian statistics to quantify the "genericity" of a view. Our analysis will favor scene interpretations for which the visual data is stable to small changes in the generic variables. This information can be used to make principled selections among competing scene interpretations where otherwise arbitrary choices would have to be made.

We show applications to the shape from shading problem. Using a two-parameter family of reflectance functions, we show how to find the probability of a shape and reflectance function combination from a single image. We rank shape probabilities corresponding to different assumed lighting directions in a case where each shape can account for the image data equally well. (See chapter 11 by Adelson & Pentland for an alternate treatment.)

We motivate our approach in the remainder of the introduction. In Section 9.3 we derive the *scene probability equation*, the conditional probability for a scene interpretation given the observed visual data. Then we show the applications to shape from shading. In Section 9.7, we frame this approach in terms of the loss functions of Bayesian estimation, introduced earlier in chapter 4. Substantial parts of this work were presented in Freeman (1993a, 1994b).

9.2 Example

A simple example illustrates the main idea. Suppose the visual data is the image of Figure 9.3 (a). Perceptually, there are two possible interpretations: it could be a bump, lit from the left, or a dimple, lit from the right. Yet mathematically, there are many interpretations to choose from under the commonly encountered conditions of linear shading[†] The image could arise from any of the shapes shown in (b), under the proper lighting conditions, which are indicated by the lighting direction arrow shown next to each shape. How should one choose between these competing explanations?

One often considers only two criteria to evaluate an interpretation: how well it accounts for the observed data, and the prior probability that the interpretation would

---

[†] In linear shading (Pentland, 1990), the image intensity is a linear function of the local surface gradient. For small surface slopes and low angles of illumination, linear shading is a good approximation to Lambertian shading.

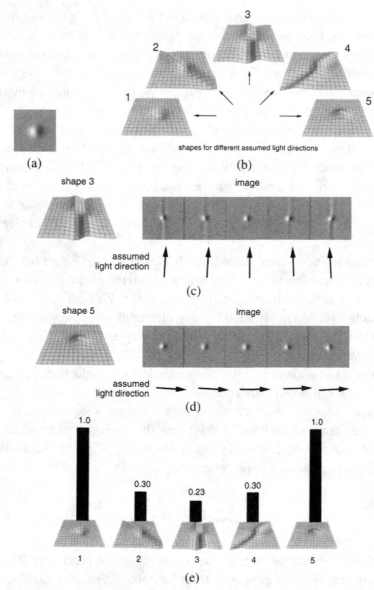

Fig. 9.3 (a) Perceptually, this image has two possible interpretations: a bump lit from the left, or a dimple lit from the right. But under the conditions of linear shading (Pentland, 1990), each of the shapes shown in (b), under shallow illumination from the direction indicated, could create the image (a). (The boundary conditions used were those described in (Pentland, 1990). Shapes 2 – 4 require coincidental alignment with the assumed light direction. We can distinguish between the explanations if we examine the image stability to perturbations in light direction. Shape 3 presents the observed image for a very small range of light angles (c), while shape 5 does for a much larger range (d). The scene probability equation, which we derive in Section 9.3, quantifies the degree of coincidence of the light direction and reconstructed shape. Using light direction as the generic variable, and shape as the scene parameter, the scene probability for each interpretation is plotted in (e). Note the preference for the bump or dimple shapes, in agreement with the appearance of (a).

exist in the world. If each shape accounts equally well for the image data, we are left with choosing based on the prior probabilities for each shape. We could arbitrarily decide that we like bump shapes more than tube shapes but we have no grounds for that. Such an arbitrary decision could easily lead to an incorrect interpretation for some other image. What is missing from this approach?

For the three tube-like shapes shown, there is a suspicious alignment between the inferred surface structure and the assumed light direction. This seems unlikely, and we would like to include this coincidence in our probability calculation. Figure 9.3 (c) and (d) give an intuition for how we might measure the accidentalness of the surface and light direction alignments. If we imagine wiggling the assumed light direction slightly, we see that for shape 3, the image changes quite a bit. For shape 5, we can observe the image of (a) over a much broader range of assumed light directions. If the light had an equal chance of coming from each different direction then there are more opportunities for shape 5 to have presented us with the image (a) than there are for shape 3.

We will quantify this intuition by taking derivatives. A small image intensity derivative with respect to light direction means that the image will look almost the same over a relatively large range of light angles. If all light angles are equally likely, then the probability of a shape is proportional to the range of light angles over which the shape looks nearly the same as the image data. In our analysis, the image derivatives will result from writing the image in a Taylor series in the generic variables.

In this way, we will exploit additional assumptions about the visual world. To the prior assumptions about what is being estimated, we add assumptions about relationships between the object, the viewer and the light source direction. This additional information may allow for weakening the prior assumptions we need to make about the scene.

This approach, and the approximation we use, comes from the literature of Bayesian statistics. Using the Taylor series approximates the likelihood term of the posterior probability as a gaussian, which gives a Bayesian version of the central limit theorem. This was done by Laplace (Laplace, 1812, cited in Berger, 1985), in the 1800's as well as Fisher (Fisher, 1959) and Jeffreys, 1961) in the first half of this century. Others have followed and extended this approach (Berger, 1985; Box & Tiao, 1973; Gull, 1989; Johnson, 1970; Lindley, 1972; Mackay, 1992; Skilling, 1989) (Berger, 1985, and Mackay, 1992 are particularly accessible references).

In the field of computer vision, Szeliski (1989) applied maximum likelihood estimation to favoring interpolation parameters which could have generated the observed data in many different ways. See Weinshall *et. al.* (1994) for a recent related non-Bayesian approach.

9.3 The scene probability equation

In this section we derive the probability densities for scene parameters given observed data. We describe the problem generally.

Let $\hat{\mathbf{y}}$ be a vector of observations. This can be image intensities, or measures derived from them, such as spatial or temporal derivatives or normal velocities. For simplicity, we will often call this "the image".

Let the vector β be the scene parameters we want to estimate. This vector can describe, for example, the object shape and reflectance function or the image velocities.

Let $\mathbf{x}$ be a vector of the generic variables – variables which we do not need to estimate precisely. For the example of Figure 9.3 this was the incident light angle. Generic variables can include viewpoint position, object orientation, lighting position, or texture orientation. For now we assume that the probability density of the generic variables $\mathbf{x}$, $p(\mathbf{x})$, is flat:

$$p(\mathbf{x}) = k \tag{9.1}$$

where k is a normalization constant. We indicate later how to generalize to the case of non-flat generic variable densities.

The scene parameters β and generic variables $\mathbf{x}$ determine the ideal observation (image), $\mathbf{y}$, through a "rendering function", f:

$$\mathbf{y} = f(\mathbf{x}, \beta) \tag{9.2}$$

For the example of Figure 9.3 the rendering function was the computer graphics calculation which gave the image as a function of surface shape, β, and incident light angle, $\mathbf{x}$.

We postulate some measurement noise, although we will often examine the limit where its variance goes to zero. The observation, $\hat{\mathbf{y}}$, is the rendered ideal image $\mathbf{y}$ plus the measurement noise, $\mathbf{n}$:

$$\hat{\mathbf{y}} = \mathbf{y} + \mathbf{n}. \tag{9.3}$$

The noise specifies a distance metric between images – the probability that the differences between the images are due to noise. We will assume that the measurement noise is a set of independent, identically distributed Gaussian random variables with mean zero and standard deviation σ. Thus $p(\mathbf{n})$, the probability density function of the noise, is

$$p(\mathbf{n}) = \frac{1}{(\sqrt{2\pi\sigma^2})^N} \exp \frac{-\|\mathbf{n}\|^2}{2\sigma^2}, \tag{9.4}$$

where N is the dimension of the observation and noise vectors and $\|\mathbf{n}\|^2 = \mathbf{n} \cdot \mathbf{n}$.

Given an observation $\hat{\mathbf{y}}$, we want to find $p(\beta \mid \hat{\mathbf{y}})$, the conditional probability of the parameters β. We first use Bayes' theorem to evaluate the joint probability of β and a particular value of the generic variables, $p(\beta, \mathbf{x} \mid \mathbf{y})$:

$$p(\beta, \mathbf{x} \mid \mathbf{y}) = \frac{p(\mathbf{y} \mid \beta, \mathbf{x}) p_\beta(\beta) p(\mathbf{x})}{p_{\mathbf{y}}(\mathbf{y})}, \quad (9.5)$$

where we have assumed that $\mathbf{x}$ and β are independent. The denominator is constant for all models β to be compared.

To find $p(\beta, \mathbf{x} \mid \mathbf{y})$, independent of the value of the generic variable $\mathbf{x}$, we integrate the joint probability of Equation (9.5) over the possible $\mathbf{x}$ values:

$$p(\beta|\mathbf{y}) = \frac{p(\beta)}{p(\mathbf{y})} \int p(\mathbf{y} \mid \beta, \mathbf{x}) \, p(\mathbf{x}) \, d\mathbf{x}. \quad (9.6)$$

From our Gaussian noise model, Equation (9.4), we have

$$p(\mathbf{y} \mid \beta, \mathbf{x}) = \frac{1}{(\sqrt{2\pi\sigma^2})^N} e^{\frac{-\|\mathbf{y} - f(\mathbf{x}, \beta)\|^2}{2\sigma^2}}. \quad (9.7)$$

$p(\mathbf{y} \mid \beta, \mathbf{x})$ is large where the scene β and the value $\mathbf{x}$ yield a rendered image similiar to the observation $\mathbf{y}$. The integral of Equation (9.6) measures the area of $\mathbf{x}$ for which the scene β yields the observation. In our example, it effectively counts the frames in Figure 9.3 (c) or (d) where the rendered image is similar to the input data. This will favor shape 5, for which the image changes little over a range of light angles.

For the low noise limit, we can find an analytic approximation to the integral of Equation 9.6 (Bleistein & Handelsman, 1986; Jeffreys, 1962). We expand $f(\mathbf{x}, \beta)$ in Equation (9.7) in a second order Taylor series,

$$f(\mathbf{x}, \beta) \approx f(\mathbf{x}_0, \beta) + \sum_i f_i' \, [\mathbf{x} - \mathbf{x}_0]_i + \frac{1}{2} \sum_{i,j} [\mathbf{x} - \mathbf{x}_0]_i \, f_{ij}'' \, [\mathbf{x} - \mathbf{x}_0]_j, \quad (9.8)$$

where $[\cdot]_i$ indicates the ith component of the vector in brackets, and

$$f_i' = \frac{\partial f(\mathbf{x}, \beta)}{\partial x_i} \mid_{\mathbf{x} = \mathbf{x}_0}, \quad (9.9)$$

and

$$f_{ij}'' = \frac{\partial^2 f(\mathbf{x}, \beta)}{\partial x_i \partial x_j} \mid_{\mathbf{x} = \mathbf{x}_0}. \quad (9.10)$$

We take $\mathbf{x}_0$ to be the value of $\mathbf{x}$ which can best account for the observed image data; i.e., for which $\|\mathbf{y} - f(\mathbf{x}, \beta)\|^2$ is minimized.

Using Eqs. (9.7)–(9.10) to second order in $\mathbf{x} - \mathbf{x}_0$ in the integral of Equation (9.6), we find the posterior probability for the scene parameters β given the visual data **y**:

$$p(\beta \mid \mathbf{y}) = k \; \exp\left(\frac{-\|\mathbf{y} - f(\mathbf{x}_0, \beta)\|^2}{2\sigma^2}\right) p_\beta(\beta) \; \frac{1}{\sqrt{\det(\boldsymbol{C})}} \qquad (9.11)$$

$$= k \,(\text{fidelity}) \,(\text{prior probability}) \,(\text{generic view}),$$

where the i and jth elements of the matrix $\boldsymbol{C}$ are

$$C_{ij} = f_i' \cdot f_j' - (\mathbf{y} - f(\mathbf{x}_0, \beta)) \cdot f_{ij}''. \qquad (9.12)$$

We call this the *scene probability equation*. We have combined the constants which do not depend on the scene β into the normalization constant k, which can be set so that the integral of $p(\beta \mid \hat{\mathbf{y}})$ over all β is one. Usually we examine relative probabilities; then k doesn't matter. The rendering function derivatives in Equation (9.8) must exist for Equation (9.11) to hold. Thus, we cannot apply Equation (9.11) to some idealized geometrical objects.

The scene probability equation Equation (9.11) has two familiar terms and a new term in computer vision. The term $\exp\left(\frac{-\|\hat{\mathbf{y}} - f(\mathbf{x}_0, \beta)\|^2}{2\sigma^2}\right)$ penalizes scene hypotheses which do not account well for the original data (hypotheses β for which the squared difference of $f(\mathbf{x}_0, \beta)$ from the image data $\hat{\mathbf{y}}$ is large). We call this the *image fidelity term*. (This may also be called the "likelihood of $\mathbf{x}_0$ and β with respect to $\hat{\mathbf{y}}$"). The *prior probability* term $p(\beta)$ came from Bayes' law and incorporates prior assumptions. These two terms (the prior and a squared error term) are familiar in computer vision. $\frac{1}{\sqrt{\det(\boldsymbol{C})}}$ is the new term, arising from the generic view assumption. If the rendered image changes quickly with the generic view variables, then $\frac{1}{\sqrt{\det(\boldsymbol{C})}}$ will be large and the scene hypothesis β will be unlikely. This $\frac{1}{\sqrt{\det(\boldsymbol{C})}}$ term quantifies our intuitive notion of generic view, and we call it the *generic view* term. Note that the generic view term depends on the best value of the generic variable, $\mathbf{x}_0$, as well as the scene parameter β, so it is not equivalent to a prior on the scene parameter, which will only be a function of β. The scene probability equation gives the probability that a scene interpretation β generated the visual data, $\hat{\mathbf{y}}$, based on fidelity to the data, prior probability, and the probability that the scene would have presented us with the observed visual data.

This quantification of the genericity of a view follows established techniques in Bayesian statistics. The matrix $\boldsymbol{C}$ is called the conditional Fisher information matrix (Berger, 1985; Fisher, 1959). It is used to approximate the likelihood locally as a Gaussian (Box & Tiao, 1973; Fisher, 1959; Jeffreys, 1961) and can be used in integration over a loss function or in marginalization (Berger, 1985; Lindley, 1972). For example, Box and Tiao (1964) employ this approximation when they integrate out nuisance parameters from a joint posterior, as we have done here. Gull

(1988) calls $\frac{1}{\sqrt{\det(C)}}$ the Occam factor and he, Skilling (1989), and MacKay (1992) use it as we have here and in other ways. This factor also arises in the context of "non-informative priors" Berger, 1985; Box & Tiao, 1973; Jeffreys, 1961).

The case of only one generic variable and $\|\hat{\mathbf{y}} - f(x_0, \boldsymbol{\beta})\| = 0$ shows the role of the image derivatives more clearly. Then the scene probability equation becomes:

$$p(\boldsymbol{\beta} \mid \hat{\mathbf{y}}) = k \frac{p(\boldsymbol{\beta})}{\sqrt{\sum_i (\frac{\partial f_i(x,\boldsymbol{\beta})}{\partial x} \mid_{x=x_0})^2}}, \qquad (9.13)$$

The probability of a parameter vector $\boldsymbol{\beta}$ varies inversely with the sum of the squares of the image derivatives with respect to the generic variable.

In evaluating the Gaussian integral in Equation (9.6) we assumed that the generic variables were separable. Generic object pose in 3-d is an exception to that and we derived the scene probability equation for that case in Freeman (1996)

9.4 Shape from shading examples

We apply the scene probability equation to some problems in shape from shading. Given a shaded image, lighting conditions and the reflectance function, there are many algorithms which can compute a shape to account for the shaded image; see Horn (1989) and Horn & Brooks (1989b) for reviews, as well as chapter 11 by Adelson & Pentland.

Most shape from shading algorithms require specification of the lighting and object surface characteristics. There are a number of methods that can infer these given more than one view of the object or other information (Grimson, 1984; Horn *et al.*, 1978; Pentland, 1990b; Woodham, 1980, Zheng & Chellapa, 1991). Finding the object shape from a single view without these parameters is not a solved problem. Brooks and Horn (1989) proposed a more general scheme that iterated to find a shape and reflectance map that could account for the image data.

However, accounting for image data is not enough. For some classes of images, many shapes and reflectance functions can account equally well for an image (although some images which are impossible to explain by Lambertian shading have been found, Brooks *et al.* (1992); Horn *et al.* (1993)). An infinite number of surface and light source combinations can explain regions of 1-dimensional intensity variations, since the solution just involves a 1-dimensional integration. The rendering conditions of "linear shading" (Pentland, 1990) can be invoked to explain any image, as we discuss later. Thus, to explain a given image, one must choose between a variety of feasible surface shapes, reflectance functions and lighting conditions.

To make such choices, one could invoke prior preferences for the preferred shapes or reflectance functions. Some shape from shading algorithms do this implicitly by using regularizing functionals. However, if one relies too heavily on the prior statistics to make decisions, that will bias the shape reconstructions. The scene probability equation enables one to use the generic view assumption to choose between shapes and reflectance functions, lessening the reliance on the priors.

We have not developed a shape from shading algorithm which uses the scene probability equation directly. Rather, we use existing shape from shading algorithms (Bichsel, 1991; Pentland, 1990) to generate hypothesis shapes and use the scene probability equation to evaluate their probability density. Future research can incorporate the scene probability equation, or an approximation to it, directly into a shape from shading algorithm.

9.4.1 Reflectance function

Figure 9.4 shows an example of a 1-d image which can be explained by several different shapes and reflectance functions. The image (a) may look like a cylinder (c) painted with a Lambertian reflectance function (b) (shown on a hemisphere). However, it could also have been created by the flatter shape of (f), painted with a shiny reflectance function (e). If both interpretations account for the data, how can we choose between them? We could invoke prior assumptions about the probabilities of various shapes or reflectance functions, but we would prefer a choice based on the image, not our prior assumptions (see Nakayama & Shimojo, 1992 and chapter 10).

Before applying the scene probability equation to this example, we provide intuitive motivation for the result. We can distinguish between the two scene hypotheses if we imagine rotating them. The Lambertian shaded image would change little for small rotations, while the shiny image would change considerably, Figure 9.4 (d) and (g). Thus, for the Lambertian solution, for a large range of object poses we would see the image of Figure 9.4 (a). For the shiny solution, we would see that image over a smaller range of poses.

One might think that the images of rotated shiny objects would always change more than those of Lambertian ones, since the diffuse reflection changes slowly with surface orientation. However, Figure 9.5 shows that this is not the case. The image data, Figure 9.5 (a), may look like a shiny cylinder, but, again, it can be explained by either a Lambertian reflectance function, shape (c) painted with (b), or a shiny one, the shape (f) painted with (e). Note that the shape for the Lambertian function is taller than that of the shiny reflectance function. When we rotate both shapes, in Figure 9.5 (d) and (g), it is the image of the Lambertian shape, (c), which changes more than that of the shiny one (f), because of the parallax induced as the tall shape moves back and forth.

To quantify these intuitions, we can apply the scene probability equation to distinguish between these shapes and reflectance functions. Our observation $\hat{y}$ is the

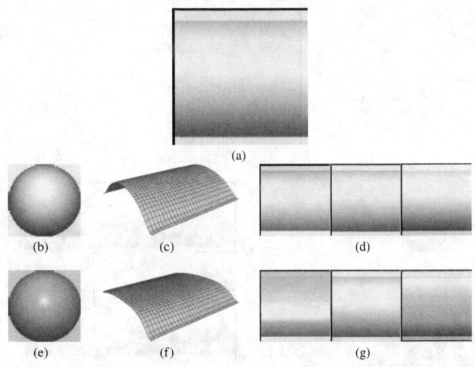

Fig. 9.4 The image (a) may appear to be a cylinder (c) painted with a Lambertian reflectance function (b) (shown on a hemisphere). However the flatter shape of (f) and a shiny reflectance function (e) also explain the data equally well. We can distinguish between the competing accounts for (a) by imagining rotating each shape. Images of each shape at three nearby orientations are shown in (d) and (g). We see that the image made assuming a Lambertian reflectance function (b) is more stable than that made assuming a shiny reflectance function (e). If all object angles are equally likely, and the shapes and reflectances of (c) and (f) are equally likely to occur in the world, then (c) should be a more likely interpretation of (a) than (f).

image data. The parameter β we wish to estimate is the shape and reflectance function of the object. We use a two variable parameterization of reflectance functions, a subset of the Cook and Torrance model (Cook & Torrance, 1981). The parameters are surface roughness, which governs the width of the specular highlight, and specularity, which determines the ratio of the diffuse and specular reflections. Figure 9.6 gives a visual key.

We want to use the scene probability equation, Equation (9.11), to evaluate the probability $p(\beta \mid \hat{y})$ for each reflectance function in our parameterized space. A shape exists for each reflectance function which could have created the 1-d images of Figure 9.4 (a) and Figure 9.5 (a). (For each shape we assumed boundary conditions of constant height at the vertical picture edge). We will consider only shape and reflectance function combinations which exactly account for the image

W.T. Freeman

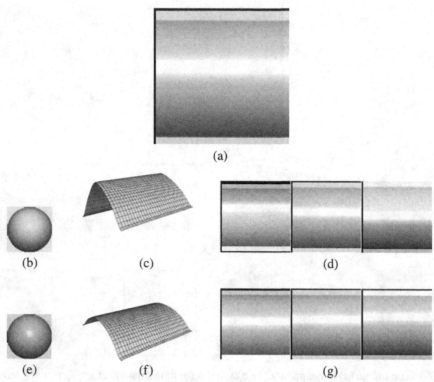

(a)

(b)   (c)   (d)

(e)   (f)   (g)

Fig. 9.5 The image, (a), can be accounted for in two different ways. The shape (c) and the
Lambertian reflectance function shown in (b) will create the image (a), as will the shape (f)
and a shiny reflectance function (e). We can distinguish between the shiny and Lambertian
explanations for (a) if we imagine rotating each shape. (d) and (g) show each shape at three
different orientations. The image made from the shiny reflectance function, (e), changes
only a little, while the parallax caused by the rotation of the tall shape of the Lambertian
solution causes a larger image change. The reflectance function of (e) provides more angles
over which the image looks nearly the same. If all viewpoints are equally likely, and the
shapes and reflectances of (c) and (f) are equally likely to occur in the world, then (f) should
be more likely than (c). The scene probability equation makes this precise.

data. Then the fidelity term in Equation (9.13) for $p(\beta \mid \hat{y})$ is 1. For this example,
we will assume a flat prior for the reflectance functions and shapes as parameterized,
$p(\beta) = c$. We used a shape from shading algorithm (Bichsel & Pentland, 1992) to
find the shape corresponding to each reflectance function.

Now we consider the generic view term. We will use both the vertical rotation
of the object and the vertical light position as the generic variables. We need the
derivative of the image intensities, I, with respect to the object rotation angle, ϕ.
This derivative is a special case of a formula given in Freeman (1996),

$$\frac{dI}{d\phi} = \frac{\partial I}{\partial Y}Z + \frac{\partial m}{\partial q}(1 + q^2), \tag{9.14}$$

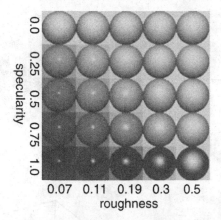

Fig. 9.6 Key to reflectance function parameters of Figure 9.7. Reflectance functions are displayed as they would appear on a hemisphere, lit in the same way as Figure 9.7 (a) and (c). The ratio of diffuse to specular reflectance increases in the vertical direction. The surface roughness (which only affects the specular component) increases horizontally. The sampling increments are linear for specularity and logarithmic for roughness.

where $q = \frac{\partial Z}{\partial Y}$, X and Y are Cartesian image coordinates, Z is the surface height, and m is the reflectance map. We calculated numerically the image derivative with respect to light position. For the z value of the axis of rotation we used the value which minimized the squared derivative of the image with respect to object rotation angle.

Using the above in the scene probability equation, we plot in Figure 9.7 (b) and (d) the probability that each reflectance function and corresponding shape generated the 1-d images, shown again in Figure 9.7 (a) and (c). Note that for each image, the high probabilities correspond to reflectance functions which look (see Figure 9.6) more like the material of the image patches in Figure 9.7 (a) and (c). We have successfully evaluated the relative probabilities that different reflectance functions and shapes created a given image. Note this was done from a single view and for a case where the reflectance function is otherwise completely unknown.

9.4.2 Why the prior probability is not enough

Figure 9.8 shows an example where both the fidelity and prior probability terms favor a perceptually implausible explanation. The generic view term biases the probabilities toward the plausible explanation. Figure 9.8 (a) shows an image, and (b) and (c) are two possible explanations for it. (The vertical scale of (b) is exaggerated by 7). (We made this example by construction. Gaussian random noise at a 7 dB signal to noise ratio was added to (e) to make (a). (b) was found from (a) using a shape from shading algorithm, assuming constant surface height at the left picture

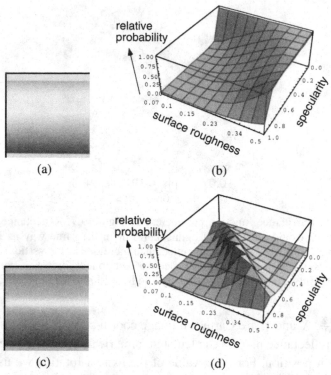

(a)   (b)

(c)   (d)

Fig. 9.7 (a) Input image. (b) Probability that the observed image (a) was created by each reflectance function and corresponding shape. The probabilities are highest for the reflectance functions which look like the dull cylinder. See Figure 9.6 for a visual guide to the reflectance function parameters of plots (b) and (d). (c) Input image. (d) Probability that (c) was created by each reflectance function and shape. The probabilities are highest for the reflectance functions which look like (see Figure 9.6) the shiny cylinder. All reflectance functions were assumed to be equally likely and all can account for the image data equally well. The distinctions between reflectance functions came from the generic view term of the scene probability equation.

edge (Bichsel & Pentland, 1992). We evaluated the probabilities of (b) and (c) assuming both generic object pose and generic lighting direction. The strength of a prior preference for smooth surfaces is arbitrary and none was included in the final densities. The actual noise variance was used for σ^2 in the fidelity term of Equation (9.11), although a wide range of assumed variances would give the preferences described here).

Perceptually, Figure 9.8 (c) seems like a better explanation of (a), even though it doesn't account for all the noise. The fidelity term of the scene probability equation Equation (9.11) favors Figure 9.8 (b). Without the generic view term, the only term left to bias the probability of an interpretation is the prior probability. A typical prior is to favor smooth surfaces, which again would favor the peculiar shape (b),

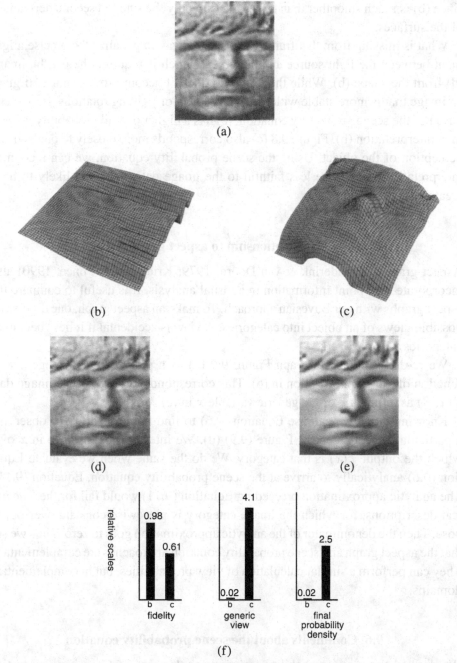

(a)

(b)   (c)

(d)   (e)

(f)

Fig. 9.8 The image in (a) can be explained by the surface (b), lit from the left (vertical scale exaggerated by 7). When rendered (d), that shaded shape accounts well for the input image, but the object and the light source must be precisely positioned. Shape (c) is another possible interpretation. When lit from above, it does not account for the noise of the input image, as shown in (e). Both the fidelity and the typical prior of surface smoothness favor interpretation (b) over the shape (c). It is the generic view term of the scene probability equation which lets us penalize the precise alignment required for shape (b) to produce image (d). The relative values of the fidelity and generic view terms are shown in (f). The large generic view contribution of shape (c) gives it a higher overall probability, in accord with the human perception in preferring interpretation (e).

since (b) is much smoother than (c), as measured by the squared second derivatives of the surfaces.

What is missing from that framework is some way to penalize the precise alignment between the light source and the object which is required the get the image (d) from the shape (b). While the shape (c) doesn't account for the noise, it gives an image that is more stable with respect to object or lighting rotations. By the criterion of the scene probability equation, (c) has a higher overall probability density than interpretation (b). Figure 9.8 (c) also corresponds more closely to one's visual perception of the object. Using the scene probability equation, we can recognize interpretations which are less faithful to the image data, yet more likely to have created the observed image.

9.5 Relationship to aspect graphs

Aspect graphs (Koenderink & van Doorn, 1979; Kriegman & Ponce, 1990) also incorporate viewpoint information in a visual analysis. It is useful to compare the aspect graphs with our Bayesian approach. To make an aspect graph, one divides all possible views of an object into categories. A view is accidental if it lies "between" categories.

We re-draw the aspect graph Figure 9.9 (a) as a plot of image category as a function of viewpoint position in (b). This corresponds to a plot of the image data $f(x, \beta)$ as a function of the generic variable x in (c).

Knowing $p(\mathbf{x})$, we can use Equation (9.6) to find the probability of observing a particular aspect category, Figure (9.9) (d). We integrate the distance in x over which the output $f(x)$ is that category. We do the same when we evaluate Equation (9.6) analytically to arrive at the scene probability equation, Equation (9.11). The analytic approximation preceeding Equation (9.11) would fail for the categorical descriptions, for which the image category is piecewise constant over object pose. Then the denominator of the analytic approximation goes to zero. Thus we see that the aspect graph and scene probability equation approaches are complementary. They can perform a similar calculation of view probabilities, but in complementary domains.

9.6 Comments about the scene probability equation

We derived the scene probability equation for the case of Gaussian observation noise. There is some physical justification for this, since Gaussian noise is the limiting case of a sum of independent random variables. However, to study the effect of assumed noise distribution, we can consider a different noise distribution for the problem of Figure 9.3. We consider uniformly distributed zero mean observation

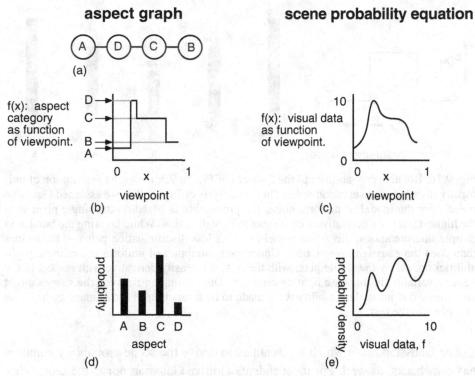

aspect graph **scene probability equation**

(a)

f(x): aspect category as function of viewpoint.

(b)

viewpoint

f(x): visual data as function of viewpoint.

(c)

viewpoint

(d)

probability

A B C D

aspect

(e)

probability density

visual data, f

Fig. 9.9 Comparison of aspect graphs and the present approach, for 1-d examples. (a) Hypothetical aspect graph of an object in a world where the viewpoint can only translate in one dimension. (b) The function relating viewpoint position, x, with aspect category is piecewise constant. In our continuous valued approach, the visual data is treated as a continuous function of viewpoint, x, plotted in (c). (d) Assuming generic viewpoint, the length of the viewpoint variable x for which $f(x)$ yields a given aspect category gives the probability of that aspect category. (e) For the scene probability equation, the local slope of $\frac{d f(x)}{dx}$ influences the probability of the observation f.

noise of amplitude γ, identically distributed at each pixel. Then $p(\hat{\mathbf{y}} \mid \beta, \mathbf{x})$ will be zero when any pixel of the rendered scene, $f(\beta, \mathbf{x})$, differs from the observed image $\hat{\mathbf{y}}$ by more than γ. Otherwise $p(\mathbf{y} \mid \beta, \mathbf{x}) = c$, a constant. Using the first order Taylor series term of Equation (9.8), we find that the value of the integral of Equation (9.6) for $p(\hat{\beta} \mid \mathbf{y})$ varies inversely with the magnitude of largest derivative at any pixel value. We calculated this for the example of Figure 9.3; the results are shown in Figure 9.10. As with guassian noise, the result favors the bump and dimple explanations. However, for this case of uniform noise, the different shape explanations are closer to equally probable. Thus we see that the assumed observation noise can change posterior probabilities. The uniform observation noise of Figure 9.10, which implies an image metric based on the single pixel of largest difference, may be a poor choice.

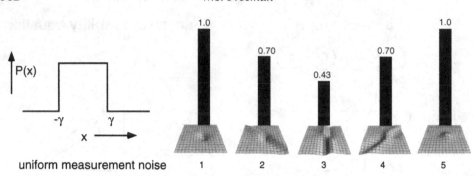

Fig. 9.10 Relative probabilities of the 5 shapes of Figure 9.3, under the assumption of uniformly distributed observation noise. (In the analysis of Figure 9.3, we assumed Gaussian noise). For the model of uniform noise, the probability is based on the single pixel with the highest intensity derivative with respect to light direction. While favoring the bump and dimple interpretations, this noise model provides less discrimination between the shapes than does the gaussian noise model. Under the assumption of uniform noise, these probabilities are set by the single pixel with the largest intensity derivative with respect to the generic variable, in this case lighting direction. Discrimination between the shapes might be increased if noise detectability were made to be a function of local image contrast, as described in the text.

The Gaussian noise which we assumed to derive the scene probability equation has drawbacks, as well. For independent, additive Gaussian noise, the probability that the difference between two images was caused by noise depends only on the sum of the squared differences between the images. Such a mean square error image distance metric is well known to be an imperfect measure of perceptual distance between images (e.g. Schreiber, 1986). The posterior probabilities of shapes 2–4 of Figure 9.3 (e) were larger than might be expected. Our Gaussian noise model may account for that. The long, linear structures of the difference images of Figure 9.3 (c) are extremely visible to people, yet not particularly improbable to the noise model. A more perceptually based image distance metric may assign greater penalty to shapes 2–4. For example, one might expect improved results by scaling the variance of the gaussian noise by a measure of the local image contrast. This would make image changes more visible in low-contrast regions than in high-contrast regions, analogously with human perception. This would give additional penalty to the tube shapes of Figure 9.3 (b) , since, when the light source moves, they introduce small changes in low-contrast regions of the image.

There is a potential computational concern regarding the scene probability equation. The approximation we made to Equation (9.6) requires that we find $\mathbf{x}_0$, the value of $\mathbf{x}$ which minimizes $\|\mathbf{y} - f(\mathbf{x}, \beta)\|^2$. This may be simple for some generic variables. It was for our examples of object pose or illumination direction, and it is for problems with bilinear structure (Brainard & Freeman, 1994). There could be cases, however, where this was a non-trivial optimization problem.

Finally, there may be cases where the denominator of the generic view term of the scene probability equation goes to zero when image derivatives with respect to the generic variables go to zero. This indicates that the approximation for the integral in Equation (9.6) no longer holds. The alternative formulation of the next section avoids this problem.

9.7 Relationship to loss functions

Another point of view from which to examine this work is that of Bayesian loss functions. I came to this viewpoint in the course of joint work with D. Brainard on a Bayesian approach to color constancy (Brainard & Freeman, 1994). Independently, A. Yuille and H. Bulthoff (Yuille & Bülthoff, 1996) have applied a related loss function analysis, described in chapter 4.

In the scene probability equation, we split world parameters into generic and scene parameters. We indicate that we do not care about the values of the generic variables by integrating the joint posterior over those variables. However, sometimes we may be interested in estimating the generic variables to rough accuracy. Bayesian loss functions provide a framework in which to specify these desired accuracies precisely.

Suppose we have a posterior distribution $P(\mathbf{x}|\mathbf{y})$ on a vector variable $\mathbf{x}$ given the observation $\mathbf{y}$. In Bayesian decision theory (e.g., Berger, 1985), one defines a *loss function*, $L(\mathbf{x}, \mathbf{a})$, which is the penalty for guessing $\mathbf{a}$ when the real value of the variable to be estimated is $\mathbf{x}$. From the posterior $P(\mathbf{x}|\mathbf{y})$, one can calculate the *posterior expected loss*, $\bar{L}(\mathbf{a}, \mathbf{y})$, for making the decision $\mathbf{a}$, conditioned on the observation data $\mathbf{y}$, as

$$\bar{L}(\mathbf{a}, \mathbf{y}) = \int_{\mathbf{x}} L(\mathbf{x}, \mathbf{a}) \, P(\mathbf{x}|\mathbf{y}) \, d\mathbf{x}. \qquad (9.15)$$

An observer will want to know what value of $\mathbf{a}$, call it $\hat{\mathbf{x}}$, minimizes the expected loss.

Figure 9.11 shows four loss functions of particular interest, illustrated for a hypothetical 2-dimensional parameter space. All the loss functions we consider are of the form $L(\mathbf{x}, \mathbf{a}) = L(\mathbf{x} - \mathbf{a})$, and the expected loss Equation (9.15) is a convolution of the loss function with the posterior.

A quadratic loss function, $L(\mathbf{x}, \mathbf{a}) = |\mathbf{x} - \mathbf{a}|^2$, Figure 9.11 (a), has many mathematically appealing properties. For example, the mean of the probability is the unique global minimum of the expected loss. However, its penalty increases without bound for outliers. It seems that a loss function for the task of perception ought to give equal penalty to all obviously wrong answers.

The commonly used MAP estimator corresponds to a minus delta function loss, $L(\mathbf{x}, \mathbf{a}) = \delta(\mathbf{x} - \mathbf{a})$. Recall that MAP estimation uses the maximum of the posterior

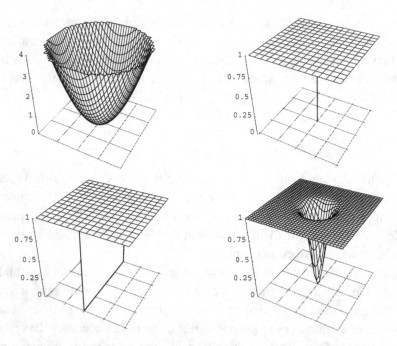

Fig. 9.11 Four loss functions for a 2-d parameter space. (a) Quadratic loss function. The loss becomes unbounded as the error increases. (b) Minus delta function loss. A constant penalty is incurred for all but *exactly* the right answer. (c) Our generic view assumption was equivalent to a constant, extended loss function in the generic variable direction, such as shown here. In this chapter we did not specify the loss function in the scene parameter direction, which is shown as a negative δ function in the figure. (d) Minus "local mass" loss function. Small deviations from the correct answer are rewarded. Incorrect answers are penalized with a saturating penalty strength.

distribution as the estimate for $\mathbf{x}$. This loss function says every guess which is not correct to infinitely high precision carries the same loss. Only *exactly* the right answer counts. Such a requirement for accuracy is not realistic for perception problems.

Figure 9.11 (c) shows a loss function related to the generic view approach of this chapter. We let the parameter vector $\mathbf{x}$ be composed of a scene parameter vector, $\mathbf{x}_\beta$, stacked on top of a generic variable vector, $\mathbf{x}_x$ (these were β and $\mathbf{x}$, respectively, in the notation of the other sections). The scene probability equation implicitly assumes a constant loss over all values of the generic parameters. Thus $L(\mathbf{x}, \mathbf{a}) = F(\mathbf{x}_\beta - \mathbf{a}_\beta)$, where F is some function of the scene parameters. To see how this assumption was made, note that in Equation (9.6) we integrated over all values of the generic variables. This corresponds to the integration of the expected loss integral of Equation (9.15) where $L(\mathbf{x}, \mathbf{a})$ is constant over the generic parameters. For the generic view work, we did not specify the loss function $F(\mathbf{x}_\beta - \mathbf{a}_\beta)$ to be applied to the scene parameters. Figure 9.11 (c) shows a delta function loss in that dimension.

Our approximation of Equation (9.8) means that we only evaluate the integral Equation (9.15) over a local area of the generic variable parameter space. Thus in practise, we only consider the effect of a small variation in the generic variables.

A potentially appealing compromise between these loss functions is what we call a minus "local mass" loss function (Brainard & Freeman, 1994; Yuille & Bülthoff, 1996). We define

$$L(\mathbf{x}, \mathbf{a}) = -e^{\frac{-1}{2\mu^2}(\mathbf{x}-\mathbf{a})^2}.$$ (9.16)

This function rewards getting approximately the right answer, and penalizes all wrong answers beyond several standard deviation with essentially equal penalty. The scalar variance μ^2 in Equation (9.16) easily generalizes to a matrix.

The local mass function can offer advantages over the generic view loss function. It does not require the separation of variables into generic and scene parameters; both are explicitly estimated. We performed an asymptotic expansion to evaluate the integral of Equation (9.6). A similar expansion may be used to find the expected loss for the local mass loss function. The asymptotic expansion used for Equation (9.6) does not hold when the derivatives $\vec{f}'$ and $\vec{f}''$ go to zero, but the analogous approximation for the local mass loss function does not have this problem. Substituting Eqs. (9.5), (9.7), and (9.16) into Equation (9.15), redefining $\mathbf{x}$ to subsume β and assuming σ^2 small (Bleistein & Handelsman, 1986; Jeffreys, 1962), we have for the expected loss:

$$\bar{L}(\mathbf{x}, \mathbf{y}) = k \, \exp\left(\frac{-\|\mathbf{y} - f(\mathbf{x}_0)\|^2}{2\sigma^2}\right) p(\mathbf{x}_0) \, \frac{1}{\sqrt{\det(C)}}$$ (9.17)

where

$$C_{ij} = f_i' \cdot f_j' - (\mathbf{y} - f(\mathbf{x}_0)) \cdot f_{ij}'' + \frac{\sigma^2}{\mu^2}\delta_{ij},$$ (9.18)

and δ_{ij} are the elements of the identity matrix. Note that the above equations are nearly the same as the scene probability equation, Equation (9.11), except that $\mathbf{x}$ now refers to a combined vector of generic and scene parameters. Also, here, $\mathbf{x}_0$, a function of $\mathbf{x}$, is

$$\mathbf{x}_0 = \arg \min_{\xi}[\|\mathbf{y} - f(\xi)\|^2 + \frac{\sigma^2}{\mu^2}\|\xi - \mathbf{x}\|^2]$$ (9.19)

The constant $\frac{\sigma}{\mu}$ in Equation (9.18) allows for use of Equation (9.17) even in cases where the image derivatives f' and f'' are zero. Equation (9.17) allows explicit estimation of generic variables as well as scene parameters, since they are both combined into the variable $\mathbf{x}$. Figure 9.12 illustrates graphically the relationship between the integrations used to obtain scene probability equation, Equation (9.11), and the expected local mass loss, Equation (9.17). The two equations reflect the similarities shown graphically.

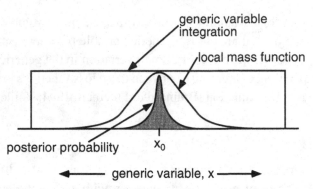

Fig. 9.12 Similarity between marginalization of generic variable, used to derive Equation (9.11), and the expected loss for a minus local mass loss function, used to derive Equation (9.17). The shaded curve is the posterior probability. Typically, for a given scene interpretation, it will be high only over a narrow range of the generic variable, as shown. The marginalization integral over the generic variable measures the probability mass under the wide rectangle shown. The expectation integral for the local mass loss function measures the area under the gaussian function shown. For local mass functions much broader than the posterior probability spikes, these can give nearly the same answer.

9.8 Summary

It is often the case that there is more than one explanation for given visual data. In those cases, assumptions about the world must be used to break ties. The generic view assumption has commonly been used to categorize scene interpretations as either "generic" or "accidental". Here we apply this powerful assumption in a complementary domain, exploiting it to make quantitative judgements about scene parameters. We show how to invoke the assumptions of generic viewpoint, lighting, or object pose to estimate parameter values of scene interpretations. This approach removes some of the decision-making burden from the prior assumptions about the quantities being estimated, for example, surface shape.

The input can be greyscale images or other visual data. We divide world parameters into two types, scene parameters, which we want to estimate, and generic parameters, which we do not. Following an approach taken in other application areas of Bayesian statistics, we write the image in a Taylor series expansion of the generic variables and integrate over the probability densities of the generic variables. The resulting *scene probability equation* gives the probability of a set of scene parameters, given an observed image. It has three major terms:

a *fidelity term*, which requires that the scene parameters explain the observed visual data;

the *prior probability*, which accounts for prior assumptions about the scene parameters;

the *generic view term*, which quantifies how accidental our view of a particular scene is. It indicates the chance that a given scene would have presented us with the observed image.

We show various applications to shape from shading. The scene probability equation gives the probability of different reflectance functions and shapes for a given image. We assign relative probabilities to different shapes, each of which would generate the observed image, for different assumed light directions. The generic view term in the scene probability is important; one can have a shape from shading solution which is faithful to the data, but unlikely, and one which is less faithful but more likely.

The loss functions of Bayesian decision theory encompass our generic view framework as a special case. We present a modified version of the scene probability equation which applies for the case of a minus "local mass" loss function. This version of the scene probability equation avoids some problems where image derivatives go to zero and allows estimation of generic as well as scene parameters.

This Bayesian approach may have many applications in vision. The scene probability equation derived in this paper ranks the relative probability densities of different scene interpretations. From such an equation, one may derive algorithms which find an optimum scene interpretation. This may result in more powerful or more accurate algorithms for such problems as shape from shading, motion analysis, or stereo.

Acknowledgements

For helpful discussions and suggestions, thanks to: Ted Adelson, David Brainard, David Knill (especially about parameter estimation), David Mumford, Ken Nakayama, Sandy Pentland, Eero Simoncelli, Richard Szeliski, and Alan Yuille (who corrected an error). Three reviewers (Knill, Yuille, and a third) gave insightful reviews. Part of this research was performed at the MIT Media Laboratory and was supported by a contract with David Sarnoff Research Laboratories (subcontract to the National Information Display Laboratory) to E. Adelson.

References

Berger, J.0 (1985). *Statistical Decision Theory and Bayesian Analysis*. Springer-Verlag.
Bichsel, M. & Pentland, A.P. (1992). A simple algorithm for shape from shading. *Proc. IEEE CVPR*, 459-465.
Biederman, I. (1985). Human image understanding: recent research and a theory. *Comp. Vis., Graphics, Image Proc.*, **32**, 29-73.

Binford, T.O. (1981). Inferring surfaces from images. *Artificial Intelligence*, **17**, 205-244.

N. Bleistein, N. & Handelsman, R.A. (1986). *AsymPtotic Expansions of Integrals*. Dover.

Box, G.E.P. & Tiao, G.C. (1970). Bayesian approach to the importance of assumptions applied to the comparison of variances. *Biometrika*, **51**(1 and 2), 153-167.

Box, G.E.P. & Tiao, G.C. (1973). *Bayesian Inference in Statistical Analysis*. John Wiley and Sons.

Brainard, D.H. & Freeman, W.T. (1994). Bayesian method for recovering surface and illuminant properties from photosensor responses. *Proceedings of SPIE*, vol. 2179, San Jose, CA, February 1994.

Brooks, M.J., Chojnacki, W. & Kozera, R. (1992). Impossible and ambiguous shading patterns. *Intl. J. Comp. Vis.*, **7**(2), 119-126.

Brooks, M.J. & Horn, B.K.P. (1989). Shape and source from shading. In *Shape from Shading*, ed. B.K.P. Horn and M.J. Brooks, chapter 3. Cambridge, MA: MIT Press.

Cook, R.L. & Torrance, K.E. (1981). A reflectance model for computer graphics. *SIGGRAPH-81*.

Dickinson, S.J., Pentland, A.P. & Rosenfeld, A. (1992). 3-d shape recovery using distributed aspect matching. *IEEE Pat. Anal. Mach. Intell.*, **14**(2), 174-198.

Fisher, R.A. (1959). *Statistical Methods and Scientific Inference*. Hafner.

Freeman, W.T. (1993). Exploiting the generic view assumption to estimate scene parameters. *Proc. 4th Intl. Conf. Computer Vision*, pp. 47-356, Berlin, Germany: IEEE.

Freeman, W.T. (1994). The generic viewpoint assumption in a framework for visual perception. *Nature*, **368**, 542-545.

Freeman, W.T. (1996). Exploiting the generic view point assumption. *Intl. J. Comp. Vis.* (in press).

Geman, S. & Geman, D. (1984). Stochastic relaxation, Gibbs distribution, and the Bayesian restoration of images. *IEEE Pat. Anal. Mach. Intell.*, **6**, 721-741.

Grimson, E. (1984). Binocular shading and visual surface reconstruction. *Comp. Vis., Graphics, Image Proc.*, **28**, 19-43.

Gull, S.F. (1988). Bayesian inductive inference and maximum entropy. In *Maximum Entropy and Bayesian Methods in Science and Engineering*, ed. G.J. Erickson and C.R. Smith, volume 1. Kluwer.

Gull, S.F. (1989). Developments in maximum entropy data analysis. In *Maximum Entropy and Bayesian Methods*, Cambridge, ed. J.Skilling, pp. 53-71. Kluwer.

Hochberg, J.E. (1978). *Perception*. Englewood Cliffs, N J: Prentice-Hall.

Horn, B.K.P. (1989). Height and gradient from shading. Technical Report 1105, MIT Artificial Intelligence Lab, MIT, Cambridge, MA.

Horn, B.K.P. & Brooks, M.J. (1989). *Shape from Shading*. Cambridge, MA: MIT Press.

Horn, B.K.P., Szeliski, R. & Yuille, A. (1993). Impossible shaded images. *IEEE Pat. Anal. Mach. Intell.*, **15**(2), 166-170.

Horn, B.K.P., Woodham, R.J. & Silver, W.M. (1978). Determining shape and reflectance using multiple images. Technical Report 490, A.I. Lab Memo, M.I.T., Cambridge, MA.

Jeffreys, H. (1961). *Theory of Probability*. Oxford: Clarendon Press.

Jeffreys, H. (1962). *Asymptotic Approximations*. Oxford: Clarendon Press.

Jepson, A. & Richards, W. (1992). What makes a good feature? In *Spatial Vision in Humans and Robots*, eds. L. Harris and M.Jenkin. Cambridge Univ. Press. See also MIT AI Memo 1356 (1992).

Johnson, R.A. (1970). Asymtotic expansions associated with posterior distributions. *The Annals of Mathematical Statistics*, **41**(3), 851-864.

Kersten, D. (1991). Transparancy and the cooperative computation of scene attributes. In *Computational Models of Visual Processing*, eds. M.S. Landy and J.A. Movshon, chapter 15. Cambridge, MA: MIT Press.

Koenderink, J.J. & van Doorn, A.J. (1979). The internal representation of solid shape with respect to vision. *Biol. Cybern.*, **32**, 211-216.

Kriegman, D. & Ponce, J. (1990). Computing exact aspect graphs of curved objects: Solids of revolution. *Intl. J. Comp. Vis.*, **5**, 119-135.

Laplace, P.S. (1812). *Theorie analytique des probabilites*. Courcier.

Leclerc, Y.G. & Bobick, A.F. (1991). The direct computation of height from shading. *Proc. IEEE CVPR*, pp. 552-558, Maui, Hawaii.

Lindley, D.V. (1972). *Bayesian Statistics, a Review*. Society for Industrial and Applied Mathematics (SIAM).

Lowe, D.G. & Binford, T.O. (1985). The recovery of three-dimensional structure from image curves. *IEEE Pat. Anal. Mach. Intell.*, **7**(3), 320-326.

MacKay, D.J.C. (1992). Bayesian interpolation. *Neural Computation*, **4**(3), 415-447.

Malik, J. (1987). Interpreting line drawings of curved objects. *Intl. J. Comp. Vis.*, **1**, 73-103.

Nakayama, K. & Shimojo, S. (1992). Experiencing and perceiving visual surfaces. *Science*, **257**, 1357-1363.

Pentland, A. (1990). Photometric motion. *Proceedings of 3rd International Conference on Computer Vision*.

Pentland, A.P. (1990). Linear shape from shading. *Intl. J. Comp. Vis.*, **1**(4), 153-162.

Poggio, T., Torre, V. & Koch, C. (1985). Computational vision and regularization theory. *Nature*, **317**(26), 314-139.

Richards, W.A., Koenderink, J.J. & Hoffman, D.D. (1987). Inferring three-dimensional shapes from two-dimensional silhouettes. *J. Opt. Soc. Am. A*, **4**(7), 1168-1175.

Schreiber, W.F. (1986). *Fundamentals of Electronic Imaging Systems*. Springer-Verlag.

Skilling, J. (1989). Classic maximum entropy. In *Maximum Entropy and Bayesian Methods, Cambridge*, ed. J.Skilling pp. 45-52. Boston, MA: Kluwer.

Szeliski, R. (1989). *Bayesian Modeling of Uncertainty in Low-level Vision*. Boston, MA: Kluwer.

Tikhonov, A.N. & Arsenin, V.Y. (1977). *Solutions of Ill-posed Problems*. Washington, DC: Winston.

Weinshall, D., Werman, M. & Tishby, N. (1994). Stability and likelihood of views of three dimensional objects. *Proceedings of the 3rd European Conference on Computer Vision*, Stockholm, Sweden, May 1994.

Witkin, A.P. (1981). Recovering surface shape and orientation from texture. *Artificial Intelligence*, **17**, 17-45.

Woodham, R.J. (1980). Photometric method for determing surface orientation from multiple images. *Optical Engineering*, **19**(1), 139-144.

Yuille, A.L. & Bulthoff, H.H. (1996). Bayesian decision theory and psychophysics. In *Visual Perception: Computation and Psychophysics*, ed. D. Knill and W. Richards. Cambridge Univ. Press.

Zheng, Q. & Chellapa, R. (1991). Estimation of illuminant direction, albedo, and shape from shading. *IEEE Pat. Anal. Mach. Intell.*, **13**(7), 680-702.

10

Experiencing and perceiving visual surfaces

KEN NAKAYAMA

Vision Sciences Laboratory, Harvard University

SHINSUKE SHIMOJO

Department of Psychology, University of Tokyo

10.1 Introduction

When we see objects in the world, what we actually "see" is much more than the retinal image. Our perception is three-dimensional. Moreover, it reflects constant properties of the objects and the environment, regardless of changes in the retinal image with varying viewing condition. How does the visual system make this possible?

Two different approaches have been evident in the study of visual perception. One approach, most successful in recent times, is based on the idea that perception emerges automatically by some combination of neuronal receptive fields. In the study of depth perception, this general line of thinking has been supported by psychophysical and physiological evidence. The "purely cyclopean" perception in the Julesz' random dot stereogram (Julesz, 1960) shows that depth can emerge without the mediation of any higher order form recognition. This suggested that relatively local disparity-specific processes could account for the perception of a floating figure in an otherwise camouflaged display. Corresponding electrophysiological experiments using single cell recordings demonstrated that the depth of such stimuli could be coded by neurons in the visual cortex, receiving input from the two eyes (Barlow *et al.*, 1967; Poggio & Fischer, 1977). In contrast to this more modern approach, there exists an older tradition which asserts that perception is inferential, that it can cleverly determine the nature of the world with limited image data. Starting with Helmholtz's unconscious inference (Helmholtz, 1910) and with more recent formulations such as Gregory's "perceptual hypotheses", this approach stresses the importance of problem solving in the process of seeing (Hochberg, 1981; Gregory, 1970; Rock, 1983). So far, however, "perceptual inference" theories have not been successfully linked to physiological findings and they are not easily distinguished from other theories of mental processes, including those which attempt to account for thinking and reasoning.

In this paper, we argue strongly for the importance of inference but provide the beginnings of what we think is a low-level mechanistic explanation of how such inferences could be learned. We argue that the observer's experience of optical sampling during locomotion provides a key to understand what will be perceived later on.

Our domain is stereoscopic vision, commonly thought to be dictated by early, pre-wired, local mechanisms. Instead, we consider stereopsis an example of surface representation, not obviously linked to currently understood properties of visual neurons[†] nor to higher stages of object recognition.

Julesz's random dot stereogram defined much of the subsequent work in the field of binocular stereopsis. Ever since, most visual scientists assumed, either explicitly or implicitly, that stereopsis depends most critically on the solution to the "matching" problem. This is indeed an important and difficult problem because the rich local texture of random dot stereograms requires that the visual system must find the correct binocular match of individual points in the face of numerous possible "false matches" (Julesz, 1960, 1971; Poggio & Poggio, 1984).

Random dot stereograms, however, are not entirely representative of the local details of everyday scenes. Such dense textures occur only occasionally in natural images and some scenes contain large regions that are effectively untextured. Whereas human perceptual systems correctly interpret such scenes, current models which were originally designed to handle densely textured stereograms do not (Jones & Malik, 1990). Thus we think it important to examine how the visual system handles image regions where texture is largely absent.

10.2 Failure of depth interpolation in untextured stereograms

Note the stereogram in Figure 10.1A and consider the binocular disparity information available (Nakayama & Shimojo, 1990). Because this cross has no interior texture, only the bounding contours are available to convey binocular disparity information. Moreover, since binocular disparity is not available from the horizontally oriented contours of the figures, vertically oriented contours provide the only source of horizontal disparity information. We have emphasized this point by constructing a partial stereogram having exactly the same disparity information as the cross. It contains only vertical lines (Figure 10.1B).

[†] Related demonstrations indicating the importance of surface representation have been summarized by Ramachandran (1986) (see also Ramachandran & Cavanagh, 1985).

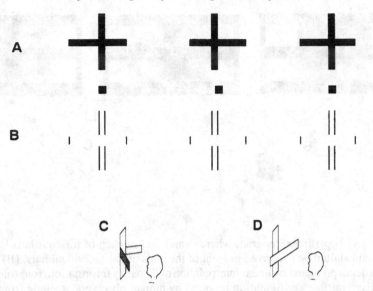

Fig. 10.1 (A) Cross stereogram. Because the outer edges of the horizontal limb of the cross have crossed binocular disparity, these edges should be seen in front. Depth of the untextured interior regions of the cross are not specified by binocular disparity. (B) Reduced line stereogram having the same disparity information as that contained in A. (C) Perceived surface interpretation predicted from linear interpolation of disparity information. (D) Perceived surface configuration reported by human observers. (In this and in all other stereograms, three binocular images are presented such that observers who converge or diverge can see the appropriate sign of depth. Convergers should fuse the two left images ignoring the right, divergers should fuse the two right images ignoring the left).

Given this paucity of local disparity information in the whole figure, one might ask how depth gets assigned to the interior portions of the figure where disparity is not explicitly defined. Classical stereopsis make no specific prediction as to the depth of these untextured regions. Yet, the least arbitrary assumption would be that the perceived depth of given positions in an untextured region is a simple linear interpolation between points having a defined disparity

The ends of the horizontal limb of the cross have crossed disparity. That should indicate that these contours are nearer to the observer than the contours defining the vertical limb.[†] Assuming depth interpolation for the stereogram in Figure 10.1A, we might expect a simple continuity of depth from the center of the cross (seen in back) to the ends of the horizontal limbs (seen in front). The observer should see a vertical bar in back flanked by horizontal "wings" that are slanted towards the observer (Figure 10.1C).

In sparsely textured random dot stereograms, perceived depth of the surface region between dots appears as smoothly interpolated between individual dots (Julesz, 1971).
[†] The technical terms "crossed" and "uncrossed" disparity refer to those disparities which would lead to perceived near and far distances respectively.

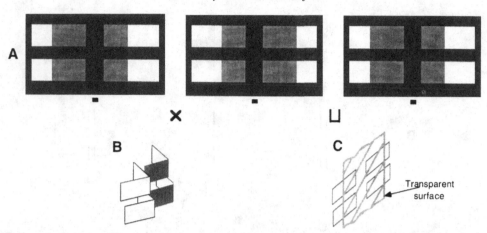

Fig. 10.2 (A) Bipartite stereogram where center line in each of the four bars has crossed disparity and should be perceived in front of the ends of the individual bars. (B) Perceived surface in depth predicted by linear interpolation of disparity information: four folded sheets. (C) Perceived surface configuration reported by human observers: a single fronto-parallel transparent surface in front of four bars in back. Note if this stereogram as well as that shown in Figure 10.6A is viewed in the reverse configuration (with right and left eye views exchanged) the red region will look opaque.

We have shown this stereogram (Figure 10.1A) to several hundred observers, and only a tiny minority observe what we have just outlined. Instead, the most frequently seen configuration is that of a horizontal bar in front of a vertical bar (Figure 10.1D). In keeping with the perception of a straight horizontal bar in front, observers also see a subjective occluding contour, which is not present in the image itself but which perceptually segregates and completes the bar in front (Nakayama & Shimojo, 1990; Shimojo & Nakayama, 1990).

In our second stereoscopic demonstration (Figure 10.2), we again show that the visual system violates the expectation of simple interpolation by allowing a break in the perceived surface pattern. This demonstration also illustrates a qualitatively different phenomenon, the perception of transparency, which is accompanied by color spreading into otherwise uncolored regions (Nakayama & Shimojo, 1990; vanTuijl, 1981). In this example (Figure 10.2A), the viewer observes a set of four bipartite bars, divided into red and white regions against a black background. The ends of the bars are in the zero disparity plane, and the dividing line between the regions has crossed disparity. Simple interpolation theory would predict that this edge would be seen in front and that the other two edges would be seen in back, forming a folded surface (Figure 10.2B).

What is seen, however, is qualitatively different. Instead of seeing a set of folded surfaces (Figure 10.2B), each visible face of which recedes back from the viewer, one usually sees this configuration as two disconnected surfaces, one transparent in front, the other opaque in back, each of which does not recede, but is fronto-parallel to the observer (Figure 10.2C). This transparent surface appears to "complete" in front and merge as a single surface which is in front of all four bars. Furthermore, it is "contained" by subjective contours, which bound the color that spreads into the black region (Figure 10.2C). (See Belhumeur, chapter 8 for related effects.)

10.3 Image ambiguity in stereograms

Depth interpolation failed to account for what is seen. Instead, it appears as if the visual system, like a clever detective, reached a conclusion with only the scantiest evidence. Are these perceptual inferences warranted? Is what is perceived consistent with the binocular image data?

In case one, the perception of surface breakage, although not predicted from depth interpolation, is nonetheless consistent with the disparities presented to the observer. A real-world bar configuration as in Figure 10.1D, as well as that in Figure 10.1C, could have given rise to the disparities seen in the stereogram. Likewise for case 2. A transparent red surface lying in front of white bars (Figure 10.2C), as well as folded surfaces (Figure 10.2B) could have given rise to the disparities seen in Figure 10.2A. Thus for both stereograms presented, the three-dimensional interpretation is ambiguous. The observer is presented with image data that can be interpreted in more than one way. Therefore, simply checking to see whether the image array is consistent with a given perceptual interpretation is not sufficient to decide which interpretation is true. Nor, can one apply a simple rule, such as depth interpolation between disparities, to reach the perceived solution.

The issues raised here are not entirely new. Both traditional and modern students of visual perception have noted the ambiguity of the visual image. For example, it has been pointed out that when presented with an image in the form of a triangle, there are an infinite number of triangles in space which could have given rise to this image (Ittelson, 1960). More recently, in studies of computational vision, it has been noted that vision is ill-posed in that the information available in the image by itself is insufficient to recover the structure in the real world (Poggio *et al.*, 1985).

10.4 Ecological optics and the importance of viewing positions

Rather than starting with an image and thinking about automatically reconstructing the surface by interpolation, we advocate a conceptual shift, arguing that the problem can be best understood from the perspective of ecological optics. As discussed by J.J. Gibson (1950, 1966). We must remember that when viewing surfaces in the world, the vantage point of the viewer is rarely stationary. The observer locomotes and new sets of image samples continuously arise. Thus, there is of necessity a one-

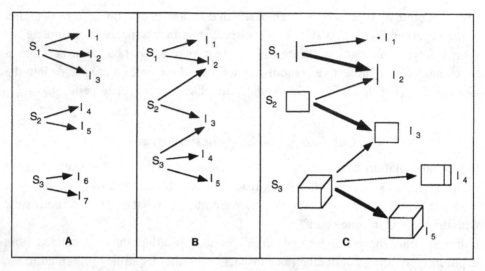

Fig. 10.3 Mapping of surfaces to images as defined by ecological optics. Classes of surface structure in the real world (S_1, S_2 and S_3), can give rise to sampled images (I_1, I_2, ...) as an observer assumes differing vantage points. (A) Image sampling without stimulus ambiguity where each image class is tied to only one surface configuration. (B) Image sampling with stimulus ambiguity where some image classes (I_2, I_3) can arise from more than one surface. (C) Specific example of line, square and cube, where thick and thin arrows indicate generic and accidental samplings respectively.

to-many mapping from the physical layout of surfaces to the image. For example, in Figure 10.3A we indicate three different sets of surfaces S_1, S_2, and S_3, each of which potentially gives rise to more than one image as a consequence of the viewer taking differing vantage points (denoted by I_1 to I_7).

If this mapping were literally as described above, the task of the visual system would be relatively easy: given a visual image, say I_1, it would simply designate the corresponding surface S_1. What makes this task more difficult is the fact that one image arising from one surface can also arise from a variety of other surfaces (Figure 10.3B). So the mapping is not only one-to-many, it is also many-to-one. To illustrate, consider a set of various real world objects: a line, a square, and a cube, labeled S_1, S_2, and S_3 in Figure 10.3C. Depending on the location of the observer's vantage point, a line can give rise to an image of a line or a point, similarly a square can give rise to an image of a quadrilateral or a line, and finally a cube can give rise to images of polygonal figures having either one, two, or three faces. Thus, changes in the visual image occasioned by differing viewer positions can be summarized in terms of particular topological classes of images as initially proposed in the important work of Koenderink and van Doorn (Koenderink, 1991; Koenderink & van Doorn, 1979).

Now, think of the various viewing positions that could have given rise to each of these images. If the observer were to assume a random position in space around the cube, image I_5 (three faces) would be much more probable than image I_4 (two faces), which in turn would be much more probable than image I_3 (one face). Furthermore, as viewer distance is increased, this inequality would be accentuated, with the likelihood of three faces tending towards unity in the limit and the likelihoods of two faces and one face tending towards zero. Thus those viewing positions in space where I_5 (three faces) is encountered are called a "generic" vantage points with I_5 designated as a generic image.[†] I_4 and I_3 are correspondingly called "accidental" images and the viewing positions in space where they are encountered are called accidental vantage points. When confronted with image I_2, it would make more sense if one sees a line rather than a square. Similarly, when confronted with image I_3, one would see a square instead of a cube. It is only when confronted with I_5 that one would see a cube.

With these ideas in mind, we return to our untextured stereograms, starting with the cross in Figure 10.1. The surface arrangement that would result from linear depth interpolation is the vertical bar flanked by the horizontal wings. Let us apply ecological optics to understand how these real world surfaces might give rise to images sampled. If an observer were to view the configuration with the horizontal wings, he could encounter the binocular image in question (I_2), but only from a restricted set of vantage points (Figure 10.4A). The observer is required to be at the same vertical level of the surfaces, neither above or below, otherwise the horizontal wings would no longer appear collinear.[‡] As a telling comparison, consider the horizontal bar in front of the vertical bar (Figure 10.4B). Here all images (I_4, I_5, I_6) arising from this pair of surfaces is qualitatively the same as I_2. Instead of arising from just one particular viewing position, the image in question can arise from a wide range of elevations. The image sampling process is very different in each case, even though the same image can arise from two different surface layouts. The sampling is accidental for the situation depicted in Figure 10.4A (bar with wings), whereas it is generic for the case shown in Figure 10.4B (crossed bars).

The same analysis applies to the stereograms shown in Figure 10.2. The surface arrangement that is predicted from linear depth interpolation is depicted as Figure 10.4C (folded surface). The image I_8 could arise from a folded surface but only from a restricted set of vantage points. The observer is required to be just at the same vertical level of the surfaces, neither above or below, otherwise the horizontal boundaries would no longer remain collinear. In contrast, in the case of the

[†] Although the terms "generic" and "accidental" have been borrowed from the mathematics literature, its exact meaning here and in computer vision has strayed from the precise mathematical definition originally assumed. In our usage, we consider an image I_1 more generic than the other image I_2 when the volume or area in space in which the vantage point can randomly move without causing qualitative change in the image is larger (see Koenderink & van Doorn, 1979).

[‡] The observer should also be relatively far from the display, such that it is effectively a plane parallel projection, otherwise the horizontal limbs will not be collinear because of perspective. Furthermore, the head must not be tilted.

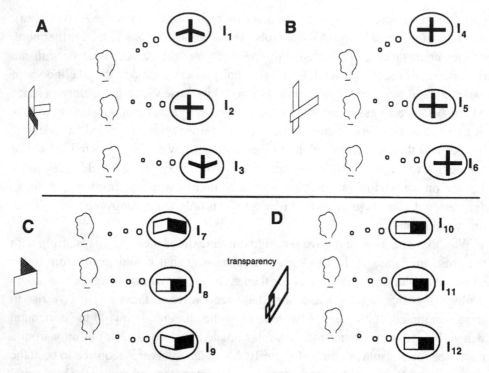

Fig. 10.4 Changes of image as the location of the observer's vantage point changes. Real-world surface structure is illustrated on the left, while changes of views with differing vertical elevations are shown on the right of each figure. (A) For the cross with wings bent. (B) For the horizontal bar in front of the vertical bar without a bend. (C) For the prism-like folded surfaces. (D) For a transparent surface in front.

transparent surface in front of a white bar on a black background (Figure 10.4D), all images sampled (I_{10}, I_{11}, I_{12}) are qualitatively the same. Thus in this case, changes in viewing position have very little effect and a sampled image which is categorically identical to I_8 can arise frequently. Again, there is a large difference in image sampling between the two surface layouts: in the first case the image I_8 being accidental, in the second the same image being generic.

10.5 The principle of generic image sampling

One of the major themes of this paper is that the observer's experience of optical sampling during locomotion provides a key to understanding what will be perceived later on. Here we develop this idea by applying the principle of generic image sampling. The principle can explain most of our findings and others to be described: *When faced with more than one surface interpretation of an image, the visual system assumes it is viewing the scene from a generic, not an accidental, vantage point.*

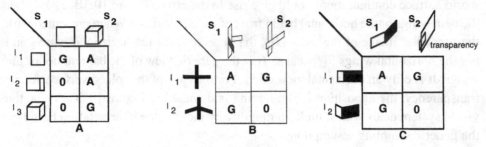

Fig. 10.5 Image sampling matrices for (A) cube vs square, (B) crossed bars vs bent wings, (C) fold vs. transparency. Potential surface sets in the real world are denoted at column headings (S_1, S_2) and possible images are denoted by row headings (I_1, I_2 ...). The likelihood of a given surface will give rise to a given image is categorized as either generic and very likely (G), accidental or rare (A) or impossible (zero).

This principle is not entirely new. It has been one of the core assumptions of machine vision algorithms (Malik, 1987) as well as a theory of human object recognition (Biederman, 1985; see also Richards *et al.*, 1987). The previous chapter 9 by Freeman is a refinement of this principle. Here, however, we use the generic view idea to explain psychophysical phenomena that are generally thought to be part of early visual processing, namely the encoding of depth in simple stereograms.

To develop this line of thinking in a more general framework, we summarize the relations between surfaces and images in the form of contingency matrices, which indicate the likelihood of sampling images, given certain real-world surfaces. To illustrate, consider the two by three array in Figure 10.5A. On top are possible sets of surfaces in the real world: a cube and a square. Along the side are the image classes that one might encounter (containing one, two and three faces, respectively). In this array, we label the likelihood of images, as either likely (G, generic), unlikely (A, accidental), or impossible (zero).

So to enumerate the possible images that can be sampled from a square, we examine the cells in the first column corresponding to images (I_1, I_2, I_3). Only I_1 could have arisen from a generic vantage point. As such, it is labeled as G. The other two images I_2, I_3 could not have arisen, and these cells are thus labeled 0. The second column outlines the possible images that could arise from a cube. Image I_1 and I_2 can arise only from privileged viewpoints and are thus accidental and labeled A. I_3 can arise from many viewpoints and is thus generic and labeled G accordingly. Applying the principle of generic image sampling is now straightforward. When I_1 (the single face) is presented, it is clearly a generic view of S_1 (the square) and, as such, a square is perceived. S_2 (the cube) is not perceived because I_1 is an accidental view of it, not a generic one.

Having introduced these contingency matrices using familiar objects, we can now provide a framework to understand the two stereograms presented. At least two real-world surface configurations could give rise to the cross (Figure 10.5B, I_1), either the bent wings or the horizontal bar in front of the vertical bar. When presented with the binocular image of the cross (I_1), the observer sees the horizontal bar S_2 and not the horizontal wings S_1, because I_1 is the generic view of the bar and not of the wings. It is only an accidental view of S_1. For the case of the folded surface versus transparency, the exposition is similar and is depicted in Figure 10.5C. Thus, the visual system deals with stimulus ambiguity by picking the interpretation based on the generic sampling assumption.

To provide an even stronger case for the principle of generic image sampling, we add a third demonstration where the identical crossed bars of Figure 10.1 can give rise to an entirely different global configuration, that of a transparent disk. All that is required is that the same cross be embedded in a new context. Consider the stereogram in Figure 10.6. The inner red portion of this figure is geometrically identical to the stereogram shown in Figure 10.1. Thus, the ends of the horizontal limbs of the cross have crossed disparity with respect to the vertical limbs and should be seen as closer. However, this red cross is now embedded in a larger white cross that has zero disparity.

What should we expect to see? We already know from Figure 10.1 that the familiar bent bar configuration (Figure 10.6B, S_1) is not seen. Instead, one sees the cross as a horizontal bar in front of a vertical one. As such, we might expect to see this same configuration embedded in the middle of a white outer cross (Figure 10.6B, S_2).

The actual perception of this stereogram is totally different from either of these expectations (Nakayama *et al.*, 1990). What is seen is a transparent red disk, hovering in front of a white cross (Figure 10.6B, S_3). So why do we see a transparent disk when earlier, we just saw a horizontal bar in front of a vertical one in an essentially identical configuration?

Again, we appeal to the principle of generic image sampling, arguing that the visual system's preference is based on the likelihoods of images arising from different sets of surfaces (Figure 10.6B). For the case I_2 and I_3, the task for the visual system is easy because only one surface interpretation is possible for each (see horizontal arrows). For the case of I_1 (Figure 10.6B), many surface interpretations are possible and here the principle of generic image reveals its predictive power. I_1 is only an accidentally sampled image of S_1 and of S_2, whereas it is a generically sampled image of S_3. Therefore, the transparent disk (S_3) has priority over S_1 and S_2 as a surface interpretation of I_1.

While this third case provides very powerful support for the generic sampling idea, it is even more revealing if we focus more closely on specific local aspects of the configurations, searching for local primitives upon which surface perception may depend. Transparency is seen in cases 2 and 3. Can we identify a local feature common to both yet absent from the other case? Indeed, each has a specific type of

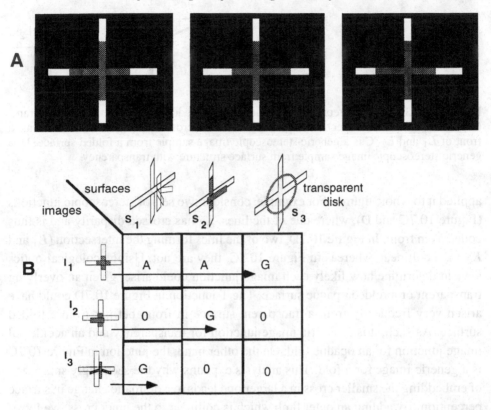

Fig. 10.6 (A) Stereogram where the inner red cross is geometrically identical to that shown in Figure 10.1A and is embedded in a larger white cross having zero disparity. (B) Image sampling matrix for this case. As in Figure 10.5, surface classes are illustrated in columns and sampled image classes are listed in rows. S_1, S_2, S_3, refer to three possible surface configurations which could have given rise to this binocular image. I_1, I_2, I_3 refer to images which could be possibly sampled.

stereoscopic T-junction. These are shown inside of the circles of Figures 10.7A and 10.7B which reproduce relevant portions of case 2 and case 3. The stem of the T has a crossed disparity in relation to neighboring contours and the transparent side of the stem is darker.

Monocularly viewed T-junctions have long been considered as evidence for occlusion with the top of the T interpreted as occluding the stem (Helmholtz, 1910; Guzman, 1971). No explicit formulation, however, has been made for the stereoscopic T-junctions, particularly where the stem is in front. In contrast to the monocular version, such a junction is incompatible with occlusion because the top of the T can not act as an occluding contour if the stem is in front of it. Yet, the principle of generic image sampling can apply to this local configuration in the same way as we have

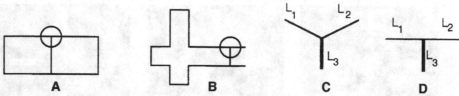

Fig. 10.7 (A,B) Local stereoscopic "T" junctions embedded in the previous stereograms (Figure 10.2 and 10.6 respectively). Thick line, L_3 has crossed disparity and is coded as in front of L_1 and L_2. C is a generic stereoscopic image sample from a folded surface, D, a generic stereoscopic image sample from surface structure with transparency.

applied it to whole figures. For example, consider two sets of stereoscopic junctions (Figure 10.7C and D), where one of the lines, L_3 has crossed disparity and is thus coded as in front. In Figure 10.7D, two of the lines forming the intersection (L_1 and L_2) are collinear, whereas in Figure 10.7C, they are not. Using ecological optics we can determine how likely each image junction could arise, given an overlying transparent or a folded opaque surface. The T-junction in Figure 10.7D could have arisen very frequently from a transparent surface in front, but not from a folded surface. As such, it is a generic image junction for transparency and an accidental image junction for an opaque fold. On the other hand, the junction in Figure 10.7C is a generic image for a fold. This analysis explains why the seemingly small step of embedding the smaller cross in a larger one leads to a dramatic change in surface perception. By adding an outer limb which is collinear to the inner cross, we introduced a very powerful local feature, a stereoscopic T-junction, which was essentially incompatible with opacity.

10.6 Role of visual experience

When the observer locomotes in the world, new images arise (Gibson, 1950, 1966), with each class of image corresponding to a certain range of vantage points that the observer can assume in space (Koenderink & van Doorn, 1976). Thus, given a particular surface layout S_n, the probability that a class of image I_m will arise can be plausibly estimated from geometry: from considering the spatial range of vantage points under which a given image class is sampled divided by the totality of possible vantage points. This is roughly equivalent to the quotient of two solid angles; the numerator being the solid angle under which a given image class is sampled, the denominator defining the solid angle from which the surface can be viewed. Thus, the viewer's experience can be is expressed as a conditional probability $p(I_m|S_n)$, the probability of a given image I_m given a real-world surface layout S_n.

We may formalize our analysis in a more general contingency table (Figure 10.8). For each column, identified by a surface S_n, the likelihoods or conditional prob-

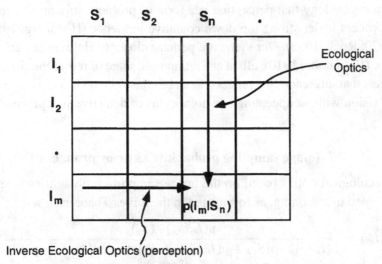

Fig. 10.8 Top: Generalized form of the image sampling matrix.

abilities of all possible image samplings $(I_1 \dots I_m)$ are listed, thus forming the exhaustive sample space of possible images. This analysis summarizes the totality of image sampling for the mobile observer. We argue that $p(I_m|S_n)$ is represented in the nervous system as an associative strength, between the perception of a surface and a visual image.

From this associative strength to perception is a short step, for the task facing the visual system is inverse ecological optics. Given an image I_m, it must decide which surface structure is the best candidate for what actually exists in the external world. Then given an image I_m, the probability of S_n being the cause of I_m can be determined from a comparison of these learned conditional probabilities, $p(I_m|S_1)$, $p(I_m|S_2)$, $p(I_m|S_3)$ or associative strengths. In terms of our matrix in Figure 10.8, this passive process acts as if it selects the cell having the highest probability in the same row, thereby finding the appropriate surface.

If we think of perceptual learning, the conditional probability terms assume special importance as they provide an opportunity for us to estimate visual experience simply from geometry. We suggest that these image sampling probabilities could be learned passively as the moving organism assumes essentially random positions with respect to real surface configurations. *It follows therefore, that the principle of generic image sampling emerges from this associative process.*

The critical cues, such as collinearity, binocular disparity and luminance contrast, are all local and primitive visual properties, the kind of selectivities commonly observed at early stages of the cortical visual processing. This implies that inverse ecological optics could be implemented in a strictly bottom-up, retinotopic representation, not requiring "higher order" inference. This view goes against the classical notion in psychology that perception is a form of problem-solving or hypothesis-testing process under strong top-down cognitive influence (Hochberg, 1981; Gregory, 1970; Rock, 1983). Our views are perhaps closer to Helmholtz' unconscious inference (Helmholtz, 1910), albeit at a retinotopic stage of representation, because we suggest that inference-like processes can be constructed via associative learning in early vision without appealing to a homoculus or detective-like processing.

10.7 Image sampling probability vs prior probability

Inverse ecological optics based on the image sampling probabilities is similar in part to Bayesian reasoning, as formulated in the Bayes Theorem.

$$p(S_n|I_m) = \frac{p(I_m|S_n) \cdot (S_n)}{p(I_m|S_1) \cdot p(S_1) + p(I_m|S_2) \cdot p(S_2) + \ldots p(I_m|S_n) \cdot p(S_n)} \quad (10.1)$$

where image sampling probabilities are denoted as conditional probabilities $p(I_m|S_n)$, and the posterior probability of surface S_n is denoted as $p(S_n|I_m)$. The major difference between Bayes theorem and our formulation (see matrix and equation in Figure 10.8) is our omission of prior probabilities or base rates $p(S_n)$. Conceivably, this term could be added to our framework, rendering it consistent with a full Bayesian approach. In terms of our matrix, each column could be multiplied by a factor proportional to the base rate of each surface structure to obtain the posterior surface probabilities described in equation (10.1). In terms of a neural network represented by such a matrix, base rates could be incorporated by increasing excitation along the corresponding vertical columns in proportion to prior probability. Yet, for many reasons, we do not think that this strategy is appropriate for the visual perception of surfaces.

First, in contrast to the learning of image sampling probabilities, the estimation of prior probability is problematic. Let's consider this in the context of transparent surfaces. Because transparent surfaces are generally infrequent, one would need a large period of time over which to obtain a sufficiently large set samplings for a reliable measure of their prior probability. In addition, the frequency of transparent surfaces can change over varying environmental contexts, suggesting that a single general estimate of prior probability is likely to be meaningless. This necessitates that the estimate be obtained in varying environmental contexts and that these contexts be tagged for future use. Moreover, the fact that prior probabilities for transparency are likely to be very small, combined with the fact that $p(S_n|I_m)$ in equation (10.1) is a product, makes Bayesian decisions extremely unstable, particularly when estimates of prior probabilities are not immune to noise.

Even if such an estimate were made and could be assumed to be reliable and valid, its not clear that such knowledge actually biases our perception appropriately.

Many studies have shown that perception is largely impervious to prior knowledge, that seemingly compelling counter evidence at the cognitive level does not destroy strong perceptual illusions and other perceptual phenomena. Kanisza, for example, has shown many cases where local perceptual rules essentially dominate our cognitive understanding of a scene (Kanisza, 1979). So in broad agreement with others (Poggio *et al.*, 1985; Marr, 1980), we suggest that the visual perception of surfaces is an autonomous process, minimally subject to object-specific knowledge about the world. Thus, our proposal is similar to a degenerate form of Bayesian inference where prior probabilities are unknown, set to equality, and ignored. This directly corresponds to inverse ecological optics as we have outlined it in the generalized matrix in the top half of Figure 10.8.[†]

10.8 Need for perceptual categorization

For simplification, an important step has been missing in our discussion so far. We have suggested that sampled images can be associated with surfaces, not mentioning the representation of surfaces themselves. By designating S_n as a real world surface, we have glossed over the fact that it too must have a neural representation. In particular, we need to ask what kind of neural organization emerges for the perception of surfaces so that they are seen as either connected, folded, disconnected, transparent, opaque, etc? For example, what gives transparency its characteristic appearance, identifiable even from opaque patches in a stereogram (Figures 10.2 and 10.6)?

Because we have no specific data to address this issue directly, we can only speculate. Consider the various distinctive properties of images which are related to surface transparency. This would include say, stereoscopic T-junction, contrast relationships which satisfies Metelli's rule (Metelli, 1974),[‡] simultaneous depth coding from a front and a back plane (Nakayama *et al.*, 1990), and semi-specular reflection at the surface. Given the associative power of theoretical neural networks (Anderson, 1972; Kohonen, 1984), we hypothesize that if these properties occur simultaneously when the observer locomotes in front of a transparent surface, an associative linkage is formed across these features. Then later, when an image

---

[†] The neglect of prior probabilities may be related to recent findings in the animal conditioning (Rescorla & Holland, 1982). These studies show that it is not simple contiguity between events that forms associations, but rather that the conditioned stimulus (CS) and unconditioned stimulus (UCS) must be correlated such that the CS provides unique predictive information about the US. Thus sheer frequency of pairing alone is not a sufficient precondition for learning. This suggests that if the frequency of transparent surfaces were extremely rare, these properties of association would enable the generic view of a transparent surface to call forth the perception of transparency even though the number of pairings of an accidental view and an opaque surface were actually more frequent.

[‡] Our neglect of prior probabilities should also be contrasted to the very different approach taken by Barlow (1990), where prior probabilities of images are explicitly registered by changes in neural connection strengths.

contains a subset of these co-occurring features, the visual system can recall the whole pattern of features. This is presumably why we see transparency in our stereograms even though no transparency exists in the literal sense. Most important for our present discussion, it provides a plausible cluster of neural connections to represent a surface which can then be associated with specific image classes sampled.[†]

Acknowledgments

This research was supported in part by grant 83-0320 from the Air Force Office of Scientific Research. S.S. was supported by the Ministry of Education, Sciences, and Culture, Japan. Reprinted by permission from *Science*, **257**, 1357-1363. Copyright 1992 by the American Association for the Advancement of Science.

References

Anderson, J.A. (1972). A simple neural network generating an interactive memory. *Mathematical Biosciences*, **14**, 197-220.

Barlow, H.B. (1990). Conditions for versatile learning, Helmholtz's unconscious inference, and the task of perception. *Vision Res.*, **30**, 1561-1571.

Barlow, H.B., Blakemore, C. & Pettigrew, J.D. (1977). The neural mechanism of binocular depth discrimination. *J. Physiol. Lond.*, **193**, 327-342.

Biederman, I. (1985). Human image understanding: recent research and theory. *Computer Vision, Graphics & Image Processing*, **32**, 29-73.

Gibson, J.J. (1950). *Perception of the Visual World*. Boston, MA: Houghton-Mifflin.

Gibson, J.J. (1966). *The Senses Considered as Perceptual Systems*. Boston, MA: Houghton-Mifflin.

Gregory, R.L. (1970). *The Intelligent Eye*. New York: McGraw Hill.

Guzman, A. (1969). Decomposition of a visual scene into three-dimensional bodies. In *Automatic Interpretation and Classification of Images*, ed. A. Grasselli, pp. 243-276. New York: Academic.

Helmholtz, H. (1910). *Handbuch der Physiologischen Optik*. Hamburg: Verlag. (*Helmholtz's Treatise on Physiological Optics*, ed. J.P.C. Southall. New York: Dover.)

Hochberg, J. (1981). Levels of perceptual organization. In *Perceptual Organization*, ed. M.Kubovy and J.R. Pomerantz. Hillsdale, NJ: Lawrence Erlbaum.

Huffman, D.A. (1971). Impossible objects as nonsense sentences. In *Machine Intelligence 6*, ed. B. Metzler and D. Michie, pp. 295-323. Edinburgh: Edinburgh University Press.

Ittelson, W.H. (1960). *Visual Space Perception*. New York: Springer.

Jones, D.G. & Malik, J. (1990). Computational stereopsis – beyond zero-crossing. *J. Invest. Ophthal. & Vis. Sci.*, **31**, suppl. 529.

[†] In a similar vein, we have previously proposed the importance of associative learning for the perception of subjective contours and surfaces arising from binocularly unpaired image points. It is also noteworthy that the same principle of generic image sampling can apply to these varieties of surface phenomena (Nakayama & Shimojo, 1990b).

Julesz, B. (1960). Binocular depth perception of conputer generated patterns. *Bell Sys. Tech. J.*, **39**, 1125-1162.

Julesz, B. (1971). *Foundations of Cyclopean Perception.* Chicago, IL: University of Chicago Press.

Kanisza, G. (1979). *Organization in Vision: Essays on Gestalt Perception.* New York: Praeger.

Koenderink, J.J. (1991). *Solid Shape.* Cambridge, MA: MIT Press.

Koenderink, J.J. & van Doorn, A.J. (1976). The internal representation of solid shape with respect to vision. *Biological Cybernetics*, **32**, 211.216.

Kohonen, T. (1984). *Self organization and associative memory.* Berlin: Springer-Verlag.

Malik, J. (1987). Interpreting line drawings of curved objects. *International Journal of Computer Vision*, **1**, 73-103.

Marr, D. (1982). *Vision: A Computational Investigation into Human Representation and Processing of Visual Information.* San Francisco: Freeman.

Metelli, F. (1974). The perception of transparency. *Sci. Amer.*, **230**, 90.

Nakayama, K. & Shimojo, S. (1990a). Toward a neural understanding of visual surface representation. *Cold Spring Harbor Symposia on Quantitative Biology*, **40**, 911-924.

Nakayama, K. & Shimojo, S. (1990b). Da Vinci stereopsis. *Vision Res.*, **30**, 1811-1825.

Nakayama, K., Shimojo, S. & Ramachandran, V.S. (1990). Transparency: relation to depth, subjective contours, luminance and neon color spreading. *Perception*, **19**, 497-506.

Poggio, G.F. & Fischer, J. (1978). Binocular interaction and depth sensitivity of striate and prestriate cortical neurons of the behaving rhesus monkey. *J. Neurophysiol.*, **40**, 1392-1405.

Poggio, G.F. & Poggio, T. (1984). The analysis of stereopsis. *Ann. Rev. Neuroscience*, **7**: 379-412.

Poggio, T., Torre, V. & Koch, K. (1985). Computational vision and regularization theory. *Nature*, **317**, 314.

Ramachandran, V.S. (1986). Capture of stereopsis and apparent motion by illusory contours. *Perception & Psychophysics*, **39**, 361-373.

Ramachandran, V.S. & Cavanagh, P. (1985). Subjective contours capture stereopsis. *Nature*, **317**, 527-530.

Redies, C. & Spillmann, L. (1981). The neon-color effect in the Ehrenstein illusion. *Perception*, **10**, 667.

Rescorla, R. & Holland, P.C. (1982). Behavorial studies of associative learning in animals. *Ann. Rev. Psychol.*, **33**, 265-308.

Richards, W., Koenderink, J.J. & Hoffman, D. (1987). Inferring three-dimensional shapes from two-dimensional silhouettes. *J. Opt. Soc. Amer. A.*, **4**, 1168-1175.

Rock, I. (1983). *Perception.* Cambridge, MA: MIT Press.

Shimojo, S. & Nakayama, K. (1990). A modal representation of occluded surface. *Perception*, **19**, 285-299.

vanTuijl, H.F.J. (1975). A new visual illusion: neonlike color spreading. *Acta Psychologia*, **39**, 441-445.

11

The perception of shading and reflectance

E.H. ADELSON

Department of Brain and Cognitive Sciences, Massachusetts Institute of Technology

A.P. PENTLAND

Media Laboratory, Massachusetts Institute of Technology

11.1 Introduction

The luminance of a surface results from the combined effect of its reflectance (albedo) and its conditions of illumination. Luminance can be directly observed, but reflectance and illumination can only be derived by perceptual processes. Human observers are good at judging an object's reflectance in spite of large changes in illumination; this skill is known as "lightness constancy".

Most research on lightness constancy has used stimuli consisting of grey patches on a single flat plane. The models are typically based on the assumption that slow variations in luminance are due to illumination gradients, while sharp changes in luminance are due to reflectance edges. The retinex models for use with "Mondrian" stimuli are good examples (Horn, 1974; Land & McCann, 1971). But in three-dimensional scenes, sharp luminance changes can arise from either reflectance or from illumination, as illustrated in Figure 11.1. The edge marked (1) is due to a reflectance change, such as might result from a different shade of paint. The edge marked (2) results from a change in surface normal which leads to a change in the angle of incidence of the light – an effect that we may simply refer to as "shading." As Gilchrist and his colleagues have emphasized (Gilchrist *et al.*, 1983), three-dimensional scenes introduce large and important effects that are completely missed in the traditional approach to lightness perception.

11.2 Intrinsic image analysis

Using the terminology of Barrow & Tenenbaum (1978) we may cast the perceptual task as a problem of computing intrinsic images – images that represent the underlying physical properties of a scene. To correctly interpret the scene of Figure 11.1(a), one must derive a reflectance image, as shown in Figure 11.1(b), and a shading

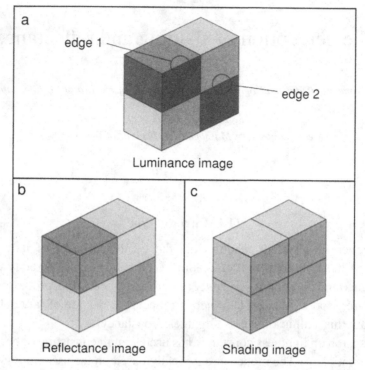

Fig. 11.1 (a) The two luminance edges marked 1 and 2 are exactly equivalent at a 2-D level, but are given different perceptual interpretations. Edge 1 is seen as a change in reflectance, while edge 2 is seen as a change in illumination due to a change in surface orientation. In an intrinsic image analysis, the image would be decomposed into the reflectance image (b) and the shading image (c).

image, as shown in Figure 11.1(c). In addition one may derive images representing surface depth and orientation, which Marr called the 2 1/2 D sketch (Marr 1982).

In a scene consisting of Lambertian surfaces illuminated by a single distant light source, the observed luminance image $I(x, y)$ is the product of the reflectance image, $r(x, y)$, and the shading image (also termed the illuminance image), $s(x, y)$,

$$I(x, y) = r(x, y)s(x, y) \qquad (11.1)$$

where the variables (x, y) index the various points in these images. The shading image itself is the product of the luminous flux, l, and the cosine of the angle of incidence, i.e. the dot product ("·") of the surface normal, $N(x, y)$, and the illumination direction , L. Thus,

$$s(x, y) = \lambda N(x, y) \cdot L \qquad (11.2)$$

Note that both the surface normal $N(x, y)$ and the illumination direction L are

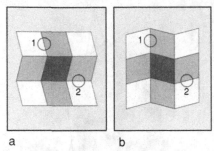

a   b

Fig. 11.2 (a) When the parallelograms are skewed horizontally, edge 1 is seen as a re-flectance edge, while edge 2 is seen as a shading edge. (b) When the parallelograms are skewed vertically, edge 1 is seen as a shading edge, while edge 2 is seen as a reflectance edge. (b) Subjects adjusted the center-most patch to match the apparent reflectance of the patches above and below it. The matches were very different for the two images.

three-dimensional vectors, but because they are defined as having unit length they have only two degrees of freedom.

A visual system must begin with the observed luminance image, $I(x, y)$, and infer the underlying shading and reflectance images, $s(x, y)$ and $r(x, y)$. Since there is no way to undo the multiplication by which the two images were combined, any mechanism for achieving the decomposition must make assumptions about regularities in the natural world.

The importance of three-dimensionality is further illustrated in Figure 11.2. Figure 11.2(a) and (b) each consist of 3 x 3 arrays of grey parallelograms, with the same shades of grey and the same adjacency relationships. The only difference between the images is the direction in which the parallelograms are skewed: horizontally in Figure 11.2(a) and vertically in Figure 11.2(b). If considered as mere 2-D arrangements of grey polygons, these images are quite similar. But our perceptual readings of these images are quite different.

In Figure 11.2(a), edge 1 is interpreted as a reflectance edge, while edge 2 is interpreted as a shading edge. On the other hand, in Figure 11.2(b), edge 1 is interpreted as a shading edge, while edge 2 is interpreted as a reflectance edge. The edges themselves, at the level of a local 2-D analysis, are equivalent. But the perturbations in the 2-D geometry lead to large changes in the 3-D interpretation, and these in turn lead to large changes in the way the edges are perceived.

The perceptual effects can be described in terms of intrinsic images. The Figure 11.3(a) the central vertical strip is seen as consisting of a single color in the 3-D object, while in Figure 11.3(b) the central vertical strip is seen as consisting of three distinct sections, the middle section being darker than the top or bottom.

It is worth nothing that the Retinex model will not correctly parse this image. It interprets sharp edges as belonging to reflectance boundaries, and since all of the

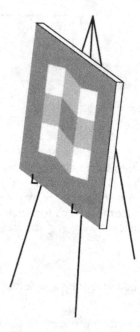

Fig. 11.3 The solution proposed by the painter. The scene consists of a flat surface, uniformly illuminated. All the image information is accounted for by variations in the grey
tone (reflectance) of the paint.

edges are sharp they will all be interpreted in terms of reflectance. In essence, the
Retinex model interprets the image as a set of grey polygons on a flat surface, as it
knows nothing about three dimensionality or the sharp illumination edges that can
exist in 3-D scenes.

   To deal with scenes in a three-dimensional world, one must employ three-dimensional constraints. We now discuss some approaches that can analyze polyhedral
scenes of the sort shown in Figures 11.1 and 11.2. (See chapter 6 by Knill *et al.* for
the use of the geodesic constraint.)

11.3 The workshop metaphor

We begin by describing a "workshop" metaphor. Suppose that we are given the
task of constructing a physical scene that will produce the image of Figure 11.2(b).
We go to a workshop where a set of specialists build the scenery for the stage sets
used in dramatic productions. One is a lighting designer; another is a painter; and
a third is a sheet-metal worker. There is also a supervisor who can coordinate the
actions of the individual specialists. We show them the desired image, and ask them
to determine how to build a scene that will look the same. They are faced with a

problem analogous to the one faced by the human visual system: given an image, try to figure out how it could have come about.

Let us imagine that the specialists charge according to a set of fixed prices. Simple and common operations are cheap, while more complex and unusual operations are more expensive. We can then cast the problem in terms of minimizing a cost function. The notion that a percept should correspond to the simplest or likeliest explanation of a scene has a long history in the perception literature (Attneave, 1959; Helmholtz, 1962; Hochberg & McAlister, 1953; Leeuwenberg, 1969; Restle, 1982;), and it has more recently been shown that formal concepts of simplicity (e.g. minimal length descriptions) and likelihood (e.g. maximum likelihood estimators) are fundamentally related (Pentland, 1989; Leclerc, 1989). These approaches can both be formalized as minimizing a cost function.

Consider the following fee structure:

Spray Painter Fees:

Paint a rectangular patch	$5 each
Paint a general polygon	$5 per side

Sheet metal Worker Fees:

Right angle cuts	$2 each
Odd angle cuts	$5 each
Right angle bends	$2 each
Odd angle bends	$5 each

Lighting Designer Fees:

Flood light	$5 each
Custom spot light	$30 each

Supervisor Fees:

Consultation	$30 per job

Now there will be many different ways of constructing scenes that produce the same image. Indeed, each of the specialists can construct a model almost entirely without the help of the other specialists. For example, the painter could simply paint the appropriate arrangement of parallelograms on a flat sheet of metal and ask the lighting designer to illuminate it with a single flood; this solution is illustrated in

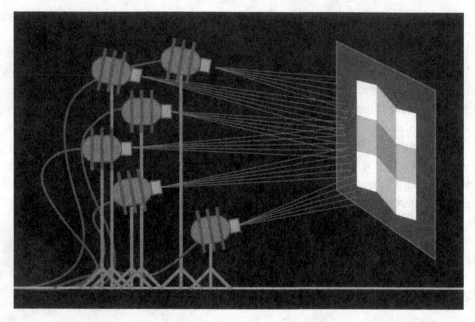

Fig. 11.4 The solution proposed by the lighting designer. The scene is assumed to be flat and of constant reflectance. All the image information is accounted for by variations in local illumination.

Figure 11.3. The lighting designer could start with a plain white sheet and project a set of nine custom spot lights onto it, having constructed a set of masks with just the right shapes, and projected at just the right positions and intensities so as to produce the desired image. Figure 11.4 shows this solution. It is also possible for the sheet metal worker to bend some metal sheets into very special shapes so that, when illuminated and viewed from precisely the correct angle, they will give rise to the desired image. This solution is shown in Figure 11.5. Finally, of course, the image could be produced by painting a square of metal with strips of two different shades of grey, and then bending the square into a zig-zag shape; this is the solution that leaps immediately to mind for a human observer. This last solution depends on the cooperation of the various specialists.

The prices for these solutions will be as follows:

Painter's solution:

Paint 9 general polygons	$180
Setup 1 flood light	$5
Cut 1 rectangle	$8
Total	$193

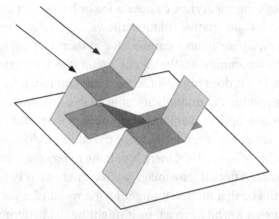

Fig. 11.5 The solution proposed by the sheet-metal worker. The scene is assumed to be of constant reflectance, illuminated by a single distant light source. All the image information is accounted for by the shading that results from the different surface normals. This scene can only be viewed from a single position, in order for the surfaces to line up properly.

Lighting Designer's solution:

Cut 1 Rectangle	$8
Set up 9 Custom spots	$270
Total	$278

Sheet metal worker's solution:

Cut 24 odd angles	$120
Bend 6 odd angles	$30
Set up 1 flood light	$5
Total	$155

Supervisor's solution:

Cut 1 rectangle	$8
Paint 3 rectangles	$5
Bend 2 right angles	$4
Supervisor's fee	$30
Total	$47

It is clear that when each specialist tries to generate a solution on his own, the result works but is expensive. The lowest cost solution is the one suggested by the supervisor, which involves the efficient combination of all the skills of the specialists. Although the supervisor charges a fee of his own, it is more than offset by the savings that his cooperative solution allows.

The workshop metaphor is an example of a system that evaluates the cost of solutions and seeks the minimum. We do not intend it as a serious model of visual perception, but we feel it does highlight some important issues in vision.

One interesting point is the multiplicity of available solutions. This is related to the problem is inverse optics: there are many scenes that could produce a given image. And there are some solutions that are trivial to produce. Once we allow a painter into our stable of specialists, there is nothing to prevent him from explaining everything with paint. After all, any image we see might merely be a skillful piece of trompe de l'oeil. For that matter, it might be the result of a pattern of light cast by a slide projector on a white screen, or it might be the pattern of self-luminous dots on a CRT. Since these are legal solutions that are easy to construct they must be discouraged by other means. In terms of cost functions, we must make them expensive, indicating our preconception that they are less likely or less useful than other solutions. At the same time we must not make paint or light so generally expensive that they are never used; we need to find a balance in which they are used appropriately.

Another issue is how to assign the costs. In the example above the costs were simply chosen to make the story come out right. In a real system assigning the costs would have to be done more carefully. There are several ways that one might proceed. First, one could try out various cost schedules, tweaking them experimentally to see which ones led to the "right" answers, meaning the answers that humans see when they look at the same images. Second, one could do psychophysical experiments on humans, attempting to determine the costs that they assign to various aspects of the solutions. Third, one could empirically or theoretically determine the conditional probabilities that relate images to objects, and thereby estimate the proper costs that should be assigned so as to encourage likely interpretations and discourage unlikely ones (Dickenson *et al.*, 1992). These all represent interesting avenues of exploration, but no one has yet undertaken them for the painted polyhedral objects we are using here.

Another problem becomes evident from the workshop metaphor. We have a well-defined cost function, which allows us to evaluate possible solutions, but we have no way of generating promising candidate solutions to be evaluated. When each specialist operates alone it is fairly easy to find a candidate solution but these solutions are usually poor. The good solutions – the cooperative ones – are much more difficult to find. In our story above the correct solution was simply announced by the supervisor, who unfortunately did not tell us how he found it. The problem can be described as one of searching the solution space and finding the point with minimum cost. But the space is enormous and there is no hope of simply searching it.

We have devised an algorithm that can correctly interpret images like those of Figure 11.2. It begins with a description of the image in terms of a set of 2-D grey polygons, and generates a description of the 3-D shape, along with intrinsic images of the reflectance and the shading. The algorithm attempts to construct an internal model that accounts for the image data with minimum cost, where cost is defined so as to capture some of the intuitive notions of "simplest," or "most likely."

Our algorithm is based on a set of specialists, each of which is a subprocess utilizing knowledge about some particular aspect of visual scenes. For the problem at hand we employ a shape specialist, a lighting specialist, and a reflectance specialist. Each specialist seeks to explain what it can within its particular domain of expertise, and the three converge on a single solution.

The system that we will describe here is not actually cooperative across specialists. The shape process goes to work first and generates its best guess about the shape, seeking the 3-D configuration that explains the 2-D shapes with minimal cost. Then the lighting specialist seeks to explain as many grey-level edges as possible by adjusting the light source direction. Finally the reflectance specialist is allowed to explain whatever is left over. This particular hierarchy gives good solutions to many simple polyhedral images.

(1) *The shape specialist*: We assume the image was created by orthographic projection. The shape process is constrained by the observed (x, y) coordinates of edges and vertices, but it is free to vary the z coordinates, since these are not observed. The operation of the shape process may be understood by reference to the example in Figure 11.6. The input stimulus is shown in Figure 11.6(a); it is a 2-D image consisting of two parallelograms. Observers typically interpret this figure three-dimensionally, seeing it as folded in space. How can the 3-D percept be generated from the 2-D image? Our shape specialist uses a representation like that shown in Figure 11.6(b). The vertices are like beads sliding on rods, and the lines between them are like infinitely elastic strings (cf. Arnhiem, 1954; Barrow & Tenenbaum, 1981; Ullman 1984). The beads are constrained to maintain the observed (x, y) coordinates, but are free to move along the z-coordinate. The shape specialist can explore these configurations at will, since they all project orthographically to the same 2-D image.

We have experimented with various simplicity measures. In the case of quadri-laterals, such as the grey patches of Figure 11.2, one plausible notion of simplicity is that angles tend to be 90° angles, since squares and rectangles are the simplest quadrilaterals. A penalty (cost) is assigned to non-right angles, and the shape process seeks the 3-D configuration that minimizes this cost. This mechanism leads to the correct behavior for Figure 11.2, but it leads to incorrect configurations for other figures.

Barrow & Tenenbaum (1981) and Marill (1991) have proposed to interpret wire-

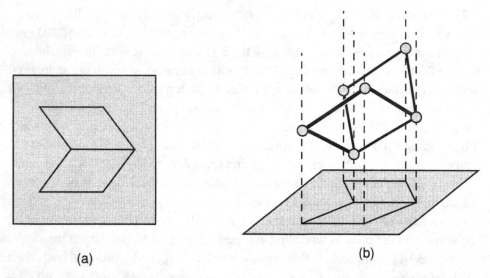

(a)   (b)

Fig. 11.6 (a) This 2-D image could be the result of projecting many possible 3-D shapes into the plane. In orthographic projection, the x and y coordinates are completely constrained by the image, but the z coordinate is completely unconstrained. (b) One may imagine a set of beads sliding on pegs, where the pegs constrain the beads to remain in the correct (x, y) position, but allow them to assume arbitrary z positions. All such configurations are legal interpretations of the image, but some configurations are simpler or more likely than others.

frame drawings by minimizing a cost function that is proportional to the variance of the vertex angles. In the special case of quadralaterals it tends to prefer rectangles, and more generally it favors regular interpretations. But this approach leads to unsatisfactory configurations for many wire- frame figures. The main problem seems to be that humans prefer interpretations with planar faces, whereas the angle-variance cost function takes no account of whether the faces are planar or not.

We have found that by combining the angle-variance constraint with a planarity constraint, the behavior of the model is much improved. It is also advantageous to add a compactness constraint, so the the algorithm does not select configurations that are elongated along the line of sight (Sinha & Adelson, 1992, 1993). A similar algorithm has been described by Fischler & Leclerc (1992).

(2) *The lighting specialist*: The lighting specialist knows about the interaction of light with reflectance and surface orientation, as embodied in equation (1). It is given a single distance light source and is permitted to move it around so as to illuminate the object from various directions. (See chapter 9 by Freeman.)

The lighting specialist also knows about the shape specialist's current estimate of 3-D shape, and it uses that estimate to calculate the effects of different lighting directions. The optimal lighting direction is the one that explains as much of the luminance variation as possible in terms of shading, thereby minimizing the need for reflectance edges.

The lighting specialist starts by assuming the current estimate of surface reflectance $r(x, y)$, surface normal $N(x, y)$, and illuminant intensity L. Then for each image edge the specialist produces two equations, one for each side of the edge:

$$I_1 = r_1 \lambda N_1 \cdot L \qquad (11.3)$$
$$I_2 = r_2 \lambda N_2 \cdot L \qquad (11.4)$$

Each variable in these two equations is known except the two components that make up the light direction L so that for each edge we have two linear equations in two unknowns and so may directly solve for L. By combining the equations from all the image edges into a single linear regression we can, therefore, determine the best overall estimate of L.

(3) *The reflectance specialist.* This process assigns a reflectance to each region of the image. It must take care of any image data that is not explained by the shape process and the lighting process. The cost associated with reflectance edges is not explicitly evaluated. It is the responsibility of the lighting specialist to minimize the need for paint; it is the responsibility of the reflectance specialist to take care of any luminance variation not explained by the lighting specialist.

11.4 An example

We ran the algorithm on the zig-zag shape shown in Figure 11.7(a). The starting interpretation is shown in Figure 11.7(b-e). The 3-D shape, shown in an oblique view in Figure 11.7(b), is initially assumed to be flat, as if the object were merely a 2-D painting lying on a table. (The image in Figure 11.7(b) may appear to be slightly folded, but it is actually flat, consisting of a set of adjoining parallelograms). The light source is initially assumed to be head-on, from the direction of the eye, as indicated in the spherical plot of Figure 11.7(c). In these conditions there is no opportunity for shading to produce luminance variation, and so the shading image is completely uniform, as in Figure 11.7(d). The reflectance specialist is therefore initially responsible for explaining all of the image luminance information, which in this case means that it replicates the original image, as shown in Figure 11.7(e). In summary, when the algorithm begins it assumes that the image is just a painting that is flat and uniformly lit.

After the algorithm is run, the interpretation settles into the configuration shown in Figure 11.7(f-i). The shape specialist finds a 3-D shape, shown in side-view in Figure 11.7(f), in which the panels are square in shape, and the folds are at right angles, and which therefore has minimal cost. The lighting specialist finds that by

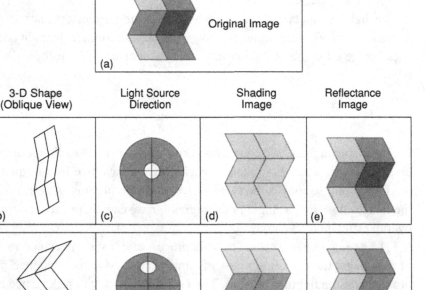

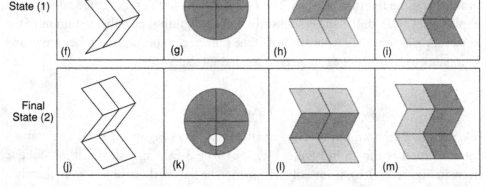

Fig. 11.7 (a) The original image that is to be analyzed. (b) The algorithm initially represents the object as being flat; the observed parallelograms are assumed to be actual parallelograms which are literally the shape of the panels in the image. The shape is shown here from an oblique view (c) The light source direction is initially assumed to be head-on, as diagrammed here by position on the surface of a sphere. (d) Since the object is initially taken to be flat, there is no variation in illumination across the surface, and so the shading image is constant. (e) The reflectance image is left with the task of explaining all of the luminance variation. (f) After the algorithm has arrived at a minimal cost configuration, the object is represented as a set of square panels which join each other in a zig-zag configuration. (g) The light source moves up into a position such that shading can account for as much luminance variation as possible. (h) The shading image accounts for the horizontally oriented luminance edges. (i) The reflectance image accounts for the remaining luminance variation. Only two colors are required. (j) An alternate final state, with the same minimum cost, occurs when the object is reversed in depth. (k) The light source moves down, rather than up, in this case. (l) The shading image and (m) the reflectance image are exactly the same in the depth-reversed case as they are in the first

placing the light at the position shown in Figure 11.7(g), a maximum number of luminance edges can be explained in terms of shading rather than reflectance. This leads to the shading image of Figure 11.7(h). Finally, the reflectance specialist takes care of the remaining luminance variation by assigning the reflectances shown in Figure 11.7(i). The final interpretation is similar to that reported by human observers.

Another interesting aspect of the human percept is bistability: if one looks at the figure for a while it will spontaneously reverse in depth. Although our algorithm does not undergo spontaneous reversals, it does assign the same cost to each of the reversed states, and considers each to be an equally good global minimum. It will randomly settle into one or the other interpretation depending on the starting conditions. The reversed-depth percept is shown in Figure 11.7(j). When the shape specialist chooses this interpretation, the lighting specialist automatically moves the light source to the correspondingly reversed angle, thereby maintaining a consistent interpretation, as shown in Figure 11.7(k). This again is consistent with the perceptual reports of human observers. Note that when the 3-D shape and the light source direction both reverse, the shading and reflectance images, Figure 11.7 (l) and (m), settle into the same states as before, as they should.

The search for a minimum cost in the above example is particularly simple because the cost function for this scene has no local minima, and has only two global minima, corresponding to the two depth-reversed solutions. For this reason we were able to solve the example without confronting the complexities that will necessarily emerge with more convoluted cost functions. (In this respect, the outcome resembles the "categorical" approach presented in chapter 3.) In order to deal with more complex scenes, such as those involving curved surfaces or occlusions, as well as complicated forms of lighting, one will need more sophisticated specialists and more sophisticated control structures. Nonetheless we are encouraged by the capabilities of the simple algorithm described here.

11.5 Conclusions

Most models of human lightness perception have been designed to deal with images consisting of simple arrays of grey patches on a flat field. These stimuli are devoid of cues about three dimensionality, and the corresponding models are unable to deal with the percepts of reflectance edges and illuminance edges as they are seen in ordinary three dimensional scenes.

At the same time, models for shape-from-shading typically assume that the world is all of a constant reflectance, and that three- dimensional shape is responsible for all the luminance variation observed. Such models cannot deal with patches of varying reflectance.

To model the perception of lightness and shading in three dimensional scenes, we must turn to systems that have richer vocabularies. This means that there are many ways to explain the luminance variation in a given image; the representation language is highly overcomplete. We introduce the "workshop" metaphor as a way of exploring the possibilities and problems of such systems. We imagine a set of specialists who have particular expertise about paint, or lighting, or 3-D shape, and each of which can explain the observed images without the help of the others. The problem then becomes selecting a description that makes proper use of these various sources of expertise. We have also developed an algorithm based on these ideas to illustrate one concrete instantiation. The output consists of a three- dimensional model, a reflectance image, a shading image, and a light source direction. For some simple scenes, the algorithm can produce interpretations similar to those reported by human observers; it is also consistent with the perception of reversible figures, and when depth reversal occurs it infers an appropriate change in lighting conditions.

References

Arnheim, R. (1954). *Art and Visual Perception.* Berkeley: University of California Press.

Attneave, F. (1959). *Applications of Information Theory to Psychology.* New York: Rinehart and Winston.

Barrow, H. G., & Tenenbaum, J. M. (1978). Recovering intrinsic scene characteristics from images. In *Computer Vision Systems*, ed. A. Hanson and E.M. Riseman, pp. 3-26. Academic Press.

Barrow, H. B. & Tenenbaum, J. M. (1981). Interpreting line drawings as three-dimensional surfaces. *Artificial Intelligence*, **17**, 75-116.

Dickenson, S., Pentland, A. & Rosenfeld, A. (1992). 3-D shape recovery using distributed aspect matching. *IEEE Transactions on Pattern Analysis and Machine Intelligence*, **14**(2), 174-198.

Fischler, M. A. & Leclerc, Y. G. (1992). Recovering 3-D wire frames from line drawings. *Proceedings of the Image Understanding Workshop.*

Gilchrist, A., Delman, S. & Jacobsen, A. (1983). The classification and integration of edges as critical to the perception of reflectance and illumination. *Perception & Psychophysics*, **33**, 425-436.

Helmholtz, H. von (1962) *Treatise on Physiological Optics*, Vol. III (trans. from the 3rd German ed., J.P.C. Southall), New York: Dover.

Hochberg, J. & McAlister, E. (1953). A quantitative approach to figural goodness. *J. Exp. Psych.*, **46**, 361-364.

Horn, B.K.P. (1974). Determining lightness from an image. *CGIP*, **3**, 277-299.

Land, E.H. & McCann, J.J. (1971). Lightness and retinex theory. *J. Opt. Soc. Am.*, **61**, 1-11.

Leclerc, Y., (1989). Constructing simple stable descriptions for image partitioning. *Intl. J. Comp. Vision*, **1**, 73-102.

Leeuwenberg, E. (1969). Quantitative specification of information in sequential patterns. *Psych. Rev.*, **76**, 216- 220.

Marr, D. (1982). *Vision.* San Francisco: Freeman.

Marill, T. (1991). Emulating the human interpretation of line- drawings as three-dimensional objects. *Intl. J. of Comp. Vis.*, **6**, 147-161.

Pentland, A. (1989). Part segmentation for object recognition. *Neural Computation*, **1**, 82-91.

Restle, F. (1982). Coding theory as an integration of Gestalt psychology and information processing theory. In *Organization and representation in perception*, ed. J. Beck, pp. 31-56. Hillsdale NJ: Erlbaum.

Sinha, P. & Adelson, E.H. (1992). Recovery of 3-D shape from 2-D wireframe drawings. *Assoc. for Res. in Vision & Opth.*, May 1992, *Inv. Opth. and Vis. Sci.*, (supp.) **33**, p825.

Sinha, P. & Adelson, E.H. (1993). Recovering reflectance in a world of painted polyhedra. *Proc. Fourth Intl. Conf. Comp. Vision*, Berlin, May 1993.

Ullman, S. (1984). Maximizing rigidity: the incremental recovery of 3-D structure from rigid and rubbery motion. *Perception*, **13**, 255-274.

12

Banishing the homunculus

HORACE BARLOW

Physiological Laboratory, Cambridge, England

12.1 The role of the homunculus

Ideas about perception have changed a great deal over the past half century. Before the discovery of maps of sensory surfaces in the cerebral cortex the consensus view was that perception involved "mind-stuff", and because mind-stuff was not matter the greatest care was required in using crude, essentially materialistic, scientific methods and concepts to investigate and explain phenomena in which it had a hand. One approach was to reduce the role of this mind-stuff to a minimum by designing experiments so that the mind was used simply as a null-detector, analogous to a sensitive galvanometer in a Wheatstone bridge, which had to do no more than detect the identity or non-identity of two percepts. Those who followed this approach might be termed the hard-psychophysics school – exemplified by people such as Helmholtz, Stiles, Hecht and Rushton – and it had some brilliant successes in explaining the properties of sensation: for instance the trichromatic theory; the relation between the quality of the retinal image and visual acuity; and the relation between sensitivity and the absorption of quanta in photo-sensitive pigments. But it left the mystery of the mind-stuff untouched.

Others attempted to discover the properties of the mind-stuff by defining the physical stimuli required to elicit its verbally recognizable states – a soft-psychophysics approach that could be said to characterize the work of the Gestalt school and, for example, Hering, Gibson, and Hurvich and Jameson. This approach has successfully described many phenomena relating subjective perceptual experience to physical stimuli, but it cannot really be said to have explained anything at all.

In the years after about 1940 the discovery that a map or copy of the responses of sensory receptors was formed in the cerebral cortex started to make a difference, because it became obvious that the ethereal, non-material, mind-stuff was associated with a real, material, pattern of neural activity. The homunculus had been around for a long time, but he suddenly became a more pressing problem because there

425

seemed to be something for him to look at, and as a result he became a disreputable irritant: he was obviously a figment, and yet none of us could dispense with him. The problem was less severe for the hard psychophysics school, whose reduction of the role of mind-stuff to a null-detector minimized his importance; in fact this successful minimization is perhaps a major factor in the continued vitality of this school. But the replacement of mind-stuff by a homunculus put the soft-psychophysicists into a difficult position: it is one thing to say that you are investigating the psycho-physical correlates of perception if this is thought to be mediated by a non-material mind-stuff, but it becomes uncomfortable if perception depends upon the properties of a homunculus that no-one really believes in.

One attempt to avoid this dilemma was to explain the properties of perception in terms of the transformations to the patterns of excitation representing the image brought about by neural interactions in retina, LGN, and cortex. For instance these transformations emphasize temporal and spatial discontinuities, such as those that occur at the onset of a stimulus and at the borders of objects, and it seems natural to relate these to the successive and simultaneous contrast phenomena that are subjectively observable. Qualitatively this is a step in the right direction, for the phenomena that were successfully explained did not depend upon the homunculus, but there are two problems: first, attempts to explain contrast phenomena in this way have not been quantitatively successful; and second, these attempts do not go nearly far enough in explaining what we do with images.

What hinders a more radical solution is the fact that we don't know what the cortex – agreed by most to be the organ of perception – does. All those intricately interconnected neurons must surely be doing useful computational work on the sensory messages, and if we understood this work better, the homunculus might be banished from much of the realm where he is now such a nuisance.

The main purpose of this paper, then, is to define the computational goal of the cerebral cortex. Section 12.2 does this by combining the biologically based view of comparative anatomists with modern neurophysiological knowledge, and the result is to define a challenging and difficult computational task. In Section 12.3 some of the implications of the hypothesis are set out. The value of an idea of this sort is to prompt new questions about perception and cerebral cortex, so in Section 12.6 some other jobs that we might take over from the homunculus are briefly described, together with some that it may take longer to take over.

12.2 A hypothesis about the computational goal of neocortex

A widely accepted idea, derived from comparative anatomy, is that our enlarged cortex is responsible for the fact that we know more about the world than other animals. It is believed that the selective advantage conferred by this greater knowledge underlies the progressive evolutionary enlargement of the cortex, and that this in turn has led to the overwhelming evolutionary success of the human race, as judged by our domination of the world and our explosive and overwhelming population growth.

Now if these statements are true, the account of cortical function given by current neuro-physiology is highly unsatisfactory. Something like 60% of the monkey cortex is directly connected with vision (Van Essen & Maunsell, 1980), but the neurophysiological account tells one only about *representing* the current visual scene. The same is true in other modalities – it is the function of representing the current input that has received attention. But as we have seen we do not have a homunculus inside our heads to look at these representations: common sense tells us that our cortex and associated structures must not only form the representation, they must look at it, analyze it, store results about it, use it, and continuously add to it. It may be knowledge of the world that has given us our dominant position, but the mechanisms for acquiring, storing and utilizing this knowledge have certainly not yet been discovered by neuroscientists – in fact they have hardly even been considered.

12.2.1 *The biological view*

How does the neocortex, together with the structures associated with it, confer the great selective advantage that lies behind the rapid evolution of the human race? Herrick (1926) said that the cerebral cortex provided the "filing cabinets of the central executive", and he also called it the "organ of civilization". Jerison (1991) summarized its role as "knowing about the world", so the comparative anatomists seem in little doubt that it stores our world knowledge, but this view made no impression on neuro-physiologists, and for almost two decades even psychologists paid little attention to it. However Craik (1943) and Tolman (1948) eventually pointed out the importance for higher mental function of forming working models and cognitive maps of the world, and although these ideas were regarded as heretical in their time, they fit the view from comparative anatomy very well and are now widely accepted.

Tolman was thinking primarily of representing the geographical layout of the world, while Craik's working models imitated the physics and dynamics of interactions in the material world, but a third aspect must also be included. Humphrey (1976) has pointed out that we are strongly dependent upon the people around us and we have to understand them in order to survive and flourish. If we could measure it objectively this would surely be a more difficult task than mastering the local geography or the dynamics of the material world, and one must face the fact that the properties of people are the major determinant of the complex forms of social life that distinguish the human race, which are in turn major factors in our domination of the world. The modelling of other minds and their interactions must therefore occupy an important place among the tasks the human cortex performs.

Thus the hypothesis is that the cerebral cortex confers skill in deriving useful geographic, physical and social knowledge from the uncertain evidence of our senses; furthermore it must not only derive this knowledge, it must also store it and give access to it when required. This obviously involves more than mere representation, and it specifies a definite computational goal for neocortex that not only provides a useful framework for thinking about its structure, organization and function, but also suggests some operations that we have previously left to the homunculus, and which we must now try to take away from him.

12.2.2 Seeing structure

We understand the problem of acquiring knowledge better now than in Herrick's day. It is not a matter of simply recording or video-taping the succession of messages from the outside world that our senses provide, but is a much more analytic process that requires identifying structure in these messages and separating this structure from the irregular, unpredictable parts. Structure is anything that is regular, repeating, or symmetric, and Figure 12.1 provides some examples.

Look for a moment at the top left part which consists of a random array of dots, then compare it with the top right, where a regular rule has been applied:- each dot is paired in a position symmetric about the centre line. The random parts of these two figures are identical, but I doubt if you noticed that fact. It is the symmetric structure on the right that leaps to the eye, while the random array means nothing to us - unless we look at it long enough and start to impose structure on it, such as faces or other imaginary forms. In the lower two figures the structure resulting from other pairing rules stands out equally clearly. Although it is pretty obvious what these pairing rules are, I don't think it is at all obvious that a pairing rule is solely responsible for the structure seen; it is hard to believe that the vivid streaks and swirls result just from pairs of dots, with no longer concatenations, but that is the case.

These figures were first described by Glass (1969), and one can detect them when they are overlaid by a huge number of completely randomly placed dots (Maloney, Mitchison & Barlow, 1987). Furthermore the absolute efficiency for detecting mirror symmetry is high under the appropriate conditions (Barlow & Reeves, 1979). It seems that our perceptual system grabs symmetry or structure in sensory messages, and uses instances of its occurrence as building blocks to construct its representation of the world.

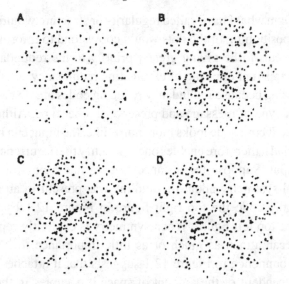

Fig. 12.1 (A) An array of 200 randomly positioned dots. (B) Each dot in the array of A has been paired at a position mirror-symmetric about the vertical midline. (C) Each dot has been paired at a position up and to the right of the original position. (D) Each dot has been paired at a position displaced radially and tangentially from the centre. It is the structure that leaps to the eye, though this is technically a form of redundancy; the random positions of the dots contain much more information, but the eye gives them less prominence.

12.2.3 Information and redundancy

The structure and randomness in Figure 12.1 are related to redundancy and information. As Shannon told us (Shannon & Weaver, 1949), the true information in a message can generally be encoded on to a channel of much lower capacity than is required for the raw stream of data, because the raw data almost always contains redundancy. It will be argued that finding a redundancy-reducing code is a powerful analogy for sensory coding and perception (Attneave, 1954; Barlow, 1959; Atick, 1992), and that finding the structure and regularity in sensory messages is the analytic operation needed to do this. This is the job that I suspect the neocortex performs better than other brain structures: it gives meaning to the stream of sensory data and it must be an important part of the job the homunculus currently does, which we wish to take away from him.

Unfortunately the model of a transmitter, a channel, and a receiver that Shannon set up for his mathematical analysis is in some ways a poor analogy for the perceptual brain, partly because we must rid ourselves of the idea that there is a homunculus to receive the messages, but also for several other reasons. As we have seen, the brain is interested in the structure in Figure 12.1, and tends to dismiss the random element (the positions of the dots in top left of Figure 12.1) as noise; in contrast, in

Shannon's paradigm what I have called regularity or structure would be redundancy, and the random positioning of the dots would correspond to information, so at first sight the brain seems to be giving greater priority to the redundancy than to the information, the apparent opposite of eliminating redundancy.

This is misleading because redundancy reducing codes are reversible, so they do not eliminate one type of message and preserve another type. Although the output of a redundancy reducing code looks more noise-like, the input can be reconstructed from the output, and it therefore enables one to identify the occurrence of a redundant feature in the input. Suppose for instance that we had a one-bit signal that told us when bilateral symmetry about the midline was present in an image; then we could economically code the top right figure in Figure 12.1 by combining this single bit with the top left figure. When symmetry is explicitly represented in this way the system can attach as much or as little importance to it as it likes, and the subjective prominence in Figure 12.1 suggests that it attaches quite a lot; but this is quite independent of the amount of space it occupies in the message. The occurrence of symmetry is no longer signalled by a bulky pattern in the message that uses up much of the capacity of the channel, but by a compact signal that is not in any way predictable from other parts of the output. Thus in some forms of redundancy reducing code one expects the redundant features of the input to be explicitly represented in the output.

The sensory system certainly loses a great deal of the information available in the physical stimuli that it receives, but this is not the result of redundancy reduction. Some of this irreversible loss (for instance that caused by low acuity in the periphery of vision) results from fixed neuro-anatomical arrangements that cannot change during the life of the individual, and in such a case there is no discrimination between redundancy and information in what is lost. But changes in coding occur, as with the adjustments of the dynamic range of retinal ganglion cells during light and dark adaptation, and these are sometimes thought of as preserving signals in the important range and discarding unimportant signals. I think it is better to regard adaptation as a redundancy-reducing step, for it preserves information about the stimuli that occur frequently, and the potential losses occur for ranges of stimulus intensity that occur infrequently or not at all under the conditions adapted to. Of course we do not know that this is the case for all types of coding change, but a case can be made that pattern-contingent adaptation is also information-preserving, though by decorrelating representational elements from each other in response to a changed associative structure in the sensory messages, rather than by simply adjusting dynamic ranges (Barlow, 1990).

Discussion of adaptation brings up another way in which Shannon's model is a poor analogy, for it assumes a static situation; it is supposed that the forms of re-dundancy are known beforehand, and that their properties remain constant, whereas redundancy in sensory messages is not necessarily known beforehand, and there is no guarantee that it will remain constant. One of the most important characteristics of perception is the ability to distinguish what is new and unexpected from what is known and normal, and this implies that new forms of redundancy are continuously being recognized. This is crucially important, because these new regularities betray the presence of new causal factors in the environment. In Shannon's terms, what was previously information (i.e. unpredictable) becomes redundancy (i.e. something regular or predictable) once the presence of the regularity has been established.

12.2.4 Structure, redundancy and knowledge

Because information and redundancy are so confusing in the context of perception it may be helpful to use different terms that are equivalent, but more intuitively meaningful. Structure and regularity in the stream of data, if they belong to categories that are already known about, are redundancy in terms of information theory, but this part constitutes the knowledge that the neocortex must continuously acquire and use. The part that is unpredictable is information in Shannon's terms, but it contains the unidentified redundancy from which new knowledge can be derived, as well as an unknown amount of new information and genuine noise. It is important to note again that a redundancy reducing code is reversible, so that the occurrence of a pattern or regularity in the input can be identified in it.

The fact that sense organs and pathways are specifically adapted to handle biologically important stimuli is well recognized, and rewards and punishments are also likely to influence the organization of sensory information. The importance of redundancy reduction is that it does not depend upon reinforcement or the specific biological importance of stimuli; it is a general principle for reorganizing sensory information that is independent of these factors. However it cannot by itself prescribe the exact form of the recoded messages, and it has nothing to say about the selection or rejection of information, so it is worth asking if there are other general principles that could help us understand these aspects of perception and representation in the cortex.

12.2.5 Sparse coding with symbols of high relative entropy

Shannon's analysis of information and redundancy showed how to make optimum use of channel capacity, and since the cost of a channel was proportional to its capacity, his analysis showed how to save money. (See chapter 1 for relation to Bayes and MDL coding.) In the brain we do not know how to assess the cost of representations of different sorts. We cannot simply assume that biological cost is proportional to the number of nerve cells required, nor is it plausible to assume that it is proportional to the number of active nerve cells, or the total number of impulses required. But without making some such assumptions we cannot really talk meaningfully about what representations are redundant or non-redundant biologically; we need to know how the representation is used before we can do this. So far this difficulty has been circumvented by referring to the physical cause of sensory messages, for we can talk meaningfully about the information, redundancy and capacity of the physical representations of pictures and sounds, but sooner or later the biological issue must be faced. Here again the notion that the perceptual representation's primary role is to facilitate learning is helpful.

To illustrate this let us start by considering the type of representation that the redundancy-reducing hypothesis in its baldest form might lead one to expect. This would consist of a large number of binary elements, each with a probability 1/2 of being active, and each becoming active totally independently of every other element. It would be a nightmare to use this for learning: learning first requires recognising that some natural object or event has occurred, ie that the current sensory input is a member of a particular subset of possible input messages; then co-occurrences of such events either with other events, or with a class of reinforcing stimuli, must be counted. Given the typical size of biological representations (e.g. 10^6 optic nerve fibres), this is a horrendous task, and the form of the representation does not facilitate it in any way, except by being the most compact possible representation.

The following argument for sparse representation is one that I have attempted to present previously (Barlow 1972, 1985a), but I have not yet succeeded in putting it in a satisfactory quantitative form. There are advantages in coding information sparsely using what I termed "cardinal cells", that is by representing a scene by the activity or a small proportion of active units selected from a large population most of which are inactive. One advantage comes from the intuitive feeling that the elementary decisions in perception are usually worth more than one bit: for instance identifying a face must be worth more like 10 bits, since it is a selection from more than 1000 possibilities. The information conveyed by a unit when active could be as high as this if it was only active rarely, but it would only be 1 bit if it was active half the time, as in the first representation considered above.

There are other advantages of sparseness connected with information storage in associative nets (Longuet-Higgins *et al.*, 1970), and I shall mention another one later in connection with learning in distributed representations. At an intuitive level again, the process Bartlett (1932) used to refer to as the "effort after meaning" seems to me to correspond to collecting together related items that individually have low information value to create symbols that have high informational value, and I cannot think of any better way this could be done neurophysiologically than by ensuring that a neuron, when it fires, carries a substantial amount of information. In our thinking we do not seem to be able to use "microconcepts", which we would have to use in their hundreds, thousands, or millions in order to represent a substantial scene, but instead we use concepts of the order of complexity of words; with a few of these we can express anything that we need. Shannon (1951) suggested that a word in English corresponds to half a dozen bits on average, and that is within the reach of a single neuron provided that it forms part of a fairly sparse representation in which the probability of being active is of the order of 1%.

These ideas have been set out in somewhat greater detail previously (Barlow, 1985a) and initial steps in developing a more quantitative argument are described in Section 12.6.4 below.

12.2.6 Is redundancy a principle of selection?

We have seen that a redundancy reducing code does not select or reject information because it is reversible, but a case can be made for using redundancy, not only to recode economically, but as a criterion for selecting what a perceptual system should represent; information which is non-redundant, and therefore indistinguishable from noise, would be rejected. The argument goes like this.

The system cannot accept all the information it receives, but it should represent as high a proportion as possible of the input, and this proportion can only be assessed as a fraction of the raw, unprocessed input. If there are redundant features, like the mirror or translational symmetries of Figure 12.1, these offer the opportunity of accepting a portion of the input at a relatively low cost in terms of the representational space they occupy. Just as a shoe-shop with a small stock-room containing the common sizes in several patterns will satisfy more customers than one that stocks the full range in a single pattern, so would such a redundancy-selecting system reversibly encode a higher proportion of the energy in the input. The principle has its dangers, for if it was carried to the extreme the perceptual system could only represent redundant features that it had already recognised, but this could be avoided by not applying the principle too rigorously. It is actually true that we tend to see what we already know, but we can also see new things, and perhaps this is because our perceptual system is cautious in rejecting what appears to be unstructured, or non-redundant. The principle may explain why we accept the Bellman's claim that "what I tell you three times is true" (Dodgson, 1876), and why there is some validity to the Kantian fear about the dominance of the a priori in our perception and reasoning, but it also shows why these should be only limited fears (Barlow, 1974).

It is obvious that we are here getting involved in deep problems, but we do not need to resolve them all in order to understand the importance of identifying regularity and structure in sensory messages, and the equal but different importance of identifying what is not accountable for by regularity and structure that has already been identified. This is the essence of the message that redundancy reduction is important in sensory coding. Finding the structure and regularity is the analytic part of dealing with the succession of sensory impressions that the brain receives, and this is the part that I suspect the neocortex performs better than other brain structures: it gives meaning to the stream of sensory data. Furthermore this must be an important part of the job the homunculus currently does, which we wish to take away from him.

12.2.7 The salience of repeated forms

Now it is plausible to suppose that the mirror symmetry and translational symmetry illustrated in Figure 12.1 are so abundant in our sensory diet that an animal is *certain* to encounter them; hence mechanisms for detecting these forms of symmetry will always prove useful, and their universal provision by ontogenetic mechanisms has selective advantage. But much of the knowledge we acquire is not like this at all; it consists of arbitrary forms whose regularity or structure results simply from the fact that they recur often, or are repeatedly associated with reward and gratification. Each individual system has to discover these for itself, and we spend our lives finding, storing and using knowledge of these regularities in our sensory diet. They range from the often-repeated experience of our parent's smell, voice, and appearance, through the geographical details of our environment and the acoustical specificities of our language, to the customs, myths, and true knowledge of our culture. Much of this process of acquisition is fostered by teaching, but each individual brain has to do a lot of discovering for itself.

I used to think this sorting of the sensory input by association and repetition was the main task that the neocortex excelled in, but for the following reasons I now think it is likely that it also excels in the genetic acquisition of world knowledge.

12.2.8 Evolutionary learning and neocortex

Most people will accept the fact that there is such a thing as inherited knowledge of the world. Many of the most striking examples are found in insects - for example the yucca moth could not fertilize the yucca plant and use its ovaries as incubators for its own eggs without such knowledge, nor could the ichneumon select a particular species of caterpillar to lay its eggs in. But it occurs in mammals too – the specialized behavioural skills of a retriever are quite different from those of a sheepdog or a greyhound – and no-one doubts that these skills have a large inherited component.

Now a characteristic cannot play an important role in the evolution of a species unless it is controlled genetically and subject to genetic variability. Therefore the view that neocortex is partly responsible for our rapid evolution implies that certain aspects of its function must be controlled genetically, for otherwise it could not, by the selective survival of genetic variants, have brought us to the position we are in. The full hypothesis must therefore be that the neocortex gives us useful knowledge of the world in two ways; not only does it discover the structure of its world by experience during its lifetime, but it has a headstart for it has mechanisms adapted through the process of genetic selection that confer skills, sometimes highly specialized ones, for doing this.

These mechanisms and skills amount to inherited knowledge of the world. On this view both extreme schools of thought about the origin of our mental powers are correct: the neocortex acquires knowledge of the world by nature as well as by nurture, but these methods work towards the same end rather than being the mutually exclusive alternatives that we tend to think. For this reason they can be considered together when trying to define the computational goal of the neocortex.

12.2.9 Reconciliation with neurophysiology

What we know of the neurophysiology of neocortex does not at first suggest that it is concerned with acquiring, storing and utilizing knowledge of the world. As we have seen, it seems instead to form representations of the current scene in the sensory areas, and perhaps the motor area could be thought of as carrying a representation of current motor actions. But this representational function does not necessarily conflict with the hypothesis about acquisition of knowledge. Different types of representations are suitable for different purposes, and it will be argued that the cortical representation is one that continuously adjusts itself to past associative structure, and thereby simultaneously stores knowledge of this past associative structure and facilitates the identification of new associations. Suggestive evidence in support can be found from the changes in neural connectivity that occur in the sensitive period (Hubel & Wiesel, 1970; Movshon & Van Sluyters, 1981), and in the known phenomena of pattern-selective adaptation, which I have enlarged on elsewhere (Barlow, 1990, 1991).

It will be shown next that storage and utilization of knowledge about the world are necessary in order to form a representation that facilitates learning, so the comparative anatomists' view that neocortex provides the filing cabinets of the central executive does not contradict the neurophysiological facts about representation, though it does imply that there is more to this representation than has yet been discovered.

12.3 Representations designed to facilitate knowledge acquisition

This amalgamation of the comparative anatomist's and the neurophysiologist's views of the cortex also fits the notion I've developed (Barlow, 1991) about the nature of perception, and Figure 12.2 illustrates a flow diagram according to this

SUGGESTED FLOW DIAGRAM FOR
INFORMATION PROCESSING IN PERCEPTION

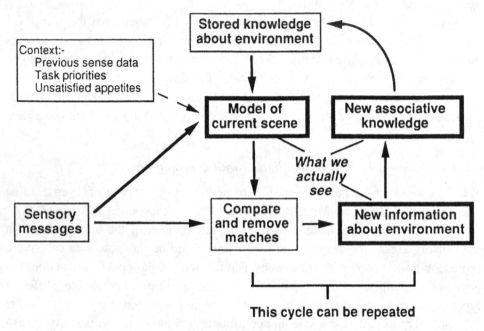

Fig. 12.2 Flow diagram for perception suggested by the hypothesis that the cerebral cortex creates a representation of the current sensory scene that facilitates the identification of new associations. In order to separate new information from knowledge (i.e. redundancy) there must already be a store of the known structure and regularities found in sensory inputs, and this must be used to form a model that accounts for as much as possible of the current sensory input; what this accounts for can then be explicitly represented and will occupy less space in the input representation. Though we think we experience sensory messages directly, what we see corresponds better to the contents of the heavily outlined boxes.

hypothesis. The sensory messages are combined with a store of knowledge of the world to find the best model of the current sensory scene. This model is then compared with the actual sensory messages, and those parts that match are eliminated from it. The residue represents the part of the current sensory input that is unaccounted for by pre-existing knowledge. Ideally this would correspond to new information, together of course with noise of random origin.

In this flow diagram the part we are consciously aware of corresponds to the model we construct by combining our stored knowledge of associative structure with the current sensory input; items that have been successfully modelled are removed from the flow, but their identification is probably the most useful part of the scheme, and also the subjectively salient part. The fact that redundancy is simultaneously reduced and exploited may appear paradoxical, but this is what happens in a redundancy reducing code. We can also be aware of the residue unexplained by this initial model, and of new regularities or structure in this part, but what we think we experience – the sensory message itself – is only indirectly accessible.

This flow diagram has features related to the "matching response" of MacKay (1955), the adjusting feedback of Daugman (1989) and Pece (1993), the thalamic "active blackboard" and the "matching templates" of Mumford (1991, 1992; see also chapter 1), and perhaps it also captures one aspect of the "counter stream" schema of Ullman (1993). It must be added that the operations in the boxes of Figure 12.2 are not like those of a program flow-diagram, for they are not well-defined algorithms but complex operations that are not fully understood.

12.3.1 *Changing the code stores associative structure*

One can think of the suggested operation in a different way. If one has a complex set of data in which there are certain known dependencies, it will often help to display them in a form in which the known dependencies have been eliminated. For instance body weight increases with height, so to bring out other factors affecting weight it would be worth expressing it in a form that removes the correlation with height, such as the ratio (True weight/weight expected from individual's height). Notice that this can be done with no loss of information provided that the expression giving the expected weight is available

I don't know if it is universally true that removing a known type of associative structure makes it easier to identify a new type, but it is certainly very often the case, and Figure 12.3 provides another illustration. The left part is a normal image and thus has an auto-correlation function that extends over a large fraction of the whole image. This can be removed by the process of "whitening", which levels the power spectrum of the Fourier transform and reduces the correlations, estimated over the whole image, between pairs of points with any fixed separation. The result is shown on the right. I think it is clear that the higher order structures that correspond to borders and edges in the image, whatever they are, are genuinely more prominent in this image in the sense that a higher proportion of the contrast energy is located at the edges.

In outline then, the idea is that associative structure one already knows about should be removed from the data stream in order to make it easier to detect new associative structure. Knowledge of the old associations should be used to change the code and thus modify the representation so that these old associations are no longer present. This is the same as the original idea of recoding to reduce redundancy (Barlow, 1959; Watanabe, 1960), and subtracting the regression that corresponds

Fig. 12.3 The image on the left was "whitened" by making the power spectrum level, thus producing the image on the right. The types of statistical structure that occur at the borders of objects survive whitening and can be more easily analyzed and detected in the absence of the autocorrelations that whitening removes. (From Tolhurst & Barlow, 1993).

to an already recognized correlation in order to find further relationships in the residuals is a simple example. Of course the modifications will not generally be as simple as subtracting out an expected regression or flattening a power spectrum, but these examples illustrate how an operation that accounts for and reduces the known structure in a set of observations simultaneously stores knowledge about that associative structure, recognizes the existence of that structure, and uses it to make the detection of new structure easier.

To an outside observer, a system performing these operations would look like one that constructed Craik's working models (Craik, 1943) and Tolman's cognitive maps (Tolman, 1948) of the environment, for it would show evidence of finding and using the associative structure that underlies such models and maps. Obviously this store of knowledge has many other potential uses, particularly in the processes of imagination and recall where we experiment and play with what we know (Kosslyn & Koenig 1992). In order to pursue this possibility further we would have to postulate means of access to the stored knowledge, perhaps by lowering thresholds in the box marked "Stored knowledge about the environment" in Figure 12.2, but I don't want to go into such possibilities now, nor to discuss what this information processing scheme might seem like subjectively. For the present argument, the point is that the automatic use of this stored knowledge to account for expected features in the current scene simultaneously allows those features to be used, and improves the acquisition of new knowledge. Anything that improves the appropriateness and

Remove evidence of the associations you already know about	*To facilitate detecting new ones*
Make available the probabilities of the features present	*To determine chance expectations*
Choose features that occur independently of each other in the normal environment	*To help determine chance expectations of combinations of features*
Choose "suspicious coincidences" as features	*To reduce redundancy and ensure appropriate generalization*

Table 12.1 *What would make it easier to identify new associations?*

speed of learning must have immense competitive advantage, so this proposal could explain the enormous selective advantage of the neocortex. With appropriate genetic variation of the details of this process, this could in turn account for its very rapid evolution and the subsequent growth of our species to its dominant position in the world.

The new hypothesis can give us a fresh viewpoint on poorly understood aspects of the evolution and neurophysiology of the cortex, but the process of knowledge acquisition must be examined in more detail to bring this out.

12.4 Requirements for knowledge acquisition

Acquiring knowledge means finding out about the regularities and patterns in the sensory input. It's a vast task to determine the associational structure of the continuous stream of sensory messages that we receive, and Table 12.1 lists some of the requirements (Barlow, 1991), starting with the point above about the desirability of removing evidence for the associations that are already known.

We need an agreed vocabulary in order to discuss various ways of representing scenes. Suppose that the representation consists of reports of *features*, of which there can be a wide variety. For instance one of them might be a point in the image having a luminance value above the mean for the neighbourhood of that point, and this would correspond approximately to the feature that causes the firing of an on-centre ganglion cell in the retina. Or it might be the occurrence of a visual pattern resembling a monkey's face, which would correspond to the occurrence of the trigger feature of a so-called face cell in infero-temporal cortex. Any representation one can imagine can be described as reporting the occurrence of features, but the number of features and their frequency of occurrence will vary.

There must be many levels in the actual representational system in the brain, and more complex features are presumably represented at higher levels, but for present purposes let us consider a single level. The first item in Table 12.1 is recoding to take account of identified regularities or associative structure, for the operation of identifying associations is required at all levels.

12.5 Need for probabilities of representational elements

The logical basis for identifying a new association in traditional, Fisherian, statistics is as follows:

(i) If two occurrences U and C *are not associated* they will occur together with the probability $p(U\&C)$ expected for the random co-occurrence of two independent variables; that is, if the individual probabilities are $p(U)$ and $p(C)$

$$p(U\&C) = p(U)p(C) \tag{12.1}$$

(ii) When we count the number of joint occurrences we find that they occur significantly more often than predicted from this probability.

(iii) Therefore the hypothesis that they *are not associated* is false, and the complimentary hypothesis that they *are associated* is true. So in this framework, knowledge of $p(U)$ and $p(C)$ and all other individual occurrences is necessary in order to identify new associations reliably.

In the currently fashionable Bayesian formulation the same probabilities $p(U)$ and $p(C)$ are necessary; they should not be confused with the prior of the hypothesis ($p(H)$, which is also needed. The probability of the hypothesis, given the data is:

$$p(H|\text{data}) = p(\text{data}|H)p(H)/p(\text{data}) \tag{12.2}$$

The "data' are the number of co-occurrences of U and C, and one will need $p(U)$ and $p(C)$ to in order to calculate the first term on the right hand side of this expression, that is the probability of obtaining this number if they have the degree of dependence specified by the hypothesis.

Where can this knowledge come from? We commonly assume, I think, that if the occurrences of U and C can be identified in the representation, then they can be counted; in fact this is a simpler job than counting their co-occurrence, which has got to be done anyway. From these counts the probabilities can be estimated, but this amounts to giving both jobs to the homunculus, which is the very thing we want to avoid.

Notice that the probabilities of the individual occurrences are required whatever hypothesis about association we want to test; $p(U)$ is needed to identify an association with C, or D, or E, or any combination of them, and so are $p(C)$, $p(D)$ etc. In contrast, we only need to estimate $p(U\&C)$ when testing that particular association. In a representation that facilitates the detection of new associations it is just as important to know the probabilities of the primitive events as it is to know about the actual moment of their occurrence, and giving access to these probabilities seems to be the first job we should take out of the hands of the homunculus. Doing this in a physiologically plausible way is not as difficult as it seems. It might be done by adjusting the threshold for a unit so that, averaged over a long period, it fires once in a particular period; then when it fires, it signals an event that has a probability of occurring once in that period. Alternatively, the number of impulses in the volley signalling an event might be an inverse function, such as $-\log p$, of its probability. Both of these would appear experimentally as forms of habituation, which is often observed in the neurons of sensory pathways.

Of course one still needs to detect co-occurrences and find out how often they happen, but if the probability of an event is implicit in the way it is signalled, this solves the problem of assembling at one locale in the brain all the information required to make an inference, for at any point in the brain reached by signals for U and signals for C, all this information is present and potentially available. The conclusion is that a representation designed to facilitate the detection of new associations should somehow signal, not just the occurrence of an event, but what the probability of that event having occurred is.

Three points may need clarifying. First we are assuming that the probability of occurrence of a feature can be estimated from its rate of occurrence over some period in the recent past. This would not always be justified, but in some cases it will be and to let the argument proceed let us confine ourselves here to these cases. Second, the features we shall be dealing with will usually have probabilities of occurrence well below half; this means that the predicted rate of occurrence of *joint* features will be low, and their expected number may be close to zero. Under these circumstances it becomes difficult to establish a *negative* association, and one must therefore look for joint features that occur *more often* than expected by chance. That's why we called them suspicious coincidences or clichés (Phillips *et al.*, 1984; Barlow, 1985), but the basic property is their non-accidental nature.

Finally it is sometimes suggested that statistical considerations are unimportant in learning because it often occurs with a very small number of trials, or even a single one. This is a misguided objection, because statistics are even more important when the numbers are small than when they are large. With large samples it is possible to obtain reliable results using statistically inefficient methods, but with small numbers efficient methods are essential.

12.5.1 Need for independence

Another highly desirable property of a representation that is to be used for detecting new associations is that the features represented should occur with statistical independence in the environment to which the system is adapted. Suppose we want to test whether the joint occurrence $C\&D$ is associated with U: to test the null hypothesis that they are not associated we now need $p(C\&D)$, just as we previously needed $p(C)$, in order that we can calculate the expected number of occurrences of $U\&C\&D$. This can be done if C and D are independent of each other, for then

$$p(U\&C\&D) = p(U)\, p(C)\, p(D) \qquad (12.3)$$

but this estimate may be seriously wrong if C is not independent of D. Markov random fields have had considerable success in modelling patterns of dependence (Geman & Geman, 1984; Marroquin, 1993), but it is surely impractical to store and have access to comprehensive estimates of the degrees of dependence among representational elements, simply because there are too many quantities involved, even among small groups of variables.

Notice however that we do not need each representational element to be independent of all others, which is obviously impractical. We only need independence between those representational elements among which conjunctions or other logical functions are to be tested. These elements are likely to be fairly close to each other in the cortical representation, so we only need independence between elements in each neighbourhood.

Are we actually able to detect new associations with logical functions of representational elements? For simple functions, surely we can, and so can most animals. We learn to stop at red traffic lights and not at green ones, for example. In this case one might suppose that there are different representational elements for red and green lights, but it would be a great restriction on the utility of a representation if this was always necessary before separate associations could be formed. Charlie Harris (1980) brought this out very nicely when discussing contingent adaptation, for he noted that almost any contingency that had ever been tested seemed to produce adaptive effects. How could this be, he said, if contingent adaptation required neurons specifically sensitive to each contingency? We might have neurons signalling *yellowness*, and perhaps *volkswagens*, but surely we cannot have neurons reserved for signalling *yellow volkswagens*!

This is an extremely important point because the advantage that is usually cited for distributed, as opposed to grandmother-cell, representations is their ability to utilize combinations of active elements, rather than single active elements, since vast numbers of these combinations are available. But this supposed advantage would vanish if one could not form associations with these combinations efficiently, either

1 SEPARATING REDUNDANCY (KNOWLEDGE) FROM INFORMATION (UNACCOUNTED-FOR MESSAGES)

2 FINDING REPRESENTATIONAL PRIMITIVES

3 MAKING THESE PRIMITIVES INDEPENDENT

4 IDENTIFYING NEW ASSOCIATIONS

5 MAP AND MODEL MAKING

6 MODELLING OTHER PEOPLE

7 MODELLING SOCIETY

8 TAKING ADVANTAGE OF GEOGRAPHIC, PHYSICAL AND SOCIAL KNOWLEDGE OF THE WORLD

Table 12.2 *Jobs the homunculus performs.*

because their prior probabilities were unavailable or grossly misleading, or for an additional reason to be outlined in the next section.

12.6 More jobs to take from the homunculus

The current hypothesis about the computational goal of the cortex has given an idea of some of the jobs the homunculus has to do when he looks at a sensory representation in one's head, but I think there are other tasks he does, and we shall have to understand these before we can get rid of him entirely. I shall conclude by sketching some of them.

12.6.1 Separating information and redundancy

Table 12.2 lists some of the jobs that we now think the homunculus performs, and which we should be able to take away from him. It starts with the task of separating redundancy (i.e. knowledge) from information (i.e. what cannot be explained by pre-existing knowledge). This is the job so far described and summarized in Figure 12.2. The next job listed, finding representational primitives, is part of this process and is listed separately because David Tolhurst and I recently tested the following prediction from the general hypothesis.

12.6.2 Finding good primitives

The presence of redundancy is shown by the elements of a representation not being independent of each other. One way to code to reduce this is to detect the presence of this mutual dependency when it occurs, and to signal this occurrence in the recoded representation; the presence of bilateral symmetry has been given as an example, and edges (see below) provide a simpler one. Notice that this tactic not only reduces redundancy, but also captures a high proportion of the input at low cost in terms of channel capacity, as described in Section 12.2.2. Thus the primitives used in a representation should be *suspicious coincidences* or *clichés* of the sensory diet that an animal is adapted to, ie they should be events that occur more often than would be expected from the frequencies of their constituent elements.

We have made measurements on natural images testing whether edges, which are certainly used by the brain as primitives, qualify as suspicious coincidences (Barlow & Tolhurst, 1992; Tolhurst & Barlow, 1993). We took a selection of digitized images and removed the correlations between pairs of points, averaged over the whole image, by the "whitening" process the result of which was shown in Figure 12.3; this leaves behind the image structures we are now interested in that occur at the borders of objects. The distribution of pixel values in such whitened images gives us the basis for the chance expectation of combinations of pixel values, and what the hypothesis says is that at the borders of objects we shall find combinations of pixel values that occur more frequently than this chance expectation.

Perhaps it's already obvious by inspection of the whitened figure that this is the case, for you would not expect to find by chance the rows of high or low values you can see in Figure 12.3. To confirm this we measured the distribution of the sum of 9 pixel values, either selected at random from all over the whitened image, or from a row of 9 adjacent positions. Figure 12.4 shows the result: the distributions are strikingly different. The sum of 9 randomly selected pixels gives the distribution of expected values, and the range is from about 1050 to 1300 on the horizontal scale, but as you can see values outside this range are very common for the sum of nine pixels in a row.

It is easy to show that these unexpected extreme values of the sum of pixels in a line occur at the borders of objects, and by looking at a varied selection of 15 images, and estimating the kurtosis excess for the sums in a line compared with randomly selected pixels we confirmed that the result is generally true. These facts vindicate the hypothesis that the features we use to represent an image are suspicious coincidences – at least in the case of the orientationally selective units of V1 – and suggests the general rule that good primitives may be patterns in images whose distributions show strong kurtosis.

12.6.3 *Ensuring independence*

The third job is to make the primitives independent of each other, at least locally in each neighbourhood of the representation. Ways of devising codes in which the

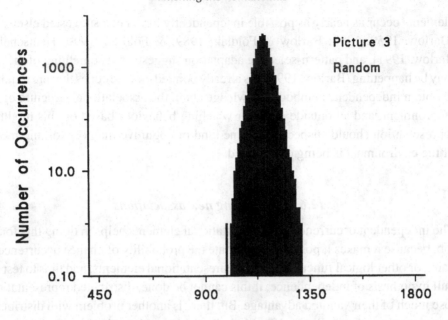

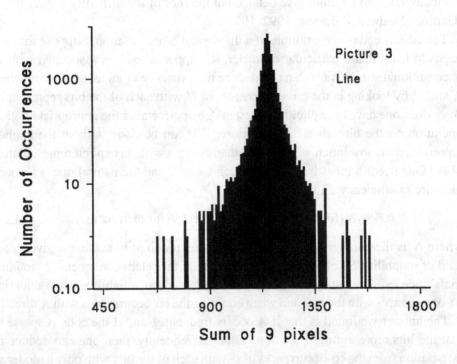

Fig. 12.4 Distributions of the sum of 9 randomly selected pixels (top), and 9 pixels in a line at 4 orientations (bottom). The lower distribution has an excess of extreme values – that is values unexpected on the basis of the distribution of individual pixel values (Tolhurst & Barlow 1993).

elements occur as nearly as possible independently have been suggested elsewhere (Barlow, 1959, 1989; Barlow & Földiák, 1989; & Földiák, 1990; Hentschel & Barlow, 1991), and pattern-selective adaptation suggests that something of the sort may be happening (Barlow, 1990). As already pointed out, the codes that are required to obtain independence embody knowledge about the associational structure of the environment, and an outside observer watching behaviour based on this modified representation should suspect that some kind of cognitive map or working model of the environment is being constructed.

12.6.4 Identifying new associations

The independent occurrence of representational elements helps in doing this fourth job, because it makes it possible to estimate the probability of chance occurrence of pairs, or other logical functions, of the representational elements, and thus to test the null hypothesis of independence; if this cannot be done, distributed representations lose much of their vaunted advantage. But there is another problem with distributed representations that A.R. Gardner-Medwin and I have been looking into; the work is incomplete and I cannot give details, but the root of the difficulty is easy to see (Gardner-Medwin & Barlow, 1992, 1993).

The ASCII code is an example of a distributed representation. Suppose that one needs to learn that a particular character, say upper case A, is associated with an unconditional stimulus U: Can one deduce the existence of an association between A and U by looking at the co-occurrrences of U with each of the bits representing A, or does one have to explicitly represent A by performing the appropriate logical operation on the bit values? Furthermore, if it can be done without the explicit representation, how much worse is this than doing it with an explicit representation of A? One needs a measure of "how much worse", and the natural one is Fisher's measure of efficiency $\mathcal{F}$, namely:

$$\mathcal{F} = N(\text{for fully efficient method})/N(\text{for method used}) \qquad (12.4)$$

where N is the number of trials, or sample size, required to achieve a given standard of reliability. So efficiency tells one directly the relative numbers of "training trials" needed to identify the association with a given reliability when counting co-occurrences with the bits and when counting the co-occurrences with A directly.

The answer we found is that if A occurs frequently, and if the code is sparse so that the bits representing it are "on" rather infrequently, then one can deduce an association from the co-occurrences of U with each of the bits with only a moderate loss of efficiency. Conversely if the code is not sparse (which is the case in the ASCII code itself), or if A occurs infrequently, then learning is very inefficient. What causes the loss of efficiency is the fact that, in a distributed representation, the representational elements are active for inputs other than the particular event of interest, and these excess occurrences increase the variance and hence necessitate a larger sample to obtain equal reliability. We think that the requirement for independence, and the difficulties of forming associations in distributed representations, are important and should be more widely recognized.

The remaining items in the table are included partly to serve as a reminder that we still have much to learn about the jobs we currently leave to the homunculus, and also because they raise issues of a rather different kind that are unlikely to be solved within the information processing paradigm.

12.6.5 Consciousness and the social role of the homunculus

So far the tasks considered for taking over from the homunculus are ones that do not seem to be beyond the scope of information processing and artificial intelligence, provided that they can be clearly and properly defined, but the situation changes when we come to the 6th and 7th items of Table 12.2. These tasks, the modelling of other people and society, raise new issues.

The homunculus looking at the image is a little man, not just an information processing device. Initially we may suppose that his skills in human communication simply provide our own consciousness with knowledge of the image, but by postulating a little man to do this, are we not recognising that our conscious experience involves more than the passive receipt of sensory impressions? Why do we postulate a little man to do it, rather than a little computer or other information-processing device? I think the homunculus is human because he has to put these sensory messages into a form that helps us share them with other humans. The role we are now considering is not just to process the representations of the outside world carried by the sensory maps in our own heads, but also to help us share the results of these analyses with other people. Furthermore, as an outsider with knowledge of other people, he introduces the results of other people's analyses into the interpretation of our own sensory representations. In other words, he translates the sensory representations in one's own mind into a form in which we can share it with other conscious minds. "Redness" is not just a raw feel, nor is it simply a processed sensory message, for to experience it as we do experience it requires a learning phase in which other humans have participated (Barlow, 1987, 1990). What the homunculus does goes beyond the realm of information processing, and is connected with the mysterious phenomenon of conscious experience. I think we shall probably need him in this role for a considerable time, but we may ultimately rid ourselves of him here too, if we can start to think of consciousness as the means by which humans enlarge the scope of their social intercommunication, rather than as a curious property of a single, isolated brain.

The overall conclusion is that we are beginning to banish the homunculus by subsuming some of his functions into our theories of perception, but we shall need to understand his role in consciousness and social communication before we can get rid of him altogether.

Acknowledgements

Some of the material in this article has previously appeared as "What is the computational goal of the neocortex?" in *Large Scale Neuronal Theories of the Brain*, Christof Koch (Ed.), MIT Press, 1993.

References

Allman, J. (1987). Evolution of the brain in primates. In *The Oxford Companion to the Mind Oxford*, ed. R. L. Gregory, Oxford University Press.

Atick, J.J. (1992). Could information theory provide an ecological theory of sensory processing? *Network*, **3**, 213-251.

Attneave, F. (1954). Informational aspects of visual perception. *Psychological Review*, **61**, 183-193.

Barlow, H.B. (1959). Sensory mechanisms, the reduction of redundancy, and intelligence. In *The Mechanization of Thought Processes*, pp. 535-539. London: Her Majesty's Stationery Office.

Barlow, H.B. (1972). Single units and sensation: a neuron doctrine for perceptual psychology? *Perception*, **1**, 371-394.

Barlow, H.B. (1974). Inductive inference, coding, perception, and language. *Perception*, **3**, 123-134.

Barlow, H.B. (1985a). The role of single neurons in the psychology of perception (Bartlett Lecture, 1984). *Q. J. Expl Psychology*, **37A**, 121-145.

Barlow, H.B. (1985b). Cerebral cortex as a model builder. In *Models of the Visual Cortex*, ed. D. Rose and V.G. Dobson, (pp. 37-46). New York: John Wiley & Sons Ltd.

Barlow, H.B. (1987). The biological role of consciousness. In *Mindwaves*, ed.C. Blakemore and S. Greenfield. Oxford: Basil Blackwell.

Barlow, H.B. (1989). Unsupervised learning. *Neural Computation*, **1**, 295-311.

Barlow, H.B. (1990). A theory about the functional role and synaptic mechanism of visual after-effects. In *Vision: Coding and Efficiency*, ed. C.B. Blakemore. Cambridge University Press.

Barlow, H.B. (1991). Vision tells you more than "What is Where". In *Representations of Vision*, ed. A. Gorea, pp. 319-329. Cambridge University Press.

Barlow, H.B. & Földiák, P. (1989). Adaptation and decorrelation in the cortex. In *The Computing Neuron*, ed. R. Durbin, C. Miall and G. Mitchison, pp. 54-72. Wokingham, England: Addison-Wesley.

Barlow, H.B. & Reeves, H.B. (1979). The versatility and absolute efficiency of detecting mirror symmetry in random dot displays. *Vision Research*, **19**, 783-793.

Barlow, H.B. & Tolhurst, D.J. (1992). Why do you have edge detectors? In 1992 Optical Society of America Annual Meeting, 1992 Technical Digest Series Volume 23, pp. 172. Albuquerque, New Mexico: Optical Society of America, Washington DC.

Bartlett, F.C. (1932). *Remembering: A Study in Experimental and Social Psychology.* Cambridge: University Press.

Craik, K.J.W. (1943). *The Nature of Explanation.* Cambridge University Press.

Daugman, J.G. (1989). Entropy reduction and decorrelation in visual coding by oriented neural receptive fields. *IEEE Transactions on Biomedical Engineering,* **36** (1), 107-114.

Dodgson, C.L.(alias Lewis Carroll) (1876). *The Hunting of the Snark.*

Elliot Smith, G. (1924). *The Evolution of Man.* Oxford University Press.

Fisher, R.A. (1925). *Statistical Methods for Research Workers.* Edinburgh: Oliver and Boyd.

Földiák, P. (1990). Forming sparse representations by local anti-Hebbian learning. *Biological Cybernetics,* **64**, 165-170.

Gardner-Medwin, A.R. & Barlow, H.B. (1992). The effect of sparseness in distributed representations on the detectability of associations betweeen sensory events. *Journal of Physiology,* London, **452** 282P.

Gardner-Medwin, A.R. & Barlow, H.B. (1993). The factors determining the efficiency of associative learning. (In preparation),

Geman, S. & Geman, D. (1984). Stochastic relaxation, Gibbs distributions and the Bayesian restoration of images. *IEEE Trans, PAMI-6,* 721-741.

Glass, L. (1969). Moirée effect from random dots. *Nature,* **223**, 578-580.

Harris, C.S. (1980). Insight or out of sight? Two examples of perceptual plasticity in the human adult. In *Visual Coding and Adaptability,* ed. C. S. Harris, pp. 95-149. New Jersey: Laurence Erlbaum Associates.

Hentschel, H.G.E. & Barlow, H.B. (1991). Minimum entropy coding with Hopfield networks. *Network,* **2**, 135-148.

Herrick, C.J. (1926). *Brains of Rats and Men.* Chicago: University of Chicago Press.

Hubel, D.H. & Wiesel, T.N. (1970). The period of susceptibility to the physiological effects of unilateral eye closure in kittens. *Journal of Physiology (London),* **206**, 419-436.

Humphrey, N.K. (1976). The social function of intellect. In *Growing points in ethology,* ed. P.P. Bateson and R. A. Hinde. Cambridge University Press.

Jerison, H.J. (1991). Brain size and the evolution of mind (The fifty-ninth James Arthur Lecture on the Evolution of the Human Mind 1989). New York: American Museum of Natural History.

Kosslyn, S.M. & Koenig, O. (1992). *Wet Mind: The New Cognitive Neuroscience.* New York: The Free Press, Macmillan.

Longuet-Higgins, H.C., Willshaw, D.J. & Buneman, O.P. (1970). Theories of associative recall. *Quarterly Review of Biophysics,* **3**, 223-244.

MacKay, D.M. (1955). The epistemological problem for automata. In *Automata Studies,* ed. C.E. Shannon and J. McCarthy, pp. 235-250. Princeton: Princeton University Press.

Maloney, R.K., Mitchison, G.J. & Barlow, H.B. (1987). The limit to the detection of Glass patterns in the presence of noise. *Journal of the Optical Society of America A,* **4**, 2336-2341.

Marroquin, J.L. (1993). Deterministic interactive particle models for image processing and computer graphics. *CVGIP: Graphical Models and Information Processing,* **55** (5), 408-417.

Movshon, J.A. & Van Sluyters, R.C. (1981). Visual neural development. *Ann. Rev. Psychol.,* **32**, 477-522.

Mumford, D. (1991). On the computational architecture of the neocortex. 1. The role of the thalamo-cortical loop. *Biological Cybernetics*, **65**, 135-145.

Mumford, D. (1992). On the computational architecture of the neocortex II. The role of cortico-cortical loops. *Biological Cybernetics*, **66**, 241-251

Pece, A.E.C. (1992). Redundancy reduction of a Gabor representation: a possible computational role for feedback from primary visual cortex to lateral geniculate nucleus. In *Artificial Neural Networks 2*, ed. I. Aleksander and J. Taylor, pp. 865-868. Amsterdam: Elsevier Science Publishers.

Phillips, C.G., Zeki, S. & Barlow, H.B. (1984). Localisation of function in the cerebral cortex. *Brain*, **107**, 327-361.

Shannon, C.E. (1951). Prediction and entropy of printed English. *Bell System Technical Journal*, **30**, 50-64.

Shannon, C.E. & Weaver, W. (ed.) (1949). *The Mathematical Theory of Communication*. Urbana: Univ. Illinois Press.

Thatcher, A.R. (1983). How many people have ever lived on earth? In *44th session of the International Statistical Institute*, Vol. 2, pp. 841-843. Madrid.

Tolhurst, D.J. & Barlow, H.B. (1993). The kurtotic statistical distribution of pixel values at edges. (In preparation)

Tolman, E.C. (1948). Cognitive maps in rats and men. *Psychological Review*, **55**, 189-208.

Ullman, S. (1993). Sequence-seeking and counter streams: a model for information processing in the cerebral cortex. In *Large Scale Neuronal Theories of the Brain*, (ed.) C. Koch. MIT Press.

Van Essen, D.C. & Maunsell, J.H.R. (1980). Two-dimensional maps of the visual cortex. *Journal of Comparative Neurology*, **191**, 255-281.

Watanabe, S. (1960). Information-theoretical aspects of Inductive and Deductive Inference. *I.B.M. Journal of Research and Development*, **4**, 208-231.

Commentaries

Chapter 6:
Ideal observers, real observers,
and the return of Elvis

RON RENSINK

Knill, Kersten & Mamassian (Chapter 6) provide an interesting discussion of how the Bayesian formulation can be used to help investigate human vision. In their view, computational theories can be based on an ideal observer that uses Bayesian inference to make optimal use of available information. Four factors are important here: the image information used, the output structures estimated, the priors assumed (i.e. knowledge about the structure of the world), and the likelihood function used (i.e. knowledge about the projection of the world onto the sensors). Knill *et al.* argue that such a framework not only helps *analyze* a perceptual task, but can also help investigators to *define* it. Two examples are provided (the interpretation of surface contour and the perception of moving shadows) to show how this approach can be used in practice.

As the authors admit, most (if not all) perceptual processes are ill-suited to a "strong" Bayesian approach based on a single consistent model of the world. Instead, they argue for a "weak" variant that assumes Bayesian inference to be carried out in modules of more limited scope. But how weak is "weak"? Are such approaches suitable for only a few relatively low-level tasks, or can they be applied more generally? Could a weak Bayesian approach, for example, explain how we would recognize the return of Elvis Presley?

The formal modelling of human perception

To help get a fix on things, it is useful to examine the fate of an earlier attempt to formalize human perception: the application of information theory. It was once hoped that this theory – a close cousin of the Bayesian formulation – would provide a way to uncover information-handling laws that were largely independent of physical implementation. In this approach, the human nervous system was assumed to have communication channels of limited bandwidth; if data transfer were sufficiently slow, delays in reaction times would be measurable. By mapping out delays as a function of the probabilities of alternative inputs (i.e. the information they contained), it was hoped that the channel bandwidths could be determined, along with the amount of information associated with each stimulus (e.g. Gregory, 1986; Pierce, 1980).

As it turned out, information theory did not live up to these hopes. Although in principle it provided a general framework in which to explore information handling, in practice it was relevant only for highly-constrained tasks where relatively little practice was allowed, where stimuli were simple, and where strategy could not be used (e.g. Gregory, 1986).

What went wrong? In retrospect, it is clear that at least three factors were at play:

(i) The basic units in the perceiver were ill-defined. Not only were these units entirely internal, but they were unstable: new, more efficient units could be learned with practice (i.e. "chunking").

(ii) The probabilities attached to these units were ill-defined.

If something occurred only once, what probability would it be assigned? How would probabilities be updated when new input was received? Frequencies might be used, but under what condition were the counts "reset"?

(iii) The structures actually used could not be controlled. Although the members of the input set might be clearly defined, attentional effects could restrict the units being used or even bring in extraneous ones (Gregory, 1986).

Looked at more generally, it is evident that formalisms such as those based on information theory (or on Bayesian inference) implicitly constrain a process, since its structure must conform to the structure of the formalism if relevance is to be maintained (see e.g. Pierce, 1980). In particular, at least three conditions must be met:

(i) The basic terms can be reliably mapped to structures in the perceiver.

(ii) The relations between the terms (including probabilistic ones) match the relations between the corresponding structures in the perceiver.

(iii) The resulting structures are independent of all other factors (i.e. independent of context).

From the ideal to the real

Knill *et al.* manage to avoid many of the difficulties that plagued information-theoretic approaches, since unstable subjective quantities are now replaced with stable objective ones. But this alone does not guarantee the suitability of their ideal observer, for a real observer is constrained by much more than just available information. First of all, *physical* limitations on available time and space constrain the amount of information that can be stored and transformed. Next, *biological* factors (both developmental and phylogenetic) constrain process formation – it might not be possible to have priors and likelihoods wired into the neural hardware, much less learn them from experience. Finally, *ecological* factors limit the kinds of tasks that are carried out. It is only important that an organism do the right thing; this does not necessarily require Bayesian inference.

Given these considerations, what kinds of perceptual process might be suited to an ideal-observer analysis? To begin with, "ideal" inputs and outputs must correspond to structures in the real observer. But such correspondences can be difficult to establish. For example, the external world might serve as its own representation, being sampled whenever detailed information is required (O'Regan, 1992). If the return of Elvis were recognized in this way (e.g. by verifying a few key image properties), it would be difficult to determine exactly what was involved. Furthermore, the combinatorial explosion of possible objects and events (see e.g. Tsotsos, 1987) means that – for the most part – increasingly complex structures are increasingly rare. If input and output structures are formed via learning, large differences could then arise between observers with different histories. Space limitations might also force rarely-used structures to be discarded, leading to history-dependent differences within observers. The existence of stable, well-defined structures common to all observers is therefore not guaranteed, especially at higher processing levels.

It can also be difficult to determine the kind of inference actually used. Optimal information usage does not necessarily imply Bayesian inference: other techniques exist (such as those based on signal-detection theory), and these cannot be easily (if at all) reconciled with Bayesian inference (Gigerenzer *et al.*, 1989). Thus, for example, it would be necessary to show that recognizing the return of Elvis does not simply require Elvis-detection of some kind, but requires determining the posterior probability of this event. And because Bayesian priors are based on event frequencies, it would also be necessary to explain how priors would be assigned to a once-only event never observed before. Furthermore, there is also the matter of computational resources. The lowest levels of visual processing involve the detection of photons, a relatively simple task best analyzed using signal-detection theory (e.g. Barlow, 1962). Indeed, detection tasks are common in low-level vision, and it may be that the time and space limitations typical of these levels prohibit the use of (more sophisticated) Bayesian inference.

A final consideration concerns the priors. Given some well-defined prior probability of encountering Elvis, this value would certainly be higher in Tennessee than in Finland. More generally, priors are often functions of several variables – indeed, Knill *et al.* use such a "conditional" prior in their analysis of contour interpretation. Unless the prior is a true invariant, information will be thrown away by use of a context-free prior (essentially an average over all conditions). But using a context-dependent prior requires knowing the context. If this involves other inferred properties, further inference will be required, which in turn might require still more inference, and so on. This could lead to a set of strongly-coupled equations in which nothing can be determined until everything has been determined. The application of ideal observers must therefore be limited to tasks involving priors that are invariant, or at least that depend upon each other in a non-recursive way.

Problems and possibilities

Insofar as a task avoids ill-defined structures and resource-limited processes, and has well-defined priors that are relatively invariant (at least under some set of conditions), there is a chance that it can be analyzed by a weak Bayesian approach. The tasks discussed by Knill *et al.* are exactly of this type. Subjects in their experiments are given ample time to respond, and the structures involved are relatively simple ones (transparent or painted surfaces, shadows) that are meaningful and that the subjects have often seen before.

But notice that complications arise even here. For example, even the task of interpreting surface contours is too complex to be handled in its most general form. Instead, analysis is restricted to a few "modes" corresponding to special contexts that are particularly easy to handle. Knill *et al.* make the important point that their approach allows generality to be gradually increased, but it is not clear how much generalization can be done in practice. The authors also show how knowledge about the priors can be gradually refined by use of "well-formed" constraints, but again, it is not clear how far this can be taken. Their approach therefore runs the risk not only of being unsuitable for processes at the upper and lower ends of the processing stream, but also of being unsuitable for many interesting processes in between.

However, all is not lost. Although time and space limitations may intrude upon some processes, these are not always arbitrary "tricks", but rather can be graceful adaptations that make good use of available resources (see e.g. Enns & Rensink, 1991). Many take the form of rapid processes specialized for particular modes of the priors. Thus, although it might not always be possible to generalize computational models in the way envisioned by Knill *et al.*, it might still be possible to make use of their framework. In particular, a Bayesian analysis of a world might uncover modes corresponding to common contexts (e.g. direction of lighting from above) which could then be used as bases for the specialized processes. It is important to notice the shift of emphasis here – specialized problems (and processes) would no longer be convenient methodological stages, but would be true entities in their own right. In other words, ontology would recapitulate methodology.

Similar considerations apply to the variations in individual observers. These variations could be captured in a natural way by relatively coarse devices, such as the monotonicity relationship used by Knill *et al.* in their model of contour interpretation, or the lattice framework of Jepson & Richards (1992). Again, this coarseness would not just be a methodological convenience, but would reflect the true variability of the process (due to accidents of history, variations in values, etc.). Note that this variability could be more than simple variation in the values of priors and likelihoods – it could also include variation in the structures used, or the procedures applied. Taking this view, of course, does not rule out a progressive refinement of priors. But such refinement will often stop well short of a quantitative formulation. A systematic comparison of the variations present at different levels might then serve as a new source of insight into the relation between the observer and its environment.

References

Barlow, H.B. (1962). A method of determining the overall quantum efficiency of visual discriminations. *Journal of Physiology*, **160**, 155-168.

Enns, J. T. & Rensink, R. A. (1991). Preattentive recovery of three-dimensional orientation from line drawings. *Psychological Review*, **98**, 335-351.

Gigerenzer, G., Swijtink, Z., Porter, T., Daston, L., Beatty, J., & Krüger, L. (1989). *The Empire of Chance*. Cambridge University Press.

Gregory, R.L. (1986). Whatever happened to information theory? In *Odd Perceptions*, R.L. Gregory. London: Routledge.

Jepson, A. & Richards, W. (1992). A Lattice Framework for Integrating Vision Modules. *IEEE Transactions on Systems, Man, and Cybernetics*, **22**, 1087-1096.

O'Regan, J.K. (1992). Solving the "real" mysteries of visual perception: The world as an outside memory. *Canadian Journal of Psychology*, **46**, 461-488.

Pierce, J.R. (1980). *An Introduction to Information Theory: Symbols, Signals, and Noise.* 2nd edition. New York: Dover.

Tsotsos, J.K. (1987). A "Complexity Level" Analysis of Vision. *International Journal of Computer Vision*, **1**, 346-355.

Chapter 7:
Shape from texture: Ideal observers and human psychophysics

DAVID KNILL

Introduction

In their chapter on the perception of surface shape from texture, Blake *et al.* describe the direct application of a Bayesian paradigm to psychophysics. Using statistical methods, they derive limits on the reliability with which different texture features support the performance of a shape estimation task. These limits provide summary measures of the information content of the different features for the specified task (estimating the elongation of an elliptical cylinder). The authors use comparisons of human performance with these measures to make inferences about which features of a texture pattern human subjects use as cues to perform the task, and by extension, about which texture features the human visual system commonly uses to perceive surface shape from texture. The approach fits generally into the ideal observer paradigm which has been historically used to investigate issues of sensory coding (Barlow, 1980; Kersten, 1990) and is just now being extended to higher level perceptual function (Braje *et al.*, 1994; Harris & Parker, 1992; Liu *et al.*, 1994). I will therefore focus my commentary generally on the application of the ideal observer paradigm to perceptual studies.

In so much as it relies on explicit calculations of stimulus information, the ideal observer approach to psychophysics pushes the Bayesian paradigm to its logical limits as a way of doing psychophysics. Ideal observers provide an absolute performance benchmark for a given perceptual task. As such, they effectively specify the information available in the stimuli for doing the task. By comparing human performance to that of an ideal observer, one can compute a measure of the "efficiency" with which human subjects use stimulus information to perform a task. The efficiency measure provides a common currency for comparing subjects' performance across different psychophysical tasks, conditions and stimuli. Moreover, it can be used to discount effects which are due more to changes in stimulus information than internal visual processing. Using ideal observers as the basis for computing common measures of performance can add rigor to the design and analysis of experiments on higher-level perceptual function (see for example Liu *et al.*, 1994, for an application of this approach to object recognition); however, limited to this application, it remains essentially a data analysis technique. The work in Blake *et al.*'s chapter points to a much richer use of ideal observers – as a tool for directly assessing the visual information used by the visual system for perception. Since they did not do so in their chapter, I will discuss the ideal observer approach in the general context of studying higher-level perception and highlight some of its advantages and shortcomings.

Variance, bias and information

The term "Bayesian," when attached to a theory of perception, makes one immediately think of perceptual bias, since Bayes rule specifies how to incorporate prior assumptions about the world into a statistical inference. Thus Bayesian theorists often use phenomenally apparent biases like the tendency to see shapes as flatter than they are as arguments for the usefulness of a Bayesian approach (see for example, Chapter 4 by Yuille & Bülthoff). This reflects the inclination of many perception researchers to study the modal properties of perceptual performance - "Why do we see a Necker cube as a cube?" Much less emphasis has been placed on studying the variability of perception - "Why is our percept of the shape of a Necker cube so stable, while shape percepts of distorted cubes are fuzzy?"; yet such questions interesting in their own right and have important implications for theories of perceptual performance (see Chapter 3 by Richards *et al.* for a detailed discussion of this point).

In contrast to research in high-level perception, work on sensory coding has placed a great deal of emphasis on the variability of subject performance, a natural result of the types of questions considered, which revolve around not only the mechanisms of sensory coding, but also the resolution with which image information is coded. Ideal observer analysis reflects the focus on variance, being in one form or other a computation of lower limits on the variability with which psychophysical tasks can be performed; that is, ideal observers provide a way to measure the reliability of stimulus information for performing a psychophysical task. As suggested above, variability, or reliability, is also of fundamental importance for higher level perception, and I will argue that it provides the phenomenal tap into many of the questions which must be answered to build comprehensive functional theories of perception. These include, but are not limited to,

- What image features does the visual system use as information for perception?
- What world properties are perceived?
- What priors does the visual system use for perceptual inference?
- How does low-level visual coding of image information constrain higher-level perception?

Blake *et al.*'s chapter deals with the question of what image "features" (global properties of texture patterns) are used for the perception of shape from texture. Different image features provide information of varying reliability about the world; therefore, perceptual variability is of significant importance for understanding which image features the visual system uses as information for perception and how it combines the information from different features. Comparing subject variability in perceptual tasks with that of ideal observers designed to use different image features can shed light on such questions. Blake *et al.* show that the reliability with which subjects estimate the elongation of an elliptical cylinder is better than that supported by the cue of texture density alone. In particular, they show that the variance of subjects' estimates of elongation was often lower than the lower limits defined by the performance of an ideal observer which uses only density information. The result indicates that subjects used more information than just that provided by texture density to perform the task. Furthermore, in some conditions, subjects performed with an astoundingly high efficiency (they quote 25-100% efficiencies for using density and compression information together).

The inference made by Blake *et al.* regarding human use of texture information is the simplest possible within the ideal observer paradigm. If human subjects perform better than some putative ideal, then one can infer that they are using stimulus information not provided to the ideal, or that they have, or gain knowledge of, constraints on the stimuli which the ideal is not given access to. Thus, Blake *et al.* argue that because human subjects "beat" the density ideal, they must use some other source of information for performing the experimental task, and texture compression is the only other reliable information available. Liu *et al.* (1994) make a similar inference when they show that human performance on a 3D object recognition task is better than that of an ideal observer constrained to use only 2D image information.

The style of experimental inference used by Blake, et. al. and Liu, et. al., looking for conditions in which human observers outperform information-limited ideal observers, is quite strong, but very restricted. The domain of tasks for which human observers will be able to beat even information-limited ideal observers is, I expect, rather small. More subtle forms of analysis, in which the patterns of behavior of ideal and human observers are compared, are needed to make ideal observer analysis generally useful to the psychophysicist. Blake *et al.* explicitly recognize this when they show how texture cue informativeness varies as a function of field of view and suggest comparing patterns of human and ideal performance as a function of field of view. They do not, however, specify how to use such a comparison in making inferences about perceptual processing.

The degree to which ideal observer analysis is useful to the perceptual psychologist depends critically on either the development of new tools for such detailed analyses of experimental results, or the extension of existing tools to the analysis of high-level perception (e.g. the intrinsic noise analysis of Burgess (1981) and others). To give a flavor of what such tools might look like, I will briefly, and qualitatively, describe a simple experimental technique which could be applied to problems like shape from texture. Consider the problem of how the visual system weights the information provided by different visual cues for surface shape. One way to study this problem would be to measure how human performance varies the reliability of the individual cues varies. In particular, through simulations of an ideal observer, one can systematically manipulate the reliability of the cues (without necessarily making them unnatural) and look at the effects of these manipulations on subjects' performance. Thus, for example, one could make the density cue more or less reliable independently of other texture cues by varying the regularity of spacing of the texture elements. At the extreme, a finding that human performance changed only with changes in reliability of one cue but not others would suggest that cue was the dominant source of information used by subjects for a task. Intermediate results would require more quantitative analysis of how human performance varied relative to the different ideal observers for the different cues.

Sources of differences between ideal and human performance

Of fundamental importance in drawing inferences from comparisons between ideal and human performance is an understanding of the factors which would "pull" human performance away form that of an ideal observer. I will briefly consider some of these factors, and in the process, hopefully suggest interesting ways to apply ideal observers to the study of perception. An ideal observer for the estimation of a world property like surface slant requires a specification of what image features the observer has access to, how the world property maps to those image features (the likelihood function) and some prior knowledge about the simulated world from which the stimuli were created. Together these specify a posterior probability distribution for the world property given the image data, which forms the basis of making an optimal psychophysical judgment. The combination of these things determines the uncertainty with which an ideal observer performs a task. Similarly, as we have described it, Bayesian models of human perception are descriptions of the image features used by the human visual system for a perceptual task, what the visual system assumes about how those features are formed as a function of some world property, or properties, and the prior knowledge about the world which is implicitly or explicitly built into perceptual processing (see Chapter 6 by Knill *et al.*). These factors, and others to be described below, determine the reliability with which humans can perform a psychophysical task. Human performance can differ from that of an ideal observer because of differences in any of these areas; that is, because of mismatches between the definition of an ideal observer and analogous characteristics of human visual processing. The point behind ideal observer analysis is to isolate and characterize the factors which determine human uncertainty in the performance of a psychophysical task; therefore, understanding where and why differences between human and ideal performance can occur is fundamental to using an ideal observer analysis.

Differences in the image features used

Human performance can differ from an ideal observer's because human subjects use more or less image information than is provided to the ideal observer. Blake *et al.* base their methodology on this simple observation. They purposefully build ideals which use partial stimulus information as a way of probing what information the visual system uses. They found that human subjects actually outdid one of these information-limited ideals, indicating that humans use either more information than just texture density for their task or don't use texture density at all, but rather use more reliable information (e.g. compression). The inference regarding the use of compression information for their task must be qualified, however, because subjects may have used a source of information which they did not account for in any of their ideal observer calculations: the shapes of texture elements. They purport to have removed this cue by randomizing the shapes of texture elements (presumably length and width of rectangles), but I have found in my own development of ideal observers for the perception of shape from texture that even with a large variation in the shapes of texture elements on a surface (on the order of the 2-to-1 figure that the authors use), the shapes of the imaged elements provide a highly reliable cue to surface shape. While the authors avoid using this information because it requires making restrictive (and seemingly arbitrary) assumptions about the distribution of element shapes, there is nothing to say that the visual system does not make such assumptions in order to use element shape to perceive surface shape from texture (and, as it turns out, the assumptions don't have to be that restrictive). Thus, the data presented in the chapter only suggest that the visual system uses more than just density to perceive shape from texture, but it may be relying on texture element shape and not on the particular form of compression the authors describe (though change in shape is a form of compression). Moreover, subjects' use of this cue would partially explain the inordinately high efficiencies found relative to the authors' proposed compression ideal.

Another form of under-utilization of image information involves inefficient spatial integration of information. The ideal observers derived for shape from texture use the information provided by each and every texture element in the stimulus displays. Human performance, however, is undoubtedly limited to some extent by constraints on the spatial integration of such information. Such effects are further compounded by the use of a global shape measure (a necessary experimental condition), so that, even if the human visual system were to use all the texture information available for local estimates of surface shape, the task requires integrating these local estimates into an estimate of a global shape parameter, a process which may lead to loss of efficiency. Ideal observer analysis is well-suited to studying the limits on spatial integration of information. Work on symmetry detection by Barlow (1980) is one example of this, and Blake *et al.* make similar suggestions for the study of texture integration in large field of view displays of textured, planar surfaces.

Finally, it is often impossible to completely eliminate contradictory cues for performing a task. In the texture experiments, for example, surface shading indicated a flat surface. Typically, ideal observers do not take these cues into account. Blake *et al.* discount the biasing effects of such cues (and other, non-image based biases) by rescaling their variance measures by the bias determined from mean estimates of cylinder elongation. Such a rescaling is appropriate under limiting assumptions about the nature of the unaccounted for information and biases; for example, that the likelihood function associated with shading is Gaussian, when expressed as a function of elongation. For other tasks, however, one has to be careful to study the potential, non-linear affects of such information or biases. Ideal discrimination performance, for example, would be reduced in the presence of flatness cues or a strong probabilistic bias towards flatness, though it would be independent of a constant additive response bias. Parceling out the sources of uncertainty in human performance requires careful consideration of effects such as this.

Differences in prior assumptions

Human performance may differ from an ideal's because the visual system assumes a different prior then is built into an ideal observer (and presumably also used to generate experimental stimuli). Thus, for the case of texture, the performance of the ideal observers derived in the chapter may degrade markedly as one changes the assumed texture statistics away from those used in the derivations. If human performance does not similarly degrade, one might infer that the human visual system employs different, or less restrictive assumptions about texture (e.g. homogeneity vs. isotropy). Thus, for example, ideal observer performance will degrade if stimuli are used which have orientation biases (since the ideal observer assumes no bias), but human performance may not if the human visual system simultaneously estimates texture orientation bias and surface shape; that is, if the human visual system assumes a more general prior on the structure of textures. This naturally suggests the possibility of using ideal observer analysis to investigate the nature of the priors assumed by the human visual system.

Other sources of differences between human and ideal performance which may be generally categorized under the label of prior assumptions are experiment-specific constraints on stimuli which are not incorporated in an ideal observer, generally because they are created by pragmatic considerations. Subjects could improve their performance relative to that of an ideal simply by learning such constraints. Typically, an experimenter will do all in his or her power to minimize the possibility of subjects' using such constraints. A close look at the experimental methodology of

Blake *et al.* suggests this may have played in their experiment (though we one could not say one way or the other without careful control experiments). Their ideals all assume a uniform prior on cylindrical elongation, yet they only test at four elongations. Such a coarse sampling of the elongation space leaves open the possibility of learning a categorization strategy for doing the task, which would tend to lower the variance of subjects' estimates. This could help explain the high efficiencies, but would also put into question the inferences the authors make about texture cue utilization.

Differences in what is measured and what is perceived

Human performance on a task is naturally dependent on how "natural" a task it is for them to perform. In the context of estimating scene parameters, this generalizes to the issue of what representations of scene parameters are derived perceptually. I have alluded to this issue as it relates to the texture work of Blake *et al.* in the discussion of spatial integration. There, I suggested the possibility that subjects may have had to perform the task by integrating local measurements of surface shape to arrive at a judgment of cylindrical elongation. I do not mean by this to take a stand in favor of local vs. global shape representations, but merely to point out how this issue can be confounded in studies like this. The extent to which perceptual representations differ from those required to perform a psychophysical task determine in part the added uncertainty subjects will show in performing the task. The notion of how much a perceptual representation differs from an abstract parameter we use to characterize a property of the world is difficult to pin down, and while I don't have a clear definition, one would intuitively think of it in terms of the added processing of the perceptual representation which must be performed to do a task. Blake, *et al.* might argue that they sidestep this issue by matching the perceived shape of a textured cylinder to that of a cylinder with a more complete assortment of image cues (in particular, stereo). Thus, subjects are matching two internal representations rather than one internal representation with an objective measure of a shape parameter. The possibility exists, however, that the visual system maintains multiple shape representations and the form of representation derived from texture information differs from that derived from information like stereo, which would in itself tend to increase subjects' uncertainty in performing the matching task. Perhaps more important is the fact that the ideal observer has a highly constrained model of shape on which to base its judgments, and one would expect judgments based on a less constrained model, as may exist perceptually, to be more uncertain.

Considering the question of what tasks the visual system is designed to perform and what representations it constructs leads to another potential use of ideal observer analysis. Arguably, tasks on which human subjects are more efficient relative to an ideal better reflect the natural functions of the visual system than tasks on which they are less efficient. Thus, for example, one might find, using the same class of stimuli, that subjects are more efficient at discriminating some shape parameters than others (say, orientation vs. elongation of an ellipsoid), suggesting the relative perceptual salience of those parameters. One has to be careful, however, in making such inferences, as other factors may determine performance; for example, image coding uncertainty might degrade the information relevant to estimating one parameter more than the information relevant to estimating another parameter.

Image noise

Ideal observers derived for tasks like shape from texture typically do not take into account the effects of image noise; that is, the uncertainty induced by early visual coding of the image information relevant to performing a task. In the case of shape from texture, this might be the uncertainty in coding the positions and orientations of texture elements. While the ideal observers derived by Blake *et al.* do not take this into account, we should note that noise would worsen ideal observer performance; thus, their efficiency measures are lower limits, and their inference about the use of compression information is made stronger by recognizing that the ideal observers they derive are not affected by image noise.

Considering the effects of image coding uncertainty raises the possibility, suggested by Geisler (1989), of extending the ideal observer approach to explicitly modeling image coding uncertainty within ideal observer derivations in order to "subtract" its effects from human performance, leaving a measure of performance which better reflects the characteristics of higher-level perceptual function. Suppose, for example, that one had a good model of the uncertainty in texture element orientation which is inherent in the image code, at the level of LGN. The differences between human performance and that of an ideal which takes this uncertainty into account would provide a better reflection of the effects of higher-level processing than comparisons with the type of ideal computed in Blake *et al.*'s chapter. The problem with this approach, however, is that we do not have a good enough physiological model of image coding beyond the retinal level (and our knowledge is not complete there) to build such an ideal. An alternative would be to use psychophysical data on the discriminability of image features such as line orientation to construct an approximate model of coding uncertainty for use in an ideal observer formulation. Geisler has used such an approach for the study of visual search Geisler, 1989), but it remains to be seen how useful it will be. At first blush, it seems fraught with difficulties, since "low-level" psychophysical data of the sort described does not necessarily isolate low-level sensory coding constraints, but reflects high-level processing constraints as well. It would only be useful to the extent that the coding constraints dominate for the tasks used.

Conclusion

Many factors are confounded in determining the efficiency of human performance, making interpretation of simple comparisons between ideal observers and human subjects a complex affair. The technical toolbox available for separating the effects of these multiple factors is still relatively empty, but this is largely because little effort has been made in applying ideal observer analysis to high-level perceptual behavior. I am hopeful that a concerted effort to develop novel techniques applicable to the types of problems described in this commentary will provide the tools necessary to broaden the domain of application of the ideal observer paradigm within perception.

References

Barlow, H. (1980). The absolute efficiency of perceptual decisions, *Philosophical Transactions of the Royal Society London*, **290**, 71-82.

Burgess, A. E., Wagner, R. F., Jennings, R. J. and H. B. Barlow (1981). Efficiency of human visual signal discrimination, *Science*, **214** (4516), 93-94.

Kersten, D. (1990). Statistical limits to image understanding, in *Vision: Coding and Efficiency*, ed. C. Blakemore. Cambridge University Press.

Liu, Z., Knill, D. and Kersten, D. (1995). Object classification for human and ideal observers, *Vision Research*, **35** (4), 549-569.

Harris, J. M. and Parker, A. J. (1992). Efficiency of stereopsis in random-dot stereograms, *Journal of the Optical Society of America A*, **9**, 14-24.

Braje, W., Tjan, B. and Legge, G. (1994). *Vision Research*, in press.

Geisler, W. S. (1989) Sequential ideal- observer analysis of visual discriminations, *Psychological Review*, **96**, 267-314.

Chapter 8:
A computational theory for binocular stereopsis

DAVID KNILL

In Chapter 8 Peter Belhumeur elegantly applies a principled Bayesian approach to a "real" problem in visual perception, the reconstruction of surface shape and depth from binocular information. His detailed construction of an imaging model and progressive refinement of prior models for surfaces in the world demonstrates the usefulness of the Bayesian approach for making explicit the assumptions about the world which one necessarily incoprorates in models of visual function. This allows us to concentrate, not simply on shallow measures of his model's performance, but on a deeper analysis of the nature of the "world" for which his model works and the differences between that world and the real world, or, for those interested in human visual processing, the world which the human visual system implicitly assumes in its performance of shape from stereo. In keeping with the spirit of the chapter, I will focus on the priors which Belhumeur uses in his theory and on the representations of shape he assumes the model must estimate.

Local constraints

As Belhumeur points out in the chapter, the algorithms he studies for solving the shape- from-stereo problem fall broadly into the category of energy minimization models commonly used for similar surface reconstruction problems in vision (Blake & Zisserman, 1987; Poggio *et al.*, 1985). These models are typically motivated by their phsyical analogues; constrained minimization of tensile energy in thin membranes, thin metal plates plates and so on (Terzopolous, 1986). These analogies provide insight primarily into the dynamics of the minimization process from which solutions are derived. They do not provide a direct means for analyzing why the constraints they embody are a good model of surfaces in the world (one would be mistaken, for example, to assume that they correspond directly to worlds made up of thin membrane or metal plate surfaces). Rather, relations between the energy functions and the prior assumptions they embody are made in an ad hoc way by noting that the functions impose some form of smoothness on solutions; for example, a function which is the sum of squared derivatives (thin-membrane model) punishes large changes in surface depth and clearly biases the solution toward fronto-parallel surfaces. An energy function which is the sum of squared second derivatives punishes large changes in a viewer-centered measure of curvature, thus biasing the solution towards planarity, but not toward the fronto-parallel. While useful, such insights are vaguely unsatisfying, because they refer only to the modal properties of the world modeled by the constraints and tell us little more about the world; that is, they tell us only about the surfaces which best match the constraints .

A Bayesian formulation of the energy minimization solution directly characterizes the worlds for which the algorithms are optimal estimators, allowing us to analyze the appropriateness of the modeled constraints for solution of a surface reconstruction problem in our world. In the case considered by Belhumeur, the "world" consists of 2D, opaque surfaces, represented in a viewer-centered coordinate frame. He carefully derives progressively more constrained models of surfaces in the world in the form of the stochastic processes which generate them. This is important, because it provides synthetic models from which we can generate random samples of surfaces in the world and which we can use to examine the statistical properties of the modeled world to compare with our intuitions about surfaces in the real world.

Belhumeur models the process which generates surfaces between boundaries and creases as a mixture of summed Brownian motion processes. In terms of the "energy function" which he minimizes to find the most likely surface to have given rise to a set of stereo data, the Brownian motion processes contribute the smoothness terms, corresponding to sums of squared derivatives of surface depth. Belhumeur's analysis makes clear how weak the constraints imposed by such smoothness functions really are. Figure 8.1 shows some sample paths drawn from fine-scale simulations of the stochastic process he models (His World III, without the crease and surface boundary processes). Depending on the parameters of the process, the sample pathes have varying degrees of smoothness, but one can generally conclude that the modeled surfaces are quite a bit rougher than many of the surfaces in our world, though they may approximate some natural surfaces. This is not necessarily bad, however. As long as a prior model subsumes the "true" model of surfaces in the world, as I suspect is largely the case here, using the prior amounts to using less prior knowledge than one potentially could; that is, the constraints imposed in the prior are accurate, but there exist further constraints that could be imposed but aren't. In this case, using the mixed Brownian motion prior is similar to assuming knowledge only of the correlations between neighboring depths and orientations on a surface, when some classes of surfaces have a considerable amount of higher order structure. This may have the unwanted effect of giving too much weight to the data (in the presence of noise), but it may also be better than imposing a more constrained prior model without sufficient justification. In the latter case, one may impose unnatural and thus "incorrect" biases in the prior model.

An important feature of Belhumeur's prior model of surfaces is the inclusion of Poisson jump processes for modelling creases and surface boundaries. The jump processes contribute what are often referred to as line processes, used to "break" smoothness constraints between neighboring points in a surface map when a line is turned on. The Poisson processes have a strong intuitive appeal, particularly when presented for the one- dimensional case. By limiting the development to one-dimension, however, Belhumeur misses out on an important source of constraints on the structure of creases and surface boundaries; namely, the relations between the appearance of neighboring breaks in 2D. Clearly creases and surface boundaries do not occur at isolated points on a surface but extend in space through and around surfaces. Incorporating such constraints would greatly help in the discovery and reconstruction of creases and boundaries in surfaces. Various prior models have been proposed and used for such edges (Kass *et al.*, 1987) and could do well to be integrated into the prior surface model. Interestingly, just as the energy functions used to reconstruct surfaces in many computer vision models correspond to Brownian motion or fractal priors, the energy functions often used to reconstruct edges or image contours have similar priors in one dimension. Their use would therefore be consistent with the Brownian motion surface models used here, as the curves formed by slices through 2D Brownian processes are themselves Brownian (Mandelbrot, 1977).

Priors, representation and global constraints

One problem with the stochastic processes Belhumeur uses to model surfaces is that they are anisotropic in the sense that they are not invariant to 3D rotations of surfaces or the viewer. This is less of a problem for World III than World II, which has a mode for fronto-parallel surfaces, but a problem nonetheless. The prior on second derivatives in world III does impose a viewer-based constraint on surface shape. While the mode of the prior is viewpoint independent (it gives equal probabilistic weight to planar surfaces of all orientations), the distribution itself is anisotropic. This is demonstrated by the fact that a spherical surface segment oriented at 45 degrees to the viewer has a lower prior probability than a similar segment oriented towards the observer. The anisotropy problem could be resolved by modeling surfaces using stochastic processes defined in a spherical coordinate system (a non-trivial problem in itself), which, I imagine, would result in energy functions based on something like the sums of squared principal curvatures of a surface, a viewpoint invariant measure (see Koenderink, 1990, for some interesting proposals of viewpoint- invariant shape measures). Such a representation, however, is computationally unwieldy, and formulating an energy function which incorporates viewpoint independent measures of curvature within a viewer-centered Cartesian representation, while possible, results in a highly non-linear form of the smoothness constraint, a problem for implementation. Moreover, a non-Cartesian representation does not easily support a formulation of the occluded surface constraint which Belhumeur uses so effectively in his model. Considerations such as these illustrate the tight connection between prior models and representations. It is possible that the human visual system uses multiple, perhaps redundant, representations which allow the imposition of different forms of constraints; thus, for stereopsis, the visual system may have a coarse, viewer-centered representation of the depth differences between different objects, while maintaining an object-centered representation of each object's internal surface shape. Estimates of depth for internal surface points may be used solely to help segment a scene into objects, and not as an intermediate step to estimating surface shape.

The connection between representations and priors becomes all the more clear when one considers how to impose global constraints, a point made in Chapters 4 and 6 of this volume. By using a single layer representation of surface depth, Belhumeur is forced to go to seemingly extraordinary means to impose global constraints on surface shape. In fact, the model he presents to do so steps away from the strict Bayesian formulation he has presented up to that point. It is not clear what the global prior is that he implements. By iteratively adapting the "prior" on the basis of image data in the course of reconstructing his solution, he hides some of the structure of the global prior in the iterative adaptation process, thus we do not have, as we had in his Worlds I - III, a neat model of the structures he models with the adaptive priors. This points out a challenge to Bayesian modeling of scene structure for vision: linking priors which capture local structure, which are naturally expressed in Cartesian data structures such as depth and orientation maps, with global priors, which are naturally expressed in more abstract model parameters (e.g. the orientation of a planar surface or the elongation of an ellipsoid). The standard paradigm for linking such prior models is to map low-level to high-level representations and model the prior constraints imposed independently at each stage. Incorporating feedback is clearly an advance over the simple serial processing approach; however, one is still left with a model which blends algorithmic descriptions of feedback with partial descriptions of priors.

This leaves us with the question: Can we formulate fully Bayesian models which characterize both local and global constraints, or will we always be forced to resort to embedding some of the structure of the prior in algorithms we build to combine the two types of constraint? I suspect that the latter will often be true, as the formalisms available for modeling prior probabilistic structure, while having been broadened considerably over the last few decades, are still relatively limited. Perhaps the best hope for building functional models of perception is to work from both directions – Bayesian theory to implementation, and implementation to Bayesian theory. The latter approach has proved profitable, for example, in the study of neural network algorithms (Golden, 1988; Kersten *et al.*, 1987; MacKay, 1992). It remains to be seen to what extent it will be useful for broader classes of algorithms.

References

Blake, A. & Zisserman, A. (1987). *Visual Reconstruction.* Cambridge, MA: MIT Press.

Golden, R. (1988). A unified framework for connectionist systems. *Biological Cybernetics*, **59**, 109-120.

Kaas, M., Witkins, A. and Terzopolous, D. (1987). Snakes: Active contour models, *Proc. ICCV*, **1**, 259-268.

Kersten, D., O'Toole, A.J., Sereno, M.E., Knill, D.C. & Anderson, J. A. (1987). Associative learning of scene parameters from images, *Applied Optics*, **26** (23), 4999-5006.

Koenderink, J.J. (1990). *Solid Shape.* Cambridge, MA: MIT Press.

MacKay, D.J.C. (1992). A practical Bayesian framework for backpropagation networks, *Neural Computation*, **4** (3), 448- 472.

Mandelbrot, B. (1977). *Fractals: Form, Chance and Dimension* San Francisco: Freeman Press.

Poggio, T., Torre, V. and Koch, C. (1985). Computational theory and regularization theory, *Nature*, **317**, 314-319.

Terzopoulos, D. (1986). Regularization of inverse problems involving discontinuities, *IEEE Trans. Pattern Anal. Mach. Intell.*, **8**, 413-424.

Chapter 8:
A computational theory for binocular stereopsis

WILLIAM FREEMAN

I found Belhumeur's chapter to be an elegant, principled approach to the problem of stereopsis. He developed algorithms for well defined, ever more complex worlds, yielding ever better results on the test example shown. I was particularly impressed with his treatment of half-occlusion, turning what can be a problem for stereo matching into a rich source of information. The way he constructed his prior probabilities for disparity from combinations of random processes is a model for how that should be done.

I was not so satisfied with his World IV, where he modifyied the prior assumptions based on the image data. The underlying priors used are hidden by the resulting iterative calculation; I don't think "iteratively adapted priors" should be called "priors". Perhaps a multi-scale approach (Burt & Adelson, 1983; Szeliski, 1989) could have been used to treat the long-range correlations and the short-range effects within the same Bayesian framework.

I would have liked to have seen more examples or comparisons to see how the care Belhumeur took in developing the priors paid off in performance. I would like to see the result on the bulldog image, or a performance comparison with standard stereo algorithms.

It might give insight to compare Belhumeur's algorithm with the more descriptive work of Grossberg (1994) on similar problems in stereo reconstruction.

Representation and priors

It would be nice to know how rich a representation to use. Belhumuer argued that it was important to explicitly represent discontinuities in the surface shape and its first derivative. Should one stop there, or is there a benefit to explicitly representing ever more complex features? Chapter 2 by Jepson *et al.* is relevant to this question.

Using a Bayesian approach, it may be that there are many free parameters to be set in the prior probabilities, as there seem to be in Belhumeur's alorithm. One might question the benefit of using such a principled approach if the result is an algorithm with many parameters to adjust in an *ad hoc* fashion.

However, the Bayesian method may make explicit assumptions which are kept implicit in other approaches. Furthermore, the probabilistic development gives meaning to the parameters which need to be set; they can be related to the statistics of the visual world. Characteristics of the algorithm can be linked to characteristics of the world.

In addition, there may be principled ways to set the free parameters. Belhumeur mentioned one approach, "generalized cross-validation". In theory, it may be possible to set the parameters from a statistical analysis of visual scenes, although that is seldom done. One could find plausible distributions for the parameters through "non-informative priors" (Box & Tiao, 1973; Berger, 1985; Jaynes, 1986; Jeffreys, 1961); Mackay (1992), Gull (1989), Skilling (1989) and Szeliski (1989) have proposed methods based on the visual data to set the parameters of the priors. (Although those approaches are not without controversy (Strauss *et al.*, 1993). Perhaps the assumptions of generic viewpoint or object pose could be exploited to lessen the influence of the priors in the final reconstruction (Freeman, 1994, 1994e).

How far can a Bayesian approach go?

Belhumeur and others (for example, Geman & Geman, 1984; Jepson & Richards, 1992; Kersten, 1991; Szeliski, 1989) have shown a Bayesian approach can be successful for low-level perception in simple worlds. Can it be used to study higher-level perception, or or to integrate perception with action? Perception can be tied to actions via the utility functions of Bayesian decision theory (Berger, 1985) by assigning an expected benefit to given perceptual decisions. For some preliminary applications, see Brainard & Freeman (1994) and Chapter 4, this volume. It remains to be seen how far one can take analytic approaches to these complicated problems.

References

Berger, J.O. (1985). *Statistical decision theory and Bayesian analysis.* Springer-Verlag.

Box, G.E.P. & Tiao, G.C. (1973). *Bayesian Inference in Statistical Analysis.* Wiley & Sons.

Brainard, D.H. & Freeman, W.T. (1994). Bayesian method for recovering surface and illuminant properties from photosensor responses. *Proc. SPIE*, **2179**, San Jose, CA, February 1994.

Burt, P.J. & Adelson, E.H. (1983). The Laplacian pyramid as a compact image code. *IEEE Trans. Comm.*, **31**, 532-540.

Freeman, W.T. (1994). The generic viewpoint assumption in a framework for visual perception. *Nature*, **368**(6471), 542-545.

Geman, S. & Geman, D. (1984). Stochastic relaxation, Gibbs distribution, and the Bayesian restoration of images. *IEEE Pat. Anal. Mach. Intell.*, **6**, 721-741.

Grossberg, S. (1994). 3-D vision and figure-ground separation by visual cortex. *Perception & Psychophysics*, **55**, 48-120.

Gull, S.F. (1989). Developments in maximum entropy data analysis. In *Maximum Entropy and Bayesian Methods*, ed. J. Skilling, pp. 53-71. Kluwer.

Jaynes, E.T. (1986). Bayesian methods: general background. In *Maximum entropy and Bayesian Methods in Applied Statistics*, ed. J.H. Justice. Cambridge Univ. Press.

Jeffreys, H. (1961). *Theory of probability*. Oxford: Clarendon Press.

Jepson, A. & W. Richards (1992). What makes a good feature? In Spatial Vision in Humans and Robots, ed. L. Harris and M. Jenkin. Cambridge Univ. Press. See also MIT AI Memo 1356 (1992).

Kersten, D. (1991). Transparancy and the cooperative computation of scene attributes. In *Computational Models of Visual Processing*, ed. M.S. Landy and J.A. Movshon, chapter 15. Cambridge, MA: MIT Press.

MacKay, D.J.C. (1992). Bayesian interpolation. *Neural Computation*, **4**, 415-447.

Skilling, J. (1989). Classic maximum entropy. In *Maximum Entropy and Bayesian Methods*, ed. J. Skilling, pp. 45-52. Kluwer.

Strauss, C.E.M., Wolpert, D.H. & Wolf, D.R. (1993). Alpha, evidence, and the entropic prior. In *Maximum Entropy and Bayesian Methods*, pp. 113-120. Kluwer.

Szeliski, R. (1989). *Bayesian Modeling of Uncertainty in Low-level Vision*. Boston: Kluwer Academic Publishers.

Chapter 9:
Are "generic variables" regularity-free?

JACOB FELDMAN

Freeman's version of the genericity principle requires, in essence, that the perceiver's estimate of the value of some parameter should not depend on an unlikely or "accidental" value of a "generic" variable – that is, that the estimate should be robust under small changes in the generic variable. Freeman defines a "generic" variable to be one that the perceiver "does not need to estimate precisely." The principle itself seems so sound, though, that one wonders why it should matter whether the perceiver cares about the generic variable or not. What, then, is the actual difference between generic variables and others?

One possible answer is this: vaguely, generic scene parameters are those that are *unlikely to be causally connected to others parameters*. Less vaguely, generic parameters are those for which the perceiver does not entertain the possibility of regular or lawful relationships with other parameters.

In a Bayesian framework, these "special relationships" may be encoded as elevated priors on certain points in the configuration space representing the relationship between the parameters in question (see Richards *et al.*, 1994 [this volume]). For example, say we have two parameters, x and y (these can be scene parameters, viewing parameters, or in fact any parameters that characterize the overall observer-environment situation), with joint prior density $f(x, y)$. Say x and y are *mutually regular* if there exists some point (x_0, y_0) (a "regularity") such that $f(x_0, y_0)$ is greater than both

$$\int_{y=y_0, x \neq x_0} f(x, y) dx$$

and

$$\int_{x=x_0, y \neq y_0} f(x, y) dy.$$

This will generally entail that (x_0, y_0) is the preferred *a posteriori* solution, i.e. that

$$p(x = x_0 | y = y_0) > p(x \neq x_0 | y = y_0),$$

and vice-versa, i.e.

$$p(y = y_0 | x = x_0) > p(y \neq y_0 | x = x_0).$$

This means that if the perceiver observes that (x, y) falls on the line $x = x_0$, then it may safely infer that (x, y) actually must fall at the regularity (x_0, y_0); similarly with the line $y = y_0$. (Note that this definition is both too strong and insufficiently general to capture the idea of "mutual regularity," but will suffice for present purposes; again see Richards *et al.*)If x and y are mutually regular we write $x \sim y$.

The relation $\sim$ is clearly reflexive. It is not transitive in general, but is so for an important subclass: if $x \sim y$ due to regularity (x_0, y_0), and $y \sim z$ due to regularity (y_0, z_0), and there are no other regularities on x, y, and z, then $x \sim z$. In this case a common process at (x_0, y_0, z_0) generates all three regularities $x \sim y$, $y \sim z$, and $x \sim z$.The number of distinct parameters involved in a special configuration like this (corresponding to the "codimension;" again see Richards *et al.* is a measure of just how "special" the configuration is.

Now consider the graph of the mutual regularity relation for an arbitrary observer-environment situation expressed by parameters $\{x_1, x_2, \ldots\}$ and the observer's global joint density $f(x_1, x_2, \ldots)$. Clearly there will be clusters of connected nodes, corresponding to those sets of parameters for which the observer postulates close causal connections (in the sense defined). In fact, in a tightly stuctured environment, the graph might be dominated by a single central cluster in which many of the nodes were all connected.

Now we can return to Freeman's distinction between generic variables and others. What Freeman is claiming, in terms of $\sim$, is that there will exist some *isolated* nodes in the graph of $\sim$ (i.e. nodes that are not connected to any of the others) – e.g. viewpoint, object orientation, lighting position, and so forth: the "generic variables." Again, reflecting the original vague suggestion above, these nodes are parameters for which the observer (as reflected in its global prior f) does not hypothesize any regular causal relationships to any other parameters. Notice that this situation strongly suggests that the observer would not much care about the values of these variables, since it attaches no particular causal significance to any particular values of them; but this disinterest is a symptom rather than a cause of the essential distinction between them and other parameters.

Normally the viewpoint vector would be considered generic with respect to arbitrary scene-dependent vectors (e.g. the normal to an arbitrary surface), as in Freeman's examples. But generalizations such as "viewpoint is always generic with respect to all other parameters" cannot be made too readily; it depends on the context. The point can be made most strongly by several (somewhat morbid) counterexamples, in which one viewpoint does *not* appear to be a be a generic variable in this sense. Consider the relationship between the viewpoint vector $\vec{v}$ and the cylindrical axis of the barrel of a gun $\vec{g}$ in the field of view. Certainly the case $\vec{v} = -\vec{g}$ is a special case of great interest to the observer(!). More particularly, though, it is a special configuration to which the observer attaches a special interpretation, and to which it must attach a non-zero prior in order to infer it when it happens.

Similarly, consider the direction $\vec{l}$ of the gaze of lion who has wandered into the field of view. Again the case $\vec{v} = -\vec{l}$ is special, suggesting that the lion has noticed the observer. But even more dire (and even higher codimension) is the dynamic regularity $\vec{v}(t) \equiv -\vec{l}(t)$ over time t (i.e. the case in which the lion's gaze continues to track the observer even after movement of one of the two parties) – *confirming* that the lion has noticed the observer. In this context, clearly, the observer does *not* want to follow the usual policy of always inferring a generic relationship between scene parameters and viewpoint.

References

Richards, W., Jepson, A., and Feldman, J. (1994). Priors, preference, and categorical percepts, chapter 3 this volume.

Chapter 9:

ANDREW BLAKE

(Reprinted by permission from *Nature*, **368**, 498-499. Copyright by Macmillan Magazines Ltd. 1994)

The problem of *shape from shading* analysis – estimating the relief of a visible surface from its pattern of light and shade in an image – has been vexing researchers in vision for around twenty years (Horn & Brooks, 1989). From an experimental point of view, psychologists seem to disagree whether the human visual system can

Fig. 1 *The assumption of generic viewpoint* The drawing in (a) may be interpreted as a line drawing of a three-dimensional object such as (b). The drawing in (c) could be a line-drawing of an object such as (d). This interpretation implies however a special viewpoint in which two vertices coincide in the image. A more plausible interpretation of (c) therefore would be one that involves no accidental alignment, for instance a planar shape (e).

(Bülthoff & Mallot, 1988) or cannot (Mingolla & Todd, 1986) make effective use of shading information to estimate even the orientation of a surface, let alone its entire shape. Horn's (Horn, 1986) elegant demonstration of the reconstruction of a human face by growing height contours outwards from shading highlights showed that inferring shape from shading is theoretically possible, at least under certain conditions. The problem comes when, as is usually the case, some parameters of the physical environment are unknown. An example of relevant parameters that are usually unknown *a priori* are the directions and strengths of the sources of illumination. It has been established that the parameters of a single light-source can be recovered if certain fairly strong assumptions (isotropy (Pentland, 1982) or smoothness (Horn & Brooks, 1986)) are made about the shape of the surface. Now Freeman (1994) has devised a theory founded on the far more general assumption of *generic illumination*, described in detail in Chapter 9.

The generic illumination assumption is akin to the concept of generic viewpoint, already familiar from computational and psychological theories of vision, which is illustrated in figure 1. A viewpoint is *generic* if it avoids accidental alignments, in the image, of features on a visible object. The assumption of generic viewpoint seems to underly human visual analysis, explaining why certain line-drawings, for example the well-known *Penrose triangle*, are perceived as paradoxical Sugihara, 1986) or "impossible". The assumption is so strong that, even for a solid object, if it is seen from a certain, special viewpoint, an "impossible" object may be perceived in preference to the real one (Gregory, 1970). Early theories of generic viewpoint applied only to line-drawings of polyhedra; more recently they have been generalised to include drawings of curved surfaces (Malik, 1987).

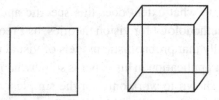

Fig. 2 *Generic illumination*. Just as the viewer can be in a special position with respect to an object, so also can the source of illumination. The image (a) consists of two regions of constant-intensity shading. This could have arisen as the image of a cone (b) but only if the light-source is in a special position, on the axis of the cone. Any perturbation of the light-source's position away from the cone axis will lead to shaded regions whose intensity is no longer constant. A more likely explanation is that (a) is the image of a planar pattern such as (c).

The *generic illumination* assumption can be regarded as the *dual* of the generic viewpoint condition. The light source and the viewer are dual concepts, as table 1 illustrates, each being defined in terms of a cone of light-rays.

In principle, this assumption can be invoked to rule out certain interpretations of a shaded image which, whilst being physically consistent, are nonetheless highly improbable. Even still, the generic illumination assumption is not quite in the form that Freeman requires for his theory. It is known, in the case of generic viewpoint, that a "soft" form of the assumption (Witkin, 1981). can be obtained to define, for all views, not just one pathological view, the *degree* of genericity of a given viewpoint. This is a numerical measure that is greater for more probable views but approaches zero as the viewpoint approaches an accidental alignment. It can be used, in a measure of probability, to evaluate competing hypotheses for the shape of a particular visible surface. What Freeman has achieved, this time for generic illumination, is an analogous softening of his assumption, again leading to a measure of probability for competing hypotheses of surface shape. Now the generic illumination assumption is applicable to shaded images rather than simply to line drawings, and this is beautifully illustrated in Figure 9.3 of his chapter.

Viewpoint	Illuminant
viewer position	light source position
visible surface	illuminated surface
silhouette	cast shadow
blurred image outline	penumbra

Table 1 *Viewer-illuminant duality*

By analogy with generic viewpoint, generic illumination is the assumption that there are no accidental alignments of object features along illuminant rays (Figure 2).

The question arises, to what extent does this specific and elegant achievement prefigure a powerful methodology for vision theories, as Freeman believes it does? Whilst it is true generally that probabilistic models of visual processing are having increasing impact, their application in his paper is somewhat limited in scope. First, the approach has been shown to work only for the simplest of physical models of reflectance, a single point light-source without shadows or surface patterning. This is a limitation common to many theories of shape from shading. Secondly, although *construction* of the theory is based on generic illumination, free of specific assumptions about surface shape, they may emerge nonetheless. Probabilistic measures of generality of illumination like Freeman's can depend, after all, on surface smoothness, having large values for surfaces that are close to being planar or cylindrical. Indeed it does appear in Freeman's Figure 9.3 that the less plausible surface shapes are also less smooth – a greater area of the planar background is disrupted.

One explanation of the link between surface smoothness and generality of illumination is as follows. For diffuse ("Lambertian") illumination, image-intensity is given by the "rendering function" $l \cdot n$ where n is the surface normal vector at each image position and vector l represents the strength and direction of the light source. In that case Freeman's measure of genericity of illumination (equation 9.11 in Chapter 9 is $1/\sqrt{\det(< nn^T >)}$, where $< .. >$ denotes spatial averaging over the image. This measure becomes unboundedly large as the visible surface approaches planarity because the normal vectors n span a space of only 1 dimension, so the $\det(..)$ term approaches zero. (Something similar also happens as the surface becomes close to cylindrical.) After all, therefore, as the underlying surface becomes smooth in the sense of approaching planarity, the measure of generality of illumination becomes large. The question is, does this link suggest that Freeman's approach might somehow be limited to smooth surfaces?

In conclusion, Freeman's specific achievement is impressive, in seeing a way to express probabilistically the general illumination assumption and in verifying experimentally, to some degree, its power to reject incorrect hypotheses about surface shape. His claim for greater generality is not altogether convincing as yet. It will be interesting to see whether future computational experiments can establish more precisely what is the breadth of conditions over which his theory is viable.

References

Bülthoff, H.H. & H.A. Mallot, H.A. (1988). Integration of depth modules: stereo and shading. *JOSA A*, **5**, 1749-1758.

W.T. Freeman, W.T. (1994). The generic viewpoint assumption in a framework for visual perception. *Nature*, **368**, 542-545.

Gregory, R.L. (1970). *The Intelligent Eye*. London: World University.

Horn, B.K.P. (1986). *Robot Vision*. New York: McGraw-Hill.

Horn, B.K.P. & Brooks, M.J. (1986). The variational approach to shape from shading. In *Computer Vision, Graphics and Image Processing*, vol. 33, pp. 174-208.

Horn, B.K.P. & Brooks, M.J. (eds.) (1989). *Shape from Shading*. Cambridge, MA:MIT Press.

Sugihara, K. (1986). *Machine interpretation of line drawings*. Cambridge, MA: MIT Press.

Malik, J. (1987). Interpreting Line Drawings of Curved Objects. *Int. Journal of Computer Vision*, **1**, 73-103.

Mingolla, E. & Todd, J.T. (1986). Perception of solid shape from shading. *Biological Cybernetics*, **53**, 137-151.

Pentland, A.P. (1982). Finding the illuminant direction. *J. Optical Soc. of America*, **72**(4), 448-455.

Witkin, A.P. (1981). Recovering surface shape and orientation from texture. *Artificial Intelligence*, **17**, 17-45.

Chapter 10:
Experiencing and perceiving images

HORACE BARLOW

I think this chapter gives very persuasive and elegant demonstrations that take one a big step beyond Helmholtz, who said "The general rule determining the ideas of vision that are formed whenever an impression is made on the eye . . . is that such objects are always imagined as being present as would have to be there in order to produce the same impression on the nervous mechanism under conditions of normal use". Nakayama & Shimojo show that the class of objects that are imagined is more restricted than Helmholtz said; they are the class that, given the geometry of objects and surfaces would *most often* produce the same impression under conditions of normal use. But I am puzzled by the suggestion that what most often produces the impression is determined by experience.

In order to estimate $p(I_m | S_n)$ one has to know when the given surface S_n is present, but all the sensory messages tell you is that I_m has occurred. In the matrix of figure 10.8 how do you determine which column the present experience belongs to? Have I missed or failed to understand some suggested mechanism for bootstrapping the accumulation of experience by means of inherited knowledge of probabilities or values deduced geometrically? This ought to be possible, for it would be safe to assume that the actual surfaces change less often than the viewpoint, so the system should be unwilling to change the column assignment as the changing image causes the row to shift up and down. But such a mechanism needs to be spelt out.

Chapter 10:

ALLAN JEPSON

Nakayama & Shimojo consider the visual interpretation of sparsely structured stereo images. The critical issue, common throughout this text, is how different interpretations for the same image should be compared. To do such comparisons the authors appeal to the notion of accidental views of a scene. The motivation for this is primarily scepticism that the visual system could gain, through experience, any accurate quantitative information about the prior probabilities of different scene interpretations. Indeed the generic view approach ignores the prior probabilities and treats every scene interpretation as equally likely a priori. I am sympathetic to this concern about the availability of accurate priors, especially considering the range of different and typically unknown contexts our visual systems must face, including various artificial contexts presented in psychophysics laboratories. But, as I discuss below, the generic view approach has some serious short comings, some of which can be traced back to this decision to ignore the priors.

Finally, I argue that there is a middle ground, which seems to me to be compatible with Nakayama's & Shimojo's general intuition, but does involve the use of some prior information. The critical point here is that the approach I suggest requires only rather general, qualitative properties of the various prior distributions. This latter part of the commentary is intended to be a carrot, enticing researchers such as the Nakayama & Shimojo to put a little structure in their priors (and just a little). But first we need the stick.

Against the generic view principle

The principle of generic views does not, by itself, explain the preferences for the interpretations of several stereo displays in the target article. There is a technical loophole in the argument which is due to the absence of a precise definition for what constitutes an accidental view or, conversely, a generic view. As we mention below this particular loophole could easily be plugged, but the more serious issue of the lack of a precise and well-founded definition remains.

What is a generic view?

It is useful to formalize the notion of a generic view. To do this the critical concept involves the set of images, say $E(I)$, which are considered to have the equivalent structure as some given image I. In particular, the set of all possible images is to be partitioned into equivalence classes, with any two images from the same equivalence

Fig. 1 Divergers should use the right pair of stereo images, convergers the left. Observers report multiple, relatively discrete interpretations when this pair is viewed at arm's length with roving fixation.

class having the same structure. According to the target article, such a partitioning may be done on the basis of various topological properties of images. Let us ignore, for the moment, the details of the definition of these equivalence classes.

Equivalent viewpoints of a 3D scene can now be defined through the use of such a notion of image structure. To do this, consider a given image I_0 and a given 3D scene structure S. We assume that I_0 is a possible image of the scene S in that, when we view S from some viewpoint v_0, we obtain the image I_0. The set of equivalent viewpoints, namely $V(S, I_0)$, is then defined to be the set of all viewpoints, v, such that the image of S from viewpoint v is in the same equivalence class, namely $E(I_0)$, as the original image I_0.

The last component required for a formal definition is a way to measure the size of various subsets in the space of viewpoints. For example, for orthographic projection the set of viewpoints can be represented by a sphere, with the projection direction represented by the vector from the center to a point on the sphere. Given a subset of viewpoints on this sphere it is standard to use the area as the appropriate measure of the size of the subset. Perspective and/or stereo views require a larger dimensional viewpoint space and, similarly, the associated uniform volume measure could be used. Given these ingredients we can now define a generic view.

Generic view definition: Given a particular image I_0 and a 3D scene structure S, suppose v_0 is a viewpoint such that the image of S from viewpoint v_0 is just I_0. This viewpoint of S is said to be generic if the set of equivalent views, namely $V(S, I_0)$, has positive measure on the set of all possible viewpoints.

For a concrete example consider the image given in Figure 10.1A along with the two interpretations displayed in Figure 10.1C and D. I refer to these interpretations as the folded cross and the floating bars, respectively. In order for the viewer to see the folded cross as depicted in the stereogram in Figure 10.1, the viewer needs to be positioned in the plane of the horizontal edges of the cross. Suppose that the notion of equivalent images mentioned above is defined so that straight lines are preserved within any one equivalence class. In particular, any viewpoint of the folded cross which is not in the plane of the horizontal edges would show the horizontal bar to have non-colinear edges in the image and, as a result, such a viewpoint is not considered to be equivalent. Therefore we find that the set of equivalent views is confined to the plane of the horizontal edges of the folded cross and must have measure zero. So the conclusion is that the the folded cross interpretation involves a non- generic (i.e., accidental) view, as desired.

But what about the floating bars interpretation, can we conclude that the viewpoint for this is generic? The issue is that we do not have a specification for the set of equivalence classes $E(I)$ and, moreover, some choices for $E(I)$ lead to the conclusion that the viewpoint of the floating bars interpretation is also accidental. For example, suppose I consider the points defined by the centers of the horizontal and vertical bars in the floating bars interpretation. Such a point can be obtained, for example, by the intersection of straight lines connecting the opposite corners of the rectangle. Given that the our equivalence classes preserve straight lines, and without explicit directions to the contrary, this could be a valid construct from image data. If we allow such a construct, then we should note that these center points coincide in the fused stereo image. But this means that the viewer must be situated on the line passing through the centers of these two bars, which amounts to an accidental view. Almost any perturbation of the viewpoint would change this topological property of the center points projecting to the same point in the cyclopean image, and therefore change the image equivalence class. As a result, we would have to conclude that the viewpoint is accidental. But then both interpretations involve accidental views, in which case the principle of generic image sampling has nothing to say about the preference of one interpretation over the other.

This same situation holds for the disk illusion shown in Figure 10.6, with the perception being that the viewer is on the line passing through the center of the cross and the center of the transparent disk. Therefore the view of this interpretation could again be considered accidental, and the generic view principle fails to account for the preference of the disk interpretation.

The glitch mentioned above relies on the use of the centers of the various parts in the scene. One could work around this by refining the definition of an accidental view so that part midpoints are not considered in the various equivalence classes $E(I)$. But without a theoretical foundation as to why such a definition is appropriate, such a step seems arbitrary. The question remains, which image features should take part in deciding topological changes, which ones shouldn't, what topology should be used, and why? For that matter, it also seems arbitrary to restrict the definition of accidental views to *topological*[†] changes in the image structure. Why not include categorical changes which are not captured by standard image topologies? For example, could

---

[†] Here I am referring to the use of topology in the third paragraph of the section titled "Ecological Optics and the Importance of Viewing Position" of the target chapter.

one usefully consider the categories of acute, right, and obtuse angles at various V-junctions in the image? The main point is that, in order to proceed, we need to have a clear definition of the equivalence class, $E(I)$, to be associated with any given image I. Moreover, one would hope that such a definition could avoid becoming a set of seemingly arbitrary criteria, and instead be well motivated from first principles.

A probabilistic perspective

In order to compare this with Bayesian approaches, it is useful to first relate the generic view principle to a probabilistic form. To do this, suppose we are given an image I and two possible scene structures S_1 and S_2. The principle of generic views considers only the likelihood of generating an image equivalent to I. That is, using the notation above for the set $E(I)$ of equivalent images, we consider the likelihoods $p(E(I)|S_i)$ for each scene interpretation S_i. The only random variable remaining in this expression is the viewpoint, which is taken to have a uniform prior. In fact, assuming that the viewpoint is selected independently of the scene S_i, this likelihood $p(E(I)|S_i)$ is just the prior probability of selecting a viewpoint v from the set of equivalent views $V(S_i, I)$. Moreover, given a uniform viewpoint distribution, this prior probability is proportional to the area of $V(S_i, I)$ on the viewing sphere. In these terms, the generic view principle dictates that we should prefer S_2 over S_1, say, whenever the likelihood $p(E(I)|S_2)$ given S_2 is positive while that given S_1 is zero. The principle can therefore be understood as special form of the maximum likelihood method applied to an extremely weak model of the world.

An alternative approach for choosing between two possible interpretations S_1 and S_2 is to compare their posterior probabilities given the observed image I. By Bayes rule this is equivalent to comparing the products of the likelihood and the prior, as in $p(I|S_i)p(S_i)$. Note that there is no need here for the contentious set of equivalent images $E(I)$, but now we do require an estimate of the prior probability of the scene S_i. As we discussed at length in Chapter 2, the inclusion and qualitative form of this prior probability term can be critical in determining which interpretation is more probable given an observed image. We illustrate this in the following two subsections.

No accidental view, no preferences

One consequence of neglecting the prior probabilities is that the generic view principle does not account for many of the preferences exhibited by observers in the absence of accidental views. That is, observers can exhibit preferences for various interpretations without any accidents in the viewpoint position. For example, consider a modified version of the cross display, as depicted in Figure 1. Here I have destroyed the colinearity (and the parallelism) in the edges of the horizontal bar. This colinearity was the critical factor, according to the argument in the target chapter, for determining that the viewpoint of the folded cross interpretation was accidental. For the display in Figure 1 observers report up to three interpretations (although most observers do not report all cases, and many complain that the percepts are quite fleeting). One interpretation is similar to the folded cross, but with tapered wings. A second interpretation is similar to the floating bars interpretation with a flat horizontal bar, but now it is shaped like a bow tie in outline. The third interpretation is again similar to the folded cross, but with the vertical bar separate from and in front of the two receding wings.

   The issue here is not so much why are these three interpretations distinguished, but rather why don't we get a continuum of possible interpretations? For example, we could parameterize a family of interpretations by the depth of the middle point of the horizontal bar. For all these solutions, the argument in the target chapter would conclude that the viewpoint is generic. Thus the generic viewpoint principle would not distinguish any of these possibilities. However, a central theme of this text is that such preferences can be represented within a Bayesian framework according to various prior models the observer has about the world. For example, the above three interpretations could arise from priors which distinguish flat surfaces, connected surfaces, and rectangular surfaces (respectively), as structures which occur relatively frequently in our world. The point here is simply that the generic view principle is clearly not enough on it's own to explain how we see; some other principles and preferences would need to be added. Presumably such preferences are also active in cases for which there is an accidental view, and a more complete theory would need to spell out how the various preferences interact with the generic view principle. In contrast, the Bayesian story emphasized elsewhere in this text, and discussed further below, attempts to gain a more unified perspective.

A preferred but accidental view

A related difficulty, caused again by ignoring the priors, is that some implausible interpretations end up being preferred according to the generic view principle. For example, the standard perception of the blocks world figure given in my commentary on Chapter 11 involves a highly accidental view. But there is an alternative interpretation of the scene for which all the colinear line segments may be taken as colinear in the world. In this interpretation various blocks must be floating in space, in special alignments, and at least one of the two cylinders must be distorted. Nevertheless, the view for this "floating blocks" interpretation is generic, while the common perception involves an accidental view. According to the principle of generic views, then, one should prefer the "floating blocks" interpretation over the standard perception of this figure. However, our visual systems do the opposite, and thereby violate the generic view principle in this example.

It is worthwhile to consider why the generic view principle fails in this example. The difficulty rests with ignoring the prior probability for the "floating blocks" interpretation. Given a simple qualitative model with smooth prior distributions for the viewpoint and for blocks floating freely in space, one can conclude that the posterior odds are strongly against any interpretation which involves the blocks aligned. Rather, the odds favour the interpretation that the viewpoint is accidental. The reason is that, even though the likelihoods favour the non-accidental view, the prior probabilities are more extremely skewed in favour of the other interpretation. As a result, the posterior probabilities turn out to be strongly against the non-accidental view. (The necessary calculations are similar to the discussion in Chapter 2, and are omitted here.) This is in accord with the standard perception of the blocks world figure.

The addition of a prior probability distribution may cause some concern. For example, the authors of the target article argue that it is implausible that the visual system has access to detailed knowledge of the prior probability distribution. I agree with this. But, as we discuss in Chapter 2, qualitative properties of the prior distribution can be sufficient to reliably select one interpretation over another. Moreover, since this required qualitative structure is rather simple, it seems plausible that our visual systems could learn it and make use of it. To illustrate this point further I outline in the next section a qualitative Bayesian formulation for the situation depicted in figure 10.1.

Modal analysis

My emphasis in the discussion below is on the mathematical properties of inferences that can be made given a qualitative model of the prior probabilities for situations such as those depicted in the stereo examples of the the target chapter. The goals are to sketch the application of modal analysis to such a domain and to study the resulting inference problem. In other words, if we postulate that our perceptual systems perform Bayesian inference, and have priors of the form described below, then we can mathematically derive a certain set of results. Our goals here are to illustrate the approach, spell out the results, but not necessarily validate these postulates about our visual systems.

Consider a qualitative probabilistic model of the scene and the viewpoint geometry for situations which encompass the stereo examples in the target chapter. In particular, we consider scene models of the form described in Chapter 2, with the various prior distributions specified by qualitative probability distributions. Following my commentary on Chapter 11, we might frame such a prior in terms of a modal workshop. The intuitive idea is that the workshop can generate rectangular strips, fold them, hang them in place, and so on.

The important observation is that it is natural to assume that the prior distributions for various operations are modal. For example, a polygonal part may be constructed over a wide range of shapes, which might be modeled by a smooth distribution on the set of vertices. However, in addition to this smooth distribution, polygonal parts may be constructed in a variety of special ways, such as rectangular, symmetrical, or square. These latter shapes are represented by lower dimensional subsets of the overall imbedding space of polygons and, since they have nontrivial prior probability of occurring, we see that an appropriate prior distribution has the original smooth distribution in addition to various delta function distributions spread over these lower dimensional sets. Other examples of modal distributions occur with the relative positioning of two parts in space (where possible modes of positioning include various alignments of the part axes), and with the place and manner parts are folded (with modes in which straight folds made parallel or in line with other structures). In addition to qualitative priors for the various operations of the workshop, we also require a qualitative prior distribution for the viewer position. Here a natural prior is to assume the viewpoint is independent of the object in the scene and to use a smooth distribution over the space of viewpoints.

In Chapter 2 we define a context C to be a set of such prior models, which includes a specification of the various modes that are expected to occur, along with various non-degeneracy conditions. We avoid the details of such a specification here and instead concentrate on the various inferences that are sanctioned once a context has been chosen.

Defining accidents

Given a context such as the one described above, we can define a notion of one scene being accidental relative to another. This is quite different from the generic view approach described above, in that it is addressing the relative sizes of the priors for two scene interpretation, say $p(S_1|C)$ and $p(S_2|C)$, without regards to an image or an observer. An accidental scene is easiest to illustrate by suppressing one of the modes we have already assumed to exist. For example suppose we modified the context such that, when objects were floating in space their relative positions did not have any alignment modes, but rather consisted of only a smooth distribution. Let us denote this modified context by C_m instead of C. For context C_m the orthogonal alignment of the floating bars would have to arise by chance, while that of the folded cross could be explained by the remaining modes of the context (i.e. cuts can be made orthogonally to other cuts, and folds can be made along the edge of the vertical bar). Thus, in such a context, the prior probability of the floating bars interpretation, say $p(S_2|C_m)$, is vanishingly small relative to that of the folded cross (here, as in Chapter 2, we are considering the limit as an error tolerance goes to zero.) It is convenient to express this in terms of the ratio of priors, as $p(S_2|C_m)/p(S_1|C_m) \to 0$. As a result, this floating bars interpretation is said to be accidental relative to the folded cross in this modified context.

For the original context, C, there are sufficient modes to account for the various structures in both the folded cross, S_1, and the floating bars, S_2. As a result, the priors $p(S_1|C)$ and $p(S_2|C)$ are comparable. That is, the prior ratio does not go to zero, or grow unbounded, as the error tolerance is refined. Therefore, in the context C, neither interpretations is (a priori) accidental relative to the other.

Another example of an accidental structure occurs in this original context C when a new piece of data is considered. Suppose that we are told that the distance from one tip to the other in the horizontal bar, in either interpretation, has to be just the same as the length of the vertical bar. To account for this observation using a folded cross interpretation, the length of the folded horizontal segments and the fold angle need to be chosen in such a way as to arrive at the correct length. The prior probability for doing this, in our current context, turns out to be vanishingly small (again, in the limit as the error tolerance goes to zero). However the same property can be explained in the floating bars interpretation by appealing to the mode that the two bars are cut into the same shape. As a result the folded cross has a vanishingly small posterior probability relative to the floating bars, given this additional observation, and would therefore be considered to be accidental relative to the floating bars.

The effect of being given an image instead of a single observation can be viewed in a similar way. That is, given the two scene interpretations S_1 and S_2, we wish to compare their posterior probabilities given the context C and the image I, namely $p(S_1|I, C)$ and $p(S_2|I, C)$. We say S_1 is accidental relative to S_2, given I and C, if $p(S_1|I, C)/p(S_2|I, C)$ is vanishingly small in the limit as the error tolerance goes to zero. In such a case, it is appropriate to prefer the story told by S_2 over that of S_1, at least for sufficiently small errors in this context C. Recall from Chapter 2 that the ratio of posterior probabilities is just the product of the ratio of likelihoods with the ratio of the prior probabilities. That is

$$\frac{p(S_1|I, C)}{p(S_2|I, C)} = \frac{p(I|S_1, C)}{p(I|S_2, C)} \frac{p(S_1|C)}{p(S_2|C)},$$

where the first term on the right hand side is the likelihood ratio and the second term is the ratio of prior probabilities.

How does this formulation work out for the stereo display in Figure 10.1? The answer turns out to be interesting in that it depends on how well the viewpoint can be estimated from the observed position of the vertical bar and the ends of the horizontal bar. Note that these positions are common to the folded cross and floating bars, and thus any estimate obtained from just this data is not dependent on the choice between the two. There are two possible scenarios.

In the first case we assume that the information available from the disparity of the vertical bar, and the endpoints of the horizontal bar is sufficiently accurate to narrowly constrain the viewpoint around the fronto-parallel direction. Moreover, the uncertainty in the viewpoint position is sufficiently small that we cannot reliably resolve the distinction between the folded cross and the floating bars from a significant fraction of viewpoints within this range. From this property alone it follows that the likelihoods, $p(I|S_1, C)$ and $p(I|S_2, C)$, are comparable. Since the posterior probability ratio is equal to the product of the likelihood ratio times the prior probability ratio, it follows that the posterior probability ratio is essentially the same as the prior ratio. As discussed above, this ratio is not extreme in the context C. Therefore, in this case, no information is gained about which of the two interpretations, S_1 or S_2, should be preferred!

In the second case, we assume that we cannot reliably estimate the viewpoint position. Moreover, the derived set of possible views is sufficiently broad so that only a small fraction are consistent with the folded cross. This is the classic case in which the generic view assumption applies. Here the likelihood ratio is determined by the fraction of views which are consistent with the folded cross interpretation, and we are assuming that this ratio strongly favours the floating bars interpretation. Also, because the prior ratio is not extreme, we can in this case reliably prefer the floating bars interpretation.

One difference between these calculations and the standard generic view assumption is that image data is being taken into account to first limit the set of viewpoints. The appropriate likelihood ratio depends on this limited set of viewpoints, not on the overall space of views. If this limited set of views is sufficiently small we may gain no information regarding the choice of S_1 or S_2. Various quantities can be expected to have an effect on the accuracy of the estimate of the viewpoint, such as the visual angle of the display and the presence of other structures such as the bounding boxes in Figure 1. These are testable predictions of the qualitative probabilistic model.

Telling stories

In a sense, the selected scene interpretation S_i and the context C together tell a story about how an image arose. This story goes considerably further than just the description of scene structure, provided by S_i, in that the context C includes a specification of various modes that are present in the current domain. The context C can be thought of as describing the 'modal workshop' (see my commentary on Chapter 11) which generated the scene; it specifies which world properties can be generated non-accidentally in the specific domain. In particular, in order to arrive at a percept, some simple qualitative properties of the prior distribution must be represented and used to compare different scene interpretations.

This picture of the perceptual system as a story teller raises several issues. The first of which is how the various modes are indexed in order to construct the particular context. For example, in the context C discussed above, the orthogonal alignment of various parts floating in space was assumed to be modal. Somehow such a mode must be recovered from a knowledge base of possible modes. Perhaps an associative memory could form the basis of a suitable indexing scheme for individual modes. A second issue is how the various modes in our environment may be learned, that is, how our knowledge base of modes is built up in the first place. This involves the construction of mixture models (see Chapter 2) for the probability density functions of various scene properties, and perhaps the work on soft competitive learning in the connectionist literature could be applied (for example, see Jacobs *et al.*, 1991).

Finally, a third issue involves the apparent preference of some contexts over others. For example, many possible contexts could be assumed for Figure 1 above. In particular, why not choose any subset of the modes in context C rather than the whole set? Suppose, for the sake of the argument, we eliminated folding from the context. This alone would rule out the folded cross interpretation. Alternatively, a different (but still seemingly arbitrary) assumption is that the context could lack the operation of aligning separately floating parts (see the discussion of C_m above). Such variations in context eliminate modes required to plausibly construct particular artifacts, and can thereby change which interpretations are most probable. Given this variability it is critical for a perceptual theory to provide a basis on which one context can be preferred over others.

The straight forward Bayesian approach would be to supply priors on these contexts, say $p(C_k)$. The estimation problem is then replaced by one in which one seeks the maximum a posteriori probability of both the scene interpretation and the context, namely $p(S_i, C_k | I)$. By Bayes rule, we would only need to compare products of the form $p(I | S_i, C_k) p(S_i | C_k) p(C_k)$. Here the first two terms are the familiar image likelihood and the scene prior given the context C_k, while the latter term is the prior for the context C_k. This is appealing in terms of it's simplicity, but I find it daunting to begin to specify priors on all possible contexts. Certainly some sort of constructive process would be needed to compute a prior for a novel context, such as the various contexts described above. But what is the nature of such a constructive process? What sort of output can be expected; presumably not quantitative prior probabilities, but rather qualitative probabilities or alternatively just a preference ordering? What are the implicit assumptions and constraints behind such a constructive process? These are some of the issues raised in Whitman Richards' commentary on Chapter 5, although he does not take a Bayesian perspective.

The importance of context selection, and the difficulty in providing reasonable priors, is highlighted further when one considers enlarging the context to include things like communication conventions or the purpose of the people showing you the artifact. In terms of communication conventions, one argument might be that if the demonstrators wanted to communicate the folded cross then they would display it using a representative view. Roughly speaking, a representative view could be defined as a viewpoint from which our perceptual systems will typically recover the folded cross interpretation. The fronto-parallel stereo view is not representative for the folded cross, but it is for the floating bars. In fact, it might be ideal for the floating bars, in terms of communicating the shape of the two bars. Thus, if we assume a context in which the demonstrators are attempting to clearly communicate an artifact, then it make sense to select the floating bars interpretation. Of course an alternative purpose, and an alternative context, is that the demonstrators wish to show you an ambiguous view, maybe to see how you cope with it. But, you should ask, what is the prior probability of a context as convoluted as that?

References

Jacobs, R.A., Jordan, M.I., Nowlan, S.J. & Hinton, G.E. (1991). Adaptive mixtures of local experts, *Neural Computation*, **3**(1).

Chapter 11:
The perception of shading and reflectance

ALLAN JEPSON

Adelson & Pentland discuss the issue of selecting a particular interpretation for a given image from the set of interpretations which are consistent with the image data. Indeed, the authors argue that there are often several alternative interpretations for any single image and that it is the perceptual system's job to choose one or more preferred interpretations from within this set of possibilities. To motivate their approach to this selection problem the authors present an elegant metaphor of a workshop whose task involves minimizing the overall cost of reconstructing the scene. The interpretation that minimizes this cost over the set of consistent interpretations is chosen as the 'percept' for the image. This same issue of selecting a low cost or preferred interpretation from the set of possible interpretations is addressed in each of the other chapters in this text, although the currencies used in the other chapters are not workshop dollars. Rather the other chapters consider cost functions based on probability estimates or, in some cases, concepts built on top of probability, such as utility and risk.

In view of the fact that this selection problem appears throughout this text, it is useful to reformulate Adelson's and Pentland's workshop metaphor in terms of the common Bayesian framework used elsewhere. The specific problem domain addressed by the target chapter, namely that of interpreting shape, pigmentation, and lighting from images, provides an excellent concrete example of many of the issues brought out in other chapters. Moreover, the reformulation of the workshop raises a few points about Bayesian models which have not been highlighted so far. My intention with the reformulation presented below is to keep the general spirit of their metaphor, as developed in their fee schedule, but not necessarily the details of the reported algorithm.

Modal specialists

The most direct way to construct a Bayesian model is to replace the three specialists in the workshop metaphor with stochastic specialists. For example, the stochastic painter would, with a particular probability, spontaneously paint a rectangular patch. Also, with a lower probability, it can paint a general polygon. Moreover, by setting the cost of an operation (according to the reported fee structure, say) to be proportional to the negative logarithm of the probability of that operation occurring in our stochastic workshop, we can directly associate costs of producing an item in the target chapter's workshop with the probability of the item being randomly produced by our stochastic workshop. That is, in the stochastic workshop the probability of independently selecting operations to form a sequence is just the product of the probabilities of selecting each operation. By identifying the cost to be proportional to the (negative) log probability we see that the total cost of the sequence is then just the sum of the costs for each step. Note that we use the negative of the log probability so that high costs are associated with scenes that are produced only rarely by the stochastic workshop.

These first steps in mapping the workshop to a stochastic model immediately bring forward one aspect of Bayesian models which has so far been neglected in this book. For example, our percept of the zig-zag shape depicted in the target chapter includes a description of the artifact's structure and a description of some of the steps in a process for generating that structure. The important point, vividly brought out by the workshop metaphor, is that our percepts not only include a description of what is in the scene and where things are, but also at least a partial description of a process for the construction and placement of the various objects in the scene (see Leyton, 1988).

Returning to our reformulation, consider the structure of the probability distributions appropriate for each stochastic specialist. In particular, we argue that it is natural to take these probabilities to have a modal structure, as defined in Chapter 2. For example, there is a significant probability that a rectangle is painted, rather than a more general four sided polygon. Moreover, the sides of a painted rectangle can be made parallel to other lines within the artifact. Similarly, cuts are straight, often at right angles to other cuts, and bends can be precisely at right angles. In all these cases we have events occuring with a nonzero probability, but which exist on smaller dimensional sets than some more general embedding space. Thus our stochastic workshop is indeed a 'modal workshop' in that the prior distributions for the basic operations performed in the workshop have a modal structure. Therefore an approach of the form considered in Chapter 2 could be used to specify the modal structure of the various specialists.

The presence of modal properties suggests that various reliable inferences can be made from image data. The flip side of this coin is that some sets of interpretations should be extremely improbable. A classic example of an improbable inference is shown in Figure 11.5 of the target chapter. Given the processes assumed to exist in our modal workshop, we might expect an extremely small probability for generating the depicted arrangement of three strips, arranged in a precise way, and viewed from a particular position so that the image matches that in Figure 11.2. For example, given that there is no mode for arranging the leading edges of each of the three strips to be coplanar, and so on, these structures would have to arise simply by chance. This is improbable and, since a small probability corresponds to a large cost, we expect the cost of the structure depicted in Figure 11.5 to be extreme.

Interestingly, this extreme cost is not reflected in the given fee schedule. Notice there is no cost for the precise positioning of various parts, nor for positioning the observer, nor for making accurately specified cuts or folds. A consequence of the lack of charging for accidental views, and so on, is that there can be some surprising minimal cost solutions within the provided fee schedule. A simple example is provided by an image consisting of a rectangle partitioned into a dark square and a light square. The minimal cost solution is the spatial expert's solution ($15 for a rectangle bent at right angles, illuminated with a flood light and viewed from an accidental position). Our percept is instead of a painted rectangle ($18, by painting only one of the squares, along with using a flood light and a fronto-parallel view). The lack of charges for making improbable inferences given the assumed modal structure of the domain therefore appears to be an oversight in the fee structure suggested in the chapter. The alternative approach of starting with a probabilistic model, for which the various modes are included in the basic formulation, appears to be a principled way to keep track of such large costs.

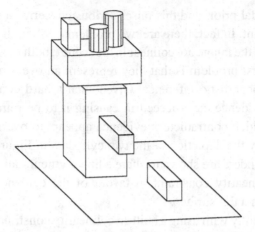

Fig. 2 An accidental view of an accidental scene. In this image there are four pairs of colinear line segments, plus a set of three colinear segments, none of which are perceived to be colinear in the scene.

Hidden costs

Some of the large costs associated with modal structure do appear implicitly in the algorithm suggested for solving the problem, even though they are not explicitly listed in the fee structure. For example, the difficulty with the interpretation of the half-painted rectangle, as discussed in the previous paragraph, is avoided in the proposed algorithm through the use of the constraint that lines which are straight in the image are actually straight in the scene. This is done by allowing the surface model depicted in Figure 11.6 to have corner beads only at places which are not junctions of two colinear line segments. By setting up the problem in this way the algorithm effectively implements a hard constraint that colinear line segments in the image are necessarily colinear in the scene.

Alternatively, one might imagine that the algorithm imposes an arbitrarily large cost on breaking this colinearity constraint, which is related to an extremely low probability within our stochastic workshop. But does a Bayesian model support such a property? In fact, the appropriate Bayesian analysis of the colinearity inference is given by the discussion of key features presented in Chapter 2. This analysis shows that, given an appropriate modal prior distribution, colinear line segments in the image provide reliable evidence for the colinearity of the corresponding lines in the scene. That is, the probability in favour of the colinear interpretation can indeed be extreme or, equivalently, the costs associated with breaking such a constraint can be taken to be extreme. Therefore it may seem natural to rigidly impose this constraint in the actual formulation of an algorithm.

But the same Bayesian analysis of key features shows that the situation is not quite that simple. In particular, it highlights the requirement that there must be an appropriate modal prior, and this raises serious concerns about using a built-in colinearity constraint. In fact, there are two problems with built-in constraints such as "colinear lines in the image are colinear in the scene", both of which are illustrated in Figure 2. The first problem is that they represent an over-commitment to what is essentially a probabilistic inference. Given such a hard constraint, no amount of contradictory evidence can succeed in causing it to be retracted. An example of a situation in which contradictory evidence appears to override the colinearity property is given by the depiction of the two cylinders in Figure 2. Note that even though the two cylinders are shown to share a line segment, our perceptual systems can break the colinearity constraint in favour of the evidence for two separate cylinders resting on a flat surface.

The second difficulty with using a built-in colinearity constraint is that such a hard constraint ignores the possibility that the required modal prior may be conditional on other aspects of the interpretation. Again this situation occurs in the preferred interpretation of Figure 2. In particular, note that there are five different colinear alignments between edges of different blocks, none of which are perceived to be colinear in the scene. In each case, the missing modal property would require a block to be floating freely in space but nevertheless be precisely positioned to have one of it's edges colinearly aligned with the edge of another block. Such a mode can be safely assumed not to exist. Moreover, without this mode the appropriate inference to make is that the line segments should be interpreted as accidental alignments of non-colinear segments in the world (see Chapter 2). That is, the odds are strongly against the colinear pair of lines in the image actually being colinear in the world, but rather favour the viewer being accidentally aligned. (The detailed Bayesian analysis for this case is similar to the discussion in Chapter 2, and is left to the reader.) Thus our common perception of Figure 2 shows that, at least in some situations, our perceptual systems can effectively take the intricacies of the appropriate Bayesian analysis in stride.

The stochastic supervisor

In addition to the specialists, Adelson and Pentland also introduce a supervisor. In their metaphor the supervisor simply charges a flat rate whenever there is cooperation amoungst the specialists. For the modal workshop we imagine a stochastic supervisor which randomly chooses a sequence of operations (according to some constraints on what operations are feasible for the various specialists). The supervisor then issues this sequence to the specialists. Given these commands, the stochastic specialists would then perform the operations according to probability distributions which are conditioned by the commands. For example, returning to our stochastic painter, when it is told to paint a rectangular patch it could choose the location, orientation, size, and aspect ratio from some probability distribution, and then paint the chosen rectangle to within some random error. Alternatively, the supervisor could completely specify the rectangle, and the only randomness introduced by the painter would be errors in precisely executing the command. In either case we see that the appropriate charge to associate with the supervisor alone is just the negative log probability of it generating a particular sequence of commands. Therefore the flat rate charged by the supervisor in the target chapter can be interpreted as a stochastic supervisor which simply randomly selects a command sequence from a large finite set of equiprobable sequences.

The stochastic supervisor and modal specialists together define the prior distribution for the sequences which the workshop can execute. This distribution, in turn, specifies the prior distribution for the various artifacts that are produced by the workshop. But how should we view these distributions? Clearly, with the supervisor simply picking a sequence of operations from a huge set of equiprobable possibilities, the model does not describe a competent prop department of any particular theatre company. Presumably the prop department would have been asked to make something like a set of steps before coming out with the zig zag shape shown in the target chapter. Do we need to incorporate such higher level constraints into our stochastic model of the prop department's workshop? If one was attempting to model the annual output of the prop department of a particular theatre company then the unavoidable answer is that we do need to consider the sorts of props required, the sorts of plays performed, and the various styles of staging used. In other words, if the probabilistic model is meant to describe the world then all these factors appear relevant. However, as pointed out in the introductory chapter by Knill *et al.*, there is a second way to view these prior distributions. In particular, the modal workshop described above can be viewed as a specification of a perceiver's model of what to expect in its world. That is, the distributions are not meant to accurately model the world, but rather serve to specify thee perceiver's model for what is more or less probable in its world (see introductory chapter). If we pursue this second line of reasoning the remaining question is, of course, how does the perceiver get away with using the wrong priors? Why doesn't the perceiver exhibit significant biases or even hallucinate objects according to it's incorrect prior distribution?

There are three inter-related reasons that a perceiver might be able to function appropriately with incorrect priors. The first is that, because of the structure in our world and the information available about that structure from a typical image, there may be a large amount of evidence available for a given interpretation and this evidence dominates any bias introduced by the prior model (see Chapter 2 and 4). The second reason is that the priors used by the perceptual system can be expected to be considerably less structured than priors that more accurately describe a particular domain in the world. Here the stochastic supervisor provides a perfect example, with any one of a huge set of processes treated as equally probable (see also Chapter 10 where the priors are taken to be uniform). In contrast, we might expect the supervisor in a theatre company's prop department to make some choices much more often than others. By choosing a flatter prior the perceiver may avoid the introduction of strong biases simply by avoiding the introduction of unwarranted structure within it's prior distributions. The cost of using flatter priors is that, in cases where more detailed and structured priors are available, the perceptual system will not be as statistically efficient as it might be (see Chapters 7 and 12 for a discussion of efficiency). Finally, the third reason a perceptual system may perform adequately given incorrect priors is that, in cases where there are several different solutions with comparable posterior probabilities (or costs), the perceptual system need not commit to the single most probable (or minimal cost) interpretation but rather might choose to explicitly represent ambiguities through the appropriate choice of resolution for various parameters (see the use of loss functions for light source location in Chapter 4). Moreover, further ambiguity may be explicitly represented by attempting to provide all the categorically distinct interpretations having roughly comparable posterior probabilities (see Chapter 3 for an approach which emphasizes this).

Can your supervisor add?

This latter point about uncertain priors raises the possibility that the analogue of Adelson's and Pentland's supervisor, which attempts to minimize the overall cost, simply cannot add. The issue has been discussed in Chapter 3, where we considered the several modes for the construction and placement of a handle. In order to compare the probabilities of interpretations incorporating one or another mode, it was shown to be necessary to know the relative probabilities of the priors for these modes, along with measurement resolutions, and so on (see Table 3.4a). One approach to this problem would be to pick a flat prior, such as is used by the stochastic supervisor discussed above. A second approach is to treat the actual prior as uncertain, but nevertheless attempt to obtain an ordering of the various possible interpretations despite this uncertainty. For an example of this second approach, assume that the three specialists in Adelson's and Pentland's metaphor use three different currencies, one for each specialist, and for which there are no known exchange rates. In such a case the supervisor is faced with three bottom lines, with no information about how to convert to a common currency.

Indeed the algorithm actually implemented by the authors is perhaps more appropriately thought of in terms of precisely these three distinct currencies. Recall that in the implemented algorithm the shape expert gets the first crack at minimizing costs, then the lighting expert has a chance, and finally the painter touches things up. As a result, the effective cost function being minimized by this algorithm treats any savings created by the shape expert as more valuable than any extra expenses that might be incurred by the lighting and paint specialists. The supervisor is therefore minimizing the costs reported by the three experts by using a priority ordering, treating the spatial expert as first priority and the painter last. We note in passing that this nicely illustrates how the specification of an algorithm might radically change the effective cost function which is being used to compare various interpretations.

The ability to compute a single 'bottom line' through the use of a common currency, or a priority scheme, is central to the workshop metaphor presented in the target chapter and also to the Bayesian approaches described in most other chapters of this text. Such a cost function, after all, forms the basis of the ordering of the set of possible interpretations. Having access to such a cost function may appear to be both simple and intuitive, at least from the perspective of a theoretician attempting to model perception. But is it simple from the perceptual system's point of view? To get a glimmer of what this might look like to our perceptual system, imagine that we had just such a cost function to make common decisions. For example, who should I hire for that research assistantship? Why can't we just crunch some numbers and get a simple total ordering of the candidates? The knowledge requirements that would go into computing such a cost function are, of course, overwhelming. It is for just this reason that in Chapter 3 we attempt an alternative approach to the problem of ordering the various possible interpretations for the purpose of selecting one or more as the 'percepts' of a given image.

References

Leyton M. (1988). A process grammar for shape. *Artificial Intelligence*, **34**(2), 1988, 213-247.

Chapter 11:
The world, the brain and the speed of sight

RONALD A. RENSINK

Adelson & Pentland use an engaging metaphor to illustrate their position on scene analysis: interpretations are produced by a workshop that employs a set of specialists, each concerned with a single aspect of the scene. The authors argue that it is too expensive to have a supervisor co-ordinate the specialists and that it is too expensive to let them operate independently. They then show that a careful sequencing of the specialists leads to solutions of minimum cost, at least for their world of Mondrian panels.

The authors admit that their approach is based on a relatively simple domain, and will have to be developed further if it is to be applied to more realistic situations. But can it really provide the basis for a better understanding of more general-purpose vision? In what follows, it will be shown that this approach is based on several rather strong hypotheses, some of which will have to be seriously modified or even replaced if an extension is to be made to more general domains. Three sets of issues are of particular concern here: the kinds of scenes that can be accurately interpreted this way, the relevance of such models to human vision, and the trade-offs between interpretative power and processing speed.

Scene domain

The operation of the workshop begins with a specialist that uses contour information to recover the three-dimensional (3D) shape of the surface. Since there is no feedback from the other specialists, error here is irreversible. The potential therefore exists for these errors to cascade through the subsequent stages and lead to large inaccuracies in the final interpretation. Shape recovery must be accurate enough to prevent such cascades.

From the description of the shape specialist, it is not clear whether planarity is enforced absolutely, or is only maximized. If planarity is simply maximized, a region could correspond to a nonplanar surface, and so would not have the uniform luminance assumed in the analysis. This in turn could lead to serious inaccuracies in the final interpretation. However, these problems can presumably be avoided by invoking the appropriate planarity constraint.

A more serious concern is that the shape specialist operates on contours alone. This amounts to a claim that (at least for the world of Mondrian panels) there is no need for shape from shading. Indeed, shading is to be completely disregarded. If true, this would be a most interesting result, and so must be carefully verified. However, shading cannot be ignored for more general domains. Such information can help to establish which areas in the image belong to the same surface in the scene, and this in turn can have serious consequences for the recovered 3D structure. For example, shading can influence the perceived ordering of depth (Figure 1a) and the perceived completion of edges and surfaces (Figure 1b). To get around this problem it is necessary to somehow take reflectance into account, possibly by having reflectance estimates be directly proportional to intensity (as is done for the lighting direction). But whatever the method used, it will still be necessary to verify that shape recovery remains accurate.

More generally, if Adelson and Pentland's approach is to be extended to larger

 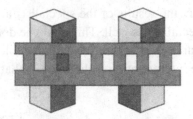

a) Depth ordering   b) Surface completion

Fig. 3 Influence of shading on 3D surface structure. In (a), the pattern of shading determines which of the oblique panels is perceived as being immediately behind the occluder. In (b), the pattern of shading determines whether the occluder is perceived as obscuring one long post (surfaces completed) or two short cubes (surfaces left incomplete).

domains, it will need to determine the kinds of interpretations generated by the fixed sequence of specialists, and to determine how well these capture the (statistical) structure of the domain under consideration. Ultimately, the relevance of this approach will depend on the existence of a world sufficiently "friendly" that its structure can be reasonably approximated by the relatively restricted set of "sequence-generated" interpretations.

Relevance to human vision

For Adelson & Pentland, the criterion for a "correct" interpretation is that it corresponds to what humans perceive. Although this is fine for purposes of general discussion, more detail is needed if their approach is to be put on a more rigorous basis.

To begin with, it is important that the solutions be tested against the results of controlled psychophysical experiment. Although Adelson and Pentland have proposed one particular set of constraints, it is possible that others are used instead. For example, the shape specialist could maximize the number of orthogonal corners (Kanatani, 1990), and the lighting specialist could be based on a nonlambertian reflectance function. It is only by a careful quantitative comparison with the results of controlled studies that the actual set of constraints used can be definitively established.

It is also necessary to specify the kind of task to be used in these experiments. What humans "perceive" depends to a large extent on what they are asked to do, since different kinds of tasks can access different kinds of representations. For example, the interpretation of line drawings as 3D objects at preattentive levels differs considerably from that based on "casual" viewing (Enns & Rensink, 1991). The criterion for a "correct" interpretation must therefore be tightened up.

Finally, if the workshop metaphor is taken to heart, it is also important to test not only the results of the specialists acting together, but the results of the individual specialists as well. This could be done, for example, by presenting actual 3D polyhedral objects (with or without colored faces) to the observer, and determining if the interpretation is the same as that based on a picture or drawing of the scene.

Processing speed

Given that each of the specialists can be based (at least potentially) on different constraints, it is apparent that the power of Adelson & Pentland's approach does not depend strongly upon the particular form of these constraints. But what then is the critical factor?

A closer look at the workshop shows that an important element in its operation is the *sequencing* of the specialists: The slants of the planes are first recovered from image measurements, the lighting direction is then recovered from the slants, and the reflectances are then recovered from the slants and lighting directions. This is an instance of *dynamic programming* (see, e.g., Kumar *et al.*, 1994), a technique that breaks a task down into a sequence of nested subtasks, arranged such that the solutions of the earlier subtasks help solve those later in the sequence. The unidirectional flow of information from the earlier subtasks to the later ones allows iteration to be avoided, which keeps computational complexity low.

Thus, the difference in "cost" between fixed sequencing and direct supervision (i.e., optimal interaction among the subtasks) involves processing effort rather than quality of solution. Since the cost of the supervisor differs in kind from the cost of the other specialists, adding these costs together is like adding apples and oranges. What is required instead is a framework that shows how processing effort can be traded off against quality of interpretation (see, e.g., Rensink, 1992). This could then serve as the basis for a true computational analysis, which would explain not only the reasons for the particular structure of the specialists, but also the reasons for the particular pattern of their interactions.

References

Enns, J.T., & Rensink, R.A. (1991). Preattentive recovery of three-dimensional orientation from line drawings. *Psychological Review*, **98**, 335-351.

Kanatani, K. (1990). *Group-Theoretical Methods in Image Understanding*. Berlin: Springer.

Kumar, V. Grama, A., Gupta, A., & Karypis, G. (1994). *Introduction to Parallel Computing: Design and Analysis of Algorithms*. Redwood City, CA: Benjamin/Cummings.

Rensink, R. A. (1992). The Rapid Recovery of Three-Dimensional Orientation from Line Drawings. Ph.D. Thesis (also Technical Report 92-25), Department of Computer Science, University of British Columbia, Vancouver, BC, Canada.

Chapter 12:
The logic of the homunculus, and the closed world assumption

JACOB FELDMAN

Barlow proposes a general principle for the inferential competence of the neocortex: (1) find some structure – i.e. some symmetry or regularity – in the sense data; (2) extract the regularity, and examine the residual for latent structure; (3) repeat, presumably recursively, until no more regularity can be extracted. The final result of this process ought to be an ultimate residual which is devoid of evident structure, i.e. is "generic". This general framework can be worked out in a logical framework, which I attempt to sketch briefly.

Imagine that in some domain X of perceptual data, a given input $x \in X$ may or may not exhibit some finite set of properties $p_1 \ldots p_k$. These predicates correspond to the symmetries, regularities, etc., the job of searching for which Barlow would like to banish the homunculus. Notice that these predicates divide the domain X into categorical regions, each corresponding to that subset of X in which a particular p holds. Thus there would be (possibly nested or overlapping) regions $p_1(x)$; $p_2(x)$; $p_1(x) \wedge p_2(x)$; etc.

Particularly interesting from the point of view of Barlow's idea, there would also be *negative* or complementary regions $\neg p_1(x)$ [$= X - p(x)$] etc. A predicate region and its negation represent stimuli that do and do not (respectively) exhibit a particular symmetry or regularity. Hence while the "regular" region $p_i(x)$ represents the set of stimuli on which p_i holds, the complementary region $\neg p(x)$ correspond to the more generic set of stimuli after the said regularity has been extracted (like before-and-after snapshots). The set of predicate regions can be thought of as a qualitative map of the possible outcomes of Barlow's recursive regularity extraction process. Hence negation and complementation are critical in enumerating the qualitative categories of final solutions to the interpretive process Barlow describes.

What is especially intriguing, then, is the fairly complex nested negation structure that Barlow's deceptively simple idea ends up imposing on the categories of solutions – in particular, on the most generic, least "regular" of them. For example a simple domain with k "crossed" predicates $p_1 \ldots p_k$ has a most generic category

$$\neg p_1 \wedge \ldots \wedge \neg p_k.$$

A completely nested domain, for example $p_1 \ldots p_k$ such that $p_1 \rightarrow p_2, p_2 \rightarrow p_3, \ldots, p_{k-1} \rightarrow p_k$, has a most generic category $\neg p_k$. But concluding p_k entails having rejected the nested regularity p_{k-1}, which in turn requires rejecting p_{k-2}, and so forth. Hence the most generic category $\neg p_k$ can be rewritten as

$$\neg(p_k \wedge \neg(p_{k-1} \wedge \ldots \neg(p_2 \wedge \neg p_1))).$$

These recursively nested negations correspond to the repeated cycle marked in Barlow's Figure 12.2. The ultimate interpretation of the stimulus is a stable solution under which the sense data is generic – that is, a "residual" in which the homunculus (or its replacement!) can find no additional regularity.

Negation and the Closed World Assumption. This prominence of negation in this process is particularly interesting from the point of view of Logic Programming (e.g. see Apt, 1994), in which the epistemological basis for logical negation is a central concern. The question, in essence, is whether a perceiver can safely infer that a given stimulus has a particular description, simply from its own failure to demonstrate that it has any more regular description.

We might assume the predicates are computable on X, i.e. each can be written as

$$p_i(x) \leftarrow c_i(x), \tag{0.1}$$

where the "$\leftarrow$" can be read as "if", and $c_i(x)$ is some conjunction of computable clauses. We might think then that the negation $\neg p_i(x)$ would naturally correspond to the subset of X on which the corresponding $c_i(x)$ does not succeed, namely $X - p_i(x)$. This simple meta-axiom is called the "Closed World Assumption" (Reiter, 1978) since it holds (in our terms) that those inputs for which we cannot demonstrate a given regularity in fact do not have that regularity.

Typically, however, the $p(x)$ might actually correspond to some productive language that is recursively enumerable but not decidable (e.g. finding a model that satisfies some first-order sentence). The unfortunate result is that the complement of the predicate region is not enumerable – an untenable situation for our homunculus whose ability to mechanically extract regularities presumably requires that negation be computable. For our purposes, we could easily assume that each regularity predicate always either succeeds or halts with failure. But since the algorithms at hand are generally substituting for regularity notions that have more abstract definitions, we must legitimately wonder whether a halt with failure necessarily means that the regularity is not in fact present in some subtle form that our algorithm could not detect.

In either case, the standard solution is simply to assume that when our attempt to find a particular regularity fails finitely, the regularity can be positively asserted to be absent; this is the so-called "negation as failure" rule. Under this rule, the negation $\neg p(x)$ is a computable (possibly improper) subset of the complement $X - p(x)$, and a hence a practical mechanism by which our homunculus may arrive at its desired generic interpretation. Equivalently, we may think of the Closed World Assumption as augmenting the left arrow ("if") in Eq.(0.1) above with a right arrow ("and only if"), an augmentation known as "Clark's completion" (Clark, 1978). Inference with this logical structure has been successfully applied to a perceptual grouping problem (see Feldman, in preparation). In this scheme the interpretive process ends with a cascade of failure, culminating in a stable model in which the data are generic – and which, by dint of the Closed World Assumption, the mechanism hypothesizes is the *correct* model, given all the possible regularities that it knows about.

A connection to Bayesian reasoning? How might this logic-flavored analysis above be connected to the probability-flavored analysis that is the subject of this volume? One connection is in the construction of prior probability distributions, in which the Bayesian perceiver, like our logical perceiver, must make an early – and quite speculative – commitment about the extent of the range of hypotheses that it is willing to entertain. The Bayesian perceiver, like the homunculus with and its Closed World, can perceive no regularity for which it has no prior concept (see Chapter 3, this volume). The ability of the perceiver in either case to characterize its environment usefully, then, will depend on the intimacy of the connection between its prior concepts and the regularities or patterns that actually obtain in its environment. What is especially interesting about Barlow's proposal is that it turns out that one can say something definite about the tacit assumptions of the homunculus – such as the Closed World Assumption – based on a consideration only of the "control structure" of perceptual interpretation, independent of investigation of the particular definitions of the particular regularity concepts (the various p_i or the various priors) that presumably consitute the heart of what the perceptual apparatus actually does.

References

Apt, K.R. (1990). Logic programming. In *Handbook of Theoretical Computer Science,* (ed.) J. van Leeuwen. Elsevier.

Clark, K.L. (1978). Negation as failure. In *Logic and Data Bases*, (ed.) H. Gallaire and J. Minker. New York: Plenum Press.

Feldman, J. (in preparation). Regularity-based perceptual grouping.

Reiter, R. (1978). On closed world data bases. In *Logic and Data Bases*, (ed.) H. Gallaire and J. Minker. New York: Plenum Press.

Chapter 12:
Banishing the homunculus

DAVID MUMFORD

Feedback and the homunculus

The problem of the homunculus is usually presented in the following setting: an information processing agent is described which has senses and effectors. The input from the senses is led to an intial processing stage, where significant features are

Commentaries

extracted; these are led to a higher stage of processing, and to another, perhaps multi-modal integrative stage. At some point a decision is made about what the stimulus 'means' to the agent and now the process is reversed. The decision leads to a choice in a large plan, which in turn is translated into a current step in a finer grain plan. Eventually, specific muscle/motor commands are issued to the effectors. In this architecture, one has the feeling that the essential component of thought has not been analyzed and that at the decision stage, there is still the need for a little man to look at the refined description of the sensory input, to think it over and decide how he wants to modify his master plan. If not that, then we seem to be thrown back on a Rod Brooks-style finite state automata at the top level, and this seems awfully stupid compared to our image of ourselves.

Unfortunately, much of the theorizing of neurophysiologists and psychologists has reinforced this architectural view of what the brain does. Time and time again, we see flowcharts in which the retina sends data to the LGN which sends data to V1 which sends data to V2 and MT leading, for instance to the dorsal and ventral pathways through posterior cortex, then to frontal lobe, etc. One example which is explicitly in the homunculus tradition is that a window of attention is superimposed on the low-level image pyramid and that this window is *copied* into IT for analysis and, hopefully, object recognition. This approach would then say that the role of V1 is to provide a massive filter bank, extracting important local features of the 2-space-dimensional and 1-time-dimensional visual signal. Although more and more properties of V1 single-cell recordings are complicating this model, it is still the dominant paradigm.

I would like to make a hypothesis for the role of V1 which is very different from the above and which deflates substantially the role of the homunculus (without, however, explaining the computations needed to replace him). This hypothesis is that the role of V1 in the neocortex is not as the first processing stage for vision, but as *the one and only high-resolution visual buffer in the neo-cortex, which is involved in all computations which need high-resolution, such as recognizing objects and discovering differences between memories and current stimuli, when details are crucial.*

We have to be careful about what this means and how it might be possible. Firstly, feedback pathways are absolutely essential in order that V1 play a continuing role in the high level processing as well as the low level processing of an image. These are, of course, found in rich abundance in the cortex. Secondly, it does imply that V1 single cell responses will be affected by high level aspects of the image, but it does not mean that V1 is doing object recognition all by itself. Some integrative mechanism which forms temporary cell assemblies, linking V1, V2, V4 and IT for example would be needed to coordinate cell activity during such a computation. In this integrated activity, the role of V1 (and perhaps the LGN) is to provide the buffer in which detailed visual structure is identified and placed into complex global structures, involving lighting, depth, object classes and the like. Recent experiments (Zipser *et al.*, 1994) can be interpreted as lending support to this hypothesis, but the crucial tests have not been done.

Where is the homunculus in such a model? Clearly, the little guy can no longer sit in a small room at the top of the information processing pyramid. He must now have a hundred TV cameras checking out all the low level buffers, the intermediate areas where global structures are tracked and the higher areas where multi-modal interpretations are weighed. Do we really need him then?

Markov random fields and sparse coding

Sparse coding, e.g. the hypothesis that one or a small number of cell's firing signifies the presence of grandmother, is very attractive, but a clear computational reason for believing in it has been elusive, as Barlow points out. I would like to argue that the computational model provided by Markov Random Fields presents one possible explanation. Most of the analysis of sparse coding has been done using information theory in an abstract setting divorced from details about the world. A totally different approach is to start with the premise that the brain's task is to infer hidden facts about the state of the world and that how to accomplish this task depends on the nature of the probability space defined by possible world states. I will argue that if this space is appproximated by a Markov Random Field, such inferences can only be done efficiently using sparse coding.

It may be helpful to review what Markov Random Fields (MRF's) are. Let us assume that we have a large collection $\{X_v\}$ of variables, which could be light intensities at different pixels, edge or filter strengths, lighting directions, Boolean variables expressing things like 'granny present' or 'patient has bacterial infection'. Some of these may be known in the current situation, some unknown, but all vary from time to time. We want to use statistics to estimate them, so we need to make a probability space out of the set of all possible sets of values $\{X_v = a_v\}$ they may have, i.e. give a big table of probabilities of all such assignments. As is well-known, this is impossible to do by storing the table, which gets vastly too large to store for even tens of variables. MRF's provide one of the few ways to effectively define probabilities on such ensembles. What makes the concept natural is that MRF's may be defined in two equivalent ways: by an abstract requirement of certain conditional independencies or by a simple concrete formula for the probability of each assignment. It works by assuming that the variables can be thought of as the nodes of a graph, in which edges join any pair of variables *which are directly dependent*. The important point is that the graph is sparse: each variable has only a relatively few edges. (By relative, I mean, e.g. that if there are a hundred million variables, then perhaps the maximum number of edges at one node – the degree of the graph – should be bounded by ten thousand.) The abstract definition of a MRF is that if some set of variables $\{X_w\}_{w \in W}$ is fixed and if any path in the graph joining X_a and X_b must cross W, then X_a and X_b are to be conditionally independent, given $\{X_w\}_{w \in W}$. The concrete definition says that

$$- \log Pr(\{X_v = a_v \text{ all } v\}) = \sum E_C(\{a_v\}_{v \in C}) + \text{cnst}$$

where C ranges over the 'cliques' of the graph, the clusters of totally connected nodes and E_C, called the 'energy', is a local interaction term, involving only the variables in the clique.

The basic hypothesis of those who apply MRF's to modeling thought – whether in speech recognition, vision or medical expert systems – is that MRF's are a good approximation to the true probability distibution of the random variables of the world. This is the strongest form of the hypothesis. It is certainly possible to believe in modified or weaker forms of the hypothesis: to extend MRF's with pointers (as in the point process models of (Ripley & Kelly, 1971)), or to merely ask that this approximation is usable even when inaccurate, or to fall back on saying that the part of the world with enough independencies to be MRF-like is the only one we can think about.

If we accept the above *MRF hypothesis*, then what are its neural implications? Clearly the brain must be able to learn and store the local energy terms E_C in some way. Given that the set of neurons in the brain is also a relatively sparsely connected graph, this suggests that some kind of rough correspondence exist between the two graphs. Let's look at two possibilities:

Consider the extreme case where there is no correspondence. This means that we have a fully distributed representation of each hidden variable X_v in the firing patterns of millions of neurons. To express a direct link between two such variables, which does not involve any other variables whose representations overlap extensively with the first two, we must extract some invariant from the whole firing pattern which signifies the individual variable. This would seem to be a decoding problem as hard as calculating X_v in the first place.

The other extreme version is to make the MRF graph and the neuronal graph isomorphic. This is the ultimate grandmother cell theory, with 'grandmother synapses' as well, i.e. two cells linked if and only if the corresponding random variables are connected by an edge in the MRF. An example of such a theory is Hopfield's symmetric weight neural net theory. Less extreme would be a theory in which a small number (e.g. 100) of neurons carried the value a_v. This is a sparse coding theory in the sense that some small cluster of cells somewhere expresses the presence of grandmother. It seems consistent not only with Hopfield-style nets, but with other theories in which individual pulses carry information such as the theory of synfire chains (Abeles, 1991). I believe that accepting the MRF hypothesis drives you strongly to some form of sparse coding.

References

Abeles, M. (1991). *Corticonics*, Cambridge Univ. Press.
Ripley, B. & Kelly, F. (1977). Markov point processes, *J. London Math. Soc.*, **15**:188-192.
Zipser, K., Lamme, V., Lee, T.S. & Schiller, P. (1994). A role for primate striate cortex in cue-independent scene segmentation (submitted to *Nature*).

Author index

507

Subject index